Managing the
Software Enterprise

Managing the
Software Enterprise

Software Engineering and Information
Systems in Context

Patrick A. V. Hall and Juan Fernández-Ramil

THOMSON

Australia • Canada • Mexico • Singapore • Spain • United Kingdom • United States

Managing the Software Enterprise, Software Engineering and Information Systems in Context
Patrick A.V. Hall and Juan Fernández-Ramil

Publishing Director John Yates	**Commissioning Editor** Gaynor Redvers-Mutton	**Editorial Assistant** Charlotte Loveridge
Production Editor Lucy Mills	**Manufacturing Manager** Helen Mason	**Marketing Manager** Leo Stanley
Typesetter KnowledgeWorks Global Ltd., Chennai, India	**Production Controller** Maeve Healy	**Cover Design** Jackie Wrout Landsky Designs
Text Design Design Deluxe Ltd, Bath, UK	**Printer** C & C Offset Printing Co., Ltd	

Copyright © 2007
Thomson Learning

The Thomson logo is a registered trademark used herein under licence.

For more information, contact Thomson Learning, High Holborn House; 50-51 Bedford Row, London WC1R 4LR or visit us on the World Wide Web at:
http://www.thomsonlearning.co.uk

ISBN-13: 978-1-84480-354-5
ISBN-10: 1-84480-354-6

This edition published 2007 by Thomson Learning.

British Library Cataloguing-in-Publication Data
A catalogue record for this book is available from the British Library

Contents

Preface ix
Acknowledgements xi

1 Introduction: Software within the information society 1

  1.1 Problems with software 1
  1.2 The ubiquity of software 4
  1.3 A changing world 7
  1.4 Rationality and its limitations 9
  1.5 How this book will address this issue 15
      Exercises 17

I   **The social and organisational context**   **19**

2 Organisation and business context 21

  2.1 Modelling organisations 22
  2.2 Inside organisations 24
  2.3 New and evolving systems 29
  2.4 Return on investment 31
  2.5 Relationship between software and the organisation 35
  2.6 Knowledge management and learning organisations 38
  2.7 Change and learning 41
  2.8 Software enterprise learning 43
      Exercises 48

3 Economic and social context 52

  3.1 Individual motivation to work 53
  3.2 Global views of motivation 57
  3.3 Human resource development 63
  3.4 Organisational motivation and market forces 65
  3.5 From market failure to the gratis economy 67
      Exercises 72

4 Ethics, codes, and standards 75

  4.1 Introduction 75
  4.2 Ethics and morality 76

4.3   Self-regulation and voluntary codes 80
4.4   Standards 84
       Exercises 91

5 Software and the law 94

5.1   Why law is necessary 94
5.2   Intellectual property rights 96
5.3   Contracts 111
5.4   Responsibilities to employees and the public 117
5.5   External threats 122
       Exercises 124

II   Processes for acquiring and evolving software   127

6 Software acquisition 129

6.1   Finding software 129
6.2   Legacy software 132
6.3   Buying software off the shelf 136
6.4   Obtaining 'free' software 142
6.5   Acquiring software as a service 148
6.6   Bespoke development, outsourcing and offshoring 151
6.7   Software acquisition decisions 157
       Exercises 160

7 Software activities 163

7.1   Introduction 163
7.2   Requirements elicitation 165
7.3   Initial estimates of cost 170
7.4   Requirements specification 171
7.5   Cost–benefit estimation 173
7.6   Architectural design 174
7.7   Work breakdown and scheduling 176
7.8   Detailed design 177
7.9   Progress monitoring 178
7.10   Coding and unit testing 179
7.11   Integration testing 181
7.12   System testing 182
7.13   Acceptance and system release 183
7.14   Maintenance and evolution 184
7.15   Quality assurance 185
       Exercises 187

8 Software processes 190

8.1   Introduction 191
8.2   Classic process models – sequential and incremental 193

8.3 Resolving uncertainties – iteration, evolution and participation 198
8.4 Resolving uncertainties – formal methods 205
8.5 Flexible about functions – timeboxing and rapid application development 205
8.6 Design-driven processes 207
8.7 Open Source methods 213
8.8 Agile processes 215
Exercises 220

9 Maintaining and evolving software 223

9.1 Introduction 223
9.2 Long-life software 225
9.3 Software decay and death 229
9.4 Software recovery and rejuvenation 236
9.5 Maintainability and evolvability 242
9.6 Management guidance 247
Exercises 255

III Managing software processes 259

10 Managing resources 261

10.1 Introduction 262
10.2 Setting up a project 264
10.3 Setting project budgets and timescales 269
10.4 Scheduling and controlling projects 285
10.5 Managing the project in context 291
Exercises 300

11 Managing work-products and digital assets 303

11.1 Introduction 303
11.2 Software configuration management 304
11.3 Change control 318
11.4 Configuration management tools 325
Exercises 332

12 Managing quality 335

12.1 Introduction 335
12.2 Quality and what it means 337
12.3 Quality frameworks 353
Exercises 364

13 Managing uncertainty and risk 366

13.1 Introduction 366
13.2 Types of risks 367

13.3   Causes and consequences of failure 369
13.4   Software risk management 374
13.5   Risk identification 377
13.6   Risk mitigation 380
       Exercises 384

14   Conclusion: The way forward 387
       14.1   Beginning with problems 387
       14.2   Change is inevitable 389
       14.3   The controlling response 390
       14.4   Value from the human component 391
       14.5   Build on top of past great products 392
       14.6   Pervasiveness, mobility, and nomadic IT 392
       14.7   Going with the flow 393

Appendix A: Modelling notations 395
       A.1   Modelling with diagrams 395
       A.2   Data-flow modelling 396
       A.3   Data modelling 402

Appendix B: Measurement theory 406

Glossary 409
Index 429

Preface

W riting this book has been the culmination of our lives of studying and doing to date. The writing process has enabled us to order our experience and understand how it all fits together, and see how it might help others. We hope that what we have to say will prove of value to you too. A lot of what we cover in this book will, we expect and hope, seem obvious to the experienced reader. But even for these readers, we hope to give them many surprises as we juxtapose viewpoints that are often distinct, and out of this synthesise a new viewpoint that illuminates software and its production and use.

While computer hardware engineers have been extremely successful in scaling down costs and in bringing about the continual improvement of the computer's capacity and performance, many software engineers still struggle and software projects continue to fail. What makes software development difficult is its complexity. This is more than mere technical complexity: it reflects the complexity of the world which computing software aims to automate, support, inform, and control. Software is a mirror, reflecting the reality surrounding as it is and as we want it to be.

Fred Brooks inspired us and many others, first in his book *The Mythical Man-Month* and then in his article 'No silver bullet'[1] twenty years ago when he said that there was no single technical or managerial approach within a decade that promised an order of magnitude improvement in software development. The process improvement 'problem' remains intractable despite the advances of formal methods, high-level languages, O-O, components, and reuse. Each single 'panacea' has fallen when confronted by real 'hard' software problems. These problems stretch the abilities of engineers, where individual ability for handling these complexities varies significantly. It is worse than that: software needs to be changed and changes need to be systematic and controlled, otherwise the software will become even more complex and even more difficult to change. We augment the ability of individuals and teams using sophisticated notations and reasoning systems and methodologies, but in doing this we are always in danger of losing the power of very able individuals, reducing them to the level of the least able. The 'Agile' response has been to minimise bureaucracy, but this does not always work: do not try it in safety-critical applications. So, where to go?

We believe that if there is a hope, it is in sound software management, recognising the inherent difficulties of the problem to be tackled. A successful software manager makes it all happen, finding some thread of stability in a world that is constantly changing. She or he must know how software fits into the human, social, and economic world, but also know where software comes from, how it can be acquired, and then changed. A software manager must know where the software fits (Part I), how to get and keep his or her software (Part II), and how to make it all happen (Part III). This book provides a principled yet gentle introduction to software management for the novice, but also challenges the preconceptions of any seasoned readers.

Software has become ubiquitous. Yet the understanding of what software is and what its inherent difficulties are is not so common, even amongst software professionals, in an era in which technological hype seems to govern. We have tried to focus on fundamental principles and have covered – we hope – many subtleties that will save the reader from more than one disappointment. However, a book on management is unlikely to be either definitive or complete. We recognise that many of the topics touched on in this book are issues of current and future research. Nevertheless, we hope that this book will stimulate the reader to continue his or her own learning and self-reflection in this important field of software engineering and software management.

Both of us have had varied careers moving between industry and academe, between learning and practising engineering while learning on the job, and teaching and research and learning in the ivory tower. Both of us realise just how much more we have to learn. Our careers span almost the whole history of software development, during which time the industry has grown and changed enormously, from a time when all the computers in the UK could be listed in a single annual publication to the time when computers are in most homes of the wealthy across the world, towards a time we foresee when computers will be accessible to all.

Pat Hall was born in Zimbabwe, educated in southern Africa and then in England, and worked about half his time in commercial organisations and half in universities, mostly within the UK but with some time outside in the Middle East, and now lives in Nepal. Juan Fernandez-Ramil was born in Caracas and spent part of his childhood in Spain. He completed secondary and university studies in Venezuela, where he worked in industrial organisations. He then studied and worked further in the UK. He now lives in Brussels. We met at the Open University, as members of the team running a postgraduate software engineering course, and then worked together to write a new course on software management. Our personal backgrounds, and our employment at the Open University, have given us a global outlook which we hope has been reflected adequately in the book. Software is now a global enterprise.

Visit the companion website at www.thomsonlearning.co.uk/hall_ramil.

Endnotes

1. F.P. Brooks (1986) No silver bullet – essence and accidents of software engineering, in H.J. Kugler (ed.) *Information Processing 86*. Elsevier Science (North Holland), pp. 1069–1076.

Acknowledgements

We would like to thank the many people who have made this book possible. Firstly our employer the Open University who has been so supportive in the writing of this book, enabling us to take material that we had previously written for teaching purposes, unchanged or through suitable transformations, into the book. We both think of many individual persons whose wisdom has moved us forward, either in direct contact or indirectly through words written or spoken: we debated whether to name the most significant among these, but have refrained, since to name some is not to name the many others. This book has benefited from insightful comments of critical readers and anonymous reviewers to whom we are specially grateful. We want to thank our publishers for believing in the book and helping us to see it through. And finally we want to thank our families for their patience and support as we wrote and rewrote the text, and all other material required for a successful book.

Pat Hall, Lalitpur, Nepal, April 2006
Juan Fernandez-Ramil, Brussels, Belgium, April 2006

Software within the information society

What we will study in this chapter

This chapter motivates the book by looking at a number of case studies and examples.

We will see that the application of software does not necessarily lead to benefit; even though software is used increasingly in many applications, it is not clear that it does us good!

This situation is made worse by the continual changing of the environment in which software must operate – so that even if it delivers benefit today, it may not do so tomorrow.

In trying to exert managerial control over the situation we would naturally turn to precise software applications and methods, but these scientific methods are limited; rationality has its bounds.

We will see that this leaves us with a paradox: the need to control the unpredictable using precise methods. In this chapter, we will explain how the book aims to address this paradox.

1.1 Problems with software

In 1995 Thomas Landauer published a book, *The Trouble with Computers*,[1] that acquired some notoriety. In this book Landauer gave an analysis of the benefits of computers which showed that investment in computers had not delivered the benefits that were widely believed should flow from such investments. Now there was nothing new in this conclusion: people in the software industry had been concerned for many years that having made a case for a **system**[2] based on the benefits and savings that would result, many of these benefits and savings did not materialise. Other analysts such as Paul Strassmann[3] and Manuel Castells[4] had also noted this. But Landauer set out the evidence very clearly, bringing together evidence from many quarters. This gained the book exposure in the media, questioning the unquestionable, that computers were good for us. What was going on?

The evidence came from economic studies of national productivity of the US and other nations. For economists, productivity is measured by the value of output in dollars for each dollar spent on inputs of labour and capital combined. This is termed *multifactor productivity*, while if we focus purely on labour it would be termed *labour productivity*. Over the last century the prosperity of the US and other

Software has not returned the benefits to the economy that we had anticipated.

countries, as measured by gross national product (GNP), grew and along with it national productivity and the standard of living also grew. Labour productivity grew year on year by around 2 per cent in the US, less in some other countries, and as high as 7 per cent in Japan. And then from 1970 onwards the steady increase in labour productivity dipped to half its former growth, at precisely the time when investment in information technologies began. A deeper analysis showed that while farming and manufacturing productivity continued to increase, elsewhere there was no growth, and the labour categories such as clerks that were supposed to have been displaced by computers in fact increased.

While there have been many studies in the area, a graph by Franke[5] shown in Figure 1.1 captures what has been happening. His figures comes from the financial sector of the US, but could have come from other sectors. It shows with depressing clarity the fall off in productivity around 1960 as investment in information technology surged.

Figure 1.1

Productivity changes with the introduction of computers in the US financial sector

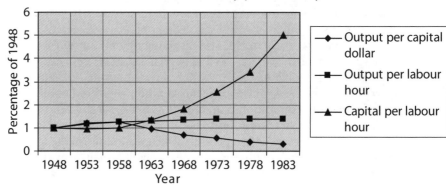

Financial industry productivity

Reprinted from Technological Forecasting and Social Change, vol. 31, Franke R.H., Technological revolution and productivity decline: Computer introduction in the financial industry, pp 143–154, 1987, with permission from Elsevier.

Landauer concluded that 'The low return on investments in computers, and IT generally, appears to be the missing piece in the productivity slowdown puzzle' (p. 45), a view strongly echoed by Castells: 'Even if we account for the specificity of some countries, what appears clearly is that we observe a downward trend of productivity growth starting roughly around the same time that the Information Technology Revolution took shape in the early 1970s' (p. 71).

Software can fail in service, often with disastrous results.

This concern about the use of computers and their effectiveness is manifest in many other ways. Software failure has been implicated in crashes of aircraft and other losses of life, such that safety-critical software became a major concern during the 1980s and 1990s. Case Study 1.1 gives one example; the books by Flowers[6] and Neumann[7] give many more.

Case Study 1.1 *The Therac radiation treatment disaster*

The Therac series of machines had been highly successful radiation treatment machines, and were electromechanical devices until the 1980s when the new Therac-25 was developed to be controlled by software. Once in service, defects in the machine became apparent, leading to the deaths of several patients. The results of a thorough investigation were reported by Nancy Leveson and Clark Turner in 1993,[8] and the following description is taken from their report.

Five machines were installed in the United States and six were installed in Canada. Between 1985 and 1987, six accidents were reported involving massive radiation overdoses, but the machines were only withdrawn from service in 1987. Several successful legal cases followed, suing the manufacturer for damages resulting from the failure of the Therac machines.

Several problems related to system use and the hardware and software were discovered. Each Therac-25 machine had a turntable that rotated equipment into the x-ray beam to produce different modes of operation when the beam was directed at a patient. The computer was used to position the turntable and set the radiation doses. The operator positioned the patient, set the treatment parameters manually, and then also entered the information at a console; the system then compared the values set manually with the values entered at the console.

Three technical flaws in the system were identified:

- The operator could edit a command line to change the state of the machine such that the execution of the radiation commands took place before the change in the state of the machine was complete. So, after the operator entered the treatment data – mode, energy level, position, and so on – he or she could then alter the data, by moving the cursor to the field to be changed, without having to start the data entry procedure from the beginning. If this was done too quickly, the new values were shown on the screen, but the internal treatment parameters remained unchanged.

- The software contained a counter that increased by one every time a treatment was performed. Before each treatment, safety checks, such as ensuring that non-lethal radiation dosages had been chosen, were per-

formed. However for the special case of the counter being zero, no safety checks would be performed, to enable specialist engineering tests to be performed. Unfortunately the counter could only take on 256 values since it was represented by a single byte within the machine – so that whenever the counter reached the value 255 and then increased by one it returned to zero – and thus on every 256th treatment no safety checks were performed.

- Hardware safety interlocks present in earlier versions of the Therac machine had been removed during the design of the new machine because they were supposed to be done in software. The machine was made to rely entirely on software for safety.

However the failure was not simply a matter of software. The engineer who had developed the software was an electronic engineer, very experienced in designing radiation treatment machines but completely untrained in software engineering. When the first few incidents were reported the manufacturers denied that they could be caused by failure of the machine.

In their report of the investigation, Leveson and Turner reflected on the lessons that should be learned:

Most previous accounts of the Therac-25 accidents blamed them on a software error and stopped there. This is not very useful, and, in fact, can be misleading and dangerous: If we are to prevent such accidents in the future, we must dig deeper. Most accidents involving complex technology are caused by a combination of organisational, managerial, technical, and, sometimes, sociological or political factors. Preventing accidents requires paying attention to all the root causes, not just the precipitating event in a particular circumstance.

Accidents are unlikely to occur in exactly the same way again. If we patch only the symptoms and ignore the deeper underlying causes or we fix only the specific cause of one accident, we are unlikely to prevent or mitigate future accidents. The series of accidents involving the Therac-25 is a good example of exactly this problem: Fixing each individual software flaw as it was found did not solve the device's safety problems. Virtually all complex software will behave in an unexpected or undesired fashion under some conditions – there will always be another bug. Instead, accidents must be understood with respect to the complex factors involved. In addition, changes need to be made to eliminate or reduce the underlying causes and contributing factors that increase the likelihood of accidents or loss resulting from them.

Although these accidents occurred in software controlling medical devices, the lessons apply to all types of systems where computers control dangerous devices. In our experience, the same types of mistakes are being made in non-medical systems. We must learn from our mistakes so we do not repeat them. (p. 41)

1.2 The ubiquity of software

Software and computers are all around us. This ubiquity of software, and information carried by software, is a relatively new phenomenon. It was not always like that: until the 1990s software was something exceptional. Have a look at Case Study 1.2[9] about payroll systems to see how these developed and are now viewed as unproblematic and the only way to do things, while historically it was 'simply' the automation of highly routine clerical processes.

Case Study 1.2 *Payroll calculations*

Fifty years ago, up until the 1950s, the wages and salaries paid to people in factories and offices was calculated manually by clerks, who consulted records of attendance and rates of pay, carrying out simple calculations, deducting fixed payments like insurance and tax, to arrive at the sum of money due to each worker. Money was counted out into envelopes that were then distributed at the end of each week or month to the workers concerned.

Some companies might even then have partially automated this process, using punched card machines like those from Hollerith and IBM (International Business Machines) in the US, or ICT (International Computers and Tabulators) in the UK.

Then during the 1950s computers, great big machines filling large rooms, using thermionic valves, paper tape or punched cards, and magnetic tape for storage of data, were adapted from scientific computers to serve the needs of peace and business. A pioneer here was the Lyons Electronic Office, who built the LEO computers to serve the needs of a chain of food shops and restaurants.[10] While the LEO interest was to control food stocks and orders, of course the LEO computers were also applied to calculating employees' pay. Soon most large companies were using computers to support their businesses to 'automate' such mundane tasks as payroll and invoicing.

While one company's payroll is much like another, there are differences, but differences that can be served by simple adaptations of other payroll programs. Companies, such as Peterborough Software founded in 1963, arose to specialise in payroll, able to supply the software to carry out this important function, adapted to the needs of the particular customer. Obtaining your software from an external supplier like Peterborough Software, rather than building it yourself, has the advantages that the experts will have thought of almost all contingencies, and organised the software to make changes in taxation and similar easy to implement. Peterborough Software is estimated today to handle the payroll of 25 per cent of the UK's working population.

Soon every company of any size was using computer software to work out their payroll payments. If they did not own a computer themselves, they used the services of a computer bureau that handled the payroll data on their behalf, or used spare computer time at a neighbouring company that did own a computer. The bureau customised the software to their needs, ran it using their data, and delivered the results to them.

Instead of money being counted out into envelopes, payment was soon being made directly into employees' bank accounts, using the data communications networks that arose in the early 1960s, and transferring money digitally using systems like BACS.

The payroll clerk in major Western companies disappeared, automated out of existence by a machine that could do the equivalent work faster, cheaper, and more reliably. But this was hardly a social revolution, just a small increment of the Industrial Revolution that had started a hundred years earlier. When you work in a company and get paid, you are hardly aware that behind the scenes a computer is dispensing your pay. It might as well be payroll clerks dispensing your pay for all the difference it makes to you. Indeed, in some small companies and in some developing economies it may well still be.

For contrast look at Case Study 1.3 about distance education, based upon the authors' experiences at the Open University – here we see a very rich and complex situation where the Internet has changed the nature of the way the **organisation**[11] continues to do its business and educate at a distance.

Case Study 1.3 *Distance education*

Universal education in Europe and the US was gradually introduced during the late 1800s, in part to provide labour for the Industrial Revolution and commercial and state bureaucracies. As the demand for education beyond the compulsory period at school arose, people began to study further, doing this full time, or part time at night or weekends. Not everybody could attend classes at local institutions, and correspondence courses arose, teaching vocational skills like book-keeping or journalism.

With the growth in university level education in the UK in the 1960s, the UK government founded the Open University in 1969,[12] to offer university education to anybody who had missed out. The model of provision they adopted was the well-developed correspondence education, but with some enhancements involving:

- very high quality learning materials with high publishing values and content written by a team of leading academics, using a course-writing process that comprehensively reviewed and tested the learning material-

ials to remove many of the barriers to learning before the course began;

- support from a tutor for the student during study, to focus on the student's own particular learning problems, giving students more personal support than had been possible in conventional face-to-face institutions.

Materials were sent to the student through the post, and learning support by a tutor was provided by a mixture of the post, telephone, and face-to-face meetings. Many courses also used broadcast television, though because courses at that time (in the 1970s) could not rely on students having television, the transmitted material was never a mandatory part of the course.

Email and the Internet began to be used in trials in the early 1990s, and ten years later most courses used the Internet in some form, with a web presence and digital communication between student and tutor. The introduction of digital communication was not just the use of postal services by other means; the whole character of distance education was – and is –

▶

changing. The Internet can reach places where conventional postal services cannot, into communities where rapid political and social change has led to a breakdown in the infrastructure, into communities where poverty had meant the absence of all infrastructure until wireless telecommunications arrived. It also enables the adoption of discussion and argument methods of education not previously possible at a distance, through online chats and conferences, by email or web pages or using special software.

Underpinning all this use of the Internet is software, and here any distance-education provider faces a dilemma. The operations of the university become critically dependent on communications and other software. The Internet and bulk standard browsers and emailers can be relied upon to work correctly, with all the software required being available on the student's computers as standard. But what about more specialist software, like conferencing or meeting software? This will need to be sent to the student for installation on their own computer, but as a distance provider the university has no control over what computer their customers, the students, use. Of course some constraint, like the use of a Wintel[13] platform, is possible, but even this would leave a challengingly large variety of systems to be coped with, made worse by the planned obsolescence policies of the suppliers with new systems every few years. Besides, Unix-based systems like Linux and Macintosh are making substantial inroads upon Microsoft's markets, and cannot be ignored. Any software provided must run on all these platforms, and given the variety of these, this may be very difficult to achieve. Does the university take a commercial product, or does it build its own? In normal software sales, the provider of major software products like data management systems would expect the customer to buy the right computer, or for commodity software the supplier might expect to lose up to 20 per cent of sales though failure of the customer computer to execute the software. But can an educator afford to dictate extra costs for its students, or lose 20 per cent of enrolments, particularly if part of its mission is to be inclusive? The pressure to develop their own software, with the requirement for it to execute on all computer platforms, may be irresistible. But this may also be impossible.

> **Software began as the automation of clerical functions justified by the saving of labour costs and the increased accuracy and reliability of the results.**

In both case studies, the organisations involved face finely balanced decisions about selection of software and whether to build or buy or hire; this is something we will return to in later chapters.

> **Software offers new opportunities for enterprises to deliver their services and products more effectively and more efficiently.**

Activity 1.1	*The information society*

In the above two case studies we focused on the contrasts between them: payroll programs were seen historically as the automation of clerical functions made in the interests of speed, accuracy, and cost savings; by contrast communications technologies and associated software have changed the way distance education is conducted.

What about automatic teller machines (ATMs) and Internet banking – how do these fit in? And what about Internet insurance, is that different again? Think about other computing systems that you have come across in your daily life, whether at work or at leisure. Can you imagine life without them now?

Discussion

We cannot comment on systems you might have met in your own life, but let's discuss those other examples.

Automatic teller machines crept into our lives in the 1990s as 'holes in the wall', a convenient way of withdrawing money outside normal banking hours. Getting to the bank had always been a problem for those in 9–5 work, so these were a great help. Thus from our perspective as customers of banks they had significantly enhanced the service that banks delivered to us. Maybe that was also the perspective of banks, though our own impression has also been that the banks gained important cost savings by reducing the staffing costs of bank tellers – the phrase 'automatic teller' is significant. From the bank's perspective, ATMs have simply been the continuation of traditional practices by other means, as was seen in Case Study 1.1 on payroll software.

A far more significant development for the information society has been the reduction in the dependency upon cash. ATMs perpetuate the use of cash, but the coming of credit cards and inter-bank transfers of money has had the opposite effect – so much so that in the US offering payment in cash seems now to be treated with suspicion. Internet banking facilitates the cashless society. Cash has become information, and life has become different.

As an aside it is interesting to look at the use of ATMs in non-European cultures. In Japan ATMs are able to accept cash as well as dispense cash – Japanese shoppers use cash, but like to return any surplus cash to the bank after their shopping trip. In India people share banking cards and openly help each other use ATMs.

So the use of ATMs and other banking systems have a much larger impact on society at large than just those perceived by the banks, just as the use of communications in the distance education Case Study 1.2 has changed the nature of the service provided.

1.3 A changing world

It has become an everyday observation that we live in a rapidly changing world, and that this is a new phenomenon. This observation was a founding claim in Alvin Toffler's seminal book *Future Shock*[14] – the future is coming at us so fast that we don't have time to adjust, just as when travelling and settling down in some new location we might suffer from 'culture shock'.

If we look at the companies and institutions around us, we will find many organisations that appear to have been in existence for a long time. But we will also see many newer organisations that come and go, as if in the 'old days' they made institutions to last, but today that is not so. However this is an illusion, for we just cannot see all those that have disappeared. In 1983 the Royal Dutch Shell company estimated that the average life of the largest industrial organisations was just forty years.[15] Case Study 1.4 illustrates this from the insurance industry.[16] Today we accept that change has become a way of life. It is no longer possible for an organisation to establish a way of doing business, and then to continue conducting its business in this way in perpetuity. Influences from outside will make it critically important to change, and keep on changing. Adapt, or die.

Case Study 1.4   *The evolving insurance industry*

Insurance in the UK began in the sixteenth century and developed significantly following the
Great Fire of London in 1666. By the end of the nineteenth century many great insurance

▶

companies had been created, and we will look at the evolution of one of these, Royal Insurance in Liverpool, from its origin through mergers to the present day.

On 11 March 1845 a group of prominent Liverpool merchants and businessmen formed a company – 'a Joint Stock Fire and Life Insurance Association' – called Royal. Nine days later they placed an advertisement in *Gore's Advertiser* inviting all those wanting to subscribe for shares in the company to apply in writing to the company's solicitor. The offer was heavily oversubscribed. The sponsors of the company met first at the office of Josias Booker at 46 Castle Street and then at the offices of the solicitor, Thomas Lee, in Cook Street to allot shares and elect a chairman. The chairman elected was Josias Booker himself, who had been a cotton planter in Demerara and whose company, Booker Bros, was one of the leading trading companies in Liverpool. His fellow directors were all men prominent in business circles in Liverpool.

Within a few days a subcommittee of the sponsors met to appoint a bank, find office premises, and make enquiries about an actuary and general manager. The Royal's first bank was the Bank of Liverpool, one of the newly established joint stock banks. It was later to take over Heywood's and other private banks and amalgamate with Martins Bank. Martins was still the Royal's principal bank when it was absorbed by Barclays in the 1960s. The close-knit nature of Liverpool's top businessmen lasted until the 1960s and partly because of this the Royal made strong overtures to Martins Bank in the 1960s. It is believed that the Bank of England indicated it would not view with favour any merger between a bank and an insurance company.

Since then, and particularly since 1990, a series of factors have led to increased competition and changes in the wider European insurance market. The main stimuli for change have been technological advances and the removal of European trade barriers as a result of the Single European Market. The European Commission legislation contains significant provision for the development of the European banking and financial services industry, with greater international competition and the insurers' traditional customer base eroded by banks and building societies offering insurance. Advances in computing and communications have enabled new ways of selling insurance business – for example Direct Line, which began by selling car insurance by telephone in 1985 and now sells a broad range of products and services internationally over the phone and online.

One response to these pressures is for insurance companies to merge and thereby reduce costs as a whole, with valuable resources directed at developing new markets rather than fending off competition.

Within the UK the first of these large mergers was between Royal Insurance and Sun Alliance in 1996. This was a significant landmark in the UK insurance industry because, despite the fact that there had been plenty of mergers in the past, this merger was the first to place a UK insurer on a similar size and scale as its European counterparts. Furthermore, it looked likely that there would be several more large scale mergers or takeovers within the next five to ten years.

Two of Royal and Sun Alliance's leading competitors planned to merge in a £14.1 billion deal. General Accident and Commercial Union would, once combined, make one of Europe's biggest insurance and asset management groups. It was expected that 5,000 jobs would be lost over two years out of a workforce of 53,000. Sixty per cent of these losses would be in the UK. Considerable savings would come from a switch to common information technology systems.

When Royal Insurance and Sun Alliance merged in 1996, Royal had already decided to adopt the financial management part of the enterprise resource planning (ERP) system by business software company SAP. Royal had had a single financial system underlying all their operations, partly a bought-in general ledger system and partly software built in house. Sun Alliance had been updating their financial systems too, but with a rival ERP system from PeopleSoft. A major challenge for the merger was the integration of these very different information systems, leading eventually to the choice of just one ERP supplier.

One aspect of recent change has been the globalisation of the world economy and the demands this makes upon the application and development of software. While economic activity has always been global in the sense that international trade has taken place by moving physical goods around the world, exploiting an international division of labour, the coming of the Internet has changed the nature of this globalisation. Production facilities can respond to changing demands in markets at the opposite end of the world, with those changes in demand being communicated through the Internet. A company can sell its products globally, retaining its product data and sales data captured online through the Internet and then placed in databases which themselves could also be made available globally. In communicating around the world, the language used for communication has become an issue, and the localisation of software to work in languages other than English has become important. We can even move software services around the world, locating these services where the labour is of high quality and relatively cheap, like India.

> Change is always with us, but has become more frequent and pervasive with the advance of technology and the globalisation that accompanies it.

1.4 Rationality and its limitations

The economic figures that form the basis for the concerns of Landauer, Castells, and Strassman cited earlier are averages, but in managing software in our organisations we might reasonably expect to do better than average. We might also reasonably expect to avoid the disasters that have arisen from earlier software failures. Over the decades many prescriptions have been advocated. In the 1980s safety problems were to be overcome by the application of mathematics, and each decade has seen a new wave of software development methodologies: 'structured', 'clean room', 'object oriented', and most recently 'Agile'. Landauer's own prescription is to focus on usability: he gives many examples of failures of usability before proposing:

> What we need now are techniques for managers and other innovators to apply to the design and deployment of computer applications that will ensure that they [computers] fulfil their promise. They are available. I've called them user-centred methods. (p. 193)

The aspiration was that through the power of reason, applying a scientific approach, the various difficulties would be removed, and software that was error-free and suitable for its intended purpose would be produced as a matter of routine. The alternative to focusing on usability as Landauer and others did, was to focus on the use of scientific and engineering methods, as illustrated in Case Study 1.5.

Case Study 1.5 *Modernism in computing: Mathematical approaches to Program Construction*

Computing as a diverse and rich field emerged from many disciplines, including mathematics and logic, electrical and electronic engineering, psychology, and linguistics. However, mathematical logic has played the predominant role since the beginning in formally specifying computing languages, designing compilers, and so on, viewing programming as a branch of mathematics.

One of the most influential groups during the late 1960s and early 1970s was the IFIP Working

▶

Group 2.3 on Programming Methodology. This group persists today, with its current aim 'to increase programmer's ability to compose programs'. The current scope of this group, quoted from its website, is (note that they start counting from 0):

0 Identification of sources of difficulties encountered in present day programming;
1 the interdependence between the formulation of problems and the formulation of programs, and the mapping of relations existing in the world of problems into the relations among programs and their components;
2 intellectual disciplines and problem-solving techniques that can aid programmers in the composition of programs;
3 the problem of achieving program reliability;
4 the consequences of requirements for program adaptability;
5 the problem of provability of program correctness and its influence on the structure of programs and on the process of their composition;
6 guidelines of partitioning large programming tasks and defining the interfaces between the parts;
7 software for mechanized assistance to program composition.
(See http://research.microsoft.com/~leino/ifip-wg2.3/.)

The mathematical logic influence can be seen in some of the scope items (emphasis on intellectual discipline, program correctness, etc.). The members past and present contain most of the leaders of mathematical approaches to computing, and we quote below excerpts from two of these distinguished members.

Tony Hoare, who has been honoured in many ways, including a UK knighthood for Services to Computing Science in 2000, wrote a paper in 1984 titled Programming: Sorcery or Science? (*IEEE Software*, April, pp. 5–16) in which he stated that software development would use mathematics to produce

a complete, unambiguous, and provably consistent specification for the entire end product (p. 8).

and mathematical proof that if each of the components meets its specification, then when all the components are assembled, the overall product will meet the overall specification agreed to by the client (p. 9).

so that

we hope to eliminate the so-called system integration phase of many current projects, in which bugs are painfully detected and laboriously removed from the interfaces between the components (p. 10).

Summarising, Hoare stated:

I believe that in our branch of engineering, above all others, the academic ideals of rigor and elegance will pay the highest dividends in practical terms of reducing costs, increasing performance, and in directing the great sources of computational power on the surface of a silicon chip to the use and convenience of man.

In 1989 another IFIP WG 2.3 member, Manny Lehman, wrote an article stating that:[17]

Recognition of the need to define and follow a disciplined process is perhaps the most important advance in system development of recent years. To achieve it one first needs to develop a process model . . . to define a systematic and coherent path from formulation of an application concept via realisation of a usable system to its subsequent evolution. . . . The introduction of defined and disciplined methods permits the application of computer-based development tools. These provide mechanised support for individual activities and their systematic control. If appropriately conceived, the totality of methods and tools provides support for all aspects and stages of system evolution. This is why techniques and tools to facilitate and control planning and management of a group and its activities, the project, must be included when planning and implementing integrated lifetime development support.

Such strong belief in the power of rational thought and science and progress, seen in Case Study 1.5, is historically not new, and can be reasonably interpreted[18] as forming part of what philosophers call the **enlightenment project**, dating back to the seventeenth century and the pioneering work of great scientists like Newton, Leibnitz, Gauss, Galileo, and Pascal. The following quotation from 1632 by Galileo[19] will suffice to represent the thinking of that age:

> If what we are discussing were a point of law or of the humanities, in which neither true nor false exists, one might trust in subtlety of mind and readiness of tongue and in the greater experience of the writers, and expect him who excelled in those things to make his reasoning most plausible, and one might judge it to be the best. But in the natural sciences, whose conclusions are true and necessary and have nothing to do with human will, one must take care not to place oneself in the defence of error...

Some of the ideas of the enlightenment project persist today as **modernism**, perhaps most visible to all of us in architecture and the built environment described in Case Study 1.6. We are all familiar with glass-encased skyscrapers with gleaming metal adornments, and with systematically laid out cities of rectangular blocks with housing segregated from shopping malls segregated from office zones and light industry. That is modernism made visible. However this link to architecture is more important than this – architecture is often used as a metaphor for software design, and we will return to analogies between software and architecture at various points within this book. In particular we will see the importance of matching a software solution to the needs and requirements of all its stakeholders, so manifestly absent in some of the building projects described in Case Study 1.6.

Case Study 1.6 *From modernism to postmodernism in architecture*

Charles Jencks has written a number of accounts of the development of modern architecture and its successors.[20] The architecture that we would now characterise as 'modern' arose in the early part of the twentieth century along with the modern design schools like the Bauhaus founded in 1919 by the architect Walter Gropius. Buildings drew upon new materials, eschewing decoration for simple lines. While many monumental buildings were produced, and whole cities were planned, modern architects also turned to mass housing in response to the housing crises following the First and the Second World Wars. A renowned leader in this was Charles Édouard Jeanneret-Gris, commonly known as 'Le Corbusier', whose 1947 development in Marseille, France, for 1,600 people is shown in Figure 1.2. Le Corbusier described such housing as 'machines for living in'.

However, such high-rise mass housing proved less popular with their residents than with their architects, and housing estates decayed and in the end had to be torn down. One such demolition in 1972 became symbolic of this 'end of high rise housing' and marked for Charles Jencks the onset of the postmodern era – 15 July 1972 at 3.32 p.m., when the Pruitt-Igoe Housing in St. Louis, Missouri, US, designed by Minoru Yamasaki, was dynamited. See Figure 1.3.

How did architects respond to this apparent crisis? Well, some architects, like Richard Rogers and Norman Foster, continued as 'late-modern' high-tech architects; Figure 1.4 shows the Lloyd's building in London, designed by Rogers in 1979. Other architects turned to classical themes and coded these into modern buildings, such as Philip Johnson's Sony building (formerly the AT&T building) in New York (see Figure 1.5), which has a capital (the top) inspired by a

▶

Figure 1.2

Modern housing by
Le Corbusier : Unité
d'Habitation in
Marseilles of 1947–
52.

Copyright Donald Corner and Jenny Young GreatBuildings.com.

Figure 1.3

The end of
modernism ? Pruett-
Igoe in 1972.

Image is taken from a report Creating Defensible Space, originally published by the U.S. Department of
Housing and Urban Development, Office of Policy Development and Research, and is reproduced here
with the Department's Permission. Defensible Spaces, www.defensiblespace.com/book.htm.

Figure 1.4

Richard Rogers'
Lloyd's building in
London – modernism
continues.

Copyright Howard Davis/GreatBuildings.com.

Figure 1.5

Philip Johnson's Sony
building (formerly
AT&T building) –
doubly-coded post-
modernism

Aerial photograph copyright Stephen Amiaga, http://www.amiaga.com.

Chippendale tallboy and a Rolls-Royce radiator, a shaft based on classical Louis Sullivan skyscrapers, and a base (not visible) based on Brunellechi's Pazzi Chapel in Florence, Italy.[21] A critic, David Harvey, has quipped that the house is no longer a machine for living in but an antique for living in. In postmodern architecture, science and technology find their place in embedded features of the building, such as in sophisticated elevator controls, ventilation, new materials and other high-tech features. A central element in architectural postmodernism is that science and technology is used to *serve* human needs and requirements (and not determine or simplify them, as in architectural modernism).

The other response to this crisis in modern architecture has been **community architecture**, designing in consultation with the people who will inhabit the buildings. When the Byker slums in Newcastle, England, were cleared and their replacement designed in 1968, Ralph Erskine set up an office on site for people to drop in and discuss the planned replacement. While the site was cleared and the replacement built (the so-called Byker Wall shown in Figure 1.6), the community was kept intact in temporary accommodation.

Figure 1.6

The Byker Wall: post-modern community architecture

Source: Part of the Byker Wall, Newcastle-upon-Tyne, copyright Leslie Garland/theimagefile, www.theimagefile.com

One aspect of the scientific method requires the decomposition of some phenomenon into its constituent parts, with this decomposition continuing until the parts can be well understood, and when recomposed the whole can similarly be understood. The process is known as **reductionism**, and is a cornerstone of modern science along with experimental methods supported by statistical analysis.

A great deal has been achieved by science and modernism, and our lives are all the better for their achievements in transport, medicine, and computers. And yet there have been problems.

Many architectural projects, particularly in mass housing characterised by Le Corbusier's 'machines for living in', have failed, as we saw in Case Study 1.5. People just did not like living in machines, and housing estate after housing estate has been demolished, to be replaced by community projects in which the inhabitants play an active part in determining the architectural outcomes.

Even science has had to recognise its own limits in admitting dual descriptions of light, in accepting fundamental limits to scientific measurement in Heisenberg's **uncertainty principle**, and in the need to think of the whole with hypotheses like Lovelock's **Gaia**. We talk of the **emergent properties** or **emergent behaviour** of large and complex systems, properties and behaviour which we did not predict, and maybe could not have predicted, from our knowledge of the parts and how they were composed.

There have been many responses to the limits of the enlightenment project and the methods of modernism. Postmodernism – as described in Case Study 1.6 is a controversial set of philosophical views but is often associated with two important forms of reality – an objective reality that exists independently of ourselves and a subjective reality and social reality that is constructed by us as we make sense of the world. The advocates of "**constructionism**" such as Latour and Woolgar in their Laboratory Life[22] argue that even objective scientific reality is in some measure socially constructed. However, other people strongly disagree.

In computing there has been a gradual awareness that approaches rooted in modernism are problematic. In 1986 Terry Winograd and Ivan Flores[23] turned to hermeneutic philosophy and Heidegger to understand problems of the relationship between people and computers, but this book was peripheral to the main thrust of computing research, and it took a paper in the leading academic computing journal, the *Communications of the ACM*, to signal the change. In his paper James Fetzer[24] concluded:

> As Einstein remarked, insofar as the laws of mathematics refer to reality, they are not certain; and insofar as they are certain, they do not refer to reality. (p. 1060)
> The operational performance of these complex systems should never be taken for granted and cannot be guaranteed. (p. 1062)

At the time there were rumours of attempts to suppress this paper by leading academics, and was a vigorous published debate afterwards. That the rationalist agenda pursued for so many years was limited was hard to accept.

As this book progresses, we will see other examples of software projects that have failed, and we will see that the responses within computing to this crisis of modernity has parallels close to the responses within architecture described in Case Study 1.6. Continued work on formal mathematical methods parallels late modern high-tech architecture, participative software development parallels community architecture, while agile methods possibly parallel multiple coding.

Rational and scientific approaches to developing software have their limits, limits often characterised under the postmodern banner that are matched in other areas of human activity.

1.5 How this book will address this issue

We see then that the world in which computers and software work is uncertain, constantly changing, and not necessarily amenable to rational and scientific processes. Yet software is pedantic and precise, founded on certainty. We want to use software to help us control our organisation in this uncertain world, using management instruments that themselves are also dependent upon certainty and predictability. How can we do that? That is what this book is all about.

We will build up concepts to help you manage the software of your enterprise in three stages.

In Part I, Chapters 2 to 5, we look at the social and organisational context within which software is developed and deployed, including sufficient aspects of economics, sociology, organisational theory, and law to be able to understand software and its use. While many of the things that happen using software will seem strange and different, they mostly are instances of much more general social and economic phenomena. We look at the relationship between an enterprise and its software and how this relates to institutional learning; we look at individual motivation and development and relate this to institutional change and learning and the wider economic processes that shape those changes. We look at regulation, from the ethics and professional societies through standards to the law.

In Part II, we focus on software and the processes involved in acquiring and evolving software. This can involve the purchase of commercial packages, use of free and open source software, use of software as a service via the Internet, and the bespoke development of software. We look in detail at the activities involved in developing software or customising and integrating software, and the variety of processes that can be used to overcome or at least live with the difficulties inherent in the environment described in Part I. We continue the thread started in Part I, discussing intellectual property from its economic role and the alternatives of private property versus public goods, through to its protection in law and the exploitation of those laws, to the free and open source software movement.

In Part III we then pick up the management processes needed for acquiring and evolving software as described in Part II: the use of projects as a management practice involving estimation, planning, and control; human resource development; managing and controlling changes; assuring quality following standards like **CMMi** (Capability Maturity Model integrated); and controlling risk and uncertainty. We control the processes discussed in Part II that control the external environment which would otherwise destroy us.

The Conclusion, Chapter 14, sums up the whole book.

> How can we as managers assure the economic and operational success of the software we deploy?

> By understanding the potential negative impacts of the environment upon us we can design processes for acquiring and using software that overcome the limits of rationality and the forces of change.

Summing up

In this chapter we have established the critical need that this book addresses:

- How can we as managers assure the economic and operational success of the software we deploy?

We arrived at this characterisation of this need by looking at a number of case studies and reports about software and the economy. We saw that:

- Software has not returned the benefits to the economy that we anticipated, and indeed if anything the large expenditure on software and computers has led to a decrease in national productivity. Worse still, software can fail in service, often with disastrous and very costly results, yet software is all around us.

- While software began as the automation of clerical functions justified by the saving in labour costs and the increased accuracy and reliability of the results, it also offers new opportunities for enterprises to deliver their services and products more effectively and more efficiently, and even create new products and services. We can do things now with computers and software that we could not do before.

- Stability cannot be relied upon; change is always with us, but has become more frequent and pervasive with the advance of technology and the globalisation that accompanies it. This needs to be managed.

- Rational and scientific approaches to developing software have their limits, limits often characterised under the postmodern banner that are matched in other areas of human activity. New approaches to developing software need to be explored.

This left us in the paradoxical situation of wanting to use rational, precise, and certain software applications and management methods to control and guide an organisation operating in an uncertain and unpredictable and changing world. This book aims to help you do this:

- By understanding the difficulties that the environment can impose upon us, we can take measures to overcome those difficulties and retain control of our organisation and its software.

Exercises

1. Find out what you can about the World Summit on the Information Society (WSIS) and the why people believe that developing countries should invest in information technology. How will they benefit? If you can, find case studies of actual benefit achieved on particular projects. Would you advise a developing country to spend money on IT?

2. Investigate examples of software failure, either using one or more of the books we have cited here, or by searching on the Internet, and see if you can discern any trends. Is the failure rate getting better or worse? Is any class of system more prone to failure than others – perhaps government projects, or safety-related systems, or systems where there is a large degree of innovation? Explain any trends you discover.

3. Read the paper by Fetzer cited in the text and the follow-up discussion edited by Brian Randell and published in the *British Computer Journal*. You may also find other discussions of this paper. What conclusions do you draw about this controversy? How can the various points of view be reconciled?

Endnotes

1. Thomas K. Landauer (1995) *The Trouble with Computers: Usefulness, Usability, and Productivity*. MIT Press.
2. We will use the term 'system' for any configuration of business procedures, hardware, software, and other equipment that serves some combined purpose. Where more particular characterisations are intended this will be made clear, for example 'software systems' to indicate a focus on software.

3. Paul A. Strassman (1985) *Information Payoff: The Transformation of Work in the Electronic Age.* Free Press.

4. Manuel Castells (1996) *The Rise of the Network Society.* Blackwell.

5. R.H. Franke (1987) 'Technological Revolution and Productivity Decline: Computer Introduction in the Financial Industry', *Technological Forecasting and Social Change*, 31 , 143–154.

6. Stephen Flowers (1996) *Software Failure: Management Failure.* Wiley.

7. Peter Neumann (1995) *Computer-Related Risks.* Addison-Wesley.

8. N. Leveson and C. Turner (1993) 'An Investigation of the Therac-25 Accidents', *IEEE Computer*, July, 18–41.

9. In this very brief case we have taken a user's view of software. For the software industry's view look at the comprehensive book by Martin Campbell-Kelly: *From Airline Reservations to Sonic the Hedgehog: A History of the Software Industry.* MIT Press.

10. See the book by David Caminer, John Aris, Peter Hermon, and Frank Land (1998) *L.E.O.: Incredible Story of the World's First Business Computer.* McGraw-Hill Education.

11. We will use the term 'organisation' for any group of people and their associated systems that have some permanence and share a collective purpose. Examples are administrative institutions and commercial companies, but also parts of these where this is appropriate. Organisations are distinct from teams, which may have a relatively short life.

12. See Ian Mugridge (2003) *The Open University after Thirty Years.* Routledge.

13. 'Wintel' is the conjunction of Microsoft Windows software and Intel computer hardware, and arose as a widely used acronym following an agreement between these two major corporations to collaborate such that Intel chips contained special features to support Windows software.

14. Alvin Toffler (1984) *Future Shock.* Bantam Doubleday Dell.

15. Arie de Geus (1988) 'Planning as Learning', *Harvard Business Review*, March–April, 70–74.

16. This account is based on a privately circulated paper by Matthew Hinton, Overview of Insurance and the Insurance Industry, written for the EPSRC funded EMTECH project, grant GR/L42353/01.

17. M.M. Lehman (1989) 'Uncertainty in Computer Applications and its Control Through the Engineering of Software', *Software Maintenance: Research and Practice*, 1, 3–27.

18. H. Robinson, P. Hall, F. Hovenden, and J. Rachel (1998) 'Postmodern Software Development', *The Computer Journal*, 41, 6, 363–375.

19. G. Galileo (1632) *Dialogue Concerning the Two Chief World Systems – Ptolemaic and Copernican.* University of California Press, 1967.

20. For example, Charles Jencks (1993) *Architecture Today.* Academy Editions London , 1988 and 1993.

21. From Jencks *Architecture Today*, p. 126.

22. B. Latour and S. Woolgar (1986) *Laboratory Life: The Construction of Scientific Facts.* (2nd edn). Princeton University Press.

23. Terry Winograd and Ivan Flores (1986) *Understanding Computers and Cognition: A New Foundation for Design.* Addison-Wesley.

24. J.H. Fetzer (1988) 'Program Verification: the Very Idea', *Communications of the ACM.* 31, 9, 1048–1063.

The social and organisational context

2 Organisation and business context

3 Economic and social context

4 Ethics, codes, and standards

5 Software and the law

Where does software fit in ?

Software does not happen in isolation; it is produced for social and economic reasons. To understand software we must understand these reasons. Part I of this book looks at the social and organisational context within which software is developed and deployed, including sufficient aspects of economics, sociology, organisational theory, and law to be able to understand where software fits into society and what the societal constraints on software development are. Part I consists of four chapters, Chapters 2 to 5.

Chapter 2, Organisation and business context, relates software to the organisation that it supports, drawing on basic ideas from organisational theory and management. We see how organisational practices become embodied in IT systems, and how practices that had previously been part of people's tacit expertise become externalised and codified in procedures and software. The software and its relationship to the organisation are constantly changing as part of a process of organisational learning.

Chapter 3, Economic and social context, looks at the critical human element of organisations, what motivates people, and how this motivation varies across cultures. We will see that the financial motive is not important for people, particularly software people, providing remuneration is sufficient; what they need is intellectual growth. This contrasts significantly with organisational motivation, which aims at profit-making through the exploitation of property rights. But property need not be private, and the highly successful open source movement has thrived on making software into public goods.

Chapter 4, Ethics, codes, and standards, relates business practices and personal behaviour to ethics and voluntary codes. These ethical codes are established by professional societies, modern day successors of medieval guilds and caste systems. Or these codes can be standards promulgated nationally and internationally that are important for the success of the technology – compliance with these is voluntary but non-compliance may be self-defeating.

Chapter 5, Software and the law, looks at regulation of software and its use by the law, where moral argument and codes of conduct are not sufficient to curb the misuse of software. We look at those parts of the law that are important for software, particularly intellectual property, but also at contracts, privacy, and misuse.

2 Organisation and business context

What we will study in this chapter

To understand software we need to understand how organisations that use and produce software work, drawing on basic ideas from organisational theory and management, and from economics. Organisational practices and knowledge become embodied in IT systems, and practices and knowledge that had previously been part of people's tacit expertise become externalised and codified in procedures and software.

This chapter looks at:

- how organisations and the work they do can be modelled by diagrams and measurements;

- the limitations of diagrams and measurements, which cannot be taken to fully represent what happens in the organisation;

- the modelling of work as business processes, as a sequence of interacting activities;

- the specialisation of these activities to enhance efficiency by Taylorist (or taylorist) 'scientific management' methods that lack flexibility and humanity;

- the embedding of software in organisations and artefacts so that it is inseparable from them, and all must be developed and evolved together;

- the paradoxical need to treat the software separately from other resources used in the business process in order to acquire software and later evolve it;

- how systems embody some of the knowledge of the organisation, but cannot embody all of that knowledge, some of which must remain tacit within the people involved;

- how new systems are introduced and existing systems are changed because of problems internal to the organisation, external business opportunities, or external demands;

- the role of rational decision-making processes and return on investment calculations to help justify a proposed acquisition or change;

- the process of introducing new systems as adaptation or learning;

- how cycles of organisational learning take place when business processes are changed, knowledge is externalised, examined, restructured, consolidated, and then re-internalised;

- the critical role of people in the organisation as part of the assets of the organisation, its human capital.

2.1 Modelling organisations

We are going to introduce some very basic ideas, but will take a slightly different perspective on these basic ideas than you may be used to, so please do read this chapter. We are going to dig behind established practices and make connections that are not usually made.

If we are going to be able to understand and reason about **systems** and the way they fit into **organisations** we need to be able to model the organisation and its work.[1] We will do this using diagrams, as is commonly done for business and software – we will discuss the strengths and limitations of this later. We will use the simple **process models** and **data models** that emerged in the 1970s using the diagramming styles of Tom DeMarco and Charlie Bachmann – please refer to Appendix A for details if you are not familiar with these. These are well established and widely used, and we have chosen them for their simplicity, avoiding the complexities of more recent notations like **UML** (**Unified Modelling Language**) that obscure understanding.

Figure 2.1a gives a simple view of the world divided into two parts:[2] the organisation undertaking activities and the environment with which it is interacting. This gives equal weight to both environment and organisation, though it is more common to draw these diagrams focusing on the organisation as in Figure 2.1b, overlooking what is happening outside.

The organisation can interact with its environment either **proactively** or **reactively**. If the interaction is proactive, the organisation takes the initiative and communicates with the environment to serve the needs of its activities. If the interaction is reactive, the organisation does nothing until some stimulus from the environment demands that the organisation undertakes some activity. Of course activities are normally a composite of both of these – initially the organisation may be reactive and then, while responding to a stimulus, change to proactive behaviour. For example, a request for some service arrives unsolicited, but thereafter the service organisation takes the initiative, creates an internal project to handle the service request, and proactively supplies the service asking for further information from the requester as required.

For both reactive and proactive interactions we can build process models to describe what is happening. In many cases, once the organisation has agreed to provide some service, the work of providing the service may well be viewed as a **project** with a defined outcome and possibly defined timescale and cost. We will look at projects in much greater detail in later chapters, since these are a common organisational device used for acquiring, producing, and evolving software.

Implicit within our understanding of what an organisation is and does, is some idea of the organisation having a purpose which it fulfils to a greater or lesser

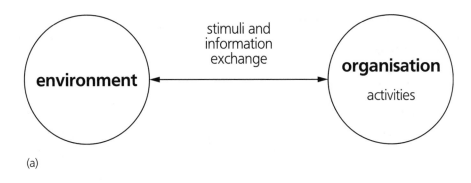

(a)

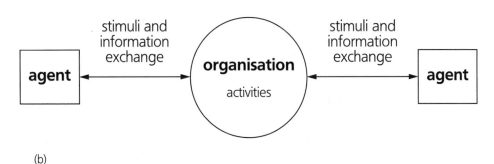

(b)

Figure 2.1

An organisation undertaking activities in interaction with its environment. (a) The organisation and environment viewed as equal partners; (b) The more conventional way of drawing these diagrams as *context diagrams*, in which the environment consists of a number of agents* interacting with the organisation. *These agents could be people, machines, or other organisations, drawn as boxes if we are not interested in their internal workings, or as circles if we are.

extent. This purpose may be implicitly understood by everybody and not be questioned, or it may be made explicit as a **vision statement** or **mission statement**. We can talk about the **performance** of an organisation as the extent to which if fulfils its mission. We may even attempt to measure the performance using a number of **performance indicators**; an accountant may use a profit and loss account or some similar financial statement, a marketing director may look at market share, a customer may look at the speed at which a request for service is met or the quality of the goods or services supplied.

We see in the example in the last paragraph that different people have different interests, as represented by the different performance indicators they choose. These people with an interest in the system are called **stakeholders**, and can include not just people but also other organisations.

The performance indicators that we saw above are a form of **measurement**. Appendix B contains a short account of the theory of measurement – it is important that the assumptions embedded in the use of measurements are well understood if serious misuses are not to occur. Here we have assumed that we can quantify the performance of an organisation, and the contribution of the software to that performance, so that when we plan a change we can quantify the modified performance that will result. However the idea of a measurement includes not only **quantitative** measures that produce numbers, but also **qualitative** non-numerical measures. This is all explained in Appendix B.

Measurements cannot capture everything we might want to know about a phenomenon, but we might be able to capture enough for us to be able to make useful judgements about the phenomenon. This use of a set of measurements to characterise some larger whole is an example of **reductionism**, central to the **scientific method**, which we discussed in Chapter 1. While we can make useful judgements based on a small set of measurements, we need to be careful because if some essential facet has been left out we can easily come to the wrong conclusions.

In the discussion above we have produced a high level and highly simplified model of the world. This model consists of the parts of interest to us, the organisation and its environment, and the interactions between these parts; later we will add the internal workings of the parts. To facilitate understanding we drew a diagram, though we further enhanced this model with a number of concepts like measurement, which we did not represent on the diagram.

In computing we often use diagrams to represent our thinking. While on occasion these might represent quite concrete objects like computer systems and their interconnection with cables, they usually are more abstract than this, showing functional units and their interactions. Diagrams are always open to some interpretation, and we will see that being open to interpretation is both a strength and a weakness.

> Organisations and the work they do can be partially modelled by diagrams and measurements.

2.2 Inside organisations

Let's look a little deeper into organisations and the way they organise their activities. In a later section we will see the importance of knowledge and how this relates to those activities.

All organisations do work, undertaking coherent sequences of activities in order to achieve the objectives of the organisation. The sequences of activities that constitute the work are usually referred to as **business processes**. These business processes may in turn be subject to **business rules** that constrain aspects of their operation – for example who is allowed to access particular information. We are interested in this work and its constituent business processes and business rules for two reasons:

- the computer and software systems of the organisation are intended to support this work, and the relationship between the organisation and this work is important in selecting and maintaining those software systems;
- these software systems themselves need to be acquired and supported, kept in service, and replaced as necessary; this in turn constitutes work, the work that a software manager may be directly responsible for.

The business processes can take various forms, and these forms in turn determine the way the work can be changed in order to respond to demands for change. We have already seen that the work can be either reactive or proactive, though both lead to a business process as a sequence of activities. As an example, consider a distance education provider that is starting delivery of its educational services in a developing country and needs to attract students. It decides to advertise, giving a postal address to which prospective students can write expressing their interest in distance study. In response they are sent a prospectus and an application form. On receiving the completed application form, they are formally registered for the course and are sent a letter requesting the fee, and sent joining details. On receipt of the fee they are sent the materials for the course. This involves the business process shown in Figure 2.2.

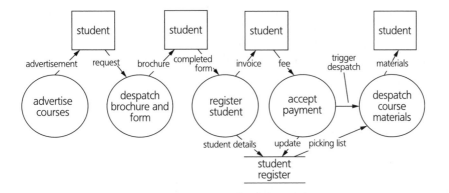

Figure 2.2

Example business process expressed as a DFDDFD data-flow diagram; see for a full definition. Recruit Students for a Distance Education Provider

Activity 2.1 *The limits of diagrams*

Consider the business process Recruit Students shown in Figure 2.2. What other information important for this business process has been left out? How much of this information could be included by extending the diagram or drawing another diagram? Is there any information that in principle could not be put on any diagram?

Discussion
This diagram does not show any detail about the information being moved around and stored in the student register, and does not show how long the process takes. Neither does it show what resources are used – who undertakes these activities, using what computing systems? We will look at these issues in more detail later.

In some cases further detail about the activities would be useful. For example, advertising courses probably involves somebody who knows what courses are on offer to draw up the advertising copy. This person may then arrange for the advertisements to be placed, but may call upon a specialist to design the advertisement and another to place the advertisement. Thus the 'advertise courses' activity might be decomposed into three subactivities: in diagrams using DFDs, using a subdiagram at a lower 'level' is a perfectly proper thing to do. See Appendix A.

The work of organisations can be modelled as business processes, a sequence of activities that interact with each other.

Note that the discussion following Activity 2.1 points out that Figure 2.2 does not show the people and other resources within the business assigned to the particular activities. Activity 2.2 will ask you to do this, but first we introduce some concepts about the assignment of work to people.

With business and manufacturing processes it is very tempting to assign different individuals to each activity in the process, enabling them to specialise and increase their skills. This in turn should lead to efficiencies in the process, with companies able to achieve lower costs and therefore sell at lower prices and at higher profit. This idea goes back to manufacturing processes and production lines of over one hundred years ago. Most production lines break down work into a series of small steps, with a succession of persons working on the line, each person carrying out just one specialised action on the assembly as it passes them. Production lines have been the focus of management experts aiming to reduce production costs, and owes much to the management theories of Frederick Taylor at the start of the twentieth century. Case Study 2.1 tells you more about Taylor's theories, and one particular interpretation of these theories that is now known as **Taylorism**.[3]

Case Study 2.1   *Taylor's scientific management*

Frederick Winslow Taylor was born in Philadelphia, USA, in 1856, and has become one of the most influential, and most reviled, management scientists. He had a privileged upbringing leading to training in engineering and a rapid rise in the emerging US steel industry to become chief engineer at Midvale Steel. He turned to 'scientific' time-and-motion studies to assess the capacity of various steel cutting machines, and through that made startling improvements in production efficiency, improving workers' pay while more than proportionately increasing output and profit.

Taylor's approach to the management of industrial processes was based on four principles or 'duties':[4]

- 'the deliberate gathering in on the part of those on the management's side of all of the great mass of traditional knowledge, which in the past has been in the head of workmen, and the physical skill and knack of the workman, which he has acquired through years of experience'; (p. 125)

- 'the scientific selection and then the progressive development of the workman' to 'enable him to do the highest and most interesting and most profitable class of work for which his natural abilities fit him'; (p. 126);

- 'the bringing of the science and the scientifically selected and trained workmen together'; and (p. 126)

- 'an almost equal division of the actual work of the establishment between the workmen, on the one hand, and the management, on the other hand'. (p. 126)

A modern paraphrase might be: find the best practice and document it, decompose a task into its constituent steps, match the worker to the job, and get rid of things that don't add value.

However, when other managements have attempted to apply Taylor's methods they often ran into problems with significant labour unrest. This has led to the generally held view that 'pure Taylorism views workers simply as machines'[5] where the work is decomposed into small steps, which workers then enact repeatedly and mechanically. Because this was applied to the manufacturing production line of Henry Ford, this is also often called **Fordism**. Taylorism and Fordism typify one extreme form of work organisation that is important historically.

However many people, such as the management gurus Peter Drucker and Gary Hamel, argue that this is a gross misunderstanding of what Taylor stood for. Clearly we should not view Frederick Winslow Taylor as being responsible for Taylorism and Fordism.

We will frequently refer to Taylorism or Fordism in our discussion of work, often writing these with lower case letters as taylorism and fordism, indicating the extent to which these have become part of the regular vocabulary of the discipline. Taylorist ideas are equally applicable to all business processes. Most of the software development methodologies of the 1970s to 1990s were taylorist in their view of work, and, as we will see later, the proponents of newer methods like **eXtreme Programming** have tried to differentiate themselves from taylorism based on the interpretation that it reduces people to machines.[6]

We can view Figure 2.2 as showing a 'taylorised' process, by assigning different people to each activity in the sequence.

Activity 2.2   *Assign resources to a business process*

How might the resources, people, and computing systems, of the distance education provider of Figure 2.2 be deployed to enact the business process Recruit Students? Assign resources to each stage of the business process of Figure 2.2 using ad hoc diagramming conventions improvised for this purpose. Note that some proprietary software development methods include special notations for this, though most do not and we have not adopted any here.

Discussion
A possible solution is given in Figure 2.3.

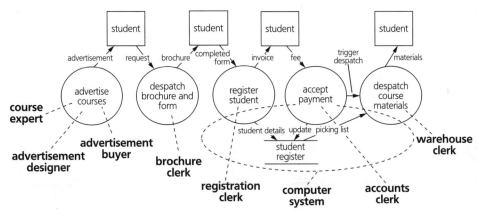

Figure 2.3

Resources assigned to business process Recruit Students

Because of simplistic interpretation of Taylor's scientific management as making human work routine and mechanical, taylorism has had many critics, and alternative ways of organising work have been actively pursued. These alternative post-fordist methods would usually be more holistic, involving everybody working together – for example car assembly is usually taylorised, but Volvo arranged its car assembly with a team of people working together to assemble a complete car, and claimed quality improvements as each member of the team identified with the complete car. The claim of eXtreme Programming, to be covered in detail in Chapter 8, is that it is holistic, involving all people in all parts of the process.

Software systems can be used to reinforce the taylorisation of working procedures, ensuring that work is carried out in the correct sequence by the specialist concerned. These systems arose in the 1980s as **workflow systems** described in

Case Study 2.2. The taylorism illustrated in Figure 2.3 could be reinforced by introducing a workflow system to move digital copies of all forms around and further entrench this business process.

Case Study 2.2 *Workflow systems*

Ideas of collaborative work have been around for many years, taking force with the introduction of networked computers into offices. CSCW (Computer Support for Collaborative Work) systems arose in the 1980s and were aimed at individuals loosely cooperating, for example writing and commenting on a document. These systems are now known as groupware and should be contrasted with workflow systems that arose about the same time. By contrast, workflow systems start with a process as a sequence of activities, and aim to ensure that these activities are carried out in the prescribed order.

To understand these workflow systems, we turn to the international authority, the Workflow Management Coalition (WfMC),[7] founded in August 1993, with more than 300 member companies and institutions in 2005. It defines workflow as 'The computerised facilitation or automation of a business process, in whole or part.'

An item of work is manifest in one or more documents that need to undergo a sequence of processes which might involve a human clerk or a computer application or search of a database. Figure 2.4 shows an example, applying the WfMC's workflow reference model (their Figure 2, p. 9).

The workflow of the business process is turned into a 'process program' that ensures the clerk at the first computer has the information presented to him/her to work on. When complete and any required elements have been added, it is passed onto the second clerk at the second computer, and so on. This is termed 'workflow enactment'.

Workflow systems have since developed further in the US through the commercial Workflow Institute[8] which couples e-learning with workflow management, making available training 'just in time' as part of the system to ensure that the human resources in the workflow optimise their performance.

Figure 2.4

Workflow enactment of an insurance claim

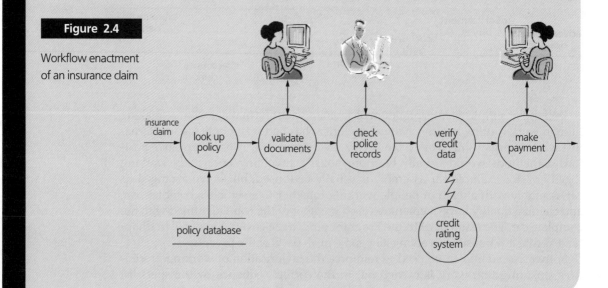

Workflow clearly fits well with taylorism! However the high degree of special-isation implicit in taylorism, and the fine division into small steps, make these pro-cesses very rigid and difficult to change. As we will see later, the ability to evolve processes in response to changes imposed from outside has become critically im-portant over recent decades.

2.3 New and evolving systems

In Chapter 1 we discussed the rapidly changing world and how changes in the environment drive changes in an organisation. These pressures are of five kinds:

1. external demands, which could be changes imposed by directives from government, such as new financial regulations or a new law;

2. external opportunities, particularly where technological developments enable new services, or new ways of doing old business, like e-shopping and tele-banking;

3. external problems, such as falling market share or profitability, requiring that the organisation change to operate more efficiently;

4. internal opportunities – quite independently of external forces, an opportunity might be seen to do things differently and enhance the organisation in some way; and

5. internal problems might arise within the organisation, for example if the software system is found to be unusable.

When a change is proposed it would be normal to define the **scope** of the pro-posed change, defining what can be changed and what should not be changed. Sometimes this definition of scope is called a **change charter**, and if we start with a business process described by a suitable diagram such as a DFD, we would typical-ly mark those parts than can be changed.

We show this in Figure 2.5, where a change has been triggered by a techno-logical opportunity, the opening up of the country for telephone connections. With the coming of readily available telephones for prospective students, the business process needs to be adapted or re-engineered to include advertising which gives telephone numbers to call, and the processing of the telephone enquiry. As shown in the DFD of Figure 2.5, the changes are minimal, with the

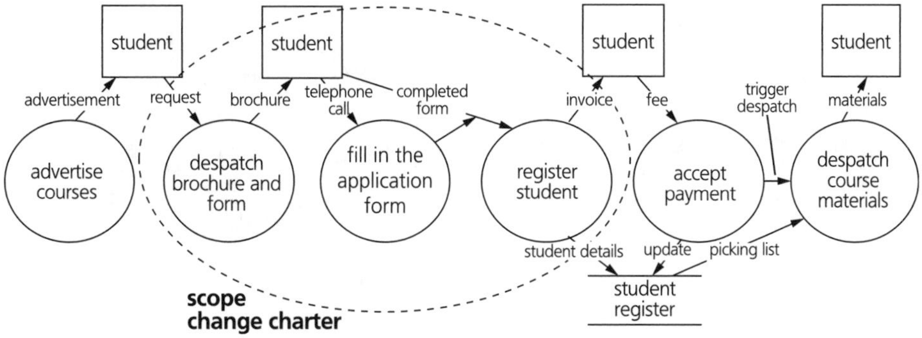

The people in a business process can become highly specialised, and can even be treated as machines. The process itself then becomes less amenable to change.

Figure 2.5

Example of a small change from Figures 2.2 and 2.3

person answering the phone filling in an application form after which processing continues as before.

Changing a business process for any of the reasons we have given above is usually known as **business process re-engineering**[9] or **BPR**. BPR arose in the 1980s as one way of responding to the need for change, with slogans like 'if it ain't broke, break it' and related methods like 'downsizing'. All it really means is changing your business processes to better fit the current environment in which you operate. The changes described as BPR would usually be much larger and more radical that that illustrated in Figure 2.5 – Figure 2.6 shows something more typical, where the changes make selecting a distance education course into a process similar to the e-commerce selection and purchase of a product. The Internet has become readily available to prospective students, and thus the business process needs radical overhaul to enable registration and payment online. Prospectuses no longer need to be posted – they can be browsed online, and if paper copies are required, the printing can be done at the cost of the enquirer. This re-engineering could have gone further, to make advertisement entirely via the web, and making course materials entirely digital and despatched via the web.

Note how in Figure 2.6 the previous taylorised process has been completely thrown away, with most processes now mediated by Internet software.

Whenever changes are made, there will be some kernel processes that are central to the organisation that won't change, like time-recording and payroll systems (though of course under some circumstances these do change). These processes often encapsulate the basic way the organisation works, and are often characterised as **legacy systems**. The legacy systems would contain a mix of human procedures and software systems. We have represented legacy systems here as containing the valued essentials of the organisation, but the much more common (mis)understanding of the term is that it is an attempt to make respectable the ancient computing systems built on out-of-date technology. Whatever. The key thing is that during re-engineering these legacy systems would need to be preserved. Unless of course you are following the advice 'if it ain't broke, break it'. We will come across legacy systems at various points in this book.

New systems are introduced or changes made because of internal problems or external demands and opportunities.

The business processes within the scope of the change charter are re-engineered.

During re-engineering, legacy systems need to be preserved.

Figure 2.6

Example of BPR from Figures 2.2 and 2.3

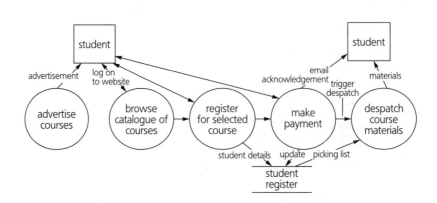

2.4 Return on investment

We have already seen in Chapter 1 that at the macro level of the whole economy there seems to be little or no return on the investment in computer systems. We expressed there the hope that in individual cases we might be able to justify a return on the investment before making that investment.

In making decisions about investment for acquiring or changing software, we are concerned with two kinds of performance indicator: the **costs** of the proposed investment, and the **benefits** that might accrue from that investment.

The cost will be made up of direct and indirect costs. The **direct cost** of making a change to both human and software systems can be estimated, and we will see established methods for cost estimation for developing and changing software in Chapter 10. **Indirect costs** include factors like management, office space, and similar, but also include benefits that would have been gained from the workers if they had not been working on the changes – called **opportunity costs**.

Benefits can be a lot more difficult to determine, but we need to try, and to express these in financial terms. In simple automation projects where software takes over the role of people, the benefits will be the saving in labour costs, and those are relatively easy to identify. Those savings are **tangible**, but very often there are also **intangible** benefits, difficult to identify let alone quantify. We have already seen the intangible benefit of computing enabling an organisation to join the information society, though if this means that the organisation could develop Internet-based sales, there might be a claim of tangible benefit in increased sales. We will see much more of this as we go along.

The **return on investment (ROI)** then is the ratio

$$ROI = \frac{(\text{benefits} - \text{costs})}{\text{costs}}$$

What the ROI gives us is a means of deciding whether a proposed investment is worth doing. But ROI is not the only way to do this, and Don Reifer[10] describes eight different options.

As our understanding of computers and software has developed and we have been able to achieve more using computers, and at lower cost, organisations have invested more and more heavily in computers. In spite of many highly publicised failures, like that described in Case Study 2.3,[11] organisations have continued to invest. After all, the failure of somebody else's software investment project does not mean that you will not succeed!

Case Study 2.3 *The London Stock Exchange's Taurus system*

In early 1993, the London Stock Exchange abandoned the development of its Taurus (transfer and automated registration of uncertificated stock) paperless share settlement system. Taurus was intended as a computerised database of investors and their holdings, leading to paperless trading in the securities industry with reduced costs for the share registrars, institutions, and

▶

brokers and for future account controllers of share transactions. Share ownership would be stored electronically and investors would not receive share certificates. Taurus would be linked to some 280 financial institutions, serving a range of stakeholders from registrars, brokers, market-makers, and custodians, to large investors.

Initially in the early 1980s the plan was to cover all share dealings with a single computerised register of shareholdings maintained by the stock exchange. But some of the main banks, who controlled over 80 per cent of the share registration business, did not want to see a centrally based database register, and so the most obvious and easiest way to develop Taurus using a centralised database register was ruled out. The stock exchange had discovered that it was not possible to propose a solution that ignored the interests of any significant part of their community of stakeholders.

The Bank of England intervened and set up the Securities Industry Steering Committee on Taurus (SISCOT), which reported how a paperless settlement system should work even while the City and thus its needs were changing. Even so, the stock exchange pushed ahead with three risky, expensive, and uncertain but pioneering imaginative proposals. The safest option of modifying the stock exchange's existing settlement system, Talisman, was not even considered. Original figures from the SISCOT cost–benefit report put minimum development costs at around £14.5 million with additional capital costs of about £3.5 million. Software costs would be recovered over a five-year period on the basis of 20,000 transactions a day through Taurus. Even though the figures were only indicative, the benefits were widely announced publicly – Taurus would bring down the cost of dealing in shares, save £54 million a year by cutting thousands of jobs, and secure London's future in world markets as a premier financial centre. The costs could not be fixed because the design could not be fixed. In the end the City chose a US software package, but rather than adapt City procedures to fit it, they chose to change the software to fit the UK.

Once work had started, progress was not visible and project deadlines slipped, with major reorganisations of the stock exchange taking place in 1989, and conflicts of interest arising between committees, and between management consultancies, with Andersen Consulting running the stock exchange's day-to-day computer operations and Coopers and Lybrand trying to run Taurus.

The project was finally killed in dramatic fashion by a combination of critical reports and memos from the two competing consultants at the stock exchange, Andersen and Coopers and Lybrand. Ten years' development effort had been wasted. The Taurus project manager, Eliott Manley, estimated that, when the project was abandoned, it had cost the City of London over £800 million (although the *Financial Times* of November 3, 1993 reported losses of 'only' £400 million – this also points out how hard it is to get accurate financial figures on IT project cost, especially failing IT projects). With its original budget slightly above £6 million, it ended up 132 times over budget with no prospect of a solution in sight.

Eventually the stock exchange did acquire a new system – bought from another stock exchange in Europe.

During the first decades of software, it was routine practice to make the case for any particular investment by carrying out a cost–benefit analysis to justify the expenditure: typically this would be justified in terms of saving in labour costs, and when considering the potential investment in computers following the identification of some problem or opportunity, there would be a **feasibility study** in which various alternative actions are considered, including the option of doing nothing. This then led to a decision concerning which course of action to follow.

This micro-economic argument was made on a case by case basis, and would include a predicted return on investment. After the completion of the investment, it would have been good practice to include a **post-implementation audit**, to identify any residual problems and to check that the intended benefits had been achieved. Both feasibility studies and post-implementation audits were excellent stages in the overall process, but seem to have disappeared from common accounts of software development,[12] as if it were unquestionable that the system should be implemented and unquestionable that it would achieve its intended benefits.

At feasibility stage we can only predict the costs and benefits, and would expect a profile like that in Figure 2.7. Looking at curve 1, we see that monthly costs are incurred gradually at first as the details of the changes to be made are worked out, the system requirements are determined, and the software designed; then costs increase rapidly as the software is implemented, integrated, and tested; and then costs decrease again as the system is completed and goes into service at release date R. Curve 2 shows the monthly benefits (returns) only starting after the release of the changes or product. However the returns will only have paid off the investment some time later, when curve 3, the accumulated costs, is overtaken by curve 4, the accumulated benefits.

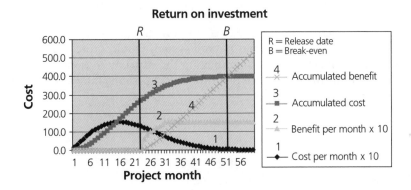

Figure 2.7

Investment and return on investment curves

Because of the delay in recovering the investment, these cost curves really should be handled using some method of analysis which takes into account inflation and opportunity costs – a dollar, euro, or pound in ten years' time is worth less than one dollar, euro, or pound is today. Such a method is **net present value** (**NPV**), also known as **discounted cash flow** – see the excellent text by Kathy Schwalbe[13] or any book on accounting for full details, or look up the NPV function in a spreadsheet package such as Excel.

Often the payback period, the time between starting the investment and recovering that investment through benefits, may be considerable. Accounting practices have become increasingly prone to **short-termism** in their outlook, and the traditional payback period may be viewed as too long – and the investment proposal rejected in consequence. We will see illustrations of this in software use, and particularly for maintenance practices, later in this book.

Our accumulated cost curve is sometimes known as the **total cost of ownership** (**TCO**) and would include other costs like that of the hardware on which to run the software and the accommodation to house it.

For a particular proposed investment, we may not be able to predict a positive return on investment. This may be because we have been unable to place a value on some of the intangible benefits, and our judgement might be that those benefits more than compensate for any apparent loss on the investment – and there are other good reasons for investing in software.

The above basis for investment has been financial, but that may not be the only basis for guiding an investment. Here are some broader issues to consider:

- **Ethical decision-making**[14] has become increasingly important. In this we take into account other factors such as whether the goods being considered were produced with exploited labour and their production could have a negative impact on the environment. We will consider ethics in more detail in Chapter 4.
- The reliability of the software, though this might have entered the calculations of the likelihood of loss resulting from using the software.
- The **trustworthiness** of the supplier – the likelihood that the supplier will still be in business in twenty years' time to support you then.
- That employees and customers support the investment.
- The competitive advantage that might be lost by using commodity software or gained by using bespoke software, as seen in Case Study 2.4.

In some cases, such as payroll systems, the software is simply a cost, and an investment decision to replace an old payroll system would quite rightly be based on minimal cost subject to the system having the capacity to handle the payroll. More generally enterprise resource planning (ERP) systems may also be procured on the basis of cost alone.

Case Study 2.4 *Competitive advantage in insurance*

Some years ago we studied the use of ERP software in a major UK insurance company that had recently been formed by the merger of two companies. Constituent insurance company 'A' had chosen financial subsystems from SAP and a human resources subsystem from PeopleSoft, while constituent company 'B' had chosen financials from PeopleSoft and human resources from SAP. Both ERP suppliers offered insurance models, but these were rejected on the grounds that the suppliers did not understand the flexibility required in insurance to move customers between policies and to produce new financial products at short notice.

When we interviewed the key insurance executive it transpired that he saw his company's uniqueness as bound up in its flexibility in the insurance-specific areas of business, and while they might buy software from an insurance-specific supplier, they would undertake significant customisations of that software, as well as producing software in house for key insurance functions. It was not so much that SAP and PeopleSoft's insurance offer was not appropriate as insurance, but that as an insurance company you would not want to be the same as every other insurance company. You want your distinctiveness as an insurer to be supported by distinctiveness in your software.

Having determined the range of factors that need to be taken into account, some way of combining these to guide a decision needs to be found. One method is the **weighted scorecard**, in which the various factors are given a weight to indicate their relative importance. A measurement for each factor is obtained, the factor measurement is multiplied by the factor weight, and all these are added up to arrive at a figure of merit for the proposed investment. If several alternatives are being assessed, each is scored in this way, and the final values are used to inform the final decision. Figure 2.8 shows the idea.

	Weight %	As is	External service	Open CMS in house
Projects our products favourably	30	50	90	60
Will not lead to increased costs (i.e., NPV is positive)	25	50	30	60
Is as attractive as the competitions' websites	10	10	90	60
Only uses established technologies	15	70	80	90
Low risk of failure	20	100	90	50
Weighted project scores	100	59	73.5	62.5

Figure 2.8

Weighted scorecard example: Project to replace current manually driven website by data-driven solution.

An important variant of the weighted scorecard is the **balanced scorecard**,[15] which builds upon business values. Both the weighted scorecard and balanced scorecard are examples of rational decision-making. Thinking back to our discussion in Chapter 1 about the limits of rationality, we must appreciate that this method is necessarily reductionist. The numbers that they arrive at cannot make the decision for us; they simply help us make an essentially human decision.

From the above we see that if we can make reasonable predictions about both cost and benefits for an investment, we can arrive at a predicted return on the investment. However in practice an investment in software seldom turns out as predicted; typically costs escalate as difficulties are found in the process of acquiring the software that were not anticipated and these only add costs, while benefits are not achieved as more staff are required to maintain the new system.

Even though overall it may not be possible to demonstrate that for an organisation there has been a return from investment in information technology, there are still good reasons for investing in software, such as providing a higher quality service to customers, or simply keeping up with the competition. Maybe we need to think about justification for investment in software differently.

Rational decision-making using ROI provides evidence to help a decision, but cannot take into account all factors and cannot determine the decision.

2.5 Relationship between software and the organisation

An organisation is made up of both people and software, as well as other resources like buildings. We can decompose the organisations into two interacting subsystems, the human subsystem and the software subsystem, as shown in Figure 2.9. Software is **embedded** in the organisation, the external environment interacts with either the human or software subsystems in the organisation, receiving input stimuli and information from the environment and responding with output stimuli and information. The precise form of these interactions will depend upon the nature and purpose of the organisation and its systems – all we are concerned with here is that this interaction takes place.

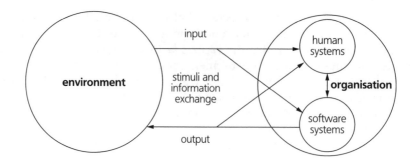

Figure 2.9

Software within organisations

While some of the interactions between the environment and the organisation may take place directly with software embedded in the organisation, other interactions will be mediated by human agents within the organisation. In responding to the stimuli the humans and software will follow appropriate business processes. These business processes may be tacit, developed by the people over many years of experience and passed on from experienced worker to new recruit, or they may have been made explicit and be set out in procedure manuals or be embedded in the software of the organisation. In many cases the business process will be a combination of all three – actions by people based upon **tacit knowledge**, actions by people following explicit procedures, and actions by software executing part of the explicit procedures. We will discuss the relationship between tacit and **explicit knowledge** in greater detail later in this chapter.

What is the relationship between the software and the organisation it seeks to serve? One tradition in developing software to support organisations has been to talk of the software constituting a model of the organisation. When non-computer processes are 'automated,' the various paper records and manual processes to handle and update those records of the pre-computer system are represented directly in the computer.[16] This representation of the organisation in the computer is a very conscious process, but the organisation may be reflected in the computer systems in more subtle ways, as is seen Case Study 2.5.

Case Study 2.5 *Social construction of technology*

Social scientists became interested in computers and software during the 1980s, studying the development and use of these as sociological phenomena. These studies followed on from social studies of science, with the sociologists taking a constructionist stance – what the technology was, was determined by the people using it or building it. A very early account of computing which encouraged this constructionist view was the book by Tracy Kidder, *The Soul of a New Machine*,[17] which gives a highly readable account of the computer manufacturer Data General (DG) and its commercial battles with the larger and more established rival, the Digital Equipment Corporation (DEC). DEC had just launched their first 32-bit machine, the VAX, and DG were lagging behind, so a DG designer, West, arranged to covertly inspect a VAX. Kidder writes:

> Looking at the VAX, West had imagined he saw a diagram of DEC's corporate organisation. He felt that VAX was too complicated. He did not like, for instance, the system by which various parts of the machine communicated

with each other; for his taste there was too much protocol involved. He decided that VAX embodied flaws in DEC's corporate organization. The machine expressed that phenomenally successful company's cautious bureaucratic style. (p. 36)

This example showed that the technology was not determined, at least not entirely, by its own inner rationality, but that social factors were also important in shaping it. Since this book was published by Kidder, the sociology of technology has

developed and grown – see for example the edited collections by Paul Quintas[18] and by Bill Dutton,[19] which report a variety of ways in which the structure and use of software is determined socially.

Data General went out of business shortly after the events recorded by Kidder. DEC was eventually acquired by Compaq, which in turn merged with Hewlett Packard. Computer companies come – and go.

The software systems used by an organisation are as much part of the organisation as the people, physical records, and buildings are. So in a sense the software is inseparable from the organisation it serves, and yet as managers with a concern for software we need to be able to treat software as a separate entity. However this may not always be the best thing to do – look at Case Study 2.6 for a cautionary tale.

Case Study 2.6 *Flight control software*

Historically, controlling aircraft in flight needed the pilot to constantly make adjustments to maintain the stability of the aircraft. Today much of this function has been taken over by computers, and primarily computer software. The computer can react much faster than a human pilot, so much so that some modern military aircraft are inherently unstable, and depend on the computer making constant adjustments to compensate for this inherent instability and thus maintaining the stability of the aircraft.

The conventional approach to designing this software would be to look at the interfaces between the hardware and the software, and specify the software in isolation in terms of the input–output functions required. Yet for the

important property of stability, the software must be treated as part of the complete system of aircraft: its flaps and other flight control surfaces, the instruments that detect the trajectory of the aircraft, and the controller including the software that connects these; what matters is the dynamics of the complete aircraft, and not the behaviour of the software in isolation. It is incredibly difficult to think about the software in isolation, let alone argue in isolation that it will function correctly in flight.

Recent moves have been to consider the overall system using control theory, taking into account the digital nature of the software and the analogue nature of the overall aircraft with what has come to be called 'hybrid' theory.

Software like the flight control software of Case Study 2.6 is usually termed *embedded*, meaning that it is integrated with various physical devices to form the complete engineering artefact. In this case, when we attempt to separate the software from the hardware, we lose the ability to analyse and understand the overall system, and it is the overall system that really matters. It has been a frequent experience in developing software for embedded systems that whenever the hardware designers run into problems, they simplify the hardware and require the software to pick up the more complex functions. The hardware and software should evolve together, thus people talk of hardware/software co-design.

There is a more general lesson to be drawn from this example: in many cases it may also be inappropriate to separate the software from the people that are using it. All software is embedded and inseparable from the engineering artefact or human organisation in which it is embedded. This combination of people and software and other systems is often referred to as a **socio-technical system**. We will come across socio-technical systems again in Chapter 8. To understand what the software does you have to understand the complete context within which it operates – and yet it is also extremely useful to treat the software separately as well.

This basic model of an organisation interacting with an environment, with some of those interactions by the organisation being supported by software, will be used and extended in later parts of this book.

Complete socio-technical systems, not component parts such as software, should be developed and evolved.

A key focus for us is the interface between the software and the rest of the organisation, and, if appropriate, with the outside world. During normal routine operation this interface will be manifest implicitly in what the system does, and how it is used by those who operate it. There may be explicit accounts of the interface and its use in user guides, and in training programs. There may also be a more abstract description of the relationship between the software and the organisation in a **requirements specification**, but the chances are that even if such a document existed when the software was originally being acquired, it will be out of date. The fact is, so often, that the interface and the relationship between the software the organisation that it supports will have simply become part of the tacit knowledge of the organisation.

2.6 Knowledge management and learning organisations

As people, either singly or in groups, we have acquired a lot of knowledge that enables us to operate effectively in the world. Originally this knowledge was personal and shared through spoken language, which limited the extent to which such knowledge could be distilled and communicated. However the emergence of writing from around 3,000 years ago changed this, enabling knowledge to be stored and re-examined, combined, and developed. Written knowledge did not then make the personal knowledge of people irrelevant, for each has different properties and together contribute to the richness of human knowledge.

We refer to this knowledge held by people, as individuals or in groups, as **tacit knowledge**, or **implicit knowledge**. This knowledge may be in the memory of people, but may also be implicit in their languages and in their social organisations. Implicit knowledge is contrasted with **explicit knowledge**, knowledge which has been **externalised** in writing or other recordings or in artefacts.

Activity 2.3	*Tangible and tacit*

How do the concepts of tangible and intangible benefits relate to tacit and explicit knowledge? Illustrate this with examples.

Discussion

When contemplating a change we will generally know why we wish to make the change, though this knowledge may be tacit. In order to be able to make a case for the change we will need to make these tacit reasons explicit. These reasons for the change then lead us into the potential benefits, though this connection may be tacit and be very difficult to make explicit. Even if we could make the benefits explicit, we may still be unable to make them tangible, though we cannot make them tangible without making them explicit.

For example, this book has been written using an industry-standard proprietary word processor. While this word processor contains lots of features that are very useful to us as authors, it also has features that make it more difficult, and also things which just don't work. We have considered changing to an XML-based authoring system. Our basic measurement would be our speed of writing and amending our document, and this is quite explicit and tangible – we could measure it. But we also feel some general stress about continuing to use the software from a supplier who has an effective monopoly and want other suppliers to benefit from our trade, and because we don't like the policy of planned obsolescence that this company practices. Even if we could make these stress factors explicit, they would still be intangible, and we could not quantify them within our cost–benefit analysis of what authoring software to use.

We see from this discussion that the distinction between knowledge being tacit and being explicit is about the relationship between what is in our brain and what is represented and recorded outside of us. Whether a benefit is tangible or intangible goes further than this, and is concerned with whether our knowledge about the benefit can be made explicit enough for us to be able to actually measure the benefit.

We saw earlier how organisations have a goal that is shared by all parts of the organisation. We talked about the degree of achievement of that goal, describing it as the organisation's performance. We saw how the goal and performance could be tacit, or could be made explicit in mission statements and performance indicators. We have also seen just how limited such attempts to make implicit knowledge explicit can be.

At its simplest, we can think of the act of writing or drawing diagrams like DFDs as making tacit knowledge explicit, and the act of reading and understanding as making explicit knowledge tacit once again. Of course it is not that simple, since some writing may be so obscure as to continue to lock up the knowledge it was supposed to release. Other activities may also make knowledge explicit, as in giving a demonstration, or constructing an artefact.

This simple model will suffice, and leads us to the simple concept of the knowledge creation cycle shown in Figure 2.10. The knowledge creation cycle was created by two Japanese management scientists, Ikujiro Nonaka and Hirotaka Takeuchi[20] as part of their explanation of the success of Japanese industry.

They called successful Japanese organisations 'knowledge creation companies', viewing tacit knowledge as existing uniquely within people, and explicit knowledge that recorded in external systems such as company manuals and information systems. Knowledge moves between these two states, growing as it cycles round.

Also important is the distinction between small 'islands' of knowledge, and integrated and shared knowledge. In organisations tacit knowledge must be shared to be effective, with the individuals in an organisation sharing a common base of knowledge and common way of working. We talk of shared cognition, shared values and beliefs and ways of viewing the world. This sharing happens through processes of 'socialisation' in which the tacit knowledge is shared – this may happen informally, but may be formalised as coaching and mentoring. We sometimes talk of the group of people with a common shared cognition as a community of practice – we will return later to this important understanding.

Some tacit knowledge may be able to be externalised, to be recorded in external media during some process of codification which at the same time abstracts from various versions of the knowledge to 'systematise' the knowledge. Tacit knowledge is externalised in small chunks, and these must then be integrated to form a coherent body of knowledge that is of value to the organisation. This act of integration or 'composition' may be undertaken explicitly, or may just happen as part of the process of using the information.

Bodies of knowledge may then be passed on to individual people as part of training or education programmes, making this knowledge tacit once again. Each stage in this cycle may generate new knowledge, to be added to the body of pre-existing tacit and explicit knowledge, and hence the title 'the knowledge creation cycle'.

This knowledge creation cycle is one view of how knowledge works within an organisation and is important for the success of the organisation. Management can focus explicitly upon the organisation's knowledge – this has come to be known as **knowledge management**.[21] Santosus and Surmaz,[22] writing for CIO.com, an ezine for chief information officers (CIOs), have commented:

> KM is the process through which organizations generate value from their intellectual and knowledge-based assets. Most often, generating value from such assets involves sharing

Figure 2.10

The knowledge
creation cycle

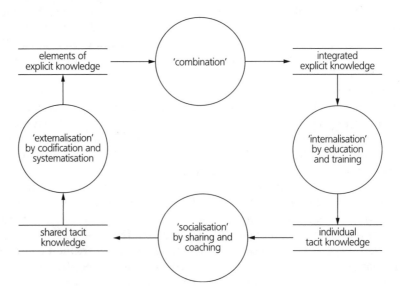

them among employees, departments and even with other companies in an effort to devise best practices.

KM is not a technology-based concept. Don't be duped by software vendors touting their all-inclusive KM solutions. Companies that implement a centralized database system, electronic message board, Web portal or any other collaborative tool in the hope that they've established a KM program are wasting both their time and money.

Some people would take the view that in principle all tacit knowledge can be externalised – once the knowledge has been externalised, the people holding the tacit knowledge then become redundant: and an example of this is described in Case Study 2.7. Others would deny this, and accept that some tacit knowledge cannot and could never be externalised. The failure of expert systems[23] to capture expertise can be taken as evidence supporting this second point of view. We talk about institutional memory, and the loss of institutional memory that results from high staff turnover. One of the negative effects of **BPR**[24] with its downsizing and 'delayering' (removing a complete level of management) was the consequential loss of institutional memory.

> Organisations operate cyclically, as business processes are analysed and described and restructured, then established through training and re-embodied in new business process and their supporting software.

Case Study 2.7 *Schlumberger's technology books*

An interesting example of knowledge management in computing was undertaken by Guillaume Arango and others in Schlumberger, coming to the problem from a software reuse perspective.[25] Faced with engineers coming up to retirement, and the prospect of losing vital knowledge about electrical devices made by the company when these employees left, Schlumberger's company management asked Arango and colleagues to capture this knowledge for later reuse. They came up with the idea of a series of 'technology books', which externalised engineers' knowledge and made it available to the rest of the company. Clearly these technology books contained information that was important competitively to Schlumberger, and could not be released outside the company. Inevitably, subtle details of tacit knowledge will not have been adequately recorded, but what was recorded proved very valuable.

2.7 Change and learning

We noted in Chapter 1 that the world outside organisations, the environment in Figure 2.1, is constantly changing. These changes in the environment may occasionally lead to beneficial effects, and an organisation thrives, but more typically the changes in the environment will damage the organisation unless it in turn changes to adapt to the new environment.

A knowledge-creating company is an example of a **learning organisation**. Just as an individual person acquires knowledge and learns, and through that improves his/her performance, so too can we attribute the improving performance of an organisation to **organisational learning**. Chris Argyris, one of the international experts on the subject, contrasts *learning organisations*, a practical business-led debate about how organisations should change and do change, with *organisational learning*, an academic area of research that should question the very idea that an

> Vital tacit knowledge can be lost through personnel turnover. Knowledge management systems can help by making tacit knowledge explicit, thus preserving it.

organisation can learn.[26] However we will take the view that the concept of organisational learning is perfectly sensible, following the view of Peter Senge,[27] another founding expert of this area: 'Learning organisations are possible because deep down we are all learners.' (p. 4)

However, it would be quite wrong to attribute organisational learning solely to the learning of the individuals within the organisation – the organisation itself can learn, as when having documented best practices (as Schlumberger did in Case Study 2.7), it later amends that documented best practice in the light of later experience; this will be seen later in quality improvement processes in Chapter 12.

Organisations learn through a process of **feedback**[28] in which the objectives and intended performance of the organisation are matched against actual performance, any mismatches are analysed, and this analysis is used to modify the internal business processes in order to reduce the mismatches. This continues in a never ending cycle. This simple model has come to be known as **single-loop learning**, illustrated in Figure 2.11.

Figure 2.11

Single-loop learning

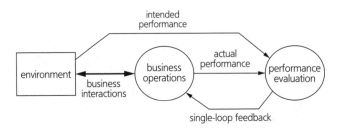

Based on this very simple model we can explain organisational behaviour that is observed in practice. The need to change, discerned in the mismatch between intended and actual performances, typically arises from changes external to the organisation in the environment, or from errors within the organisation; the feedback of the performance evaluation should lead to corrective action that moves the actual performance closer to the intended performance and enables the organisation to track the environmental changes. This situation, where the action reduces the difference between the intended performance and the actual performance, is termed **negative feedback**. However, determining the appropriate corrective action is not easy; adaptations may not work and the situation may even get worse as the action reinforces the gap, making the gap between intended performance and the actual performance even greater – when it is termed **positive feedback**. Or the adaptations may work for a while, and then get stuck at some position where business performance never is able to attain its targets.[29] Carrying through this feedback always takes time, and it is easy to overshoot, to overcompensate, and then have to readjust only to overshoot once again; engineers have the very graphic and appropriate term for this – **thrashing**. Examples of these abound in the literature of learning organisations.

However, the behaviour of learning organisations can be more subtle, which has led to the formulation of a more complex model of learning – **double-loop learning**, illustrated in Figure 2.12.

The organisation's ability to adapt itself may need to change over time. Single-loop learning ensues adherence to procedures; double-loop learning changes the

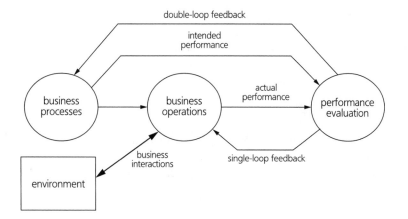

Figure 2.12

Double-loop learning

procedures so that adherence continues to be appropriate. In education double-loop learning would be recognised as 'learning to learn'.

The single-loop and double-loop learning models may still not explain all phenomena, and Argyris[30] has written at length about the difficulties and the need to formulate yet richer models. In particular he and his colleague Donald Schoen attribute organisational learning to individual learning; we will return to this line of reasoning in the next chapter.

Organisations learn through a process of feedback that adapts their internal processes to a changing environment.

2.8 Software enterprise learning

We will look in considerably more detail at how the organisation may adapt to changes in later chapters. Here we want to make some simple observations about the different ways in which the various components of the organisation interact and can be changed.

A need for change will most likely be identified by an individual who is having difficulties completing some business process. This person makes personal adaptations to the problem, and if the problem does not arise from some misunderstanding of the system, they might introduce personal **work-arounds**, using the system in unintended ways and augmenting this with personal notes and records outside the system.

If the problem identified needs to be tackled on a wider scale, other people and management would become involved, and personal adaptations would be shared and harmonised. An immediate response might be to change the software system, but even if a change were accepted, it could take a considerable time to be implemented. So some interim solution at least must be sought through human adaptation.

The harmonisation of people's personal work-arounds and solutions might well happen entirely through interpersonal interaction, debating best solutions, and arriving at an agreed solution for general adoption. The agreement may, however, be documented and existing documents changed.

The organisation may decide to stay with personal and procedural adaptations, but may decide to modify the software so that it directly supports the problem area identified. This would take them into the change control procedures discussed in Chapter 11, and requires work to agree what the changes to the software system should be, followed by the costs and delays of actually making those changes.

In this scenario we see components of change:

1. change the human system, modifying tacit knowledge with experience, possibly working around problems posed by the formalised processes;
2. once changes have stabilised, externalise these into the business procedures and manuals; and
3. modify the support software systems.

In our discussion we implied that changing the tacit human system was easier than changing the documented business processes, which is easier again than changing the supporting software system. Of course none of this is easy, and that relationship may not always apply. The option of changing only part of the system does always exist. In the following two activities we will relate the above to the various concepts we have encountered in this chapter.

Activity 2.4   *Relating change to knowledge creation*

Relate the description of change happening at three levels described above to the concepts of tacit and explicit knowledge, the knowledge creation cycle seen in Figure 2.10, and the ideas of single- and double-loop learning in Figures 2.11 and 2.12.

Discussion

The scenario begins with the tacit knowledge of individual users, with a mismatch between intended and actual performance. Single-loop learning ensures that individual use is successful until a problem is encountered where the system cannot support the business process and the single-loop feedback cycle breaks down.

At this stage the person looks for **work-arounds**, updating their tacit knowledge in localised double-loop learning.

Once other people become involved we move into socialisation of tacit knowledge where it is integrated and harmonised.

Then, as people become involved in documentation, they begin externalising that tacit knowledge, and further combining it with other documented procedures. All of this is changing the documented business process and is part of the double-loop learning cycle. Once established, people will need to be trained, internalising the documented procedures into their tacit knowledge.

Single-loop learning, once in use again, takes over to ensure adherence to the procedures.

To change the software, we get into another round of double-loop learning with a software development process, and in due course new software is produced to form a part of the composite externalised work practices. Training will need to be carried out to ensure that the use of this new software becomes internalised. Finally, single-loop feedback ensures the successful use of the new system.

Activity 2.5   *Modelling knowledge creation change cycles*

Re-express as a data flow diagram (DFD), or set of DFDs, the account discussed in Activity 2.4 relating change to knowledge creation.

Discussion

This is much trickier than at first it seems: the written description seems to make it obvious. Here is one possible way of representing this as a DFD:

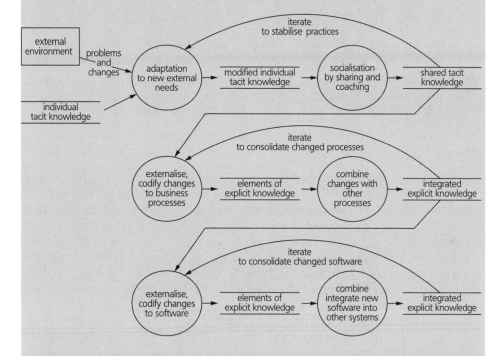

Note the use of feedback cycles to show what we know happens in practice – we make changes, try them out, and then make minor adaptations in practice and try those out, and so on until we are satisfied.

We see how critically important it can be to retain some level of human processes within our business system and not completely automate everything, because we would otherwise lose our flexibility and ability to adapt to a changing environment. Case Study 2.8 introduces the idea of **situated action** – every detail of work cannot be planned and made explicit, and in some circumstances at least people must draw upon their tacit knowledge to respond to situations as they arise. We will draw on this idea of situated action later because it plays a critical role in the development of software systems.

Case Study 2.8 *Situated action*

One very significant outcome of the reaction against reductionism and taylorism has been the questioning of planning. Laying down plans for the production of software or undertaking other work requires that all elements of work can be anticipated and their interdependencies spelled out, and the resources for each element of work be reasonably accurately estimated.

This assumption about planning was first questioned by Lucy Suchman in her doctoral research at Xerox, published as *Plans and Situated Actions*.[31] Suchman illustrates the planning dilemma graphically with the example of navigation in the Pacific, contrasting European methods with the methods of Pacific Islanders. Europeans plot the course on charts and then follow the plan by taking readings from various instruments (chronometers, compasses, theodolites) to ensure that the planned course is indeed travelled. Pacific Islanders set off in the right direction, responding to observations of the sea and of the atmosphere around them. Both arrive, but by very different means.

Suchman carried out her researches on the use of guidance shipped with Xerox copiers, and applied her researches to human machine communication more generally. But her observations are much more general than that, and apply to any complex human activity which could be planned, but for which plans could fail due to a range of unanticipated and unanticipatable circumstances. Instead of having recourse to some pre-planned and explicit response to these circumstance, the people involved have to react on the basis of the situation as it arises, drawing upon their tacit knowledge in order to do so.

The people in the organisation and their embedded tacit knowledge are critical for the success of the organisation, part of its assets: its human capital.

When we consider change, we will be faced with a range of choices concerning what is actually changed. Which of these choices we decide upon will depend upon both the cost of making the change and the expected benefit from that change. In analysing a proposed change it would be usual to include some form of cost–benefit analysis. Usually a number of change scenarios would be considered, including the null scenario of making no changes, and full cost–benefit figures would be derived for two or three of these. That is the received wisdom – though in practice decisions may be made in other ways. We have already discussed these issues in section 2.4.

However we attempt to estimate them, neither the cost nor the benefit can be known precisely and will be subject to some uncertainty, which means that there is a chance that the cost will be much greater than expected, or the benefit may be far less than expected, or there may even be a net disbenefit. These uncertainties usually arise from things not working out as envisaged in our scenario, and consideration of these uncertainties is usually tackled as risk assessment.

The idea in **risk assessment** is to consider all places in the scenarios where assumptions have been made, and then consider how things could go wrong. The next step would be to consider how the effect of the risk could be reduced, and in Chapter 13 we will see a number of risk mitigation techniques. Risk must always be considered: it is part of the external changing world with which we must cope.

Change needs to be carefully managed and planned. Cost–benefit analysis and risk assessment will guide what changes can be made, but ultimately a decision will need to be made. This decision should be made at a level commensurate with the projected scope and impact of the change – many large organisations follow a

change management strategy, and operate a system of change control boards. This will be discussed in detail in Chapter 11. Organisations, whatever their size, are relatively complex, with their business processes made up of many parts. When changes to a system are made, some selection of this totality of parts will need to be changed, and these changes need to be tracked and coordinated. The changes may not immediately be made correctly, and the changed components may evolve through several versions. We need to ensure that changes are made consistently and that a consistent set of versions of the changed parts of the system are integrated to form the new system. All this means that the change management strategy needs to be complemented by a configuration management or version management strategy. This would be usually done for changes to business software systems and software products, but it would be unusual to do this for purely manual processes, though perhaps it should be.

Summing up

In this chapter we have seen the intimate embedding of software into organisations and artefacts, which means that though we might separate these for the practical purposes of acquiring software, that separation is synthetic, and we must always be ready to look at the overall system when we evaluate the role of software embedded in an organisation or an engineering artefact and make decisions about changes and replacements. We saw that people play a critical role in the learning organisation as it evolves.

We arrived at this conclusion by the following argument:

- organisations and the work they do can be modelled by diagrams and measurements;
- but these models are necessarily partial, and should not and cannot be taken to fully represent what happens in the organisation;
- the work of organisations can be modelled as business processes, a sequence of interacting individual activities;
- the activities in these processes can be made highly specialised to enhance efficiency by 'scientific management' methods;
- these taylorist processes lack flexibility and humanity;
- organisations contain computing systems and software embedded within them and are inseparable from them;
- the software and the business processes to use that software must necessarily be developed together, and though the software can be defined by a requirements document, the software cannot be understood in isolation;
- yet in order to acquire software and later evolve it we must be able to treat the software separately from other resources used in the business process;
- the software systems embody some of the knowledge of the organisation, but cannot embody all of the knowledge, some must inevitably remain tacit within the people involved;
- new systems are introduced either because of internal problems, because of external business opportunities, or because of external demands;

- rational decision-making processes and return on investment calculations can only partially help justify the acquisition;
- the process of introducing new systems can be viewed as a process of adaptation or learning, and the organisation that does this as a learning organisation;
- organisational learning takes place in cycles as business processes are changed: knowledge is externalised and examined and restructured and consolidated and then re-internalised;
- the people in the organisation are critically important in this process, and should be viewed as part of the assets of the organisation, the human capital.

This left us focusing on the human side of organisations, which will be pursued further in the next chapter. These two chapters will then leave us with an underpinning view of software in organisations that will inform our analysis of the more technical processes of acquiring and sustaining software covered in Chapter 6 and onwards.

Exercises

1. Think of a process that you are involved with and you wish to improve in your work or your daily life (e.g., the way the local council deals with queries). Draw a context diagram and a level 1 DFD of the process as it currently is, using the conventions indicated in the Appendix A of this book. Then apply some form of re-engineering to this process and show the result by drawing a modified level 1 DFD.

2. A software enterprise may have several software projects happening at the same time. The collection of projects of an organisation is sometimes called the 'project portfolio'. Make a list of the additional types of costs and benefits that emerge from having a portfolio of projects that should be considered when making a cost–benefit analysis of a newly proposed project.

3. The net present value (NPV) of a sum of cash $F(n)$ received or paid in n years time is given by the formula

$$\text{NPV} = F(i)/[(1 + (r/100)]^i$$

   where r is the discount rate (interest rate) in percentage (e.g., 5 per cent).
   Based on the original figures for the Taurus system given in Case Study 2.3 and using the NPV formula, calculate how much the minimum income per year would have to be in order to break even and recover the development and capital costs after five years. Assume a discount rate of six per cent. (Hint: create a simple spreadsheet with the NPV formula and manually adjust the yearly income so that NPV approximately matches the initial costs).

4. Discuss how you would use NPV calculations (see exercise 3), and in particular a target discount rate, in order to accept or reject individually each project in a set of projects to be evaluated.

5. Computers and software not only automate processes, but also provide or make accessible to people more information than would otherwise be available. Such extra information can be essential for the survival of a business. However, there is a danger of information overload of personnel using computers. Relate this to the limitations of a taylorist approach when applied to the staffing of computerised activities.

6. The following expression represents the Rayleigh curve for staffing a software project (discussed, for example, in DeMarco's *Controlling Software Projects*):

$$PT(t) = 2^*K^*a^*t^*exp(-a^*t^2)$$

where PT is the person-time (e.g., person-months) t is the time in months, K and a are parameters of the model (K is the total person-time allocated to the project and a is a parameter which controls the shape of the curve). Assuming that $K = 500$ person-months and $a = 0.01$, find out in which month of the project the effort will reach a peak. What are the implications for staffing and training?

7. According to Robert Glass in his book *Facts and Fallacies of Software Engineering*, one of the most important facts is that 'For every 25 per cent increase in problem complexity, there is a 100 per cent increase in complexity of a software solution'. Explain why this argument can be used to justify the need to re-estimate the costs and benefits of an automation project after any significant change in scope and to find an appropriate balance between human-based and computer-based activities.

8. One of the reasons why some apparently simple activities cannot be fully computerised is the need for tacit knowledge. Consider, for example, a hotel receptionist who has to rapidly identify whether a person checking in is part of a family coming together, a group of travellers, or the owner of the hotel, and how quickly he/she adapts to the needs of the situation. A simple activity like this may involve visual, hearing, and other clues which are learnt over many years and are difficult to elicit and formalise in any notation and implement in any computer algorithm. Think, for example, of other activities you are familiar with that involve tacit knowledge. Based on these, list some of the advantages of retaining some level of human processes within a business system.

9. The World Bank's website interfaces into the World Bank's knowledge management system. This site and its underlying knowledge management systems has been highly acclaimed and won many awards. Visit their website, http://www.worldbank.org/index.html, find the various papers that explain the theory underpinning the site, searching on 'knowledge management' and 'knowledge sharing' and similar terms. Study these documents and explore the website, then write an evaluation of the World Bank's knowledge management system. To what extent does the website form an integral part of the knowledge management system?

Endnotes

1. Modelling an organisation is seen as an important a step towards understanding it and managing it – see the Gartner report by Jim Sinur (2004) Drivers for BPM: 11 Money-Relevant Reasons to Start, 25 February 2004, Note Number: COM-21-9991. ('BPM' is an abbreviation for business process management.)

2. Note that as soon as we divide a system into parts we are creating the illusion that such a division is possible and that the parts are separate and that the whole can be described in terms of the behaviour of the parts and their interaction. Even though we know that this is an illusion, we will still do this, for creating such abstractions is extremely useful.

3. Frederick Winslow Taylor (1911) *The Principles of Scientific Management*. Available from http://www.marxists.org/reference/subject/economics/taylor/principles/index.htm.

4. Quoted from Taylor's testimony to the House of Representatives Committee, 1912.

5. Quoted from the entry on Taylorism and Scientific Management in the US-based Labor Law Talk encyclopaedia at http://encyclopedia.laborlawtalk.com/Scientific_management.

6. See for example: Kent Beck (2000) Fred Taylor, Making Software, and Conversation. CSE'00 Software Productivity in a Changing World, and JAOO conference Aarhus Denmark Sept 2000. The summary of his keynote at JAOO claims: 'Many of the dysfunctional patterns of software development can be traced directly back to Fred Taylor and Scientific Management.'

7. The Workflow Management Coalition's website is http://www.wfmc.org/.

8. The Workflow Institute's website is http://www.workflowinstitute.com/.

9. See, for example, Michael Hammer and James Champney (1995) *Reengineering the Corporation: A Manifesto for Business Revolution* (revised edn). Nicholas Brealey.

10. Donald Reifer (2002) *Making the Software Business Case: Improvement by the Numbers*. Addison-Wesley.

11. Condensed from an account posted at the University of Wolverhampton on http://www.scit.wlv.ac.uk/~cm1995/cbr/cases/case02/NINE.HTM and a number of other sources.

12. For example, the popular 900-page textbook on software engineering by Pressman (R.S. Pressman (2000) *Software Engineering: A Practitioner's Approach* (5th edn, European Adaptation, adapted by D. Ince). McGraw-Hill) devotes just one page to concerns of technical feasibility and nothing to benefits.

13. Kathy Schwalbe (2004) *Information Technology Project Management* (3rd edn). Thomson Course Technology.

14. See, for example, the Josephson Institute of Ethics guide Making Ethical Decisions, on http://www.josephsoninstitute.org/.

15. The balanced scorecard system was developed in 1990s as a means of measuring the non-financial performance of private sector companies, but has since been made much more generally applicable. Thus it is much more general than its suggested use here in making decisions about investment. See the Balanced Scorecard Institute's website at www.balancedscorecard.org.

16. See, for example, Michael Jackson (1983) *System Development*. Prentice Hall.

17. Tracy Kidder (1981) *The Soul of a New Machine*. Allen Lane.

18. Paul Quintas (editor) (1993) *Social Dimensions of Systems Engineering: People, Processes, Policies and Software Development*. Ellis Horwood.

19. William H. Dutton (1996) *Information and Communication Technologies: Visions and Realities*. Oxford University Press.

20. Ikujiro Nonaka and Hirotaka Takeuchi (1995) *The Knowledge-Creating Company*. Oxford University Press.

21. See, for example, http://www.kmresource.com/ for a broad coverage of the area.

22. The ABCs of Knowledge Management, at http://www.cio.com/research/knowledge/edit/kmabcs.html.

23. Expert systems were a class of systems pursued in the 1980s and 1990s by the artificial intelligence community who hoped to capture human expertise by a set of rules – while some expert systems proved very successful, in general they were judged to have failed in their goal of automating human expertise.

24. Business process re-engineering – see glossary.

25. G. Arango, E. Shoen, R. Pettengill, (1993) 'Design as Evolution and Reuse in Advances in Software Reuse', *Selected Papers from the Second International Workshop on Software Reusability*. IEEE Computer Society Press. March 24–26, 9–18.

26. See Chris Argyris (1999) *On Organizational Learning* (2nd edn). Blackwell Business.

27. Peter M. Senge (1990) *The Fifth Discipline: The Art and Practice of The Learning Organisation*. Random House Business Books.

28. The concept of feedback was first articulated in electronics by Norbert Wiener, though feedback is basic to much of life and engineering. This history has persisted in learning organisations through the use of the terms 'single-loop' and 'double-loop'. A comprehensive history is given by George Richardson (1991) *Feedback Thought in Social Science and Systems Theory*. University of Pennsylvania Press.

29. The feedback learning cycle can be formulated as an optimisation problem, that of making organisation performance as high as possible. The cycle of feedback and improvement would then be viewed as 'hill-climbing' optimisation, where a standard problem is getting stuck at the top of a 'foothill'; in order to reach the 'peak' you must start reasonably close to it!

30. See Chris Argyris (1999) *On Organizational Learning* (2nd edn). Blackwell Business. See in particular Chapter 3, pp. 67–91.

31. Lucy A. Suchman (1987) *Plans and Situated Actions: The Problem of Human Machine Communication*. Cambridge.

3 Economic and social context

What we will study in this chapter

Software is developed and evolved by people. Software is used in organisations and organisations are made up of people whose work is supported by that software. When software makes organisations more productive, it does so by making people more productive. People are critically important, and we need to understand people, what motivates them, and what demotivates them. People respond well to situations that could not have been characterised and turned into procedures beforehand. We saw in the previous chapter that the use of tacit knowledge and the ability to take situated action nevertheless can be shared and managed, and valued as human capital by the organisation.

We will see that not all activity is done for financial reasons, and that there is in fact a large 'gratis' sector of the economy of which the important Free and Open Source software movement is part. Labour for software development and evolution is provided freely and without charge, and yet businesses can be built around this.

This chapter looks at:

- the motivation of people in the workplace: the classical theories of McGregor and Herzberg and Maslow, and the apparent paradoxes of the Hawthorne effect;

- the aspects of these theories that apply to creative people working with and on software;

- how motivation varies across cultures, looking at the theories of Hofstede and others;

- the critical nurturing of people as 'reflective practitioners' working in 'communities of practice' able to take 'situated action';

- the interplay between personal and organisational motivation;

- simple models of the market and the profit motive;

- market breakdowns, externalities and public goods, monopolies, planned obsolescence;

- the free software movement.

3.1 Individual motivation to work

We began this book in Chapter 1 by looking at why we invest in software, looking further in Chapter 2 at productivity and return on investment. We found that a justification based purely on the direct benefits of the use of computers was difficult. We saw how software could embody part of the knowledge of the organisation, but that other important knowledge remained tacit within the people working in the organisation: people remain critical to the success of organisations.

In this chapter we focus on people and how they can become more effective, starting with the factors that might motivate them both individually and within a group. This leads us into the consideration of economics, finding that simple arguments based on markets and profit are not adequate to account for movements like Open Source that are important in software. But first we look at people's motivation to work.

Why do people work? The simple answer might be so that they can earn sufficient money to be able to meet their needs. But if that were the case, would paying them more make them work harder? Why do some people choose less highly paid jobs, and why do some people work for nothing? Clearly there is more to this than simple money. The reasons for people working are important for organisations and for the economy, since these depend upon people's work. Why people work, or do anything else, has been studied for many years as 'motivation'. How can we motivate them to do the work that we want them to do?

To understand the issues involved, let us start with the classic discussion by McGregor in 1960[1] – 'Theory X' versus 'Theory Y'. In this seminal paper McGregor describes a traditional view of how you direct and control workers, his **Theory X**, as:

- the average person has a dislike of work and will avoid it if at all possible;
- because of this dislike of work most people must be threatened and coerced in order to ensure that they put in adequate effort for their employer;
- even the promise of rewards is not sufficient;
- the average human prefers to be directed, avoids responsibility, has little ambition, and wants security.

He contrasts this with his **Theory Y** which is characterised by:

- the average human being does not dislike work, the expenditure of physical and mental effort in work is as natural as play or rest;
- people will exercise self-direction and self-control in order to achieve objectives to which they are committed;
- commitment to objectives depends on the rewards for their achievement, rewards such as self-fulfilment and not just money;
- people learn to accept and even seek responsibility;
- most people like to exercise their imagination and ingenuity in their work for an organisation;
- the intellectual potential of people is frequently only partially utilised.

McGregor realised that motivation was deeply rooted in human biology, and there was a hierarchy of human needs that underpinned their behaviour in organisations. Deploying the Theory Y potential of people required them to be integrated into an organisation, to become part of that organisation, and this view of the relationship between employees and the organisation that employs them underpinned the discussion around learning organisations in Chapter 2.

McGregor's line of reasoning that motivation is deeply rooted in human psychology has been picked up by other theorists, and we will look at the seminal studies of Herzberg and Maslow.

People work because they enjoy it, requiring an adequate financial compensation to meet their 'hygienic' needs, but after that it is other, non-financial, factors that create motivation.

Herzberg was researching at the same time as McGregor, with much interaction between their ideas. Herzberg is most famous for his motivation-hygiene theory,[2] based upon studies in US industry investigating the factors that led to satisfaction and dissatisfaction at work. He and his co-workers found that the factors that gave most satisfaction were achievement, recognition of that achievement, responsibility, advancement, and the work itself. The factors that led to most dissatisfaction were company policy and administration, supervision, salary, interpersonal relations, and working conditions. The first set of factors relate to what the person does, the second to the circumstances under which they do it. Herzberg described this first set as motivation factors, and the second set as hygiene factors. The hygiene factors need to be sufficiently good in order to avoid dissatisfaction (i.e., avoid pain from the work environment). After that it is the motivating factors (seeking personal growth from the work) that make the difference. Note particularly the place of salary as a hygiene factor.

Both McGregor's and Herzberg's theories are in some sense monotonic – the more you have of a motivating factor, the better the result at work. However this is not always the case, as is seen in Case Study 3.1.

Case Study 3.1 *The Hawthorne effect*

The Hawthorne Effect[3] is named after a factory of the Western Electric Company in the US which was studied in the 1930s. Systematic experiments were conducted to determine the range of factors that affected worker productivity. Among these was the level of lighting in the factory – the results were perverse: when lighting was improved productivity went up, but it also went up in a second room where the lighting had remained unchanged. When lighting was reduced, productivity again went up, as it also did in the control room where lighting had not been changed. When other factors, like rest periods were studied, similar seemingly perverse results were found. What was producing this?

It seems that the interventions and the changes that were having the effects observed were not the changes in lighting level or rest periods at all, but the fact that they were being observed. You could interpret this as showing the need to include surveillance equipment to watch workers ever more closely. However we and others interpret this as showing that it was the management displaying interest and concern through making the interventions and interviewing the staff involved that produced the effect. Further, in order to obtain worker participation in these investigations, people had had to be handled in teams and gained a sense of community from this.

Activity 3.1   *Hawthorne, Theory X or Theory Y?*

Discuss the Hawthorne result, as described above, in terms of Theory X versus Theory Y.

Discussion

The original hypothesis at Hawthorne was clearly a Theory X view of workers: if you adjust lighting levels, and workers can see their work better, their performance should improve. However the full sets of results, and the interpretations given to these, clearly fit better into Theory Y. Caring for the workforce helps them align with organisational objectives, with their participation in the experiments giving them some autonomy and responsibility.

Our view of people, particularly those working in the 'knowledge industries' and those involved with software, is now much richer. It is the research of Abraham Maslow that have proved most useful here, for his recognition and elaboration of the need for people to be able to grow and develop through their work. Surprisingly his work[4] was actually conducted earlier than that of McGregor and Herzberg, but has been much slower in gaining recognition.

Maslow's idea was that there is a hierarchy of needs, **basic needs** and **growth needs**. Basic needs are the physiological needs of sleep and rest, food and drink, shelter, and air; and safety, freedom from harm in a stable and secure environment. Growth needs include love and belonging, self-respect and the respect of others, knowledge and aesthetics, self-fulfilment. Maslow developed and refined this view over many years, and others since have added to it.

It is usual to draw this hierarchy of needs as a pyramid, as in Figure 3.1 which shows a current view of the hierarchy. Without the foundation of basic needs being met, satisfying the higher growth needs is not effective.

Figure 3.1

Maslow's Hierarchy of Needs

People are motivated by opportunities for self-development and social interaction and contribution to their organisation and society.

Motivation is an important part of obtaining productive work from a person. However motivation is by no means the only factor involved. Productivity studies of people working in the software industry have shown individuals vary enormously in their performance: however, as team sizes grow, individual variation becomes less important, though for critical roles, like product architect, employing the best is essential.

The three studies we have looked at are all classical studies undertaken in the US more than fifty years ago, but which are still referred to and form the springboard for more recent studies of motivation. In the next section we will look at more recent studies, and ones that look more globally at motivation. But before going on, do Activity 3.2 to consolidate what you have learnt.

Activity 3.2   *Maslow*

How could you manage people working with software so that you address the needs identified in Maslow's hierarchy? Comment on each of the needs in turn, though you can ignore the foundation layer of physiological needs and the pinnacle layer of self transcendence.

Discussion

Stability and security
Maslow has shown that there is a basic need for stability and security, a need whose breach can lead to the stress so common in recent decades. Security of employment is critical, though note that this security can be found as a freelance contracting in a market where the demand is high.

Belonging
Ensure good communication so that everybody feels involved at every level, and if people work in teams make sure that the teams gel so that the members identify with the team.

Self-respect and the respect of others
It is important that everybody feels competent and that their competence is recognised by their colleagues, so people should not be too challenged and led into failure (but they must be challenged enough for self-fulfilment); ensure adequate training.

Understanding and knowledge
Ensure that everybody has the opportunity to extend their knowledge and learn new things, and apply that knowledge.

Aesthetics
Some people, like Donald Knuth[5] who wrote about literate programming, find software beautiful. Others take aesthetic pleasure from good human–computer interfaces; Jakob Neilsen[6] has written about the art in interfaces.

Self-fulfilment
Various management methods encourage people to set themselves objectives and to regularly review whether they have met those personal targets.

Knowledge workers have a need to develop their knowledge and skills and to develop their social relationships.

3.2 Global views of motivation

All the research on motivation in section 3.1 was undertaken in the US (a Western developed country) over fifty years ago. More recent studies have built on these seminal studies, but almost inevitably as a result of globalisation have a multi-national and multicultural aspect to them.

That people from different nations and different cultures have different attitudes and behave differently is a commonplace observation, but the first systematic study was by Geerte Hofstede,[7] followed shortly by Fons Trompenaars.[8] What Hofstede did was to study the attitudes and values of people within a single organisation, IBM, at locations around the world, sending a wide-ranging questionnaire which he then analysed statistically to extract just four 'dimensions' of significant variability between the groups in the various countries studied. He called these dimensions:

- power distance;
- individualism–collectivism;
- masculinity–femininity;
- uncertainty avoidance;

though please don't read anything into these names. (In particular the masculinity–femininity dimension does not have anything to do with the sex of the people concerned!) Hofstede claimed that his dimensions were reflected in the social fabric of society, in the relationships between the individual and the family, school, work, and the state.

Power distance is concerned with the inequality between people. Hofstede wrote:

> Power distance can . . . be defined as the extent to which the less powerful members of institutions and organisations within a country expect and accept that power is distributed unequally. (p. 28)

In a country with a high power distance, people expect and accept that power is invested in a few individuals or an elite. This elite expects respect and obedience from others, and in return will take responsibility for and protect these others. Hofstede claims that in such a culture, there is a 'pattern of dependence on seniors which pervades all human contacts' (p. 32), and that 'this pattern establishes a need for such dependence: inequalities among people are both expected and desired' (p. 37).

By contrast, in a country with low power distance people aspire to equality and to the sharing of responsibility and power. In cultures with a high power distance, the ideal boss is a benevolent dictator; power is centralised and power structures hierarchical. In cultures with low power distances, workplaces tend to have flatter hierarchies and more democratic institutions.

Hofstede found that Malaysia, Guatemala, and Panama have the highest power distances of the fifty-three countries surveyed, while Denmark, Israel, and Austria have the lowest.

Individualism–collectivism is concerned with the relationship between the individual person and the people around them. Thus Hofstede writes:

Individualism pertains to societies in which the ties between individuals are loose: everyone is expected to look after himself or herself and his or her immediate family. Collectivism as its opposite pertains to societies in which people from birth onwards are integrated into strong, cohesive in-groups, which throughout people's lifetime continue to protect them in exchange for unquestioning loyalty. (p. 51)

Collectivist cultures, scoring low on the individualism index, have these characteristics:

- the collective interest is valued more than the individual interest;
- fitting in with the social group is very important, personal opinions are suppressed;
- harmony and the avoidance of conflict are valued;
- pride is taken in the achievements of the group, and the collective shame of the whole group must be avoided.

Individualistic cultures on the other hand have these characteristics:

- individual interests take precedence over collective interests;
- personal opinions are valued as a sign of sincerity and honesty;
- the ability to handle conflict is valued over the ability to avoid it;
- individual qualities such as self-respect and guilt are more important than their collective equivalents (group pride and shame).

Thus in the workplace in an individualistic society, the individual's self-interest is paramount and work should be organised so that the interests of the individual and the organisation coincide. The organisation will:

- give enough time for personal life;
- provide a personal sense of achievement;
- provide flexibility in how the job is done.

In a collectivist society, employees are members of a group and have a duty of loyalty and protection to each other; this duty might influence who gets hired and who gets fired. A collectivist society values:

- training opportunities;
- good working conditions;
- full use of the individual's skills and abilities.

Hofstede ranked the USA, Australia, and Great Britain as the most individualistic of the countries surveyed, with Panama, Ecuador and Guatemala as the most collectivist.

The **masculinity–femininity** dimension is concerned with roles normally related to gender: the 'masculine' traits of aggression and competition, etc., as opposed to the 'feminine' ones of caring and nurturing. In some cultures these roles are polarised, in others less so. In his IBM survey, Hofstede found that one cluster of people valued jobs which provide opportunities for:

- high earnings;
- recognition;
- personal challenge;
- personal advancement.

Another cluster placed more value on:

- good working relationships with a boss and with colleagues;
- employment security;
- the location of the job.

These clusters statistically differentiated between nations, and nationwide, between men and women.

Hofstede found that in countries with high overall scores on masculinity, the difference in the survey responses between males and females was higher than in countries which scored lower. That is, in cultures which were overall quite aggressive and competitive, the differences between men and women were more pronounced than in cultures which were overall more caring. He also found that this gulf was age dependent, with men and women converging on the more caring 'feminine' attitudes with age. In cultures with a high masculinity score, Hofstede claims that relationships between management and workers are more likely to be confrontational, whereas in cultures with a low score, they are more likely to be cooperative.

Japan, Austria, and Venezuela topped the masculinity index (and thus had the largest difference in responses between men and women), with the Scandinavian countries coming lowest.

Uncertainty avoidance is concerned with how a society copes with unpredictable events: whether such events are avoided as much as possible or are welcomed as providing new opportunities and challenges. Hofstede notes that technology might go some way towards alleviating unpredictable environmental events; laws and social norms might make human behaviour more predictable, and some forms of religion might be regarded as providing answers as to why unpredictable events happen.

In countries with a high uncertainty index people find that:

- their jobs are very stressful;
- they intend to remain with the same employer for some time;
- company rules should never be broken.

In high uncertainty avoidance countries, where there is a cultural need for frameworks and rules, people might be better at implementation than innovation, with managers better at operational details than strategy. In low uncertainty avoidance countries, where people seem more eager to explore the unknown, the reverse might be true: innovation might blossom and managers might be better at strategy.

Greece, Portugal, and Guatemala came top of this index, and Denmark, Jamaica, and Singapore at the bottom.

How effective would you expect a staff appraisal system to be, based on an honest exchange of views between appraiser and appraisee, in cultures across the four Hofstede dimensions?

Discussion

Staff appraisal works best in a society with:

- low power distance, where the appraisee can express views openly and frankly, even when the appraiser is their manager;
- high individualism, since the views expressed may be contrary to general opinion which would need to be suppressed in a collectivist society;
- low masculinity, because the society needs to be caring and supportive of divergent opinions;
- low uncertainty avoidance, since expressing contrary views can be unsettling and lead to results that are not anticipated.

Various people have proposed other dimensions. The most interesting of these have been to do with time: whether people have a long-term or short-term orientation; and whether they are mono-synchronic or poly-synchronic – mono-synchronic people can only concentrate on one thing at a time, while poly-synchronic people thrive on having many things going on at the same time.

Hofstede has been very influential, even though he has rightly been criticised for being overly reductionist. There have been attempts to use Hofstede's dimensions to predict whether particular software would be acceptable in a particular market, and even to design systems for a particular market, but these have singularly failed. Human behaviour cannot be reduced to a few simple dimensions, it is much more complex than that, and yet these simple dimensions do seem to embody within them some truth, if only that people from different cultures can be very different.

Hofstede has also explored what his dimensions might mean for organisations in their employment of people. This has led to six organisational interpretations of his data, classifying organisations as follows:

1. Process-oriented versus results-oriented: differentiates between those organisations that avoid taking risks by regulating their practices and those that set goals even in challenging circumstances.

2. Employee-oriented versus job-oriented: concern for the welfare of people as opposed to completing the job.

3. Parochial versus professional: parochial employees identify with the organisation with a sense of belonging while professional employees only identify with doing their job.

4. Open systems versus closed systems: open organisations welcome newcomers and the external public.

5. Loose control versus tight control: loose control means little control of time and costs, while tight control means accurate timetables and budgets.

6. Normative versus pragmatic: pragmatic organisations change according to the 'needs' of the market while normative organisations implement inviolable rules.

Fons Trompenaars[9] has focused much more on organisational issues and inter-cultural cooperation. He believes there are three basic categories of problem:

1. those arising from an individual's relationships with other people;
2. those arising from the passage of time;
3. those relating to the environment.

These problems lead to seven fundamental dimensions of culture:

1. Universalism versus particularism: universalism assumes that there is some right way of proceeding in a given situation, while particularism emphasises that context fashions behaviour, that is, the right way of proceeding depends on the particular situation.[10] A culture with strong social norms might be universalist; one allowing more individual behaviour, particularist.

2. Individualism versus communitarianism: similar to Hofstede's individualism–collectivism.

3. Neutral versus emotional: in the former case, it is expected that the nature of our transactions will be objective and detached: in the latter, the showing of emotion is expected or, at least, not deprecated. For example, you might expect that the British are likely to be detached in their transactions; people from Latin American countries are likely to be more emotional.

4. Specific versus diffuse: this relates to the degree to which people's roles are separated. In a specific culture, your boss may behave as you would expect a boss to behave in the workplace, but if she/he meets you in a café after work, she/he might behave as you expect a friend or acquaintance to behave. In a diffuse culture, a friend behaves like a friend at all times; a boss behaves like a boss at all times; the role diffuses through all behaviour.

5. Achievement versus ascription: in the first case, individuals are judged by their individual achievements, their record of accomplishments. In the second, they are judged by the group they are associated with, for example, by kinship, age, connections, or education.

6. Attitudes to time: this appears similar to Hofstede's short-term/long-term orientation. Some cultures emphasise the present and the future, the new and the innovative; others, the past and tradition.

7. Attitudes to the environment: should the focus of concern be on the individual or the environment around him/her? Trompenaars and his co-author Hampden-Turner give the examples of an individual wearing a face mask, or listening to a personal stereo with headphones. In Japan, the reason for a face mask might be to stop an individual's cold from spreading to other people; the use of a personal stereo with headphones might be so as not to disturb people nearby. In Great Britain, according to Trompenaars and Hampden-Turner, the reason for wearing the face mask is more likely to be to protect the individual

from pollution; the use of the personal stereo with headphones, so that the individual is not distracted by the noise of people nearby.

Activity 3.4

Match the seven cultural dimensions identified by Trompenaars with his three categories of problems, and relate them to Hostede's dimensions.

Discussion
Here are some of our thoughts: you may have others, or may disagree with ours.

We think that dimensions 1–5 all address problem category A concerning personal relationships. Dimension 6 clearly addresses problems relating to time; dimension 7, problems relating to the environment.

Turning to the relationship with Hofstede, the numbers below are the numbers we have given to Trompenaars' dimensions.

1. A universalist culture with strong social norms might be one with strong uncertainty avoidance and weak power distance. A particularist culture might be associated with weak uncertainty avoidance.

2. Matches with Hofstede's individualism dimension.

3. We can't think of any obvious relationship between neutral–emotional and Hofstede's dimensions.

4. 'Specific versus diffuse': perhaps there is a relationship here with individualism–collectivism: in a collectivist culture, a friend (member of your in-group) is always your friend and protects your interests, whatever his/her role.

5. 'Achievement versus ascription' seems to relate to individualism–collectivism. The valuing of individual achievement may also correlate with high scores on the masculinity index.

6. Attitudes to time – relates to the short-term/long-term orientation dimension.

7. Attitudes to the environment. A collectivist culture might subscribe to a collectivist ideal, preferring concern for the environment rather than for individual comfort. This might also reflect a culture which scores low on the masculinity index.

We commented earlier that the classical studies of motivation were based in the US, but indicated that more recent studies have built on those early works but also taken a more global view of motivation. We have seen from the studies of Hofstede and Trompenaars that there can be a great diversity across cultures. The 1992 study of cross-cultural psychology by John Berry and colleagues[11] looks at a number of studies of motivation and needs. One interesting study[12] used a simplified version of Maslow's needs hierarchy to survey managers and found that self-fulfilment and the need for autonomy was important for everybody, but that job satisfaction varied widely, with the most satisfied in Japan and the Nordic countries, and the least satisfied in Latin America and developing countries.

A quite separate line of research, discussed by Berry *et al.*, has been the 'Meaning of Working,' begun by Weber in 1905. Since 1978 a number of researchers around the world have collaborated under the general heading of the Meaning of

Working International Research Team to find out how working fits into people's lives. The principal finding was *work centrality*, that work has value in people's lives. Work was important in people's lives, second only to the family, and people would continue working even if they had enough money to be able to stop work. They distinguished between entitlements, the right to meaningful and interesting work, and obligations, the duty to contribute to society by working: we see a strong echo of the individualism–collectivism divide here. Working was considered most important in Japan, and least important in Britain.

Both of the studies reported by Berry *et al.* indicate that a long history of industrialisation is significant in shaping attitudes to work in national cultures.

3.3 Human resource development

We saw above that people have a need for social interaction, and providing this is one important aspect of motivation. This social need is also important in establishing teams and enabling these teams to gel. However, there is another very important benefit to be gained from personnel socialisation and team organisations – they can be central to the development of the people within their workplace.

When staff are not able to perform their work adequately, the conventional solution is to undertake staff training, and it would be normal in most organisations for staff to undergo several weeks of training a year. Depending upon the particular job being undertaken, this training might be technical and skills based, such as training in particular software development methods or the use of software applications. Alternatively, the training might be more management focused, developing generic conceptual tools to aid the manager perform more effectively. This book has elements of both of these.

However, training has its limitations, for it presupposes that all possible contingencies can be known beforehand and be anticipated in the training. We have already seen that such planning is not in general possible, and that many activities are 'situated' with the actions that need to be taken contingent on factors which could not have been anticipated. We need people who have learnt how to learn, who can go on learning and enjoy that learning. Case Study 3.2 illustrates this with findings from studies of expert engineers.

> The relationship between people and their work varies considerably between communities and countries, and it would be wrong to transfer organisational structures and processes unchanged between countries.

Case Study 3.2 *The discipline of expertise and innovation*

Marian Petre has spent many years studying experts in order to uncover how they work and consistently create innovative solutions. Here is what she has discovered.[13] Innovative expert teams and individuals:

- acquire knowledge systematically from patent searches, reading relevant journals and books and attending conferences, monitor-

ing legislation changes, and monitoring the competition;

- habitually solve problems and store the solutions for later use;

- keep records of all work they do;

- reflect on newly completed projects and related projects, and general themes as they emerge;

▶

- reuse and reapply recent innovations;
- identify barriers to what is wanted, and re-move them;
- focus on conflicts between competing re-quirements and analyse these;
- regularly brainstorm to generate new ideas;
- look for gaps in knowledge and under-standing seeking to find new possibilities;
- work through scenarios to explore the con-sequences of design proposals;

- abstract away from real problems to focus on the essence of the problem;
- explore constraints on a design and aim to reduce these;
- play with toys as a way of discovering solu-tions to real problems.

Experts are highly disciplined individuals who do not sit around waiting for inspiration, but sys-tematically develop their capabilities and seek out that inspiration.

Personal development of knowledge and skills can only be partly met through formal training, and also depends upon self-reflection and social interaction within a community of practice.

Donald Schoen has noted the importance of reflection in the process of devel-oping expertise, and has coined the term 'reflective practitioner' to denote the in-dividual who does this.[14]

As well as learning individually by reflecting on their experience as discussed above, people also learn very effectively together as part of a team. They share knowledge related to their work, learning new things together to construct a com-mon understanding.

A group of people engaged in this social learning has been called a **community of practice** by Etienne Wenger.[15] Communities of practice cannot be designed or imposed, but they should be nurtured and encouraged. They are, in effect, the non-technical mechanism for knowledge management that we discussed in Chapter 2.

One very important social group to which people belong is the organisation for which they work. This is explored in Activity 3.5.

Personal motivation fits well within learning organisations.

Activity 3.5	*People in learning organisations*

Given the preceding discussion of human motivation and the need for growth, how well do people fit into learning organisations discussed in Chapter 2?

Discussion

We saw at the end of Chapter 2 that in order for organisations to learn, the people within them need to learn, and through them the business processes of the organisa-tion can change.

We saw in this chapter that people are motivated by opportunities for personal de-velopment, for growth, and that learning forms an important part of this. Thus there is a powerful willingness for people to learn along with the organisation that employs them.

We can extend this argument a little further and conjecture that a learning organisa-tion constitutes a community of practice within which the development and growth of that organisation and its employees can take place to mutual benefit.

However, organisations are not created just to learn, and we need to look a little deeper into organisations and their motivations.

3.4 Organisational motivation and market forces

Markets have become the foundation of most western economies, based on the idea that if individuals pursue self-interest this leads to an appropriate use of limited resources (economists terms this an 'optimal' use, but that clearly is not a correct use of the term 'optimal', meaning best possible). To see how markets work to achieve this, look at Case Study 3.3.

Case Study 3.3   *The market in personal computers*

Personal computers can be bought through a wide range of retail outlets, or directly from companies that assemble them to order. There is fierce competition, with an abundant supply of computers, so that the price is kept down and the customer has a wide range of choices. People who own PCs may elect to sell them second hand, advertising them in local newspapers or across the Internet.

This free market in personal computers is characterised by three related key features:

- use of the personal computer is exclusive to one owner or a few owners at a time either through constraints on physical access to the computer or the use of passwords;

- the benefit gained from sharing the PC would be reduced if the other rival users/owners were also competing for access to the computer and thereby limiting your use of it;

- the right of ownership of the PC is recognised in law, with proof of ownership resting partly on the fact of possession and partly in the documents recording purchase.

The features seen above in the PC case study are characteristics of markets in general, and will be important later when we come to look at market failure and markets associated with software, and particularly open source software. But first let us turn to some basic ideas of economics[16] to set all of this in context.

In any society (or economy) a large range of goods and services (we will call these collectively **goods**) are required. What particular goods are produced and consumed may be determined by some process of central planning in a **command economy**, or may be determined by a system of trading within a **market economy**.

In economics a **commodity** is a standardised and undifferentiated non-perishable good, with an abundant supply and a potentially fluctuating price, capable of being traded both for current ('spot') delivery and for future delivery. Its value arises from the owner's right to sell rather than from their right to use. Commodity markets focus on raw materials from agriculture and mining possibly with some intermediate extraction process, so oil, metals, rubber, wool, and even electricity are traded as commodities. However the term 'commodity' is used more widely to mean any good produced for sale in a market, and in Marxist political economy theory the value of a commodity is equated with the labour required to produce it. In our discussion of software as a commodity we mean that the software is a marketable good that can be bought and sold in shops, distinguishing it from a be-spoke product that is built for a particular purpose and that will not be traded.

In a market a number of buyers (consumers) and sellers (producers) of the commodities interact to determine the price of the commodities being traded. If the price is high, buyers will reduce their demand for the commodity, while sellers will produce more to increase the supply of this commodity and hence the volume of their sales. However if the price is low, buyers will wish to buy more and increase their demand, while sellers will produce less because their profits are not adequate. Providing there is no interference with the market mechanisms, an equilibrium is reached in which resources are used optimally. This is the **perfect market**, which works as if some 'invisible hand'[17] were regulating it, whereby prices, supply, and demand are kept in balance. Every commodity has a price which reflects not just the cost of production but more importantly the willingness of the market to pay for that commodity. Resources are attracted to their most valuable use. Implicit in this is a **law of scarcity**, that there are not enough resources to be able to produce enough commodities to meet each and every demand.

Goods can either be **consumables**, or **capital** goods. The production of commodities can be direct, simply relying on labour and other basic resources like land, or can be indirect, relying on the input of both basic resources and on capital goods. Capital goods are durable and enable human labour to be more productive.

The use of capital goods constitutes an investment, withholding immediate consumption in favour of saving to increase production and gain future consumption. In Chapter 2 we studied return on investment; now we see how this fits into the free market view of economic activity. When an organisation wants to make an investment to improve its performance it must choose among investments such as hiring more people, training existing people, purchasing software to enhance their productivity, and so on. For each choice there will be some predicted benefit or saving or other return, and some cost which must be offset against this – this net return on investment will be used to make a decision. Note that from the point of view of the organisation this is a rational decision-making process, with no evidence of an invisible hand, but from outside the organisation this is seen as rigorously competitive and subject to the invisible hand of the market.

Basic to the above is the idea that the commodities are owned individually, with the ownership rights or **property rights** recognised within the communities. This ownership allows the goods to be traded within the market. Also important is the property of **excludability** – the benefits of a particular good can be denied to other parties by the owners. We call commodities which are excludable and have property rights **private goods**.

Private goods are to be contrasted with **public goods**, where the benefits are spread throughout the community and it is difficult or impossible to give exclusive benefit to one or just a few people. Examples of public goods are the health service (in countries which have a public health service), the military protection of the armed forces, public land, and the open oceans. The property rights of public goods would be held in common and are normally administered by the state, which decides who can and cannot benefit from them (e.g., through granting citizenship). Public goods are also often known as the **commons**.

The failure of exclusion leads to public goods, as seen above, though of course public goods may well be desirable in their own right and it would be wrong to see them as lesser than private goods. However public goods do have their own problems. Where the public good is a natural resource with open access this can lead to the 'tragedy of the commons'.[18] If we assume that individuals simply pursue self-interest and exploit their open access to the limit (examples are fish stocks at sea or firewood on community land), then together they could deplete the natural resource to the point where it cannot recover: thus some regulation of open access to shared resources is necessary.

Activity 3.6   *Software services and software products*

To what extent do software services and software products constitute perfect markets as described above?

Discussion

Software services will be offered at a price appropriate to the particular market, and the price will be adjusted in the face of vigorous competition. These services are often labour intensive – examples are consultancy or bespoke software development. Being labour intensive, consultancy services are naturally excluding – a consultant cannot be in two places at once.

By contrast a software product has difficulty with excludability, since software is so easily copied unless significant technical measures are taken to overcome this. If a copy is made, the user of the original copy is not damaged in any way, except in special circumstances. An example of those special circumstances is where the competitive advantage to the owner of the original software relies upon a rival not using the product or system or an equivalent.

Software products have been made subject to property law, as we will see at length in Chapter 5.

> Modern economies are founded on free markets, which in turn are based on the ownership of private goods and property, which can be exchanged between free agents.

However, these free markets often fail, as we shall see in the next section. This may lead to government interventions in various forms.

3.5 From market failure to the gratis economy

The basic assumption of free markets is that the only parties involved are those who are undertaking the trade of the goods. Many agents might be involved, but the role of each will be represented in some manner in the prices in the exchange of goods. However, sometimes agents who are external to the transaction are affected either beneficially or detrimentally. In this case, the market is said to have failed and the causes that brought about the failure are called **externalities**.

We have already seen examples of externalities. First, if goods are not excludable, then people who have not purchased a good may still be able to benefit or suffer from it. The usual example given of positive benefit is firework displays, where it is difficult to prevent people from viewing the display: the person who benefits is often called a **free-rider**. The usual example of negative effects given is pollution from factories. We have already seen the example of software products in the discussion following Activity 3.6, where it is difficult to exclude people from copying software and then benefiting from it. We will see in Chapter 5 that intellectual property law can provide exclusion, but where such laws have not been enacted, or have been enacted but are not enforced, the market fails and producers of software cease their activities.

Case Study 3.4 *Software assets and reuse*

During the 1980s and 1990s, software reuse became very fashionable. Why didn't software have a thriving industry of component suppliers like other branches of engineering? Various research projects sought to address this with sophisticated technical solutions for defining and interconnecting software components.

Industrial programmes sought to create component repositories, often referring to the components as 'software assets' to emphasise the value to the enterprise. Software is typically produced by projects where the success criteria for the project is to produce the software for which they have been chartered within time and budget. Now project managers were being asked to identify components for incorporation into the asset repository, and to develop software using components from the repository. The demand that an asset repository is used required extra effort to generalise the project's components, and to describe them so that they could be reused. It also required searching the repository for useful components, which might not quite meet the need. Who would pay for all this? Project managers rejected the asset repository system and these failed. This has happened even where there were internal payments for adding assets to the repository and payments for use of assets from the repository, for they were not made within a free internal market but under some level of duress.

However, another approach has proved viable. Many software applications are similar to each other and can be understood as software product lines – essentially the same software product with small variations that are easily understood and readily changed.

We will see more of this in Chapters 6 and 8.

Software reuse was seeking a limited public good within the bounds of a particular organisation. The asset repository is a form of open access commons, but it needs to contain goods that are both useful and used. It starts empty, and while it may become populated, it remains a desert of useless artefacts. The internal market within the organisation fails; this is not the tragedy of the commons, but a tragedy nonetheless.

For a perfect market to work, it requires a number of small players, none of whom can unilaterally determine the prices for goods and services. All too frequently markets are not perfect, and one or a few players can determine price and rig the market – this is **imperfect competition**. When a single player can control the market we have a **monopoly**. Many countries have laws to prevent monopolies – in the US these are called anti-trust laws. Even where there is not a monopoly some players may collaborate in a cartel to effectively create an monopoly. A monopoly or near monopoly can arise naturally, due the relative efficiency of a larger firm benefiting from **economies of scale** – this can be seen in the retail grocery trade in most countries.

Imperfect competition can come about due to legal constraints, perhaps introduced to reduce imports or protect particular markets, like supplies to government. In the US AT&T used to use government-sanctioned entry barriers to prevent competition in long-distance telephone calls, and similar practice has been seen in many countries where the government suppresses VOIP – voice on Internet protocol. The use of patents is an important constraint on competition, backed up by the law – see Chapter 5 for details about patents and other intellectual property protection.

A simple but common source of imperfect competition is product differentiation – products are not identical and substitutable, having features that distinguish them. Differentiating software products in this way is perfectly normal – but distorts the market since for each differentiated product the supplier creates a monopoly! Product differentiation can further distort the market, since once a customer has bought the product the cost of repeat purchases can be significantly lower than purchase from an alternative supplier, making this a captive market.

Software never 'wears out', and some products don't become useless fast enough, which has led to planned obsolescence. This is the way the haute-couture clothing industry works, where it is important to have the latest fashion, and has been practiced in the motor industry by frequent changes in the external appearance of motor vehicles. In the software industry some element of fashion prevails, for example in naming products with the year embedded, but planned obsolescence is achieved in other ways, as picked up in Activity 3.7.

Activity 3.7   *Product differentiation and planned obsolescence*

In what ways do software suppliers exploit product differentiation and planned obsolescence in order to ensure repeat purchases of essentially the same product?

Discussion

Software does not 'wear out', so in principle once you have obtained software that meets your needs, you need never buy that type of software again. Software suppliers take measures to ensure that you will need an upgrade to the next version.

Product differentiation in software is created not only by offering different facilities and user interfaces, but also by not supplying easy data exchange between different products of the same type: items produced by one package must be maintained by that package. However, a product may include ways of importing data from other packages, but often only into the package and not out again. Though the rival product may have similar import facilities, there is no guarantee that data or its structure will be preserved if a round-trip is made. This traps customers into using software produced by the original supplier because movement to an alternative can only be made at considerable extra expense of data conversion as well as learning new interfaces.

Planned obsolescence is assured by a policy of new releases with limited backwards compatibility every two years or so. Because software is never delivered defect-free, products in service will be subject to updates relatively frequently, particularly if a security loophole has been discovered and needs to be plugged. Updates for earlier releases may be stopped after a short period once a new version has been released. New releases may contain new functions, but often these seem to add limited extra value, so while the manufacturer may claim to give continued product improvement, this may well not be the case.

Markets fail when agents external to the transactions are also affected, either positively or negatively: when product differentiation occurs, when one agent dominates the market and has a monopoly, or when the goods concerned are public and open access.

Some measures have been taken to counteract software marketing practices like those discussed above. Conformance to standards for data interchange is particularly important, and could be enforced in procurement agreements, though the market may also insist on conformance standards – as for example the continued use of Rich Text Format (RTF) for word-processed documents. Adherence to standards can also be token, for example in the claimed conformance to HTML where suppliers of Internet browsers differentiated themselves by supporting non-standard extensions with all the anti-competitive effects discussed in Activity 3.7.

One significant measure in Europe has been to support third-party suppliers who integrate their software with the software of major companies. Companies do publish application program interfaces (APIs) to support this integration, but often with insufficient information, and programmers have been in the practice of reverse engineering code using various techniques so as to understand what facilities are actually provided or required at the interface. The major companies did not like this, claiming that attempts were being made replicate their software, and appealed to the European Union, who, after consultations, issued a directive permitting the continued use of limited reverse engineering.

Case Study 3.5 *Free Software Foundation*

The Free Software Foundation (FSF) was founded in 1985 by Richard Stallman.[19] Twenty years later its website, http://www.fsf.org, proclaims:

> *Free Software is a matter of liberty not price. Free software is a matter of the users' freedom to run, copy, distribute, study, change and improve the software.*

Stallman had previously been working at the MIT AI laboratories on special purpose computers to support the AI programming language LISP, disagreeing with colleagues who left MIT to commercially exploit what became the Symbolics computer. Stallman by contrast wanted software to benefit people and society, and published the GNU[20] Manifesto and then established FSF in 1985.

The FSF is best known for its GNU project which produces 'free' editors and compilers, and for its very important and influential license GPL (GNU Public License) – we will look at this in detail in Chapter 5. The FSF and Stallman campaign for the free software ideal.

Related to the idea of free software is the Open Source model of software development. These are different concepts, though they are often combined, even coming together in the acronyms FOSS (Free Open Source Software) or FLOSS (Free/Libre Open Source Software). We will see a lot more about OSS in Chapter 6 as one important method of acquiring software, and Chapter 8 as one method of developing software.

The Free Software Foundation proclaims that software is a public good, and that everybody should be given open access to the software source so that they can change it, adapt it, and improve it. Software, unlike natural resources, cannot be depleted; there can be no scarcity of copies; it cannot suffer the tragedy of the commons.

However it can lead to similar tragedies if changes and evolution are unregulated. Look at the evolutions of Linux. Many distributors offer slightly different flavours of Linux, the complexity of which are then compounded in further adaptations to make Linux work in languages other than English (known as **local-isations**). Software designed to run on one flavour of Linux may not run on another flavour of Linux, and the ideal of a general public good is diminished.

While the 'free' of Free Software connotes freedom, it is nevertheless also associated with low or no cost. People develop the software and then effectively give it away. They may constrain the further uses that can be made using a license agreement, but they encourage its use and change. They do it out of a desire to do public good, but how does its original development and further evolution get paid for? The answer is simple: people give their time for free. This donation of voluntary labour has a very long tradition, as part of what Andras Kelen calls the '**gratis** economy'.[21]

Public goods and services in modern states would normally be provided by government and paid for by taxes, but there is long tradition of these being provided privately through voluntary work, perhaps operating through non-government organisations (NGOs) or other not-for-profit organisations (emphasising their gratis nature). However public goods might well be provided privately by individuals, for example in fostering children or giving **pro bono** legal advice; or developing software. But why do people do this, and how do they gain sufficient income from other sources?

As to motivation, we have already seen this in growth-need and social-need. Contributing to the development of open source software is intellectually challenging and stimulating, it is fun, and brings people into a small and dedicated social group. There may also be some *social obligation* that is discharged to some degree – the work is done for the good of the wider community, just as giving alms to charity discharges such a social obligation. There is a long established theory of the *social contract*, dating back to Jean-Jacques Rousseau in 1762.[22] The FOSS community of today invoke this concept to support their conditions of distribution.

The one aspect of motivation that is missing in the gratis economy is financial remuneration, Herzberg's hygiene, though there may be some payments of costs for public-spirited activities like child fostering or representing your country in sport. The financial needs of the volunteers would be met from other employment, or from sponsorship, where the provider of this sustenance may itself benefit through commercial exposure and projection of a positive image.

People's main employers may well agree with them undertaking voluntary work, and may even encourage it. This happens in particular when software engineers participate in open source development, since by doing so the software engineers work with very able people and learn much from their exposure as participants in the OSS community of practice.

> Organisations and people may operate outside the normal market within the gratis economy of voluntary labour and free use of products and services.

Summing up

In this chapter we have looked more deeply into the motivational factors at play in individuals and then in organisations. However, these are not antagonistic with one another, but can align with the organisation providing a stimulating environment within which the individual can learn and grow through exposure to advanced technology and knowledgeable colleagues. This applies equally well to voluntary work within the gratis economy and open source software.

We arrived at this point of view by noting that:

- people are motivated by factors other than money, providing that they get enough money;
- important motivation comes from the need for personal development and social contact;
- motivation may vary between nations and organisations;
- personal development can be partly achieved by training to meet the employer's needs;
- training must be supplemented by learning from experience and socially from others within communities of practice;
- organisations are also motivated by the need to survive and grow within some wider national and international economy;
- modern economies are based on free markets, which are in turn based on the exchange of private goods between free agents;
- markets adjust themselves through signals of prices, interest rates, profits, and wages to achieve optimal use of limited resources;
- markets fail when agents external to the transactions are also affected, either positively or negatively;
- markets also fail when the goods concerned are public and open access;
- organisations may operate outside the normal market within the gratis economy of voluntary labour and free use of products and services.

In the next two chapters we will look at how societies regulate the behaviour of their citizens to ensure that markets operate properly, focusing of course on software. This will include consideration of ethics, guilds and professional societies, standards, as well as the law.

Exercises

1. Some time ago, in a talk given at Imperial College London, Tom DeMarco argued that managers need to know how to praise the work of their workers and give thanks. He gave examples of how different ways of praising the work can be more appropriate than others. Saying, for example, 'I think that your report is good' sets the person who says it as the judge and in a position of superiority. However, saying 'I learnt much from what you wrote, for example, the insight about how we should test our requirements early in the process is something I did not think of before.' Discuss how DeMarco's recommendation relates to McGregor's Theories X and Y and Maslow's views of human needs.

2. Suppose that you are a researcher working in a large software department, with hundreds of engineers who develop embedded software for a range of telecommunications equipment. Plan an empirical study using your company's data to study how the motivation of the developers impacts on software quality. You wish to be able to report the results in a highly reputable journal so you plan to follow a disciplined approach using state of the art methodologies. But

you also want to be able to inform management practice in your company. Write a preliminary plan of your research project (in no more than one page of A4) addressing the following issues: relevant theories that will inform your research, whether you will use observations or experiments, use of qualitative or quantitative data including metrics, possible threats to internal and external validity, ethical issues including confidentiality, and resources you will need.

3. Imagine that you are the chair of an appointment committee in a university which is committed to ensuring equal opportunities for all candidates. You are hiring professional software engineers for appointments in an organisation in charge of customising open source software to the university's needs. You want the person to fit well in the culture of the team. Use the concepts discussed in Chapter 3 to write a 'person specification' and a questionnaire for the interviewees, focusing on the human, as opposed to the technological (e.g., expertise with a given programming paradigm) aspects. Consider that any item in the person specification should be 'testable' against objective evidence. Match the questions in the questionnaire to the person specification, so that all the critical aspects are covered.

4. Identify the specific differences between software and traditional goods and services. Discuss how these may affect the classical view of the functioning of the market.

5. Look up Moore's law on the Internet. You will see that the cost of hardware has fallen dramatically. However, the cost of software has not followed the same trend. Why?

6. Consider accounting practices, in which some purchases are viewed as capital investment to be written off over a number of years, while other purchases are viewed a consumables to be written off in the year of purchase. Software can be considered as an expense, as capital investment, or something in between. Find out the book-keeping conventions in the country where you live or work, with respect to internally developed software and to software acquired from others. In some economic regimes software is viewed as a consumable, while people are viewed as an investment. How do these practices distort the market for software and for labour?

7. A group of university colleagues have implemented the prototype of a tool for requirements representation and management and are debating whether to make it available as open source or opt for some form of commercial exploitation. The intellectual property office in your university has invoked the small text in your contracts, claiming that if the tool has any commercial value, it should be exploited and part of the benefits should go to the university, who in turn will use the money to fund further research. As academics you see it as your social obligation to make the software a public good and to ensure that others can freely benefit from it. Explain this conflict by comparing and contrasting the motivations of the academics as individuals and the motivations of a university as an organisation.

8. For some years the traditional view of the long-term evolution of software systems has been that their growth is constrained by increasing complexity, to a point at which they stagnate and become a 'legacy system'. According to some researchers, a number of open source systems, including Linux, have been

experiencing superlinear growth. This means that when the size of the system in number of files or lines of code is measured over time, the rate of growth itself increases. Based on what you have learned in this chapter about the human, social, and economic context of software, give an explanation of why this may happen.

Endnotes

1. D. McGregor (1960) *The Human Side of Enterprise*. McGraw-Hill, Chapters 3 and 4, pp. 33–57.
2. F. Herzberg (1966) *Work and the Nature of Man*. World Publishing Co, Chapter 6, pp. 71–91.
3. See, for example, the account by E. Mayo (1949) Hawthorne and the Western Electric Company. In *The Social Problems of an Industrial Civilization*. Routledge, Chapter 4, pp. 60–76.
4. The original account was given in A.H. Maslow (1943) 'A Theory of human motivation', *Psychological Review*, 50, pp. 370–396. Available online at http://psychoclassics.yorku.ca/Maslow/motivation.htm. This was later developed into a book: A.H. Maslow (1954) *Motivation and Personality*. Harper.
5. Donald Knuth was a pioneer of computing who developed many early algorithms for solving basic computing problems. He is most famous for inventing the TeX method for typesetting mathematics still widely used today as LaTeX.
6. Jakob Neilsen is an international authority on human–computer interaction who writes a regular column in the IEEE journal on HCI.
7. G. Hofstede (1991) *Cultures and Organizations: Software of the Mind*. McGraw-Hill; and G. Hofstede (2001) *Culture's Consequences: Comparing Values, Behaviors, Institutions and Organisations across Nations* (2nd edn): Sage.
8. F. Trompenaars (1993) *Managing Across Cultures*. Business Books (Random House).
9. F. Trompenaars and C. Hampden-Turner (1997) *Riding the Waves of Culture: Understanding Cultural Diversity in Business*. Nicholas Brealey Publishing.
10. We saw this in Chapter 2 as situated action, following Suchman.
11. John W. Berry, Ype H. Poortinga, Marshall H. Segall, and Pierre R. Dasen (1992) *Cross-cultural Psychology, Research and Applications*. Cambridge University Press, Chapter 13, Organisation and Work, pp. 315–338.
12. M. Haire, E. E. Ghiselli, and L. W. Porter (1966) *Managerial Thinking: An International Study*. New York: Wiley.
13. Marian Petre (2004) 'How Expert Engineering Teams use Disciplines of Innovation', *Design Studies*, 25, 477–493.
14. Donald Schoen (1983) *The Reflective Practitioner*. Basic Books.
15. Etienne Wenger (1998) *Communities of Practice: Learning, Meaning, and Identity*. Cambridge.
16. See, for example, Paul A. Samuelson and William B. Norhaus (1992) *Economics* (14th edn). McGraw-Hill.
17. The term 'invisible hand' originated with Adam Smith, the person who first studied market economics described in his book *The Wealth of Nations* (1776).
18. Garrett Hardin (1968) 'The Tragedy of the Commons', *Science*, 162, 1243–48.
19. Stallman was born in New York in 1953. His life up to 2002 is told in the book by Sam Williams (2002) *Free as in Freedom*. O'Reilly.
20. 'GNU' is a TLA (three-letter acronym) constructed recursively – it stands for 'GNU is Not Unix'.
21. Andras Kelen (2004) *The Gratis Economy: Privately Provided Public Goods*. Central European University Press.
22. See, for example, http://www.constitution.org/jjr/socon.htm.

4 Ethics, codes, and standards

What we will study in this chapter

Any activity can have a negative affect on other people, on society, or on the environment. This is equally true for the use of software. Clearly decisions about which actions should be taken should be influenced by these potentially negative outcomes. But how do we decide? This chapter and the next chapter address this from the point of view of regulation.

We start by looking at the principles of **ethics** and moral philosophy as the basis for making decisions. This leads us then to rules and those particular rules that are mandated by professional societies as codes of conduct. Some actions clearly should not be undertaken since they are unethical, or contravene an agreed **code of conduct.** In special cases only practitioners who are licensed to practice should be able to undertake certain activities.

A particularly important form of regulation is conformance to standards. We look at how these are produced and what the advantages, and disadvantages, are.

In the next chapter, Chapter 5, we will look at the role of the law in regulating activities concerned with software.

4.1 Introduction

In Chapter 1 we saw that software can fail, sometimes so disastrously that it can result in death. We looked in detail at one example in Case Study 1.1, the Therac radiation machine that led to a number of deaths and maimings. When systems fail, details may never become public, because a person's or company's reputation may be put at risk, and because the public admission of failure may involve legal proceedings. Any such failure of software in service should trouble us, for it may have damaged people or the environment, and revealing of details of the incident should also trouble us, for that in turn can damage other people. How can we manage our organisations and our lives to minimise the problems and losses that these system failures lead to?

Of course any particular incident can be very complex, and the problems arise from a combination of many factors. In the Therac radiation treatment case the causes were a combination of changing technology, an inappropriately trained

Decisions concerning software need to be regulated with respect to their social and environmental impact.

engineer, a management that denied first and assessed later – a combination that led Leveson and Turner to conclude that it was a system failure. We are concerned in this book with the underlying principles that would help us as individuals and members of organisations involved in software to avoid such incidents and to respond responsibly if such incidents do occur. In this chapter we will look at the responsibility that individuals and organisations bear for their actions and inactions in such incidents, and the extent to which individual and organisational behaviour must be regulated in order to avoid such incidents. We view regulation as a form of **public good**[1] embracing voluntary constraints on behaviour covered in this chapter, as well as constraints imposed through the law covered in the next chapter.

We will start in section 4.2 by considering the need to constrain individual and organisational behaviour as an issue of morality and ethics. If taking some action is unethical then it should not be done. Deciding not to do the action might be entirely voluntary, or it could be governed by codes of conduct laid down by some professional society. In section 4.3 we look at professional societies and the historical genesis of these, and the codes of conduct that they generate. A particular kind of code is the Standard; this will be covered in section 4.4.

All of the guidance on behaviour covered in this chapter is voluntary, but it could be that a society needs to enact laws in order to mandate certain behaviours and punish others. We cover the various areas of law related to software and its use in Chapter 5 – the important area of intellectual property, including copyright, patents, and trademarks – at length, before looking at contracts and tendering, care for employees and the public, and the malicious use of computers.

4.2 Ethics and morality

Constraints on our behaviour can be seen as a limitation of our freedom. There is always a balance to be struck here. As a first step it is useful, following the nineteenth century philosopher John Stuart Mill, to distinguish between behaviour which only affects us ourselves, and that which affects others. One reason, and a very basic reason, for limiting the freedom of action of others is self-protection, and this leads to a reciprocal constraint on your own freedom; your actions should not harm others since that action if undertaken by others could harm you. 'Do as you would be done by.' This principle represents the ethics of reciprocity and is found in one form or another in several major religions and many cultures.

The **deontological** approach to ethics, sees duties as the source of morality, to be undertaken regardless of the consequences. These duties could arise from religious beliefs, or from moral reasoning such as that of Immanuel Kant. Kant saw the basis of action as doing things only if they should be done universally, that people should never be seen as a means but as an end in themselves, and that all action should be relative to a community which itself is also an end of that action.

For many centuries people have debated **moral philosophy**:[2] what should be the basis for our behaviour; what actions are good and should be encouraged; what actions are bad and should be discouraged? Some people would argue that some actions, such as taking a life, are objectively wrong and should never be condoned, while others would say that it all depends on the circumstance, and thus life could be taken in self-defence or on behalf of the nation as punishment. Issues arise from the diversity of approved behaviours: a behaviour condemned in some societies could be approved in others – for example copying the written work of others might be seen as the positive sharing of knowledge in one community, as the acknowledgment of the words of the master in another, while in yet other cultures it might be condemned as plagiarism or theft, unless done so with permission. Thus while some people may accept **cultural relativity** in issues involving morality, we must not accept that people decide individually the moral fitness of their actions (i.e. individual relativity) and the free-for-all that this might lead to.

The major assumption in moral philosophy is that the consequences of all action and inaction can be evaluated, and even measured, and a judgement reached as to whether or not the action should be undertaken. An example of this is Bentham's 'greatest happiness to the greatest number' (**utilitarian ethics**). A simple criterion sometimes used to judge whether an intended behaviour raises potential ethical problems is whether it could potentially harm anybody or damage the environment.

Being able to reason ethically about potential actions is useful. We will see an example of this kind of reasoning in Activity 4.1. Some people would want to make this reasoning process into a formal procedure, as seen in Case Study 4.1. This can be useful, though you may have reservations about this since any codification of such processes can remove flexibility by constraining the power of human reasoning.

Questions of moral philosophy are deep and important issues, but regrettably there are significant disagreements between philosophers about them. When faced with a new moral dilemma involving the proper use of computers, we may need to take recourse to these basic philosophical principles, so as to be able to think clearly and objectively about the issues raised. Fortunately we can generally fall back on **normative** views of behaviour, what we ought to do, looking to agreements within our social group. These agreements might be passed down to us as part of our national heritage and culture, communicated to us in stories, codified in sets of rules like professional codes of conduct, or be spelled out for us in the laws of our country. Even where the exact action being considered is new, it might be similar to other actions for which we do have a normative view, and from which we can argue by analogy. Normative ethical analysis is described in Case Study 4.2.

> Any situation can be analysed ethically, working from first principles of moral philosophy.

Case Study 4.1 *A procedure for making ethical decisions*

Kallman and Grillo in their book *Ethical Decision Making and Information Technology: An Introduction with Cases* set out the following procedure. Note how this procedure is deontological in its approach, focusing on consequences of actions in the form of rights and duties.

Step I. Understanding the situation

A. *List and number the relevant facts.*
B. *Which of these raises an ethical issue? Why? What is the potential of resulting harm?*
C. *List the stakeholders involved.*

Step II. Isolating the major ethical dilemma
What is the ethical dilemma to be resolved NOW? State it using the form: Should someone do or not do something? Note: Just state the dilemma here; leave any reasoning for Step III.
Step III. Analyzing the ethicality of both alternatives in Step II

Consequentialism.
A. *If action in Step II is done, who, if anyone, will be harmed?*
B. *If action in Step II is not done, who, if anyone, will be harmed?*

▶

C. Which alternative results in the least harm,
    A or B?

D. If action in Step II is done, who, if anyone,
    will benefit?

E. If action in Step II is not done, who, if
    anyone, will benefit?

F. Which alternative results in the maximum benefit, D or E?

Rights and Duties

G. What rights have been or may be abridged? What duties
    have been or may be neglected? Identify the stakehold-
    er and the right or duty. When listing a right, show its
    corresponding duty and vice versa.

Kant's Categorical Imperative

H. If action in Step II is done, who, if anyone, will be treated
    with disrespect?

I. If action in Step II is not done, who, if anyone, will be treat-
    ed with disrespect?

J. Which alternative is preferable, H or I?

K. If action in Step II is done, who, if anyone, will be treated
    unlike others?

L. If action in Step II is not done, who, if anyone, will be treat-
    ed unlike others?

M. Which alternative is preferable, K or L?

N. Are there benefits if everyone did action in Step II?

O. Are there benefits if nobody did action in Step II?

P. Which alternative is preferable, N or O?

Step IV. Making a decision and planning the implementation

A. Make a defensible ethical decision. Based on the analysis
    in Step III, respond to the question in Step II. Indicate the
    letters of the categories that best support your response.
    Add any arguments justifying your choice of these ethical
    principles to support your decision. Where there are con-
    flicting rights and duties, choose and defend those that
    take precedence. (Note: Just make and justify your choice
    here; leave any action steps for parts B and D below.)

B. List the specific steps needed to implement your defens-
    ible ethical decision.

C. Show how the major stakeholders are affected by these
    actions.

D. What other longer-term changes (political, legal, tech-
    nical, societal, organizational) would help prevent such
    problems in the future?

Source: John Kallman and James Grillo (1996) *Ethical Decision Making
and Information Technology: An Introduction with Cases*, Second
Edition. McGraw-Hill, p.34.

Case Study 4.2 *The normative approach for making ethical decisions*

McFarland[3], in his IEEE Computer article 'Ethics
and the Safety of Computer Systems' (1991)
describes four basic principles that need to be
considered in any given situation:

1. Beneficience: "to do good"

2. Nonmalfeasance: "not to harm"

3. Autonomy: "respect for freedom and self-
    determination of all people"

4. Justice: "the fair distribution of benefits
    and burdens"

Problems arise when an ethical decision is
based only on a subset of these principles. For
example, liberalism, based exclusively on (3),
fails when the decisions of autonomous
people or organisations bring harm to others.
Utilitarian approaches, illustrated by Bentham's idea of 'greatest happiness to the

greatest number' are based exclusively on (1)
and (2) and, hence, fail to take into account
the fundamental human rights in (3) and (4).
Despite the importance of the four principles,
no ethical system has achieved their unifica-
tion. This means that when facing a practical
situation one needs to prioritise the principles,
which is often challenging and difficult. McFarland quotes the following four guidelines
given by Childress[4] in order to apply the normative approach "to the use of risky technology in critical applications":

a. 'Proportionality', meaning that good origin-
    ated through a technology must be larger
    than any associated harm or risk. In add-
    ition, no alternative is available that pro-
    vides similar benefits with less harm or risk.

b. 'Informed consent' of anybody affected by
    the technology.

c. *'Justice', implying a fair sharing of benefits and risks. Particularly, those not benefited should not suffer an increment in their risks.*

d. *'Minimized risk'. In addition to satisfying (a) to (c), the implementation of the technology should seek to minimise all risks, including avoidance of those risks which are unnecessary.*

Activity 4.1   *Applying ethical reasoning*

Evaluate the moral fitness of continuing the Therac 25 machine in service following the sixth incident in 1987 (see Case Study 1.1 in Chapter 1). Note that it was after this incident that the machine was actually withdrawn. Consider the various stakeholders in the machine – e.g. the patients who have already been treated by the machine, the patients who might be treated in the future, the engineers who developed the machine, the management of the Therac company, and the shareholders of the Therac company. Base your answer on the description in Case Study 1.1, making any reasonable assumptions you need to. If you can, get hold of the article by Leveson and Turner, or any other description of this case. How would things have been had the machine been withdrawn earlier?

Discussion

Apply either or both

   a) simple criterion judging potential harm to people or the environment,

   b) the normative approach, following the Childress guidelines described in Case Study 4.2

Simple "consequential" or utilitarian approach

'For the patients (and their relatives)' already affected: it is too late, though they may gain some comfort from knowing that if the machine is withdrawn then at least nobody else would suffer.

'For patients who may be treated in the future': withdrawing the machine will save them from the great pain and possible death suffered by earlier patients, so the gain is significant, particularly if we assume that other equivalent machinery was available to treat them anyway.

'For the engineers and managers (also the shareholders) of Therac': withdrawal will mean loss of revenue, but much more seriously the admission of a failing machine will lead to loss of reputation and direct financial loss in subsequent lawsuits. However if withdrawal were delayed, the situation would get far worse, so relative to that there is positive benefit to withdrawing the machine immediately.

Normative approach

'Proportionality': the decision of continuing the Therac 25 machine is not proportionate. The harm to their patients (and emotional distress to their relatives) was larger than any good arising from the use of the machine. Moreover, there were safer alternatives, notably the older machine type which included electromechanical interlocks as safety measures.

'Informed consent': neither patients and their families nor health personnel where informed of the previous accidents and of the potential risks so that they could give their consent.

'Justice': for the patients (and their relatives) who have already been treated it is too late, though they may gain some comfort from knowing that if the machine is withdrawn, then at least nobody else would suffer. For patients who may be treated in the future, withdrawing the machine will save them from the great pain and possible death suffered by earlier patients, so the gain is significant, particularly if we assume that other equivalent machinery was available to treat them anyway. For the engineers and managers of Therac, and also the shareholders, withdrawal of the machines will mean a loss of revenue, but much more seriously the admission of a failing machine will lead to loss of reputation and direct financial loss in subsequent law suits. However if withdrawal were delayed, the situation would get far worse, so relative to that there is positive benefit to withdrawing the machine immediately. For engineers who will be designing new machines it is important that the lessons learnt from the Therac 25 are documented and publicised so that new designs do not repeat the same mistakes. For society at large it is important that any technical and managerial lessons are identified and shared.

'Minimised risk': continuing the use of the Therac 25 did not minimise risk, there were less risky alternatives to the Therac 25, as for example the older machine type.

Situations can be pre-analysed to give sets of rules that can be applied whenever those situations arise.

We will refer to these agreed normative behaviours as **rules**. Rules might be purely personal, such as never telling a lie or only lying to protect your family; or collective, as in the codes of conduct of a professional society and in the laws of a country or region. The rules may be voluntary, as in personal codes and the codes of conduct of professional societies, or be enforceable as laws.

Personal codes may well not be written down, but be kept tacit and reinterpreted at each use. Codes of conduct and laws are written down and need to be understandable, promulgated and thus widely known, accepted by those to whom they apply, and enforced when not adhered to. However we must recognise a major limitation. Rules may not be able to be precise and characterise every possible situation in which they are to be applied: they need to recognise the need for interpretation at the point of application. There have been a number of attempts to mechanise the law, to make it subject to machine interpretation, and it should not surprise you that these attempts failed. The interpretative elements cannot be mechanised, and indeed in these attempts at mechanisation the existence of the interpretive elements was not even recognised.[5] Of course in some exceptional cases mechanisation is possible, as in tax law, though even there a good tax accountant may be able to vary the final tax to be paid through suitable interpretation.

4.3 Self-regulation and voluntary codes

While legal systems have arisen because of the interest of the state in controlling its citizens' behaviour, usually in the public interest, a number of other organisations have also taken an interest in the regulation of society. Early examples were the medieval **guilds** widely distributed across Europe. The caste system of India seems to have had similar origins to the European guilds, and arose at around the same time. These European guilds were originally founded as religious or faith guilds during the ninth century ACE[6] for the general governance of small town and city communities. However in time these gave way to merchant and craft guilds where the emphasis was much more on the sectional interests of the members of the guild.[7]

The merchant and craft guilds aimed at:

- an exclusive right to practice for members of the guild, to monopolise all wealth from activities in their field so that it accrued to guild members alone;
- ensuring the quality of goods and services in their area against the inferior work of outsiders;
- educating and training members of the guild, including the induction of new members of the guild through apprenticeship schemes;
- helping impoverished members of the guild and their families.

While the power of the guilds in Europe diminished over time with the rise in power of the nation state, the idea of such associations was a powerful one, and in altered form persists in, for example, the **professional society** of today.

Activity 4.2   *Professional jargon*

All professions include their own jargon. When is the use of this professional jargon appropriate, and when should it not be used?

Discussion
Jargon has often arisen because it represents concepts that are important for the profession, and in discussions and debates within the profession it is perfectly appropriate to use jargon. However, this jargon may not be understood outside the profession, and should be avoided in communication outside the profession, or be explained within that communication. It is very easy for jargon to become a barrier dividing those inside the profession from those outside. Regrettably, jargon is also one way to hide uncertainty or lack of knowledge.

Activity 4.3   *What is a professional?*

Some people describe themselves as being 'professional'. Is it important to be regarded as a professional? If so, why? If not, why not?

Discussion
Reasons for wanting to be regarded as a professional may include increased earning capacity, marketability, greater respect from colleagues, trust (an individual known to operate under a consistent code of professional ethics is one who can be relied upon), security (employment as a professional is often perceived as offering more security) and comfort (this is admittedly subjective, but peace of mind may be an important benefit).

In some professions, being admitted as a formal member of that profession is an essential prerequisite for being allowed to practise. It is easy to see why this is important for doctors, but wouldn't it also make sense for software professionals, particularly those who are concerned with safety-critical and mission-critical systems?

Reasons for not wanting to be seen as a professional are perhaps harder to find. Not wanting to cut oneself off or be regarded as part of an elitist group might be a motivation for some.

The liveried companies of the City of London form an interesting modern-day continuation of the ancient merchant guilds, primarily continuing the charitable functions of those ancient guilds. While many of the companies date back to the eleventh century, they have continued to be created, with a surprising one being the recent Worshipful Company of Information Technologists described in Case Study 4.3.

Modern professional societies have developed from the medieval trade and merchant guilds.

Case Study 4.3 *The worshipful company of information technologists*

The City of London liveried companies are so called because of the distinctive badges and clothing used. The Worshipful Company of Information Technologists was founded in 1992 as the 100th livery company of the City of London. Its website tells us that:

The Company's work covers three broad areas:

- *Promoting the IT profession – increasing awareness and understanding of the IT industry, raising issues that are relevant to the industry's future and supporting the development of qualified IT professionals*

- *Education and Training – helping young people acquire IT skills through projects such as the apprenticeship scheme.*

- *Charitable Activities – using members' experience and skills to benefit charitable projects related to IT.*

The Company also organises a programme of events to bring together like-minded people and to encourage the greatest possible support and participation from the liverymen and freemen of the Company.

4.3.1 Software professional organisations

Most countries will have a number of organisations who act collectively for segments of the software industry. These range from trade associations that are concerned with the commercial and industrial aspects of computing and software, to professional (or learned) societies who look after the advancement of knowledge and the adherence to standards. We will focus on professional societies, and in particularly on their codes of conduct or equivalent. All these software professional societies take their duties to the public very seriously, and have expressed this in codes that they expect their members to follow.

In Europe the professional societies for IT organise as the Council of European Professional Information Societies (CEPIS), and the mission and goals of CEPIS[8] capture the general objectives of professional societies well:

CEPIS Mission Statement (Council Meeting April 2000)
CEPIS is a non-profit organisation seeking to improve and promote high standards among informatics professionals in recognition of the impact that informatics has on employment, business and society.
CEPIS Goals (Council Meeting April 2002)

1. To be the European IT professional network for Member Societies
2. To become the European IT certification organisation, working with educators, industry and other certification organisations
3. To be recognized by EU / European institutions as the leading independent IT Professionals organisation
4. To help ensure an adequate supply of competent IT professionals.

Activity 4.4   *Professional societies*

As well as newly founded professional societies specifically for computing and software, societies concerned with electrical engineering and electronics have also taken on a significant interest in software. For example in the United States as well as the Association for Computing Machinery there is the Institute of Electrical and Electronic Engineers (IEEE), and in the United Kingdom, as well as the British Computer Society, there is also the Institution of Electrical Engineers.

Why should this be? Look these societies up on the Internet to find out more about them.

Discussion

Computers arose within electronics, so electronic engineers very naturally migrated towards software engineering. Devices like telephone exchanges which had formerly been purely electrical and electronic devices, gradually began to incorporate computing micro-processors where much of the functionality was created in software. The division between which functions were hard-wired and which functions were executed in software was a decision for the designers of devices, and as more and more of the functions were moved to software, more and more electronic engineers found themselves developing software. But the fact that functions were created in software does not mean that the concern for quality of the overall device is absolved, and thus these electronic societies have developed very active subgroups concerned with software.

Case Study 4.4 shows the **Code of Ethics** of the US IEEE. This code is comparatively short, whereas other codes while largely covering the same ground can be five to ten times longer. This extra length is because of the explanatory guidance given, and possibly because there is a move from principles to particular practices that may change over time.

Case Study 4.4 *The US IEEE Code of Ethics*[9]

Reprinted with the permission of the IEEE © 1990.

This code applies to all of the engineering covered by the Institution, and thus does not mention software directly. It was approved by the IEEE Board of Directors in August 1990.

We, the members of the IEEE, in recognition of the importance of our technologies in affecting the quality of life throughout the world, and in accepting a personal obligation to our profession, its members and the communities we serve, do hereby commit ourselves to the highest ethical and professional conduct and agree:

1. *to accept responsibility in making engineering decisions consistent with the safety, health and welfare of the public, and to disclose promptly factors that might endanger the public or the environment;*

2. *to avoid real or perceived conflicts of interest whenever possible, and to disclose them to affected parties when they do exist;*

3. *to be honest and realistic in stating claims or estimates based on available data;*

4. *to reject bribery in all its forms;*

5. *to improve the understanding of technology, its appropriate application, and potential consequences;*

6. *to maintain and improve our technical competence and to undertake technological tasks for others only if qualified by training or experience, or after full disclosure of pertinent limitations;*

7. to seek, accept, and offer honest criticism of technical work, to acknowledge and correct errors, and to credit properly the contributions of others;

8. to treat fairly all persons regardless of such factors as race, religion, gender, disability, age, or national origin;

9. to avoid injuring others, their property, reputation, or employment by false or malicious action;

10. to assist colleagues and co-workers in their professional development and to support them in following this code of ethics.

Software professional societies help regulate professional practice through codes, and support this through events and activities that share and promulgate best practice.

In addition to codes of conduct aimed at regulating professionals in their area, professional societies will actively promote the advancement of software and its production practices, fostering groups and running conferences that share knowledge, and participating in the formulation of standards.

The critical role of software in safety has led to concerns that software engineers should be licensed to practice, at least for particular classes of systems. This has been most strongly pursued in the US, under the rubric of 'the establishment of software engineering as a profession'.[10] Part of this process is seen as the establishment of codes of practice, such as that seen in Case Study 4.4, but does this really require the move to licensing practitioners?

4.4 Standards

Standards are important in the regulation of the production of software and its deployment. They may be used within a company to regulate its development and use of software:

- in the procurement of individual items of software, to help ensure that they are fit for the purposes that are intended;
- across areas of technology, to ensure the successful interoperation of independent pieces of equipment, as in communication standards;
- within markets, to ensure a free market for third party suppliers, as in operating systems and support environments.

Standards are in general associated with official standards-making and promulgating bodies, from the quality assurance (QA) department within a company to national and international standards bodies.

In standards we draw a number of distinctions:

- *de facto standards* (versus *de jure* standards) are usually associated with a dominant commercial interest that determines the structure of the market. This form of standard will not be addressed in this chapter, though it must be recognised that de facto standards frequently themselves become the subject of standardisation.
- *reference models* (versus actual standards) lay a framework within which other standards will be formulated.
- *product standards* (versus process standards): some standards are concerned with specific software products, such as compilers and communications

equipment, while other standards are concerned with the process whereby a software product is developed. Within product standards, one distinguishes interface standards, which determine purely what happens at the interface and not what happens within the product as a whole.

- *codes of practice, guidelines, and specifications*: under the general term of 'standard', a number of levels of enforcement are distinguished, though these do not seem to be officially defined. Broadly speaking, codes of practice and guidelines indicate desirable good practice to which conformance cannot be precisely determined, whereas specifications are precise, with conformance determinable by appropriate tests or analyses.

- *prospective standards* (versus retrospective standards): if standardisation is undertaken too early, the technology may not have advanced enough and standardisation may fix on practices which are not adequate. It may be best to develop a prospective standard alongside the technology, or an intercept standard (sometimes called a 'draft for development') may be published. If standardisation is undertaken retrospectively once the technology has been advanced, then several incompatible practices may have become established with significant costs required in order to change to conform to a single standard.

- *functional standards* ('profiles') – groups of interrelated standards which together service a user need (function).

The critical aspect that needs standardisation in both product and process is the interface, the part of a product or a process that connects to another part. Clearly if the parts are to work together successfully they need to conform to the same conventions of representation and protocol. If the parts are being made by private agreement between two parties then all we need is some formal agreement, but if the parts can potentially be made by a number of parties operating within an open market, then a public official standard is required.

The consumer's interest is in the quality (fitness for purpose) of software products; thus it is the prospective specification product standards that are of concern. Process standards are only of value when there are insufficient product standards to enable the proper assessment of the quality of a product. For example, in accounting software, some aspects concerned with meeting financial regulations may be subject to product standards, but other attributes like the user interface will not be subject to standardisation and either a process or quality standard (see Chapter 12), or the reputation of the supplier, will be appealed to. We must appreciate that even the highest quality development process will not necessarily deliver a high-quality product – it is a necessary but not a sufficient condition. In addition to a quality develoment process, we require well-trained engineers following best practice methods using leading tools to enact the process, and high-quality information about what is needed in order to meet the customer's requirements.

> Standards for software take many forms, the ideal of which is product specification standards.

4.4.1 Standards-making bodies

Standards-making today is dominated by international standards organisations, reflecting the international nature of trade. The most significant of these organisations are:

- ISO, the International Organisation for Standardisation, founded in 1947.
- IEC, the International Electrotechnical Commission, founded in 1906.

The ISO and IEC have a formal agreement that their activities should be complementary and together provide a comprehensive standardisation service. Other international organisations are important in the standards-making process; principally those concerned with telecommunications, where it is essential that interface standards are conformed to. The international body concerned is the International Telecommunications Union (ITU) (formerly known as CCITT, the Comité Consultatif International de Télégraphique et Téléphonique). Most countries have their own standards bodies, and many groups of countries also have group or regional organisations: Comité Européen de Normalisation (CEN) and CENELEC, the electrotechnical counterpart of CEN, in Europe.

> Standards are becoming international, with ISO being increasingly important in information technology standards.

Trade associations and professional societies of various kinds also participate in the formulation and promulgation of standards. In the US these are the IEEE and the Computer and Business Equipment Manufacturers' Association (CBEMA); and in Europe the European Computer Manufacturers' Association (ECMA), and the European Workshop on Industrial Computer Systems (EWICS).

Military standardisation has proceeded largely independently of the civil effort outlined above, and is described in further detail later. Duplication between organisations is avoided by many coordination and liaison functions, as well as a lot of cross-membership of committees. There are also continuing moves towards harmonisation across industries and across countries, and between military and civil procurement.

ISO

The technical work of ISO is carried out by technical committees (TC), which are each responsible for an area of technology.[11] There are around 200[12] technical committees altogether, with one of these, JTC1, being responsible for whole range of information technology. JTC1 was established in 1987 as a joint committee of ISO and IEC to integrate the work of the previous ISO committee TC97 Information Processing Systems and IEC technical committee Information technology equipment and subcommittee IEC/SC 47B Microprocessor systems. Among the other technical committees in ISO, only one other is of interest to the software engineering community: ISO/TC176 Quality management and quality assurance, concerned with standardisation of generic quality management, including ISO 9000 series to be discussed in Chapter 12.

Technical committees in turn establish subcommittees (SC) and working groups (WG) to cover different aspects of their work. JTC1 has a number of subcommittees that are concerned with software development – it is useful to look at these subcommittees to see the breadth of standardisation work undertaken for IT, and the way historical divisions now can impact current work. Table 4.1 lists these – the subcommittees of particular interest to readers of this book would be JTC1/SC7 on software and systems engineering.

When a new area of concern is identified, a new work item (NWI) is raised and assigned to a particular subcommittee. A draft proposal (DP) is developed and circulated. When agreement has been reached, the draft proposal is registered as a Draft International Standard (DIS) and voted upon, and if successful, becomes an international standard. All ISO standards are subject to a periodic review at not more than five-year intervals, when they could be confirmed for a further period, be withdrawn, or be revised. This whole process of initial standardisation, and of later revision, may each take many years!

Committee	Title
JTC 1/SC 2	Coded character sets
JTC 1/SC 6	Telecommunications and information exchange between systems
JTC 1/SC 7	Software and system engineering
JTC 1/SC 17	Cards and personal identification
JTC 1/SC 22	Programming languages, their environments, and system software interfaces
JTC 1/SC 23	Digital storage media for information interchange
JTC 1/SC 24	Computer graphics, image processing, and environmental data representation
JTC 1/SC 25	Interconnection of information technology equipment
JTC 1/SC 27	IT security techniques
JTC 1/SC 28	Office equipment
JTC 1/SC 29	Coding of audio, picture, multimedia, and hypermedia information
JTC 1/SC 31	Automatic identification and data capture techniques
JTC 1/SC 32	Data management and interchange
JTC 1/SC 34	Document description and processing languages
JTC 1/SC 35	User interfaces
JTC 1/SC 36	Information technology for learning, education, and training
JTC 1/SC 37	Biometrics

Table 4.1

JTC1 subcommittees concerned with software development

United Kingdom

Information technology standards in the United Kingdom are largely produced through the British Standards Institute (BSI). The committee structure shadows that of the ISO.

The work on BSI standards is initiated within a technical committee, which drafts the standard for public comment. Drafts are circulated normally only once. All comments must be properly taken into account, and the technical committee must reach consensus before the standard is published. Note that there is no voting procedure within BSI. When guidance is required urgently, but it is too early for standardisation, a Draft for Development might be prepared.

United States

Standards-making in the United States follows quite a different pattern. The official standards body of the United States is the American National Standards Institute (ANSI), which represents the US on international standards bodies. Policy in software engineering is determined by the Information Systems Standards Board (ISSB). The actual formulation of standards is carried out by accredited agencies:

- IEEE, which covers the JTC1 areas of work of SC7, SC83, SC47, POSIX, and LAN;
- the X3 committee, with secretariat CBEMA which covers all other areas of ISO JTC1 work.

The IEEE works by raising projects charged with preparing standards and guidelines in its particular area. As projects complete their standard they are closed off, while new projects are raised regularly. The IEEE is very active in standards-making, particularly in development process and communications.

The X3 committee has a number of subcommittees charged with standardisation in particular areas, and thus is similar in its approach to ISO or BSI. Another important organisation is the National Institute of Standards and Technology (NIST), formerly known as the National Bureau of Standards (NBS), which is charged with developing standards, providing technical assistance, and conducting research in diverse areas including computers and related systems. It formulates Federal Information Processing Standards (FIPS) and issues these for conformance in US federal government work.

> As with the UK, the US also organise themselves to relate effectively to the ISO.

Military standards

Military systems are very large and complex, typically either custom-built for a particular defence force, or built in relatively small numbers. Military systems will frequently have very long lives, continuing in service for perhaps twenty-five years or more, with later systems being functionally compatible but built on a technological base that will have advanced with the technology. Quality is a very important issue in military procurement, and most of the concerns about quality systems and project management began here. A major mechanism in the control of procurement has been the use of standards. Thus military administrations have established standards-making processes and enforcement mechanisms. All too frequently the separate branches of the armed forces – land, sea, and air – have proceeded independently and duplicated the work of each other, and clearly in the area of software they do overlap. Over many years there has been a strong move to harmonise work on standardisation, to bring the separate armed forces within a single defence force together, and to bring separate forces within a military alliance together.

> Much of the bureaucracy of software development standards began with the military.

There is an international effort in military standardisation within NATO (the North Atlantic Treaty Organisation), with preference in those countries that are members to use NATO standards where these exist. NATO standards are promulgated as 'AQAPs' – Allied Quality Assurance Publications.

4.4.2 Software technical standards

Some of the first standardisation in software was in programming languages. The purpose of standardisation is to ensure portability of complete software from one hardware plus operating system to another, and to ensure the interworking and interoperation of separately developed software when brought together for integration into a new system. As the definition techniques used attain maturity, formal definition of programming languages is becoming increasingly important. Other techniques are currently subject to standardisation.

With distributed systems becoming ever more widespread, communications and data interchange standards are important, so that communications sent from one system can be correctly interpreted by the receiving systems.

There are many standards aimed at guiding practice in the process of software development. Some standards attempt to give a complete view of the whole process, but many only focus on a part of the overall process. None of these focused standards conform to a cohesive view of the total development process – there is no reference model for software development standards such as that which would be provided by the many commercial 'methods' such as **SSADM** (Structured Systems Analysis and Design Methodology). The nearest that any collection of standards comes to having cohesiveness is that from the IEEE.

Of importance are 'safety-critical' systems, whose failure could lead to loss of life, damage to the environment, or severe financial loss – these systems need yet higher quality, and special standards have been developed here. Particular programming languages, or subsets of them, might be mandated because it is easier to formally reason about the correctness of the code. Other practices, like **failure mode analysis**, may be required.

> There are many internationally approved technical standards for software that should be consulted and used in procurement and software development.

4.4.3 Process certification

Regulation of the overall process of software development has drawn upon general engineering methods. There has been persistent scepticism about the extent to which these do apply, but nevertheless interpretations of the generic engineering standards for software have been commonplace. These either take the form of separate standards (such as the UK Def Stan 00-16 *Guide to the Achievement of Quality in Software*) or as guides to be used during certification of an organisation for software (such as ISO 9000 Part III, which gives guidance on how ISO 9001 should be interpreted for the software industry). The more detailed practice of software development has also been directly addressed through standards. While the ultimate objective of all such standards must be to ensure that high and consistent quality software is produced, the emphasis has been on bringing in managerial control over cost and timescale. Of course the two are related, and with loss of control over cost and timescale, quality is all too frequently also lost.

Organisations involved in software development and use can seek certification as conforming to ISO 9001 or similar quality standard. Process certification must necessarily be by audit, inspection, and review, and takes the following form:

1. The company establishes a quality system which is intended to conform: this includes the complete documentation in a quality manual or similar document. The quality manual may cite some of the more detailed international standards or include organisation-specific standards.

2. A team of inspectors visits the company for several days, assessing that the quality manual conforms with ISO 9001 or other generic quality systems standard, viewing the quality department at work, and viewing projects in progress to make sure that the documented procedures are actually carried out.

3. Any appropriate corrective actions to the quality system are made, and the company is registered or certified as conforming to the quality systems standard for the particular branch of engineering concerned.

4. At intervals the company will be audited for continued conformance – audit visits may be unannounced or arranged well in advance.

> Companies can gain certification of their software processes if they are carried out in conformance to relevant standards.

This will be covered in much greater detail in Chapter 12.

Case Study 4.5 *HTML development*

Let's turn to the Internet for an example of the role of standards in the face of commercial pressures.[13]

Sending information across the Internet so that it would appear properly formatted at the other end needs agreement at both ends. Following early ideas about the Internet in 1989 from Tim Berners-Lee, this led to the standard, HTML, HyperText Mark-up Language, with tags embedded in the text to define the format. HTML was based on the then-existing SGML, Standard Generalised Markup Language, and developed rapidly from 1989 to 1994 when HTML 2.0 was released. HTML 2 aimed at consolidating a great number of ideas proposed at the time, with the intention that many of the web browsers being developed then should conform to HTML 2 and thus be able to exchange data. However, the developers of browsers realised that HTML 2 had limitations and invented new tags for new features, and full interoperability was not achieved.

In March 1995 a draft HTML 3 was published, and an immediate problem arose with tables, since HTML 3 tables differed from SGML. This was reconciled in HTML 3.2. HTML 3 was seen by many as too large, and browser developers only implemented subsets – and different subsets, so interoperability was still not achieved.

Then in August 1995 Microsoft launched its Internet Explorer with its own extra tags and features like Active X, aimed at establishing its own commercial share of the Internet market, in competition with the then-dominant browser, Netscape. As soon as a new feature was launched by one browser developer, the others found ways of handling it and launched their own features. In September 1995, Netscape launched frames. That led to heated debate. In November 1995, others proposed style sheets and internationalisation of the web.

The HTML working group, which had served as the forum for debate and agreement for such proposals could not handle all of this, and was dismantled in December 1995. The replacement HTML Editorial Review Board (ERB) was launched by the World Wide Web Consortium (W3C) in February 1996. The HTML ERB proved successful, and HTML 3.2 was formally endorsed by the W3C in January 1997. Work had been progressing on HTML 4, with a large range of innovations, and it was eventually published as a proposal in 1998.

Meanwhile XML had been under development in W3C as a next generation of SGML, and it is now XML that is the basis for document interchange on the web, though HTML is still widely used. Formally HTML is viewed as a special application of XML, now captured in XHTML, eXtensible HTML.

Note that all of this was done through academic and industrial collaborations, and that the formal standards-making bodies were not involved.

Activity 4.5   *Innovation versus regulation*

Concern has been expressed that with the over-regulation of the use of software, innovation will be suppressed and opportunities to benefit from rapidly developing information technologies may be missed. Do you think that there is a balance to be struck between innovation and regulation?

Discussion

Clearly some aspects of the use of software that impact on human lives need to be regulated, but even then market forces might be sufficient, since software failure can lead to loss of reputation and thus loss of market share. Being innovative does not necessarily mean risk-taking, and being too cautious could mean organisations and whole societies do miss opportunities.

The HTML case study above gives a nice example where agreement and standardisation was clearly in the best interests of all parties concerned, but developments were moving so fast that, had a formal standardisation process been joined, all the innovative energy involved would have been lost.

Summing up

We have seen a range of informal regulation of software development processes and practices. We saw that:

- decisions concerning software need to be regulated in areas affecting people and the environment;
- situations should be analysed ethically from first principles of moral philosophy;
- sets of rules can be applied instead whenever pre-analysed situations arise;
- professional societies provide a set of rules as codes of conduct;
- professional societies support software practices through events and activities that share and promulgate best practice;
- standards for software provide extra guidance, with ISO being increasingly important;
- process standards can be bureaucratic, displaying their military origins;
- internationally approved technical standards should be consulted and used in procurement and development work;
- overall processes can be certified if they comply with the relevant standards.

We will see more of this with backing by the law in the next chapter.

Exercises

1. A colleague of yours, who is a software engineer in a software house, tells you confidentially that she has received indications from her line manager that she should release an information management system that, to her view, is still not sufficiently reliable. The customer, a local hospital who is paying for the software, has been informed that all is according to schedule and that software will be released in just a few days. Use the procedure for making ethical decisions given in Case Study 4.1 to analyse the situation and recommend what your colleague should do, making any reasonable assumptions.

2. Central to the argument of this chapter has been the need to constrain individual and organisational behaviour to minimise the risk of damage that

software may cause to people and the environment. However, there will be cases in which the individual and the organisation have a duty to act, instead of passively accepting an outcome or situation. Look at the IEEE Code of Ethics and classify each of the numbered items as a constraint or a duty. Does the number of duties surpass the number of constraints? Are some items in the IEEE Code of Ethics easier to comply with than others? Order the items in terms of the difficulty that each of them personally represents for you. For example, if you do not know how to perform estimations, number 3 may be high in your scale. Then use the ordered list for planning your future professional development needs.

3. Technical standards are particularly important for software because they limit variability, facilitating reuse and interoperability of components. They can also help to stabilise the evolution in particular domains. However, technical standards represent the state of the art at a particular point in time, which may well subsequently move on. From the list given in the chapter, identify one standard that you do not know and that you think you should know. Order one copy of the standard for your personal library and study it.

4. Some software vendors oversell their products as a matter of routine. This has led to the term 'vapourware', the promise of features and characteristics that do not exist. Discuss the ethical validity of such an approach to marketing.

5. Two very common ethical rules are 'do unto others what you desire them to do unto you' and 'the end should not justify the means'. Discuss these in relation to utilitarian ethics. Give examples of two 'extreme' situations in which the utilitarian view will contradict each of these rules.

6. UML, Unified Modelling Language, is a de facto standard for modelling when developing object-oriented sofware. Identify other de facto standards in the software field. Discuss how the use of de facto standards will help to avoid software failure and its consequences.

7. In different domains (e.g., aerospace, medical instruments, oil and chemical industries, and automobile manufacturing) different approaches to safety have emerged. These have sometimes been triggered by accidents, which have hit the headlines, followed by commissions who investigated these accidents and produce recommendations that then become embedded as rules. These rules are then enforced by administrative personnel without adequate knowledge of software. Suppose that a software expert in a particular domain feels that the rules imposed by a certification agency (e.g., the use of a particular type of documentation) are out of date or not justified for the newest technology. Discuss the options that could be taken in this situation, considering any ethical or moral implications.

8. Since software involves the work and activity of people at many levels (users, developers, etc.), managing software and managing people are inseparable activities. The work of the enterprise software manager has a high ethical content: almost all decisions may affect people's feelings, and some decisions may even affect people's lives. Based on her personal religious beliefs and her experience, a manager has developed an approach which combines rules and,

when the rules are not adequate, applies moral reasoning based on those rules as principles plus relevant facts. Compare and contrast her approach to the 'pure' normative approach and the 'pure' moral philosophy approach in a situation where there are a high volume of ethical decisions.

9. Investigate the emergence of Windows-based interfaces as 'standard', and write a short report on the way commercial interests operated in the development of these interfaces, and the extent to which such interfaces should be subject to *de jure* standardisation.

Endnotes

1. The economic concept of 'public good' is central to many of our arguments, and is discussed in detail in Chapter 3. 'Good' here is not a moral concept, but a product or service.
2. See any of the many books on ethics applied to computing or business, or even medical ethics, such as: Deborah G. Johnson (1985) *Computer Ethics*. Prentice-Hall; Elizabeth Vallance (1995) *Business Ethics at Work*. Cambridge University Press; Duncan Langford (1995) *Practical Computer Ethics*. McGraw-Hill; Ernest A. Kallman and Jhon P. Grillo (1996) *Ethical Decision Making and Informaton Technology: An Introduction with Cases* (2nd edn). McGraw-Hill; Judith Hendrick (2000) *Law and Ethics in Nursing and Health Care*. Nelson Thornes Ltd.
3. M C McFarland, Ethics and the Safety of Computer Systems, IEEE Computer, February, 1991, pp. 72–75.
4. J. F. Childress, Priorities in Biomedical Ethics, Westminster Press, Philadelphia, 1981, pp. 98–118. Quoted by McFarland (ob.cit).
5. In one controversial case an academic computing researcher proposed using logic programming in Prolog to formalise and mechanise the then-new British Nationality law, to be roundly criticised by a researcher in computers and the law: see Philip Leith (1986) 'Fundamental Errors in Legal Logic Programming', *Computer Journal*, 29, 6, 545–552. Leith's analysis was deprecated by computer scientists who did not like this kind of argument, but also in part because the author of the attempt being criticised was himself subject to the nationalisation law he was trying to formalise.
6. ACE = 'after the common era', BCE = 'before the common era'.
7. See, for example, the comprehensive entry on Guilds in the New Advent Catholic Encyclopaedia, available from http://www.newadvent.org/cathen/, or the book by Elliott Krause (1996) *Death of the Guilds*. Yale University Press.
8. From the CEPIS website, http://www.cepis.org.
9. See http://www.ieee.org/.
10. Nancy Mead (2002) *Issues in Licensing and Certification of Software Engineers*. Carnegie-Mellon Software-Engineering Institute.
11. ISO MeM, ISO Dir.
12. In 2005 there were 192.
13. For further details see: Dave Raggett, Jenny Lam, Ian Alexander, and Michael Kmiec (1998) *Raggett on HTML4*. Addison Wesley Longman, Chapter 2.

5 Software and the law

5.1 Why law is necessary

In looking at the embedding of computers in society, we saw in Chapter 3 how some transactions between people or organisations could affect other people – what economists call externalities. Sometimes these externalities are positive and good, and lead to the free-rider 'problem'. In other cases the effects can be negative and bad, and even the seemingly beneficial free ride can have negative effects, for example where software is easily copied (a free ride) with the consequence that invention and production stops.

We analysed these negative effects as questions of ethics and morality in Chapter 4. We studied ethical principles and their embodiment in professional codes of conduct. We also looked at more strongly formulated regulations in the form of technical standards, aimed mostly at helping technology and people work together.

All of the above were voluntary. However, sometimes we need the full might of the state in order to ensure that harm is not done and that society and the economy operate in the way intended. The instruments used by the state are the law and law enforcement. Look at Case Study 5.1.

Case Study 5.1 *Fonts and software in South Asia*

Personal computers have been used in South Asian countries like India and Pakistan since the 1980s. While the hardware clearly must be bought, the ease of copying software has meant that software has seldom been bought. For basic software like operating systems this has meant a loss of revenue for major suppliers like Microsoft, but has also meant that there has been little incentive to produce software locally. Most use of computers takes place in English and pirated software has met local needs; the only exception has been software that is required to work in local languages.

Since the 1980s and the arrival of desktop computers, individuals have created fonts for the local writing system, to facilitate desktop publishing in the local language. The production of such fonts takes many months, even years, of effort, but as soon as a font is produced, it becomes freely copied and distributed: companies who assemble computers locally will include such fonts to enhance the appeal of their product. In Nepal there is a delightful typing tutor based on the traditional tale of the Ramayana, commissioned by one of the local pioneering IT companies, and written by a local expert, which was afterwards copied shamelessly by local distributors.

Fonts for local languages and software that works in local languages using those fonts has produced little income for their originators, with the result that such work is only undertaken for love rather than for financial return.

It has only been in the first decade of the twenty-first century that serious software for Indic languages has been produced, following the adoption of open source methods. The move to open source has been partly to gain the freedom to localise in whatever language is desired, unfettered by considerations of markets. But this also tacitly recognises the realities of the market, that without intellectual property law and its enforcement, fonts and software are effectively public goods.

We will look at a range of legal areas where most legislation has been created, starting with an extended account of **intellectual property** law. Our treatments will necessarily be brief and focus on principles, independent of any particular legal jurisdiction and its laws, statutes, and legal precedents. Many books have been written on how the law affects software and what special measures have been introduced for new problems created by software,[1] made more complex as older laws, enacted prior to the coming of software and the Internet, are reinterpreted.

The coming of the Internet in particular has caused the law to become more international, for when crimes happen on the Internet it is frequently not clear *where* the crime has happened. Normally the physical location of the crime determines the jurisdiction, and therefore the particular set of laws that should be applied. But when a person in North America posts information on an Internet site in Asia that is offensive to a person in Europe, where did the alleged crime take place?

In any particular case, the advice of an appropriate specialist lawyer should always be sought. We will devote a section to each broad area of law.

5.2 Intellectual property rights

Software can be expensive to produce. A substantial piece of software like a database management system or an operating system can take many hundreds of person-years of effort to produce and a large team of engineers to maintain and evolve the software afterwards. How will this be paid for?

We have already looked at general concepts of property and the difference between private property and **public goods** in Chapter 3. We saw there that a key issue was the economic conditions surrounding the production of goods, and whether production should be based on the market and an economic return acquired through sales of the goods. An important issue in enabling a market to function is **excludability** – people who don't pay should not be able to use the goods. Software and information goods are extremely easy to copy and distribute, and their use by one person has little or no impact on others (indeed it might even be beneficial, since it widens the community of practice for that software or information, and the community within which data can be exchanged). One way to ensure excludability is to use technical measures, like encryption and license codes, or to use the Internet to check that people are properly licensed (as it is rumoured one major supplier does). We will not look further at such technical measures, though we will come back to the use of the Internet to police the use of software and information.

The other measure in wide use is the law, itself a public good, created to protect private goods. We will look in detail at the use of the law based on private goods and markets. Later we will return to consider software and information as a public good, and what is being done to use the law to protect this approach – the most common manifestation of this public goods view is the Free/Libre and Open Source Movement (**FOSS**), as we saw in Chapter 3 and will see again below.

Activity 5.1	*Why have intellectual property rights laws?*

Why do people in Europe and North America regard intellectual property law as so important? Why might people in Asia or Africa take a different view?

Discussion

The usual Western response is to treat software and information works like other property. We saw this in Chapter 3. The idea of property rights, where that property is physical in nature, like a house or motor vehicle or a television set, is well established. It would be generally agreed that such objects can be owned by a person or an organisation for their exclusive use, and that the owner is free to sell the object, hire it out, or profit from it in other ways. This economic activity would be seen as a fair recompense for the labour in building the house or other goods or the capital outlay in purchasing the house, motor vehicle, or television set. Most people in North America and Europe would agree that the law should protect the rights of the owner to undertake this economic activity and prevent the theft of such property, but also that the law should regulate the activity, for example to limit monopolistic and extortionate activity.

What about the fruits of creative activity, like the composition and performance of music, the writing of a novel, the invention of some new device, or the writing of software? These have come to be known as intellectual property, property that has resulted from the work of the intellect. Most people now agree that this form of property also needs to be protected and regulated. The argument is that if we do not, people will then stop producing such works – an argument that we questioned in Chapter 3.

Elsewhere in the world, in Africa and Asia, people might think differently. The idea of private property is very individualistic, for example, we saw in Chapter 3 that some cultures may well be collectivist and wish to see as many goods as possible shared as public goods. In such communities we might expect open source software to be popular, not because of its low cost but because it aligns with cultural beliefs.

Developments in technology have made the need for protection of intellectual property ever more urgent. With software and now books, music, and film available digitally, replication and distribution is both easy and cheap, and the financial barriers to copying no longer apply. Some technical measures, such as the need to enter long license keys or the use of digital watermarking, throw up barriers, but they still need to be complemented by legal protection.

Over the past two hundred years two different legal approaches have developed: **copyright** to protect written works, music, and similar; and **patent** to protect inventions and their subsequent exploitation in manufacture. *Copyright* protects the expression of an idea, while *patents* protect the idea itself. Different countries have enacted slightly different laws, but generally these kind of laws have been thought to be beneficial and have been widely adopted, and have become the subject of international agreements.

Having resolved that intellectual property rights (IPR) are desirable, it is believed that all countries should enact and enforce these laws. If a country does enact IPR law to protect the IPR of other countries, their own IPR would also be protected within the country and in export sales, which would help them obtain foreign investment. Investors want the protection of the law for the products they produce in that country, for without it a return on their investment is difficult.[2] In the short term there might seem to be benefits from avoiding copyright, particularly on material that would otherwise have to be imported at great cost, however, the country would benefit from other countries implementing copyright so that their exports could in turn generate income.

There are strong arguments against the protection of intellectual property based on ideas of common good that should not be withheld: if an invention protected by IPR could save a life, should it be withheld? To some, the protection of IPR, particularly for technology and science, by the more developed North and West mitigates too strongly against less developed countries.

If a software enterprise is seeking to operate internationally, it is important that intellectual property issues and the different views of intellectual property in different countries are taken into account. We will start by looking at international bodies and agreements to establish concepts and set a context within which copyright, patents, and other aspects of IPR can then be described and discussed.

> Intellectual property needs the protection of the law if copying is easy and cheap. This protection needs to be international.

5.2.1 International organisations and agreements

Intellectual property rights have become the focus of much debate internationally. With the coming of digital media and software, and digital communication networks facilitating cross-border flows, the need for international harmonisation and agreement has become ever more pressing. Commercial parties can exploit variation in national laws and the lack of an international authority with jurisdiction across countries, or attempt to flout the law altogether through the uncertainty as to where exactly an illegal copy was being held. The idea of cyberspace as a territory in which the law should operate has therefore become established.

This need for international agreement led first to the Berne Convention for copyright, and then to subsequent conventions to further elaborate and refine Berne. Other conventions addressing other parts of intellectual property law have followed. The European Union as a collaboration between countries with advanced economies but very different legal systems[3] has been important in movements towards international agreements. This section briefly summarises those international conventions and highlights current debates and open issues.

The Berne Convention

The original Berne Convention took place in 1886, focusing on the protection of 'literary and artistic works'. It was reviewed in Paris in 1896 and again in Berlin in 1908, before being completed in Berne in 1914. The year 1928 saw a further review in Rome, followed by reviews in 1948 in Brussels, 1967 in Stockholm, and 1971 in Paris. Its most recent amendment was in 1979.

Countries sign up to this agreement, but may not select the whole of the agreement. So, for example, Canada has signed up to the Rome version, and has then moved to the more exacting 1971 Paris version. Some 120 countries have now signed up – the United States was very late in doing so, having only signed on 1 March 1989.

The Berne agreement lays down three basic principles and a minimum level of protection that its signatories must grant. The three principles are:

- the protection given an original work in one Berne country must also be given that protection in all other Berne countries;
- protection should be automatic and not contingent upon any formalities like marking the work as copyright with the special © symbol;
- the protection given in a Berne country should not depend upon that same protection existing in the country of origin.

Because many important countries (like the US and countries in Latin America and Asia) did not join Berne until very late, the Universal Copyright Convention (UCC) was created in 1952 to build a bridge between the copyright systems of these countries and Berne members. With the US joining Berne in 1989, the importance of the UCC has diminished.

GATT and TRIPS

The General Agreement on Tariffs and Trade (GATT) was established after the Second World War to regulate world trade. In 1995 it was replaced by the World Trade Organisation (WTO). GATT and the WTO hold regular negotiations, a series of meetings called 'rounds', in order to reach agreements on areas of world trade. A number of rounds have addressed intellectual property rights.

The Uruguay Round of GATT (1986–1994, which led to the establishment of the WTO) developed its own view of copyright, different from Berne in important ways. This view has now become enshrined in TRIPS (Trade-Related aspects of Intellectual Property Rights) administered by the World Trade Organisation.

TRIPS introduces a 'most favoured nation' (MFN) requirement on copyright, so that a member of GATT/WTO must be given the same copyright treatment as any other member. GATT-style dispute settlement and enforcement procedures are introduced. TRIPS is generally seen to favour developed rather than developing countries in increasing protection, with the only accommodation being that developing countries could take five years instead of one year to move to the TRIPS agreement.

More recent WTO meetings, notably Doha in 2001, have focused on pharmaceuticals. We must anticipate that future meetings will focus on software.

WIPO

The World Intellectual Property Organisation (WIPO)[4] acts as the secretariat for the major intellectual property conventions, including the Berne Convention, and the more specialised Brussels, Geneva, and Rome Conventions. WIPO's role is to provide its members with information and assistance about intellectual property, to ensure that international and regional agencies cooperate on intellectual property issues, and to help developing countries in protecting their own intellectual property and in obtaining the intellectual property of developed countries on favourable terms.

On 20 December 1996, the members of WIPO adopted two new treaties: the WIPO Copyright Treaty for the protection of authors, and the WIPO Performance and Phonograms Treaty. The Copyright Treaty updates the last Berne Convention (1971) to cover digitisation, and in particular the availability of work online, but a resolution on reproduction rights in this environment was not reached.

At the general assembly meeting of WIPO in Geneva in September 2004, a proposal[5] from Argentina and Brazil was accepted, in which economic development depends upon a freer use of intellectual property than normal IPR regulation expects. A very strong and cogent argument supporting the Argentinean and Brazilian 'Friends of Development' proposal was given by India, as seen in Case Study 5.2. This important area will clearly continue to develop over the coming decades.

> Property rights law may protect the parties directly involved, but may not be in the wider social interest.

Case Study 5.2   *The imbalance of IPR protection*

Statement by India at the Inter-Sessional Intergovernmental Meeting on a Development Agenda For WIPO, 11–13 April 2005.

Mr. Chairman,

. . .

As pointed out in the two documents presented by the Group of Friends of Development, we agree that much more needs to be done in WIPO to reach the effective results that meet the challenges of development. 'Development', in WIPO's terminology means increasing a developing country's capacity to provide protection to the owners of intellectual property rights. This is quite the opposite of what developing countries understand when they refer to the 'development dimension'. The

▶

document presented by the Group of Friends of Development corrects this misconception – that development dimension means technical assistance.

The real 'development' imperative is ensuring that the interest of Intellectual Property owners is not secured at the expense of the users of IP, of consumers at large, and of public policy in general. The proposal therefore seeks to incorporate in international IP law and practice, what developing countries have been demanding since TRIPS was forced on them in 1994.

The primary rationale for Intellectual Property protection is, first and foremost, to promote societal development by encouraging technological innovation. The legal monopoly granted to IP owners is an exceptional departure from the general principle of competitive markets as the best guarantee for securing the interest of society. The rationale for the exception is not that extraction of monopoly profits by the innovator is, of and in itself, good for society and so needs to be promoted. Rather, that properly controlled, such a monopoly, by providing an incentive for innovation, might produce sufficient benefits for society to compensate for the immediate loss to consumers as a result of the existence of a monopoly market instead of a competitive market. Monopoly rights, then, granted to IP holders is a special incentive that needs to be carefully calibrated by each country, in the light of its own circumstances, taking into account the overall costs and benefits of such protection.

Should the rationale for a monopoly be absent, as in the case of cross-border rights involving developed and developing countries, the only justification for the grant of a monopoly is a contractual obligation, such as the TRIPS agreement, and nothing more. In such a situation it makes little sense for one party, especially the weaker party, to agree to assume greater obligations than he is contractually bound to accept. This, in short, is what the developed countries have sought to do so far in the context of WIPO. The message of the De-velopment Agenda is clear: no longer are developing countries prepared to accept this approach, or continuation of the status quo.

Even in a developed country, where the monopoly profits of the domestic IP rights holders are recycled through the economy and so benefit the public in varying degrees, there is continuing debate on the equity and fairness of such protection, with some even questioning its claimed social benefits. Given the total absence of any mandatory cross-border resource transfers or welfare payments, and the absence of any significant domestic recycling of the monopoly profits of foreign IP rights holders, the case for strong IP protection in developing countries is without any economic basis. Harmonisation of IP laws across countries with asymmetric distribution of IP assets is, clearly, intended to serve the interest of rent seekers in developed countries rather than that of the public in developing countries.

Neither intellectual property protection, nor the harmonisation of intellectual property laws leading to higher protection standards in all countries irrespective of their level of development, can be an end in itself. For developing countries to benefit from providing IP protection to rights holders based in developed countries, there has to be some obligation on the part of developed countries to transfer and disseminate technologies to developing countries. Even though the intended beneficiary of IP protection is the public at large, the immediate beneficiaries are the IP rights holders, the vast majority of whom are in developed countries. Absent an obligation on technology transfer, asymmetric IP rent flows would become a permanent feature, and the benefits of IP protection would forever elude consumers in developing countries. As pointed out in the proposal by the Group of Friends of Development, technology transfer should be a fundamental objective of the global intellectual property system. WIPO is recognised as a specialised agency with the responsibility for taking appropriate measures for undertaking this and we expect the 'development agenda' to address this issue.

Technical assistance should be primarily directed towards impact assessment and enabling the developing countries, including LDCs to utilise the space within the prevailing arrangements in multilateral IP treaties and conventions.

The current emphasis of Technical Assistance on implementation and enforcement issues is misplaced. IP Law enforcement is embedded in the framework of all law enforcement in the individual countries. It is unrealistic, and even undesirable to expect that the enforcement of IP laws will be privileged over the enforcement of other laws in the country. Society faces a considerable challenge to effectively protect, and resolve disputes over, physical property. To expect that the police, the lawyers and the courts should dedicate a sizable part of society's enforcement resources for protecting intangible intellectual property is unrealistic. Therefore, WIPO's current focus of Technical Assistance should be shifted to other areas such as development impact assessment. This would, inter alia, inspire civil society and others to play a supportive role, if the impact is seen to be favourable to the community.

In conclusion, it is important that developed countries and WIPO acknowledge that IP protection is an important policy instrument for developing countries, one that needs to be used carefully. While the claimed benefits of strong IP protection for developing countries are a matter of debate – and nearly always in the distant future – such protection invariably entails substantial real and immediate costs for these countries. In formulating its IP policy, therefore, each country needs to have sufficient flexibility so that the cost of IP protection does not outweigh the benefits. It is clearly in the interest of developing countries that WIPO recognises this and formulates its work program accordingly – including its 'technical assistance' – and not limit its activities, as it currently does, to the blind promotion of increasingly higher levels of IP protection. This is where WIPO, as a specialised UN agency, can make a major impact – by truly incorporating the development dimension into its mission – in letter and in spirit, so that it is appropriately reflected in all its instruments. Certainly it will result in a revitalisation of WIPO as an organisation sensitive to integrating the development concerns of developing countries into all areas of its work.

Text taken from http://lists.essential.org/pipermail/ip-health/2005-April/007753.html.

5.2.2 Copyright

Copyright has been of central importance to publishing for two hundred years, and now to software and the Internet. Copyright gives the right to the 'originator [of a work], or his or her assignee, for a fixed number of years, to print, publish, perform, film, or record literary, artistic, or musical material, and to authorize others to do the same' (definition from the *Concise Oxford Dictionary*, ninth edition).

It is important to note that copyright law does not protect the ideas underlying the work, but only the expression of those ideas. This means that having examined a work, or a number of works, an author is free to create a new work through the re-expression of the ideas underlying those other works. However this does not mean that the simple rekeying of text with small changes is permitted, and nor is the redrawing of a diagram or reimplementation of an animation. Note also that compilations and databases are explicitly protected as intellectual property.

When software became a concern in the second half of the twentieth century, it was copyright that was originally used for the protection of software. In 1991 the

European Union issued a directive[6] requiring all member states to use copyright law for the protection of software, spelling out the rights and exceptions; in 2000 they reported[7] on the success of this initiative. Nevertheless, although not everyone agrees with this statement, we would argue that copyright has not proved adequate, since it only protects the way the software is written and not the underlying algorithms. In consequence, software is increasingly being protected by patents (see next subsection). Copyright is now also very important for the protection of Internet websites and for documentation.

Traditionally the different kinds of artistic work have been protected by different legislation – so music has been protected separately from literature and from film, and so on. However, recent theory has emphasised 'convergence', as everything becomes digitised and intermixed within multimedia products. Beyond this convergence, digitisation has raised new problems and the need to protect works against new actions. Thus the treatment of all rights under the general heading of intellectual property rights, or at least general copyright, is the only reasonable way forward. Further, the ability to distribute digital material over the Internet makes intellectual property rights a global problem, requiring international resolution; we saw some of these actions earlier in this chapter.

Under copyright, the author or originator of the intellectual property is given a number of legal 'rights'. These then circumscribe what the owner can do (and in some cases cannot do), and what other people can do with the intellectual property. The details of how the right is claimed and what it gives the owner of the IPR varies between legal jurisdictions.

In some cases the right has to be explicitly claimed or registered, as was the case in the US before 1989; while elsewhere, as in the UK, the very act of creating the work automatically gave the creator the rights. The move is now towards the latter through decisions taken at various international agreements described earlier – the Berne convention, the Uruguay round of GATT, and its TRIPS. Note that even though it may not be necessary to place a copyright line on the work, this is still advised.

The actual right given is exclusive use for the life of the creator plus seventy years. The US and others had previously limited rights for life plus fifty years, but moved to life plus seventy years to match the European practice as part of the process of harmonising copyright law internationally. Some cynics claim that the US made this move to protect Disney!

There are exceptions to granting of exclusive rights recognised by the law that will be covered in greater detail later. Where exceptions are made it is generally done to protect the public interest; what is allowed here varies – for example in the US a teacher can read from the work in the classroom but not distribute copies, while in the UK a researcher can make a copy of part of a work for personal use. Very limited quotation from works is accepted as 'fair use'.

Copyright protects the expression of an idea, but not the idea itself.

All other use requires a request to the copyright owner for permission, and possibly the payment of a fee. Finding out who are the rights owners can be very complex, and even a simple request can involve more copyright owners than you might imagine. Rights can be assigned to other persons or legal entities, which is a common practice – in some jurisdictions like the US all rights can be assigned, while in others like France some rights are inalienable, such as authorship and the look and feel of an artistic work.

Any breach of an intellectual property right can be viewed as theft, just as under the law the taking of another's physical property is theft. Yet many people see the kinds of works protected by copyright laws as different from physical property, and the introduction of new technologies is making the breach of copyright easier.

How breaches of copyright are dealt with varies between jurisdictions. In some places, such as the US, breaches are largely handled through the civil courts and owners claim statutory damages: owners of copyright often group together in societies and make random checks to see if copyright is being breached; if it is, they then take joint action to recover the money lost and punish the offender. In the US, the music industry associations conduct around 500 lawsuits per year to enforce the copyright interests of their members. In other countries enforcement might be through the criminal law, which investigates to deter major and systematic infringers.

Case Study 5.3 *Software copyright in the courts*

Over the period 1970 to the present, court cases have set a variety of precedents, and the following four examples, taken from David Bainbridge's book *Software Copyright Law*,[8] illustrate some of the judgments given:

1. *Digital Communications Associates* v. *Softklone Distributing Corporation* [659 F Supp 449 (ND Ga 1987)]
   The plaintiff (DCA) designed a screen display for a communications program which showed a list of commands with the first two letters highlighted and in block capitals; the user selected a command by entering its first two letters. The defendant (SDC) developed another communications program with a similar display. The court upheld protection of the screen display, saying that the idea was the concept of such a screen (and therefore not copyrightable), and the expression (that is, the use of highlighting and capital letters, and the organisation of the command) was the means to communicate the idea (and hence was protected by copyright).

2. *Broderbund Software* v. *Unison World* [648 F Supp 1127 (ND Cal 1986)]
   This case also concerned screen displays. In this instance, it was argued by the defendant (UW) that there was only one way to structure the screens and input, thus they were part of the idea, and not simply expression. In fact, other versions of the screens were produced as evidence, and it was ruled that the screen displays were indeed part of the expression used by BS, and thus copyrightable.

3. *Ibcos Computers Ltd* v. *Barclays Mercantile Highland Finance Ltd* (UK) [1994, FSR 275]
   A programmer had worked on an accounts package for the plaintiff (Ibcos), and subsequently marketed a competing accounts package for the defendant (BM). Copyright was held to subsist in the individual program and in the entire software package as a compilation. This case showed that, as well as individual computer programs being protected by copyright, the way they are linked together (structured) may, in some cases, also be protected. In other words, depending on the skill and judgement involved in selecting and arranging the individual programs, copying structural and design features may infringe copyright.

4. *Lotus Development Corporation* v. *Paperback Software International* [740 F Supp 37 (D Mass 1990)]
   This case showed that overall organisation and structure, the content and structure of commands, and the user interface (choice of words or symbols) are protected by copyright, but the judge in this case said that it does not follow automatically that every expression of an idea

►

is protected by copyright. He listed four things that must be considered:

- originality – the expression must originate from the author
- functionality – if the expression simply embodies functional elements of an idea, it is not copyrightable

- obviousness – if the expression is inseparable from the idea, it is not protected
- merger – if the particular expression is one of a quite limited number of expressions, then it is not copyrightable.

There are a number of quite distinct rights, and we will discuss each kind of right in turn, to point out some of the specific problems and issues raised by that right. Because this is an evolving area, particularly for digitised material, it is always advisable to seek expert legal advice when considering intellectual property rights in general and copyright in particular.

Moral rights

Moral rights are concerned with the artistic integrity of the intellectual property and the right of its creator to be acknowledged as that creator. In Anglo-American law these moral rights have in the past been neglected, with emphasis being placed upon the economic or pecuniary rights, but this has now changed. Moral rights may be waivable, but they are never assignable.

The moral right of attribution is clear – the originator must be attributed with authorship if anybody is, though the originator may choose to remain anonymous. In some jurisdictions, such as France, this right is inalienable. In others it may be waived, so in the UK the originator has to positively declare this right of 'paternity', otherwise a publisher could in principle (but never would) drop the name of the author from the work. However, they may not substitute another person's name. When intellectual property is created under contract, the attribution often gets dropped.

It is common practice to credit the developers of computer games, but less so for software – for example, although the Eudora email package credits its developer the policy at Microsoft is not to do this (though in some Microsoft products, if you know how to find them, you can find the names of the developers).[9]

The position on integrity is less clear. The most common breach of integrity occurs in television and film, where the colourisation or aspect ratio may be changed. A famous case in Canada concerned a sculpture of Canada geese that was draped in red ribbons by its owner, which led the sculptor, who was no longer the owner, to sue for damages to his reputation. Again in France this right is inalienable, while elsewhere it may be waivable – there is a strong case that this should be so, for example to handle cases where a publisher might want to edit an author's work or where a film might be distributed in a range of different cultures where particular colours have cultural significance. For Internet sites it could be desirable that properties like font size and picture resolution can be changed.

Economic rights

The most fundamental economic right is that of controlling the **reproduction** of the work. When publishing a work through some other party, it is important to license the publisher to print (and distribute) the work; this is done either by assigning (transferring) copyright to the publisher, or by giving the publisher a license to print and distribute the work as part of the publishing contract. Once a work has been printed, the publisher may assume a 'typographical right' in the printed material, generally for a shorter period than the copyright itself.

Reproduction with computers may now also cover the initial digitisation of the work, and uploading or downloading of the work.

All of these acts of reproduction may only be carried out with the permission of the owner of the copyright, who may also require the payment of some suitable fee.

The most common point at which people meet the copyrighting of text and print is in photocopying, for which, in principle, a license is always required. Recovery of fees from photocopying is an important source of income for copyright holders.

Distribution and communication of copies

Having made a copy of a work, you may typically want to further reproduce it and distribute it to others. The right to distribute also belongs exclusively to the owner of the intellectual property rights, and distribution and communication have a broad interpretation covering anything that enables members of the public to access the intellectual property at a time and place of their choosing.

Thus, distribution and communication includes the performance of plays, the reading of poetry, and the on-demand transmission of film and audio across communication networks. But it also includes any display of material where the public can access it, particularly on the Internet.

'Communication to the public' is a new right under the Geneva Convention and is contained in the EU harmonisation directive, though it may not yet be incorporated into law. This is a complicated right that includes concepts like 'performance' and 'broadcasting', and is inconsistent or incomplete with regard to electronic publishing.

The exercise of the right of distribution and communication may involve sale or hire, but does not require it. It also includes the right to prohibit unauthorised distribution and communication. These rights normally cannot be 'exhausted' except by transfer of the ownership of the right to some other party. This idea of 'exhaustion' has been present in some jurisdictions, such that some particular action by the owner can terminates their right.

In linking websites together it is very easy to embed material from some other site within your site, and pass it off as part of your site; to do this would be a breach of copyright. The usual advice is to make such links to the home page of the site being linked to – this may make the link much less useful, since you then have to find the part of the site you need, but it does avoid breaching distribution and communication rights.

> The rights protected by copyright law include the moral right to be known as the author and the right to economic benefit.

Exceptions and exemptions

It is recognised that there need to be some exceptions to the intellectual property rights of the owner. This need arises for a number of reasons, to support the wider public interest, because of market failure, and to support the exercising of licences granted by some previous copyright holder.

It is clear what we mean by making copies of printed and other creative physical works, and it is widely accepted, but not universally so, that you may make single copies for the purpose of research, private study, criticism and review, and the reporting of current events. This is termed 'fair dealing' in the UK and 'fair use' in the US, where it would be argued that it is in the wider public interest, since it facilitates the education and development of society. However, the idea of fair dealing is not accepted in many European countries, and is still the subject of much debate. Where fair dealing is referred to in national laws, it tends not to be very explicit and publishers and users have had to resort to drawing up consensus guidelines to guide actual day-to-day practice.

It is less clear when considering the copying of digital works. There are no guidelines yet for the electronic environment and really no clear agreement of what the digital equivalent might be. Exceptions may be taken further in a number of ways. It may be permitted to make copies of audio and audiovisual materials for personal use – so called 'private copying'. In some jurisdictions it may even be permitted to use materials in TV transmission for educational purposes, although normally this would require a license. The European directive on the use of copyright for software includes exemptions for making back-up copies and for limited decompilation[10] of software at the interface to facilitate the interoperability of the software with other software.

Libraries may also be exempted from the constraints of copyright for particular actions like archiving – this is called library privilege in the UK, and is not part of fair dealing. Libraries make extensive use of fair dealing in supplying copies of materials to scholars, particularly between libraries – in the UK this forms part of the 'inter-library loans' system. It is not clear what the equivalent of an inter-library loan is in the digital world, and the remote delivery of library services in digital libraries would not be exempt from intellectual property law.

In many technical processes involving digitised copies, temporary intermediate copies are inevitably produced, and legislation has been proposed to exempt these copies. However, the purposeful making of copies for the purposes of security or back-up may not be exempt – though typically a license would grant this right while prohibiting making copies for other purpose.

It is clearly unwise to assume an exemption exists, and when in doubt, a license should be sought.

Berne and TRIPS

The minimum protection required for all literary, artistic, and scientific works is:

- the rights include translation, adaptations and adjustments, public performance and recital, reproduction, communication and broadcast;
- moral rights of paternity and integrity; and
- a minimum duration of protection.

TRIPS adopts the Berne principles and requires countries to adopt Articles 1 to 21 of the Paris 1971 protocol, with the notable exception of Article 6 on the moral rights of paternity and integrity. TRIPS extended copyright coverage to computer programs (as literary works) and to databases, and required that a rental right is established for computer programs and for recordings.

Activity 5.2   *Intellectual property rights*

You have been teaching mathematics for a number of years and have developed your own individual way of explaining the key concepts of set theory, which involves the students playing a game. You now decide to publish this method of teaching and the game as a multimedia product with an accompanying book. You will write the book, but will need to hire a multimedia developer to produce multimedia to your specification. You will then sell this through a well-known publisher. What rights do you believe you should have, and what rights do you believe the multimedia developer and the publisher should have?

Discussion

Since the basic ideas are yours, it would seem sensible to retain these. As the employer of the multimedia developer you may well automatically own the actual multimedia software produced and the employee would gain no rights over the software – but it would be wise to spell this out in the contract of employment.

When entering into the agreement with the publisher, all you need grant are the copying and distribution rights, retaining all other rights for yourself. Standard publishers' agreements are very likely to demand assignment of copyright to the publisher, but this is not necessary and some publishers are happy not to demand this.

5.2.3 Patents

In contrast to copyright, patents are explicitly intended to protect ideas or inventions. Patents in the UK go back to the Statute of Monopolies in 1623, and in the US the first patent law was enacted in 1790. Since then the need to protect inventions and similar creations has become recognised around the world, first in national legislation and now in global agreements, such GATT discussed earlier. An excellent discussion of patents is given by Gordon and Cookfair in their book *Patent Fundamentals for Scientists and Engineers*[11] and much of that advice is relevant to software managers – except that the book predates recent moves to make software patentable.

The US Patent Act describes the position very well:

> Whoever invents or discovers any new and useful process, machine, manufacture, or composition of matter, or any new and useful improvements thereof, may obtain a patent, subject to the conditions and requirements of this title.

To be patentable the invention must be novel and not already exist. Existing inventions are known as 'prior art' and have been disclosed and become public, perhaps in a publication or embodied in a product or an earlier patent. If novel, it must not be obvious 'to one of ordinary skill in the art', and though it may be similar to some pre-existing invention, it must contain non-obvious new features. Further, the invention must be useful and operable.

Patent laws usually circumscribe what can be patented. Historically they have been inventions and discoveries, human-made products, compositions of matter, and processing methods. To this have been added designs (in the sense of ornamental appearances) and more recently plants following developments in genetic engineering. Software was initially explicitly excluded, as was methods of doing business, and 'mere printed matter'. However, following initiatives in the US and then in Europe, software seems likely to become patentable subject to international agreement.

To obtain copyright requires no particular action by the author or creator: the very act of creation is sufficient, though insertion of a copyright statement is advised, as is commonly seen at the front of books. By contrast, acquiring a patent can be a lengthy and expensive procedure. Because the process can take considerable time, immediate protection can be obtained by filing a provisional patent. As an alternative to filing a patent (for example if the cost makes the investment unacceptable) it is always possible to disclose it, and thus avoid others patenting the same idea. It has become standard practice in many major industrial companies to have a 'technical disclosure' publication for this purpose.

A patent is applied for by the inventor from the national patent office, following procedures and regulations laid down by national or international law. The invention needs to be specified in sufficient detail for anybody in the technological area to be able to build the invention, include any appropriate drawings, and describe one means of actually constructing the invention. The actual novelty needs to be claimed explicitly; this is what will be examined during the registration process. Thus, to establish a patent an extensive search must be made of prior art in order to establish novelty.

If successful, a patent is granted to the owner of the patent for a period of twenty years from the date of filing. During this period the patent holder has the exclusive right to exploit the patent commercially, to make, use, or sell the invention.

Software patents have become established slowly as court rulings attempt to decide what is and what is not patentable. The patenting of software in the US became regularised in 1996. There are now many thousands of software patents, including the well known GIF compression patent, the algorithm for reducing the size of images encoded in the GIF manner. But software patents remain controversial, and many trivial and obvious algorithms have been given patent protection in the US. The Software Patent Institute[12] in the US, supported by most major organisations involved in software, is systematically setting out to document prior art to bring some order to the current situation. Nevertheless, many parts of the software industry, particularly outside the US, remain concerned lest much obvious and useful software should be prevented due to claims of patent infringement.

> Patents protect the ideas themselves, and are now applicable to software. This is controversial, especially concerning prior art.

5.2.4 Trademarks, service marks, and brands

Brands have become an important component of commercial activity: they identify a product or service and represent the quality of that product or service. International brands like CocaCola and Nike are instantly recognisable and attract customers.

Brands are recognised in law as 'marks' for which special protection is given. A **trademark** is defined by the US Patent and Trademark Office:[13]

> A trademark includes any word, name, symbol, or device, or any combination, used, or intended to be used, in commerce to identify and distinguish the goods of one manufacturer or seller from goods manufactured or sold by others, and to indicate the source of the goods. In short, a trademark is a brand name.

This clearly identifies trademarks with brands. Service marks identify and distinguish the services of a particular provider. The US also recognises two further marks: collective marks for societies and certification marks to indicate that products conform to particular standards.

International agreement on trademarks was reached in April 2002 under the Madrid Protocol, managed by WIPO. The US contracted into this treaty in November 2003.

Brands, and their associated marks, need to be managed through advertising and refreshing them through suitable changes. While this makes sense commercially, it is also necessary from the trademark perspective, for a trademark to remain protected it needs to be maintained and in active use – otherwise some other body could be authorised to use it.

Activity 5.3   *Patents, trademarks, and markets*

To what extent might the use of patents and trademarks distort the market as described in Chapter 3?

Discussion
Patents are intended to distort the market and create a monopoly for the owner of the patent for the life of that patent. This means that the price of the goods based on the patent might be inflated, but the counterargument would be that it is necessary in order to recover the costs of developing the patent and to support continuing invention for future exploitation. Once the patent has lapsed, the market should revert to its normal competitive state.

People do not buy goods solely on the basis of price, but also on quality and trust, and brands and trademarks help in this. So in this way trademarks help the market rather than distort it.

5.2.5 Common and public goods

An alternative approach to the one described above, based on private property and market forces protected by both copyright and patent, is that software and information should be public goods and be freely available. We discussed this view at length in Chapter 3, where we saw how in general economic terms this works. How does it work legally?

The idea would be to freely distribute software for use by whoever wishes, without any hinderance of having to pay fees or constraints on what the software can be used for. However, this free distribution would be happening in an environment in which software copyright and patents are established and in active use. The free distribution of software could still run into problems as people attempt to take ownership of the software as private property and use the law to give themselves exclusive rights to the intellectual property.

Thus it has become common practice to use intellectual property law to protect 'free software', software as a public good. This turns out to be desirable anyway, since there may be some basic rights, like moral rights, that you would always want to protect – so that for those jurisdictions that do not treat such rights as inalienable, these rights have to be respected anyway. These protections are set out in standard licensing agreements, of which there are two in increasingly widespread use within the Free and Open Source movement.

The GNU General Public License and Free Documentation Licences were established by the Free Software Foundation[14] for software and documentation respectively. The intention is to ensure everybody is free to copy and redistribute the work, with or without modification, commercially or non-commercially, while crediting the original authors without making them responsible for any modifications. These are the original public goods licenses, though they have evolved over the years. These licenses contain a number of specific stipulations that must be adhered to.

Software as public goods can use intellectual property law to protect itself.

The creative commons license[15] for a copyrighted work is somewhat less restrictive than the GNU licenses, but is gaining considerable popularity. This license enables you to reproduce and distribute the work, incorporate the work into a larger collection, and create and reproduce and distribute derivative works. This can be done in any medium. The creative commons license must be passed on to recipients of the distributed work without any further imposed conditions. The original copyright notice must be passed on intact, in particular to identify the original creator of the work. The distribution of a work should not be one primarily for commercial gain, and where such gain is made, the licensor retains the right to collect royalties.

The use of GNU and creative commons licenses has been contested in disputes between the commercial software development industry and the Open Source movement. The claim has been that the conditions laid down are infringements of human rights. The debate about public goods had led to interest by the United Nations, where it is believed that many services like education and the use of the Internet should be viewed as public goods. This is clearly going to be an area of change and great growth in the decades ahead. Fortunately you will be able to track those changes through the Internet, where so much valuable information is posted as a public good.

Case Study 5.4 *Microsoft versus Linux using software patents*

Microsoft claims that their software patents are violated by the Linux kernel. The following article about this was published on *The Register* in 2004.[16] Reprinted with permission of John Lettice.

Use Linux and you will be sued, Ballmer tells governments

By John Lettuce

Published Thursday 18th November 2004 10:34 GMT

Asian governments using Linux will be sued for IP violations, Microsoft CEO Steve Ballmer said today in Singapore. He did not specify that Microsoft would be the company doing the suing, but it's difficult to read the

claim as anything other than a declaration of IP war.

According to a Reuters report (which we fervently hope will produce one of Ballmer's fascinating 'I was misquoted' rebuttals*), Ballmer told Microsoft's Asian Government Leaders Forum that Linux violates more than 228 patents. Come on Steve, don't hold back – what you mean 'more than 228' – 229? 230? Don't pull your punches to soften the blow to the community. 'Some day,' he continued, 'for all countries that are entering the WTO [World Trade Organization], somebody will come and look for money owing to the rights for that intellectual property.'

This reference is possibly more interesting than the infringement number scare itself, because it suggests that Microsoft sees the wider implementation of corporation-friendly IP law that is part of the entry ticket to the WTO as being a weapon that can be used against software rivals. More commonly, getting WTO members to 'go legit' is viewed as having a pay-off in terms of stamping out counterfeit CDs, DVDs and designer gear, but clearly Microsoft's lawyers are busily plotting ways to embrace and extend this to handy new fields. It could be used to throttle emergent OSS companies, and it could conceivably be used to take the new generation of US (and maybe EU too) anti digital piracy and IP laws global.

The venue for Ballmer's menacing claims was nicely judged. Microsoft's Government Leaders Conferences are pitched as select events where chosen senior representatives and influencers from target governments are wined, dined, schmoozed and impressed by the cream of the Microsoft high command (we've explained them before.) They'll be intended to take away the message from this dynamic, hospitable and successful company that OSS is dangerous and will make you poor.

But if countries who want to join the WTO and get developed and rich should consider the dangers inherent in OSS, what about all of those countries who're already members of the WTO? They should perhaps also get the message about how Microsoft sees IP law being used in the future. Which might well have a helpful collateral damage effect in Europe, if Europe's leaders are paying attention. Yesterday the Polish Government backed out of support for the EU patents directive, in a move which threatens to derail it (because the directive may not now achieve a qualified majority in the council of ministers).

This on its own may be no more than a temporary setback for the patents lobby (prominent members in Europe include Microsoft and Sun), but the sound of Microsoft threatening all-out IP war really ought to strengthen the opposition's hand, and make the European Parliament, which opposes software patents, more determined to fight. So well done, Steve, we look forward to the rebuttal. Reuters report here.

*You can set your watch by him. A couple of hours later, we have this. Note that the denial simply amounts to Microsoft denying that Steve said that Microsoft believes Linux violates 228 patents. Steve, allegedly, was merely citing an OSRM report saying Linux might be vulnerable over 283 patents. The 'you will be sued' threat, as far as we can make out, stands. How 283 could have got to be 228 we do not grasp – Fear, Uncertainty, Dodgy arithmetic?

Text taken from http://theregister.co.uk/2004/11/18/ballmer_linux_lawsuits/.

5.3 Contracts

Contracts are very frequently entered into as part of software management: for employing personnel and for hiring consultants, for purchasing hardware and software, for software developments contracts, and for hardware and software maintenance, for example. Contracts are agreements between two (or more) parties that are legally binding. If one of the parties fails to fulfil its agreements then the other party can obtain redress through the courts. The central importance of contracting in computing can be seen in the monograph published by the British Computer Society[17] which spends more than half its pages on issues around contracting, giving much useful detailed guidance, with the underpinning guidance that when in doubt expert legal advice should be sought.

The contract needs to set out what the parties to the contract will do and when they will do it. Typically this involves the payment of money in return for the supply of goods and services. We need to make sure that our contracts are well formulated so that we do not find ourselves in difficulty later; some of the issues that need to be addressed in any contract are described below.

The goods to be supplied might be computer and communications hardware as part of some major development of the IT infrastructure of your organisation. In this case it would be normal to specify delivery dates, and include the procedures for commissioning and acceptance of the new equipment. The supplier might depend upon us to prepare our premises to receive the new hardware systems. Alternatively the goods might be software – we will see in Chapters 6 to 9 a number of ways this might be supplied, from off-the-shelf products to bespoke development. Software which involves customisation of some pre-existing software or the bespoke development of new software is notoriously difficult to specify precisely enough for a simple contract to suffice, and we will see variations of software development process models in Chapter 8 that aim to address this.

Over the past few decades there has been a move to supply 'total solutions', both hardware and software, responding to a organisational need. In these cases it can be easier to define what must be delivered and to identify failures under the contract. There have been some cases of failure to deliver systems that have led to successful lawsuits for breach of contract. An example of a lawsuit settled out of court to illustrate the kind of issues that could lead to litigation is given in Case Study 5.5.

Case Study 5.5 *PeopleSoft charged with contract breach*[18]

Cleveland Sate University is a public university founded in 1870 in the state of Ohio in the US, with approximately 16,000 undergraduate and post graduate students in 2002. Like all universities, administering student records is important, and in 1997 they licensed the ERP supplier Peoplesoft's student administration system - and tried for 7 years to get it to work for them. Eventually on Jan 30th 2004 the Ohio attorney general filed a lawsuit against Peoplesoft for $510 million damages suffered at Cleveland State University. The also filed a lawsuit against Kaludis Consulting who had advised the selection of Peoplesoft and managed the project in its early days. In the end these lawsuits were settled out of court following the take over of Peoplesoft by Oracle in December 2004, and Oracle's

undertaking to continue support for Peoplesoft ERP systems.

Cleveland Sate was the first university to select Peoplesoft's student administration system. Later in 2000 Stanford University also adopted Peoplesoft's student administration system and also struggled, though the difficulties were attributed to interactions with Oracle's Financials that Stanford had also adopted. The CIO (Chief Information Officer) at Stanford, Chris Handley, has commented negatively about ERP systems as 'a collective hallucination'. Stanford has had to change its practices (re-engineer their business processes) to fit. Fred Gage at Cleveland State has commented that had Cleveland State also re-engineered their business processes they would not have had the problems that they did.

When hardware is supplied, it is usual for the purchaser to own the hardware, as with any other physical property. However when software is supplied, the property rights may not be bought, just licensed, as in Case Study 5.6, with ownership remaining with the supplier, or some other party who supplied them. Only in the case of bespoke development might the intellectual property become the purchaser's, though even then the agreement might entitle the supplier to further develop the software and sell it to other clients where this does not lead to loss of competitive advantage for the original purchaser. The details need to be spelled out in the contract.

Case Study 5.6 *Red Hat Linux service contract*

Each of Red Hat's software products is covered by a Subscription Agreement including an End User License Agreement. All agreements are governed by the contractual laws of the State of North Carolina and the intellectual property laws of the United States of America, unless otherwise indicated. In the following extracts taken from the Spanish version of the contract, we concentrate on the Appendix that contains the clauses that interest us (all Red Hat agreements have similar appendices). We will also show a few others clauses that are typical of such agreements. Where passages of text have been left out these have been indicated by '· · ·'.

Services Agreement
This Services Agreement (the 'Agreement') is between Red Hat, Inc. ('Red Hat') and any purchaser or user ('Customer') of Red Hat products and services that accepts the terms of this Agreement ('Customer').

· · ·

I. Terms and Conditions
A. GENERAL TERMS AND CONDITIONS

The term 'Services' as used in this Agreement means, collectively, the Support Services provided under the purchased subscription and defined herein and the RHN Services as defined herein. The term 'Software' means the software products purchased under this Agreement and defined herein. The term 'Installed Systems' means the number of Systems on which Customer installs the Software. The term 'System' means any hardware on which the Software is installed, which may be, without

limitation, a server, a work station, a virtual machine, a blade, a partition or an engine, as applicable. The initial number of Installed Systems is the number of copies of the Software that Customer purchases.

· · ·

II. Support Services Service Levels
A. SUBSCRIPTION TERMS AND CONDITIONS

· · ·

'Software' means the software purchased under this Agreement, which is provided under Red Hat's trademarks and is subject to the applicable end user license agreement attached hereto as Appendix. . .

· · ·

4. SUPPORT SERVICE CONDITIONS:

4.1 Red Hat may, at its discretion, decline to provide Support Services for Software that has been modified or changed by Customer in any way, except as directed by Red Hat. Red Hat will provide Support Services for Supported Hardware and Platforms only. Red Hat will only provide Support Services for those Installed Systems for which Customer has subscribed under this Agreement.
4.2 Red Hat may, at its discretion, decline to provide Support Services for the packages included in the Software which are designated as 'kernel-unsupported.'
Appendix 1

LICENSE AGREEMENT AND LIMITED PRODUCT WARRANTY
RED HAT® ENTERPRISE LINUX®

This agreement governs the use of the Software and any updates to the Software, regardless of

▶

the delivery mechanism. The Software is a collective work under U.S. Copyright Law. Subject to the following terms, Red Hat, Inc. ('Red Hat') grants to the user ('Customer') a license to this collective work pursuant to the GNU General Public License.

1. The Software. Red Hat Enterprise Linux (the 'Software') is a modular operating system consisting of hundreds of software components. The end user license agreement for each component is located in the component's source code. With the exception of certain image files identified in Section 2 below, the license terms for the components permit Customer to copy, modify, and redistribute the component, in both source code and binary code forms. This agreement does not limit Customer's rights under, or grant Customer rights that supersede, the license terms of any particular component.

2. Intellectual Property Rights. The Software and each of its components, including the source code, documentation, appearance, structure and organization are owned by Red Hat and others and are protected under copyright and other laws. Title to the Software and any component, or to any copy, modification, or merged portion shall remain with the aforementioned, subject to the applicable license. The 'Red Hat' trademark and the 'Shadowman' logo are registered trademarks of Red Hat in the U.S. and other countries. This agreement does not permit Customer to distribute the Software using Red Hat's trademarks. Customer should read the information found at http://www.redhat.com/about/corporate/trademark/ before distributing a copy of the Software, regardless of whether it has been modified. If Customer makes a commercial redistribution of the Software, unless a separate agreement with Red Hat is executed or other permission granted, then Customer must modify the files identified as 'REDHAT-LOGOS' and

'anaconda-images' to remove all images containing the 'Red Hat' trademark or the 'Shadowman' logo. Merely deleting these files may corrupt the Software.

3. Limited Warranty. Except as specifically stated in this agreement or a license for a particular component, to the maximum extent permitted under applicable law, the Software and the components are provided and licensed 'as is' without warranty of any kind, expressed or implied, including the implied warranties of merchantability, non-infringement or fitness for a particular purpose. Red Hat warrants that the media on which the Software is furnished will be free from defects in materials and manufacture under normal use for a period of 30 days from the date of delivery to Customer. Red Hat does not warrant that the functions contained in the Software will meet Customer's requirements or that the operation of the Software will be entirely error free or appear precisely as described in the accompanying documentation. This warranty extends only to the party that purchases the Software from Red Hat or a Red Hat authorized distributor.

4. Limitation of Remedies and Liability. To the maximum extent permitted by applicable law, the remedies described below are accepted by Customer as its only remedies. Red Hat's entire liability, and Customer's exclusive remedies, shall be: If the Software media is defective, Customer may return it within 30 days of delivery along with a copy of Customer's payment receipt and Red Hat, at its option, will replace it or refund the money paid by Customer for the Software. To the maximum extent permitted by applicable law, Red Hat or any Red Hat authorized dealer will not be liable to Customer for any incidental or consequential damages, including lost profits or lost savings arising out of the use or inability to use the Software, even if Red Hat or such dealer has been advised of the possibility of

such damages. In no event shall Red Hat's liability under this agreement exceed the amount that Customer paid to Red Hat under this agreement during the twelve months preceding the action.

5. *Export Control. As required by U.S. law, Customer represents and warrants that it: (a) understands that the Software is subject to export controls under the U.S. Commerce Department's Export Administration Regulations ('EAR'); (b) is not located in a prohibited destination country under the EAR or U.S. sanctions regulations (currently Cuba, Iran, Iraq, Libya, North Korea, Sudan and Syria); (c) will not export, re-export, or transfer the Software to any prohibited destination, entity, or individual without the necessary export license(s) or authorizations(s) from the U.S. Government; (d) will not use or transfer the Software for use in any sensitive nuclear, chemical or biological weapons, or missile technology end-uses unless authorized by the U.S. Government by regulation or specific license; (e) understands and agrees that if it is in the United States and exports or transfers the Software to eligible end users, it will, as required by EAR Section 741.17(e), submit semi-annual reports to the Commerce Department's Bureau of Industry & Security (BIS), which include the name and address (including country) of each transferee; and (f) understands that countries other than the United States may restrict the import,*

use, or export of encryption products and that it shall be solely responsible for compliance with any such import, use, or export restrictions.

6. *Third Party Programs. Red Hat may distribute third party software programs with the Software that are not part of the Software. These third party programs are subject to their own license terms. The license terms either accompany the programs or can be viewed at http://www.redhat.com/licenses/thirdparty/eula.html. If Customer does not agree to abide by the applicable license terms for such programs, then Customer may not install them. If Customer wishes to install the programs on more than one system or transfer the programs to another party, then Customer must contact the licensor of the programs.*

7. *General. If any provision of this agreement is held to be unenforceable, that shall not affect the enforceability of the remaining provisions. This agreement shall be governed by the laws of the State of North Carolina and of the United States, without regard to any conflict of laws provisions, except that the United Nations Convention on the International Sale of Goods shall not apply.*

Software or hardware would normally be given a warranty during which any defect identified after delivery would be fixed free of charge. In hardware this may be one year, but in software it might be significantly shorter. A warranty period of just three months is far too short for many defects to have arisen (such as those related to large volumes of data that only builds up over several years), let alone be demonstrated unambiguously. Software supply contracts would usually be followed by maintenance contracts. There is some justification for the joke that software is the only industry that requires the customer to pay for the supplier's mistakes – this is not a situation that we can expect to continue, and nor should we want it to, for it simply encourages irresponsible and cavalier software supply practices. We will pick this up again in later chapters of this book as we discuss what can be done on the software development and supply side.

In any contract for the supply of goods or services there is a danger that the supplier might go out of business, and the contract should include clauses about what happens then. With the supply of software, especially where this involves continued maintenance or licensing, a useful fallback position would be to have access to the source code of the software so that alternative developers and maintainers could be found. This can be arranged through an **escrow** agreement, which arranges for a copy of the source code to be held by some third party, perhaps a bank, to be released if certain conditions like the bankruptcy of the supplier arise. The escrow clause would normally require that the supplier place new releases in escrow, so that should the need arise, the latest copy is available.

Payment for products or services under a contract will usually be staged so that some initial payment might be made, and then subsequent payments at key milestones in the project, like the delivery of hardware and then its commissioning, or for software at the agreement of functional requirements or the delivery of the software into alpha trials. Payments may be for time and materials, and for covering costs, maybe with a small allowance for profit in a 'cost plus' contract. However in order to avoid cost escalation, the contract may specify a fixed cost, or a maximum acceptable cost as a 'limit of liability'.

In addition there may be other standard clauses that need to be included in the contract. You may need to declare that the only agreements in force are those in the contract, that it constitutes the **entire agreement**. Some things can go wrong on a contract that the parties to the contract cannot be held responsible for, such as flood destroying the supplier's premises – these are called *force majeur* – and what happens then needs to be covered in the contract. If there should be a dispute, it is important to declare which legal system should apply (the **jurisdiction** for any settlement of a dispute). In some cases it might be appropriate to include a **restraint on trade** following the contract – for example, to prevent a supplier or employee working for a rival company for a number of years.

Because setting up a contract may take considerable time, and work needs to start immediately, it is common practice for a purchaser of goods or services to issue a **letter of intent**, indicating that a contract will be issued and work can begin. However it is important to make the work **subject to contract**, so that when the contract has been agreed and signed the contract is the only document that counts.

Prior to the letting of a contract, there will very likely to be a tendering stage in which those responding to the tender can invest a considerable amount of money – perhaps as much as ten per cent of the contract value – developing partial solutions to the requirements of the contract. It is important that if you are tendering you take steps to protect this investment – it has been known for the designs proposed by one tenderer to be given to another tenderer for implementation in the contract, with the creator of these designs receiving no recompense for them.

Activity 5.4	*Contract analysis*

Take any contract for the supply of software or services related to software, and analyse it for the issues described above. Does it grant unreasonable powers of termination to the supplier? Are you protected should the supplier go out of business?

> **Discussion**
> We can see some of the standard contract elements in the examples we have given in the Case Studies above. If you can, get hold of the complete contracts – you will find clauses about jurisdiction and entire agreement, and about termination of the contract from the supplier's end. However, you may not find any escrow protection or favourable clauses for termination from your side.

Contracts need to be drawn up carefully to protect the interests of all parties against a range of contingencies.

5.4 Responsibilities to employees and the public

In carrying out our activities using IT we have a responsibility of care for our employees, our customers, and the general public. While these responsibilities would be clear from ethical argument, some aspects have been cast into law. Whenever we gather information about people we must be sure that the information is correct and used appropriately – data protection legislation enacted in many jurisdictions ensures this, and more generally laws of libel and defamation regulate the promulgation of false information. The use of computers can lead to physical injury to their users, and legislation concerning health and safety of working environments could apply.

5.4.1 Data protection legislation

In the past, organisations retained information about people in their manual filing systems: records of employees, customers, students, hospital patients, and so on. While this information could have been misused, for example, by being passed on to others who had no right to such information (e.g., passing the medical history of a patient to an insurance company considering insuring her life), these misuses were limited in their scope by the limitations of manual filing technologies. Focused legal measures and codes of practice usually sufficed.

Information technologies changed this completely. IT enables the much more rapid searching and collating of information, and its transmission around the world. The concerns found their focus in data protection legislation first enacted in the United Kingdom in 1984 and updated later. Similar laws have now been enacted in many jurisdictions, all embodying essentially similar principles. Case Study 5.7 quotes the principles of the 1998 UK law.

> **Case Study 5.7** *The UK Data Protection Act 1998*
>
> The essence of this Act is encapsulated in eight principles, quoted below:
>
> 1. *Personal data shall be processed fairly and lawfully and, in particular, shall not be processed unless –*
>
>   *a. at least one of the conditions in Schedule 2 is met, and*
>
>   *b. in the case of sensitive personal data, at least one of the conditions in Schedule 3 is also met.*
>
> 2. *Personal data shall be obtained only for one or more specified and lawful purposes, and shall not be further processed in any*

manner incompatible with that purpose or those purposes.

3. Personal data shall be adequate, relevant and not excessive in relation to the purpose or purposes for which they are processed.

4. Personal data shall be accurate and, where necessary, kept up to date.

5. Personal data processed for any purpose or purposes shall not be kept for longer than is necessary for that purpose or those purposes.

6. Personal data shall be processed in accordance with the rights of data subjects under this Act.

7. Appropriate technical and organisational measures shall be taken against unauthorised or unlawful processing of personal data and against accidental loss

or destruction of, or damage to, personal data.

8. Personal data shall not be transferred to a country or territory outside the European Economic Area unless that country or territory ensures an adequate level of protection for the rights and freedoms of data subjects in relation to the processing of personal data.

These eight principles are given in Schedule 1 of the Act, together with guidance in the interpretation of these principles. Schedules 2 and 3 further elaborate what is meant by personal data being processed 'fairly and lawfully', and various legal judgements have further helped the interpretation of the act.

Crown Copyright material is reproduced with the permission of the Controller of HMSO and the Queen's printer for Scotland.

Data stored in computer systems should be accurate, appropriate, and only used for the purposes for which it was gathered.

What data protection law is concerned with is that when personal data is gathered, it is only done so for a particular purpose with only sufficient data being gathered for that purpose. Once the intended use is complete, the data should be deleted. No other use may be made of the data, and the person who is the subject of the data should be able to inspect and if appropriate challenge what is recorded. The data needs to be kept securely so that no other person can obtain and then misuse the data, particularly when the data is moved between countries. All this makes good moral sense, but not everybody will necessarily act morally.

5.4.2 Libel and defamation

Whenever material refers to people and organisations it is possible that what is published may give offence and lead to other people holding the person or organisation referred to in low esteem. If what is portrayed is not capable of defence in a court of law, severe damages may result.

When material is thought to be sensitive, as for example in material about disasters where blame for them is attributed, publishers will necessarily go to great lengths to ensure that they will not be liable for damages. Some publishers in their agreements with authors will deflect this onto the author, just as they will deflect onto the author responsibility for copyright clearances.

5.4.3 Product liability and negligence

When a piece of physical machinery causes damage most people would regard it as reasonable that the person suffering the damage should be able to seek redress from the manufacturers and suppliers of that machinery. In particular, for machinery that is faulty through negligence on the part of the manufacturers or suppliers, the case would seem clear. We saw this in the earlier Therac example in Case Study 1.1.

Consider the following famous urban legend. A woman in the US, so the story goes, decided to upgrade the way she cooked her food, and purchased a microwave cooker. But she had also been used to using her previous conventional cooker for another purpose, to dry her favourite poodle after giving it its regular wash. Next time she washed her dog, she popped it into her new cooker, with the unfortunate consequence that the dog was killed. She sued the manufacturers for negligence in not warning her that a microwave could not be used for drying pet animals – the courts agreed with her, and awarded significant damages. Well, that is just a myth, but as with many myths, it contains a grain of truth.

Losses resulting from 'faulty' goods may not necessarily result directly from failure of the machinery. It could be argued that published material containing no physical machinery could also lead to damages, to consequences for which the author and publisher of the material could be held responsible. For example, an academic discussion of software viruses might include sufficient information about the construction of viruses to enable somebody to construct one for themselves. If somebody then constructs a virus following the guidance in the book, and damages somebody else's software, the author and publisher could be claimed to be liable.

In 1985 the European Community passed a directive[20] concerning the strict liability for defective products regardless of whether the defect arose from negligence or not – anybody in the supply chain could be sued. When this directive was first promulgated the UK software industry protested and petitioned the UK government to make software exempt. When the UK law to embody this directive was enacted, software was not made explicitly exempt, but 'product' was defined in such a way that it is not clear whether software is included or not. The difficulty with software is its 'floodgate risk', that if faulty it can lead to unlimited liability through its widespread use.

Even though there are doubts about the applicability of negligence laws to software, suppliers often do attempt to limit their liability through clauses in their contracts of supply, an example of which is seen in Case Study 5.8. These clauses may themselves be unlawful and thus void, but it would be unwise to rely on this when accepting such exclusion clauses.

Case Study 5.8 *Disclaiming warranties*

Many commercial software licenses disclaim all warranties, such as the one below, part of the License Agreement for Microsoft XP Service Pack 3 – March 2004.

DISCLAIMER OF WARRANTIES. TO THE MAXIMUM EXTENT PERMITTED BY APPLICABLE LAW, MICROSOFT AND ITS SUPPLIERS PROVIDE THE SUPPLEMENTAL SOFTWARE AND SUPPORT SERVICES (IF ANY) AS IS AND WITH ALL FAULTS, AND HEREBY DISCLAIM ALL OTHER WARRANTIES AND CONDITIONS, EITHER EXPRESS, IMPLIED OR STATUTORY, INCLUDING, BUT NOT LIMITED TO, ANY (IF ANY) IMPLIED WARRANTIES, DUTIES OR CONDITIONS OF MERCHANTABILITY, OF FITNESS FOR A PARTICULAR PURPOSE, OF ACCURACY OR COMPLETENESS

▶

OF RESPONSES, OF RESULTS, OF WORKMAN-LIKE EFFORT, OF LACK OF VIRUSES, AND OF LACK OF NEGLIGENCE, ALL WITH REGARD TO THE SUPPLEMENTAL SOFTWARE, AND THE PROVISION OF OR FAILURE TO PROVIDE SUPPORT SERVICES. ALSO, THERE IS NO WAR-RANTY OR CONDITION OF TITLE, QUIET ENJOYMENT, QUIET POSSESSION, CORRESPONDENCE TO DESCRIPTION OR NON-INFRINGEMENT WITH REGARD TO THE SUPPLEMENTAL SOFTWARE.

Software and the digital content it stores can cause harm; harm for which anybody in the supply chain could be held liable.

5.4.4 Health and Safety

We saw in Chapter 3 how the working environment can affect productivity. In addition to the motivational importance of the working environment, there may be legal constraints on the working environment. These will differ considerably between jurisdictions and relate to office space allocated; temperature, humidity, and air quality; and maybe equipment layout. Historically, during industrialisation health and safety legislation was important and is still vitally important in developing countries, to help prevent unscrupulous employers from exploiting their workers.

Today, with modern office work accommodated in a clean and reasonably safe working environment, could there be a problem? Of course there are new health problems like Legionnaire's Disease in air-conditioning, but modern office equipment and computers have also created their own concerns. Could prolonged attention to a screen or use of a keyboard and mouse lead to problems? Muscular injuries like RSI (repetitive strain injury) have been attributed to computer use. Concerned about this, the European Union decided to act to require employers to follow best industrial practice, and they issued the Display Screen Equipment directive in May 1990. This is detailed in Case Study 5.9 and gives an example of how good practice might be brought into regulations. If a worker suffered ill health and it was found that the laws related to health and safety at work had been flouted, the worker would have a case for compensation.

Case Study 5.9 *European Directive on Display Screen Equipment*

The substance of this directive is the Employer's Obligations, Articles 3 to 9, quoted below.

Article 3 Analysis of workstations

1. *Employers shall be obliged to perform an analysis of workstations in order to evaluate the safety and health conditions to which they give rise for their workers, particularly as regards possible risks to eyesight, physical problems and problems of mental stress.*

2. *Employers shall take appropriate measures to remedy the risks found, on the basis of the evaluation referred to in paragraph 1, taking account of the additional and/or combined effects of the risks so found.*

Article 4 Workstations put into service for the first time

Employers must take the appropriate steps to ensure that workstations first put into service after 31 December 1992 meet the minimum requirements laid down in the Annex.

Article 5 Workstations already put into service

Employers must take the appropriate steps to ensure that workstations already put into service on or before 31 December 1992 are adapted to comply with the minimum requirements laid down in the Annex not later than four years after that date.

Article 6 Information for, and training of, workers

1. Without prejudice to Article 10 of Directive 39/391/EEC, workers shall receive information on all aspects of safety and health relating to their workstation, in particular information on such measures applicable to workstations as are implemented under Articles 3, 7 and 9.
   In all cases, workers or their representatives shall be informed of any health and safety measure taken in compliance with this Directive.

2. Without prejudice to Article 12 of Directive 89/391/EEC, every worker shall also receive training in use of the workstation before commencing this type of work and whenever the organization of the workstation is substantially modified.

Article 7 Daily work routine

The employer must plan the worker's activities in such a way that daily work on a display screen is periodically interrupted by breaks or changes of activity reducing the workload at the display screen.

Article 8 Worker consultation and participation

Consultation and participation of workers and/or their representatives shall take place in accordance with Article 11 of Directive 89/391/EEC on the matters covered by this Directive, including its Annex.

Article 9 Protection of workers' eyes and eyesight

1. Workers shall be entitled to an appropriate eye and eyesight test carried out by a person with the necessary capabilities:

   – before commencing display screen work,
   – at regular intervals thereafter, and
   – if they experience visual difficulties which may be due to display screen work.

2. Workers shall be entitled to an ophthalmological examination if the results of the test referred to in paragraph 1 show that this is necessary.

3. If the results of the test referred to in paragraph 1 or of the examination referred to in paragraph 2 show that it is necessary and if normal corrective appliances cannot be used, workers must be provided with special corrective appliances appropriate for the work concerned.

4. Measures taken pursuant to this Article may in no circumstances involve workers in additional financial cost.

5. Protection of workers' eyes and eyesight may be provided as part of a national health system.

This directive makes good sense, and European national governments have absorbed this directive into their laws, and issued guidance.[21] We will come back to the topic of the working environment in Chapter 10 when we discuss the management of resources.

5.5 External threats

The act of using computers and software in the workplace may also do their users harm, and needs regulation.

The law can also be useful to us in protecting us from people outside our own organisation, or indeed from people within our organisation acting against our interests. Because information and communications technologies (ICTs) are relatively new, laws here have only recently been enacted, and are still undergoing development.

We have already seen one example: the potential theft of our software and other intellectual property. We saw how copyright and patent laws could protect us, though it would be up to us to detect infringements and to take legal action ourselves in the civil courts.

With the coming of ICTs, new opportunities for threats to ourselves and our organisations have arisen. We need the protection of the law, so old laws have had to be reinterpreted for new technology, and a whole range of new crimes have had to be recognised and legislated against.

Computers can be used for communications between criminals and terrorists, and these communications can be made secret through encryption. This prospect has proved to be so threatening that some countries like France prohibit the use of encryption in any communication, while other countries like the US prohibit the export of any foolproof encryption technology – any encrypted message could in principle be decoded by a powerful enough computer given enough time, and the intention here has been to only permit encryptions that the security forces in the US could break. However this is rather futile, since the alleged enemies in time will produce their own secure methods of encryption, and any encryption method that is breakable today by the US Pentagon but not by anybody else will soon be able to be broken by everybody as home computers become ever more powerful.

This communications issue is one of a class of older crimes simply conducted by newer means. We will ignore those examples, and focus on the newer crimes peculiarly to computing. So computer-aided fraud, such as a person siphoning off money from his employer, will not be addressed further. However in many cases attempts to reinterpret old laws, such as those of theft, in the new context, have failed. Theft involves the removal of some physical property, and simply accessing information without changing or removing anything may not be interpretable as theft. Examples might be hacking into a person's mailbox and reading what is there, or hacking into a university's file systems and copying an exam paper.

This has led to the formulation of new laws, focusing completely upon computers, communications, and information. What can malevolent people do with computers and communications? The cases are common news items, such as the breaking into private networks using the facilities of the Internet and other networks, and the propagation of computer viruses. While these acts are often simply intended to display the prowess of the perpetrator, they can be used with malevolent and criminal intent: for example, viruses can send personal financial information to external agents. The outcome has been to make the unauthorised access to computer-based information or software illegal. This has been enacted in many different countries under the title of 'hacking' or 'computer misuse', as seen below in Case Study 5.10.

Case Study 5.10   *The Singapore Computer Misuse Act*

In 1993 the Singapore government enacted the Computer Misuse Act,[22] amended in 1998. Part II of the original act listed the following offences:

1. Unauthorised access to computer material
2. Access with intent to commit or facilitate commission of offence
3. Unauthorised modification of computer material
4. Unauthorised use or interception of computer service
5. Unauthorised obstruction of use of computer
6. Unauthorised disclosure of access code
7. Enhanced punishment for offences involving protected computers
8. Preparation or furthering of an offence.

Computer misuse acts have been strongly criticised for being technically inept, making them overly restrictive given current security technologies, and for jeopardising human rights.

> Harm may be caused deliberately, and actions which cause harm should be criminal offences.

Activity 5.5   *Computer viruses and spyware*

A recurrent fear with computer installations connected to the Internet is that computers are sending private information to people outside using computer viruses or Internet 'cookies'. If a computer virus infects your computer, and then broadcasts personal information about other people that you happen to store on your computer for perfectly legitimate reasons, what areas of law would apply to this unfortunate incident?

Discussion

There is clearly a data protection issue here, and while you did not misuse the data you may be deemed to have not kept the data secure enough. The person who sent the virus is also guilty of computer misuse, and could be charged if they are caught.

Summing up

In this chapter we saw how the state regulates the use of software in the interests of the wider community. However, this legal regulation does not always obtain wide support, and in discussion around these laws we saw a number of problems. This area of law will continue to develop over the years ahead.

In particular we saw that:

- intellectual property – software and digital content – needs the protection of the law because copying it is easy and cheap; however, while this protection might benefit the those directly involved with exploiting the intellectual property, it may not be in the wider interests of society to grant this protection; this could be particularly true for developing countries, where ideas that have been found useful elsewhere should be capable of free exploitation;

- copyright law protects the expression of an idea, but not the idea itself; the rights protected by copyright law include the moral right to be known as the author, and the right to economic benefit; patents protect the ideas themselves, and are now applicable to software, but this is controversial, especially concerning prior art;
- software as public goods can use intellectual property law to protect itself;
- contracts need to be carefully drawn up to protect the interests of all parties against a range of contingencies;
- software and the digital content it stores can cause harm indirectly and anybody in the supply chain could be held liable; data stored in computer systems should be accurate and appropriate and only used for the purposes for which it was gathered; the workplace in which computers and software is used also needs regulation to protect those required to use computers;
- harm may be caused deliberately, and actions which cause harm should be treated as criminal offences.

When acquiring and deploying software and computer systems all of these legal matters must be taken note of. Expert legal advice should also be sought.

Exercises

1. Suppose that your organisation is planning to commercialise a software product in a country in which the IPR legislation differs substantially to any other country in which you have been doing business. Based on what you have learnt in this chapter, make a list of the issues that you need to check before the release of your software in the new country.

2. If you are a salaried employee, check that you know and fully understand the clauses in your work contract that relate to the intellectual property rights arising from any work you do for your organisation.

3. Suppose that you work for a company that develops software that is embedded in their own proprietary hardware. The software contains concepts that are considered intellectual property and a key asset of the company. Discuss the issues that will need to be addressed for this company to be able to use open source software.

4. Familiarise yourself with the health and safety regulations for computer users and health workers, and with the statistics of office workers injuries in your country or region. How do your local regulations and statistics compare to international best practice? If the difference is alarming, seek to raise the issue in local professional associations or elsewhere applicable.

5. The vast majority of 'shrink-wrapped' software contains non-liability clauses in their license agreements. Is the software profession being responsible enough? Discuss.

6. Are data protection regulation and anti-spam measures an obstacle for doing business?

7. Privacy and data protection are also subject to the cultural differences discussed with reference to organisations Chapter 3. What would be the implications for a multinational organisation which handles data of customers in many different countries? How could the problem be practically addressed?

8. Your company is hosting email services for a variety of international users. What precautions you should take in handling personal data? List three of your duties and three of the things that never should be done.

9. Write an essay on the issue of 'software idea patents'. Take a position and justify your points.

Endnotes

1. We have consulted widely, including the following texts, as well as others some of which are cited in other endnotes: Chris Edwards, Nigel Savage, and Ian Walden (Eds) (2000) *Information Technology and the Law* (2nd edn). Macmillan; Jeremy Holt and Jeremy Newton (Eds) (2004) *A Manager's Guide to IT Law.* The British Computer Society.

2. See, for example, Jonathan Zavin and Scott M. Martin (1997) 'The Value of Intellectual Property Rights Enforcement in Developing Countries', *Economic Perspective, an Electronic Journal of the US Information Agency,* Vol. 2, No. 3, June, 13–15.

3. There are two major forms of legal system: common law, based on arguments from previous cases made by knowledgeable and powerful independent judges; and civil code (introduced widely by Napoleon), based on carefully formulated laws that can form the basis for a judgement by magistrates. England and the US epitomise common law, while France and Germany epitomise the civil code. These two systems now form the basis for many legal systems around the world, spread by European colonial activities during the fifteenth to nineteenth centuries.

4. See WIPO website http://www.wipo.org/, with the WIPO Treaty at http://www.wipo.org/eng/diplcon.

5. See http://www.wipo.int/documents/en/document/govbody/wo_gb_ga/pdf/wo_ga_31_11.pdf.

6. Council Directive 91/250/EEC of 14 May 1991 on the legal protection of computer programs, Official Journal L 122, 17/05/1991, pp. 0042–0046; Finnish special edition: Vol. 1, Chapter 17, 0111; Swedish special edition: Vol. 1, Chapter 17, 0111.

7. Report from the Commission to the Council, the European Parliament, and the Economic and Social Committee on the implementation and effects of Directive 91/250/EEC on the legal protection of computer programs identifier /* COM/2000/0199 final */.

8. Adapted from D. Bainbridge (1994) *Software Copyright Law* (2nd edn). Butterworths, pp. 50, 58–9, 92–3, 96–7.

9. If you would like to find these, look at Alan Cooper (1995) *User Interface Design.* IDG Books.

10. Software is usually delivered as an 'executable', with guidance on how to connect to it at particular points in particular ways. To be able to make this connection effectively, it can be helpful to know what the original programming language code of the software was, particularly of those parts being connected to. This source code can be abstracted from the executable through a process of decompilation or reverse engineering. We will come back to consider reverse engineering in Chapter 9, as part of the process of evolving and sustaining software.

11. Thomas T. Gordon and Arthur S. Cookfair (2000) *Patent Fundamentals for Scientists and Engineers* (2nd edn). CRC Press and Lewis Publishers.

12. See http://www.spi.org/.

13. See http://www.uspto.gov/main/trademarks.htm.

14. See Chapter 3 and http://www.gnu.org/.

15. See the Creative Commons Legal Code at http://creativecommons.org/.

16. The Register, November 2004: http://www.theregister.co.uk/2004/11/18/ballmer_linux_lawsuits/. We quote this as an illustration of the use of patents in commercial positioning, and the difficulty in determining prior art in the retrospective granting of software patents. This also illustrates the strong invective that can flow in such debates, a style of argument that we, the authors of this book, do not condone.

17. Jeremy Holt and Jeremy Newton (eds) (2004) *A Manager's Guide to IT Law*. The British Computer Society.

18. This description is based on various reports in Computerworld at http://www.computerworld.com/softwaretopics/erp/story/0,10801,91720,00.html, in the Christian Science Monitor http://www.csuohio.edu/aaup/news/peoplesft.htm, the Chronicle of Higher Education at http://chronicle.com/free/2000/01/2000011101t.htm as well as many other sources including the web site of Cleveland Sate University itself and an article by Fred Gage at http://www.educause.edu/ir/library/html/cnc9862/cnc9862.html.

19. See http://www.redhat.com/licenses/rhel3_spain.pdf?country=Spain&.

20. Council Directive, 25 July 1985, Product Liability.

21. See, for example the, UK's Health and Safety Executive website: http://www.hse.gov.uk/.

22. See http://unpan1.un.org/intradoc/groups/public/documents/apcity/unpan002107.pdf.

Processes for acquiring and evolving software

6 Software acquisition

7 Software activities

8 Software processes

9 Maintaining and evolving software

How to get the software you need and keep it

If we are to use software within our enterprise, we need to acquire it, and then sustain it. Part II of this book looks at what is involved in acquiring and sustaining software, whether by using existing systems or by developing a system just for our purposes. However software is obtained, it needs to be sustained in service after that, evolving alongside the organisation that it serves.

Chapter 6, Software acquisition, describes how it is increasingly rare for software to be purpose-built by organisations for their own use, and instead existing software is often rejuvenated and continued in use, obtained ready made and adapted to. This software may be proprietary and be bought, or may be obtained for lesser cost as open source, or as a service. Software development and integration may be outsourced or even offshored.

Chapter 7, Software activities, looks at the activities that are typically undertaken when developing or integrating any software. These activities may be undertaken to different degrees and in different orders, depending upon the actual software being produced and the development process being followed. Each activity produces particular representations of the system with the various representations fitting together within a particular development process. These stereotypical activities are illustrated with a simple application following a simple sequential process.

Chapter 8, Software processes, considers the many alternative software development processes that use the typical activities in Chapter 7 in an order which overcomes some particular hazard of software development. Iterative methods aim to minimise risk, timeboxing aims to overcome cost and timescale escalation, open and agile methods focus on creativity and motivation, design-centred methods address feasibility, and participative methods are concerned with user acceptance.

Chapter 9, Maintaining and evolving software, accepts that existing software needs to be kept in service as the user organisation develops and evolves. The software co-evolves with the organisation. Conventional software development processes cannot necessarily handle this situation and need to be adapted.

6 Software acquisition

What we will study in this chapter

While software was originally purpose built by organisations for their own use, this is now becoming rare. Instead, a number of sources may be tapped in a search for software that will fulfil the needs of the organisation. Each source has its own characteristics, advantages, and disadvantages that one must know.

In this chapter we will look at:

- keeping old 'legacy' software in service, 'wrapped' in other software to integrate it with newer software;

- procuring software 'off the shelf' as packages or components which may be subject to some customisation;

- integration of systems from packages or software components;

- use of open source software, obtaining it from public distribution, customising it for local use, and contributing to its development;

- outsourcing of software development versus development in house;

- offshoring of software development;

- the use of software remotely as a service, accessed via the Internet.

6.1 Finding software

We now come to consider how we can acquire the software we need for our enterprise. This chapter and the next two chapters address this, with this chapter focussing on the sources that you need to consider before acquiring and deploying software, while Chapters 7 and 8 will address the development of 'bespoke' software specifically to meet our needs.

We will start this chapter in this section by considering the market for ready-made software, how it has developed, and what it now offers us. We will then look at how we need to approach this market to be sure that we do obtain software that meets our needs – how requirements should be formulated and the goodness of fit of a particular offer assessed. We then go on to look at the major sources of software:

- redeploying existing in-house legacy software;
- selecting a ready-made package from among those on offer in the market 'off the shelf';
- selecting an open source system and how to assess its real costs;
- meeting our needs through a service rather than ownership of the solution technology;
- in-house development of software.

6.1.1 The software marketplace

We saw aspects of the history of computing in Chapter 1:

- how software initially focused on scientific and military and then specific clerical functions, but has now become ubiquitous, embedded in everything around us and around the world,
- how this spread of software has been accompanied by changes in the way organisations and people work, to create the 'information society'.

Let us turn again to that history to consider how software was acquired in the past and contrast that with the situation that we find today. At the beginning of the software industry during the 1950s and 60s most software was written from scratch and for use by a single person or within a single organisation. Computing hardware came with a large number of peripherals for inputting and outputting information and for storing it – in order to be able to use all the hardware effectively, the hardware supplier had to supply software to organise the hardware to do routine work. This software was the **operating system**, originally also known as the 'master program'. Users of computers expected the manufacturer to provide a working operating system so that the machine could actually be used.

At that time there was little compatibility between different computers, and software developers had first to select a supplier of hardware and then limit themselves to what software was offered for that particular computer in terms of operating systems and other utility software such as text editors and compilers. In most cases the software was 'free', being 'bundled'[1] with the hardware. The hardware was the major cost. The lack of compatibility between computers made it difficult to share applications. This meant that software to solve essentially the same problem had to be rewritten whenever there was a change in the underlying hardware. Software engineers resented being asked to repeat the same development over and over again – we saw in Chapter 3 the need for personal growth by software engineers, the need to learn new things. In many cases the engineers refused to build the same system repeatedly, and moved employers. And the software industry acquired a reputation for waste and inefficiency. Concern about this was raised at the very first conference on software engineering, in 1968,[2] by Doug McIlroy,[3] arguing that at least some software, like scientific calculations, could be standardised and written once and shared thereafter.

However it was not nearly as bad as it seemed, and in 1984 Peter Wegner[4] argued that operating systems, referred to above, exemplified an industry that did apply the same software very many times over, and in order to facilitate the development of software made significant investment in tools like compilers to reduce the cost of production – making it a capital-intensive industry.

However it was even better than Wegner indicated. Software applications as commodity products did gradually emerge, as we saw in Case Study 1.2 about payroll software developed in the 1960s. Compatibility between computers has improved over the years with the emergence of **standards** for hardware (for example the IBM-compatible PC) and for information representation (for example Unicode and XML), enabling a software market to emerge. **Infrastructure software**, such as operating systems and communications software, and **applications software** could be acquired from different sources, with confidence that they would work together. In some domains, such as database management, users will very rarely consider developing a system on their own, when they can buy powerful database management software that has taken hundreds of person-years to develop and evolve.[5]

While much software has originated in the US, a significant amount is being produced elsewhere, in Europe, in Asia and elsewhere. For example, the dominant supplier of enterprise resource planning software is German, and many computer games are made in Japan. Software has become an item that can be acquired independent of other software or of hardware, and nowadays there exists a global market in software.

We refer to this process of obtaining software by whatever means as **software acquisition**, but it is also referred as **IT provision** or **IT procurement** in other texts. This chapter is about different ways in which software or software-related work may be acquired by a user or an organisation that needs it. Ideally this software should be ready made, a package to which we can adapt, or a service we can employ – it is only if this acquisition process fails that we turn to **bespoke development** solutions, building the software ourselves in house, or having it built for us through an outsourcing or offshoring contract.

> We should aim to acquire software ready made, and only if that fails, should we have it purpose built.

6.1.2 How to approach the marketplace

The software required may range from an inexpensive software license for a personal firewall program bought over the Internet, to a contract for the provision of an air-traffic control system. When we acquire software we might be purchasing a license to use the software or we may be acquiring the right to use source code that we will incorporate into a larger software system. Software can be seen as a product, as a service, or both.

Before we set about acquiring software, we had better know what it is that we want. The overall process we must go through is known as **requirements elicitation**, the first part of **requirements engineering**. We will describe requirements elicitation more fully in Chapter 7, and here we give a brief overview of what must be done. The various stakeholders in the software will have their own views about what is needed, and these views need to be elicited: the techniques to be used can range from brainstorming sessions to interviews to observation of people at work. Inevitably the different stakeholders will have different needs, and any conflicts and disagreements must be reconciled. This agreement is formally documented in a requirements statement. This statement might be discursive text, but for our purposes in judging whether candidate software does meet our needs, a list of required functions or features, with some indication of how critical they are, would be more useful.

For large and complex software systems the acquisition decision is not simple and may need to consider many issues: human, technical, financial, managerial, cultural, social, etc. Usually software forms part of wider systems involving the activity of humans, hardware, and complex processes. The acquired software must match the wider context within which software will be used. After acquisition, the software and its environment should co-evolve smoothly, but this is not easy to achieve: the acquisition decision must be accompanied by decisions about how the software is to be installed, operated, and further enhanced. The acquired software needs to be sustained and this leads either to further acquisitions or to software-related work in house – this will be explored further in Chapter 9. The issue of long-term support is important and needs to be taken into account during the acquisition decision.

6.2 Legacy software

6.2.1 Old software may be a valuable legacy

A lot of the software that you already have and use may still be capable of providing a valuable service. The term **legacy software** emerged in the late 1980s as a euphemistic way of referring to software running on mainframes and minicomputers which still performed a useful function in spite of being very old and built to conventions and using tools that had long since been superseded. COBOL programs, for example, still represented a significant portion of the software upon which businesses relied in 2005.

One of the characteristics of the computing field is that it evolves rapidly. Paradoxically, some old programs and technologies survive far beyond their creators' expectations. There are applications supported by software developed ten or twenty years ago based on technologies that are now completely out of date. The initial development and evolution of these systems may have involved considerable effort and these software systems may still support a part of the business which is stable and hasn't changed since that legacy system was built. The total replacement of the software may not be justifiable, unless it can be predicted that it will become completely inoperable.

Case Study 6.1 *The COBOL programming language*

Much of the code running in the world was written in COBOL. This programming language dates back to 1959, when the US Department of Defence set up a committee for the creation of a programming language for business applications. Preliminary specifications of the language were made and compilers for the new language soon become available for several brands of computers. In 1960, the US government indicated that it would not buy or lease computers which could not support COBOL. This endorsement and the wider adoption of the language made it popular.

The person principally associated with COBOL was Admiral Grace Hopper (1906–1992), the 'Mother of COBOL', and it is claimed that COBOL-inherited features can be traced back to her experience with UNIVAC compilers. Also due to Grace Hopper are the long-variable names which enabled meaningful names. However, this was far away from making programs self-documenting, as some initially had claimed. One of the advantages of COBOL programs was their ability to run, with some amendments, in computers of different manufactures in which each computer manufacturer had different programming conventions, a great achievement in the early 1960s. The COBOL programming language hit the press headlines once again in the late 1990s as the year 2000 approached and with it the growing concern for the 'Y2K bug' – see Chapter 9. However, at the beginning of the twenty-first century, COBOL programs are still being used – examples of legacy systems.

One such COBOL program is BT's customer services system, called CSS. In 2005 BT was one of Europe's largest telecommunication companies, with more than twenty-one million customers, to whom it provides phone and data connections, along with other services. One of the most important software systems for BT is CSS. This system was initially developed in the mid-1980s, and orchestrates the interaction of the company with its customer base and the running of all the services (setting up telephone lines, changes in numbers, line repairs). It generates the phone bills that are sent to homes and businesses in the UK. The CSS system holds over eleven terabytes of data in its database on IDMS (integrated database management system) originally developed by Cullinet Software in the 1970s. The CSS system, mainly written in COBOL, has evolved over nineteen years to keep pace with the changes in the telecommunications industry, for example the de-regulation of the telecommunications sector in the UK during the 1990s. The CSS architecture, based on the separation between the business logic and the presentation logic, had to do with its survivability. BT added interfaces between many other applications and CSS, as many as 500, using middleware, software which sits between the business logic and data, on the one side, and the data presentation, on the other. A variety of mechanisms have been developed[6] which include the so-called robots, software which emulates the data entry that would have been performed by humans.

Legacy software is business-critical software (e.g., the software-holding customer's account details in a bank), based on old, now superseded, technologies, for example COBOL or other languages from the 1960s, 70s, and 80s.

Any sufficiently complex software will be difficult to change, but legacy software may include additional characteristics:

You may already have the software you need. Keep useful legacy software in service.

- The first operational release of the software was developed a long time ago. However, time is relative in the computing domain. Even relatively young software can be considered a legacy if the original developers of that software have moved and the people currently responsible for maintaining the system do not understand it sufficiently well to be able to evolve it rapidly and confidently.

- The original architecture of the system has deteriorated as a result of the implementation of change upon change upon change and/or by the departure of the original architects and/or lack of compliance with the original architectural principles (this is sometimes referred to as violating the architectural and conceptual integrity of the software).

- The interactions between the different subsystems, files, and functions of the system are very complex. Small changes then have large ripple effects through the system. There are parts of the system which are extremely complex (e.g., algorithms with branching which is difficult to understand), and dare not be changed.

- The documentation of the system is out of date or inconsistent with the code, the test cases, etc.

- There is a growing gap between the stakeholder's needs, including the users' requirements, and the legacy software.

All business-critical software systems are likely to become a legacy unless the organisation in charge of them actively works to avoid the above symptoms or characteristics. In Chapter 9 we discuss these activities from the perspective of maintenance and evolution. Despite careful evolution, the legacy syndrome may be difficult to avoid, simply due to changes in the wider environment or because of the following paradox: a successful application can attract many new requests for further functionality after the system is initially released which, if applied without due care, are likely to increase the complexity of the system and turn it into a system that is less useful.

A legacy system usually involves more than legacy code. The software may run on computers (e.g., mainframes) now no longer available or for which spare parts are becoming difficult to obtain (this is less an issue with the emergence of computer hardware standards, particularly in the personal computer market). The legacy system relies on infrastructure software (e.g., operating system, compilers) no longer supported by the hardware manufacturer or whoever provided them in the first place. In some cases it was cheaper to emulate the old hardware on a new computer than to port the old software to the new hardware or re-implement the software to be 'native' to the new hardware.

As well as legacy software, we must also consider **legacy data**,[7] the information manipulated and held by the legacy software. Such data may be an important asset. Data transformation or migration needs to be considered in any plan dealing with a legacy system.

The legacy application embeds and reflects the business's processes – sequences of activities followed by the user organisation in order to fulfil its mission and achieve its goals. In some cases, the business process may require the continued use of the legacy application. The legacy software will embed these business processes and business rules, many of which may not be documented or be only partially documented elsewhere. The legacy code becomes the best documentation of the business practices. This is why if a legacy system is to be replaced, the business processes and rules must first be identified or extracted from the legacy software.

> We need to work to counteract the appearance of legacy symptoms, and to save business-critical software from becoming legacy systems.

6.2.2 Wrapping legacy software

Wrapping of legacy software is an alternative to complete replacement of the legacy software. The idea is to acquire (or develop) new software which will sit between the existing legacy software and other applications or between the legacy software and its users – this is illustrated in Figure 6.1. The wrapping software can simply serve as an interface, include additional functionality (e.g., support of communications standards), or provide graphical user interfaces (GUIs) and other

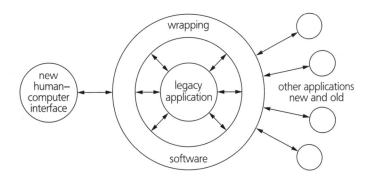

Figure 6.1

Legacy wrapping

features whose implementation directly in the legacy software could have been expensive or simply impossible.

Wrapping of legacy software is generally cheaper than a complete replacement of the old legacy software. It involves less risk as the legacy software continues its operation as in the past. However, the legacy software functionality may remain undocumented or only partially documented. Moreover, some new requirements may not be capable of implementation even with the wrapper software. Legacy data can also pose problems to those in charge of wrapping the legacy system, with incomplete or duplicate records and data formats which are incompatible with the new requirements. Data transformation can consume a considerable part of the effort of wrapping legacy software.

Thus we see that legacy software involves many issues. Changes to some of the parts (for example, hardware replacement) may solve some problems (for example, improve performance) but also bring about new challenges (for example, some of the support software may not run in the new hardware). The legacy problem may also involve a whole set of human and organisational issues, rather than merely being a technical problem. Case Study 6.2 illustrates some of these problems.

Case Study 6.2   *Deutsche Bank Luxembourg*

By Kenny MacIver, first published in Information Age.[8]

Deutsche Bank Luxembourg had a challenge that will be familiar to many. It wanted to integrate a new package – in its case, a portfolio management system – with existing COBOL applications, especially one named 'Mozart' which handled securities orders. It also wanted to improve communications between Mozart and external systems, such as the Swift inter-bank payment system.

As a prelude to that, though, the bank had decided it needed to adopt a strategic, integration standard and chose XML as the interface medium for new data interchange. XML was chosen for a number of reasons: to reduce implementation costs of future integration projects; to deliver improved capabilities more quickly; to reduce deployment costs; to lower the total cost of ownership of the application; and to reduce the operating costs per transaction.

But achieving interoperability between XML and COBOL systems looked daunting. 'At first sight, integrating XML and COBOL seemed rather bold,' says Roger Engel of the the bank's IT development team. Just as the team was wondering if such a thing could be done successfully, it stumbled on Net Express, a newly launched tool from COBOL specialist Micro Focus that provides interoperability between XML and COBOL.

In a matter of weeks, the bank was able to create a new XML I/O module in COBOL that 'consumed' the XML document from the portfolio management system, fed that data through to Mozart and then, when Mozart had completed the transaction, updated the XML document for return to the portfolio management system. As that might suggest, COBOL applications are being re-invigorated. '[We have] modernised our COBOL and turned it into a high-tech solution,' says Engel.

©Infoconomy 2004.

Activity 6.1   *Legacy wrapping*

Suppose you are a software manager in an insurance company and that you are in charge of a project that involves wrapping a business-critical legacy application in COBOL. You have already signed a contract with a specialised company which provides tools and consultancy to perform the work, which is about to start with a briefing meeting. Consider the various issues that will need to be discussed at the meeting.

Discussion

Presumably the contract must stipulate what the duties and obligations of the contractor are, how the performance of the work will be measured (for example by acceptance testing), and any other relevant technical and economic issue. The briefing meeting should enable the personnel of the contractor and the insurance company to meet each other and through this facilitate later cooperation. Issues that will need special attention are the confidentiality of the data (e.g., personal data held by the insurance company in the legacy system), security, and dealing with contingencies. The contractor will need to access domain specialists in the insurance company and the people who best know the legacy application. Similarly, it must be clear how the newly wrapped system is to be tested and made operational, and how the responsibility of its further evolution is to be transferred to the insurance company, including the necessary training. It is important to establish good communication between the consultants and the client. In particular, you want to make sure that if there is a technical or a managerial problem, you are the first to know about it.

Wrap legacy software to enable its integration with other software.

6.3 Buying software off the shelf

If there is no legacy system that meets the need established by the requirements elicitation, then the first alternative might well be the procurement of an existing system off the shelf, either the purchase of a proprietary package considered in this section, or the adoption of an open source system considered in the next section.

Systems bought off the shelf are known as **packages**, or now commonly as **commercial off the shelf (COTS)** software.

6.3.1 Why buy off the shelf?

Let's start by looking briefly at the advantages and disadvantages of acquiring software from a third-party supplier. Assuming that suitable suppliers exist, the advantages of acquiring software externally over in-house or bespoke development include:

- Lower costs: the development and evolution costs, sometimes substantial, are shared amongst the many users to whom the package is sold.

- Increased functional power: the shared software incorporates requirements from many users. This results in the software having much more functionality than the minimum required by the average user.

- Increased quality: the testing and other quality-assurance costs can be shared amongst many users. The intensive use of the software by many users makes it easier to achieve a high level of coverage of the testing of the functionality in real operational conditions. Defects tend to be identified and fixed earlier in the life cycle.

- Better use of specialist knowledge: specialist knowledge can be shared in a more effective way when it is encapsulated in software which is shared amongst many users.

- Easier compliance with standards: this can be achieved through the acquisition of software built to conform to certain standards. For example, a particular software system may already comply with a data exchange format or with a particular type of human interface which is then homogeneous across a family of software products.

- Speed of acquisition of the software: acquisition time is reduced by the external acquisition of software as opposed to in-house and bespoke development.

> Buy COTS packages for lower costs, higher functionality, and quality.

Some of the drawbacks to the external acquisition of software, as opposed to bespoke development, are:

- the systems you run will not give you any competitive advantage, since your rival companies could also be running the same systems;

- some degree of mismatch between what is needed and what is available, which in turn may require the development of wrapping software;

- dependence on an external supplier for implementation and adequate testing of changes and enhancements may be risky, since the business goals of the supplier may be driven by the market and the needs of other clients;

- software supplied as a black box may only include documentation about the interface, and will almost certainly forbid the reverse engineering of the code;

- lack of long-term support since the supplier may go bankrupt, decide to phase out the system or to further evolve the software in directions which are incompatible with your user requirements.

> COTS means compromises.

6.3.2 How do you choose?

We have already seen in section 6.1.2 that any acquisition of software must start with some appraisal of need, balancing the needs of various stakeholders, and leading to a list of functions or features together with a view of their relative importance.

The COTS selection process then starts with the exploration of what's on offer in the marketplace. Morisio and his colleagues[9] studied NASA COTS-based projects and found that the requirement process involves the traditional steps plus an additional step, consisting in the identification of candidate COTS products and their preliminary evaluation. This step is accomplished through vendor demonstrations, study of the relevant literature, and building and evaluating prototypes. In COTS-based projects the requirements are limited, shaped and conditioned by what the COTS vendors can offer. Morisio *et al.* point out that the availability of support from the COTS vendor (e.g., existence of a help desk) is a critical issue. To this we would add access to reference sites at which the product is in use.

We cannot expect an exact match with our set of requirements, but want to find the best match. We have already seen how to do this in Chapter 2, by using a weighted scorecard. Of course the use of a weighted scorecard is not perfect, and can only guide our decision, but it does make sure we take into account all our needs and makes explicit any compromises we make. Case Study 6.3 shows an example: note the general categories like the reliability of the supplier, as those specific to the particular software being selected. Weighted scorecards or their equivalent have been used for package selection since the 1970s or earlier.

Select COTS using a weighted scorecard.

Sometimes the cost of the selection process may exceed the cost of the actual software procurement when that is made. This is justifiable since a bad decision followed by a period of attempting to make the choice work can be very expensive indeed.

Case Study 6.3 *Selecting project management software*

One of the authors has, on a number occasions over the past thirty years, set out to choose adequate project management software, and here we abstract the process used. On the first occasion in the mid 1970s in a R&D organisation he and colleagues had hoped that the product chosen would embody best practice and from that introduce quality project management into the organisation – but without success, and it was clear that knowing what to do for good project management must come first, with a solid statement of requirements. On later occasions, in software companies and later in universities running large collaborative projects he used a list of criteria like that set out as a weighted scorecard in Figure 6.2. In Figure 6.2, product X is an international best seller from a major company and product Y is from a start-up company and is under development so we could influence its facilities.

We see that the product Y is favoured by the score card, perhaps too optimistically assuming that the facilities needed will be delivered. As a start-up they must also be viewed as high risk, and this is not very strongly weighted in the score card. The key functional criterion is the ability to record the work content of tasks independently of how the work is assigned, and then use this in consistency checking. Most project management tools just do not offer this, it is not clear why, though the best, aimed at the management of very large projects in engineering and construction, do. It is lack of this capability in product X that has counted strongly against this, and yet product X is widely used. Perhaps there are ways of working around this deficiency that should be explored. Further interviews with the suppliers and a range of customers would seem to be necessary – though most customers interviewed were found later to have abandoned use of product X on the grounds of the heavy workload it generated. A simple spreadsheet might well provide all that is necessary, and that is what was selected by the author in the most recent acquisition trail to help him run a large international IT project.

	Selection criteria		Product X Scores		Product Y Scores	
Figure 6.2	**Feature**	**Weight**	**Score**	**Weighted Score**	**Score**	**Weighted Score**
Weighted scorecard	Maturity of product	2	1.0	2.0	0.0	0.0
for project	Reliability of supplier	4	0.8	3.2	0.8	3.2
management	After-sales support	6	0.8	4.8	0.5	3.0
software	Task hierarchies (or just single level)	8	0.5	4.0	1.0	8.0
	Work content of task recordable	12	0.0	0.0	1.0	12.0
	Resource hierarchies	6	0.4	2.4	1.0	6.0
	Multiple granularities of time	2	0.0	0.0	1.0	2.0
	Task dependencies	4	0.6	2.4	1.0	4.0
	Milestones	6	1.0	6.0	1.0	6.0
	Resource assignment hierarchy	6	0.0	0.0	1.0	6.0
	Sub-projects and plan combination	2	1.0	2.0	0.0	0.0
	Resource levelling	0	1.0	0.0	0.8	0.0
	Consistency checking	10	0.8	8.0	1.0	10.0
	Proactive and reactive tasks	4	0.0	0.0	1.0	4.0
	Progress recording	4	0.7	2.8	0.0	0.0
	Plan change/replanning	6	0.0	0.0	0.0	0.0
	Range of plan displays	6	0.6	3.6	0.3	1.8
	Ease of use	6	0.8	4.8	0.4	2.4
	Exchange data with a spreadsheet	6	1.0	6.0	0.0	0.0
	Overall score	**100**		**52.0**		**68.4**

6.3.3 Making the software and processes fit

We saw above that while we can select a software package on the basis of needs as described in a feature list, we inevitably make some compromises. As delivered the software package may not quite fit, and we must make it fit. We do this at three levels:

- *technical integration*, to make the software communicate with other software, and in particular to work on the computing hardware and operating system that we use;
- *customisation*, to modify the functions of the package in so far as we can to perform the functions that we really need;
- *business process re-engineering*, adapting the way we work to use the package as it is or customised as far as we are able.

Technical integration

Software from different suppliers can interact with one another through defined interfaces and clear conventions of data representation and exchange. We would expect any package we choose to be quite clear about these interfaces and conventions, as we would expect it of all other software that we use. It was failure in this area that led the European Union to promulgate its reverse engineering directive and to include exemptions for limited decompilation or reverse engineering in its copyright directives, which we saw in Chapter 5.

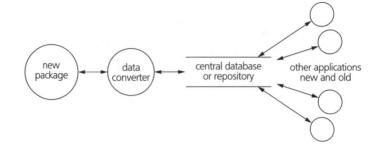

Figure 6.3

Integrating COTS
software via a
database

COTS software can be integrated with other software in various ways, but the simplest is working around a common database or set of files as illustrated in Figure 6.3. This is where clear data representation conventions are necessary – and we might have to introduce some interfacing code to convert between representations. This interfacing code is really a form of wrapper, seen previously for legacy software.

The other means of integration is connecting the software directly together through APIs (application programmer interfaces) and unless the new package was specifically built to work with our other software, we will almost certainly need to develop some interfacing or wrapping software.

Business integration by customisation

Many packages will give us the ability to modify their functions to more closely fit our needs, and the ability to do this should have been taken into account when selecting the package. Indeed trial customisations might have been undertaken as part of the process of package selection. To see what is possible consider the two contrasting case studies, 6.4 and 6.5. First of all look at Case Study 6.4.

Case Study 6.4 *The SanFrancisco project[10]*

The SanFrancisco Project (SFP) was an IBM initiative in the late 1990s, as part of its wider Java strategy, to build a Java framework, a set of configurable and extendable software units devised for integration in multiple software applications. In the late 1990s, when SFP was undertaken it was estimated that 70 per cent of critical business data resided in mainframe applications. The extension of these applications to the Internet using mainframe programming languages is laborious: one has to write software from scratch which supports application programming interfaces (API). The programming language Java supports many APIs that enable access to networks and services, so it offered advantages as

the glueware between the legacy applications and the Internet. The creation of a Java-based framework was intended to help bridge the mainframe applications to the Internet, taking advantage that Java supports many APIs.

SFP aimed to provide independent software vendors (ISVs) with the application frameworks and components they needed to build commercial applications. Some 200 organisations participated in the advisory councils of the SanFrancisco Project. The frameworks aimed at achieving cross-platform support, network enablement, localisation via support of many national languages, and multicurrency support. At that time SFP was considered the largest single Java development in the world with a team of more than 200 developers. The SFP framework was intended to be more powerful than Sun Microsystems' Enterprise JavaBeans (EJB). However, SFP did not make the expected impact, suggesting that the sought-after industrial revolution in software creation via components is hard to achieve.

The SanFrancisco project is generally viewed as an innovative step that was well worth taking, but has proved unsuccessful due to its focus on technology at the expense of application knowledge. We see this technology focus in Case Study 6.4. The customers were expected to be specialist software development companies who would then produce the tailored systems for end-users.

The fate of the SanFrancisco project should be contrasted with the resounding success of ERP systems – the leading supplier of ERP solutions, SAP, is now one the world's leading software companies, second only to Microsoft in size and turnover. Look at Case Study 6.5.

Case Study 6.5 *ERP systems*

ERP (enterprise resource planning) systems the complete range of a customer's needs – hence the word 'enterprise' in their title. The suppliers of these systems offer modules for financial management, stock control, insurance, university management, and so on. Some suppliers, like SAP, focus on support for large enterprises with their systems running on mainframes. Other suppliers focus on smaller companies, with their systems running on PC servers and workstations – these smaller systems cost a lot less, but of course you also get a lot less for your money.

The suppliers all claim that their systems embody best industrial and commercial practice, and all of these systems offer a range of customisation facilities, through:

- selection of the subsystems to be installed;
- selection of the data fields to be included in the database;
- setting parameters;
- modification of business processes and functions with specialist help.

While the selection of subsystems and data fields and setting of parameters is all part of the procurement process, the modification of functions can be expensive and the advice is to adopt the functionality as is, on the basis that it embodies that 'best practice'. However, in studying mid-range ERP system marketed globally we have discovered such wide variation in national practices as to make it impossible to capture these within a single system claiming global best practice.

As we indicated previously, ERP systems have been enormously successful, making systems that had previously been bespoke into commodities.

Customisation of any COTS package will be similar to that available for ERP systems, with basic adaptations to make the package into the kind of system you are interested in, and more detailed parameterisation to tailor the package close to your needs.

Investigate ERP systems on the Internet, considering the range of systems available, and what the various websites say about ERP systems.

Discussion

When we searched on 'enterprise resource planning' we found many entries, a lot of them descriptions of ERP to inform business who thought ERP might be the solution for them, or as resources for educational establishments teaching courses involving ERP. One website claimed that ERP had 'reached the end of its life cycle as a strategic competitive weapon', though we could never find the evidence for this claim. Not many actual suppliers came up, though an open source system, TinyERP.com did show up.

One interesting site, erp.technologyevaluation.com, asked us to describe our requirements and it would suggest possible suppliers – most of the questions, sixteen in all, were very high-level about the size of the organisation, number of ERP users expected, budgets available, and so on, with only five technical questions, though the importance of being able to customise showed up early on. We agree with this emphasis. We worked through the needs of a higher education institution of the size and nature of the Open University, our own institution, and an initial list of seventy-six ERP suppliers was reduced to just twenty potential suppliers, mostly on the grounds that they did not cover higher education, though some on the grounds of being unable to support the English language or the financial regulations of the UK. But there were some surprises, the big systems like SAP, PeopleSoft, and J.D. Edwards were included, but also mid-range systems like Exact-Macola and Sage.

No website suggested that we build our own.

Business process re-engineering

Once the new package is installed and customised, it becomes necessary to adapt working practices to use the new software effectively. After all what the software system does and what people do is open to negotiation, as we saw in Chapter 2. This is something you have to do, even for bespoke systems, since these will almost always involve some change to working practices as well. Commercial organisations who do this business process re-engineering following the installation of new software refer to the process as 'change management', though we will use that term with a different meaning in Chapter 11.

> Make your COTS package fit by customisation and business process reengineering.

6.4 Obtaining 'free' software

The idea that software should be a public good, freely available for use by everybody, has already been introduced in Chapters 3 and 5. This software is known as Free and Open Source software (FOSS):

- open source software because the source code of the software is also made available; and

- free software because there are no constraints imposed upon the use of the software – the slogan is 'free as in freedom, not free as in free beer'.

One thing FOSS is not is cost free, as we will see later.

Not all types of application are available as open source. For an open source system to be developed and sustained by a community, there must be a common need for the software and a common set of requirements that can be implemented. There are many applications which are currently outside the scope of open source. However, the list of open source software continues to grow.

6.4.1 The Open Source movement

The Open Source movement depends on the contributions of many individuals and has been made possible by Internet technology. There are thousands of open source projects available on the Internet, and websites such as SourceForge.net and FreshMeat.net provide links to a large number of open source projects, including information about releases, contact details of the key developer(s), links of one project to other projects, list of most popular open source projects and bulletin boards. The latter are a source of support, where people can post problems and get answers from the community.

| Activity 6.3 | *SourceForge* |

Obtain a feel for SourceForge and what it offers, by visiting its home page at http://www.sourceforge.net, and following some of the links there.

Discussion

At the time we visited it, there were 105,395 registered projects hosted at SourceForge, and 1,167,233 registered users. By far the majority of projects were technical, developing communications and software development aids and similar, but there were also many other applied projects, for example in education and sociology. Releases occurred frequently – but from so many projects, that is what we should expect.

What we did not find out was how active all these projects were – for that we would need to be paid-up subscribers, in which case we could have viewed the statistics of the site, and accessed yet more information. For the active user there are many (49) documents about how to use the site. The implication was that the site was multilingual, but we could not find any evidence that this really was the case – when viewing documents we were offered a pull-down menu of languages but were only offered English.

The contributions to open source software projects come from individuals, working privately in their own time, though there may also be many contributors who work as paid employees of an organisation which has a business interest and for which contributing to open source software is part of their business strategy.

Despite the large number of open source software projects, only a few attract the attention of contributors. The most well-known open source project is Linux – an operating system, initially developed by Linus Torvalds, who still is involved in its evolution. Also of great significance is the Apache web server, built on a Linux base – this is currently used by 70 per cent or so of the Internet websites world wide.[11] The Open Source movement is challenging some of the assumptions of traditional software development processes, and we will see more of this in Chapter 8. Among other distinguishing practices, defects are logged and the defect databases are publicly available; this transparency of Open Source development contrasts with proprietary software in which defect-related information tends to be confidential. Look at Case Study 6.6.

Case Study 6.6 *The two Linux Hats*

The most well known and largest supplier of Linux distributions is Red Hat, founded in 1993 with preceding operations under different names since 1993. Red Hat has supplied a number of variants of Linux and other software and services through a subscription licence – you don't buy Red Hat Linux because it is free, but instead subscribe to a range of services from online support, training, to global outreach.

Red Hat has been a highly successful company, receiving many accolades for innovation and entrepreneurship. It has also created a number of strategic alliances with other technology companies (the website lists these as 'IBM, Dell, HP, Oracle, Sun, Fujitsu, Intel, NEC, Hitachi, BEA') and key users (the website lists these as 'Amazon.com, AOL, Merrill Lynch, Credit Suisse, First Boston, DreamWorks, Lithonia Lighting, VeriSign, Charles Schwab, Lehman Brothers, UBS Warburg, Morgan Stanley, and Goodyear').

By 2002 Red Hat Linux had reached its eighth full release, with many minor releases in between. Meanwhile they had been entering the server market and in March 2002 launched their first enterprise-class Linux with this having reached release 3 by October 2003. The aim in these releases is always a highly stable system built from the stable enhancements made in the wider Linux community.

Red Hat also sponsors the Fedora project, a community-supported Open Source project. This enables Red Hat to work with the Linux community to build a complete, general purpose operating system exclusively from free software. Fedora acts a proving ground for new technology that may eventually make its way into Red Hat products, but Fedora is not a Red Hat product itself.

There is even a company, CentOS, which builds systems from Red Hat sources and gives these away. Ownership of such sources is not an issue in the FOSS world.

Red Hat has approximately 1,000 employees worldwide, with headquarters in the US, major regional headquarters in Germany and Singapore, and branch offices in many other countries: Brazil, Canada, France, United Kingdom, Ireland, Italy, India, Japan, Korea, Hong Kong, Malaysia, and Australia.

Red Hat can be taken as typical of open source developers, distributing software freely, while generating income from selling services or from subscriptions. They aim to make available regular stable releases which have been thoroughly tested. Often these releases are called **distributions** to indicate that a larger package is being made available, consisting not just of executables (the **release**) but also the sources, documentation, and maybe related software as well.

Some projects offer a set of stable and a set of unstable releases. Stable releases have been in use for some time and are offered to conservative users who are concerned about reliability. Unstable releases are available to users who are interested in the latest functionality, even though defects may still be apparent.

Organisations considering the acquisition of Free/Open Source software can benefit from the access to the source code, even though this is not necessarily the main driver: they can remove unwanted parts of the functionality, reducing vulnerabilities, leading to a more secure system than otherwise. Paradoxically, open source software may be more resilient to virus and hacking attacks because, though it may attract the attention of software virus writers just as proprietary software does, the open source code can be more transparent and subject to more scrutiny than proprietary code, supported by active communities of volunteers and businesses who provide amendments which cover vulnerabilities as these are discovered.

Expertise in open source software is needed in order to install, customise and configure the software. One of the possible deterrents to the acquisition of open source is the lack of any person or organisation legally responsible for the software and provider of support. Such support may be obtained through the effort of the personnel of the acquirer, through bulletin boards (e.g., Slashdot.org), or by hiring small- or medium-sized companies that specialise in supporting and tailoring applications based on open source.

> Open source offers a very rich source of software, mostly but by no means exclusively in the technical arena.

6.4.2 Costs and Benefits of FOSS

To appreciate what the costs of FOSS are, consider Case Study 6.7 about the experience with FOSS of a hospital in Ireland.

Case Study 6.7 *Beaumont Hospital*

Fitzgerald and Kenny[12] have documented how the Beaumont Hospital, a major health-care organisation in Ireland, adopted open source software. In the early 2000s, facing lack of cash and budget cuts after the peak IT expenses of the Y2K bug, the IT management decided to move towards the acquisition and deployment of open source software (OSS) for several of the hospital's needs, both infrastructure and applications, and to replace legacy software. The primary motivation was economic, to achieve the best possible use of taxpayers' money, the largest source of funding for the hospital. The decision to incorporate OSS was part of a move towards a 'web-based service-oriented' architecture. However, the overall hospital software acquisition strategy continued to be 'mixed-market'. The hospital maintains links to providers such as Microsoft – who had granted academic discounts in 1995, Hewlett Packard, IBM, Sun, and Linux providers such as Red Hat and SuSE. Table 6.1, quoted from Fitzgerald and Kenny, gives an overall estimate of the savings from the

move to OSS totalling around €12.9 million during a five-year period.

There was a concern at Beaumont about the level of support that it was possible to obtain using OSS applications. OSS continuing support is not undertaken, as in the case of proprietary software, by a single provider which takes responsibility for defect fixing, providing help, etc. Before the formal decision to acquire OSS software, the hospital IT team did six months' research, looking at websites such as SourceForge and Slashdot.org, and found that the level of the postings on the bulletin boards suggested that the risk of moving into OSS was 'relatively low'.

The main driver for the move towards OSS was economic. There was only limited interest in modifying the source code of the OSS even though it could be accessed and modified by the users. Beaumont Hospital, and apparently many other users, do not feel comfortable or confident enough about modifying the code: in Beaumont the only source code change reported is a five-line amendment in Linux, in order to make it

▶

Table 6.1			Initial cost		Total cost over 5 years	
Comparison of cost of open source (OSS) vs proprietary alternatives for Phase 1 of Beaumont Hospital	**Application**	**OSS**	**Proprietary (cost reflecting academic discounts)**		**OSS**	**Proprietary**
	Desktop Applications	€27,500 (StarOffice)	€120,000 (e.g. MS Office)		€34,700	€288,500
	Content Management	€20,000 (Zope)	€126,000 (e.g. Lotus Notes)		€32,100	€140,200
	Digital Imaging X-Ray	€150,000	€4.3 million		€237,000	€7.34 million
	Application Server	€10,000 (JBOSS)	€302,000 (e.g. Websphere)		€60,500	€595,300
	Email	€1,000 (SuSE Email)	€110,000 (e.g. Lotus Domino)		€8,700	€175,000
	Total	€208,500	€4.958 million		€373,000	€8.539 million

Source: B. Fitzgerald and T. Kenny, Developing and Information System Infrastructure with Open Source Software, IEEE Software, January/February 2004, pp 50–55.

compatible with the hospital's Oracle database application.

As the office application, Beaumont chose the StarOffice version of Open Office because it is supported by Sun. The IT manager pursued a thin-client strategy: the idea was that applications were downloaded from the servers whenever possible, making the administration of the package, such as updates and new releases, easier. After some users complained of losing network connections, StarOffice was installed on desktop machines for those who required it. Users feared being de-skilled with respect to popular proprietary solutions – this was addressed by Ximian, who at the time of the case study (2003) was preparing a release of Open Office that follows the MS Office user interface closely. The XML inbuilt capabilities of StarOffice has provided unexpected benefits, for example, it is being used to automatically route to the Human Resources Department online human resources request forms.

The content management system (CMS) adopted was based on Digital Creation's Zope, which can be downloaded for free. The CMS ser-ver provides management of documents such as multidisciplinary patient care documents, standard procedures, and personnel online forms. The Beaumont implementation required support from an 'OSS broker', a small software company called OpenApp, at a cost of €20,000. The IT manager recognised that there are installation and support costs associated with OSS which may be difficult to justify. He said:

If you have a product which costs €1 million – it may be appropriate to spend €500,000 on consulting. However, if the product costs nothing, then spending €500,000 somehow seems to be a more difficult decision to take, yet the saving is still €1 million.

The largest saving was achieved in a digital x-ray imaging system, which replaced the traditional printing of x-ray images on films for visualisation and diagnostics. Sun Microsystems made a donation of a Sun Fire V880 (1 Terabyte of disk space) and the Beaumont IT staff developed a solution, so that x-ray images can be viewed online. This involved the writing of Perl scripts which extract relevant information from the existing HP 3000 hospital information system. Another health-care institution in Ireland reportedly spent €4.3 million on a commercial system. Even though Beaumont needed to upgrade its network and acquire high-resolution workstations to support the radiologists using the new system (about €400,000), the expenditure is significantly below using a commercial system and is funded by savings in x-ray film (about €480,000 per year).

The fact that the deployment costs were relatively low enabled the 'quiet' deployment of OSS. The IT personnel, who already had experience with Unix – probably a key factor – adapted well to the new situation and developed new skills.

There are some concerns that the personnel may be recruited by other organisations with interest in OSS-conversant personnel.

The hospital's CEO supported the initiative of deploying OSS, because financially speaking, there were no other options. In the OSS deployment there was a lack of official maintenance contracts and help-line advice. Because of the need to rely on bulletin boards and consultancy support to effectively deploy the applications, top management backing has been crucial for the success of the first phase of OSS acquisition described here. A second phase was being planned when this case study was reported in the literature in 2003.

From this case study we see that the advantages of open source software include:

- lower costs than proprietary alternatives: in many cases open source software can be downloaded without cost, and some organisations provide support for specific versions of open source software at a small cost;
- access to the source code, which permits customisation to specific needs and selection of which parts of the software need to be installed; and in addition:
- greater degree of control of when to upgrade than when acquiring proprietary software – the hospital can wait until there is a clear benefit to do so (for example, you may not wish to replace your hardware: proprietary software upgrades often mandate an upgrade in your hardware);
- extra motivation for personnel, as they gain new skills in the integration of open source applications and deeper knowledge on how these systems work.

Open source software is not free but can reduce cost significantly.

Some of the disadvantages of acquiring open source are:

- There is a lack of anybody with legal responsibility for the software and lack of any clearly identifiable provider of support.
- It may be difficult to justify further investment in the application given that the expense in open source is generally modest when compared to acquiring commercial proprietary or bespoke software.
- If open source code is mixed with proprietary code in the same application, developers need to be trained to be disciplined and not to mix the two types of code. Hybrid applications, involving both open source and proprietary code, need to be architected so that the open source and proprietary parts are always separable and identifiable.
- It is expected that the organisation using open source should contribute back to the community in some form and not become a 'free rider'. This involves a cost, but can be also a form of motivation for the IT personnel.

- Long-term support for the software needs to be sought from a variety of sources, such as own personnel, bulletin boards, specialised consultants and firms. This can be seen as more risky than using proprietary code or developing a bespoke application.

- Some organisations wait until there is a sufficiently large community contributing to a particular software system before either acquiring or getting involved with that software in other ways.[13] Thus people hold back because the community is not growing, and the community is not growing because people hold back.[14]

There clearly is a need for senior management understanding of the situation involving use of open source – it can be very different from their experience of proprietary software.

| **Activity 6.4** | *OSS Support* |

One of the key aspects that software acquirers consider is the availability of support during deployment and later. An operating system kernel such as Linux is maintained and evolved by developers who form a loosely coupled community, with contributors sharing their knowledge and experience through bulletin boards. Since the source code is available on the Internet, in principle, anyone can implement such long-term support. Some software acquirers will prefer not to have to modify the source code. What are some of the alternative sources of support available to them?

Discussion

IT organisations which do not have expertise in coding can obtain such support in different ways: by hiring staff with specific open source knowledge and experience, or by an agreement with consultants, as a form of outsourcing. The open source model has enabled many small software companies to offer their specialised knowledge in certain applications. The reasons for choosing a specific open source distribution must also be carefully considered: some open source distributions add value with extra services provided by the distributors (e.g., Red Hat and SuSE distributions of Linux) which include support and updates.

Open source deployment requires finding your own sources of support.

6.5 Acquiring software as a service

6.5.1 Services across the Internet

A service is an act or a set of actions which one party performs for another. In general,[15] the recipient party does not have to hire or own any factor of production (hire personnel, buy hardware and software) in order to get access to the service. Usually a payment or another form of compensation is given to the party performing the service for the recipient.

The application of this basic idea is not new in computing and has its origins in the computing bureaux which were very common in the 1960s and 1970s, such as providers of payroll services we saw in Chapter 1. These bureaux owned or leased mainframe computers in dedicated computing centres (which needed air conditioning facilities, floors adapted for extensive cabling, etc.), very expensive at that time, and ran applications for a variety of clients. Nowadays, a similar idea is the hosting of Internet websites, which has become a popular business.

Case Study 6.8 *Projistics*

As part of the author's most recent round of evaluating project management software in 2004, introduced in Case Study 6.3, he considered a service-based solution, having met representatives of the company at an exhibition. The product concerned in Projistics.

From their website at http://www.projistics.com/index.asp, we learn that Projistics is a web-based collaboration and project management software for managing entire project lifecycles and logistics seamlessly, by facilitating collaboration in distributed teams. It consists of integrated applications that provide high return on investment by increasing productivity and reducing collaboration costs. Projistics provides complete support for all Project Management activities like Project Planning and Scheduling, Task Management, Time Tracking, Issue Management, Defect Management and Resource Management. It also helps facilitate Change Management processes, thus minimizing defects and disruption caused by changing requirements or business objectives.

One of the great attractions of Projistics is its emphasis on collaborative working across geographically dispersed sites, so the product is aimed at management records held in one place but accessed and updated from around the world via the Internet. So it is not surprising that it can be bought as a service.

While the website does not indicate that the system can be used as a service across the Internet, when we enquired and discussed it with a representative, we were told that our project information could be held at the company site in the US and accessed and updated globally. There was no need to buy the software and install it on our own computer, though we could choose to do that. Licensing use of the software as a service would cost per year about one-third of the outright purchase price for six users – since we needed the system for three years this made the decision balanced.

What in the end mitigated against the use of the product was the same lack of functionality that concerned us in the more general product assessments reported in Case Study 6.3. We felt positive about the product and its underlying concepts, but it was not for us.

The idea of acquiring software as a service is becoming increasingly appealing as applications become Internet enabled and relatively easy to offer in the form of **software as a service** (SaaS). There are at least three increasingly powerful modalities:

- In the first modality, the simplest, the user accesses an application, which is owned and maintained by a provider, through the Internet. He or she configures the application, provides input data and receives the output. The user may only need to have access to a web browser, and in some cases email for identity validation, in order to access and enjoy the use of the application, which runs on a remote server.
- In the second modality, it is the software of the user that interacts with the software provided by the service supplier: this is a variant of the popular **client-server architecture**, in which the client and server belong to different

organisations. There are two variants to this architecture: thin and fat clients. Under the thin-client approach, the client software runs the user interface, with both data and business logic residing at the remote server site. Under the fat-client approach, the client runs both the user interface and the business logic, with the remote server essentially only holding the data.

- The third type involves what is called **service-oriented architectures**. It consists of putting together applications based on shared services which are provided by third parties. Service requestors define and find the functionality they need when they are about to use a software product and not when it is being produced or delivered. The software suppliers produce software and make it available for service requestors when they need it. This is an approach in which applications are created by aggregating at runtime a set of services provided by various software suppliers. The linking or binding together of the services occurs when the application is to be used. There are several service models, such as web and grid services. The different services interact dynamically over the network. There are several standards (SOAP, WSDL, UDDI) which are based on XML. SOAP stands for Simple Object Access Protocol and defines how web services can exchange data between them. WSDL (Web Services Description Language) is a standard which focuses on the representation of the interfaces of the web services. The UDDI (Universal Description, Discovery and Integration) standard covers the areas of discovery of software services and establishes how the description of a service should be reflected in a software registry. Service requestors can use this information to discover and access a service. The underlying technologies and standards are still in development (as of early 2006) and its practical application is still limited.

> Instead of owning or licensing the software, rent time using it at a service provider.

6.5.2 Costs and benefits of software as a service

Software as a service (SaaS) is an area of great potential that needs to be followed closely by those in charge of defining software acquisition policies. The advantages of SaaS are:

- Users, the service recipients, have a choice of service provider which, depending on the modality, can be chosen at runtime. This can reduce lock-in, in which the user finds it is not feasible to switch to an alternative supplier: lock in can be used by the supplier to increase price and let the quality of the software deteriorate, with the user being defenceless.

> Software as a service may give clear cost advantages.

- There are economic advantages for both software acquirers and providers. In fact it creates a dynamic market in which the goods – software – can circulate between the demand and supply sides. Using a service reduces the overhead from the point of view of the user. Users pay as a function of the time spent using a particular application, the amount of data stored or transferred, or the number of program executions, which is more transparent from the economic point of view. The service requestors benefit from the use of the software only for the time needed. They do not have to fulfil the obligations of software licensee in the traditional sense, which are to keep a copy of the software even if it's not used, keep the software up to date through ordering new versions or releases, adding the latest security patches, etc.

There are also disadvantages to the SaaS approach:

- the technology may not be able to transfer code and data reliably at high speed;
- it may not be clear which organisation is responsible for the success of the application, particularly when services of different origin are opportunistically connected at runtime;
- hidden costs of transactions,[16] network performance, trust and security are factors that need to be considered.

In order to use a software service, provider and requestor may have to establish a **service level agreement**. This establishes the minimum acceptable performance of the service, based on a set of mutually agreed metrics.

Activity 6.5   *Service versus license*

Consider the business model of companies such as Adobe, which offer a client document viewer Acrobat as software that can be downloaded without payment through the Internet, and sell the server side at a price to organisations which wish to publish electronic content. Suppose that a competitor establishes an alternative scheme by which both client and server software can be acquired as services. Compare the advantages and disadvantages from the point of view of the users and of the software economy.

Discussion
The payment for the actual use of the software as a service could be a more transparent mechanism than paying for a license, particularly if the payment is proportional to the use or the value that the use provides to the user. Costs can be shared more fairly between those who make use of the software. If the software is frequently used, the payment-for-service mechanism will provide resources to the software provider in order to further evolve it. However, current administration mechanisms make it cumbersome to generate payments for every use (e.g., having to use a credit card every time one uses a software system). Moreover, the need to download the software or to access a remote service places a strong load on networks and their availability.

> Software as a service raises issues of responsibility, technical limitations, and hidden costs.

6.6 Bespoke development, outsourcing and offshoring

We now come to consider what we do if there is no ready-made solution adequate for our purpose. We must consider building the software ourselves, bespoke. The detailed processes that we must go through are described in Chapters 7 and 8. Here we will consider the more strategic aspects of this development, whether we build it in house or outsource it. And do we do either of these in-country or off-shore?

> Choose bespoke development only if no ready-made system will suffice.

6.6.1 In-house development

If we do not already have appropriate software, and cannot buy the software off the shelf or as a service, then we should consider building it ourselves in house. This was widely practised until the 1980s and 1990s, but is becoming increasingly less common.

Of course any organisation that uses software will need a number of people on site to support the use of the computers and their software, and to install and integrate any software that is acquired. But is it worthwhile going further than this and establishing a software development team? You need a continuing load of software development work to justify hiring the people, and this only makes sense for large organisations that use a lot of software that needs continuous change and replacement.

Only choose in-house development if you can retain the staff long term.

If you do establish your own software development capability, you will need to consider ways of organising the development personnel. This is covered in Chapter 10.

The alternative to building you own in-house team might be to offshore most of the work in a subsidiary company. This is becoming quite commonplace, and will be discussed below in section 6.6.3.

6.6.2 Outsourcing

Instead of building the software in-house, we could **outsource** it, and place a contract with a specialist firm to build the software for us. The duties and rewards will be reflected in the contract between ourselves the client and the external contractor. Chapter 5 has already discussed contracts and their importance.

Outsourcing to specialist firms has long been a common practice, with specialist companies originally called software houses or systems houses, or simply consultancies. Conventionally there have been two forms of this. First, contracts in which the external company supplies staff to the client who then work in house as if employed there – this is sometimes termed 'body shopping', and will come up again later. In-house development, whether with employees or contract staff, has been covered in section 6.6.1.

Alternatively the contract could be for developing the software given a requirements statement, possibly after some invitation to tender and bidding process. The contract would be formulated to ensure that the process followed by the contractor properly engages with us to ensure that the software developed does meet our needs. This might mean some small team being resident on our site to keep in contact with us and validate system requirements as these evolve during the development process; the main development process may well happen at the contractor's site following the kind of processes described in Chapters 7 and 8.

The outsourcing market is expanding in the US and Europe, as numerous reports from Forrester Research (http://www.forrester.com) and on the Internet attest. Outsourcing is increasingly becoming an alternative means of doing software-related work. Organisations looking to streamline their workforce and focus on key business activities may consider a contract with an outsourcing company as an alternative to hiring their own personnel.

The advantages of outsourcing from the point of view of the client organisation include:

- the services of a specialised company and personnel who may be very difficult to recruit and retain ourselves;
- possibly lower costs, since it may be more economical to hire personnel through a fixed-term contract than to have to hire your own personnel;
- lower risks if the contract can be fixed price or formulated in some other way appropriately;
- less management burden since management is reduced to managing a contract instead of having to manage a complete software organisation;
- higher business flexibility, since the outsourcing contract may have provisions to stop the work if market or other circumstances dictate so.

Outsourcing may also have disadvantages for us:

- less control over the actual software development, including process and programming practices;
- the contractor may have to address the needs of various clients simultaneously and the business goals of the contractor may not coincide with our goals;
- intellectual property rights need to be clearly worked out in the contract;
- knowledge about the application gained by the development personnel will be lost when the outsourcing contract ends;
- the contracted personnel may lack the incentive to produce software which is of sufficient quality or is robust enough for further evolution;
- the longer communication lines between the final user and the contractor personnel involved with the software may introduce delays in the investigation of defects or implementation of user requests. We know from the OS 360 experience of Fred Brooks[17] that the more groups there are involved with an application, the higher the likelihood of misunderstandings.

Activity 6.6   *Core competencies for outsourcing*

Visit CSC's website, http://www.csc.com, or a similar outsourcing company and browse through the different news items and reports on new contracts and agreements. Look at the descriptions. Identify what the core competencies of organisations providing outsourcing should be.

Discussion
CSC's website, indicates that its mission is

> ... to use our extensive IT experience to deliver tangible business results – enabling our clients in industry and government to profit from the advanced use of technology. We strive to build long-term client relationships based on mutual trust and respect. (Nov 2005)

This has changed over the period we have been writing this book, so you may find something slightly different if you look, though it should be essentially the same.
    Companies offering outsourcing usually highlight their understanding of the client's needs and of the market segment in which they operate. Outsourcing companies also indicate experience in linking software technology and business processes in such a

Outsourcing has
economic and
technical benefits,
but may lead to
loss of control.

way that the business processes are optimised or improved and that automation needs are satisfied. Outsourcing companies also mention in their adverts their ability to gain and retain the trust of the client and to maintain long-term collaborations.

CSC is an enormous company, with nearly 80,000 employees globally at the end of 2005, over 10,000 of these outside the US, though we could not find the exact figures. However not all outsourcing companies need be that large; they might be small and specialised, as in website development.

6.6.3 Offshoring

Increasingly IT work is being moved offshore to organisations located in India, Russia, China, Israel, Ireland, and other locations. Many companies have discovered the business advantages of relocating part of their software-related operations another country, like India, Russia, and China, where there is an educated and talented workforce, and salaries are lower than in the industrialised West. In some cases, as in Ireland, tax incentives provide cost advantages.

Contrasting with this, **onshoring**[18] is the supply of IT personnel or IT work by a local low-cost provider supplying staff of offshore origin. Some of the companies involved in onshoring are foreign firms which operate locally but bring in personnel who are paid lower salaries than the locals, using mechanisms such as the US special immigration L1 visa. This practice has created some scandal in the US, with a report at http://www.newsmax.com/archives/articles from 2003 commenting:

> The misuse of the visa system is devastating the computer job market and keeping wages artificially low and the visa holders themselves as indentured servants to the economic oligarchy.

This is clearly a high-tech form of the well-established exploitation of illegal immigrants in agriculture and other manual labouring jobs. We are not sure how much of this high-tech onshoring still goes on.

Offshoring of IT work follows in the wake of the offshoring of manufacturing which has been building up since the middle of the twentieth century, based on reliable shipping and airfreighting. However the coming of reliable electronic communications has meant that call centres have now been offshored, drawing in top graduates in English in countries like India. And with the Internet has also come the offshoring of computing work, which started to be significant around the mid-1990s and is now a global phenomenon with a great impact on how organisations supply their computing needs. The website http://www.techsunite.org/offshore/ has been recording technical jobs, mostly IT, offshored from the US since 2000, and records 469,996 jobs offshored from the US between 1 January 2000 and 4 November 2005. The underlying technologies are the communication networks, the Internet, and the various tools which support distributed software development. Nevertheless, offshoring is more than a technological phenomenon. Carmel and Tjia[19] identify six main drivers which have made it possible:

- software commoditisation,
- globalisation of trade and services,

- difference in salaries,
- decrease in the cost of the telecommunication services,
- increase in the availability of labour in offshore countries, and
- business-friendly climates.

Commoditisation means that the outcome of one activity is the same, without regard to the producer, as in the case of products such as wood and paper. This requires a level of standardisation that has only been achieved in some software activities. A survey quoted by Carmel and Tjia[20] suggests that only a subset of software-related activities tend to be located offshore: coding, unit testing, some integration and system testing, software localisation, and routine maintenance, whilst other activities which require user involvement and domain knowledge, such as requirement analysis and systems integration, tend to be kept onshore. Design activities tend to be shared between the onshore and offshore teams. However, this work division may change as software organisations in the developing world achieve higher levels of excellence – already many Indian companies are ranked as good as or better than US and European companies.

Offshoring shares all the advantages and disadvantages we already mentioned for outsourcing. The following comments apply specifically to offshoring:

- the economic advantages of offshoring can be significant, due to the lower wages in developing nations and the tax incentives which may also be available;
- offshoring can also be used as a way of searching for talent in developing countries which have a growing pool of graduates able to take up IT work;
- there are hidden costs in setting up the work relationship, such as the costs of searching for an overseas partner, setting up offices, drafting contracts and so on;
- offshoring usually involves the interaction of teams and managers with different professional and cultural backgrounds, which can be enriching in many ways but also may require special efforts in communication to avoid misunderstandings;
- there are risks regarding the sharing of confidential data which sometimes can not be adequately handled due to the supplier's operation in a different country under a different legal system;
- there is a political dynamic added to the business, as the offshoring can be perceived as a threat by the industrialised nations and may lead to protectionism, however, many large companies are behind the trend towards offshoring. Moreover, software professionals do not tend to belong to unions, and hence have limited lobbying possibilities.

Some companies have seen an opportunity in being able to work on a software project around the clock (also termed 'following the sun'), with teams located in three different time zones, so that two teams are active while the members of the other team sleep. It has been argued that the development time can be shortened. However, to make this strategy work, the coordination of the work of the three teams has to be good.

Offshoring is realised in at least four different forms: as the opening of a subsidiary, as a joint venture, as a build–operate–transfer, and as outsourcing through a contract.

The first option, opening a **subsidiary** or a local branch, involves registering a company locally, which will need to comply with local laws regulating foreign investment. These laws may impose conditions in the ownership of the subsidiary and the membership of the management board of the branch. The subsidiary will need to comply with local labour legislation and taxation rules, which need to be considered when estimating the cost of this option. Case Study 6.9 gives an example of this.

The second option, **joint venture**, involves a local provider and ourselves entering into a business agreement, so that they both share goals, duties, profits, and losses. The agreement needs to be very fully worked out for it to succeed. The joint venture may be also subject to taxation, which needs to be considered when evaluating this option.

The third option, build–operate–transfer (BOT), consists in the contractor opening an organisation which will serve our needs. We will have the option of buying the organisation once the latter has been established and is operating. This alternative gives us time to get familiar with the legal context before the transfer of the control of the organisation occurs.

The fourth option, outsourcing through a contract, is similar to what has been discussed in the previous subsection but with the implication that the two parties to the agreement are located in different countries.

Case Study 6.9   *Transferring usability expertise to India[21]*

During 1997–1999 the IT firm Baan, a Dutch company specialising in the ERP (enterprise resource planning) business, worked at improving the attention to usability at their Indian subsidiary Baan-India. Baan had had established operations in India since the late 1980s. In 1997 it opened large centres in Mumbai and Hyderabad. (Baan had financial problems at the end of the 1990s, and is now owned by the American firm SSA.)

Before 1997, only the Dutch part of Baan had a team of usability consultants that worked together with the developers to address usability concerns, how easy and natural it is for users to interact with the software, including screen layout, selection of controls, and so on. The usability consultants had to influence the software developers since they did not have veto rights over the work. This made the usability consultancy function special and different to other tasks in the software process.

In 1997 Baan-India decided to create a local usability consultancy team in India. This was done with the help of the Dutch usability team who were involved from the recruitment phase onwards. The first problem encountered was the lack of Indian applicants with a similar background to their European counterparts, who have a background in computer science and psychology. The five persons selected were graduates who had taken courses in visual communications and product design.

In order to transfer knowledge and skills to the local usability group, two persons from the Dutch branch moved to India for one year. This training year included the participation of the Indian group in the preparation of Baan's usability style guide. At the end of the year (1999), an Indian person was assigned to lead the local usability team and its work officially started.

During the training year there were two aspects which needed particular attention. One was the need for the local professionals to have a clear and straightforward communication style, that is, to be more assertive, because this is essential for the usability team to make their voice heard within the wider development team. This was not natural to the local professionals. The other aspect had to do with raising awareness of the differences that cultures place on colours and hand gestures, for example, and the need to choose interfaces and icons which are not offensive for any culture. The Dutch consultants provided advice and training in these aspects.

The local team was able to contribute from their knowledge on colour theory and product design. On a slightly negative side, the offshore team felt that it did not have as much autonomy and design freedom as they wanted, since the Dutch counterpart defined the work in such a way that the room for creativity was limited. More could have been done to improve the collaboration in this area. However, in general, the initiative was considered a success: there was an improvement of the usability features (e.g., screen navigation) of the software developed in India. The corporate-wide usability style guide was actually used by the developers. It was found that co-locating the usability team with the developers, as in the Dutch counterpart, was a good idea and made communications easier.

Activity 6.7   *For and against offshoring*

Perform a Google (http://www.google.com) search for 'software offshoring', and briefly visit some of the websites retrieved by the search engine. Look for arguments in support of and against offshoring and list them. Select one argument and consider whether, based on your own experience, it is well justified.

Discussion

Some offshore initiatives are justified on the basis that software-related work is highly mechanistic and can be safely delegated to others if it is properly specified and well defined. Those who take this view consider that software production has achieved a degree of maturity in which the software-related work can be highly systematised and predictable. However, the success of offshoring is not only based on the maturity of the software development field, but also on the capability of the local software organisations to improve their processes. In 2001, thirty-one organisations in India had achieved the highly regarded 'CMM level 5' for process capability even though CMM does not address many of the challenges of offshoring (e.g., issues emerging from the need for multicultural teams). See Chapter 12 for a discussion of CMMi, the successor of CMM.

Move offshore work that does not need user involvement and domain expertise.

6.7 Software acquisition decisions

We have described various ways in which software systems can be acquired. Each source of software has its own particular human, technological, and economic characteristics. As technology, market mechanisms, and the law evolve, it is likely that new mechanisms for acquiring software will emerge and become accepted.

We have seen that acquisition decision-making involves many factors, but primarily whether the software will meet our needs at acceptable cost and risk. We will now look at other factors that should also be taken into account: issues of interoperability, trust, and ethical decision-making.

From the point of view of the end users and their managers it is important that their various applications **interoperate**, that is, smoothly exchange data if and when required, and do not pose a threat to the reliability and security of other systems. Interoperation can add extra value to the new software. For example, in a university one would like the student records system to interact with the library system, so that when a new student is enrolled, his/her library account is set up automatically; this will save clerical effort and, hopefully, diminish data transcription errors. However, interoperation will certainly require compatibility between both systems, adding additional requirements which make the acquisition of interoperable systems more expensive. There are architectural work-arounds to the inter operability problem such as the insertion of middleware or wrapping software. However, that would be another software item to acquire. The need for interoperability explains the success and popularity of application suites that address a wide range of related business or administrative problems, such as ERP, which aims at automating all the major processes in a commercial firm, or office suites of word processor plus spreadsheet and so on. These systems are built for the interoperation of their component subsystems from a single supplier – but do necessarily interoperate with components from other suppliers.

Software is generally acquired based on certain terms and conditions expressed in a legal document, such as **contract** or a **license agreement**. Normally a license agreement limits the right of using (that is, executing) the software to the software's purchaser. In some cases other rights are transferred, such as the right to read and modify the source code, as when defect fixing is needed. However, it is often the case that the intellectual property rights in the code remain with the developers and only the right of executing the software is conferred to users. Software acquirers must be aware of these obligations and act on them. Intellectual property and other legal issues surrounding this have already been discussed in Chapter 5. Some governments have regulations and guidelines about the way in which their software should be acquired.

It is important that you trust the organisation supplying the software and the software itself. Are you confident that the supplier will respond when, for example, a serious defect or other vulnerability needs to be remedied? Is the supplier acting in good faith and protecting the interest of the user? What is the reputation of the supplier in the software business? Are they likely to continue to support the software?

Ethical decision-making is important in software acquisition – see Chapters 2 and 4. We need to take into account many factors here. Aggressive commercial practices to push products as de facto standards need to be questioned. Some users prefer to use Open Source software as a matter of principle over proprietary alternatives. Many users like to have an input into the development of the software that they are using: many users of Free/Open Source software become contributors and have their own say in the future evolution of these systems. Some governments (e.g., Brazil, China) and some regional administrations in Europe (e.g., Munich) are supporting Open Source software communities and have specific directives which favour (and even mandate) the acquisition of Free/Open Source software for the applications that they fund. Pricing of software may have been done with users in the developed world in mind, leaving users in developing countries unable to afford the software and under pressure to use illegal copies. Similarly, software developed and evolved offshore by low-paid labour in developing countries is not used by the populations of these countries, whose majority may still remain computer illiterate. Moreover, offshoring of software development may not be acceptable for users who are concerned about fair trade conditions, even though some others may argue that offshoring contributes to the wealth of the developing countries and to raising their standard of living. These are all complex issues that need to be thought about if the final decision is to be ethical.

Activity 6.8   *Wide impact software*

It has been said that 'technology makes it possible for people to gain control over everything except over technology.'[22] As software becomes pervasive, software acquirers and suppliers are involved in deploying systems which determine ever-more-important aspects of the lives of people and society. Think of software systems which may influence the lives of millions of people. Based on what you have learnt in this chapter, how should such software systems be supplied and acquired? Consider some of the risks for individuals and for society which emerge from software acquisition decisions.

Discussion
Consider these two examples:

1. *Inland revenue and taxation*: In many countries, particularly in the West, these are heavily dependent on software. Automation has reached a point at which legislators cannot make changes without consulting IT specialists, who will implement them and who will tell what is possible and what is unachievable in terms of changes to the taxation system. The organisations who acquire these systems are formed by civil servants and the software may be developed in house or acquired from a third party. National legislation establishes how the government should go about acquiring goods and services with no specific rules for software (so the legislation does not ask the procuring authority to systematically consider the advantages and disadvantages of each form of software acquisition). In general, the public has little or no access to these systems, how they are architected, validated, and verified. A calculation error could affect the finances of the whole country. One may ask whether the architecture and code of this system should be made public, so that it is open to independent verification. However, that will expose vulnerabilities and may be exploited by some for their own benefit.

2. *Electronic voting systems, which have been adopted in countries such as the US*: In general, electronic voting systems are provided by companies who supply hardware, software, and people to help run the system. In some cases, the voting is electronic without any audit record that permits checking of the results. The lack of an audit trail is justified in terms of keeping the votes secret. Even though the arithmetic involved in compiling the election results may be relatively simple, it is always a theoretical possibility that the election results may be affected by unknown defects in the software.

A software acquisition decision may have consequences that go far beyond that immediate decision.

The process of acquiring software does not end with the acquisition of the software and its documentation. The newly acquired software will need to be configured and customised in order to fit existing business processes and other software systems with which it is expected to interoperate. We saw this in section 6.3 on COTS solutions, but it is generally true even for bespoke solutions. To be able to do this may require knowledge which is not contained in the documentation and the acquirer will need external support. Users and others involved (e.g., system administrators) need training so that they can profitably use the software. Defects will need to be identified, reported, and fixed. Moreover, requirements are subject to evolutionary pressures and hence the software needs to be continually evolved. This topic is further discussed in Chapter 9.

Summing up

This chapter has looked at various ways in which you can acquire your software. What we saw was that:

- we should aim to acquire software which is ready made, and only if that fails, should we have it purpose built;
- a first source to consider is software that you already own: legacy software, if it continues to be useful or could be made to be useful; wrap it to keep it in service; work to counteract legacy symptoms, to keep business-critical software in service;
- buy COTS packages to benefit from lower costs, higher functionality and quality, but know that you will need to make compromises; select COTS and other software using a weighted scorecard; make your COTS package fit by customisation and business process re-engineering;
- Open Source offers a very rich source of software, mostly but by no means exclusively in the technical arena; it is not free but gives cost reduction; open source deployment requires finding your own sources of support;
- instead of owning or licensing the software, rent time using it at a service provider; this software as a service gives clear cost advantages, but raises issues of responsibility, technical limitations, and hidden costs;
- choose bespoke development only if no ready-made system will suffice; only choose in-house development if you can sustain the staff long term, though outsourcing has economic and technical benefits, it may lead to loss of control; offshore work that does not need user involvement and domain knowledge;
- software acquisition decisions may have consequences that go far beyond the immediate decision, and raise trust and ethical issues.

Exercises

All the following exercises are based on the hypothetical acquisiton of emailing software.

1. Develop a list of features or functions that you and a group of your friends or colleagues would require of an email package. Make sure that your list includes

not just functions but operational matters like vulnerability to virus attack and availability of support.

2. Draw up a weighted scorecard for your list, determining weights with respect to the group with whom you drew up the list. Put this list into a spreadsheet in preparation for later evaluations.

3. Find all proprietary emailers that are available, by searching the web, visiting software exhibitions, or whatever. Enter these into your scorecard, and score each one. Which is the best buy based on the weighted sums? Do you believe the result, or would you want to override this in favour of some other choice? Why – was the scorecard wrong, or were some critical factors not adequately represented on the scorecard?

4. Find all open source mailers that are available, using general searches of the Internet and looking specifically at major open source project management sites like SourceForge. If possible visit an open source exhibition and conference. Enter all of these into your scorecard. Do any open source emailers become candidate acquisitions – that is, having a score near the top?

5. Consider other decision models that more adequately cope with the issues that this acquisition has raised. Make sure that these alternatives take into account the difficulties you have had with the scorecard. Could a decision procedure ever replace your own judgement?

6. In a sense, web-based mail services like Hotmail and Yahoo are software-as-a-service solutions. Find all such services available, and add these to your scorecard. Do any of them become competitive?

7. Consider the option of developing your own email program. Imagine that this emailer would not be just for your personal use, but also sold as part of a business system that you and your enterprise are developing. Could there be any advantages in doing this? Try to give an estimate of what this might cost in person days or in money. Would you develop this in house or outsource it? Would you consider body-shopping the people to do it in house? Would there be any advantages in doing this offshore?

8. Discuss the ethical issues involved in offshoring, considering the loss of jobs in your own country, the creation of jobs in another country, and exploitation of people that might result.

9. From your reading in this book, and from reading elsewhere, discuss how the software acquisition process may develop over the next decade. Where do you think most software will come from in ten years from now?

Endnotes

1. 'Bundling' is a marketing term for any situation where independent but related products or services are sold together. Often as the market develops the offer is 'unbundled' so that the independent parts are then sold separately – typically to enable the producer to increase revenues, but also enabling third-party suppliers to also enter the market.

2. Pieter Naur and Brian Randall (eds)(1968) *Software Engineering: Report on a Conference by the NATO Science Committee*. NATO Scientific Affairs Division. Republished (1976) as *Software Engineering Concepts and Techniques*. Petrocelli/Charter.

3. M.D. McIllroy, *Mass-Produced Software Components*, in Naur and Randall (1976), pp. 88–98. See endnote 2.

4. Peter Wegner (1984) 'Capital-Intensive Software Technology', *IEEE Software*, 1, 3, 7–45.

5. As a simple guide, a multi-user database management system in the 1980s required 100 person years to develop, but today it would require much more because of the larger range of more complex systems it would have to integrate with.

6. See http://www.information-age.com/article/2003/november/legacy-salvation.

7. The term 'legacy data' may be also applied to data that needs to be retained for legal, commercial, or other reasons.

8. See http://www.information-age.com, © Infoconomy 2004.

9. M. Morisio, C.B. Seaman, A.T. Parra, V.R. Basili, S.E. Kraft, and S.E. Condon (2000) 'Investigating and Improving a COTS-based Software Development Process', *Proc. 22nd Int. Conf. Software Eng.*, ICSE 2000, Limerick, Ireland , pp. 31–40.

10. Edited from article by E. Gottshalk, *Technical Overview of IBM's Java Initiatives*, 1 April 1999 http://www-128.ibm.com/developerworks/java/library/j-tech/tech.html#2. This article also appeared in the IBM Systems Journal.

11. http://www.netcraft.com.

12. B. Fitzgerald and T. Kenny (2003) *Open Source Software in the Trenches: Lessons from a Large-Scale OSS Implementation*. 24th International Conference on Information Systems, Seattle, WA, USA, 11–14 December 2003, pp. 316–326. With permission from IEEE Software and ICIS 2003.

13. An example of another form of commitment to FOSS would be developing proprietary software which is compatible with the open source system.

14. Martin Fink refers to this in the context of Linux as the 'chicken–egg conundrum'. M. Fink (2002) *The Business and Economics of Linux and Open Source*. Prentice Hall.

15. The use of the Internet or of the phone network are example services. One uses them without having to own the complex and expensive infrastructure (routers, phone exchanges, satellites, cable networks). In some cases the user has to own some equipment in order to be able to access the service: in order to access the Internet one needs a computer and modem; for the telephone service one has to buy a handset, though in some countries even the handset is provided by the telephone company.

16. See summary of the talk Software Development Across Boundaries: Lessons from Supply Chain Management, Dr Steve New, Said Business School, University of Oxford, http://www.service-oriented.com/isen/Report2.html.

17. Frederick P. Brooks, Jr. (1975) *The Mythical Man-Month: Essays on Software Engineering*. Addison Wesley.

18. This is a confusing term, since we would want to contrast software work done offshore with work not done offshore, which we would naturally call 'onshore' without meaning that it is done by migrant exploited labour. We hope that the context will make it clear what form of 'onshore' we are writing about.

19. E. Carmel and P. Tjia (2005) *Offshoring Information Technology – Sourcing and Outsourcing to a Global Workforce*. Cambridge University Press.

20. Survey published by *Software Development Magazine*, 2004, p. 14, Figure 1.5, and quoted by Carmel and Tjia.

21. Summarised from the case study 'Offshoring Usability to India' by J. Versendaal, R. Subramanian, and K. Bapu, in E. Carmel and P. Tjia (2005) *Offshoring Information Technology – Sourcing and Outsourcing to a Global Workforce*. Cambridge University Press, pp. 193–195.

22. Attributed to John Tudor, cited in D.G. Messerschmitt and Clemens Szyperski (2003) *Software Ecosystem – Understanding Technology and Industry*. MIT Press.

7 Software activities

What we will study in this chapter

The creation of software applications, whether as original programs or through the integration of software components, requires that a number of distinct activities are undertaken. No matter what the means used for acquiring the actual application software, as covered in Chapter 6, all these activities must be carried out in some explicit or implicit form. The activities may be undertaken to different degrees and in different orders, depending upon the actual software being produced and the development process being followed. Each activity produces particular representations of the system with the various representations fitting together within a particular development process. In this chapter we look at these typical activities and their representations, illustrating them with a simple application following a simple sequential process.

We will look at activities undertaken and representations used for:

- determining what is required of the system and keeping this constantly under review;

- obtaining a sound estimate of the cost of development;

- designing the software through various levels of detail;

- encoding the design using computing languages of various types;

- testing and trialling the software at various levels;

- validation and verification of the system as its production progresses;

- tracking progress using appropriate management methods and tools.

The activity of selecting a development process appropriate to our particular circumstances will be left until Chapter 8, where the range of development processes will be described along with the circumstances that gave rise to them and the circumstances under which they would be applicable.

7.1 Introduction

In Chapter 6 we looked at a range of ways in which software could be acquired, and the relative merits of those methods. Even in those approaches where the software came ready made, or largely so, we still have some need for customisation to tailor the software to our own requirements, and may need to integrate the new software with other software. The other extreme is to develop the software specifically to meet our requirements. Whatever the approach, customisation, integration, or development of new software, we will always become involved in activities that are essentially the same. We will call these activities simply **software activities.**

Developing, adapting, or integrating software is never an easy process. When that software is large and complex, the process is even more difficult. We want to produce high-quality software, but we want to do this for some reasonable cost and within some acceptable timescale. We will see how we need to undertake a number of tasks or activities in order to construct the software, and these activities need to be managed within a project. We have already come across *projects* in Chapter 2 and again in Chapter 6 – a project is work which has a defined starting point and a defined outcome, possibly constrained by costs and timescales. This chapter will be about projects for developing software. It will lay out a number of basic concepts related to software development, concepts that will be generalised and expanded upon in later chapters.

We will see all technical aspects of software production:

- gathering requirements;
- designing solutions involving software;
- building the solution ready for operational use;
- confirming that the solution does solve the problem at hand;
- sustaining the solution through its operational use over many years;

and some aspects of software project management:

- estimating the costs and timescales for a particular development;
- planning the work to be undertaken;
- monitoring the progress of this work;

In this chapter we will look at the typical activities involved in building software, taking the very simple-minded and traditional view that they are done in sequence. An important concept is that of the **deliverable** or **work-product**. Each activity produces one or more products which are passed on to following activities. The work-products will use particular notations and may need to conform to local or industry-wide standards. They will be subject to some review before being picked up by the succeeding activities. Deliverables are important, as we will see, in marking the progress of a project. We want you to understand what is involved in developing and integrating software, and even if you personally never have developed and never will develop software, you may well be managing people who do.

In practice the sequence in which the activities are carried out may vary from project to project, with many projects following similar sequences. The activities and the sequence in which they are undertaken are known as **process models**. Because building software is unconstrained by physical factors that would demand that one activity is done strictly before another, we have great flexibility here, as we will see in Chapter 8.

In this chapter we will explain what software developers actually do through a simple case study outlined below. We will explore both the technical methods for developing the software solution, and the management processes necessary to ensure its success, seeing these as intermingled activities all of which are necessary. Further details of the management processes will be picked up later in the book in Chapter 10. All of these activities will be illustrated using a running example of a school library system and its problems – this is an entirely fictional but plausible system. The problem is posed as Case Study 7.1. The solution fragments for this system will be expressed using data flow diagrams and data structure diagrams as in Appendix A; throughout this chapter you will be asked as activities to repeat these using UML[1] **object-oriented** notation – but we will not give you the answers, leaving that to you as an exercise.

> All software development involves a number of typical activities which may be carried out in different orders depending upon the actual system and project.

Case Study 7.1 *The project brief – problems with a school library*

A school library holds a large number of books and other items which are stored on shelves that can be browsed by students at the school. Students can read books in the school library, but are also able to borrow non-reference books to read while outside the library, at school or at home or elsewhere.

The school has trusted students to return books when they have finished with them, but has always accepted that there would be a small number of replacements as books get damaged or lost. However the cost of replacements has risen sharply, with the need to buy multiple copies of popular books because they cannot be relied upon to be returned when an open request to all students to return the book is issued. The school managers now want to take control of this situation – should they just stop all borrowing, or could an information technology solution help them? Could there be some other way of tackling this problem?

7.2 Requirements elicitation

As soon as we get the project brief shown in Case Study 7.1 we need to set about understanding the problem better. This requires us to meet with the project sponsor who is paying for the system, and all stakeholders who will be affected by the system in some way or other. In doing this we are setting out on an activity known as **requirements analysis**.

Requirements are statements about what the software system should achieve for its stakeholders – the functions it should perform, the benefits that are hoped for, who is going to use the software, under what circumstances the software may need to be changed, and so on. We need to recognise that requirements do not objectively exist but are constructed through negotiation between the suppliers of the software and those who have a stake in the use of the software in expecting to benefit from it. Requirements may not be knowable beforehand, but may emerge in the process of acquiring the software, with the stakeholders making compromises determined in part by conflicting demands among the stakeholders, and in part by what is possible or available in the technology. We would typically distinguish two subactivities within requirements analysis:

- **Requirements elicitation** which looks at requirements from the point of view of the stakeholders, spending time with the stakeholders to fully understand their needs, producing a document that is often know as the **requirements statement**.

- **Requirements specification** which defines or specifies the system that needs to be produced in order to fulfil the stated requirements. These are expressed in technical terms, perhaps using specialist notations and diagrams, frequently within a document called the *software requirements specification* or similar.

At this stage all we will be doing is requirements elicitation.

That initial problem statement of Case Study 7.1 may well have started with a casual conversation, but arose out of some serious review of the organisation and the difficulties it faces. All too often such problem statements are articulated in terms of a possible solution, and we must be careful not to get trapped by any implementation details in the statement. At this point there is a problem to be solved; solutions come later.

So where do we start? If the problem is with an existing system, as in our case study, an excellent place to start is with the current system. What is done now? We document this existing system carefully looking not just at any computers being used but at the whole process surrounding the system – we call that the 'As-Is' system. To do this we will need to talk to the people involved and also sit and observe what happens – usually what people say (and believe) what happens is not what actually happens. We may document what we find using text, but may also use diagrams and other means to record what we observed. And we would check back with our stakeholders to make sure that we have documented the current system correctly.

Case Study 7.2 *The As-Is system for the school library*

Students may be sent to the library by a teacher, or may just wander in of their own accord. We group these two possibilities together as the student taking an interest in the library. Sometimes they will leave the library with one or more books, and later return these. They may also be asked to return a book by a recall message, sent to every student.

A teacher will be on hand to give students guidance. Occasionally a new book may be ordered from a bookseller, and later delivered, and a request to the library budget may be made.

Observing the library at work we observe students scanning the shelves and library catalogues before selecting a book for detailed reading in the library; this book may also then be taken out of the library.

When a book is not found, it can then either be recalled, or a new book ordered from the library budget. If there is not enough money in the library budget, then a request for more money might be made to the school's financial controller.

An administrator was often in the library, shelving returned books and new books, filling out orders, etc., but this person did not seem to be a user or stakeholder of the library but part of the library itself.

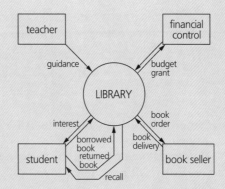

Figure 7.1

Context diagram for
the As-Is system

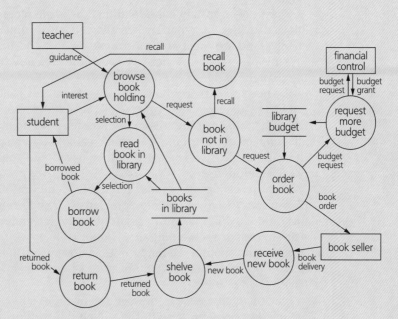

Figure 7.2

Level DFD for As-Is
system.

There is also a simple card file system with
one card for each book title in the library, with
the date purchased, from whom and at what
price. If there are multiple copies of the same
book, sometimes these are recorded on the
same card, and sometimes on separate cards.
When books get lost, or so worn that they have
to be withdrawn, the card file is often not updated and thus records books that are no longer
in the library.

Activity 7.1   *Library As-Is in UML*

Re-express the library As-Is description using UML.

Discussion

The context diagram becomes a set of actors and simple use cases, while the level
one DFD extends these use cases. You might also be tempted to draw a class diagram ▶

to account for the data stores and the actions made upon them – if you do, base your diagram on the data structures in Figure 7.5, in Case study 7.4 but consider whether you really need to do that at this stage.

Now that we have understood the problem and the system within which it arises, we can begin to explore ways of solving the problem. We are very unlikely to simply automate part of the system As-Is, and may change the way the particular area of work is done quite radically. New technologies may give new opportunities.

One very important consideration now is the **scope** of the project – who are we allowed to talk to, what are we allowed to document, what are we allowed to change, and are there any constraints on cost and timescale or technologies? We saw this in Chapter 2, where we called the area in which changes were permitted the **change charter**.

We need to explore the kinds of systems and facilities that the various stakeholders would like, being open to all possibilities. One way of doing this would be through **brainstorming**[2] sessions with each stakeholder group; aimed at involving all members of the group, fostering creativity and respecting all ideas. Afterwards the various ideas will be sifted and analysed and combined to yield one or more possible solutions.

We also need to make some initial considerations of how our ideas might be implemented. As we commented previously, new technologies give new opportunities, and we don't want to miss out on new technologies, but equally well do not want to propose something that is unfeasible or would cost too much. This is important, and though we might not need to record these considerations as part of any proposed solution, we do need to keep notes in order to come back to these later.

Once we have a clear view of one or more solutions that might be possible, we need to present these to the stakeholders. One approach might be to use a **focus group**,[3] inviting representatives to a meeting at which the various candidate solutions are presented and discussed with the aim of converging on one solution, possibly modifying this in the light of the meeting. This should end up with a requirements statement setting out what the real needs of the stakeholders are and what kind of solution will solve their problem and be acceptable to them.

Case Study 7.3 *Ideas concerning a solution*

Scope

An interview with the head teacher of the school discussed in the Case Studies above indicated that while anybody in the school can be talked to, the book procurement agents used by the local government department which finances the school cannot be contacted. No changes to school financial management or staffing can be proposed. This leads to the change charter boundary shown in Figure 7.3.

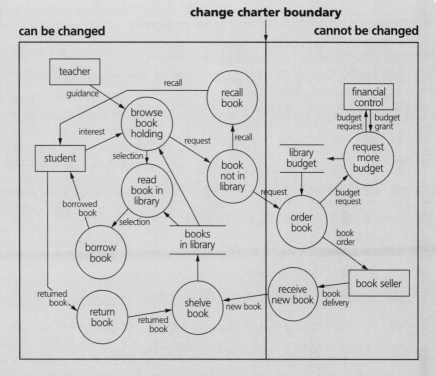

Figure 7.3

System model showing the change charter

Notes from brainstorming sessions

Governors and head teacher:

- Want students to read as much and as widely as possible, should be easy for students to borrow books.
- Want to stop all losses of books, don't mind modest investment – e.g., ten per cent of capital cost of books.
- Don't want to have to have a member of staff in attendance.

Staff:

- Cannot expect students to carry around library cards.
- Don't want to have to sit in library and control its use.
- Students must borrow a book by some positive act which establishes some form of contract between them and the library.
- Want the system to just recognise the students in the way that cameras on highways can recognise cars.

Students:

- Want more exciting books about spies and romance.
- Hate having to fill in forms, and want to just scan the book like they do in supermarkets.

Notes concerning design and implementation

While conventional library solutions of identifying books and users with barcodes and similar will be considered, we noted that items, including books, are now being tagged electronically using radio frequency identification (RFID) labels (a product supplier was found at http://www.rfidinc.com/) so that they can be tracked remotely – could we exploit this emerging technology?

Candidate solutions for focus groups

The basic data seems to be the same for all solutions – they need to record the:

- books, both titles and copies (accessions), and
- students, including the class to which they belong.

However, the bookseller who supplied the books is out of scope and should not be recorded.

Solutions representing classes of solution would be presented and preferences between these looked for.

Solution class 1 : Manual system, no computer system is necessary, but a librarian is necessary; fill in loan cards each time a book is borrowed: these loan cards are filed in simple date order.

Similar to current system. Each copy of a book has its own unique card while students have a set of library cards made up as a small envelope into which book cards can be slotted – when a student wants to borrow a book they hand over one library card, the librarian slots the books card into it, and files the card in a special tray arranged by book accession number.

Solution class 2 : Use a computer system to store the information and librarian; each student holds a card with a barcode or magnetic strip that identifies them, and each book is barcoded or magnetically coded; when a book is borrowed, the identifications are scanned by a librarian.

Solution class 3 : As solution class 2, but the student does the scanning, saving the cost of a librarian.

Solution class 4 : Issue all students with an identity card that that has been activated for RFID and which they should wear at all times. Fasten an RFID card to every book. Place an RFID detector at the library doors, and record each student and each book that passes in and out of the doors.

Outcome of focus groups – discussion

Solution classes 1 and 2 were rejected because they required a librarian in attendance, and discussion wavered between classes 3 and 4 because these did not. Everybody doubted whether solution class 4 could work at all, let alone identify accurately who had taken out the book if several students left the library at once. Solution class 4 was disliked because it had no explicit act of borrowing the book.

Then an amalgam of 3 and 4 was suggested, with an alarm triggered if a book was taken out of the library that had not been officially borrowed.

Outcome of focus groups – requirements statement

1. Record all loans of books by students with ability to recall books if needed.

2. Ability to reserve books, or request books that need to be ordered in.

3. Students are able to record loans themselves.

4. Enforceable limit on number of loans.

5. Alarm system triggered if book removed without being booked out.

6. Ideally returns also registered by students, though it is acceptable that they are just put into returns bin and staff register these later.

We must always understand what the problem is that we are trying to solve, articulating this as a set of requirements, and agreeing this and potential solutions with the stakeholders.

| Activity 7.2 | Change charter in UML |

What is the equivalent of a change charter in UML? Could you draw a diagram showing this?

Discussion
There is none, and you would need to look to a scope statement for the project.

7.3 Initial estimates of cost

The cost of the requirements elicitation work, and the following requirements specification, will almost certainly be done on a time-and-materials basis – that is, no attempt is made to fix the costs, a person or person will be employed to do the work for however long it takes, with travel and similar added to the cost as needed.

If the software we wish to build is similar to software we have built before, then we can use that experience from that previous project or projects to estimate the potential cost of this new system by analogy. Of course we must have kept records of how much that earlier development cost, what effort was used, how large the software was, as well as a comprehensive description of the software so that we can assess how well our new project matches the previous one. Alternatively we can ask several experts to make estimates, and seek convergence using the Delphi technique.

In this case we would expect to use one of the above techniques – see Chapter 10 for more detail about these, and for other methods.

> An initial estimate of costs can be made as soon as the problem to be solved has been understood.

7.4 Requirements specification

Having focused on a single solution and expressed this from the perspective of the stakeholders in the requirements statement, we are now in a position to give a fuller description in the system from the perspective of the developers of that system. One good way to do this is to take the As-Is description of the current system, and change the parts within the change charter. Some of these changes will be to business processes that are enacted by people within the organisation, and some of these changes will be undertaken by software. Those parts of the changes that are to be done by software would be marked within an 'automation boundary'.

For simplicity, in this chapter we follow the modelling conventions of DFDs and data structure diagrams used earlier in this book and described in Appendix A. These enable us to illustrate all our major points. Within the automation boundary we may choose a whole variety of description and modelling conventions that match those of the intended implementation technologies and that enable us to represent particular aspects of the problem and the solution in a clear way. The implementation technology nowadays is likely to use object-oriented methods, and we may well adopt the industry standard notation of UML. UML is really only suited to describing the software within the automation boundary – while in principle it should be suitable for describing the human procedures outside the system, this is not commonly done.

This new model is often called the 'To-Be' model, contrasting this with the 'As-Is' model.

Case Study 7.4 *Requirements specification for the library system*

Context diagram and change charter remain the same as in previous case studies.

▶

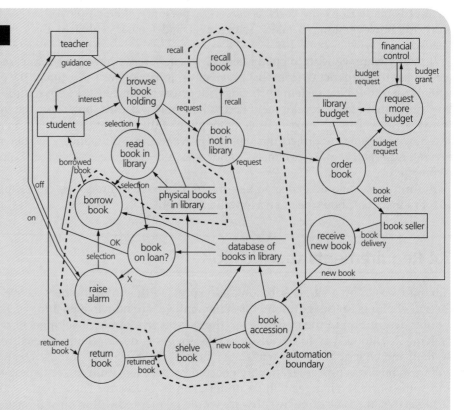

Figure 7.4

To-Be level 1 data flow, showing automation boundary

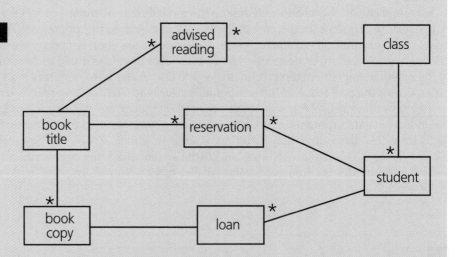

Figure 7.5

To-Be data structure model for the proposed system

Note that the functions for creating student records and setting advised readings – functions for the teachers – have not been included in the data-flow diagram of Figure 7.4. Figure 7.5 gives the database structure.

Activity 7.3   *Requirements for the new system in UML*

Draw a class diagram to capture the requirements embodied in Figures 7.4 and 7.5.

Discussion

If you got carried away in Activity 7.1 you may already have done some this. Figure 7.5 suggests the classes you might use, and all that functionality in the DFD will need to appear as methods in the classes.

Software developers need a reasonably comprehensive specification of what 'the solution' must do in order to be able to develop the software.

7.5 Cost–benefit estimation

Now that we have a rather full description of the system, we can hope to make a reasonable estimate of how much it is likely to cost. Methods for doing this evolved during the early 1980s – thus Tom DeMarco,[4] writing in 1982 observed:

> The specification model describes the requirement itself, not a particular way to meet that requirement. So, a quantitative analysis of the model will provide a measure of the true function to be delivered as perceived by the user. This is precisely . . . 'Bang'. Bang is a function metric, an implementation-independent indication of system size. (p. 80)

The current equivalent of DeMarco's 'Bang' is function points (FP), developed about the same time by Capers Jones.[5] Both Capers Jones and Tom DeMarco took their inspiration from a paper by Albrecht[6] in 1979. Albrecht wasn't really aiming at estimating the effort to develop software, he wanted to compare systems developed by different means; in doing this he came up with function points.

Albrecht counted the number of inputs to a system, the number of outputs from the system, and the number of data files or elements stored in the system. He weighted each of these by an assessment of their complexity, and then added them all up to arrive at a size measure for the software in terms of function points. He then translated from function points into effort or lines of code based upon experience of previous projects. This idea transfers very readily to modern methods of developing software, replacing inputs and outputs and data files by their modern equivalents.

It is then common practice to adjust the FP value for the complexity of the actual system to be built using a suitable formula, to produce a new adjusted function point score. Each adjusted function point is assumed to take the same effort to implement, so all we now need is a productivity figure of person-hours per function point. But this depends upon the implementation technologies being used.

The function point method is further described in Chapter 10, and enables us to estimate the cost of the proposed new system. After having done that, we are also in a strong position to estimate the benefits of the proposed solution and the system it contains. We will be able to compare the As-Is and To-Be systems and determine the saving in labour costs, and will be able to look at the costs of other items like technology.

Thus we arrive at the costs and benefits of the new system, and on this basis either buy an existing system off the shelf, commission a fixed price contract for implementing the system or follow one of the other acquisition alternatives discussed in Chapter 6.

Given a comprehensive specification of the software it becomes possible to give a reasonably accurate estimate of what it will cost to develop that software.

7.6 Architectural design

Given the requirements specification for the system, and the contract to implement the system, it could be tempting to immediately start programming and get the reward of having something working quickly. But it pays to do a little **design** work first, 'thinking on paper', to decide on what the major components of code and data will be and how they will work together, and to document these decisions and obtain agreement from all interested parties.

A first level decomposition or refinement of the design would break down the system into a number of interacting subsystems. This level would often be called **architectural design** or **high-level design**. The use of the term 'architecture' here (the people who undertake this high-level design are called 'architects'), picks up the architecture theme we introduced in Chapter 1. Researchers working to improve software engineering will frequently turn to architecture for inspiration and ideas, as will be seen later in this book.

The job of the system architect is to identify the main components of the system and determine how they interact. Typically there would be four or more kinds of subsystem components, as illustrated in the data-flow diagram of Figure 7.6a; Figure 7.6b shows a more usual way of drawing such diagrams.

The user interacts with the system through the user interface, nowadays engineered with full graphical facilities running on a PC or equivalent. This interface then communicates with the application, or applications, which receive data and requests from the user and respond with information in reply or requests for further data from the user. Communication could be locally within the same PC and

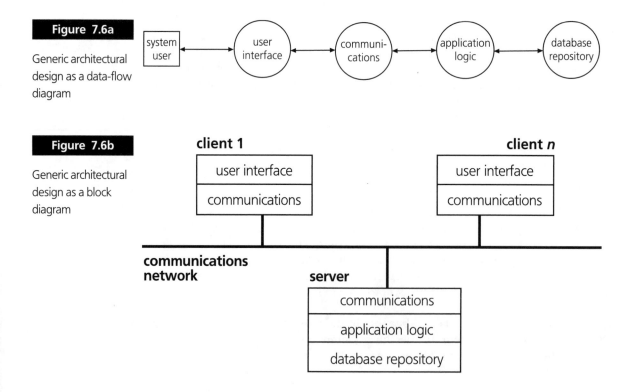

Figure 7.6a

Generic architectural design as a data-flow diagram

Figure 7.6b

Generic architectural design as a block diagram

thus in some sense trivial, or could be via some network to a local or remote '**server**' – in which case we would refer to the PC as a '**client**' for that server. The application itself will almost invariably be required to store data for long periods, and retrieve the data on demand; in some cases the data may be retained as part of the application logic, but would usually be stored separately within a **database** or **repository**.

In any actual system there would be many different kinds of users, interacting through different interfaces calling on different parts of the application logic to use the shared data, leading to a much richer and seemingly more complex architectural design.

Further, the software may be 'layered', in that each element of software developed to meet the requirements will itself depend upon general purpose or purpose-built software that forms part of the computer platform. Three levels of layering is shown in Figure 7.6b. The user interface software may use some form of **user interface management software** (UIMS) with libraries of standard components, possibly involving a browser if the interface is delivered remotely across the Internet. The communications will actually be part of the lower layer of platform software, only distinguished here to underpin the design choices of local or remote interfaces. The application logic will be written in some programming language or application generator, using sophisticated software to compile the application software into an executable form, with run time support during execution that forms part of the lower layer of the platform. The database will normally be set up using a database management system. All this lower layer software would be procured from software vendors using the methods we described in Chapter 6. You would never build these yourself – these systems require specialised knowledge and many hundreds of person-years to develop.

Any new system must fit in with other systems within the enterprise. This requires not just that it interfaces successfully with those systems so that they can exchange data and work together, but also that they share some coherent view of the overall system. This first arose as an issue in the 1960s when separately developed systems began to exchange data and found that their views of the information represented by the data were subtly different. It wasn't just that they were inconsistent, for example, recording the day somebody joined a company in two different places as two different dates – the meaning of the items may be entirely different. For example an item labelled 'joining date' could be the actual date at which they were first paid in the salary system in the payroll system, but could be the day on which the person joined the pension system at the start of the next pension year in the pension system. This led to the ideas of corporate schema which took hold during the 1970s, and which now form part of many of the software development methodologies covered in Chapter 8. One popular and influential approach has been the enterprise architectures of John Zachman[7] from 1989; this advocates a number of distinct complementary views of the system which together describe the whole system, an idea also advocated by a great many other writers of around that time and earlier.

While the need for a coherent overview of data to facilitate the integration of systems arose relatively early, the consequences of not having a coherent view of the active software were only fully analysed and described in the 1980s by Mary Shaw and David Garlan.[8] Garlan and Shaw identified a number of **architectural styles**. If different styles used in separate systems were then integrated, it led to enormous difficulties in the integration – clearly part of the overall coherence required is a compatible set of architectural styles in the various component subsystems.

This architectural level of system description is not well represented by established software engineering notations, and often the major architectural level components are simply noted as regions on the more detailed products of the detailed design that follows.

Note that the architecture is the start of an implementation and determines what is possible – and this in turn might feed back to the requirements level to influence what alternative system could have been specified! The architectural design and requirements specification cannot be completely separated.

Case Study 7.5 *The design of the library system*

A simple database architecture is needed, as shown in Figure 7.7.

Note that we have had to go beyond the simple architecture of Figure 7.6 and recognise that we now have people interacting with the system and devices like badge readers, alarms, etc.

Figure 7.7

Architectural design of school library system

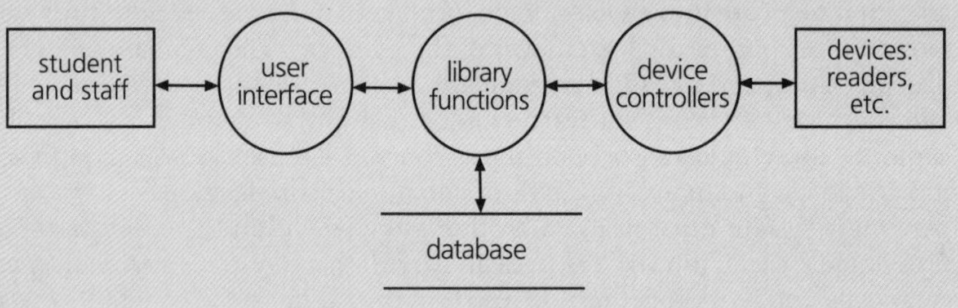

It is important to decide early on what the architectural software components are and how these fit into the overall enterprise.

Activity 7.4   *The architecture in UML*

Find out what the equivalent of an architecture in UML is, and draw the corresponding diagram.

Discussion
UML is rich in types of diagrams. What you need here is a component diagram.

7.7 Work breakdown and scheduling

Now that we are starting on the design and further stages of implementation of the system, possibly working to a fixed price contract, we should manage the process carefully, scheduling the work and assigning resources and then monitoring progress. While this will be picked up in greater detail in Chapter 10, we will give a sketch of what is normally done here.

We have produced an estimate of the overall work content of the project in person-months or equivalent, and arrived at some possible timescale for development. How do we now proceed to lay out the work over the months and years ahead?

As a start, we can look at the typical distribution of effort throughout the software development process, based on general industrial experience. We start with a relatively small number of people, then build up to a peak number around coding and the start of testing, tapering off after that through testing and into support for the software following delivery. The skills required also change: we start with analysts and designers, moving on to a preponderance of programmers and testers while retaining core analysts and designers.

To do this in any greater detail, what we really need is a **work breakdown**. We need to decompose the overall task of developing the software into many much smaller tasks. We then juggle things until the tasks can be scheduled in a sequence that honours their interdependencies and keeps the people on the project busy without overworking them. One issue that often emerges, as you will see in Chapter 10, is the handling of contingency. How do we plan for problems should they arise?

The requirements specification and architectural design enable us to break down the work and schedule a project subject to resource constraints.

7.8 Detailed design

Each of the components identified in the architecture will need further decomposition into software components or modules. This process of decomposing a component subsystem into smaller components, and maybe further into subcomponents and their interactions, is called **detailed design**, in contrast to architectural or high-level design. The decomposition continues until each component is small enough for one person to produce it in less than a month.

Architectural design and lower levels of detailed design will be undertaken in such a manner as to ensure that the subsystems and components are as independent of each other as possible. Of course they must have interdependencies, since they are designed to work together within a system, but those dependences must only be those that are necessary, and must be well documented and agreed by all parties. What we have described is just good design practice, characterised in software engineering as **encapsulation** and **information hiding**, where the modules have high internal **cohesion** and low **coupling** to other modules. This independence is important, for it enables work to be assigned to different individuals or teams who can then work largely independently of each other.

As implied above, the actual high-level and detailed design processes require different kinds of skills and design processes. They also deliver different kinds of design document to record the decisions that have been made, or proposals for which agreement is being sought. The designs themselves will be presented diagrammatically following some established convention consistent with the conventions used in the requirements specification and architectural design.

Case Study 7.6 *Detailing the design of the library system*

Figure 7.8 presents a large data-flow diagram showing one possibility for the detail design of the library system.

Note 1: While the data-flow diagram specifying requirements in Figure 7.4 uses terminators which were the human actors in the environ-ment, here, in Figure 7.8, the terminators are the physical devices that will interact with the soft-ware.

Note 2: The teacher functions for adding stu-dents and advised reading are not shown.

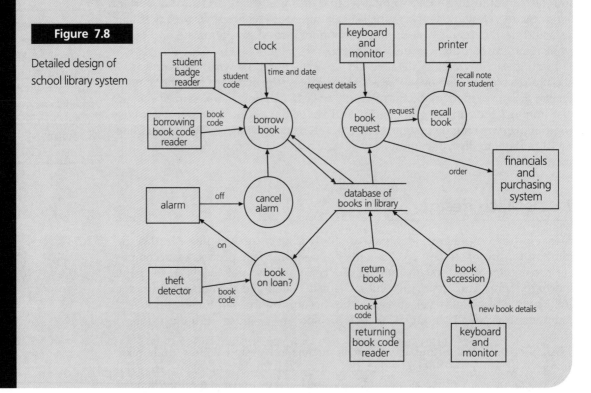

Figure 7.8

Detailed design of school library system

Activity 7.5   *Detailed design in UML*

Design needs to proceed until small independent components of software have been specified.

Revisit the class diagram earlier in which you represented your requirements, and change this and add further classes to capture this design.

Discussion
You should find that not much needs to be done.

7.9 Progress monitoring

The project is under way and you have a plan, so it should be a simple matter to assess whether your project is proceeding according to plan. But is it? This is taken up in greater detail in Chapter 10, but in this section we shall consider just some aspects of the day-to-day **progress monitoring** and tracking of the project. This may also involve the replanning of the activities and tasks, and reprioritising resources to meet new circumstances.

A first idea might be to collect data on expenditure, especially of person-time, against activities, and thus knowing for each task how much of the budget set aside for that task has been spent. This would typically be done at the end of each week using a timesheet or equivalent, and this is a widespread practice in engineering companies. When a task has been completed you will have a record of how much was actually spent in comparison to the estimates set out in the task budget. Where an activity is only partly complete, the timesheet might ask you to estimate how close to completion you believe you are, perhaps as a percentage of the overall work involved, or perhaps as an estimate of the effort required to complete the task.

But there are two problems with this approach. First, software engineers, and indeed people at large, can be hopelessly optimistic; so basing the monitoring of progress on estimates of completeness can be very misleading. If the budget has run out, people invariably claim that they are 'ninety-nine per cent complete' week after week after week. Second, simply recording time spent is simply monitoring whether you are spending to plan, not progressing to plan. You need to measure progress against budget spent and actual task completion. We give additional detail on how to do this in Chapter 10.

> Progress towards completion needs to be continually monitored both in terms of budget spent and task completion. This can signal the need for reprioritisation and replanning.

7.10 Coding and unit testing

Eventually the design process will reach the point where **coding** can take place, and the actual executable code can be produced. This code production might require programmers to create the code, but often the code will be able to be created largely automatically using an appropriate generator. It may even be possible that the required software component is ready made as part of a programme library or could be bought off the shelf from some component supplier.

Each unit of code to be produced will have been specified in terms of the input data supplied, output data expected, and what processing is required in between. The processing required might be described in natural language, or perhaps in a more formal programming-like language often referred to as pseudo-code or program design language. However if greater precision in the specification is needed, a formal mathematically based method like Z or PI might be used.

The unit will then be coded in some programming language, perhaps in C or C++ to follow existing practice, or in Java.

If a database is being used, the entities identified much earlier in the requirements specification will need to be coded, and all queries of the database will also need to be coded. This may be in some proprietary language, but today it is very likely to be in the industry standard SQL.

Once the units have been coded, they do need to be proven in some way. Almost invariably this is done by **testing**, exercising the code, running the unit within a **test harness** and supplying it with sample test inputs and seeing if it produces the correct results. Even very small units can have very complex behaviour, and cannot be tested exhaustively on all possible input combinations, but with careful design a complete representative set of test data can be constructed such that if the unit passes the test we can be very confident that the unit would perform correctly on any other input combination. At the same time we might check that every bit of code is used at some point, carrying out this check automatically using a **coverage analyser**. Occasionally the proving of units could be done through mathematical reasoning, but this would only be done in very special situations, for example with safety-critical systems.

Units should be coded and tested as a single activity.

Case Study 7.7 *Sample unit from the library system*

Unit RETURN_BOOK

(Reads the codes of the book from barcode or magnetic strip, looks this up in the database, and removes the loan record.)

Unit specification in Program Design Language

```
Procedure RETURN_BOOK
    call readBookCode (IN returnsReader; OUT accessionCode);
    call retrieveEntity (IN booksDatabase, accessionCode; OUT accessionRecord);
    call deleteEntity (IN accessionRecord.loan);
    increment accessionRecord.title.number;
end RETURN_BOOK
```

Unit code

```
/* Sketch implementation in C*/
/* Need to add variable definitions */
    ...
return_book (...) {
    ...
    accessionCode = readBookCode (returnsReader);
    accessionRecord = retrieveEntity (booksDatabase, accessionCode);
    deleteEntity (accessionRecord.loan); /*Assigns NULL value*/
    (*accessionRecord.title.number)++ ;
    ...
}
```

Unit test plan

1. Must have working database system with simple records loaded.

2. Use stub for readBookCode procedure to access reader. This removes dependency on technology of actual reader and any delays in getting actual choice working.

3. Use test cases where accession code read exists and does not exist.

4. Where it exists, use test cases where the linked records (loan, title) are present (as they should be) and where they are not to test error handling.

Activity 7.6   *Coding from UML*

Get a colleague or friend who can write Java or C++ or C# to sketch one of your classes in the chosen language.

Discussion
This should be very straightforward for your friend or colleague, but don't let them be too pedantic about your designs.

7.11 Integration testing

The unit coding activities will deliver to us small units of software that must then be assembled systematically to produce the complete system. It might seem tempting to collect all the units as they are produced, and then when you have them all, simply **link** these together to **build** the system, and try them out. The trouble is, what do you do when something goes wrong? There may be several hundreds, even thousands, of these units, any of which might contain an error. Which one is it? Are there many in error?

The process of putting the separate units together is known as **integration**. The way to proceed is to do the integration systematically, building up the system just a few units at a time. Any missing units may need to be represented by a **stub** so that the system as a whole links properly. We sometimes talk about this as 'scaffolding', drawing on the architectural analogy where scaffolds are used to support the building when only part of it is there. This integration may take place in levels, to match the levels in the design process, or may be undertaken to ensure a full function works as soon as possible, involving modules at all levels of the design.

Because this will be the first time many complex items are brought together and be required to work together, it is very likely that defects to be revealed – and hence this process is often know as **integration testing**. Whenever a problem is found we know where to look first – at the new units that have been added, and any units that have been changed.

Once integration testing has succeeded, and all units have been shown to link together successfully, we are then ready to test the complete system.

We need to integrate a new system incrementally and systematically to be sure that when a problem arises the reason can be easily located.

Case Study 7.8 *Integration test plan for the library system*

Everything depends upon the database, so implement and test this first. Then test the processes in this order:

1. add students

2. remove students

3. accession, add books – simple entry of data into the database

4. borrowing – updates the database, and uses the book code reader

5. return – updates the database and also uses the book code reader

6. advised reading

7. request – simple database query, updating to create reservation record, create recall note, or request a purchase via the financial system.

8. alarm – simple logic, but complex device since we assume that it will be able to read the book code.

7.12 System testing

Once all the software has been integrated, and later re-integrated following changes, we need to thoroughly test the complete system: we need to run a **system test**. This means exercising every function of the system in every combination. Of course in normal circumstances we cannot test real-world software such as the library system exhaustively, but we must test it sufficiently thoroughly to feel confident enough that it all works properly and as expected from the requirements specification. Even where we have decided to procure the software from outside on the basis of the requirements specification rather than develop it ourselves, we still need to carry out comprehensive system tests.

These tests would be developed systematically from the requirements specification, making sure that all functions are tested in all the contexts in which they can occur. A major problem here, less significant in unit testing, is controlling the state of the system so that you know what data a particular function is operating upon and thus what result you should be expecting.

As with unit testing, we would want make sure that our tests did exercise all major elements of code – so some **coverage measure** might be sought from the system. A suitable measure could be the proportion of units that are invoked during the tests. When you establish some coverage measure like unit coverage for the first time, you may be shocked just how little of the code is used regularly in normal operation: the good old 80:20 rule applies – 80 per cent of the operational use only uses 20 per cent of the code – only the ratios might be much more extreme than this.

Tools will be really important here, to enable us to automatically run through a large number of tests and check the results. This becomes doubly important once we are into retesting following a system change – if humans have to run the test entering data it is tempting to skip a few tests because you 'know' that it will be all right on those tests. Such tools would be called **test harnesses**, containing either a **test-scripting** capability, or a **capture-replay** facility so once the tests have been run once manually they can then be re-run automatically.

Case Study 7.9 *System test plan for the library system*

Require tests with sufficient coverage to invoke all procedures at least once, including all database procedures used. Self instrument the code, placing dummy procedures between the application code and the system code (which we cannot instrument) which can act as stubs and be instrumented and invoked by a test harness for capture-replay purposes between the application code and system code. This will add considerably to the volume of code that must be produced.

1. Functional test of library logic

Start with an empty database, then load it with five realistic titles and ten books generating accession codes, borrow some of these, and return them.

2. Robustness

As for 1, but introduce errors, such as borrowing or returning the same book code twice. Also introduce errors by changing the database directly to remove material.

3. Volume testing

See how far you can load the database before it breaks, testing for correct functioning regularly as the volume builds up.

4. Stress testing

Anticipating more than one book code reader, see how rapidly they work, and see if combinations of borrowing, returning, and raising alarms will break the system.

Activity 7.7   *Object-oriented testing*

Should the fact that you are developing your system in object-oriented style make any difference to your testing?

Discussion
It shouldn't, but it does! Because of the intimate coupling of data and function within objects, testing can be more complex, though the details of why this should be the case is outside the scope of this book.

7.13 Acceptance and system release

Before new software is put into service, it needs to tested to see if it solves the original problem as described in the requirements statement that gave rise to its procurement. This **acceptance test** could take various forms:

- **Sample realistic data**: System tests may well use artificial data, with names like Xyz and ages like 999. At the very least the system needs to be tested now with the values that the users of the system would use. This kind of data is best obtained from the stakeholders using the systems that they currently use, perhaps capturing data for a whole cycle of use (say a month) to use for the acceptance test.
- **Parallel running**: The limiting form of the sample realistic data would be to run the new system in parallel with the system it is replacing – but this is both expensive and it may well be that there is no simple one-for-one replacement.
- **Alpha test**: Trial real use within the producing enterprise who developed the software. No business-critical work should be done using the software, though its use must be serious.
- **Beta test**: Like the alpha test, but is undertaken by some customer or potential customer. If the software does fail in use, it is essential to clear the defect as soon as possible.

Real usage, particularly in alpha and beta testing, can throw up startling surprises as real users use the software in ways that the developers never anticipated. Clearly, as many defects as possible should have been cleared during system testing before any users actually use the system. Acceptance testing is made more

> New systems and changed systems need to be tested comprehensively before being made available to users.

The new system must be tested to see that it does solve the original problem before being formally accepted.

difficult by the potential confusion between defects with respect to the original requirements statement and defects in that statement indicating that the real problem had not been fully understood.

Once users get to use the system they may only then understand what it is that they really need. This simple observation will be seen in Chapter 8 to be key to some approaches to developing software.

Once acceptance testing has been judged to have been passed, the system will be formally released and move into maintenance. For bespoke development the passing of acceptance testing may mark a final payment for the development, but also the start of any period of warranty.

Case Study 7.10 *Acceptance test plan for the library system*

There is no system we could run in parallel with, so the system should be tried out with a small set of real books used by real students as a trial – that is, a beta test. This should be a small trial, perhaps lasting a week, for which fifty books suitable for a particular age group have been prepared with codes and entered in the system following which students from the appropriate class would be encouraged to borrow and return books.

It would be important that all contingencies should be tested, including triggering of the alarm. If the system works without error for that week (i.e., there are no system crashes, failures to formally borrow trigger the alarm, and all functions are found to work), the system will be deemed to have been accepted, final contractual payment should be made, and the system can move into full-scale operation.

7.14 Maintenance and evolution

Once the system has been formally released, it enters the continuing process of software maintenance and software evolution. As they are discovered, defects need to be noted and possibly repaired, and existing features may need to be changed with new features added. All of this will be comprehensively covered in Chapter 9.

One important aspect of maintenance is its link to the preceding development. As development progresses, it produces a number of intermediate abstract descriptions of the software, such as design documents, unit specifications, and so on: these descriptions become very valuable during maintenance and evolution, since they provide an overview of the software and the way the parts fit together. Before you can change the software, you must understand it, not guess what might work and then hope. Clearly these documents need to be kept up to date, and updated appropriately each time a change is made to the system.

A system is not finalised when it is first released; it will evolve, and include enhancements and changes, in order to remain useful.

During development, other practices will have been adopted to ensure that software is easy to understand and change. Software elements will be given meaningful names, layout of documents and code will follow standards, and so on, as demanded by the project's quality plan, to be discussed in more detail in Chapter 12.

Case Study 7.11 *Maintenance plan for the library system*

Outline plan

Changes will only be made with agreement of all stakeholders.

All code and documents belonging to the system will be stored in a configuration management system (see Chapter 11) and changes will be controlled through this system.

High level specification and design documents will be maintained up to date each time the system is changed.

The costs of making changes will either be met directly by the customer making the request, or if of general benefit out of the maintenance payments of those having maintenance contracts.

The system may need periodic revision to keep it up to date with changing stakeholder needs and technologies (see Chapter 9). Maintenance of the system is likely to be subject to constraints (e.g., increasing complexity) and extra activities might have to be put in place (e.g., complexity control and other quality enhancing activities) in order to avoid the system becoming difficult to maintain.

7.15 Quality assurance

Throughout the development process we have just described, quality will be critically important. We need to constantly monitor the development not only to make sure that it is proceeding to cost and timescale, but also to be sure that quality is not being compromised as we proceed. In order to assure the technical quality of the software and other changes being introduced, we will undertake a range of quality enhancing procedures.

In these quality enhancing processes we distinguish between two different aspects – verification and validation. **Verification** is concerned whether the correct technical processes are being followed and whether the deliverable output from an activity is consistent with the input to that activity – for example that a unit of code is correct relative to the specification of the unit provided by the preceding design activity. By contrast, **validation** is concerned whether what is being produced does actually contribute to solving the stakeholder's problems. This can be neatly expressed by explaining that validation is concerned whether we are *building the right system*, while verification is concerned with whether we are *building the system right*.

We have already seen the testing of code, a procedure that we might like to think is redundant, but that is nevertheless necessary since people make mistakes and we need to check for these mistakes. Testing is only possible when we have software that can be executed and thus tested. Early in the life cycle all we have is documents, but we can carry out a process equivalent to testing on these documents by reviewing them from various perspectives. In these **reviews** (sometimes called *inspections*), we serve the interests of validation by involving stakeholders, and serve the interests of verification by involving technical development people.

We will see a lot more about quality and how it can be managed in Chapter 12.

Quality enhancing procedures are important in order that the quality of the software does not regress during its development.

Summing up

In this chapter we have focused on introducing the activities that are commonly carried out during the development of software. For people who have spent some time within the software industry, these activities and associated concepts will be well understood. But for people whose experience lies elsewhere it is vital that these concepts are understood if they are to be able to manage the procurement and use of software. Throughout this chapter we have illustrated the activities and concepts using a simple example, that of a school library system.

What we have seen is:

- all software development involves a number of typical activities which may be carried out in different orders depending upon the actual system and project;
- we must always understand what the problem is that we are trying to solve, articulating this as a set of requirements, and agreeing this and potential solutions with the stakeholders;
- an initial estimate of costs can be made as soon as the problem to be solved has been understood;
- software developers need a reasonably comprehensive specification of what 'the solution' must do in order to be able to develop the software;
- given a comprehensive specification of the software it becomes possible to give a reasonably accurate estimate of what it would cost to develop that software;
- it is important to decide early on what the architectural software components are and how these fit into the overall enterprise;
- the requirements specification and architectural design enable us to break down the work and schedule a project subject to resource constraints;
- design needs to proceed until small independent components of software have been specified;
- progress towards completion needs to be continually monitored both in terms of budget spent and task completion (this can signal the need for reprioritisation and replanning);
- units should be coded and tested as a single activity;
- we need to integrate a new system incrementally and systematically to be sure that when a problem arises the reason can be easily located;
- new systems and changed systems need to be comprehensively tested before being made available to users;
- the new system must be tested to see that it does solve the original problem before being formally accepted;
- a system is not finalised when it is first released; it will be evolved, including enhancements and changes, in order to remain useful;
- quality enhancing procedures are important in order that the quality of the software does not regress during its development.

In the next chapter we see a range of life cycle models in which the activities described in this chapter are done in different orders and with different emphases in order to overcome particular problems that can arise when developing software.

Exercises

1. The following is a simplified description of the process of collecting money for a charity organisation that helps the poor in areas in need and after natural or man-made disasters:

   > The charity collects payments from donors and sends them to their partners in developing countries. There are two types of donors: those who make an occasional donation using credit card or cheques and those regular donors who have activated direct-debit payments. The charity has a connection with a bank for the processing of occasional donations. Regular donations are processed only once by sending a form to the relevant bank or building society in order to activate the direct debit. A donor can cancel their direct debit instructions at any time. Once an occasional payment has been confirmed, a thank-you letter is sent to the donor. If the payment is denied by the bank (e.g., because of lack of funds) a letter is sent to the donor. Donors can 'ear-tag', if they so wish, their donations to particular countries. On a monthly basis, a list of countries and sums to be transferred is produced. Regular donors receive an annual statement of their donation, together with the annual newsletter and Season's greeting card of the charity. Donations coming from donors who are taxpayers are entitled to a top-up contribution from the government. For this, the charity holds a register of taxpayer donors. A request for top-up contribution is sent every month to an Inland Revenue office. There are weekly, monthly, quarterly reports to the charity's Managing Director and the Finance Officer and to the Board of Trustees, totaling the amounts received under the categories of occasional and regular giving. Occasional donors that have not been making donations in the last six months received a letter and a brochure informing about the charities activities and asking for further donations. In case of emergencies and disasters, all donors are sent a letter with an special appeal. If an occasional donor has not made a donation in the last two years, his/her details are automatically erased from the system.

   Based on this problem statement, you should draw a context diagram, a level 1 data-flow diagram and a data structure diagram for a possible solution, showing the automation boundary. Make any reasonable assumptions you need.

2. A crucial step in requirements analysis and elicitation is the identification of stakeholders. Indicate different classes of stakeholders that could be present in question 1 and how you would, as a project manager or system designer, deal which each of the different types of stakeholders.

3. Boehm's win–win approach can be used to deal with multiple stakeholders with sometimes inconsistent, even clashing views. Find out about Boehm's approach and summarise it in one or two paragraphs. (See B.W. Boehm and R. Ross, Theory-W Software Project Management Principles and Examples, *IEEE Transactions on Software Engineering*, 15, 7, 902–916.)

4. At any step in the software developing process there could be several alternatives for any intermediate products. Discuss how you could use the

weighted scorecard approach discussed in Chapter 2 in order to evaluate different architectural designs for the library system described in Chapter 7 and for the system in question 1.

5. Some process steps or activities can be done explicitly and others implicitly. For example, requirements elicitation and analysis could in theory be done based on conversations only, without any written document, with all the details and agreement in people's minds and sketches on paper. In your opinion, are there essential activities, in addition to the actual implementation or coding, which should be always done explicitly and in a given sequence? Justify your answer.

6. Case Study 3.2 summarised some of Petre's findings with regards to the way in which innovative people and teams go about their work. From the list of activities listed in Case Study 3.2, indicate which are clearly reflected in the software activities described in Chapter 7 and which aren't. Based on this, propose a software process for innovative teams which reflects all the activities these are believed to perform. Use DFD notation, described in Appendix A, to present your answer.

7. Consider different ways in which a change in the process, intended to be an improvement, can be evaluated and briefly explain each of them. For doing this take into account the discussion about modelling and measurement in organisations given in Chapter 1.

8. Write an outline test plan for the system of question 1.

9. Traceability between requirements and test cases can help to show that the system does what it is intended to do. Investigate, in software engineering texts, what can be done in order to minimise the risk of the system doing what it shouldn't.

10. Following Donald Shoen's concept of a reflective practitioner in Chapter 3, consider your own experience as software developer or your work in a software organisation and contrast it with what you have learnt in this chapter. To do so, write a brief summary (e.g., a set of bullet points) of the new things you have learned in this chapter regarding software activities. Highlight things that appear to contradict your previous assumptions. In your next assignment or project, what you would be doing in a different way?

11. Brian Fitzgerald wrote a paper in 1998 (An Empirical Investigation into the Adoption of Systems Development Methodologies. *Information & Management*, 34, 317–328), which reported the results of a postal survey indicating that the adoption of methodologies is not as common as it might be commonly thought, with sixty per cent of the respondents not using them at all. Only six per cent followed a methodology rigorously. Read this paper and compare and contrast its findings with what you have learnt about Suchman's 'situated action' in Chapter 2 and the role of tacit knowledge in organisations.

12. Consult references on UML and complete all of the activities of the chapter, drawing the UML diagrams requested.

Endnotes

1. UML – Unified Modelling Language. See the UML website http://www.uml.org, or consult any of the many excellent books on UML, for example Craig Larman (2002) *Applying UML and Patterns*. Pearson Education.
2. Search for 'brainstorming' on the web; you should find a number of organisations that offer training in brainstorming, and even software that you can use to support your brainstorming.
3. See, for example, S. Vaughn, J.S. Schumm, and J. Sinagub (1996) *Focus Group Interviews in Education and Psychology.* Sage Publications. Note that while brainstorming sessions are divergent, opening up possibilities, focus groups are convergent, closing down possibilities.
4. Tom DeMarco (1982) *Controlling Software Projects.* Yourdon Press.
5. Capers Jones (1991) *Applied Software Measurement.* McGraw-Hill.
6. A.J. Albrecht (1979) 'Measuring Application Development Productivity', *Proc IBM Application Development Symposium.* Monterey, California, Oct 1979, 83–92.
7. First described in J.A. Zachman (1987) 'A Framework for Information Systems Architecture', *IBM Systems Journal*, 26: 3, pp. 276–292, this was extended in J.F. Sowa and J.A. Zachman (1992) 'Extending and Formalizing the Framework for Information Systems Architecture', *IBM Systems Journal*, 31: 3, 590–616. The original paper was republished in the *IBM Systems Journal* in 1999, 38: 2&3, 454–470.
8. Mary Shaw and David Garlan (1996) *Software Architecture – Perspectives on an Emerging Discipline.* Prentice Hall.

8   Software processes

What we will study in this chapter

The sequential development process used as an example in Chapter 7 has been widely followed as the 'waterfall model'. This has been adopted and adapted to create many alternative software development processes; in spite of being highly prescriptive and thus hopefully predictable, these methods have difficulty in building software that is effective, useful, and built within budget and timescale.

In this chapter we will look at a range of the software development approaches that have arisen as alternatives, aimed at overcoming the acknowledged shortfalls of sequential methods. We will cover:

- alternative sequential and incremental methods;

- iterative, prototyping, and evolutionary methods that explore possible solutions aiming to converge on an acceptable solution;

- participative and user-centred methods that involve the intended users and beneficiaries;

- formal methods that significantly reduce the likelihood of errors during development;

- timeboxing methods that fix the cost and timescale and vary the functionality delivered;

- design-driven methods that build on known solutions to solve new problems;

- agile methods like eXtreme Programming that focus on the software developers and the code they produce;

- open source methods that deploy many developers in a loosely controlled yet effective process.

We examine the particular strengths of each process model and discuss what new problems these create in turn.

8.1 Introduction

In managing software within an administrative or business enterprise, you may only occasionally be involved in overseeing the development of completely new software, but you will most certainly be involved in procuring software by one or more of the routes described in Chapter 6, and with integrating that software with other software. For all of this you need to know how software is usually developed, so that you may appreciate the claims being made by suppliers of software, and be able to manage the integration of your new software once acquired. This chapter gives you that understanding.

In Chapter 7 we saw a range of activities that would typically need to be undertaken when developing software or procuring and adapting software for operational use. We looked at these activities in the context of developing a simple hypothetical library management system for a school, progressing through each activity in sequence. Let us start by looking at those typical activities, focusing on their essence in order to generalise them. Then in the rest of this chapter we will consider alternative sequences in which these activities could be undertaken in the process of developing successful software. The activities were:

- **Requirements elicitation** to understand what the stakeholders' problems are that may need software solution; while this must always be done, it could be that the understanding of what is needed only emerges after the system is in operation.

- **Requirements specification** to give a precise description of the software required ready for the software developers to start building the new system – or for the evaluation of ready-made systems to be purchased and then customised.

- **Estimation** of the effort required to undertake the work required – we saw some illustrations of what was needed in Chapter 7; this will be picked up in detail in Chapter 10.

- **Architectural design**, identifying the major building blocks of the system and how they interact; this needs to be done for any system that will be composed of more than one part – the parts may be human procedures as well as software, and may be purpose built or bought in from outside; once the parts have been acquired they will need to be integrated.

- **Project planning and control**, establishing a sequence in which the work will be done and ensuring that it does get done; this will be covered in more detail in Chapter 10.

- **Detailed design** – any component that needs to be developed, whether software or procedural, needs to be designed, that is thought about abstractly in terms of its constituent parts and how they interact; the design may be documented explicitly, or may simply be implicit in the programme code and as tacit knowledge of the developers.

- **Module coding**, writing the program in some compilable and executable code; this includes designing the module initially and testing the module afterwards.

- **System integration** – the various parts need to be made to work together; this is always necessary, and how easy this will be will depend upon the software architecture and extent to which the components actually do what was specified by the architecture; inevitably one aspect of this activity is the 'testing' that the components do connect and work together – and hence the alternative name of integration testing.

- **System testing**, the technical testing of a system or a major component with respect its specification, if any; even if no specification is available standard sources of failure can be explored.

- **Acceptance testing** – any contract for work to be done or goods to be supplied as described in Chapter 5 will conclude with an activity which formally accepts the goods or services as complete and discharges the contract; for software this is usually some trial use that represents operational use.

All software development processes consist of a number of typical activities being done in some prescribed sequence.

The sequence in which we have listed the activities above is the sequence in which we presented them in Chapter 7. In section 8.2 we will see a number of established methods that do advocate the simple linear sequential execution of these activities. However we will see that this simple linear sequence creates problems, and will look at arranging the activities in other sequences in order to overcome these problems. The sequence in which the activities are conducted, and the rationale underlying that sequence, is known as a **life cycle model** or **process model**.

Each activity produces a number of **work-products**, which might be given formal status as **deliverables** whose production become the **milestones** that mark the progress through the development process. We will see more of this in Chapter 10. Each deliverable will be subject to some review or inspection that confirms that the deliverable has been produced to acceptable quality – this may lead to changes and quality improvements before final formal acceptance.

The testing and review activities form part of a larger set of activities known as **verification** and **validation (V&V)**. Verification activities focus on the technical correctness of the software and other systems, while validation activities focus on ensuring that the system being built achieves the purpose intended. We will see that validation concerns often motivate our different process models. Verification and validation in turn are often treated as parts of a larger quality management system, to be covered in depth in Chapter 12.

The work products may be documents, or software, or other items. Documents will conform to some standard which defines what should be covered in the document and what notations should be used. The notations help document the aspect of the software being described at that point – we commonly refer to this description as a **model**.

The models and notations will themselves conform to standards that cover all the models to be developed during the software development process. We have been following a simple convention in this book, using data-flow diagrams and data structure diagrams conforming to the 'standard' set out in Appendix A. Usually the set of notations to be used is much more comprehensive – an example of full data-flow and data modelling notations are included in the structured systems analysis and design method (**SSADM**[1]); developed during the 1980s and stabilised in its final version 4.2 in 1995, it is now known as 'business system development'. During the 1990s a number of proprietary methods arose to support the development of object-oriented software, and in the early 2000s the **Object Management Group** (OMG) unified these to create **unified modelling language (UML)** which standardises the modelling notations. UML does not prescribe any particular way of using the models standardised – this is done in the Rational Unified Process and to a lesser extent in OMG's Model-Driven Architecture, both of which are described later in this chapter.

Models using these notations are very likely to be produced using a software tool, which also stores them in a repository – these tools are commonly known as **IDEs** or **Integrated Development Environments**, though in the past thay have been known by the rather more all-embracing **Integrated Project Support Environments** or **IPSEs**. These IDEs and IPSEs are very likely to support not just modelling using these notations, but also to impose some process model concerned with the sequence in which the particular models are produced.

> All work products should conform to some standard and include models using some standardised notations.

8.2 Classic process models – sequential and incremental

The simplest set of life-cycle process models are based on viewing the activities described above as taking place in their 'natural' order, as listed above, followed by a process of evolution or maintenance.

When drawn out in a process diagram, as in Figure 8.1, it is known as the **waterfall** life cycle. This process model encapsulates the standard practices that arose in the early days of software development between the 1950s and 1970s, matching the views of engineering industries that were finding themselves increasingly involved in software as an important component of their engineering. This waterfall life cycle is often attributed to Royce[2] though some people claim that he should not be given the credit for inventing it – this sequential model has long been part of the tacit knowledge of engineering.

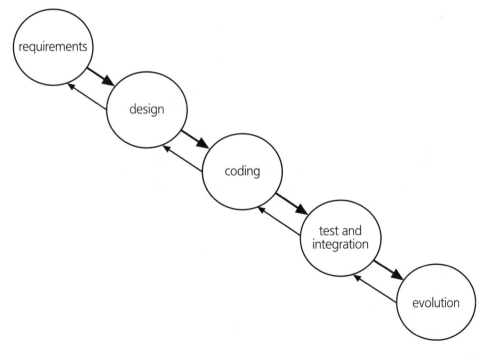

Figure 8.1

The waterfall life cycle

The main flow ('waterfall') of activity is from top left to bottom right, shown with the heavy arrows. The deliverables flow along these arrows between activities. However, we must recognise that in any process like this there will be some iteration or feedback: as deliverables get reviewed and then used, some reference back to the earlier activity and some rework, will be necessary. This is shown by the very light arrows, to emphasise the normal expectation of a smooth flow 'down the waterfall'.

An early variant on this waterfall life cycle was the recognition of parallelism in the development process, particularly with the parallel development of database and functional elements, as in Figure 8.2. The importance of the user interface was not appreciated initially, but when this did get recognised, the parallel development of user interfaces was also included. The many formalised methodologies that arose during the 1970s and 1980s allowed for these parallel developments, and this recognition persists today, as indeed it should, recognising as it does the basic generic architecture of software seen in the last chapter.

Figure 8.2 simply shows the forward flow of the work-products, but of course as before there will be some backwards flow as rework happens, and also some lateral flow between activities as the design or coding of one major component requires agreement with designers and coders of another component. Note that a small amount of architectural design will have happened during the requirements activity, sufficient at least to have identified the three architectural components for the application: its functions, its user interface, and its database.

These sequential methods clearly work for relatively simple systems, such as the library system used as the case study in Chapter 7. However, as systems have

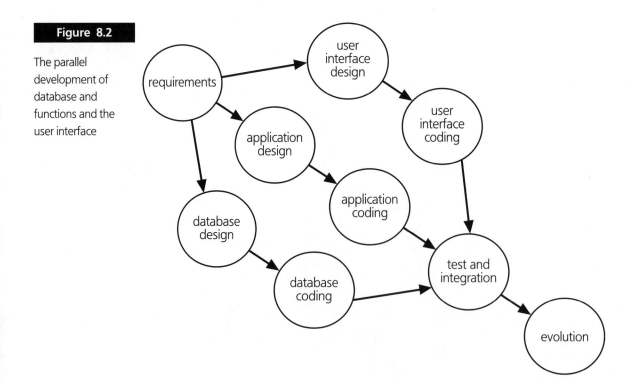

Figure 8.2

The parallel development of database and functions and the user interface become larger and more complex technically, and aimed to support less routine aspects of an enterprise's activities, they have had difficulties.

Case Study 8.1 shows a very popular sequential method, the **Rational Unified Process (RUP)**. RUP is an example of an **object-oriented (OO)** method: when object-oriented programming became popular in the 1980s through programming languages like Smalltalk, C++, and later Java, this was followed by a number of attempts to modify earlier methods for use with OO programming. What characterised many of these early OO methods was their retreat from any consideration of the total process within which a part would be automated using software, to a strong focus just upon the software system and its interaction with the external world. RUP, even in the early version given in Case Study 8.1, is better than most, and does give some regard for the business context within which the software will be used, though not nearly enough. RUP was developed by the Rational company, now part of IBM; OMG has also developed its own method for using UML in the initial development of OO systems – MDA or Model-Driven Architecture.

> Sequential process models work well for small, well-defined problems.

Case Study 8.1 *The Rational Unified Process*

Object-oriented methods arose to prominence during the 1980s, with many leading consultants advocating their own processes for doing these. The **Rational Software Corporation** was founded in 1981, and over the next four years recruited three of the most prominent experts of that time: James Rumbaugh, Ivar Jacobson, and Grady Booch. Together these 'three amigos' developed the Unified Modelling Language (UML) for representation of object-oriented software designs, and then the Rational Unified Process (RUP) to prescribe how software should be developed using UML. The RUP has evolved over the years, and the version we describe here was promulgated around 2000 as a wall chart.

The process is described at three levels: a top level in Figure 8.3 as a simple sequence drawn as a cycle, as has been done by many people before.

Figure 8.3

Top level processes of RUP

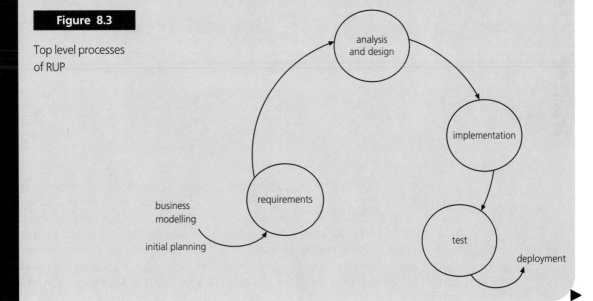

The second level is a sequential data flow with some parallelism for each of the top-level processes, indicating also the allocation of each activity to a particular class of software engineer – architect, designer, system analyst, and so on, as we saw in Chapter 2. Figure 8.4 shows the sub-process for requirements analysis. Note that beside each process activity we have placed the acronym of the class of engineer who will undertake this activity.

At the bottom level each activity is briefly described. For example, the description of 'elicit stakeholders needs' would be:

- determine sources of requirements;
- gather information;
- conduct requirements workshops;
- evaluate your results.

The Rational Software Corporation was bought by IBM in 2003, and RUP is now articulated differently as a framework which can be adapted to a particular project, in which iteration is an important feature (see later in the chapter for iterative development).

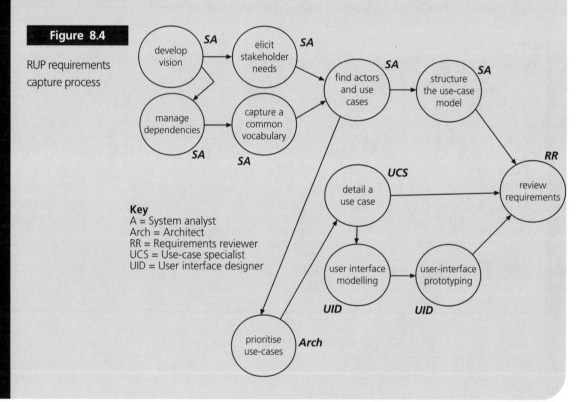

Figure 8.4

RUP requirements capture process

Key
A = System analyst
Arch = Architect
RR = Requirements reviewer
UCS = Use-case specialist
UID = User interface designer

A second variant of the sequential lifecycle arose in the early 1980s from the recognition of the importance of the levels of design and corresponding testing, as manifest in UK defence procurement engineering standards of the time. This led David Brewer to invent the **Vee life cycle** model, shown in Figure 8.5. Here we have split the requirements activity and design activity into their component elicitation, specification, architectural design and detailed (module) design activities, and have also decomposed test and integration into its sub-activities.

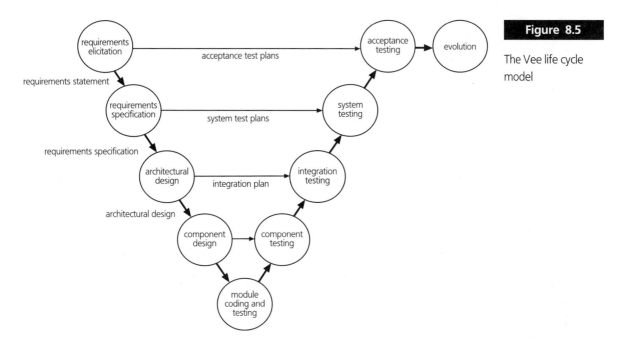

Figure 8.5

The Vee life cycle model

Note the horizontal lines showing a forward flow of test plans and test case designs; in some sense we have a process with redundancy, with two descriptions of the proposed system. One description of the system is intentional, a description of what is required in terms of rules and prescriptions. The other description is extensional, a comprehensive set of examples of the system in use. During testing the final system based on the intentional description is compared with the extensional description captured in the test scripts. This observation probably seems a little abstract here, but will take on more force later when we come to consider Agile methods and Test-Driven Development, where the initial requirement may be captured as scenarios of typical use.

So far these are all variants of that basic waterfall life cycle, making important distinctions between different parts of the system, but not changing the essential sequential nature of the process. The next step was the recognition that in practice not every aspect of the system needs to be delivered at the same time – it had become quite common to deliver a succession of releases of the system, with each successive release containing more functions while also correcting or modifying the functions of the earlier releases. This was formalised as the **incremental** process model shown in Figure 8.6.

Activity 8.1   *The limits of sequential methodologies*

The methodologies of the 1970s and 1980s were characterised by the large prescriptions of required practices, what activities should be done and when, and what should be produced, including the notations to be used. Large multivolume methodology manuals were produced, placed on shelves, and expensive tools and training courses were purchased, in the hope that through following the prescriptions good quality software would be produced at affordable cost and to a predictable timescale. Through the sheer power of rational planning and systematic work practices the difficulties encountered in projects could be overcome.

What would you expect to happen with the sequential methodologies described above, as the problems being tackled get increasingly larger and more complex? Relate your answer to your own experience of the methodologies, as well as to the discussions about the limits of rationality in Chapter 1.

Discussion

The heavy rationality and prescription is likely to alienate software developers who will feel as if they are being treated like machines. In addition the difficulties and challenges that arise naturally in software development, and which make software development an exciting activity, are not handled by the methodology, which then hinders rather than helps the software engineers. Room must be left for human insight and problem-solving, processes that cannot be automated or captured in prescribed procedures.

As a result, it is all too common for methodology manuals to gather dust on their shelves, and never be looked at, and for the software tools bought to support them to have gone largely unused. They become 'shelfware' because the difficulties being tackled are not those anticipated in the methodology.

Sequential process models and the methodologies built upon these have reached the limits of rationality, and are not able to handle very large and complex projects.

8.3 Resolving uncertainties – iteration, evolution and participation

In the sequential approaches to software development it is assumed that it is possible to identify the system requirements in full beforehand, and then to

---

Figure 8.6

An incremental process model

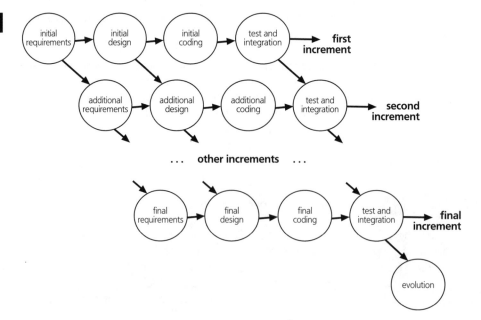

use this as the foundation for further development, the design, coding and testing. However, it may not work out like that. It may not be clear at the start what the needs of the organisation are, these needs may change with the passage of time, and new technologies may offer new opportunities. Furthermore, what the organisation really needs may not be clear until the system has been built – for most people it is difficult to envisage the way a system will work in practice simply from descriptions of the system, the new system needs to be available and in use before the full impact can be assessed. The use of the new system may suggest new possibilities. And so on. We need an approach that is more exploratory, that does not demand that immutable requirements are laid down at the start. **Iterative** and **evolutionary methods** are a response to this need.

An early idea was **prototyping**. In order to resolve problems concerning requirements the idea is to build a prototype of the system, or a part of the system, to act as a focus for discussion and agreement with stakeholders. The prototype may itself be very simple, hardly more than a few typical screens that might be encountered when using the system. Based on reviews of the prototype, further prototypes might be built, until a clear understanding of what is needed and how it would fit into the stakeholder's work has been reached. At the end of the process the prototype may form the 'agreement' or a formal requirements specification may be written – and then development continues sequentially as before. This is shown in Figure 8.7.

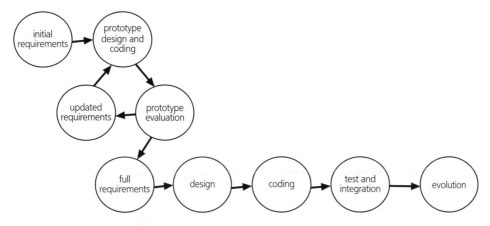

Figure 8.7

The prototyping process model

Prototyping used in this way to clarify requirements still leaves a normal development at the end with the delays that that introduces and the attendant risk that needs may have changed by the time the real system is delivered. Why not simply use the prototype? Well, this may be difficult, the prototype may not include all the functions, and it certainly will not be fully engineered with the robustness and security that would be required for the final system. But the basic idea is right, why not let the prototype evolve into the full operational system? This leads us to the evolutionary process model of Figure 8.8. Note that evolution and maintenance is not shown, since these are simple further iterations of the same process, so the process model shown in Figure 8.8 *is* the full life cycle from the cradle to the grave.

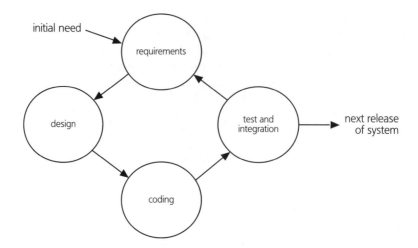

Figure 8.8

The evolutionary or iterative process model

The common practice in prototyping and evolutionary processes, apart from the iteration, is the involvement of users and stakeholders throughout the development process as part of the test and evaluation activity. This is clearly important in order to address the risk of misunderstood requirements, recognising that the software systems being built are for people, the software is but part of a **socio-technical system**. In the wider movement of the development of socio-technical systems, mostly associated with researchers and workers in Scandinavia, there has been a strong emphasis on worker participation in the design and development of systems intended to support their work. Not only would stakeholders be involved in testing and reviewing, they would also be involved in other aspects of the development, joining the team and thus adding to the team an essential usage perspective. This was very popular during the 1980s, and has come to be known as **participative design** or **participative development**, PD for short. A very active advocate of participative approaches has been Enid Mumford[3] and her ETHICS method, described in Case Study 8.2.

Case Study 8.2 *The participative ETHICS method*

The ETHICS (Effective Technical and Human Implementation of Computer-based Systems) method aims to make computer systems successful though involving people in the design and change of their own working practices. She distinguishes between consultative participation where senior management and labour union leaders reach agreement, representative participation where members from all groups involved in the change are able to influence the nature of the new systems, and consensus participation where everybody associated with the business processes involved is able to play a part in the design of the new system. No one should suffer from the changes that happen, and as many people as possible should gain. The ETHICS method has the following systematic steps:[4]

- *Diagnosing user needs and problems, focusing on short- and long-term efficiency, job satisfaction and quality.*

- *Setting efficiency, effectiveness, job satisfaction and quality objectives.*

- *Developing a number of alternative design strategies which will assist the* chosen efficiency, effectiveness, job satisfaction and quality objectives.

- Choosing the strategy which best achieves all of these objectives.
- Choosing hardware and software, and designing the system in detail.
- Implementing the new system.
- Evaluating its success once it is operational. (pp. 38–39)

ETHICS has been adopted by a number of organisations, particularly for requirements capture in its Quick-ETHICS form. Mumford in defending ETHICS wrote 'One of the most powerful counterforces to the scientific management approach has been provided by the socio-technical school of systems design.' (p. 44)

Scientific management is taylorism, as discussed in Chapter 2, and Mumford is a member of the socio-technical movement.

However, while socio-technical design and PD seem great ideas in principle, they do not always work out in practice. The participating user can 'go native' and take on the beliefs of the software engineers, or the voice of the user can still go unheard. In 1993 Clement and Van den Besselaar[5] surveyed a number of projects, arguing that

The focus of participatory design (PD) is not only the improvement of the information system, but also the empowerment of workers so they can codetermine the development of the information system and of their workplace. (p. 29)

They conclude:

The experiences from the projects reported here offer some encouragement and guidance for further development of PD. The basic tenets of PD are seen to work in a variety of settings. Researchers report that users have become better informed about the nature of information technology and more self-confident in taking initiative with it. Several of the computer systems that have resulted appear to function well from the user's perspective and are still in operation. Systems development approaches specifically suited to supporting PD activities are also gaining acceptance. However, PD is still characterised by isolated projects with few signs that it leads to self-sustaining processes within work settings. While in part this reflects short-term project aims, the reasons for this appear mainly to do with organizational inertia and resistance. The main challenge now for PD is to deal effectively with the political and ideological aspects of the broader organizational contexts on which PD initiatives depend for their long-term survival. The dilemma remains that without organizational reform in the direction of greater democratisation at all levels, the knowledge and commitment that PD can stimulate in users will ultimately reinforce patterns that limit the growth of their capabilities and thus undermine further initiative. The projects evaluated here suggest that an increased and positive role for management PD would be useful. A careful involvement with management, without abandoning the desirability of an independent perspective, could open up important possibilities for PD. Only by giving participation the meaning of full engagement in vital organizational affairs is the process likely to flourish. (p. 36)

As identified by Clement and Van den Besselaar, the main factor preventing the self-sustaining uptake of PD is the 'inertia' of organisational culture. If there are political inequalities in an organisation then PD will not work, it will become a form of tokenism, and be recognised as such, losing credibility. There are many subtle ways in which some participants may not be able to express their views, and therefore not participate fully. To expect equality of input, and, more particularly, equality of representation in the final product, would be naive.

Participative design is one form of what is now known as user-centred design. While participative design arose out of the socio-technical movement concerned with ensuring that the functions of the system were socially appropriate, user-centred design arose out of concern for the usability of systems at the level of the interactions between the computer and its user.

This whole area of system usability became crystallised in the publication of two books on user interface design, by Ben Schneidermann[6] and by Jakob Neilsen,[7] that have since become seminal. What they advocated was pretty obvious, that the interfaces should be consistent, using words and images that were understandable to the user, and in general seem natural and obvious and not require extended training. Around the same time Don Norman[8] gave us the concept of **affordance**, that an icon or interface object's visual appearance should suggest the function. Alan Cooper,[9] who developed Visual Basic, wrote an excellent book explaining the various devices that had become commonplace in interfaces.

Since then there have been some major disasters, including a near catastrophe at a nuclear power plant and the crash of an airplane, that have been attributed to inadequate design of the human interface to the software. At a more mundane level, e-commerce has led to concern about the design of websites, to turn visits to the site into purchases of the services on offer. This has led engineers involved in interface design into involving users in the design of systems, conducting usability trials with contextual enquiries, focus groups, and observations. This is in effect giving more focus in requirements analysis to the actual operators of the systems, and building the system so that the way that it will be used fits those intended users, trying out the system and changing it in response to feedback. While there are many good books about this, those by Carol Barnum[10] and Mike Kuniavsky[11] can be recommended, with the book by Helen Sharp and others[12] filling in some of the psychological and sociological background.

We see in participative development and user-centred design the software counterpart of the community architecture we saw in Chapter 1. It is one of a number of ways of responding to the problems of excessive rationality embodied in methodologies such as those described above, and particularly those in section 8.2.

Activity 8.2	*Motivation in prototyping and participation*

Drawing upon the knowledge of human motivation you gained in Chapter 3, describe how you would expect software engineers to react to prototype development processes and the participation of users in that process. What have you observed in practice, or do you think would happen in practice?

Discussion
Prototype development offers three things of importance to the software engineer:

- interaction with people and their problems;
- a reduction in uncertainty concerning the usefulness of the software;
- a short delay between producing code and seeing something working.

We saw the importance of meeting social needs in discussion around general motivation and Maslow's needs hierarchy. Making software production into a social process is very important for motivation.

We saw the other two factors in our discussion of cross-cultural factors, following Hofstede and Trompenaars. We saw there that while some people can handle uncertainty, others cannot. We saw that this ability to handle uncertainty as a general cultural trait, with members of some cultures better able to handle uncertainty, but clearly everybody in some measure has difficulties with uncertainty and would like to avoid it.

The third factor related to long-term and short-term orientation. Again we saw this as a factor that varied between cultures, but is equally appropriate when considering individuals. Everybody to greater or lesser extent wants to influence the way that they work, and prototyping offers this (as indeed do Open Source and Agile methods, to be covered later).

The evolutionary and iterative process model shown in Figure 8.8 can be viewed as a quasi-sequential model in which all the work products are passed round from one activity to the next in sequence. This means that during coding, for example, if a change in requirements or design is proposed, this must be passed on to the next iterative cycle. But it is tempting to simply change the code – and then abstract from the code the design and requirements changes that were implicit in the code. This is **reverse engineering** as seen in Chapter 6. Modern software development tools can support this, enabling developing to move forwards and backwards to give us a flexible totally iterative process that is known as **round-trip software engineering**.

Involve users in a participative process to reduce requirements risks.

When we became concerned about our requirements, concerned that we might not fully capture those at the start of a sequential development process, we were focusing on risk. What if we got the requirements wrong, and built the wrong system? We iterated around the requirements in order to mitigate that risk. But what about other risks, like adopting a new technical approach, or building a system much larger than any previous system? We also need to explore these, and this led Barry Boehm to propose the spiral model[13] for software development, a model that captured the enthusiasm of many software engineers. This is described in Case Study 8.3. This Spiral model does not yield a set prescribed practice to follow, but rather generates insight into how software is produced.

Iterate to control risk, focusing on the highest risks in early iterations.

Case Study 8.3 *Boehm's Spiral model*

The figure below shows the original form of the spiral. Many people now draw it differently to serve particular purposes, but the essence remains the same – iteration. Boehm comments in his original paper:

The major distinguishing feature of the spiral model is that it creates a risk-driven approach

to the software process rather than a primarily document-driven or code-driven process. (p. 61)

In Figure 8.9, the project progresses round the spiral clockwise, starting in the centre. The radial dimension from the centre outwards represents the accumulated cost to date, so that each

▶

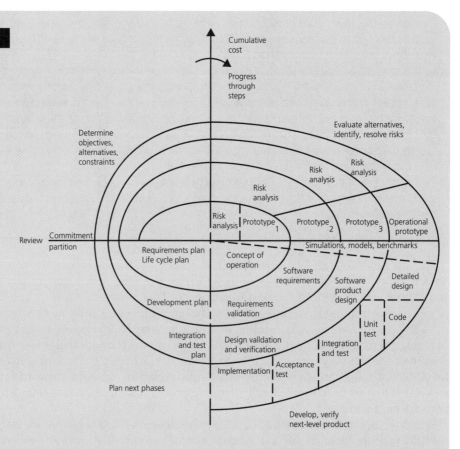

Figure 8.9

Boehm's original Spiral model. Adapted from B. Boehm (1988) 'A Sprial Model of Software Development and Enhancement, *Computer*, 21(5), May, 61–72. © IEEE 1988.

successive cycle of the spiral moves outwards as it adds to that total cost so far.

A typical cycle consists of the sequence of steps, roughly one of these steps in each quadrant of the cycle:

- identify the objectives of this cycle, and alternative solutions and any constraints;
- evaluate alternatives, identifying areas of uncertainty and resolve these by appropriate means, following up any new uncertainties revealed and in need of exploration;
- then follow normal waterfall-type activities, as seen in Chapter 7;
- end the cycle with a review of everything done in that cycle, aiming to get commit-

ment of all stakeholders to the next cycle – or to terminating the project.

The next cycle may partition the work to be done, and have many parallel spirals.

Towards the end of the paper Boehm claims:

All of the projects fully using the system have increased their productivity at least 50 per cent. (p. 69)

A claim like this made today would be viewed with great sceptism, but at that time the industry was just beginning to move from a chaotic regime to one in which management did think about the process and attempt to control it.

8.4 Resolving uncertainties – formal methods

In section 8.3 above we looked at how uncertainties with respect to requirements could be resolved by using processes which were iterative or evolutionary and involved participation. The uncertainty being addressed was that of 'building the right system', the focus of validation activities.

However there is also uncertainty in the process of building the system technically, 'building the system right', the focus of verification activities. Given a specification of the system to be built, how can you be sure that you do deliver a system that conforms to that specification? A complete strand of software engineering research and practice has focused on this, spurred on by concern for safety and mission-critical systems, and the losses that a failure of these would incur.

Good software engineers have always thought carefully about their designs and programs, reasoning about them to convince themselves that they will do what is intended before they ever try them out. This kind of reasoning is similar to the reasoning used in mathematical proof, and people very early on turned to mathematics for inspiration, to 'prove' the correctness of their software. A number of formalisms were developed to help with this: the **Vienna Development Method (VDM)**[14] arising in Europe in the 1980s, and **Z**[15] arising in the UK a little later.

Many other notations have since been developed, some of them very elegant indeed. Unfortunately there have also been exaggerated claims both about the efficacy of the approaches, and about the prospective widescale employment of mathematicians in the development of software. Clearly mathematical proofs are fallible, even when undertaken by mathematicians in the pursuit of mathematics. Proofs cannot guarantee the correctness of the software they claim to have proved. In Chapter 1 we discussed this as an example of the breakdown of rationality. The approach fails because of the size of problems in need of proof, and uncertainties where the software has contact with the physical and social world.

Nevertheless, mathematical reasoning and related notations would be used for small critical regions of code, where the extra expense in developing the software can be justified by the consequences of any failure of the software. This extra attention does seem to improve the software, though whether this is because of the mathematical style of reasoning, or just because of the extra attention paid, is not clear.

8.5 Flexible about functions – timeboxing and rapid application development

If we are going to develop a system iteratively, we know that we can always defer functions from the current iteration to some later iteration. This means that for the current iteration we can focus on the currently most important functions, and postpone those that are less important. In doing this we could fix the delivery schedule, the timescale, or even the costs, and vary just the functions that will be delivered. This is usually explained by a triangle with vertices of functions, costs, and timescale, as shown in Figure 8.10.

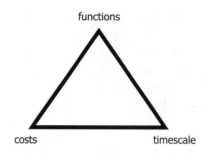

Figure 8.10

The function–cost–timescale triangle

Any software development process must deliver a stated set of functions or requirements at some cost and within some timescale. However, as we will see later in Chapter 10, it is not possible to predict accurately either the costs or the timescale for delivering a system with a given set of functions, and typically what happens is that in order to deliver the agreed functions the delivery date is extended as costs increase. However, focusing on this triangle, we realise that it need not be so: we could fix any two of the vertices and simply vary the third to fit. So why not vary the functions and fix the costs and timescales? In other words, deliver what we can by the date agreed and with the costs agreed.

This leads to the principle of **timeboxing**. We keep the elapsed time to delivery constant, as well as the resources or costs, while varying only what is delivered. Varying the functionality is justified on the basis of the 80/20 rule – that 80 per cent of the benefit from a system can be gained with 20 per cent of the development effort. Requirements are prioritised into essential, important, desirable, and deferred. All essential functions must be delivered at the end of the timebox, while as many of the important and desirable functions are delivered as possible. Each timebox is relatively short, just four to six weeks, and a complete development process model then consists of a number of timeboxes in sequence.

If we lay out each iterative cycle of the iterative development process seen in Figure 8.8, and place a timebox round each iterative cycle, we get **Rapid Application Development**, or **RAD**. RAD has had a significant impact upon software development practice, and takes a variety of different forms. One significant form is the Dynamic Systems Development Method (DSDM) described in Case Study 8.4.

Case Study 8.4 *Dynamic Systems Development Method*

The Dynamic Systems Development Method (DSDM) is owned by the DSDM Consortium, which was established in 1994 as a not-for-profit organisation. Their website http://www.dsdm.org contains a wealth of information. They see DSDM as a framework for rapid software development methods, driven by a number of principles, including:

- team effort and decision-making involving both customers and IT professionals;
- frequent delivery of products;
- quality as fitness for purpose and technical robustness;
- incremental and iterative development and delivery;

- testing integral to the process.

  The core techniques include timeboxing, but also:

- careful prioritisation of objectives;
- modelling of the software to explore business understanding;
- prototyping as part of the method;
- 'facilitated workshops';

- systematic testing throughout the process;
- configuration management;

deployed within the five phases of feasibility study, business study, functional model iteration, design and build, and implementation.

DSDM now describe themselves as an Agile method (see later in this Chapter), emphasising this on their website.

| Activity 8.3 | *Timeboxing versus the Spiral model* |

Timeboxing and RAD advocate doing the most important features of a system first, invoking the 80/20 rule, whereas the spiral view of software development would advocate doing the highest risk parts of the system first. How can these two views of the software development be reconciled?

Discussion

Superficially they do seem completely contradictory, until you realise that in timeboxing we are recognising that the major risk for a project is that it does not get delivered on time and within budget. Thus you can view each cycle of the spiral as being a timebox aimed at controlling the risk of slippage and cost escalation, delivering the most important functions at the end of each cycle before setting off on another cycle to produce then next most important set of functions.

It is very difficult to produce software to an agreed specification, timescale, and cost – vary the set of functions delivered using timeboxing to facilitate this.

8.6 Design-driven processes

As experience with software has grown over the years, it has become apparent that while most software is unique, it is also very similar to other software that has previously been developed and proven in use. How can past experience of similar systems be built upon when building a new system? Early attempts at tackling this focused on software reuse and components – the economic and quality advantages of this were focussed on in Chapter 6, as a motivation for acquiring software by buying part or all of it rather than building it bespoke. Approaches that simply focused on general-purpose components have proved unsuccessful, but the more general idea of building on knowledge and experience gained in solving earlier problems has proved fruitful.

It was realised really very early in the history of software development, as early as the 1950s and 1960s, that in programming computers you constantly came across the same kind of problem which you then solved in the same kind of way. These solutions were so common that the makers of computers then built some of these into the computer hardware itself, and others found their way into early programming languages. But this only works for common situations that repeat exactly as before.

A programmer often does not want exact reuse, but reuse of the design ideas adapted to their particular situation. Standard ideas in software design are usually passed on as tacit knowledge from experts to less experienced programmers. During the early 1990s people began to realise that this experience could be written down and passed on explicitly, using the ideas of patterns from the architectural work of Christopher Alexander.[16] Patterns[17] arose in the object-oriented programming movement, and it is usual practice to represent these using object-oriented notations, usually UML, which are very suitable for this purpose. The model–view–controller pattern of Case Study 8.5 itself arose in the earliest of object oriented programming systems, Smalltalk.

Case Study 8.5 *The model–view–controller pattern*

Suppose that you want to build a personal budgeting system that allows you to plan the way you will use your money. It should allow you to set a number of budget headings, and then to record under each the sum of money you are allocating — either the absolute amount or as a percentage of your income. The allocations should be capable of being displayed in a bar chart, in a pie chart, or as a spreadsheet. These requirements are illustrated in Figure 8.11.

The primary representation of the data at the bottom of Figure 8.11 contains the budget headings and the absolute figures in pounds sterling. The percentages and various displays are generated from this primary data. This primary representation forms the model, while the others form the views. The model can be changed through any view, for example, by changing figures in the spreadsheet view, or by dragging lines in the pie-chart and bar-chart views. This capability is the input or controller aspect of the pattern.

This is a commonly recurring problem, maintaining a number of representations or views of

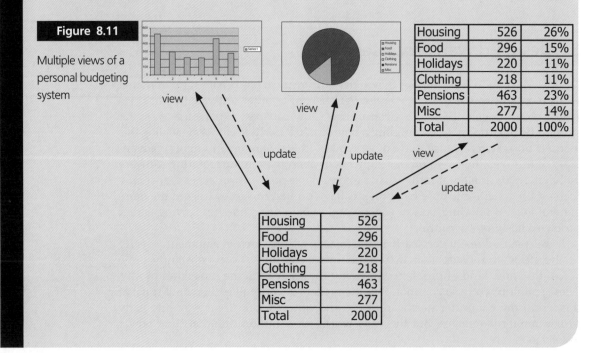

Figure 8.11

Multiple views of a personal budgeting system

Housing	526	26%
Food	296	15%
Holidays	220	11%
Clothing	218	11%
Pensions	463	23%
Misc	277	14%
Total	2000	100%

Housing	526
Food	296
Holidays	220
Clothing	218
Pensions	463
Misc	277
Total	2000

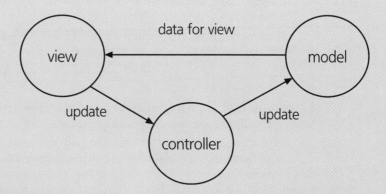

Figure 8.12

The MVC pattern

data in step with each other, while permitting updates in any representation which must then be propagated to the other representations. We divide the system into three parts as in Figure 8.12.

The basic idea here is simple — views are generated from the data held in the model, whenever some input through a controller changes the primary data of the model, the model then informs all views and all controllers so that they in turn can update their representation of the data.

Using this pattern we enable future developments of the system, for example to add figures generated in other currencies, and to allow more sophisticated interactions to happen (such as keeping some figures fixed while others vary). Porting of the software to various digital personal organisers may also be envisaged, as is sharing the system over a network. The pattern gives an abstract model of the software that enables this to be done relatively easily.

Patterns are the externalisation of the tacit knowledge of experienced designers, making them accessible to other less experienced designers as part of an industry-wide knowledge creating enterprise. At the start of their book on patterns, Buschmann *et al.*[17] wrote:

Patterns help you build on the collective experience of skilled software engineers. They capture existing, well-proven experience in software development and help promote good design practise. Every pattern deals with a specific, recurring problem in the design or implementation of a software system. Patterns can be used to construct software architectures with specific properties. (p. 1)

Software design patterns are not prescriptive — you can take them or leave them; you choose to use them only if they benefit your design or some other activity. To help you select a pattern, it is normal to catalogue them using a fixed format such as the following.

Name: And all alternative names in use.

Motivation: Why the pattern is useful and important, perhaps illustrated with a real-world example.

Applicability or *context*: The situations in which the pattern can be applied.

Problem: The actual design problem that the pattern addresses.

Solution: The principles involved in solving the problem.

Structure: The class diagram for the solution.

Collaborations or *dynamics*: One or more interaction diagrams to show how it works.

Participants: Textual definitions of the object classes involved.

Consequences: Any trade-offs involved.

Implementation: Any pitfalls you might meet, or special techniques you might use.

Sample code: Code fragments to help the implementation, originally in C++ or Smalltalk, but now increasingly in Java.

Variants and *related patterns*: Similar patterns and specialisations of this pattern; patterns that solve similar problems; patterns that could help implement this one.

Known uses: Such as reference sites, to show where used and thereby build up confidence and illustrate applicability.

Spread software
design best practice
through the use of
software design
patterns.

Patterns have given us a very powerful means of passing on best practices in software design: experienced software designers and programmers have proved very open in documenting their experience as patterns and having this published. Patterns can be used in any of the software development processes discussed within this chapter.

Most patterns are aimed at facilitating the low level design of programs, but some patterns take an overall architectural view of the software, in the way that the model–view–controller does. Another well known architectural example is **CORBA**, the **Common Object Request Broker Architecture**, developed by the Object Management Group for distributed systems. Model–view–controller and CORBA are general purpose, but often these architectural patterns become application-specific, and in this form are commonly called application frameworks or simply **frameworks**. Because of this association with applications, frameworks are often seen as commercially sensitive, capturing the know-how of the enterprise, though some have been published in sufficient detail for them to be useful for others producing similar applications.

It frequently happens that a company wants to produce many similar software systems. For example, engines in motor cars are controlled by an on-board computer using quite sophisticated software. Different engines and cars require slightly different engine-control software, but all engine-controllers are essentially the same. A manufacturer of engine-control software can produce a series of engine-controllers for different customers, reusing major parts of the software from customer to customer with only those parts peculiar to the particular customer being different. Using the jargon of engineering manufacture, this is known as a **product line**, a line of products that differ only in detail.[18]

Developing product lines for software began in the mid 1980s, mostly in the defence sector where the costs and reliability of routine weapons systems gave a lot of concern.[19] The methods moved from defence to the civil sector, and by the late 1990s the practice of product lines had become established for normal commercial systems as well, for example, in the SanFrancisco project of IBM.[20]

The way to develop product lines is to build upon the idea of frameworks. There are a number of steps that need to be undertaken.

1. *Product-line initiation and domain analysis.* Before a product line development begins, there will have been a recognition that there is a class of commonly recurring software systems where solutions do not differ much from each other. This then leads onto domain analysis, a form of requirements elicitation in which existing systems in the domain are examined and domain experts are consulted. The area in which the product line will operate is very thoroughly analysed to obtain the general customer needs and the terminology that is normally used, leading on to general models of data and process, the **domain model**.

2. *Architecture specification.* Further analysis then leads to the architecture for the product line. There may be several such reference architectures or frameworks produced. These are further elaborations of the domain model to add detail, particularly about the prospective implementation, and with flexibility in mind. Each reference architecture will include any encoding necessary to make the architecture work once components for deployment in the architecture have been decided upon.

3. *Component collection.* As with a framework, each reference architecture will be accompanied by a repository of candidate components that could be used in the architecture. Nevertheless, it must be recognized that complete coverage is not possible or desirable, and that some new components and glue code may need to be written for a particular use of the architecture. All components in the repository must be appropriately documented.

These three steps, each very complex and difficult, leave us in a position to produce software systems for which the product line was created. For this the following four further steps are required, each of which must be repeated for each new product in the line.

4. *Specific-requirements capture.* The requirements for a new product are captured, as specialisations and extensions of the domain model.

5. *Architecture specialisation.* A reference architecture is selected based on the specific requirements, and changes are made to incorporate the specialisations and extensions of the domain model corresponding to the new requirements.

6. *Component selection and specialisation.* The product that meets the new requirements is then built, selecting components from the repository where these exist, and adapting them as necessary. If there is nothing appropriate in the repository, you may request a new component to be built by those managing the repository for this product line. Alternatively, you may develop the new component yourself, if it is so specialised as to be unlikely to be required in other products.

7. *Integration and release.* Integrating the components into the architecture should be a relatively easy — if the architecture has been well designed!

To be able to operate a production line effectively you will need a lot of detailed understanding about what to do at each stage – OMG's Model-Driven Architectures has much of what is needed here.

Product lines enable us to build new systems based on success with previous similar systems.

The process model for product lines

Which process model, described in sections 8.2 to 8.4, best fits the product-line approach to software production? Draw a process model for product-line development.

Discussion

We haven't so far drawn a process model for product-line software development – had we done so, it would have looked remarkably like Figure 8.6 for incremental development, but with differences. This has been drawn as Figure 8.13.

An initial software development process along the top establishes the product line with a generic description of requirements produced by domain analysis, leading to architectural framework and detailed design, and then a library of useful components. Some trial integration and test is carried out to validate the framework and its components. Thereafter the framework and components are evolved, with major feedback from use of the product line.

When a specific requirement comes, the differences between this and the generic requirement leads to specialisation in the framework and identification of new components that need development from which the specific system can be built. This can be viewed as an increment in the overall process. This continues with successive products in the line.

Figure 8.13

The product-line process

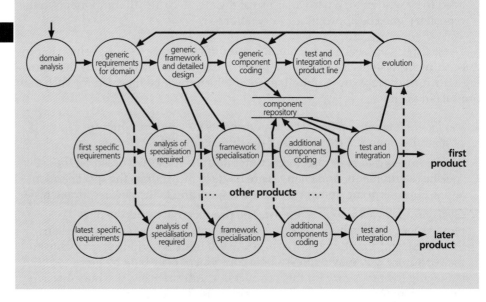

Component basesd approaches have their limitations. Components localise the functions being considered, as part of good modularisation practice based on high cohesion and low coupling.[21] However, this is not what you always need: some important aspects in software design are not localised. Usually these cross-cutting concerns like security and robustness would be handled by process standards, relying on every software engineer to properly respond to the standard. However, these cross-cutting concerns can be handled in a manner similar to components within an approach known as **aspect-oriented software development**,[22] each aspect separately described and then implemented across the software using automatic processes. While at the time of writing this book this area is very new, we can expect this to become an important approach to the design of software systems.

8.7 Open Source methods

We have seen in the preceding sections that the received wisdom in software development has been that software should be developed following sound scientific and engineering principles. When describing these approaches, we acknowledged that there were some problems with these 'best engineering practices', and saw as early as Chapter 1 that these problems were not surprising given the limitations on rationality. Best practice engineers work methodically through abstract descriptions of the software before eventually writing the code.

However there have always been people who reject this framework of software engineering best practice. These people have been derogatorily referred to as 'hackers', who simply develop software directly in code. But the work of these hackers has not been a failure, and what has evolved is a new approach to developing software, now commonly known as **open source software development**.

Open Source software has achieved enormous popular appeal as **FOSS, Free and Open Source software**, and through the **Free Software Foundation** founded by Richard Stallman in 1985 and described in Chapter 3. There are two sides to Open Source software, a use or deployment side that has already been looked at in Chapter 6, and a development side that will be looked at here. Open Source software development processes have the reputation for delivering high-quality software for only a small additional cost and thus appear very attractive, if only they could be replicated.

Eric Raymond, in his book *The Cathedral and the Bazaar*,[23] described how the open source approach to developing software arose in 1991 almost by accident when Linus Torvalds requested help from outside for the development of a Unix operating system for the 386 PC. Hackers helped out, modifying and improving his code to produce a stable and competitive system within a couple of years, and thus the Open Source movement began. However, the OS movement was only possible because of the pre-existing Free Software movement initiated by Richard Stallman that had created a culture of hackers and voluntary contributions, and because of the establishment of the world wide web that enabled easy communication between dispersed hackers.

Set in the context of the established formal methodologies of the early 1990s, characterised by Raymond so graphically as 'cathedrals', open source software development was definitely radically new, even revolutionary, and its informality warranted Raymond's term, the 'bazaar'. This new movement was largely overlooked until its products like Linux began to find favour and exhibit quality and stability attributes so often absent in proprietary products. How did they do it? How could they do it without tight managerial controls and prescribed methods and procedures? It seems that open source software development is a new paradigm, perhaps one that should be more widely adopted.

The key ingredients of open source software development[24] are worth examining:

- *Open code*[25] – software engineers other than the person who developed the code can access it freely and flexibly to propose changes at any time.
- *Established and proven architecture* that is highly modular – everybody understands what the overall system being developed is, and how the parts fit together, so that individual engineers can work on components independently of others working on the software.
- *Highly parallel development* – the independent modules enable developments and updates to proceed in parallel, unaffected by each other, enabling very rapid development of the whole system.
- *Lots of duplicate development* – multiple people can also be working on the same module, with the best solution being the one chosen.
- *Rapid peer comment and feedback* when a new module or updated module is proposed for inclusion, with the added advantages of subsequent rounds of discussion from the original contributor and reviewers.
- *Acknowledged leaders and experts* may be party to the review processes, and are often the ultimate arbiters as to whether or not a contribution is accepted.
- *Increased user involvement* because open source software is often basic software that developers themselves use for other purposes.
- *Highly talented and highly motivated developers* who are among the best available and are probably themselves also users of the software and thus beneficiaries of the high-quality development.
- *Rapid cycle of releases* – the complete system may be rebuilt daily, or even more often, to ensure that the latest improvements are available to all, and that new contributions are given that ultimate test of full use in context;
- *A very loose 'management'*, though this may vary, depending upon the particular lead person and the other people involved;
- *Support tools* (such as SourceForge.net) that enable communication and manage software versions.

If you have no proprietary interest in the software you wish to develop, then consider making it open source, inviting additions and enhancements as widely as possible.

Often open source development is characterised as using free voluntary labour, but this clearly is not essential and not always the case since major companies have also paid their engineers to work full time on open source projects subject to the controls of open source rather than the controls of the company. Rather it seems that the key features are working on exciting technology with extremely able peers, combined with a non-authoritarian management regime.

As a software development process to be managed, open source may seem very risky – you may not be able to lay out the work in a plan to ensure that development reaches predefined stages at predictable times.

Activity 8.5   *What lies behind open source?*

Discuss the open source development process using all the concepts and understandings you gained from Part I of this book. Contrast this with the use and deployment of open source software covered in Chapter 6.

Discussion

The key attribute of open source software is that all the source code is made publicly available on a website, free for anybody to copy and use subject to the license agreements attached to that source. The license agreements effectively make the source code into public goods as described in Chapter 3, unable to be exploited for private gain.

This means that if you have a use for the software, you can take it and use it. If you want to make changes and adaptations for your own use, then you are also free to do that. This is the way open source was discussed in Chapter 6, as a source of software for somebody seeking to acquire it. As we saw in Chapter 6, there is no such thing as cost-free software: you have to do some work and spend some money, even when using open source. But the overall costs can be considerably less than for proprietary software.

The second consequence of making software open source is that it becomes open to improvement by anybody who has an interest. Users of the software who are also sufficiently expert to fix defects or add new functions can do so, subject to any controls enforced by the guardians of the software, typically through a license agreement. This is the way open source can be used as a means of developing software. The effort required to improve or add to the software is given without payment, as part of the 'gratis economy', though the person giving the effort may benefit in other ways. The person benefits from the improved software, from personal development through learning from the other very able people working on the software, and may be able to sell expert advice about the software.

> Liberate your software engineers' energy and creativity by reducing bureaucracy to the minimum, making the technical work exciting, and engaging the best engineers you can.

8.8 Agile processes

All the process models in sections 8.2 to 8.6 have been developed into proprietary 'methodologies' that demand the production of particular documents conforming to particular standards, with a significant overhead in record keeping and just plain bureaucracy. Having to keep these records and follow the rules of the methodology has proved unpopular with software engineers, since this distracts them from their main pursuit of developing software. And here they may be supported by their managers: this heavy bureaucracy adds cost and thus has not been popular with managers either, yet the managers wish to maintain control of their projects. What can be done? As a manager you don't want to lose control, but you don't want to over-control and alienate the software engineers who are your most valuable resource and who you depend upon.

The response has been the emergence of **Agile** methods. These approaches realise that there is great merit in the informal approaches of small team, small company software development – what in the US would be characterised as 'skunk works'. Somehow these teams develop quality software at low cost – how do they do it? How they achieve this had remained tacit knowledge, and what Agile methods have aimed at is to make it explicit and visible and thus acceptable to managers and stakeholders.

In February 2001 a number of leaders from within the object-oriented movement and outside met to discuss what to do about the bureaucracy of current methodologies, and release the creative energy of software developers. They established the **Agile Alliance** and drew up the *Manifesto for Agile Development*[26] backed up by a number of principles well worth quoting here:

- Our highest priority is to satisfy the customer through early and continuous delivery of valuable software.
- Welcome changing requirements, even late in development. Agile processes harness change for the customer's competitive advantage.
- Deliver working software frequently, from a couple of weeks to a couple of months, with a preference to the shorter timescale.
- Business people and developers must work together daily throughout the project.
- Build projects around motivated individuals. Give them the environment and support they need, and trust them to get the job done.
- The most efficient and effective method of conveying information to and within a development team is face-to-face conversation.
- Working software is the primary measure of progress.
- Agile processes promote sustainable development. The sponsors, developers, and users should be able to maintain a constant pace indefinitely.
- Continuous attention to technical excellence and good design enhances agility.
- Simplicity – the art of maximising the amount of work not done – is essential.
- The best architectures, requirements, and designs emerge from self-organising teams.
- At regular intervals, the team reflects on how to become more effective, then tunes and adjusts its behaviour accordingly.

At that meeting were Kent Beck, Alistair Cockburn, Martin Fowler, Jim Highsmith, and Steve Mellor, but also a representative of DSDM. The DSDM consortium have since actively described DSDM as 'Agile'. People who find that they support the Manifesto are invited to 'sign' it on the Agile Manifesto website, and some 2000 people had done so by mid-2005. Among those who signed in 2003 is Eric Raymond of the Open Source movement – in signing it he wrote:

> It has become more and more obvious over the last few years that agile programming and the Unix/open-source culture are converging. A lot of what you guys are doing sharpens and articulates practices that have been part of the Unix inheritance for decades. Some of what you're doing challenges Unix assumptions in useful ways. I'm beginning to think that I see the outline of a mature, *humane* discipline of software engineering emerging, and that it will be in large part a blend of the boldness of the agile movement with the wisdom and groundedness of the Unix tradition, expressed in open source.

While a number of Agile methods have been proposed, we will focus on the best known of these, **eXtreme Programming (XP)**, described in Case Study 8.6.

Case Study 8.6   *eXtreme Programming*

eXtreme Programming was developed by Kent Beck[27] well before the Agile Manifesto, arising out of his personal experiences of developing software. The guiding principles that he lays out are:

- each release is a small increment of the previous, scoped by a combination of business priorities and technical realities; this scope can be changed if things don't turn out as expected;

- development is guided by a metaphor or story about how the whole system works;

- design is kept as simple as possible, with complexity and duplication removed as soon as it appears, redesigning if necessary;

- tests are developed by programmers and customers, and tests must be passed in order to proceed;

- coding is done as pair programming, with two programmers sharing a single computer; code is produced to standards which enhance communication through the code to other programmers; each element of new code is immediately integrated into the overall system;

- the team includes a customer, all code is owned collectively and can be changed by anybody; people only work the normal 40-hour week.

A key part of eXtreme Programming is the use of testing in what was originally known as Test-First Design but has now come to be known as **Test-Driven Development (TDD)**. TDD did not appear as part of the original XP and was added later.[28] The idea here is to express the desired functionality as a number of test cases, and then develop the software so that it executes successfully on those test cases. This is done incrementally so that the procedure becomes:

- write the test case for the next bit of functionality to be implemented;

- test the current version of the software on this – it should fail!

- update the software so that it will pass on this test case;

- reengineer the code to incorporate the new code as elegantly as possible;

- retest everything so far.

Agile methods do not include prescriptions concerning what should be done when; they do not plan in the conventional sense. They recognise that what an engineer does is contingent upon the situation the engineer finds, and this cannot be planned. The engineer's actions are situated in exactly the sense described by Lucy Suchman many years earlier, and described by us in Chapter 3.

Activity 8.6	*Human factors and Agile processes*

In Chapter 3 we saw a number of factors that affect the way people respond to work. Use these human factors to explain why XP and Agile methods should be expected to prove popular with software engineers.

Discussion

We are concerned here with person-related human factors, which arise directly from the engineer her/himself, such as the engineer's experience or abilities or motivation.

There are many person-related human factors that are important during software development and will affect the way a software engineer responds to a particular software development method. Agile methods, notably eXtreme Programming, have many aspects that are likely to cause a positive response in the engineer, as can be seen by examining these human factors.

First let us consider the individual person-related human factors, competence and motivation. Competence is not relevant here, but the use of XP could help significantly with motivation. There are two parts to motivation: intellectual growth and social contact and esteem.

XP caters well for intellectual growth, supporting skill-variety through its combination of coding and design and testing within mixed teams, involving the person in the complete process with strong links through the metaphor to the overall system; making each individual's work significant through the strong team structure; and supporting feedback through team working and frequent testing. However, XP could be demotivating with respect to personal autonomy, since all activity is undertaken by the team and not by the individual.

XP caters well for social needs through strong team working and emphasis on communication. XP emphasises team working, with pair programming and group ownership, but has no strong internal team structure that would risk arbitrary structure imposed on the software, team goals are shared through metaphor and flexible planning. However, XP is seemingly neutral on team leadership and team building. XP also emphasises communication through pair programming, and through the need to write programs conforming to standards so that others can read them.

Additionally the use of XP will be motivating, partly because it is currently fashionable, and partly because it will give the opportunity to learn a new skill.

Activity 8.7   *Agile versus open source*

How do the Agile development approaches relate to open source development?

Discussion

Both Agile and open source methods emphasise the production of code over and above the production of intermediate abstract descriptions of the software, and emphasise the importance of the people producing the software. It is surprising that they aren't more strongly linked historically, though clearly both arose out of the hacker culture that led to the Free Software Foundation.

What Agile adds is a very light process model that enables some level of predictability and control over costs, and a very clear team environment. However, open source does not demand these, and open source software developers can take on as much, or as little, social contact as they wish.

Even the older bureaucratic methods have been reconciled with the Agile methods that arose in reaction to them. Thus Barry Boehm, that long-term advocate of disciplined and controlled software engineering methods, which he terms 'plan-driven', was able to write in 2002:[29]

> Although many of their advocates consider the agile and plan-driven software development methods polar opposite, synthesising the two can provide developers with a comprehensive spectrum of tools and options. (p. 64)

Move to an Agile method if you are new to software development, or have a bureaucratic process that is proving ineffective.

Summing up

We have based this chapter on the set of typical activities identified in Chapter 7. From these we took the view that:

- all software development processes consist of a number of typical activities being done in some prescribed order;
- all work products conform to some standard and include models using some standardised notation.

In this chapter we have seen a number of software development processes, finding that:

- sequential process models work well for small well-defined problems, but have reached the limits of rationality, and are not able to handle very large and complex software development problems;
- uncertainty in user requirements means that we should involve users in a participative and iterative process to reduce requirements risks;
- all risks can be addressed by iteration, focusing on the highest risks in early iterations;
- only in special cases would formal proofs of programs be appropriate;
- it is very difficult to produce software simultaneously to an agreed specification, timescale, and cost – if something has to give, it should be the set of functions delivered, using timeboxing to facilitate this;
- software design best practice should be spread through the use of software design patterns;
- product lines enable us to build new systems based on success with previous similar systems;
- if you have no proprietary interest in the software you wish to develop, then consider making it open source, inviting additions and enhancements as widely as possible;
- engage the best engineers you can, liberating their energy and creativity by reducing bureaucracy to the minimum, making the technical work exciting, as would happen in open source development;
- if you are new to software development, or have a bureaucratic process that is proving ineffective, consider moving to an Agile method.

Exercises

1. The building of simulation models is important in much business and economic planning, as well as in applications like oil extraction planning. Sometimes these models are built directly in some general-purpose programming language, but sometimes they are built using special-purpose simulation languages or systems. In all these models there is an external reality which is characterised by a number of sets of measurements of that reality. The problem in simulation modelling is then to build a model that represents that reality from which new situations can be explored. One experienced software engineer has characterised the difference between simulation programming and conventional programming: in the conventional case the software remains unchanged but the data processed changes, while in the simulation case the data remains the same and the software changes. This characterisation may make it seem that developing simulation software is different from conventional software. However it isn't. Describe the process of developing simulation software as an iterative method, drawing a suitable data-flow diagram.

2. Many companies have been inspired by the software reuse rhetoric and established corporate component and software asset libraries. Many of these have failed. Explain why you might have expected that, and how the development of a software asset library should be approached.

3. As part of institutional practices a certain software development group supply standard code templates containing slots for descriptive information about the piece of software, and standard methods for handling errors to ensure the graceful degradation of the software when a problem during execution is encountered. Analyse this approach as an aspect-oriented method.

4. Investigate use of open source methods for the development of Linux in all its variants. Produce a catalogue of all the Linuxes you can find, characterising their differences and similarities. The production of all these variants can be characterised as a product line. Write a short report on Linux development as a product line. Could this approach be used for product lines in general?

5. It is claimed that Agile methods are fine for website design, but do not scale up for software of any substantial size. Investigate this and find out how Agile methods could be scaled up, describing a way of doing this.

6. We saw in Chapter 3 that individual software engineers can vary greatly in their abilities – this adds a dimension of uncertainty about how effective a particular software development process will be. Select two process models described in this chapter that handle this uncertainty particularly well, describing how they do so.

7. Problems requiring a solution in software can be classified into routine problems and innovative problems. For each of the methods described in Chapter 8, discuss the extent to which they are best suited to routine or to innovative problems.

8. In Chapter 7 we worked through in outline the sequential development of a school library system. Now that you have read Chapter 8, select an alternative

method of developing such a system, explaining how you would have developed the system using this method, and why your chosen method is the most appropriate.

Endnotes

1. The development of this was supported by the UK government and is mandated by them for government projects, along with the project management method PRINCE. The best sources of information about these can be found by simple web searches.
2. W.W. Royce (1970) 'Managing the Development of Large Software Systems: Concepts and Techniques', *Proc. WESCON*, IEEE Computer Society Press, Los Alamitos, CA. Reprinted at the ICSE'87, Monterey, California, USA, 30 March – 2 April 1987.
3. Enid Mumford and Don Henshall (1979) *A Participative Approach to Computer Systems Design*. Associated Business Press.
4. Quoted from Enid Mumford (1995) *Effective Systems Design and Requirements Analysis: the ETHICS Approach*. Macmillan.
5. A. Clement and P. Van den Besselaar (1993) 'A Retrospective Look at PD Projects', *Communications of the ACM*, June, 29–37.
6. Ben Shneiderman (1987) *Designing the User Interface: Strategies for Effective Human–Computer Interaction*. Addison-Wesley.
7. Jakob Neilsen (1993) *Usability Engineering*. Academic Press.
8. Don Norman (2002) *The Design of Everyday Things*. Basic Books (1st basic edn). Originally published in 1988 under the title of the *Psychology of Everyday Things*.
9. Alan Cooper (1995) *About Face: The Essentials of User Interface Design*. John Wiley and Sons.
10. Carol M. Barnum (2001) *Usability Testing and Research*. Longman.
11. Mike Kuniavsky (2003) *Observing the User Experience: A Practitioner's Guide for User Research*. Morgan Kaufmann.
12. Helen Sharp, Yvonne Rogers, and Jenny Preece (2004) *Interaction Design: Beyond Human–Computer Interaction*. John Wiley and Sons.
13. Barry Boehm (1988) A Spiral Model of Software Development and Enhancement *Computer*, May, 61–72.
14. See, for example, Cliff Jones (1980) *Software Development: A Rigorous Approach*. Prentice Hall International.
15. See, for example, John Wordsworth (1992) *Software Development with Z. A Practical Approach to Formal Methods in Software Engineering*. Addison Wesley .
16. C. Alexander (1977) *A Pattern Language: Towns/Buildings/Construction*. Oxford University Press.
17. There are two seminal books about design patterns: E. Gamma, R. Helm, R. Johnson and J. Vlissides (1995) *Design Patterns: Elements of Reusable Object Oriented Software*. Addison-Wesley; F. Buschmann, R. Meunier, H. Rohnert, P. Sommerlad, and M. Stal (1996) *Pattern-Oriented Software Architecture: A System of Patterns*. John Wiley. You might also find it useful to look at Craig Larman (1998) *Applying UML and Patterns: An Introduction to Object-oriented Analysis and Design*. Prentice-Hall.
18. See Jan Bosch (2000) *Design and Use of Software Architectures: Adopting and Evolving a Product-Line Approach*. Addison-Wesley.
19. The product-line idea for software was strongly investigated in the US military Adage project under the rubric of domain-specific software architecture (DSSA) and 'mega programming' by one of the pioneers of software reuse, Will Tracz.
20. See Case Study 6.12 in Chapter 6. This ambitious project produced frameworks for a number of industrial sectors, providing libraries of components for use within that framework. Regrettably this project was later abandoned, apparently because its frameworks did not capture enough of the subtleties of real applications.
21. Originally described by Glenford Myers (1975) *Reliable Software through Composite Design*. Van Nostrand Reinhold. Now covered in any book on software engineering.
22. See, for example, Tzilla Elrad, Mehmet Aksit, Siobhan Clarke, Robert E. Filman (2004) *Introduction to Aspect-Oriented Software Development*. Addison Wesley Professional.

23. Eric Raymond (1999) *The Cathedral and the Bazaar: Musing on Linux and Open Source by an Accidental Revolutionary.* O'Reilly.

24. This account is based on Chapter 6 of Joseph Feller and Brian Fitzgerald's excellent 2002 book *Understanding Open Source Software Development* (Addison-Wesley) tempered by other sources and our own experience of the area.

25. Open code was not new, and goes back to ego-less programming and the classic book: Gerry Weinberg (1971) *Psychology of Computer Programming.* Dorset House, now republished in a silver anniversary edition.

26. See http://agilemanifesto.org/.

27. Kent Beck (2000) *eXtreme Programming eXplained: Embrace Change.* Addison-Wesley.

28. Kent Beck (2002) *Test-Driven Development – By Example.* Addison Wesley.

29. Barry Boehm (2002) Get Ready for Agile Methods, with Care. *IEEE Computer* 35(1) Jan 64–69.

9 Maintaining and evolving software

9.1 Introduction

We have seen in Chapters 1 to 3 that organisations and the software that supports them are intimately interlinked. As the organisation is subject to pressures to change and evolve by a changing environment, so too must its software change and evolve. In Chapters 6 to 8 we looked at how software is acquired and developed, and in this chapter we look at how it is changed. What are the consequences for software of those modifications forced on it by the changing environment? As we will see, the fact that it is software that is being changed has some particular consequences.

This whole area of software change while in service has generally been referred to as **software maintenance**. During maintenance the existing software is repaired, adapted, enhanced, and modified, with the various changes analysed and prioritised so that the software keeps supporting the organisation and giving value to its stakeholders.

The term 'maintenance' came about initially because this activity was concerned with fixing defects in the software. But software does not suffer wear and tear in the way that mechanical and other physical devices do. Cars, for instance, need maintenance periodically to counteract the effects of wear and tear and bring them back to a condition which is closer to that of a newly manufactured and tested vehicle. In software there is no wear and tear and so maintenance should never need to be performed, yet the universal experience is that software sooner or later needs to be changed. Why? Because of the changing environment.

Nowadays it is widely accepted that software change is inevitable as a consequence of organisational changes, and thus modifications to software are less 'maintenance' than **evolution** or support. Some people also use the term **sustenance**, in the sense of the software being sustained in service, but because of the association in English of 'sustenance' with food, the term will not be used here. In this chapter these various terms will be used synonymously, though we prefer the term 'evolution'.

'Maintenance' has negative connotations in the software industry. Maintenance personnel often feel that they are doing low-profile tasks, lacking support from management. Maintenance programmers might have to use out-of-date technologies and work under tight budgets which do not reflect real needs.

The term 'maintenance' may not be the most appropriate term, but the term is still used in many organisations and is in the title of several conferences, such as the IEEE International Conference on Software Maintenance. However, there is a sense in which maintenance is the right term! What is maintained in software is not the software itself, but the satisfaction of the stakeholders.[1] Software maintenance is the process of keeping the satisfaction of the stakeholders at an acceptable level.

Activity 9.1	*Requirements volatility*

The need for software change is normal, part of the need for organisations to change and adapt to their environment. However, when user requirements are volatile, particularly early on in the development of the first release, this may lead to problems. Why?

Discussion
If requirements are volatile at the start of or during a developing project they will need to be addressed by selecting a development process which can respond quickly and adequately to these changes. Requirements need to be prioritised and classified according to their volatility. More volatile requirements should be responded to after the less volatile requirements have been seen to. Doing this using DSDM-style time-boxes, which we saw in Chapter 8, would be a suitable way to handle this. Deferring volatile requirements is important, because otherwise changes that happen after the

requirement has been implemented may then require amendments to other software artefacts (e.g., design, implementation, test suites), with costly ripple effects. Organisations following traditional bureaucratic processes (e.g., **waterfall** – see discussion in Chapter 8) are more vulnerable to these than those following **Agile** methods. Boehm has found that the later a defect is found in the life cycle of a project, the more expensive it is to fix (see Chapter 12). The same reasoning can be applied to any change.

In section 9.2 we will look at software as an enduring asset of an organisation, which often continues in service for twenty-five years or more to become part of the legacy of the organisation. In looking at this we will look at the processes of change that help enable this long life. However, software grows old, decays, and will eventually die. This may seem counter-intuitive, since software does not wear out. Nevertheless this cycle was discovered through a series of observations within IBM, since substantiated in other studies, and encapsulated in a number of laws that will be described in section 9.3. The processes of decay can be mitigated using a number of recovery processes described in section 9.4. The overall process of evolution needs to be carefully managed, and we pick this up in section 9.5, and again later in Chapter 11.

> Software evolution is the maintenance of the satisfaction of the software stakeholders.

9.2 Long-life software

During the 1990s, in the run up to the year 2000, there was a lot of concern about the 'millenium bug' (described in Case Study 9.1). This revealed that there was a large amount of software still in use which had been written in COBOL. A Gartner group survey in 1996[2] reported that at that time an estimated 200 billion lines of COBOL code were in existence, making COBOL by far the most widely used programming language at that time. While the response to the Y2K problem reduced this proportion significantly, we must still recognise that COBOL is very widely used for information systems and business applications today.

Case Study 9.1 *The Y2K 'millennium bug'*

As the year 2000 approached there was a world-wide concern for the possible malfunction of software that represented the calendar year with only two digits (for example, '89' instead of '1989'). For this software, crossing the threshold from 1999 to 2000 could have had unexpected consequences. It was feared that the transition from year 99 to 00 would trigger software malfunction. Some experts predicted chaotic scenarios during New Year's Eve with electricity power cuts and a collapse of the transportation infrastructure, unless proper measures were taken. Precautions were taken worldwide; some governments carried out publicity campaigns, many organisations invested heavily in making an inventory of their software and in checking the Y2K compliance of their software systems. When the year 2000 came, only minor incidents were reported, though after the event experts could not agree whether this was because of the precautions taken or because there had not been a problem in the first place. The need for

▶

modification of old software gave rise temporarily to a large demand for programmers with knowledge of COBOL and other programming languages which were popular in the 70s and 80s. The Y2K issue revealed that many software systems outlived their developers and that software tends to be used for much longer than initially expected. Anthony Finkelstein has argued[3] that the Y2K issue was used as an excuse for making major replacements of software that had been in service too long but whose replacement had been difficult to justify. The Y2K 'bug' also revealed society's dependence on software and its timely evolution.

Software is an asset of the organisation that may have a long life.

But this long life of software is not peculiar to COBOL and administrative systems. It is also true for embedded systems. Any major engineering artefact like a manufacturing plant or military system will be expected to give service for at least twenty-five years, and when software is embedded within these, that too will be expected to last for twenty-five years. Software is a long-life asset of an organisation. As with any other long-life asset, software needs to be looked after, to be maintained and sustained so that it can evolve and continue to maintain the satisfaction of its stakeholders.

9.2.1 The stakeholders and the environment

Software interacts with its stakeholders and its environment of:

- the organisation and its management who procured the software, purchasing it off the shelf or having it developed bespoke;
- the organisation that will use the software and benefit from this use;
- the people in the organisation who will actually operate the software;
- business processes followed by the user organisation;
- suppliers of the software or its components, who may have a continued commercial interest in the software;
- software developers, who also may have a property right in the system, or may simply have pride in the system as its creators;
- the actual hardware and software platform on which the software executes;
- the suppliers of this platform;
- the regulatory framework (e.g., standards and professional regulations), law, and other elements.

This environment of the software is subject to change, which impacts on the software. Software and the business it supports should be changed together, they should **co-evolve**.

During use, the users and other stakeholders may wish to give feedback of their experience, typically to raise issues concerning the use of the software. This feedback can take several forms: defect reports, user complaints, suggestions for new functionality, and so on. This feedback is a significant factor in driving the future of a software application.

Software is very malleable but its change is constrained by the existing software system, by the need to update the documentation, and by existing conventions and standards. One of the challenges in software change is the need to keep all the artefacts generated by the software process up to date and consistent with respect to each other and to their changing environment.

Software co-evolves with the organisation it supports.

9.2.2 The nature of software evolution work

Evolution work includes fixing defects, keeping the software compatible with the execution environment, adapting it to changes in other software and hardware, and keeping it up to date with the changing user requirements. This work is conventionally classified into the following types:[4]

- **Corrective maintenance**: diagnosing and fixing errors, from localised changes to more fundamental design fixes.
- **Adaptive maintenance**: changing the software so that it can work properly following changes in the environment, such as changes in other software, hardware, or user practices.
- **Perfective maintenance**: adding new functions and the enhancement and change of existing functions.
- **Preventive maintenance**: improving the sustainability of the software, so that future changes can be done more rapidly and easily. These include complexity reduction and various re-engineering processes described later, aimed at improving the understandability of software without changing the externally observed functional behaviour of the software.

Activity 9.2   *Types of maintenance and evolutionary activity*

Consider the following examples of software changes to existing software. What type of software maintenance and evolution activity does each represent?

1. An operating system needs a missing driver implemented for it.
2. A text-based word processor needs a speech recognition module implemented and incorporated into it.
3. Sales point software needs to be changed to support the latest security identification procedures for credit and debit cards.
4. An email program needs to be changed to make it robust against a new type of software virus to which it is vulnerable.
5. Spreadsheet software has a malfunction which prevents a particular function from being accessed by the user.

Discussion

These could be classified as follows, though there could be room for disagreement:

1. Perfective, since a new driver represents an improvement in capability for the operating system; however it might be considered adaptive.

2. Perfective, clearly a speech recognition module is a new function for an otherwise text-based word processor.

3. Adaptive, changes in legislation and business practices can be seen as changes in the external environment of the software and hence their implementation represents adaptive changes.

4. Adaptive, since a new software virus potentially present in the environment of the software represents a change in that environment, hence the adaptive nature of this change.

5. Corrective, since it consists of fixing a defect.

Classifying potential software maintenance work in this way is helpful in making us understand what the change requested is and why we should, or should not, make the change.

Making a change to a system has all the attributes and problems of original software development, and all the discussions of Chapters 6, 7, and 8 apply. Software evolution assumes that the changes to be implemented are small and localised relative to the whole system. When the work involved in a change exceeds a certain size or estimated cost, the change may be treated as an independent project, separate from routine maintenance. In terms of complexity, making a major modification to an existing system can be more challenging than developing a new software system.

Software changes are corrective, adaptive, perfective, or preventive.

9.2.3 Basic change processes

In order to make the changes described above, there are several basic processes that we must carry out. These will be described briefly here, and picked up in greater detail in Chapter 11.

Configuration management

When the software is changed, individual components of it will be changed and new versions created. We will need to keep track of these versions, and how particular configurations of versions fit together to implement the overall change intended. This overall process is known as **configuration management**, which is well supported by software tools. Configuration management is essential for any large system developed and maintained by a large group of people over a long period of time.

Estimation and impact analysis

We need to analyse the business case for any proposed change in terms of benefits and costs of the proposed change. How much of the existing system will be affected by the implementation of a change? What business processes need changing in consequence? This will then lead us to be able to estimate how much – and for how long – human resources will be needed in order to make a change or a set of changes to the software.

Release planning

Changes will not be released one at a time, but will be grouped together into coherent groups. This needs planning to prioritise changes into the system releases which will be delivered to users.

Regression testing

Every time that there is a change to a software artefact, it is likely that a subtle new defect will be introduced. This needs to be carefully tested for, by running a test suite after the implementation of a modification to the code, in order to establish whether previously implemented functionality still works as intended and that previously fixed defects remain fixed. This is regression testing, testing whether the software has regressed or gone backwards. The test suite itself also needs to be updated as part of the evolution work. The running of the regression tests as well as checking that the results are what should have been expected can be automated.

> Configuration management and regression testing are critically important processes in software evolution.

9.3 Software decay and death

The long life of software is not necessarily assured. As change upon change is applied to software, its complexity increases and software ageing effects emerge. Future changes to the software become increasingly difficult. If the easiness of change, the maintainability, is not kept within reasonable bounds, software can become an obstacle to business change.

It was realised relatively early in the history of computing that sustaining software for a long period was problematic. Initially this was just part of the folklore of computing, part of its tacit knowledge, but when it became a serious commercial issue for IBM and their operating systems, objective studies were commissioned and this tacit knowledge became grounded in hard evidence.

9.3.1 Empirical studies of software evolution

Starting in the late 1960s and the early 1970s Manny Lehman, Les Belady, and others conducted a series of metrics-based studies of various software systems.[5] One of the first systems studied was the IBM OS 360/370, which has been also discussed by Fred Brooks in his book *The Mythical Man-Month*.[6] The studies also explored the consequences of the findings for management of software systems. In the 1960s and 70s, maintenance had been considered a consequence of poor programming practice, but the studies of Lehman and his colleagues helped establish that in fact changes to real world applications were inevitable.

At the beginning of their studies, the focus was on 'large program growth dynamics'. When trying to explain the concept of 'largeness' for software, the investigators found that the intrinsic need for evolution did not depend so much on the size, but on the nature of the application. They classified software into three types to explain why different types of software are subject to different evolutionary pressures: fixed software (type S), variable software (type E), and pliable software (type P). We will review them now.

Fixed software (type S)

This type of software solves problems that can be completely and formally described, for example, the numerical evaluation of a mathematical equation. The essential characteristic is that fixed software can be proven to be correct with respect to its specification. Since such programs completely solve well-defined problems, fixed programs are not subject to evolutionary pressures. If the problem is changed or evolves, a new specification is derived and a new program is generated to address the new problem. The most advanced programming technology (e.g., formal methods) can be applied to fixed type software. The developer only needs the specification in order to develop the program. The implementation of the program does not depend on feedback from the environment in which the program will be used. In this sense, the development of fixed software is 'open loop' as illustrated in Figure 9.1.

Figure 9.1

Open loop
development of fixed
software

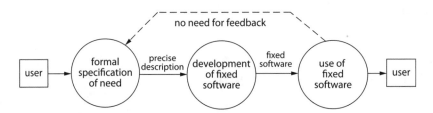

Variable software (type E)

This is the most interesting of the three types. It refers to programs that automate human activity. One characteristic of this type of software is that the application cannot be completely specified. The process of development and evolution constitutes a feedback system, in which stakeholders' reactions need to be extrapolated and predicted, and once the system is operational the stakeholders' reactions become an essential contribution to the development of further versions of the software.

The situation for variable software is even more subtle than this, since the software becomes a part of the world that it models, a source of continual evolution and pressures for change. The implementation of changes provides temporary satisfaction for the stakeholders, until the stakeholders see potential for changes in the software and the nature of the solution needed, triggered by their own learning or by exogenous factors such as functionality implemented in a competing product. Evolution is intrinsic to variable software and is inevitable.

The resulting cycle of change is shown in Figure 9.2, a simplified, high level view of the software evolution process as seen by Lehman and his colleagues. An application life cycle starts in the application domain with interaction between stakeholders, which leads to the application concept. This defines the problem that will be tackled via software. This is followed by an activity, called 'bounding' in the figure, where the problem scope and limits are established. This in itself introduces a whole series of assumptions that anything that lies outside the bounds is irrelevant. Development of the software then starts. Though any of the different processes covered in Chapter 8 could be followed in developing the software, for the sake of simplicity Figure 9.2 shows a sequential process. At the end of the first iteration the operational program is deployed in the application domain, effectively

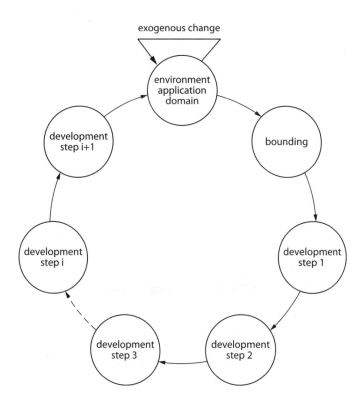

exogenous change

environment application domain

bounding

development step i+1

development step 1

development step i

development step 2

development step 3

Figure 9.2

The process of developing 'variable software' in which the installation of the software changes the domain

changing the domain. That is, the original the input to the process has changed, introducing a feedback cycle.

Exogenous changes can and will also influence the domain. Domain changes are likely to trigger the need for program changes and so lead to program evolution going round and round the circle of development steps. A more detailed view than that presented in Figure 9.2 would show many information flows connecting the activities showing that the software process is not purely sequential. A representation of the software process that better fits experience is that of a feedback system.

Examples of variable programs include air-traffic control systems, word processors, and stock control systems. IBM's OS 360, described in Case Study 9.2, gives an excellent example. Even the travelling salesmen problem, fixed-type software, when applied in the real world to an application controlling the deployment of sales personnel in a given geographical area, becomes of variable type. The vast majority of systems are of this type, particularly those which address different aspects of business processes. The need for continual evolution is intrinsic to these type of program.

> Software changes the organisation it is intended to support.

Case Study 9.2 *IBM's OS 360 mainframe operating system*

IBM OS 360 is a mainframe operating system, popular in the late 1960s and 70s, which introduced important technological innovations. Reportedly,[7] T.J. Watson said that the preparation of OS 360 involved 5,000 person years and some 50 million US dollars. Fred Brooks was for

▶

some time the manager of this massive development. His management experiences are summarised in his famous book *The Mythical Man-Month*, a software engineering management classic. It is from his IBM OS 360 experience that Brooks realised what is called Brooks' law, that 'adding people to a late project makes it later' emerged. Whilst Fred Brooks documented many interesting management aspects of the development of early releases, Lehman and Belady looked at its long-term evolution over its first twenty-six releases.

Figure 9.3 shows the growth trend from release 1 to release 19, which is almost linear, captured by the linear model $S(i) = S(i\text{-}1) + 0.19$, where $S(i)$ is the relative size of the system (measured in models) at the release i. The parameter 0.19 was obtained through a linear fit. What is remarkable is that this system achieved a linear growth rate despite the lack of evidence of any intentional control of the growth rate of the system.[9] Lehman interpreted this as an indication

that the system had its own growth dynamics, resulting from the interactions between all those involved in its evolution, the various feedback loops, checks and balances and constraints. The ripple present over the linear growth trend was interpreted by Lehman as an indicator of the feedback nature of the variable type software evolution process, based on the observation that feedback systems (systems in which the output modifies the input, studied, for example, in control theory or modelled using **system dynamics**), tend to exhibit this type of oscillatory behaviour.

What happened after release 19 was equally remarkable. A very large size increment, due to pressures from stakeholders to include certain type of functionality, led to instability and the splitting of the system into two different versions. This suggested that managers should pay attention to the historical trends and in particular to the bounds and limits suggested by the previously safe growth rate.

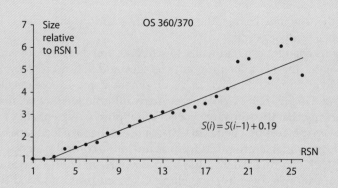

Figure 9.3

Growth trend of the IBM OS 360/370 operating system over its first twenty-six releases, as reported by Lehman[8]

Pliable software (type P)

This is an intermediate type between the fixed and variable. In pliable software, the problem can be completely specified but the solution inevitably involves approximation and is tentative, not definitive as in the fixed program. An example of pliable software is a program addressing a weather prediction problem. The solutions are approximate, and sometimes unsatisfactory, for example, when a weather prediction turns out to be totally wrong; in this case a comparison of the predicted with the actual weather would be used to improve future weather prediction programs.

9.3.2 Laws of software evolution

Lehman and his colleagues studied many systems, none of them as dramatic as IBM OS 360/370 described in Case Study 9.2, but similarly demonstrating the evolution dynamics phenomenon. They summarised their observations in a set of eight laws of variable type software evolution, called **Lehman's laws**. The term 'law' is used to highlight that the phenomena are outside the area of influence of individual software developers or their managers. The observations are also believed to be independent of the technology used. At the core of these studies are a set of similarities in the attributes of evolving systems, as behavioural invariants, that are characteristics that appear to be constant across different entities and over time.

Developers have to accept them as laws and take measures in order to counteract their impact. The number of the laws has increased over the years: the first three were formulated in 1974; a further five were added and the original three reformulated in 1996 as 'feedback system' laws, even though description of the evolution of software as a feedback system dates from the early 1970s.

A recent formulation of the laws for variable type systems is presented in Table 9.1. Each law is believed to reflect organisational and sociological forces that lie outside the realm of software engineering and the immediate control of software developers.

Despite being subject to criticisms, Lehman's laws provide useful insight for software evolution managers. This is discussed below, under management guidelines.

Software deteriorates as it evolves unless explicit action is taken to prevent this.

No.	Name	Statement
1	Continuing change	A system must be continually adapted or else it becomes progressively less satisfactory in use
2	Increasing complexity	As a system is evolved its complexity increases unless work is done to maintain or reduce it
3	Self regulation	Global system evolution is feedback regulated
4	Conservation of organisational stability	The work rate of an organisation evolving a software system tends to be constant over the operational lifetime of that system or phases of that lifetime
5	Conservation of familiarity	In general, the incremental growth (growth rate trend) of systems is constrained by need for the maintenance team to maintain familiarity with the software
6	Continuing growth	The functional capability of systems must be continually enhanced to maintain user satisfaction over system lifetime
7	Declining quality	Unless rigorously adapted and evolved to take into account changes in the operational environment, the quality of a system will decline
8	Feedback system	Software evolution processes are multi-level, multi-loop, multi-agent feedback systems

Table 9.1

Recent statement of Lehman's laws of software evolution for variable (type E) software.

9.3.3 The software uncertainty principle

In this section we look briefly at the issue of uncertainty in software evolution as captured by Lehman's Software Uncertainly Principle,[10] which constitutes another of his empirical findings. The principle states that for a variable type program, despite many past satisfactory executions, a new execution may yield unsatisfactory results. It is based on the observation that software inevitably reflects assumptions about the real world. The program is limited but the real world has an unbounded number of attributes. All real-world attributes not considered in the development of the program become assumptions, either implicit or explicit, that the attributes do not play any role in program execution. However, a single change in the application or in the real world can render an assumption invalid and render unsatisfactory the execution of the program. Case Study 9.3 gives an example of the invalidation of assumptions reflected in software and their consequences.

Case Study 9.3 *CERN particle accelerator*[11]

In 1989 the LEP new particle accelerator at the world's largest particle physics laboratory, CERN, located in Switzerland, was made operational. Particle accelerators used in high-energy physics experiments consist of tunnels several kilometres in length within which particle trajectories and acceleration are controlled using sophisticated equipment.

The software running the LEP accelerator was based on trusted software that has been used in controlling a smaller accelerator in the past. Soon after the initial experiments, the scientists were surprised at obtaining wrong results and were totally mystified by them. Replicated experiments should have given the same results as they had in the smaller accelerator but they didn't. The error values followed a regular fluctuation. Rather surprisingly, one of the scientists suggested that the regular fluctuation followed the lunar cycle. After suffering sarcasm from colleagues, it was then understood that the gravitational pull of the Moon produces a tiny deformation of the Earth's crust, which is large enough to affect the results of the experiments of the large particle accelerators with a radius of several kilometres. The tidal force of the Moon makes the particles deviate from their trajectories. It can account for up to 0.02 per cent energy variations, which is significant if one takes into account that the physicists desire a precision of 0.003 per cent.

The assumption that the Moon did not affect the experiments was appropriate for the smaller accelerators but not for the larger one. Once the software was updated to reflect this effect, scientist again obtained the expected results. However, other unsuspected factors had to be later considered and built into the corrections made by the software. One of those was the water level in the nearby lake, since the amount of water in the lake exerts pressure on the Earth which produces a tiny deformation in the accelerator's tunnel, with similar effects to the Moon's gravitational pull.

Let's briefly consider some of the assumptions of the principle. First, the principle refers to variable type software, to software systems which address a problem in the real world and that are executed in the real world. Second, it refers to satisfactory executions. Satisfaction is, in fact, the degree to which the program's execution meets the expectations of its stakeholders – this is often taken as a definition of quality, usually more succinctly expressed as 'fitness for purpose'. So one possible way of reformulating the uncertainty principle is as follows: the quality level that will be achieved by a program in the future cannot be guaranteed. Because this applies to quality it also applies to all its factors, such as reliability, safety, and fitness for purpose. According to the principle, one cannot guarantee absolute reliability and total fitness for purpose of a software system in the future, no matter how many successful executions of the program took place in the past.

Lehman's observation was triggered by Heizenberg's Uncertainty Principle from physics, which sets a limit on the precision possible in scientific observation. This uncertainty principle is often taken as evidence of postmodernism in science; we have already argued that rationality has limits and this affects software, and here we see it once again as our uncertain knowledge about the world with which our software is interacting means that we cannot be certain about the software itself.

> Software quality cannot be guaranteed.

Activity 9.3   *Testing and uncertainty*

Lehman's Uncertainty Principle expects software to fail. Why can't this uncertainty be eliminated by thorough testing? Discuss the role of software testing in the context of Lehman's Uncertainty Principle. What type of testing and how much of it would be required to counteract the uncertainty implied by Lehman's principle?

Discussion

Testing consists of executing the software (or parts of it) under certain classes of input so that errors might be discovered and fixed. The more thorough and systematic the testing, the more certain we can be that we have discovered and eliminated all the defects. However for any real software we realise that we cannot be completely certain since we cannot test exhaustively – however, if we test following the 'operational profile' of the software, testing more thoroughly in areas where the software will be used more frequently, then we can make strong statistical claims about that level of final uncertainty and that as we test more the uncertainty slowly reduces.

However this uncertainty is not Lehman's Uncertainty, but statistical uncertainty arising from the testing process itself. Lehman's Uncertainty arises from uncertainties about the environment, and arises if our testing process takes a long time, since there is the likelihood that what the software should do will change as the environment moves on and requirements change.

What we have described is system testing – if we were to move on to acceptance testing, particularly beta testing or trials, we are increasingly likely to fail the acceptance test the longer the system testing (and consequent defect removal and fixes) goes on.

Paradoxical, isn't it? The more we test and fix defects the less likely it is to fail, but the longer we test the more likely it is to fail as the environment changes.

Activity 9.4   *Formal methods and uncertainty*

Consider the role of formal methods, a topic covered in Chapter 8, and discuss whether or not a software system built using formal methods will be subject to Lehman's Uncertainty Principle.

Discussion

The idea behind formal methods is to write a software specification in some formally defined language with precise and unambiguous meaning (as we saw in Chapter 8). The formal specification can then be tested for inconsistency and other mathematical properties. Errors or ambiguities may be corrected sooner than otherwise. A program can then be built from the formal specification following some formal and rigorous process, by successive refinement, for example, so that at the end the program is 'provably correct' or 'correct by construction'.

Thus formal approaches can be seen as a means of mitigating uncertainty. However, the uncertainty they mitigate is not Lehman's Uncertainty but the uncertainties in the development process itself, that the software as delivered will meet the specification. Formal methods cannot mitigate the uncertainty that the specification is right in the first place, nor that it remains right as the environment within which the software will operate changes.

The complete mitigation of this type of uncertainty can only be possible in the realm of fixed type software. For the vast majority of software (variable type), the specification will be incomplete and becomes more so as time passes.

The discussions following Activities 9.4 and 9.5 are important, for they show that there are four sources of uncertainty concerning software:

1. from the technical development of the software, manifest in defects;
2. from the misunderstanding of the environment when building the software;
3. from the testing process itself as one of sampling and extrapolation from those samples;
4. from changes in the environment that happen after the software has been built.

The first two areas of uncertainty might be eliminated by thorough verification and validation testing, but there are limits to this as indicated in the third source of uncertainty: the inherent limitations of the testing process itself. It is the fourth source of uncertainty that Lehman's Uncertainty Principle relates to.

9.4 Software recovery and rejuvenation

Software is often used over a very long period, during which it changes, but also decays, and if nothing is done about it, will eventually die. However, Lehman's laws in Table 9.1 are hedged – decay won't happen if you do something about it. What can we do?

The first law, 'continuing change,' requires a system to be continually adapted, and for long-life software this will happen through corrective, adaptive, and perfective maintenance, as described in section 9.2. However as these evolutionary processes continue, complexity can grow and the system can become progressively more difficult to maintain, as captured by other laws, especially the second law on 'increasing complexity' and the seventh law on 'declining quality'. To combat these laws we need preventive maintenance. That is what this section is about.

9.4.1 Well engineered from the start

Well-engineered software anticipates change. We must start our evolutionary process as we intend to continue.

In a keynote address at an ICSM conference, David Parnas[12] argued that the solution to the maintenance problems lies not in maintenance, but in development. His view was that by applying software engineering design principles, such as **information hiding** and **encapsulation**, during initial development, software will become easier to maintain. During development software is subject to constant change and revision, and many of our software engineering practices are aimed at facilitating these changes. For example, the minimisation of external dependencies between our system and other systems means that it is less likely that changes in those other systems will trigger changes in our system. Similarly, fewer internal interdependencies (low coupling) between modules makes it easier to implement changes.

Parikh and Zvegintzov and others[13] have shown that software maintainers spend 47 to 60 per cent of their time understanding existing code. Programming style and conventions can help to reduce maintenance costs by facilitating this understanding. The use of meaningful names for files and variables, the prohibition of 'unstructured code' (e.g., gotos), and the writing of meaningful change records, can all help. Maintainers should not need to trace back to locate the original developer for an explanation of a particularly difficult algorithm.

Programs written in high-level languages are easier to understand and to modify than their lower-level counterparts. Some programming languages, such as Java, are independent of the operating system, making it easier to adapt the program to changes in its hardware and software environment.

The degree to which designs and programs are tested is related to the number of defects and the need for corrective maintenance. A higher level of testing will lead to fewer errors being encountered once the system has been released and hence will reduce the maintenance costs.

We would expect lower maintenance costs for systems which are adequately documented and where the documentation is kept up to date.

Evolution is much easier if the system being evolved is well engineered.

The use of a fixed and meaningful format in the change log records can also help extract historical data, which in turn could be used to build quantitative models of the evolution of a system and support decision-making.

9.4.2 Reverse engineering

We saw above that in order to change software, it must first of all be understood. We saw how important good documentation is, and that if this is available from the start, maintenance costs will be reduced. If not, more that half the maintainer's time could be spent trying to understand the software.

Unfortunately documentation all too often does not represent the system as it actually is. Perhaps the documentation was wrong in the first place, or perhaps it was correct to start with but when the system was evolved the documentation was not evolved alongside it. The system maintainer and evolver needs help, and help has been provided through programmes of research and development aimed at automatically abstracting higher-level descriptions of software from lower-level descriptions, including from the program code itself. This process is known as **reverse engineering**, but also as **redocumentation**, **design recovery**, and **design abstraction**.

Reverse engineering predates software. Engineers have long been challenged by obtaining an artefact produced elsewhere, then to try to understand and replicate that artefact. This might be done for industrial or military espionage purposes, or just out of curiosity. The process required is one of abstraction, and is similar to natural science investigations. We may proceed either structurally or functionally (behaviourally), either looking at what the object is made of, or how it does what it does; in biology this is the distinction between anatomy and physiology. We look for patterns: patterns in the object's structure or patterns in the object's behaviour that taken together match some higher-level view of structure or behaviour.

During the late 1980s and early 1990s reverse engineering was the focus of much academic study and commercial interest. Surveys were published, such as those of Chikovsky and Cross[14] and Hall,[15] and a report for commercial users was even produced by the UK IT consulting organisation Ovum.[16]

Reverse engineering software is easiest when the processes which produced the software are known, since we will then know the higher level structures and behaviour to look for. These higher structures and behaviour then give us the patterns to search for. However, the results of these processes are limited in what they produce, and tools often aid understanding by producing:

- 'call-graphs', maps of the software structure showing which other parts of the software were used by each part;
- 'execution tracers,' showing what happens as the software executes and different parts of the software are invoked.

All these tools are simply aids to understanding. Because the original knowledge necessary to create the software does not get encoded into the formal structures of the software, any tools working on the software just do not have access to

Figure 9.4		

Program in pseudo-code (Pascal) to look up a symbol in a table, with and without meaningful names

(a) *A machine-eye view of code, where the critical thing is name-matching to bind the parts together.*

```
var
  v001: array[1..v009] of record
    v002: char;
    v003: integer;
  end;
  v005: integer;
function f002 (v004: char): integer;
  var
    v007, v008: integer;
  begin
    v008 := 0;
    for v007 := 1to v005 do
      if v001[v007].v002 = v004 then
        begin
          v008 := v001[v007].v003;
          leave;
        end;
    f002 := v008;
  end;
```

(b) *The human-eye view of the code – meaningful identifiers added; comments would add yet more information.*

```
var
  table: array [1..tablesize] of record
    key: char;
    index: integer;
  end;
  lastindex: integer;
function Tlookup (key: char): integer;
  var
    i, loctn: integer;
  begin
    loctn := 0;
    for i := 1 to lastindex do
      if table[i].symbol = key then
        begin
          loctn := table[i].location;
          leave;
        end;
    Tlookup := loctn;
  end;
```

all the information required. This knowledge may, however, be given in the informal structures like the names given to elements in the code, or comments inserted into the code. This issue was very graphically illustrated by Ted Biggerstaff in an example given in 1989;[17] we give an equivalent example in Figure 9.4 in which we see the same program with and without meaningful names. If you add to the human version, Figure 9.4b, comments to further guide understanding, you can see what is missing in the encoded knowledge in software.

We thus see that understanding software, and reverse engineering it to find higher level descriptions of the software, must rest on human guidance and understanding. This will only change when all the knowledge necessary to understand the software is formally encoded in the software, and as we have discussed previously, doing this in its entirety may not be possible.

However, when the reverse engineering is associated with a formalised forward engineering process, and small changes at a low level need to be reverse engineered, it may be tractable, as we will discuss later as **round-trip software engineering**.

> Reverse engineering redocuments a system, but this cannot be fully automated.

9.4.3 Restructuring and refactoring

Restructuring is any reorganisation of the software to make the structure of the code more properly reflect the structure of the processing, placing together code that is tightly coupled, and separating it from code with which it is only loosely coupled. Exactly how this is done may be determined by the currently prevailing design fashion, so during the 1970s it would have been done in terms of 'modules', while by the 1990s it had become restricted to object classes.

Refactoring is a term that has emerged more recently, since 1990, and has become an integral part of Agile methods like **eXtreme Programming**. It is a restricted restructuring associated with more detailed and localised changes primarily in object-oriented systems.[18] There are a number of small transformations that can be made to improve the code without changing what it does – taken together quite significant transformations can be made. Some non-functional properties may be changed, for example performance may be improved by refactoring. Refactoring is done on portions of the code that are particularly difficult to understand or which display a number of topological or other characteristics, typically referred to as 'bad smells'. In general, refactoring and restructuring are done without changing the programming language or underlying technologies.

An example of a simple refactoring is the systematic changing of the variables in a program to be more meaningful. Programmers have to invent names for many things within their programs, and often will choose meaningless single letter identifiers for these, or name the elements after their friends. However if somebody else is to understand the program it is important that all these names indicate their purpose in the program and that they are meaningful. It is a very simple operation to change all the names from one meaningless symbol to something that helps the evolution programmer, and the payback is significant.

Other examples of refactoring transformations are moving methods between classes, replacing recursion with iteration, replacing error codes with exceptions, and many others – Martin Fowlers' website lists ninety of these, and there are many more available elsewhere. Not everybody agrees that these transformations make the code easier to understand. Consider, for example, two of those transformations which are particularly controversial, but which may be pushed by product salesmen:

1. *Recursion* divides a problem into parts, where the subproblems are essentially the same as the original problem and you can reapply the same software, until some primitive cases are arrived at which can be directly solved; if you understand the general idea of recursion this can be a particularly elegant and clear way of presenting the solution, and removing the recursion simply obscures the algorithm.

2. *Exceptions* are an elegant mechanism for handling error situations, leaving the main processing in the absence of errors very clean and understandable – however when errors do arise exactly what happens can be very obscure indeed. The alternative method of using error codes makes exactly what happens in the face of errors very clear, though it may obscure normal processing. Thus replacing error codes by exceptions may be a good idea, but it may not be; it certainly it is not something that should be done without deliberation.

Automatic restructuring of programs requires less human effort than manual restructuring. It has, nevertheless, limitations. For example, after re-engineering, in-line comments may be lost and existing documentation may be unrelated to the new restructured code.

Restructuring a system makes it easier to evolve.

9.4.4 Re-engineering

Refactoring and restructuring takes place at the code level, but the reorganisation of the software can take place at any level, and indeed often must. If the software architecture is inappropriate for the evolutionary changes now intended, then that must be changed.

These higher level changes would be known as **re-engineering**. In this process the software will be restructured and transformed, very likely changing to a new programming language and up-to-date technology in the process. Software re-engineering requires major effort, and would not be handled as routine work but as a major project in its own right.

Because of poor or out-of-date documentation, software re-engineering will normally first require **reverse engineering** of the legacy system as described above. We may need to reverse engineer right back to the requirements, via the architecture, data structures, and other design views of the system.

Whilst normal software development, which in this context we could call **forward engineering**, starts with an application concept or a specification and produces the design and then the executable code; reverse engineering starts with an existing system and its executable code and produces the application design and specification.

Figure 9.5 shows how re-engineering can be defined as reverse engineering followed by forward engineering. The product of re-engineering should be an improved, restructured and remodularised version of the same program, together with new documentation. Reengineering also provides an opportunity to improve functional and non-functional characteristics of the program. Usually during re-engineering of software the functionality of the system and its behaviour are not altered, though the opportunity might be taken to add or change functionality – after all we would very likely be doing the re-engineering in order to enable such changes and additions.

If we close the cycle in Figure 9.5, and overlay the re-engineered software and the existing software, we have **round-trip software engineering**. However we normally reserve this term for situations supported by software development tools, where some original system has been developed with the tools, following which changes can be made at any level, and then propagated both backwards and forwards as appropriate to create a consistent set of descriptions of the software. The changes must be sufficiently small so that the intentions underlying the changes are clear. Then it works.

Some of the disadvantages of re-engineering as opposed to carrying on with the evolution of the software without re-engineering include:

- the developers may need to become familiar with a new programming language and the changed structure of the system, and part of the knowledge of the old system becomes useless;
- the developers may not be comfortable with the automatically generated documentation;
- some of the activities of re-engineering are supported by tools but others require involvement of both the existing developers and those performing the re-engineering, and activities such as rearchitecting and data restructuring can be effort consuming.

There are limits to what technology can do. There is no tool that can take a legacy system, poorly structured and poorly documented, and produce a fully documented and adequately structured program. But there are many tools that can help, and as we have discussed so frequently throughout this book, we would expect such challenging processes to be undertaken by people assisted by tools. Re-engineering requires the involvement of experts in the use of the re-engineering tools, working together with the developers in charge of the system being re-engineered, so that both groups can share knowledge about the application.

As we saw in Chapter 2, the term re-engineering is also used for business processes as business process re-engineering (BPR). The difference between software re-engineering and BPR is that the first transforms a legacy system whilst keeping

> Re-engineering completely restructures the software to reproduce the old system in new technology.

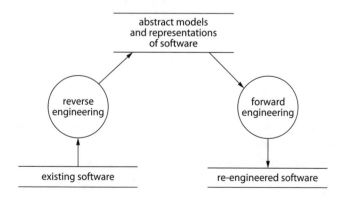

Figure 9.5

Re-engineering as formed by reverse engineering followed by forward engineering

Software re-engineering preserves the business rules within the software; business process re-engineering changes the business rules.

the functionality, as perceived by external users, as nearly unchanged as possible, while in BPR, the business process itself is changed and the functionality of the software supporting the business process needs to be changed as well. Chapter 2 provides an example of BPR: the process of registering students for distance education courses is changed by the introduction of new technology – the Internet – which leads to business process change, which then triggers the need for changing the software functionality.

Activity 9.5 *Re-engineering versus new software*

An alternative to re-engineering a legacy system is the acquisition of new software, replacing the legacy software by a completely new acquisition. Compare and contrast the process of re-engineering with the acquisition of new software.

Discussion
Total replacement by new software can be more costly and entail more risks than re-engineering. Generally an old legacy system embeds many undocumented business rules. For example, a bank may have a set of rules for a bank account to be opened. The rules are sometimes embedded in the software managing the customers' accounts. The development of a new system requires documented requirements that sometimes are not available. The existing legacy software becomes itself the documentation of the business rules. Hence, one of the characteristics of re-engineering is that the old system becomes the specification of the new re-engineered system. The old system can equally well be used as a specification when a system is completely reimplemented.

Finding general evidence to support the effectiveness of particular software engineering practices is difficult. Thus software organisations must gather their own evidence in their own organisation, and be systematic in the way they measure their products and processes, to evaluate the impact of their internal processes on product improvements.

9.5 Maintainability and evolvability

We have seen that changing software can be difficult and involve significant costs.

- As the software ages, it is more and more likely that the original developers have been assigned to other activities or gone elsewhere. The new people in charge of the work may have an incomplete and even erroneous understanding of the system.
- As change accumulates upon change, the complexity of the software is likely to increase, making it more difficult to implement changes.
- Pressures for functional enhancements make the software grow in size. All other factors remaining the same, the larger the code base the more difficult it is to understand.

- The conceptual and architectural integrity of the software is likely to deteriorate as changes are implemented by new and inexperienced personnel in a manner which does not take into account the overall system.

- The various software artefacts which were generated during the preparation of the first operational release, such as requirements documents, specifications, design, and user documentation may not be kept up to date simply because of the cost of such activity or the lack of adequate tools.

We saw that this difficulty could be significantly improved by improving the software. Can the state of the software be measured, and can improvements through restructuring and re-engineering be measured?

9.5.1 Measuring ease of change

A software system can be considered maintainable when the required changes can be easily and rapidly implemented within the available resources.

When implementing a software system for the first time and during its subsequent evolution, trade-offs must be made between maintainability and other desirable properties. Maintainability may be more important for certain types of system than for others. For example, a system which will be only used once as a prototype may not require the same degree of maintainability as another which will be in continual use and critical to the operations of their stakeholders. Moreover, maintainability is itself a complex property that could be decomposed into other properties, including the complexity of the software, the quality of the documentation, and so on.

Maintainability of software is related to the wider sustainability of a business. The evolution of software involves trade-offs, such as stopping work on new functionality and dedicating time to cleaning up the existing system and its documentation. Managing software maintainability involves attention to both technical and human factors.

A basic measurement of maintainability would be the time and effort required to fix a defect, including the diagnosis and the implementation phases. The time to fix a defect is sometime termed the 'mean time to change' or MTTC. Also of interest is the size of the backlog of user-requests, the number of defects and their severity, and the ratio between the cost of the initial development and the cost of fixing defects.

There are a number of pure software metrics that can be used during maintenance. These include design metrics,[19] which can be used to judge the quality of a design and also to identifying candidates for preventive maintenance. Some studies[20] have found that lower measures of complexity at the architectural and functional level are correlated with lower maintenance costs and defect rates. However, there are many aspects of complexity and there is no single metric which reflects them all. Case Study 9.4 provides one example of the successful use of maintainability metrics at Hewlett-Packard.

As a system is evolved, historical records such as change logs – the register of each change performed, when and by whom – and similar records provide raw data from which useful metrics can be derived. We need to accumulate data in order to identify trends; this means that we can only make real use of historical

> The ease of software change can be measured in a number of ways.

Case Study 9.4 *A maintainability index at Hewlett-Packard*[21]

Oman and Hagemeister[22] at Hewlett-Packard (HP) created a maintainability index for an entire system which was intended to capture three different dimensions: the control and information structures and level of comments by means of a particular mathematical function (a polynomial). Coleman and colleagues[23] applied this maintainability index to several software systems at HP in 1994. The first step involved the calibration of the maintainability index using several other metrics such as an extended version of the cyclomatic complexity measure, the number of lines of code, the number of lines of comments, and the effort measure as defined in Halstead's *Elements of Software Science*.[24] Coleman *et al.* studied 714 third-party components (equivalent to 236,000 lines of code written in C). The polynomial index was used to rank the components ac-cording to the expected maintenance difficulty with the result corresponding to the intuitive or 'gut feeling' appreciation by HP personnel. The maintenance index was reported to match the intuition of HP maintainers in subsequent studies. It is also reported that the additional information provided by the measurements has other uses: helping to decide whether to develop in house or to buy components, and for targeting pieces of software for preventative and perfective work. The maintenance index was also used to evaluate the impact of re-engineering. Despite the success reported in this case study, the measurement and management of maintainability is still a topic with many unresolved issues, as for example when the software is built from components using different languages and technologies.

records after several iterations of the evolution process (e.g., after several releases). These trends can help to make strategic decisions about the software. They can be used, to a certain extent, to predict productivity, defect density and so on. As a software system evolves, the historical trends provide an indication of the rate of work that the software organisation can safely achieve. The history of the system also offers a baseline against which future improvements of processes and products can be measured. Observations suggest that the level of work required for systems being continually evolved tends to stabilise, even though drastic transitions may occur, as when re-engineering or restructuring is applied.

Measurements that you can use include the growth (in lines of code or number of files) of the system over time or releases. It is also useful to plot the number of changes implemented and the portion of the system examined (added or changed) by the maintainers over a period of time (e.g., one month) or during a release interval. Long-term measurements have to be used with due care and we must avoid a blind projection of the past trends into the future.

The classification of software evolution activity into corrective, perfective, adaptive, and preventive, presented earlier, can be useful in several ways. For example, managers can quantify the different types of work and use the result in process and product improvement – a manager might desire a low level of corrective work and prefer that the majority of the work is applied to enhancement activities which are likely to provide real value to stakeholders. Managers may want to know what percentage of the maintenance budget is consumed by defect fixing, for example. A high level of adaptive work may indicate that the environment where the software is executing is volatile. It also may indicate lack of sufficient foresight in the planning of the initial architecture of the system, even though one has to recognise that future requirements are difficult to anticipate and that some changes in the environment can invalidate even the most carefully designed architecture.

Historical data gives a useful basis for predicting future maintainability.

9.5.2 Factors that influence maintenance costs

Surveys of software maintenance activity have consistently shown that it consumes a large proportion of the software engineering resources available. In 1988 Arthur[25] summarised the results of a number of surveys conducted from 1972 to 1979; these indicated that between 40 to 80 per cent of the organisation's effort went into maintenance. Observations also suggest that, on average, the expenses incurred in evolving existing systems greatly exceed the cost of developing the original software. In some domains, evolution consumes up to 90 per cent or even more of all the costs incurred during the lifetime of an application. Another observation is that corrective activities represent only a small part of the software maintenance effort, with on average non-corrective work being four times or so the level of effort applied to corrective work.

We have a general idea of the factors that influence the cost of software evolution but this remains to be quantified and encapsulated in estimation models. The vast majority of estimation models that we have for software focus on projects developing from scratch, not on continual evolution. There have been proposals to extend estimation models such as COCOMO to the maintenance phase (see Chapter 10). However, there is little evidence of empirical support and practical success of these so called 'maintenance extensions'. The majority of software organisations still rely on expert knowledge for costing and planning the work on long-lived software systems.

The fact that systems are evolved over many years, even decades, offers the opportunity for the use of historical records to identify trends and use them in planning the future of a software system. However, the study and modelling of these trends has to be done with due care. Even if a trend is apparent, changes in the software itself (e.g., due to re-engineering), in the software process, or in the environment, can invalidate previous trends. We will come back to this point later in this chapter when we discuss the presence of stages in the evolution life cycle of a software system.

Despite the lack of quantitative models, a qualitative understanding of the cost factors involved in software evolution can be useful for managers. These factors affect maintainability and hence the costs of implementing changes. Figure 9.6 shows an influence diagram of these cost factors for drivers. The major cost drivers, shown in larger type in the figure, will be discussed below. The drivers shown in smaller type are less significant, though still important.

Personnel

The motivation, knowledge, experience, and stability of personnel involved in software was discussed in Chapter 3. If a separate maintenance organisation is established it can help by spreading good practice and by making the software better understood within a community of practice. If developers maintain their own programs it is likely that they will be able to do the work faster and that costs will be less; they also then have the incentive to make their software maintainable since

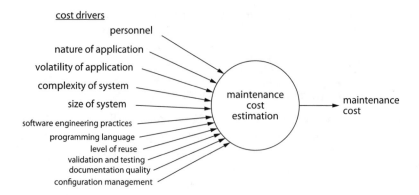

Figure 9.6

Cost drivers for
maintenance cost

it will be for their own benefit! The critical issue could be the continued involvement of the original software architects – the architectural integrity of an evolving software system is likely to suffer once the original architects leave the organisation, and this could be the critical point at which a system becomes very difficult to evolve further.

Nature and volatility of the application

Some application domains are well understood while other application domains may be new and involve much innovation. In well-known application areas it is more likely that we will achieve a set of requirements which is stable and will satisfy the majority of the stakeholders. In new areas the requirements may well be incomplete and change as we learn more, with need for adaptive work.

Level of complexity

Complex software is harder to maintain and evolve. As change upon change are implemented, the structure of the program is likely to degrade and complexity increase. This is what Parnas called the 'software ageing phenomenon,'[26] described above in section 9.3 As we saw, these effects can be mitigated by continual rework.

Size of the program

The size of the software, measured for example in lines of code or number of files, can be an important cost driver in software maintenance. In general, the larger the system, the more expensive the maintenance will be. Over time a system actively used and evolved will tend to grow in size and complexity as new functions and modifications to existing functions are implemented. Large programs are usually maintained by more than one person or even more than one group, involving at least two levels of management. This adds to the complexity of the communication and implementation of changes as these need to be agreed. Those involved need to be kept informed and this consumes time and effort.

Certain software technologies may help to make the software more maintainable, though the evidence to support claims in this area is insubstantial. We will see below that there are software product and process characteristics that help reduce the costs of maintenance; these were also shown in Figure 9.6 in smaller type. Note configuration management in Figure 9.6 – this ensures that the right version of all the software is sent to users and facilitates the traceability of changes – see Chapter 11.

Activity 9.6   *Objected-oriented maintenance*

What would be the impact of object-oriented techniques in reducing maintenance costs ? (Object-oriented approaches were discussed in Chapters 7 and 8.)

Discussion
One would expect that the use of object-oriented techniques would promote a higher degree of encapsulation and reuse than other techniques. Moreover, object-oriented languages are high level. These factors can contribute to a reduction of maintenance costs. On the other hand, one has to consider that there are many other factors such as quality of documentation, programming style, and so on, which, if they are not properly taken care of, can attenuate any possible benefits derived from object-oriented techniques.

The cost of software evolution is influenced by many cost drivers.

9.6 Management guidance

When we looked at the development of new software in Chapter 8 we saw a range of possible software processes that could be followed. A software process is a sequence of development activities. These usually ended in a simple activity labelled 'maintenance' or 'evolution'.

We need to look inside this evolution process, and through it understand how to guide the evolution process and make it effective.

9.6.1 Process models for software evolution

Software evolution processes do not remain the same throughout the life of the software. Mikio Aoyama[27] found this when he studied the evolution of mobile phone software in Japan over a period of four years. During the late 1990s, mobile phones went through extremely fast evolution from being voice communication devices to becoming mobile Internet terminals, and more recently, mobile Java-enabled terminals. The code base studied by Aoyama increased its size by a factor of four in four years.

Bennett and Rajlich[28] have also looked at a number of long-lived software systems. They concluded that a software system is likely to go through several distinct stages during its operational lifetime. Recognition of these stages can be helpful for managers since they can then adapt the management approach to a particular stage. Figure 9.7 shows their model.

According to this model, after initial development, the software enters a stage that Bennett and Rajlich call 'evolution' (though we are using this term for the complete process from first release to final close down). This stage is characterised by the implementation of a relatively large number of enhancements and adaptations to address new and changed requirements. Defects are also fixed, but during the evolution stage, the majority of the work is absorbed by changes to the system.

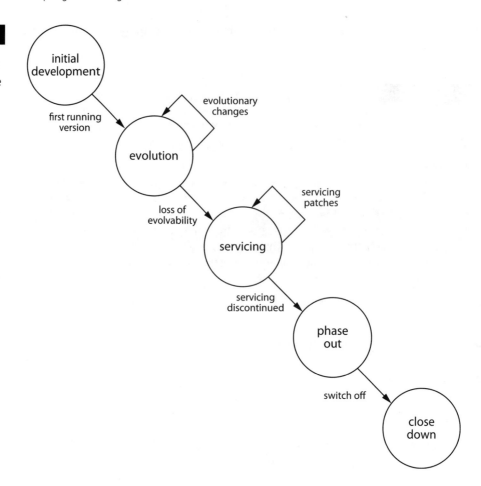

Figure 9.7

Bennett and Rajlich's staged model for the total software lifecycle[28]. © 2000 IEEE

Software evolution proceeds through a number of distinct phases from first release to final close down.

For several possible reasons (for example, the system has become very large and difficult to evolve, or key architects have left the organisation, or the organisation has lost interest in the system), the software goes from 'evolution' into a stage called 'servicing'. During servicing, only essential work is done in order to keep the system running (e.g., patches to fix defects and vulnerabilities). Servicing is followed by a stage called 'phase out', in which the system may be still used, but without any support, until the system is finally completely closed down.

A system which is actively evolved in the evolution stage is very different from another which is serviced with only minor essential changes implemented. During servicing the ultimate phasing out and replacement are being anticipated.

9.6.2 Management decision-making involving long-lived software

Even though our decision to invest in software will have taken into account evolution and maintenance costs to consider the total cost of ownership in our return on investment decision, as covered in Chapter 2, later on we may still have difficulties justifying expenditure on maintenance and evolution. Keith Bennett[29] has argued that one of the problems in justifying this expenditure is that software is then seen as an expense rather than an investment.

However, the initial purchase of software may also be seen as an expense when there is no competitive advantage in making particular choices over others, and thus the aim in acquisition is to choose the cheapest option that fulfils the requirements. What is critical is that the original decision will have included expectations of expenditure on maintenance and evolution as part of the total investment, and viewing the evolution costs later on as an expense that can be reduced invalidates that original decision.

Activity 9.7   *Saving on initial development*

Under what circumstances is it desirable, or professionally acceptable, for costs and timescales to be reduced during initial development? For example in order to deliver the product within a marketing window, is it acceptable to save on some quality-enhancing activities like thorough testing and documentation, deferring these costs until after delivery of the system? Can you compensate for this during the subsequent maintenance and evolution?

Discussion

If quality is going to be added in later during maintenance and evolution, it is likely that it will be more difficult than trying to address quality issues from the start of development. As key architectural decisions are made and the code base increases, product improvements become increasingly difficult. Once the system has become very large and complex, even a small change may have a ripple effect through the system. This makes the strategy of 'adding quality later' a risky one.

If the software is written by a contractor with a subsequent maintenance contract, one could argue that it is unethical to undertake a cheap but poor development with the view of recovering costs during maintenance. However, for a software company trying to hit a marketing window, the strategy could be acceptable, provided that the software meets its basic quality requirements, that no unsubstantiated claims are made about the software or its capability, and that none of the stakeholders of the software are put under unacceptable risk. For example, the 'adding quality later' strategy will be clearly unacceptable for safety-critical software applications.

Daniel Freedman told a story at a seminar of an election forecasting system which was still not working to the developers' satisfaction as the election date grew near and the system was required. A board meeting decided to deliver the software anyway, on the grounds that if they delayed they would lose the customer altogether, and anyway nobody believed election forecasts so it did not matter if it was wrong!

The lesson from Activity 9.7 is very important indeed for maintenance and evolution decisions, and exemplifies the issues we always face in investment. The break-even point for investment is, as we saw in Chapter 2, long after the investment has been started, or even completed. Look at Figure 9.8 to see this illustrated in a similar way to the return on investment curves of Figure 2.7 in Chapter 2. Taking action to ensure quality during initial development is a form of investment, where the payback comes later in lower maintenance and evolution costs. To be able to make such a decision we really do need to know what the relationship is between investment in quality and savings on evolution. For example, if we invest in insulating a house, we know that we will benefit from lower heating costs and a

Costs can be
moved from
development into
evolution and
maintenance.

warmer house, and can calculate relatively precisely what the relationships are. But regrettably we cannot do that for software quality and evolution.

There are no widely accepted quantitative models for the estimation of the costs of evolving a software system, and it is difficult to anticipate the level of changes in requirements that would drive that evolution. The use of techniques such as net present value, discussed in Chapter 2, can help support software life cycle decisions (e.g., replacement vs re-engineering). We will return to this problem of cost estimation and justification again in Chapter 10.

Figure 9.8

Alternative
approaches to
software
development and
evolution for a
fictitious system

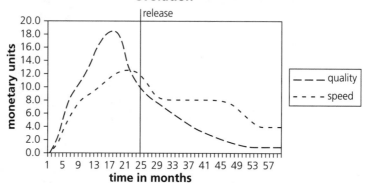

9.8a Monthly spend – note that the curve 'quality' spends more initially and saves later

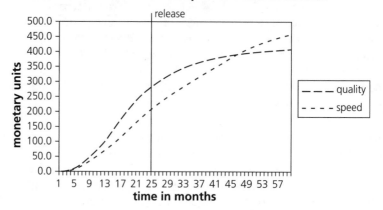

9.8b Accumulated spend – note how initially the quality curve is more expensive until the extra
      evolution costs of the 'speed' solution take over

*Note how at release at Month 24 the quality option seems significantly more expensive, but after Month
   47 it is turning out cheaper

9.6.3 Evolution management guidelines

The laws of software evolution, seen in Table 9.1 provide useful inputs into understanding the software process and form part of a theory of software evolution. One of the outputs of such theory would be a set of guidelines for management.

Tables 9.2 and 9.3 give the main management guidelines that Lehman and colleagues have given based on the laws[30] and underpinning case studies. Once set out like this, the recommendations of course seem self-evident, but the important point is that they can be linked to empirical evidence. Some of these recommendations may be difficult and too expensive to implement. All have potential long-term benefit in terms of productivity, increased predictability, maintainability, changeability, and so on. The recommendations in Table 9.2 are particularly appropriate for safety- and business- critical applications where failing to achieve an adequate evolution of software can be very serious. The recommendations in Table 9.3 are applicable to systems evolved by organisations made up of a number of different groups.

1	Prepare comprehensive specifications and maintain them.
2	Formalise specifications (long-term goal).
3	Capture, document, structure, and retain assumptions in specifications.
4	Verify assumptions as part of verifying specifications.
5	Capture, update, and fully document assumptions during design, implementation, integration, and validation work.
6	Develop and use tool support for specification work and recording of assumptions in structured form (as database), classified by appropriate categories, throughout the process.
7	Document assumptions, design, and implementation rationale underlying a change.
8	Periodically review the assumption set.
9	Validation of all changes, including local and incremental changes, must include a check of the continued validity of assumptions.
10	Assess domain and system volatility and take this into account in implementation.
11	Estimate likelihood of change in the application domain and its sub-domains, and their impact on assumptions.
12	Conduct both periodic and event-triggered reviews and assessments of likelihood of change in assumption sets.
13	Improve questioning of assumptions by, for example, using independent implementation and validation teams.
14	Provide ready access by evolution teams to all appropriate domain specialists.

Table 9.2

Lehman's main recommendations related to formalisation and assumption management

15	Create and update comprehensive documentation to minimise the impact of growing complexity.
16	Apply sufficient effort to control and reduce complexity and its growth.
17	Plan for clean-up releases after the addition of major increments of functionality and/or large functional changes.
18	Observe safe change rate limits in planning and implementing change and evolution.
19	Constrain scope and size of release-functional increments based on past successful incremental growth.
20	Alternate major (functional enhancement, extension) and minor (clean up, restructuring) releases.

Table 9.3

Lehman's main recommendations related to release management

21   Validation of all changes including local and incremental changes, must also address interaction with and impact on that part of the system that is not changed. Validation of all changes must include a check of the continued validity of assumptions.

22   Collect, plot, and model historical data to determine patterns, trends and rates of change and growth.

23   Establish baselines of key process and product measures over time and releases.

24   Use recent data to assess, recalibrate, and improve metric-based planning models.

25   Based on the incremental size of the previous releases, derive criteria to determine safe, risky or unsafe growth increments.

26   When a release with large incremental growth appears to be required, split into several releases as in evolutionary development.

27   To minimise interaction between system elements, follow recognised software engineering principles, for e.g., information hiding, when implementing and evolving functionality.

28   Consider, model, and manage the global process that embeds the technical process.

29   Consider, model, and manage formal and informal organisational links as part of the global process.

30   Model the system dynamics[31] of the global process.

32   Use dynamic models to identify interactions, improve planning, and control strategies.

33   Use dynamic models to plan further work.

34   Use dynamic models when seeking process improvement.

Activity 9.8   *Lehman's guidelines and stage evolution*

Relate Lehman's guidelines in Tables 9.2 and 9.3 to Bennett and Rajlich's staged model of evolution.

Discussion

One of the implications of Bennett and Rajlich's model of staged evolution is that evolution is not static and that management of software system evolution should be tailored to individual stages. There are two stages which are of particular interest: evolution and servicing. During evolution all Lehman's recommendations (Tables 9.2 and 9.3) are relevant. However, during servicing only Table 9.2 (management of assumptions) is really relevant. The recommendations in Table 9.3 lose relevance during servicing, since within this stage the amount of work carried out on the system is minimal and all the releases are likely to be minor defect-fixing releases and patches.

Activity 9.9   *Engineering experience and maintenance*

If you are the manager responsible for assigning software engineers to both projects developing new software and projects maintaining existing software, with a pool of both experienced and inexperienced engineers to draw from, how would you make this assignment based on their experience only?

Discussion

The assignment of technical personnel to tasks is a complex issue with many factors involved. There seems to be a natural tendency to assign the less experienced personnel to maintenance, based on the rationale that their exposure to existing code will provide them with a way to gain the experience they need. However, T. McCabe, well known for the software complexity metric he proposed in the 70s, is of the opinion[32] that those occupied with software maintenance activities should be the most skilful, well-trained, and better-supported personnel. Changing an existing software system requires at least as high a level of experience and discipline as developing a system from scratch. Software maintainers have often to implement changes to complex systems that are difficult to understand. Implementing changes to systems can lead to the introduction of new defects. If changes are done 'on the fly' to operational systems any new defects have a high risk of impacting the application, a serious concern in safety-critical and mission-critical applications. Thus maintenance requires mature knowledge about software systems and the likely impact of changes – and hence experienced engineers.

The IEEE has published a standard on software maintenance (IEEE 1219-1998) that provides guidance to organisations setting up maintenance and evolution processes.[33] The standard, however, does not cover the issues emerging in the more recent processes such as Agile and open source methods.

> The common-sense management of software evolution can be grounded empirically through Lehman's laws.

9.6.4 In house or outsourced?

In Chapter 6 we saw a range of ways in which software could be acquired, and some of those options also apply to software evolution, except that it is a little more complex now, since there is an interplay between how we have chosen to acquire the software and now how we choose to maintain and evolve it. For both acquisition and evolution, we can either do it ourselves in house, or rely on a package

Table 9.4   Acquisition and maintenance matrix

The commentary within the table shows the relationship between the maintenance organisation and ourselves the users

		Maintenance organisation		
		User organisation	Original developers	Third-party maintainers
Development organisation	User org bespoke	In-house maintenance	In-house maintenance	Outsource contract
	Package or open source	Customise in house and then maintain	Take package, update, and recustomise	Only possible for open source
	Outsourced bespoke	In-house maintenance	Original contract included maintenance	Independent contract placed

Outsourcing maintenance to third parties should be considered.

developer (whether proprietary or open source), or place a contract to outsource the work either onshore or offshore to some third party. This leads to the matrix of options shown in Table 9.4.

When maintenance is undertaken and who does it can be crucial, for if the maintenance organisation is separate from the original developing organisation, there might well be the temptation to compromise maintainability to save costs during development. There is a story, possibly a myth, that when Henry Ford was asked what to do about the waste from factories polluting a river, he replied that they should be forced to take their water from the river below their own outflows into the river. An organisation living with its own mistakes has merit!

Managing software evolution requires complex decisions involving human, business, financial, technical, and non-technical factors. Wherever maintenance happens, we need to ensure discipline in implementing changes and in maintaining the behaviour of the software within its environment to the satisfaction of the stakeholders.

Summing up

In this chapter we saw that:

- during software evolution we maintain the satisfaction of the stakeholders in the software as a long-life asset of the organisation;
- software co-evolves with the organisation it supports with changes being corrective, adaptive, perfective, or preventive;
- configuration management and regression testing are critically important processes in software evolution;
- software changes the organisation it is intended to support;
- software deteriorates as it evolves unless action is taken explicitly to prevent it; its quality cannot be guaranteed;
- evolution is much easier if the system being evolved is well engineered;
- reverse engineering redocuments a system, but this cannot be fully automated; restructuring a system makes it easier to evolve; re-engineering completely restructures the software to reproduce the old system in new technology;
- software re-engineering preserves the business rules embedded within the software, while business process re-engineering changes the business rules;
- the ease of software change can be measured in a number of ways, with historical data giving the basis for predicting future maintainability;
- the cost of software evolution is influenced by many cost drivers, and costs can be moved from development into evolution and maintenance given an appropriate rationale;
- software evolution proceeds through a number of distinct phases from first release to final close-down; with common-sense management grounded empirically through Lehman's laws;
- outsourcing maintenance to third parties should be considered.

This chapter provided you with an overview of the challenges involved; the concepts, tools, observations, and guidelines which can be useful in managing software change. The management processes for software evolution are similar to those for initial software development. Resource management issues are picked up in Chapter 10, with the important tools of configuration and change control being covered in Chapter 11.

Exercises

1. While Case Study 9.1 about the Y2K or 'Millenium bug' established that software can continue in service for many years, much software, like websites, has a relatively short life. However even in their short lives they should be a positive asset to the organisation and have to continue to satisfy their stakeholders. Discuss the maintenance problems of websites and the extent to which even these conform to Lehman's laws.

2. Consider the following events requiring changes to the school library system introduced in Chapter 7, which have arisen after one year in service:

   a. The school library is to be extended to be a community library, holding many more books and permitting many new classes of borrower.
   b. Certain books when removed illicitly from the library fail to trigger the alarm system.
   c. Government regulation is introduced that certain books considered of an adult nature are only to be allowed to be read by children while in the library under adult supervision.
   d. The radio identification system is found to have a serious defect and the manufacture of this system is no longer in business.
   e. The number of books a student is allowed to borrow at one time is to be doubled.

   For each event say what kind of change is involved: corrective, adaptive, perfective, or preventive. Indicate whether the changes required are purely to the software, or whether they will also involve the way the school is managed, thus co-evolving the school with the software.

3. You have decided to adopt a maintainability assessment method[34] based on a table of factors as shown below.

   a. Each factor is awarded a score between 0 and 10 by an engineer who knows the system, to indicate how maintainable the system is relative to that factor. For example, a relatively old system may be awarded a score of 8 out of 10 to indicate that due to its age the system will be relatively difficult to maintain.
   b. Each factor will have been assigned a weighting between 0 and 10 by a group of experienced software engineers to indicate its importance to the overall maintainability of the system – the higher the score the less maintainable the system.
   c. The scores for each of the factors assessed are then multiplied by the appropriate weighting and the resultant products are then summed to give an overall score which forms the *maintainability measure* (MM) of the system (the lower the score, the better the maintainability of the software system).
   d. If the overall score is more than 300 you need to do something about the system.

The system you are working on has been given scores as in the following table:

Factor	Weight	Actual score	Weighted score
Business requirement complexity	9	3	27
Application complexity	9	8	72
Data structures complexity	7	6	42
Code complexity	8	5	40
Change history documentation	5	9	45
Business documentation	4	6	24
Architectural documentation	6	7	42
Code annotation	7	8	56
Code size	6	4	24
Release frequency	8	2	16
Overall total MM			**388**

Explain what you should now do to your system. What tools should you use, if any?

4. Write a couple of pages evaluating the maintainability measurement of Exercise 3, explaining how it could be improved.

5. Many software technologies and tools have been advocated on the basis of reducing maintenance costs. This is the case of object-oriented programming. Do a search on the Internet for papers showing hard empirical evidence supporting these claims. You can try several searches based on keyword combinations at the site of http://portal.acm.org/portal.cfm. Read the abstracts of some of the papers with suggestive titles. What are your conclusions? (Accessing the full paper may not be possible unless you are a registered user.)

6. During the 1980s an entrepreneur in Germany, Harry Sneed,[35] set up companies in Eastern Europe to reverse engineer new systems. The sales argument was that it was common practice in software development projects to find yourself under time pressure as the planned delivery date approached. The temptation then was to compromise on documentation in order to meet the deadline. But documentation could be produced retrospectively after the delivery of the system for perhaps only 20 per cent of the overall project costs, with the added advantage that it could be guaranteed that the documentation matched the system as delivered. Imagine that your manager has asked you to investigate whether this could be done for all systems your company produces, offshoring this documentation process to Asia. Write a short report for your company senior management advising them whether or not they should set up this retrospective documentation process.

7. Look up business simulation either in a library or on the Internet, and find out how it might be applied to making decisions about how to maintain software that you have developed in house. Should it be maintained in house or outsourced to some third party? Build the relevant simulation models, and if you can, run these. What are the critical parameters that will determine your decision?

Endnotes

1. This observation is due to Manny Lehman.
2. Cited by E.S. Flint (1997) 'The COBOL Jigsaw Puzzle: Fitting Object-oriented and Legacy Applications Together', *IBM Systems Journal*, 36(1).
3. Anthony Finkelstein made this observation in an article in the *Daily Telegraph* in the UK in April 1998, and in a BBC radio interview.
4. This classification originated with B.P. Leintz and E.B. Swanson (1980) *Software Maintenance Management*. Addison-Wesley. A different classification based on objective evidence has been proposed by N. Chapin, J.E. Hale, K.M. Khan, J.F. Ramil, and W.G. Tan (2001) 'Types of Software Evolution and Software Maintenance', *Journal of Software Maintenance and Evolution: Res. and Practice*, 13(1), Jan/Feb, 1–30.
5. M.M. Lehman and L.A. Belady (eds) (1985) *Software Evolution – Processes of Software Change*. Academic Press.
6. F.P. Brooks (1995) *The Mythical Man-Month* (20th anniversary edn, 1st edn. 1975). Addison-Wesley.
7. P. Naur and B. Randell (eds)(1968) *Software Engineering* – Report on a Conference Sponsored by the NATO SCIENCE COMMITTEE, Garmish, Germany, 7–11 Oct 1968, p. 15. Available at http://homepages.cs.ncl.ac.uk/brian.randell/NATO/.
8. M.M. Lehman and J.F. Ramil (2003) Software Evolution: Observation, Practice, Theory. ESEC/FSE 2003, Half Day Tutorial, Helsinki, Finland, 2 Sep 2003, available via links at http://mcs.open.ac.uk/jfr46/710c.mml.esec.fse03.pdf.
9. M.M. Lehman and J.F. Ramil (2002) An Overview of Some Lessons Learnt in FEAST, WESS' 02, Montreal, 2 Oct 2002.
10. This Uncertainty Principle was originally proposed in M.M. Lehman (1989) 'Uncertainty in Computer Application and its Control Through the Engineering of Software', *J. of Software Maintenance: Research and Practice*, 1(1), 3–27.
11. See CERN Bulletin 09/98, 23 Feb 1998, The Earth breathes on LEP and LHC. Available at http://bulletin.cern.ch/9809/art1/Text_E.html.
12. David Parnas, Design for maintenance and maintaining design. Keynote Address, ICSM 2001, Florence, Italy, 6–10 Nov 2001.
13. See Garish Parikh and Nicholas Zvegintzov (eds)(1983) 'Tutorial on Software Maintenance', *IEEE Computer Society*.
14. E.J. Chikovsky and J.H. Cross II (1990) 'Reverse Engineering and Design Recovery: a Taxonomy', *IEEE Software*, pp. 13–17.
15. P.A.V. Hall (1992) 'Overview of Software Reuse and Reverse Engineering Research', *IST Journal*, April 1992, pp, 239–249.
16. Rosemary Rock-Evans and Keith Hales (1990) *Reverse Engineering: Markets, Methods and Tools*. Ovum.
17. T.J. Biggerstaff (1989) 'Design Recovery for Maintenance and Reuse', *IEEE Computer*, V. 22(7), 36–49, July.
18. See, for example, Martin Fowlers' website: http://www.refactoring.com/ or his book, Martin Fowler (2000) *Refactoring: Improving the Design of Existing Code*. Addison Wesley.
19. Examples of design metrics are the level of fan-in (the number of input lines on the chart) and fan-out (the number of output lines on the chart), while for a flowchart or PDL or program code the cyclomatic complexity (see McCabe, below) gives an indication of the difficulty of understanding a function by measuring how many independent paths in the control flow can be found in the code. See T. McCabe (1976) 'A Complexity Measure', *IEEE Transactions on Software Engineering*, 12(4), 308–320. See also S. Henry and D. Kafura (1981) 'Software Structure Metrics Based on Information Flow', *IEEE Transactions on Software Engineering*, 7(5), 510–518. There is an earlier slightly different definition, based on the number of calls that a module receives (fan-in) and number of calls it generates to other modules (fan-out), given in B.H. Yin and J.W. Winchester (1978) 'The Establishment and Use of Measures to Evaluate the Quality of Software Design', *Performance Evaluation Review*, 7(3–4), Nov. 1978, pp. 45–52.
20. David N. Card and Robert L. Glass (2000) *Measuring Software Design Quality*. Prentice-Hall.
21. Summarised from the account given by Shari Pfleeger (2001) *Software Engineering – Theory and Practice* (2nd edn) Prentice Hall. p. 486.

22. P. Oman and J. Hagemeister (1992) 'Metrics for Assessing Software System Maintainability', *Proc. ICSM 1992*, IEEE Computer Press, 337–344.

23. D. Coleman, D. Ash, B. Lowther and P. Oman (1994) 'Using Metrics to Evaluate Software System Maintainability', *IEEE Computer*, 27(8), 44–49.

24. M. Halstead (1977) *Elements of Software Science*, Elsevier/North Holland. This work postulated a relationship between effort applied to writing a program and various software metrics. Later this work was subject to criticism by several researchers (e.g., Gillian Frewin) in which the postulated relationships were shown not to be so clear. Software science metrics have at least one merit: they are a rare example of software metrics that are based on a set of expressions with explanatory power (a theory). It is more frequent to find empirical models derived from data, but which cannot be explained or given a meaning.

25. L. J. Arthur (1988) *Software Evolution: The Software Maintenance Challenge*. Wiley.

26. D.L. Parnas (1994) 'Software Ageing', *Proc. ICSE 16*, Sorrento, Italy, 16–21 May, 279–287.

27. M. Aoyama (2001) 'Continuous and Discontinuous Software Evolution: Aspects of Software Evolution Across Multiple Product Lines', *Proc. IWPSE 2001*, Vienna, Sept 10–11, 2001, ACM Press, 87–90.

28. K.H. Bennett and V.T. Rajlich 'Software Maintenance and Evolution: A Roadmap', *The Future of Software Engineering, ICSE 2000*, ACM Press, 2000, 73–87.

29. K. Bennett (2000) 'Software Maintenance: A Tutorial', in M. Dorfan and R.H. Thayer (eds), *Software Engineering*, IEEE Computer Society Press, pp. 289–303.

30. For details on the reasoning that led to each of these guidelines see M.M. Lehman and J.F. Ramil (2001) 'Rules and Tools for Software Evolution Planning and Management', *Annals of Software Engineering, special issue on Software Management*, 11(1), 15–44.

31. Some of the recommendations of Table 9.3 refer to system dynamic models. Such models are representations of the software process which can be executed as simulation models: managers can use these models to predict the performance of the process and to assess the impact of possible process improvements. One of the best documented software process simulation models is by T.K. Abdel-Hamid and S.E. Madnick (1991) *Software Project Dynamics: An Integrated Approach*. Prentice-Hall.

32. McCabe expressed this opinion in an informal conversation with several conference attendees.

33. A commentary on a previous version of the IEEE Software Maintenance standard is given in K. Bennett (2000) 'Software Maintenance: A Tutorial', in M. Dorfman and R.H. Thayer(eds), *Software Engineering*, IEEE Computer Society Press, pp. 289–303.

34. Adapted from http://www.testingstandards.co.uk/maintainability_guidelines.htm.

35. H. Sneed and G. Jandrasics (1987) Software recycling. *Software Maintenance Conference*, Austin 1987.

Managing software processes

10 Managing resources

11 Managing work-products and digital assets

12 Managing quality

13 Managing uncertainty and risk

Making it all happen

The acquisition processes described in Part II will happen in the context described in Part I. The processes involved with software can become very complex and need careful management. Part III considers how we can manage the software processes of Part II, ensuring the effective use of resources input into the processes, controlling the many elements produced by the processes and their configuration and change, ensuring their quality, and controlling the many risks and uncertainties involved in software processes.

Chapter 10, Managing resources, considers the management of the resources needed in the software acquisition, software development, and software evolution processes, including people and the working environment. This chapter takes projects as the basic managerial device within which these resources are deployed and managed.

Chapter 11, Managing work-products and digital assets recognises that change needs to be managed and controlled as software is evolved. This is essential to ensure that the software built from the changing parts continues to function as intended when assembled. We need to regulate changes and record versions of components and collections of these versions which belong together. Many of the concepts described in this chapter apply to the change management of any set of digital assets.

Chapter 12, Managing quality, is concerned about the quality of software and how it can be prevented from degrading as it evolves and changes. Quality is an elusive concept, difficult to define, and yet we know a lot about how to manage it. It depends upon the processes being followed, with product improvement closely linked to process improvement. Frameworks such as CMMi help software organisations produce quality software and maintain that quality during evolution.

Chapter 13, Managing uncertainty and risk, deals with the issue of uncertainty in software. Whilst many software projects need well-defined objectives, schedules, and resources, they are executed in uncertain environments where complexity and change are inevitable and risk needs to be identified and managed.

10 Managing resources

What we will study in this chapter

In Part I of this book we saw how software has become integral to our organisations and society, as integral as our buildings and roads and railways. Like the buildings that house an organisation and support its work, software and computer systems need to be acquired and maintained. In Part II we saw in some detail how this can be achieved. Chapter 6 presented different sources for acquiring software, Chapter 7 gave an example of methods for software development, Chapter 8 discussed the various processes by which software can be developed, and Chapter 9 covered software maintenance and evolution. In this chapter, the first of Part III, we consider how to make the activities and processes described in Part II work within the rich context of Part I: how to make it all happen. This chapter discusses the management of the resources needed in the software acquisition and evolution processes, including people and the working environment.

A key managerial device is the project. Projects are human activities that have a clear starting point with some objective or need to be fulfilled, and a clear end point when that need would actually be filled or a decision made not to pursue the attempt further.

This chapter will look at:

- setting up a project;

- the establishment of project objectives or requirements, balancing the competing demands of stakeholders;

- the subsequent management of project objectives and stakeholder expectations;

- the determination of constraints;

- setting project budgets and timescales;

- setting the completion criteria for the project;

- reactive processes working with limited resources;

- reaction to a particular contingency as a small project;

- the infrastructure and tools needed to support the management of projects;

- the management of the working environment;
- the management of technical people.

10.1 Introduction

It is normal to respond to a problem or opportunity by making changes in an organisation, making an investment. Resources need to be assigned to make the changes, and these resources need to be managed. This management typically takes place through a project, and this chapter on resource management mostly focusses on projects, and particularly on software development projects.

Software development involves teams, using sophisticated tools, working to achieve project objectives with limited budgets and defined timescales while interacting with a number of stakeholders.

It is frequently part of the project's work to elicit the requirements, followed by refinement and clarification until they are sufficiently clear so that implementation can start. The actual work of the project may follow a particular process. We saw a number of different software activities and processes in Chapter 8. The end of a project is marked by the achievement of the intended goals or, alternatively, when a decision has been taken to change the project or abandon it.

The kind of projects that we are interested in here, **software development projects**, have as their main deliverable outcome the operational software, together with procedures for its effective use within new or modified business processes, communicated through user documentation and user training. The software being developed may be:

- a bespoke software system to address specific internal needs of the organisation and for use only within the organisation;
- generic software for marketing to multiple users;
- a software component for some larger system such as an organisation or an engineering artefact.

Project management has become a discipline in its own right with many books that cover the topic from a general point of view.[1] Many of the concepts and tools of generic project management apply to software projects. However, some concepts and tools are specific to software, and in this chapter we will be concerned mainly with issues that are specific to software project management. The special features of software projects include the following:

- Software is invisible. This represents a challenge for those managing a software project who must use various devices such as measurement in order to make progress visible.
- Software is an intellectual product, and can be changed relatively easily, though such changes are likely to introduce defects, over time making error-free changes increasingly difficult.

- Software systems can be very complex and difficult to understand, and can include perhaps the most complex systems ever created by mankind.
- The economics of software production are very different from the economics of manufacturing physical goods.

Software projects are very difficult to manage, so much so that during the 1970s and 1980s the term **software crisis** was used to refer to the many projects which ended in failure, and to the shortage of skilled IT personnel. Since the 1990s, the software industry has become more heterogeneous, with a large variety of processes, technology, and tools. As we saw in Chapter 8, component-based development can enable small groups of developers to put together applications which in the past would have required huge amounts of development effort and duration measured in years; and we saw how Agile methods enable rapid change at the cost of less formality and documentation. We no longer talk about the software crisis, but there remains a consensus that software projects are in general difficult to manage. The typical problems that managers encounter in projects are:

- inaccuracy in estimation of cost and schedule, generally over-optimistic, leading to cost overruns and missed delivery deadlines;
- high rate of change in requirements, also known as **requirements creep** or requirements volatility;
- insufficient quality of the software, with high defect rates;
- difficulty in maintaining and evolving the software, due to 'shortcuts' having been taken during development.

Managing a software project and achieving a successful outcome can be very challenging. From time to time, software project failure stories hit the headlines. Some professional groups, such as the ACM Sigsoft, regularly publish problems that have emerged with software (see, for example, the journal *Software Engineering Notes*[2]). Each case can be individually explained and rationalised. Many of these have been attributed to management failure from misconceptions and lack of understanding of the counterintuitive consequences of their decisions. Case Study 10.1 describes some of these counterintuitive consequences.

> A project organises activities and work to achieve defined outcomes under technical, financial, timescale, organisational, and other constraints.

Case Study 10.1   *The 'laws' of software project management*

Fred Brooks in *The Mythical Man-Month* shares the experiences and insight he gained as manager of the IBM OS/360 operating system development in the early 70s, one of the largest and most complex projects of that time. One of his many useful observations, frequently quoted as 'Brooks' law', states that 'Adding people to a late project makes it later.' Brooks was referring to the fact that bringing inexperienced people into a project requires experienced personnel to stop working in the project in order to train the newcomers. The end result is that the project gets further delayed. Another useful observation is 'be prepared to throw one away'. This reflects the experience that sometimes one needs to build a system in order to clarify the requirements and test the technology. Once the learning has been achieved, this system is thrown away, and a new system is built based on the learning

▶

achieved and carefully avoiding the errors made in building the first system.

Albers Endres and Dieter Rombach in their book *A Handbook of Software and Systems Engineering – Empirical Observations, Laws and Theories* (Addison Wesley, 1st ed, May 2003), provide a useful list of insights which are derived from observation and empirical study. Some of these laws relevant to managing resources are:

- 'Individual developer performance varies considerably.' (Sackman's second law)
- 'A multitude of factors influence developer productivity.' (Nelson-Jones law)
- 'Development effort is a (non-linear) function of product size.' (Boehm's third law)

- 'Most cost estimates tend to be too low.' (DeMarco-Glass law)

For some people, these 'laws' can be seen as a set of generalities with little practical value. However, they reflect an attempt to encapsulate observation, received wisdom and experience for which there is a wide consensus. Project management must be learnt through experience and exposure to real-world situations. As empirical studies progress, it is likely that hard empirical evidence will support, refine, or even negate these law-like statements.

Ignoring these laws is to deny the experience of earlier generations of software project managers, and is likely to lead to more software project failure.

The activities involved in managing resources in a software project involve:

- setting up the project;
- establishing the project requirements;
- managing project objectives and stakeholder expectations;
- determining constraints;
- setting project budgets and timescales;
- setting the completion criteria for the project;
- organising and managing activities;
- managing the working environment;
- identifying and managing risks;
- managing technical people.

On a couple of occasions in this chapter we will refer back to the example school library system of Chapter 7 to give examples of management practices covered in this chapter.

10.2 Setting up a project

A project is usually started in response to a problem that needs to be resolved, to fill a need that has been identified – this may be internal to an organisation, or may come in an invitation to tender (ITT) from outside. Depending on the organisation, some form of business analysis will be required. Business analysis involves the recognition of a business opportunity or need, and an analysis of how much should be invested to resolve this, and what return on the investment would be required.

For software products we need to consider the market potential, possible competitors, the product functionality, the expected level of sales and selling price, and so on. Given that the majority of the resources consumed by a software system are not in its development but in its evolution, it is difficult to estimate beforehand the cost and return on investment associated with the software during its full operational lifetime. Hence business analysis most often focusses on the first operational release. Given the level of uncertainty involved in predicting the direction in which the software will be led during its evolution, it is likely that the majority of organisations will seek to recover their investment early in the life of the software.

Once a business case has been made, we start by preparing a project plan. This will be followed by the **requirements document**, elaborating in detail important aspects of the project plan.

10.2.1 The project plan

This document defines the scope, the success criteria, the schedule, and the resources needed for the particular project. Doing this properly can be a costly exercise, but is effort well spent. It can be quite common for the response to an invitation to tender to cost ten per cent or more of the overall value of a prospective contract.

Let's work through the kinds of things that should be covered in this project plan or response to an ITT.

High-level objectives and constraints

The highest level objective of the project could be to reduce costs in a particular part of the organisation or to provide a competitive advantage in some other area. This should be spelled out simply and directly in a way that is easy to understand to both technical and non-technical readers. Any constraints on the project, such as a limitation on the resources that can be used or the need for any solution to use hardware and software from preferred suppliers, needs to be made clear. Definitions of any obscure terms and the meaning of acronyms should be given. This will be elaborated in the project requirements document discussed more fully in the next subsection.

The project organisation

Each project will bring together people with different skills and expertise, inevitably more than one person will be involved, and often there will be tens or even hundreds. They need to be organised into teams that must themselves collaborate in developing the system. We could divide the people into teams following two possible criteria.

The first is separation by life cycle activity. Here the team is divided up into sub-teams with each sub-team responsible each of the different life cycle activities we saw in Chapters 7 and 8. This is illustrated in Figure 10.1.

The second possibility is to arrange the teams by subsystem, assuming that broad top-level architecture has already been determined. Subsystems often have particular skills and knowledge needs. Figure 10.2 illustrates this. Each team undertakes the full sequence of life cycle activities, working in parallel, and has to negotiate with other teams about interfaces between subsystems.

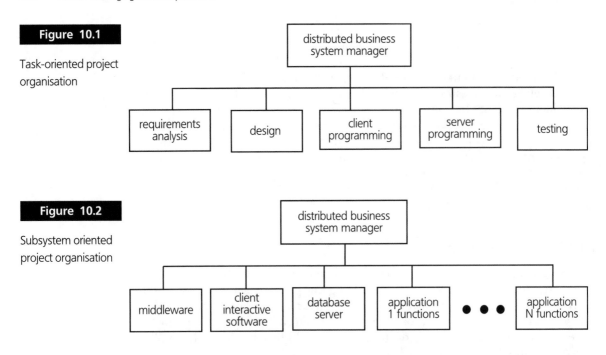

Figure 10.1

Task-oriented project
organisation

Figure 10.2

Subsystem oriented
project organisation

With any division of a project into teams, there is a danger that each team will develop its own subculture and ways of working which can endanger the integrity of the overall project. The project manager will need to set up clear lines of communication between the various sub-teams, ensuring consistency of the methods and tools used by each team.

Risk analysis

The project plan must analyse the risks that the project will have to face, and describe how these risks will be mitigated. This important topic is covered in Chapter 13 of this book.

Hardware and software resource requirements

Both hardware and software items need to be considered, as well as more general infrastructure requirements like office space and communications. Software projects use a variety of software tools: requirements representation and management, configuration management, compilers, system builders, frameworks, and so on. Furthermore software projects with longer duration may need to upgrade their software tools and adopt new releases; the impact of these upgrades on the project schedule must be taken into account, allowing for periods of adaptation to the new release and avoiding the installation of new releases close to milestones or delivery deadlines. Seemingly simple requirements, like execution on multiple platforms, will bring a whole series of hardware requirements, particularly for testing purposes.

Work content estimation and work breakdown structure

The overall effort required to accomplish the project's objectives needs to be estimated. This work must then be decomposed into individual activities which can be undertaken by one of a few people over a short period of a few weeks. Section 10.3 explores this important aspect of project management in greater detail.

Resource assignment and project scheduling

Resources, including people, need to be assigned to the activities, and the activities need to be scheduled with account for both their dependencies and availability of the assigned resources. **Deliverables**, the tangible and measurable outputs of the activities, need to be identified, with the production of the most important of these identified as **milestones** that will be used to mark the progress of the project.

Project constraints

It is important to know any constraints on the required delivery date, the availability of personnel and of total funds, so that this can be built into the plan. Organisational factors, wider corporate policy, and politics are also forces which constrain and determine the size and shape of projects.

Reuse of existing software assets can significantly reduce the cost and duration of a software project. Equally well the project may be expected to produce assets for use by other projects: this **development for reuse** with several projects' requirements in mind is more expensive than development for single use.

Any project **assumptions** must be documented either here or as part of risk analysis or as a separate section of the plan.

10.2.2 Establishing project requirements

The project objectives given in the project plan will necessarily be very brief; these need to be elaborated in some detail right at the start of the project as the **project requirements**. We have already seen the activities involved in Chapter 7, but will recapitulate them here.

During **requirements elicitation**, analysts meet with potential users and other stakeholders in order to find out their needs and wants, the functional and non-functional properties of the proposed computer system, any constraints, interfaces to other systems, and so on. Users will be interviewed and observed at work, and the system requirements documented using methods such as **scenarios** and **use cases** for discussion with stakeholders. We saw an example of this in Chapter 7 using dataflow diagrams for the school library system example that will be revisited later in this chapter.

The **requirements specification** document uses diagrams and other modelling techniques, as well as natural language. Using natural language exclusively would make it subject to ambiguity and misinterpretation.

In some projects the requirements may only emerge along with the solution, a variant of the Brooks observation 'build one to throw away'. We discussed this at length in Chapter 8, and looked at life cycle models that recognise the difficulty in specifying the requirements in detail at the start and instead let these emerge as the project proceeds.

An essential activity is **requirements validation**, checking whether the requirements are achievable or feasible, and sufficiently complete and consistent. This may involve **prototyping**, **reviews**, or **test cases**. A prototype demonstrates essential characteristics to potential users, reviews closely and examines the requirements systematically, and the writing of test cases early in the life of a project may reveal that some requirements are not testable and need either to be reformulated or eliminated from the requirements document.

Case Studies 10.2 and 10.3 give two contrasting examples, one where the requirements can be fixed from the start, and the other where the requirements will change and emerge as we proceed. In Chapter 9 we classified these as fixed and variable software.

Case Study 10.2 *Geo-stationary satellites*

The software needed for the control of a geo-stationary satellite has particular requirements in terms of stability, controllability, reliability, and so on. The inputs and outputs to the computer are well defined. The inputs are represented by the commands received from the control centre on Earth plus the inputs from various measuring devices on the satellite itself. The outputs of the control software involve the firing of rockets located at different places on the satellite in order to generate any required movement. The output also includes status information which is sent back to the Earth.

Case Study 10.3 *Plant automation*

Juan Fernandez-Ramil participated in several plant automation projects in Venezuela during the late 1980s and early 1990s. Tank farms, truck loading, and pipeline operation were to be automated. The automation included computer screens in the control room from which the operators could visualise the status of the plants (e.g., level of product in tanks, open/close status of valves, on/off status of pumps), and facilities to command the valves and the pumps. Many of the operations personnel had never been exposed to computers before. As they became aware of the potential of the new computer system, new requirements emerged, such as the need for visualisation of the status of one plant from another plant. This was useful in handling pipeline operations by which fuel is pumped from one plant to another. Some of these requirements were implemented at the cost of making changes to the designs and implementations. Other requirements had to be deferred for the project to be able to finish.

A major problem in software systems is requirements creep, the continual change in requirements during a project, and is often quoted as one of the causes of project failure. Case Study 10.3 gives a real example of requirements creep. Requirements creep is inevitable in what is in reality an evolving application, and depending on the degree of volatility of the requirements, one of the many variants of evolutionary development or Agile methods would be followed.

Scoping the project and determining its change charter (also called application bounding) limits what may be automated by the software and what may not, and helps control requirements creep and the underlying evolutionary pressures. One of the challenges of a software project manager is to address and contain the evolutionary pressures within the limits and constraints of the project.

Requirements need to be documented and their evolution managed during the fixed lifetime of a development project.

| **Activity 10.1** | *Requirements analysis in routine and radical design* |

The conventional view of projects expects that the project plan will indicate the scope and resources needed as accurately as possible. This is a reasonable expectation for normal or routine engineering design, but is difficult for innovative or radical engineering design when projects attempt to produce software that has not been previously attempted or achieved.

Compare the requirements analysis phases in routine and in radical design.

Discussion

The establishment of project requirements is considerably less burdensome for routine design than for radical design. For radical design an evolutionary process may be needed, so that the requirements are elicited through exposure of a series of prototypes or incremental versions of the software to the users or their representatives. Their feedback is then considered in the next iteration of the development cycle. The main difference between the use of prototypes and incremental versions is that prototypes are discarded, while incremental versions are progressively enhanced to incorporate additional functionality and eventually become the operational system. Deciding the scope of prototypes is also important: only some of the functional properties need to be implemented and exposed to users. The selection of the properties is based on the identification of the critical aspects of the requirements that need to be exposed to users and clarified. Sometimes it is the first occasion in which users will be exposed to such an application, so the building and exposure of the prototype becomes an experiment whose results will feed into the later phases of the project. We saw this in Chapter 8.

10.3 Setting project budgets and timescales

A critically important part of project planning is the establishment of the budget. What resources will be required, of what type, and over what period? This will then become the foundation upon which the project is executed, and errors made now may lead to major difficulties later.

How much software can a software engineer produce in a given time? The experience of the software industry is that to develop software requires, on average, roughly one person-hour of effort to deliver two or three lines of finished program code. This figure includes all the effort from requirements analysis through coding to testing and delivery. The variability in the amount of effort required comes from the type of product being developed, and its size and complexity, and also from the varying ability of individual software engineers. For very large and complex systems productivity could be as low as one line of code per person-hour of effort; while for really small and simple systems it might exceed ten lines per person-hour of effort.

The productivity figure of two or three lines per hour does not depend on what notation or language the code is written in. In this respect, software is rather like laying bricks: if the bricklayer builds with larger bricks (within reason) the walls go up proportionately faster. If the software engineer builds with 'bricks' that deliver more functionality per brick, they have to lay fewer bricks – we talk of the software engineer working at a higher level of abstraction or in a higher-level language. However it is not that simple, since these larger software building blocks will in general be more complex, and require more time in selecting the appropriate one and fitting it into place. It is rather as if the bricklayer had oddly shaped but larger bricks to use. So software productivity in terms of delivered lines per hour decreases with the use of higher-level languages – but of course the productivity in terms of delivered functionality increases.

Individual engineers vary significantly in their ability to deliver code. In the 1960s a variation of ten to one was found experimentally,[3] but as systems have become larger and more complex, more demanding upon the intellectual abilities of the engineer, the differences between the extremes has become larger, and some people claim that there is as much as a hundred to one difference between the very best and the average. This variation is really startling, and some employers will enhance their company's productivity by hiring the best at pay rates substantially higher than the norm. Can this gap be closed by suitable education or training? Clearly the gap can be narrowed in part, noting that the training takes considerable time, perhaps two to three years, to turn a novice into an expert.[4] This requires training on the job, with the novice learning from those more experienced within a community of practice, as described in Chapter 3.

The variation observed at the level of individuals tends to be 'averaged out' when one aggregates the output of many engineers in large projects and large software organisations. This explains, at least in part, why the common unit of cost estimation is normally the output of the project, not of one single individual.

10.3.1 Estimating resources and duration

The ideal is for a project to complete on time and within budget while achieving the required levels of functionality and quality and benefit. Inaccurate estimates can either set unachievable targets or waste resources.

Cost consists primarily of manpower costs for development, testing, and other activities. We must also take into account the cost of hardware and software needed for the software development, the procurement of software packages that will be integrated into the solution, and the design of new business processes.

An important issue in software development is the **diseconomy of scale** – for large systems the rate at which the software is produced is relatively slower than for small systems. This arises for two interrelated reasons:

- as the software increases in size there are more potential interactions for the software designers to keep in mind and monitor;
- as the number of people increase there are more people to talk to and negotiate with;

and hence a slowing down of the overall speed of development.

There are two broad approaches to estimation. **Top-down** or **macro estimation** provides a direct estimate for the whole project or system. By focussing on the whole project or system, they naturally take into account the issue of scale, and also tend to average out the enormous variability between people.

Within the top-down methods we will describe three approaches:

- *Expert-based*: this is the most popular approach to estimation. An expert or a group of experts estimates how much effort will be required. There are a number of techniques (e.g., Delphi) that can be applied to facilitate the expert estimation process.
- *Analogy*: given a list of past projects, the past project which most closely resembles the current project becomes the estimate, with some adjustments for the differences between the reference case and this new one.
- *Algorithmic*: based on mathematical models which are derived from historical data on project performance. Two of the most popular of these approaches have been the COnstructive COst MOdel (COCOMO) and function points.

Bottom-up or **micro estimation** breaks down the work involved to find estimates associated with individual parts, which are then combined to give an estimate for the whole. Bottom-up approaches tend to ignore diseconomies of scale, unless special measures are taken during the aggregations of the lower-level estimates to make higher-level estimates. However they can take into account special skills and strengths in particular aspects of the work and do not rely on a single average productivity figure, as we will see.

When describing these, and employing them in practice, we must be sure not to be distracted by two classic issues:

- *Parkinson's law*: 'work expands to fill the time available' – if we overestimate, we may find that all the resource allocated still gets used up, since people relax and do unnecessary things.
- *Price to win*: we need to clearly distinguish between cost and price. In order to gain a contract we may need to quote a low price, and be tempted to try to produce the system for this amount of money as if it were a proper estimate of the cost of producing the system. Clearly if the price you agree is below the cost you estimate, you are expecting to make a loss.

Activity 10.2   *Ethics of cost estimation*

Is price to win ethical?

Discussion

In principle, organisations operating in free markets are allowed to set the prices of the goods and services they provide, assuming that they comply with the law and the regulations of the profession.

Price to win could be unethical if it leads to damage or suffering of any of the people involved in the contract, including employees and software users. For example, the price-to-win strategy with the intention to recover costs through a maintenance contract can be considered unethical, as would a price to win in order to put a rival out of business.

However, a price-to-win strategy in which all those concerned are informed, no one is lying, and all have accepted the risks, could be ethical.

10.3.2 Expert judgement

As a first method of estimation, we can draw upon the experience of people who have built similar systems in the past, and ask them to make estimates. Have a look at Case Study 10.4 to see how one particular expert estimation method has been conducted, supported by meetings in which the opinions of different experts are combined.

Case Study 10.4 *An estimation session*

Look at the following text by Alistair Cockburn.[5]

Before beginning the project proper, but after spending two weeks gathering over 100 rough use cases, we made our first project estimate. Our four best OO designers, the project manager, and a few other experienced, non-OO people made up the planning team. We split the session into:

- Estimating the size of the system
- Estimating work time according to the type of person we would need
- Suggesting releases, by technical and business dependency
- Balancing the releases into approximately similar sizes

We used an 'open-auction' system to get to a size estimate. Each experienced OO designer wrote on the board the factors he thought would determine the project effort. One wrote, 'technical frameworks, use cases, UI screens'; another added, 'database generation tool'. Each added a column with his guess at how many of each type would be present. Then the first person added a new column with his revised estimates based on what he had learned during the first round. We did three rounds this way. Some used multiplication factors from the estimate of business classes, some used use cases as a base, some used UI screens as a base. There were about 20 to 25 factors in all.

We discussed whether we had achieved convergence, and what the differing factors were. In the end, we agreed on some numbers and understood where we disagreed. The key drivers for the estimates were the number of (1) business classes, (2) screens, (3) frameworks, and (4) technical classes (infrastructure, utility, etc.) created a separate lines-of-code estimate using different curves for the various productivity levels people have. Productivity per month changes over time with learning, peak productivity, and saturation as the project grows in complexity. This second estimate gave the startling prediction that six expert developers could develop the system in the hoped-for timeframe, but 4 experienced people and 15 novices could not. As it turned out, using six experts was not an option, and we were going to have to use 3 to 4 experts and 12 to 18 novices. I pulled this chart out at several times over the course of the project, and found it was tracking accurately.

As the project progressed, we learned that we could not come up with a detailed estimate from the requirements alone. . . .

The essential ingredients here are the use of experts who from experience can make reasonable judgements about the cost of the system being estimated. We need several of them, and we need a means of combining the estimates to reach one final and agreed estimate that we can act upon. Simply averaging the separate estimates is not sufficient; what we need is some process by which the experts can reach a consensus. Case Study 10.4 gives one way, and another popular method is the **Delphi method**. It is important that the view of no single dominant person should influence everybody else, a factor particularly important in some cultures. Delphi is particularly good here.

In the Delphi method the experts write down their estimates with reasons in secret, and then a moderator makes these available anonymously to the group to consider. The experts are then invited to make a second estimate based on the first round estimates and what they have learnt from any reasons advanced. These second round estimates are again secret, and revealed by the moderator later. This continues until convergence on a single agreed estimate has been achieved.

Along with the experts, there is some value in involving in the estimation everybody who will later be involved in the project. Participation of the developers in estimation and planning will help them to feel more committed to the finally agreed estimates and plans.

10.3.3 Estimation by analogy

Estimation by analogy is a natural extension of expert judgement in which tacit knowledge is made explicit and more generally accessible. Descriptions of real systems being developed are collected, together with their final sizes and costs. These are stored in a database and when faced with a new project, the database is searched for similar systems, the actual sizes and costs are retrieved and examined and modified in the light of differences between that former system and the new system. Several good matches may be used.

However, estimation by analogy faces a couple of serious problems:

- How do you match systems for similarity? After all, an air traffic control system is similar in some sense to a discrete production line, in that items flow along a reserved space separated by gaps for safety and other reasons.
- How do you use the differences in the systems to adjust the sizes and costs appropriately?

The solution to the first must be encoded in the database retrieval engine, and must be confronted. The latter can reasonably use expert judgement, albeit more focussed. It seems clear that estimation by analogy is limited in its effectiveness.

However, analogy does require real data collected from real projects, something that we will see is critical for good estimation.

10.3.4 Algorithmic estimation methods

Let us prepare for estimating the cost of developing software by thinking of the way we might estimate the effort and cost required to build a house. To do this we would identify the basic elements we use to build the house – the bricks, concrete, window and door frames, and so on. For the design of the house a quantity surveyor would calculate how many of each of these would be needed, and then we would use simple productivity figures to calculate the labour required to lay the bricks, pour the concrete, insert the frames, and so on. We would end up doing a cost calculation using a simple formula of the form:

$$\text{Total cost} = C_0 + C_1 \times N_1 + C_2 \times N_2 + \ldots + C_j \times N_j + \ldots C_K \times N_K$$

where we recognise K different elements in the construction, where we have calculated that there will be N_j of the j-th of these elements at a unit cost of C_j. This unit cost C_k would consist of two parts, the cost for initial procurement of the element, C_{j1}, plus the cost C_{j2} of integrating this into the overall construction. Expressed differently, we could separate the capital costs from the construction costs to give:

$$\text{Capital cost} = C_{01} + C_{11} \times N_{11} + C_{21} \times N_{21} + \ldots + C_{j1} \times N_{j1} + \ldots C_{K1} \times N_{K1}$$

$$\text{Construction cost} = C_{02} + C_{12} \times N_{12} + C_{22} \times N_{22} + \ldots + C_{j2} \times N_{j2} + \ldots C_{K2} \times N_{K2}$$

where C_{01} and C_{02} are fixed costs, and the C_{j2} costs are the inverse productivity figures, the cost of integrating one unit into the building. Normally we think of productivity as the number of units that can be produced with one unit of resource.

Let us apply this simple idea to software. Reduced to its simplest, the basic element out of which software is built is the programming language statement. There is no capital cost to this, and if we view that all program language statements are the same, we get the formula:

$$\text{Software construction cost} = C_0 + C_1 \times N$$

The C_1 figure is the average cost (or effort) to produce just one line of programme code – the programmer productivity. To find out what C_0 and C_1 we look at our record of past projects and their size and cost, and do a simple calculation. What we find is that the fixed cost can be ignored, but that the productivity varies enormously between projects. Let's ignore the variation between people. Part of this variation between projects is due to the size, the diseconomy of scale we mentioned previously, but mostly it is due to the type of system being built. We will come back to the variation by type of system later.

A diseconomy of scale means that there is some non-linearity whereby the larger the N gets the more the productivity decreases and the overall cost increases. We could introduce this non-linearity with polynomial formulae of the form:

$$\text{Software construction cost} = C_0 + C_1 \times N + C_2 \times N^2 + \ldots + C_j \times N^j + \ldots C_K \times N^K$$

but the non-linear form that has become preferred among most software engineers is:

$$\text{Software construction cost} = C_0 + C_1 \times N^b$$

where b is a number just greater than 1.

This idea has been applied by many authors, and Table 10.2 shows some of the formulae that have been used. Note that the size of the software is expressed in

Table 10.2 Estimation Models[6]		
$E = 5.2 \times (KLOC)^{0.91}$		Walston-Felix
$E = 5.5 + 0.73 \times (KLOC)^{1.16}$		Bailey-Basili 1981
$E = 3.2 \times (KLOC)^{1.05}$		Boehm 1981 (COCOMO simple model)
$E = 5.288 \times (KLOC)^{1.047}$		Doty (for KLOC > 9)

KLOCs, thousands of lines of code, rather than single lines, and the formulae yield the labour costs E in person-months.

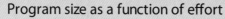

Activity 10.3   *Comparing estimation models*

If we plot the formulae of Table 10.2, we obtain the curves shown in Figure 10.3:

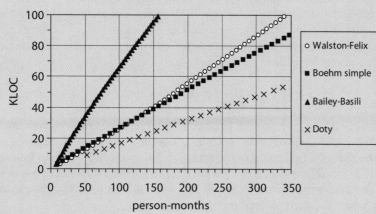

Program size as a function of effort

Legend:
- o Walston-Felix
- ■ Boehm simple
- ▲ Bailey-Basili
- × Doty

(y-axis: KLOC, 0 to 100; x-axis: person-months, 0 to 350)

Figure 10.3

Program size as a function of effort for four empirical estimation models

Why are the trajectories in Figure 10.3 so different from each other? What is the characteristic common to three of the four trends? What would you recommend your colleague in order to achieve an estimate which is more accurate than the one achieved using the models in Figure 10.3?

Discussion

The trajectories in Figure 10.3 are so different because they are derived from different empirical models, which in turn originated from regression analysis on data reflecting different past software projects. These projects may have reflected different types of system, a variety of programming languages, tools and development environment.

One characteristic of three of the trajectories (Bailey-Basili, Boehm, and Doty) is that as the size increases, the increase in effort required grows faster than the increase in size (check this by laying a ruler along the curve, or by looking at the curve at a sharp angle). This is the 'diseconomy of scale' and is generally explained in term of the increasing complexity of larger applications, and also the increasing number of communication paths as the team increases in size. The number of communication paths is generally assumed to grow as the square of the size of the team.

Ideally you should calibrate an estimation model from local conditions, by collecting data from your own projects, including the size and effort and other factors that could also be included, and fitting your data to the curve. Which curve you choose is a bit arbitrary – we will look in more detail at two of the most popular cost estimation models – COCOMO and function points.

Collect data about past projects and calibrate your chosen estimation model to this data so that it fits local conditions.

COCOMO

The COnstructive COst MOdel, COCOMO,[7] is a well documented example of an algorithmic, generic cost model. Barry Boehm, then at TRW but now at the University of Southern California, collected and analysed data on the performance of sixty-three industrial software projects, mainly from the defence and aerospace domains. This led to the COCOMO 81 model, one of the best known and the most widely used estimation models. A number of refinements have followed to account for additional data and for changes in the software process and its technology, leading to the second generation COCOMO II.[8]

For simplicity, we describe here the 1981 model before going on to the later COCOMO II. What COCOMO gives us is a simple means of converting from code size (in KLOCs, thousands of lines of code) to effort in person-months and optimal elapsed time, using formulae of the form:

$$E = a \times (\text{KLOC})^b$$

The coefficient a is the nominal productivity in terms of person months to produce one thousand lines of code (1 KLOC). Coefficient b is greater than 1 and determines the degree of diseconomy of scale. So, for example, a million lines of code (1000 KLOC) would be estimated as requiring proportionately twice as much effort if $b = 1.1$ and four times as much if $b = 1.2$, while it is estimated as requiring proportionately half as much effort if $b = 0.9$.

Optimal project duration D then is given by

$$D = c \times (E)^d$$

in elapsed months. Coefficient c is the basic elapsed months per person month while d gives the non-linearity – larger projects should take proportionately shorter time, so typically d should be less than 1.

COCOMO tackles the problem of variability in production rates for different types of software. In the simplest form of COCOMO 81, known as Basic COCOMO, a first rough cut at complexity is handled by recognising three classes of software project:

- organic – relatively small, simple projects;
- semi-detached – intermediate projects in terms of size and complexity;
- embedded – complex software projects, such as a flight control system for an aircraft.

The names organic, semi-detached, and embedded are Boehm's own terms – don't worry about their origin, just remember that we have three classes of software ranging from the relatively simple to the complex. These are not related in any way to Lehman's three classes seen in Chapter 9. The coefficients a and c, and the exponents b and d depend on the type of software being developed and may vary from organisation to organisation. Table 10.3 gives Boehm's coefficient values for COCOMO 81.

Where did these coefficients and exponents come from? Boehm based them on the analysis of many software projects. Many organisations tune these coefficients

Software type	Parameters			
	a	b	c	d
Organic	2.4	1.05	2.5	0.38
Semi-detached	3.0	1.12	2.5	0.35
Embedded	3.6	1.20	2.5	0.32

Table 10.3

The values for the coefficients for COCOMO 81

and exponents on the basis of their own software development practices, using actual project costs accumulated over many years.

A second round of adjustment can be made to the effort figure E, to take into account other factors involved with the project. These are the fifteen effort multipliers EM_i or cost drivers, each rated on a six-point scale from 0 to 5. The cost drivers are: language experience, schedule constraint, database size, turnaround time, virtual machine experience, virtual machine volatility, software tools, modern programming practices, storage constraint, applications experience, timing constraints, required reliability, product complexity, and analyst and programmer capability. The values for a particular system are determined by an expert. The nominal effort is multiplied by each of these EM_i in turn, resulting in an adjusted Effort figure:

$$E_{\text{adjusted}} = E_{\text{nominal}} \times EM_1 \times EM_2 \times EM_3 \times \ldots \times EM_{15}$$

COCOMO II uses the same method as COCOMO 81 to calculate a nominal effort using the formula:

$$E_{\text{nominal}} = a \times (\text{KLOC})^b$$

where the exponent b itself is made subject to adjustment by five scale factors W_i using the formula

$$b = 0.91 + 0.01 \times \Sigma W_i$$

These scale factors capture the COCOMO 81 ideas of organic, semi-detached, and embedded, as well as other influences. Note that under very favourable circumstances we could in principle obtain some economy of scale!

Then the nominal effort calculated above is adjusted using effort multipliers as for COCOMO 81:

$$E_{\text{adjusted}} = E_{\text{nominal}} \times \Pi_i EM_i$$

At different stages of the project a different set of effort multipliers is used – seven at 'early design', seventeen 'post-architecture' later in the development process when more is known about the system development.

Just to give you an idea, the reported predictive accuracy of approaches such as COCOMO II is within thirty per cent of the actual values for effort fifty-two per cent of the time. Recent recalibration of the model based on Bayesian techniques has led to an improvement of the predictive accuracy, achieving predictions within thirty per cent seventy-five per cent of the time.[9] These predictions made so early in the life of a project are, not surprisingly, not very accurate – no wonder expert judgement is preferred!

| Activity 10.4 | *Reducing cost by weakly coupled subsystems* |

You are the project manager for a large software development project which breaks down into five equal sized subsystems. You have estimated the size of the five subsystems at 100 KLOC each, but realise that if you developed them together certain common utilities could be identified, reducing the system size to 455 KLOC.

From the costs and timescale point of view, which should you do:

- develop the system as a single project in which the savings on the utilities could be achieved?
- develop the system as five independent projects in which the utilities would be duplicated?

Give reasons for your choice. Draw any more general conclusions.

Discussion

Use COCOMO 81 assuming system is basic organic.

For the single project of size 455 KLOC:

$$E = 3.6455^{1.20} \cong 5571 \quad \text{person-months (roughly 470 person-years)}$$

$$D = 2.55571^{0.3} \cong 40 \text{ months}$$

This implies an average team size of just over 140 engineers.

For each subproject of size 100 KLOC:

$$E = 3.6100^{1.20} \cong 905 \text{ person-months (roughly 75 person-years)}$$

$$D = 2.5 \times 905^{0.32} \cong 22 \text{ months}$$

This implies five teams of an average size just over forty software engineers each.

From this we might be tempted to recommend doing the work as five subprojects. The overall effort required is 470 person-years for a single project but considerably less, 375 person-years, for the subprojects. However this ignores the cost of the final integration of the subsystems, which could be considerable. Nevertheless, overall you might save.

If the five subprojects were done in parallel they would be delivered more quickly, even taking into account the final integration of the subprojects. Of course more people would be required, but that could be acceptable. More generally, this shows that smaller projects are desirable, that a policy of subdividing large problems can save cost.

Function-point based estimation

The trouble with COCOMO and similar estimation methods is that they require estimates of the size of the code to be produced. But how do you determine the size of the code to be produced? If you use expert judgement you will have gained very little.

So instead of focussing on lines of code as the elements to be used in estimation, several people have focussed on things that can be counted early in the development process. Tom DeMarco[10] produced a set of function metrics in 1982 that he called 'bangs', but these did not catch on, and instead an idea that began just a little earlier than this in 1979, function points,[11] has become the popular approach.

Function-point-based estimation became a well tried and proven method for systems built prior to the introduction of object-oriented methods. It starts from a description of the required functionality for the system, perhaps in the form of data-flow diagrams and entity-relationship diagrams. This description is analysed to identify the number of inputs (F_i), outputs (F_o), external interfaces (F_e), and the number of data files or elements stored in the system (F_d). You weight each of these by an assessment of its complexity (W), and then add them all up to arrive at a size measure for the software as 'function points':

$$FP = F_i \times W_i + F_o \times W_o + F_e \times W_e + F_d \times W_d$$

The idea then is that one function point on the average requires the same amount of effort regardless of what in detail the actual function is, and creates the same volume of program code on average in a particular programming language. The full IFPUG (International Function Point User Group) 'Counting Practices Manual'[12] gives a detailed account of exactly what to count.

Having calculated the number of function points, we could convert the function points to lines of code using conversion rates from our historical record of projects, and then proceed using a lines-of-code based method like COCOMO.

Alternatively, function points can become the elements used in the formulae we saw earlier. Table 10.4 shows three models for direct estimation based on function points – note that only one of these includes any non-linearity that might account for diseconomies of scale. Of course the basic elements really aren't the function points, but the inputs and outputs to the system and the stored data, etc.

Function points transfer well to object-oriented approaches to software development. In OO approaches we gain our understanding of the software functionality by producing Use Cases and Class Models – and with these we have everything that we need to count to give a function point estimate. We will give a highly simplified account[13] of how to proceed, concerned with the principles here, and not a practical method.

First, working from the requirements level Use Case Model, every use case that is connected to an actor (or maybe several actors) outside the system boundary

$E = -13.39 + 0.0545 \times (FP)$	Albrecht and Gaffney	**Table 10.4**
$E = 60.62 + 7.728 \times 10^{-8}(FP)^3$	Kemerer	
$E = 585.7 + 15.12\,(FP)$	Matson, Barnett, and Mellichamp	Function point estimation models[14]

counts as an element of functionality. This is regardless of whether the actor is a human or another system. Call this count F_U.

Second, every class in the requirements level Class Model counts as an element of stored data, regardless of whether it is party to an aggregation, association or partakes in inheritance. Call this count F_C.

Function points are then estimated from the counts by weighting them with an adjustment factor – call these W_U and W_C respectively. Some use cases or classes will be seen as large and complex, others as simple, relative to an experience of what 'average' examples are like. The actual weights will be somewhere in the range four to seven for use cases, and seven to fifteen for classes. We end up calculating the function points (FP) by:

$$FP = F_U \times W_U + F_C \times W_C$$

It would then be common practice in function-point calculations to further adjust the FP count for the complexity of the actual system to be built:

$$\text{Adjusted } FP = \text{Unadjusted } FPs \times [0.65 + 0.01 \times \Sigma F_i]$$

ΣF_i adds all the F_is together, where factors, F_i, are rated on a scale of 0 to 5. The idea is that same as in COCOMO, though the factors are different.

Originally these multipliers and weighting factors would have been derived from the analysis of a large number of projects, so they are experience-based. However, each development organisation will be different because of local development practices, experience of particular system types, etc. Some organisations tune these multipliers and weighting factors to suit their particular circumstances.

Case Study 10.5 *Costing the library system*

Estimate the cost in person-day for implementing the library system (from Chapter 7) using function-points analysis.

Step 1: carry out some preliminary analysis.

Before we can begin to estimate the cost and timescale for developing the library system, we need to analyse the problem to the point where it takes a standard form in which there are aspects of the functionality that can be counted. The data flow and data structure models shown in Figures 7.4 and 7.5 will suffice. A real library system would be much more complex than this.

Step 2: apply function points.

There are six inputs and four outputs on the diagram in Figure 7.4, with seven stored items in Figure 7.5. We apply weights to all of the these, as in the following table.

Factor	Number	Weight	Total
Inputs	6	4	24
Outputs	4	5	20
Stored items	7	10	70
External interfaces	1	7	7
Total			**121**

This gives us an FP contribution of 121 so far. We would now normally adjust the FP value for complexity, but here we will assume no adjustment is necessary.

If we look up an appropriate table relating function points to lines of code, we would find that we would write 128 lines of C on average for each function point. Thus we expect to have to write between 15,000 and 16,000 lines of C code.

If we assume that we can write twenty lines of C per person-day, this means 750 to 800 person-days are required from start to finish. Let us say 800 person-days, 53.3 person-months.

This makes it a relatively expensive system, which needs to be set against the potential savings in reduced book losses. This would only be justified if the development costs could be shared among many schools, perhaps through the local education authority.

Activity 10.5   *Calibrating the estimation process*

What form of calibration would be necessary to align this generic estimation process using function points with the particular practices of a particular software development organisation?

Discussion
We would need to collect data for a large range of systems:

- development costs in person-months, with class of person and skill levels;
- technical support, working environment, and their costs;
- technical feature of system;
- function point estimates from high-level descriptions of the system;

and from these calculate the parameters needs for adjusting for complexity

---

Some practitioners have sought to make function-point approaches independent of the particular development methodology being used. The first and most influential of these was Charles Symons' Mark II Function Point method,[15] – which talks in terms of 'Logical Transactions' rather than Use Cases or Data Flows, but the effect is the same. While this method originated with Charles Symons, its current most accessible form is the MK II Function Point Analysis Counting Practices Manual[16] which sets out very clearly what should be counted and how these counts should be used.

Estimation for maintenance and evolution
Cost estimation methods usually focus on estimation for projects started from scratch. The simplest approach to budgeting for maintenance is to allow some proportion of the original development cost over successive years – say twenty per cent reducing to ten per cent. There are, however, a number of more systematic approaches which address the problem of evolution estimation.

COCOMO 1981 has a maintenance extension, captured by the equation:

$$E_m = k_m \times T \times E_d$$

where E_m is the annual maintenance effort in person-months and T is the annual change traffic defined as: 'The fraction of the software product's source instructions which undergo change during a (typical) year, either through addition or modification.'[17] k_m is an adjustment factor that would reflect the difference in the cost effort multipliers between the development and the maintenance situation, and E_d is the effort used to develop the system initially.

In COCOMO II the annual change traffic concept has been replaced by a 'reuse model' applied to maintenance. These later refinements include 'program understanding' as an important cost factor in the maintenance context. However, these are not widely used. As an alternative, it is possible to build simple effort estimation models for evolving software based on historical data as in Case Study 10.6.

Case Study 10.6 *Simple estimation approach for evolving software*[18]

As we saw in Chapter 9, evolving software is likely go through identifiable phases. Bennett and Rajlich gave names to these phases in their staged model of software evolution. One practical way of using historical data in order to build estimation models for software evolution (e.g., for release planning) is the following:

1. Gather historical data on effort and work achieved (e.g., lines of code or files touched per month).
2. Plot the data and identify the stages.
3. Within the latest – most recent – stage, calculate the average work achieved per release.
4. Through impact analysis, calculate the size of the work that needs to be implemented, for example, the number of files touched.
5. Calculate the required duration for the implementation as:

$$\text{Duration (in number of releases)} = \frac{\text{Work to be implemented}}{\text{Average work achieved per release}}$$

This simple model assumes that the work-rate – and effort level – is constant per release. Corrections to the result are likely to be needed to take into account the increasing complexity of the software, changes in the release interval (time elapsed between releases) and changes in the level of personnel.

10.3.5 Bottom-up work breakdown

If we break down the work required to produce the system into smaller activities, we should be able to estimate the work to produce these with some fair degree of confidence, and then simply add up all these smaller estimates to obtain an estimate for the whole. So how do we break down the work into smaller activities? There are essentially two approaches to achieve this: activity-based and product-based.

In the activity-based approach, we decompose the overall task of developing the software into many much smaller activities which are well defined (typically they end with the production of a deliverable, a visible demonstration of completion of the task) and which can be assigned to individual teams or persons and which can be individually scheduled (allocated dates when the work will be done). A possible decomposition based on activities will involve work packages such as 'design', 'implementation', 'integration', 'distribution', etc. See Case Study 10.7 in the next section for an illustration of these processes in the context of project scheduling.

In the product-based approach, the decomposition of the project's work is based on the products which will be handed over to users, as reflected in, for example, the PRINCE 2 method (described later in this chapter). We use a decomposition of the system into subsystems, and so on; the difficulty is that any such decomposition we use will be notional, since the design upon which this must rest will not have been finalised yet.

We end up with a number of activities for which we will need to make work content estimates. Ideally for scheduling purposes these bottom level activities should be quite small, of the order of five to twenty person-days' effort. However for estimation purposes we may go for much larger activities, whatever we feel confident about using.

The simple-minded approach would then be to add together all the bottom level estimates G_i,

$$G = \Sigma G_i$$

but that might not work out too well since the probability distributions we are dealing with are very skewed. When people make estimates like this they choose the statistically most-likely and the result of adding them together is not necessarily the most likely value for the aggregate. We could end up with a value that is much lower that it should be. So how can we correct for this?

Instead, when making the bottom-level estimates we should not just make one most likely estimate, but also estimate the worst case and best case. Doing that enables us to combine our estimates to produce an expected value, and we can add expected values together okay. Let's denote the three estimates for activity A_i as B_i, M_i, and W_i for the best case, most likely case, and worst case respectively so that

$$B_i < M_i << W_i$$

where typically the best and most likely estimates are close together and the worst case is much larger. We produce the expected value estimate for the activity using the following calculation:

$$E_i = \frac{(B_i + 4 \times M_i + W_i)}{6}$$

Try this for values of (B_i, M_i, W_i) of symmetrical values (2, 3, 4) and skewed values (2, 3, 10). We can now add together the expected values:

$$E = \Sigma E_i$$

The danger in work breakdown approaches is that you overlook some critical piece of work, and thus end up underestimating the expected cost, though some contingency fund could be set aside for this.

Note that anyway we must eventually produce a work breakdown structure down to very small activities or tasks, so that we can schedule the work of the project. So even if we don't initially estimate by work breakdown, later in the project when we do make the work breakdown we can make a cross-check on the original top-down estimates. If the more accurate picture that you then get is wildly different from the original estimate, you may then have some radical rethinking to do!

10.3.6 General considerations

Effort is expressed in person-months, and this raises important questions about what is meant by a person-month. Is it the work that can be done by a person working flat out and thus involves twenty-two person-days, or is it an average person-month allowing for illness and leave and general company activities – say seventeen days? We need to be clear about this, and then set our models to estimate the kind of person-months we expect.

Estimation should be an ongoing activity as the project continues. For example, as the project progresses it would be useful to compare the KLOC estimate derived from the FP count to a more reliable estimate derived from estimates of the size of smaller constituents of the system. This should be done as the architecture and design of the system is being progressively defined. Generally, at completion of high-level design, one can estimate the size of the individual subsystems. Later, at completion of low-level design, we can estimate the individual size of the modules or classes which will be part of the system.

Activity 10.6 — Estimating project duration

Suppose that a colleague of yours has estimated the effort required to create a software product as twenty-four person-months. Explain how you would estimate the project duration, based on your colleague's effort estimate by discussing different ways of achieving such an estimate. Indicate two disadvantages of the methods you have discussed. (Guideline: The answer does not have to include precise numerical expressions, but should comment on them and discuss their use.)

Discussion

A straightforward way to calculate the project duration would be to allocate a number of people to the project, and then divide the effort by the number of people in the team and this will provide an estimate of the duration. For example, if the team has two members, then the duration would be

$$\text{Duration} = \frac{24 \text{ person-months}}{2 \text{ people}} = 12 \text{ months}$$

However the above approach may allocate too many, or too few, people to the project and effort required may be more in consequence. Remember, a larger team involves a higher number of communication paths between the individual members, leading to a decreased productivity.

However, the relationship between duration and effort is captured by some empirical estimation models, which were developed after collection of empirical data reflecting the performance of several projects. The COCOMO duration equation permits the calculation of duration based on total effort by means of a simple formula, with different parameters which reflect the type of application.

However, sometimes top-down models are not very precise, particularly when used in an organisation different from the one for which the model was developed in the first place. A more accurate approach would be to gather historical data and then use it as a basis for both the estimation of size and duration.

Top-down methods of estimation should be, when possible, compared to the results of bottom-up approaches, such as the ones which involve finding out and listing the different activities of a project, estimating the effort and duration that each individually involves, building a project plan and from there calculating the critical path and the expected duration of the project. The bottom-up method can be precise but requires a lot of detailed planning about the project and may not be applicable at the initial phases when the design has not been properly defined yet.

10.4 Scheduling and controlling projects

10.4.1 Project scheduling

Once we have an agreed effort and timescale that we believe are feasible, we must next schedule the work, and assign resources to carry out this work. How should we proceed?

As a start, we can look at the distribution of effort throughout the life cycle. Pressman[19] gives the following guidance figures for various activities: project planning (2 to 3 per cent), requirements analysis (10 to 25 per cent), design (20 to 25 per cent), coding (15 to 20 per cent), testing, integration and debugging (30 to 40 per cent). This draws upon general experience of the industry, and can be useful in determining a **resource profile** for the project. Generally speaking we start with fewer people, then build up to a peak around coding and testing, tapering off after that through testing and into support of the software following delivery. The skills needed also change: we start with analysts and designers, moving over to a preponderance of coders and testers while retaining core analysts and designers. We can view this as general guidance for the whole project, or as guidance for individual subsystems.

We will also need to have some idea of the order in which the activities should be done, and their interdependencies. These dependencies are important since some activities cannot start until some preceding activity has completed, or is far enough along to be able to informally supply information.

To schedule a project we must find a sequence of activities which respects their dependencies and keeps the people on the project busy without overworking them. This is known as **resource balancing** or **resource levelling**. The end result is the project plan, defining what work will be done when and by whom. Included in this plan will be a number of project milestones when key documents are completed, reviewed, and then 'frozen'.

We can represent the plan in one of two equivalent ways:

- PERT charts, which show the activities as boxes with lines joining them showing the dependencies and flow of critical information. These boxes are usually annotated with the start and finish dates.

- Gantt charts or bar charts in which the horizontal axis represents time and the vertical axis shows activities which are then laid out as bars showing when the work takes place.

PERT charts emphasise dependencies. Gantt charts emphasise the times at which things happen. Note that dependencies in software projects are often not critical, and though there might be some ideal sequence, if some work-product required is not available this can be worked around, obtaining information informally, anticipating what will be produced, building dummy software as place holders, and so on. Thus Gantt charts are to be preferred and are most commonly used. However, PERT charts do give us the opportunity to do **critical path analysis**, to find out which activities are the ones whose duration determines the duration of the project. It is important to identify these activities from the start and keep them under special review.

Building contingency plans is a common practice. Some managers will add an additional percentage to the estimates of effort and timescale in order to provide some additional time and effort to deal with unplanned activities or unanticipated events. However it would be more usual to keep a contingency fund aside for use wherever needed, to pay for extra manpower or overtime. There might also be some time contingency provided so that it does not matter if some work overruns.

Case Study 10.7 shows how this works out for our school library example.

Case Study 10.7 *Scheduling the library project*

Let us now schedule the development of the library system that we estimated earlier as requiring 800 person-days or 53.3 person-months. There are formulae which can be used to advise you on possible duration, but let us say here that we have just twelve months to do it in. On average we will need four-and-a-half people.

We shall assume that most of the project planning and requirements analysis has been done, through there will still need to be time allowed for project management and some residual requirements analysis. Using industry proportions as a guide, we could divide the effort up as follows:

- design (including some residual analysis), 225 person-days;
- coding (including some unit testing and debugging), 175 person-days;
- testing, integration, and debugging, 365 person-days;

- project management, including overall technical leadership, 35 person-days.

We can now make a first attempt at scheduling these person-days of effort over the twelve-month duration of the project. This leads to Figure 10.4 which shows not just when things happen but also the level of effort required at any time.

We need to break down these high-level activities into much smaller tasks, and also allocate particular people to do the work. The people we will require are:

- a part-time project manager who is also technically able to lead the project;
- an analyst/designer/tester who 'owns' the overall system, designs it, and then establishes an integration strategy and system test to ensure that the code produced does what was asked for;
- a programmer who codes and later debugs the code.

Figure 10.4

Gantt chart

Task	Percentage	Budget (in person-days)	1	2	3	4	5	6	7	8	9	10	11	12
			Person-days per month											
Design (and residual analysis)	28	225	30	45	45	45	20	10	5	5	5	5	5	5
Coding (and unit testing/debugging)	22	175	5	5	5	15	35	45	30	15	5	5	5	5
Testing, integration, and debugging	46	365	–	–	–	5	20	30	55	70	70	60	40	15
Project management technical lead	4	35	4	3	3	3	2	2	2	2	3	3	4	4

The tasks shown in Figure 10.4 are much too large to enable us to produce a detailed schedule, and we need to divide the work to be done into smaller chunks. One way to do it is to refine the categories of Figure 10.4:

The analysis/design tasks are:

- D1 – select the reader devices and learn about them, acquiring any software (like drivers) to help them;
- D2 – design the database, filling in all the attributes and relationships;
- D3 – design the human–computer interaction (HCI) systems for obtaining requesting books and recording new accessions;
- D4 – design the internals of the individual processes. Most of these should be relatively trivial.

The test tasks are:

- T1 – specify system tests;
- T2 – integrate the system and run the system tests;
- T3 – specify and conduct the client acceptance tests.

The programming and debugging tasks are:

- P1 – program the library functions in C;
- P2 – program the interactive systems;
- P3 – code the database in a suitable DBMS;
- P4 – debug the individual library functions;
- P5 – debug the two interactive systems;
- P6 – debug the database.

Whatever the decomposition, we need to provide individual estimates for each of the elements of work before we can schedule them and assign them to particular people.

This then leads to a detailed Gantt chart for the project, and possibly a PERT chart. To this we have also need to add milestones, critical dates in the development of the system that could make our progress visible. A key milestone would be when the design is complete, when we could have a major technical review as part of our quality assurance procedures.

Activity 10.7   Confidentiality of contingency plans

Some managers would not reveal any time or budget contingency to their staff. Why not?

Discussion

The problem is Parkinson's law – if we let it be known that more time and effort is available, then that extra time and effort would be consumed. However we can take ▶

this argument too far. So we must make our estimates realistic and achievable, expecting some to end ahead of schedule, while still recognising that the unexpected will inevitably happen and some activities will take longer than expected and that new activities will arise, and thus that contingency will be needed and used.

10.4.2 Monitoring and controlling progress

Once the initial project plans, including the schedules and resource assignments, have been approved by the relevant authority – perhaps by the client signing the contract – the plan becomes the **baseline**. Future progress is measured with respect to this baseline plan and departure from these original plans will need to be justified.

How do we know that the project is proceeding according to plan? One common practice is to require people to record how they use their time, filling in timesheets such as that shown in Figure 10.5.

If we just record the time spent, all we have is a record of whether we are spending according to plan. We need to have some record of progress and achievement, such as noting any milestones achieved.

In the plan we will have set a number of milestones, deliverables to be produced with the dates on which they should be produced. Of course if all the deliverables are produced on or ahead of schedule and under budget, we know all is going well. If all deliverables are being produced late and over budget, we know that things are not going according to plan. But normally it is not that black and white. Not all our activities will have well-defined deliverables and committed dates, and some deliverables will be produced ahead of schedule but over budget, and some may be produced behind schedule but under budget. How do we handle this?

One thing we could do is ask our engineers to record on their timesheets just how complete they are – perhaps recording what effort is still required to complete the task. But this has been found to be unreliable, engineers are usually optimistic and are nearly there, '99 per cent complete'. The best thing seems to be simply to claim progress when the task is finally completed and manifest in milestone achievement. To fully assess progress we need to be able to attribute greater value

Figure 10.5
Sample timesheet

TIMESHEET for Company Xxx
Person name: staff id:
Project name:
Task

id	description	\multicolumn{7}{Hours worked per day}	Total week	Milestones achieved
		Mon	Tues	Wed	Thurs	Fri	Sat	Sun		
nominal hours		7.5	7.5	7.5	7.5	7.5	0	0	37.5	task complete
L1	public holiday									
L2	annual leave									
L3	sick leave									
T15	DB schema									
TOTALS										

to some achievements that others. Here we can use the original budget estimates as a measure of value – so if the original planning estimated that X man hours, pounds, euros, or dollars were need to achieve a particular milestone, then once that milestone has been achieved the project can be said to have earned that amount, regardless of what it actually cost. To measure progress against budget you then compare actual spend to date with value earned to date. This idea has become very popular under the title of **earned value**, but has also been known since the 1970s as **cost-accomplishment** or **accomplishment-cost**.

Here is what we do.

1. In the work breakdown, make sure that every task has some clearly defined outcome, probably a deliverable document, with some process to verify that the outcome has been achieved. For a deliverable this might well be some final review or inspection after which the document is 'signed off' by the QA section or somebody whose work depends on that deliverable.

2. For a simple visualisation of progress, plot a graph (the earned-value chart) of expected (planned) accumulation of earned value and spend value against time. This gives us our planned progress.

3. Regularly record the time and other resources expended on each task using some appropriate method – probably weekly timesheets. Update the spend line on the earned-value chart.

4. When each task is complete and signed off, attribute the budget value for that task to the project. Update the earned-value line on the earned-value chart.

5. Report on progress relative to budget by comparing spend to date with value earned to date. You must expect some shortfall because of work in progress, but for large projects the work in progress at any one time will be a relatively small proportion of the total.

6. Report on progress relative to planned timescale using the earned-value chart.

It is useful for project participants to hold regular meetings at which progress is reviewed and outstanding issues discussed and recorded. Divergences between plans and actual progress are identified, and remedial action can be planned.

If the progress reports and meetings show that the project is not keeping up with its plan, what do we do? Almost every project falls behind schedule or goes over budget at some time in some of its activities or tasks. If these slippages are small, then they can often be made up in budget by using the underspend in other activities and in schedule by using the time saved by earlier deliveries. But what do you do if the accumulated overspend and delay cannot be made up? We have already looked at contingency budget provision and, if all else fails, the project manager would have to plead for extra resources from the contingency fund, or arrange to deliver less; or maybe completely re-estimate and replan the project, using the increased knowledge currently available. If the re-estimated duration is a lot more than the one originally planned and agreed, we may be in real trouble, for we know that we just cannot reduce the time to develop software substantially – in this case we must reduce functionality as is done in **timeboxing**. One thing we might learn from the divergence between cost and earned value is that we have systematically underestimated (or perhaps overestimated!) the effort required, and that what we need to do is update our estimation methods, re-estimate the whole project, and then replan.

> Progress is best monitored in terms of earned value, with frequent re-estimation and replanning.

In multidisciplinary projects, because software is perceived as easy to change, software engineering may be given the task of solving problems which have proven difficult to solve by the other engineering disciplines involved.

Activity 10.8	*Remedial actions*

Suppose that you are the manager of a project which is running behind schedule. The client dictates that an operational version of the product has to be released in three months' time. However, careful estimation and risk analysis indicates that instead nine months will be required. Briefly comment on the implications of Brooks' observation that 'adding man power to a late project makes it later' to this situation. List and briefly discuss steps which you could take as manager in negotiating with the client to avoid an unrealistic deadline.

Discussion

Brooks observed that adding people to a project which is running late is likely to make things worse rather than improve them. Why? Newcomers will have to be trained in the methods, tools, existing architecture, and so on before becoming productive members of the team, using the time of existing team members who are already critical to the project. Moreover, a large team involves more communication paths between team members so more time will need to be spent in keeping people up to date on decisions and so on. This suggests that for a late project with fixed deadlines it would be much better to negotiate with the client to reduce the scope of the work in a way acceptable by them.

Pressman[20] suggests the following steps in dealing with the situation similar to this one:

1. Perform a detailed estimate of effort and duration using historical data from past projects, possibly revising existing estimates.

2. Using an incremental process model, develop a strategy which will aim at delivering the critical functionality by the required date, and fully document this plan. Document the possible outcomes, based on historical data, of the following options:

   a. Increase budget and resources in an effort to try to meet the deadline.
   b. Renegotiate scope and plan for an incremental delivery strategy.
   c. Do nothing.

3. Meet with the customer, and explain to them that based on the revised estimate the original plan is unachievable (unrealistic), stressing that the estimates are based on the performance of other projects. Indicate what would be the productivity improvement rate that will be necessary to meet the deadline and that such rate is greater than any recent improvements in that rate.

4. Suggest option 'b', an incremental development strategy as the less risky alternative and show the client that according to historical data the other two options are very risky. Option 'a' may lead to quality problems as the team struggles to meet the deadline and option 'c' is unacceptable.

There could be other alternatives. The key ideas are the revision of the estimates based on historical data and the negotiation with the customer based on the risk of the alternatives.

10.5 Managing the project in context

Projects are usually managed in the context of a wider organisation which determines the practices to be followed and what tools to use.

10.5.1 The organisational context

Once a person has finished on one project, they move on to the next, maybe spending time in between developing their own skills or in helping management processes like preparing proposals in response to invitations to tender (ITTs).

A popular way of organising a software development company or division within a larger company is the matrix. Figure 10.6 illustrates this. People (human resources) are organised into 'functions' through which they find their career advancement. As new projects get started by the business manager, people are assigned to projects, as shown by the small circles on the intersections of the project and function lines. On any particular project not all functions would necessarily be present. Note in Figure 10.6 that we have placed two functions, software assets and quality assurance, outside the organisational structure of projects, since these 'staff' functions transcend any particular project.

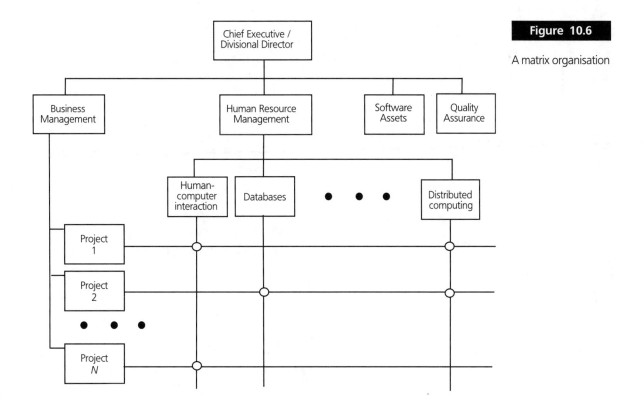

Figure 10.6

A matrix organisation

10.5.2 Standard practices

It would not be effective for each project to invent its own way of managing the project, and it would be normal for each organisation adopt a standard set of practices for internal use. These would in turn often be based on external standards, perhaps laid down by a national body like a government procurement agency.

One example of a standard project-management method is PRINCE, described in Case Study 10.8. Standard project-management methods define a project-management vocabulary and embody much common sense and good practice, giving management mechanisms and structures which can be tailored to the specific needs of the organisation. An elaborate infrastructure for project planning and control is expensive, and small organisations will need to decide which parts of the standard to follow and which ones to omit.

Case Study 10.8 *The PRINCE project-management method[21]*

'PRojects IN Controlled Environments,' PRINCE, is a project management method that was sponsored in the UK originally by the Central Computer and Telecommunications Agency (CCTA),[22] and subsequently revised as PRINCE 2.

There are eight components to the method: organisation, planning, controls, stages, management of risk, quality, configuration management, and change control. The PRINCE 2 planning phase is product-oriented, rather than activity-oriented. The project planning phase consists of seven sequential steps:

1. design a plan
2. define and analyse products
3. identify activities and their dependencies
4. estimate effort for each activity
5. schedule
6. analyse risk
7. complete plan.

The first step, design a plan, involves choosing the type and level of detail of the information that will be incorporated into the project plan.

The second step defines all the products, including management and quality documents, that will be needed. The other steps follow more or less naturally. Step six involves identifying risks, which can lead to the inclusion of extra activities in the plan. PRINCE divides large projects into *stages*, which represent subsets of the activities of the project.

PRINCE 2 goes beyond indicating how to plan a project, and provides guidance on how to start, follow up, and close a project. Each project is overseen by a project board involving the customer (or executive), users, and suppliers. Users will use the products of the project. Suppliers provide goods and services needed by the project. The executive ensures that the business requirements are met by the project. The project board delegates the day-to-day running to the project manager, who is supported by team managers when needed.

Those interested can be examined on PRINCE 2 for professional recognition as a PRINCE practitioner. PRINCE is recommended for UK government IT projects.

10.5.3 Software tools for managing resources

The whole of the area of planning and control can be strongly supported by tools. Planning work can be tedious, and tools both help to reduce errors and to reduce the tedium. This in turn means that good plans are drawn up initially, and, perhaps more importantly, are maintained up to date.

First, for estimation, historical data can be collected in a database of projects which could be used for analogical estimation, or to calibrate other methods. The actual calculation of function points and the conversion of these to work content and elapsed time figures can also be supported by tools, and there are a number of commercial tools available to help in this. Tracking the actual effort spent and the actual activities done by developers can be tricky. People can have different perceptions of their work and track activities differently. Make sure that all the personnel report their activity on the same basis and assumptions; this will improve the quality of your historical data and add confidence to your estimation methods.

If you are using commercial tools for estimation, the output of an estimation tool must be used with care, particularly if the tool has not been calibrated with your own data. When possible you should compare the output of more than one estimation method. Any large discrepancies should be explained. Check your estimates again as the project progresses. Remember that you and your team will be responsible for your estimates.

Second, scheduling projects, particularly large projects, can benefit significantly from tools. These tools allow you to record work breakdown into a hierarchy of activities, with any dependencies between these activities. Milestones will be noted. They allow a hierarchy of resources from team to individuals to be made available, and then assigned to the activities. And load balancing will be supported through the automatic summation of efforts by individual and by activity, to make sure that all activities are adequately resourced and that people are not being either under- or over-committed. Some tools will also allow some automatic scheduling, but this seems more appropriate to routine engineering work, not the development of software where the particular skills of individual engineers can be important.

Large and complex projects will benefit from specialised tools. Small projects can be managed using spreadsheets, as discussed in Case Study 10.9. For larger projects it is better to use a project management tool which will help you to achieve consistency and detect errors in your planning assumptions – see Case Study 10.10. A key issue in evaluating project management software is whether work content estimations can be done independently of resource assignment – so many leading commercial tools just cannot do this (See Case Study 6.3 in Chapter 6).

> There are many tools which can be used to help when managing resources, but you must still tackle the difficult problems of estimation and scheduling yourself.

Case Study 10.9   *Using spreadsheets to manage projects*

One of us (PH) runs research and development projects using spreadsheets, having previously used specialist project-management tools and found them laborious to use for little added benefit for a part-time project-management role. Besides directly supporting the project-management function described in this chapter, the spreadsheet can add tremendous help in other ways to a project manager.

It was a spreadsheet that was used for the Gantt charts in the examples in this chapter. We took a very simple-minded approach in those examples, analysing the underlying data analysis requirements as:

- Activities: what they are and what effort has been estimated for them, what dependencies they have with other activities,

▶

and what they deliver which may be associated with a project milestone.

- People, the basic resource that will be used: who they are, what their skills are, when they are available, and for how much time.
- Time periods, the units of time for which work will be assigned and monitored: most likely this will be weeks, but it might be months or even quarters.

These are brought together in an assignment of a person resource to an activity in a particular time period. We may also want to represent milestones.

In a spreadsheet, we create a three-dimensional data model of the management problem, with activities, people, and time periods being the three dimensions. The points in this three dimensional management space are the assignments. Gantt charts are two-dimensional projections of this 3D space.

Case Study 10.10 *Open source tools for project management*

A list of open source project management tools is available at http://proj.chbs.dk. One of these tools is Open Workbench, which is developed in C++ and Java, with translations in English, French, and German. A free version of this tool is available from the Open Workbench website at http://www.openworkbench.org. The source code of this tool is available through http://sourceforge.net/projects/openworkbench/.

The following list of key features is taken from the tool's website[23] and gives us an idea of the functionality that we could expect to find in a project scheduling and monitoring tool. Several levels of aggregation are provided for each aspect of management. So work may be aggregated as 'phases' and 'tasks' as well as 'activities'. Support for 'subprojects' can be useful in managing complex projects. The tool will enable the manager to:

- define projects and create associated work breakdown structures with activities, phases, tasks, and milestones;
- define resources as people, equipment, materials, or expense;
- assign resources to tasks;
- create dependencies as finish-start, start-start, finish-finish, or start-finish;

- schedule tasks manually or automatically using Auto Schedule;
- automatically schedule tasks forwards or backwards (the latter allowing tasks to be started as late as possible) and with or without resource constraints;
- configure resources on tasks with uniform, fixed, contour, front, or back loading;
- create subprojects and link them to master projects;
- create and manage inter-project dependencies;
- associate guidelines with tasks;
- manage advanced task properties such as fixed duration, dependency lag, imposed start/end dates, and charge codes;
- define, compare, and reset project baseline settings;
- create, edit, and delete calendars;
- schedule to general or individualised calendars;
- schedule across linked master and subprojects;
- view Gantt charts (both detail and roll-up), PERT charts, and the critical path;

- track status, percentage complete, and estimates to complete;
- conduct earned value analysis;
- customise project views including column layouts, filters, sorts, and rule-based formatting.

Note that this does most things we need, and some we don't. If you need to acquire a project management tool, this could be a good place to start.

Activity 10.9   *Simulation for decision support*

Simulation has a long tradition in engineering as a problem-solving tool. This can also be used in management decision-making, by simulating the project organisation and the work planned, and then running the simulation model under various conditions to see what might happen in practice. Using your common-sense understanding of how simulation tools might be used to support software project management, identify two advantages and three disadvantages of the use of these type of tools for managing resources in software organisations.

Discussion[24]

Some advantages are:

- Simulation models provide an objective means to justify decisions.
- Simulation models can capture more complex relationships between variables than simple estimation models such as COCOMO.
- Simulation models can explain counterintuitive or paradoxical behaviour observed in software projects (e.g., Brooks's law).

Some disadvantages are:

- A large amount of high-quality data is required in order to build and calibrate a meaningful process model.
- Building and using models requires effort and a considerable expertise which only large software organisations may be able to justify.
- Each project is different. Existing models will need to be refined and re-calibrated in order to cope with new situations.

> Project management needs to be supported by appropriate standards and tools.

10.5.4 The working environment

We saw earlier in this chapter that the productivity of individual engineers can vary enormously. While the varying productivity between engineers may be largely due to innate intellectual endowments and propensities, this is not the only factor at work. When in the 1970s and 1980s people attempted to measure the effect of factors like programming tools upon individual productivity, they found to their surprise that the general environment within which engineers worked was of critical importance.

Software developers use computers to do their work and spend a considerable amount of time inside their cubicles or offices, working at their desks. The working environment involves many factors: office space, ventilation, illumination, layout of offices, type of workstations, and so on. In some countries, there is legislation which mandates minimum requirements in terms of workstation quality (e.g., the EU Directive 90/270/EEC, which sets minimum health and safety requirements for work with display screen equipment, with measurable ergonomic properties based on the ISO 9241 on 'Ergonomic requirements for office work with visual display terminals'[25]). Such legislation is important and encapsulates collective wisdom and experience on how to arrange workstations in such a way that the risks to the worker are as low as possible.

Some versions of the Agile method involve pair programming. Two people write code together, which has particular requirements in terms of office and workstation configuration: large screens and desks with space for two chairs, etc.

But it is not just these ergonomic factors that are important. DeMarco and Lister[26] give a number of other factors that are important, like an external view, and the ability to personalise the workspace. Making people comfortable and happy also makes them work more productively. Do not forget the Hawthorne effect described in Chapter 3.

| **Activity 10.10** | *Improving the work environment* |

Refer back to Chapter 3 and the discussion of the Hawthorne experiments and Maslow's hierarchy of human needs. What lessons can we learn when we apply these findings to the work environment of software-related work?

Discussion

Maslow's hierarchy of needs suggest that work should be enjoyable and that elements such as motivation, respect, and feeling part of a community and contributing to that community are very important.

Further, the Hawthorne effect suggests that also the very fact that management is interested enough in its employees' welfare to make the work environment more interesting will also boost productivity.

The work environment is important as a motivator of people.

Case Study 10.11 *Environmental needs change as professionals mature*

Humphreys tells the following story:[27]

The case of Dan, a talented young scientist who worked for me when I first joined IBM, is a good example of the way professionals' attitudes change during their careers. Early in his career, Dan was enormously concerned about status and job titles and made a big fuss about the size of his office and the style of its furniture. At the time, office space was extremely tight, and my entire department was moved to

temporary quarters in a nearby shopping center. The entrance was at the back of the building by the trash cans, and only one of the offices had a window. My office didn't have a carpet, my furniture was scratched and dented, and no one's office even had a door. Dan saw this as a personal affront, and although I tried to convince him that these conditions were only temporary, he soon quit to join another company. In spite of this early immaturity,

> *however, Dan was highly competent and soon gained considerable fame in his specialty. In fact, he later was the principal inventor of an important new computer architecture. Years* *later, he was entirely happy with a cluttered office in a university department and felt no concern about the lack of carpets or expensive furniture. (p. 51)*

10.5.5 Getting the best performance from your team

An organisation could be a small company of two or a large corporation with several thousand employees. Managing resources in the software enterprise involves achieving the best possible work with the available skills and talents.

Watts S. Humphrey shares his experience of many years as an IBM manager in his book *Managing Technical People – Innovation, Teamwork and the Software Process*. He points out, as we have so frequently throughout this book, that human creativity is essential for software development and humans are the critical resource. Despite all the care put in preparing plans and estimates, things may change during the course of a project, and it is the people's commitment to successfully achieving the project goals which makes all the difference. In order to be committed, people need to believe in the goal and have a strong desire for its achievement. Humphrey warns that there is no recipe for obtaining the best performance of a team; in order to achieve such dedicated performance, the manager needs to 'respect the employees and follow sound management principles' (p. vi). The elements identified by Humphrey which need to be combined in different degrees, in order to achieve superior performance are (p. vii):

- a challenging and worthy goal;
- talented, motivated, and capable people;
- the training and support to enable the work to be properly done;
- a manager with the drive and vision to make it happen;
- a leader who understands and cares about his or her followers.

Managing resources involves not only the successful achievement of the work goals but also contribution to the personal and professional development of the individual team members. The best professionals operate at the self-fulfilment level of Maslow's scale. Managers need to know what motivates people, how people's expectations may change as they move on in their careers and how to provide them with challenges and rewards and the appropriate environment.

Activity 10.11   *Failing your human resource*

Many organisations claim that people are their most important resource. However all too often the actions of management do not live up to this claim. Give examples of such actions.

Discussion
Answers might include the following:

- Failure to assign clear roles and responsibilities within a team.

- Interference with technical decisions.
- Not listening to technical advice, including enforcing effort and duration estimates which are clearly unachievable.
- Lack of proper facilities, formal training, tools and support for the professionals as part of a community of learning.
- Permitting members of the team to be overloaded without doing anything about it.
- Not sharing with the team members the plans, news, and expectations about a project.

The Software Engineering Institute (SEI) at Carnegie Mellon University has proposed the People Capability Maturity Model (P-CMM), which provides a road map for organisations wishing to make progress in the way they manage people. This model is related to the wider SEI's process improvement model (**CMMi**) which we will cover later in Chapter 12.

Case Study 10.12   *The People Capability Maturity Model (P-CMM)*[28,29]

P-CMM is a road map for organisations to improve the way they manage their workforce and help to develop technical and managerial excellence and leadership. The most important resource in software-related work is the people. The first step in improving an organisation is to improve the way the organisation deals with people. As any improvement effort, P-CMM starts with an assessment of the current state of the organisation. P-CMM identifies five levels, each of which is associated to a set of priorities. In level 1, organisations do not have basic people-management practices. The move from level 1 to level 2 requires establishing a fair compensation (salary and grading) system and effective two-way communication by which individuals and managers share views of performance and expectations. To pass from level 2 to level 3, organisations must start identifying the core human resource competencies that are necessary in order to meet business needs, focussing on developing the talents and potential of the existing personnel. An organisation at level 3 will help employees to achieve competencies and mastery of technology in areas which are key for the business. The organisation will support career development and motivate individuals to improve their knowledge and skills. Level 4 focusses on the management of human resources at the team, unit, and organisation-wide levels. The idea is to facilitate, support, and measure team-based performance. It also involves alignment of goals at the individual, team and unit levels. Finally, level 5 focusses on coaching and continuous improvement of the people-management practices. As with any such scheme, organisations can select from frameworks such as P-CMM the elements they need for their particular situation.

Activity 10.12   *Management skills*

In order to carry out the responsibilities of managing resources, what skills would you see as necessary to meet the project manager's responsibilities?

Discussion

Just being a good programmer or analyst is not enough to be a good project manager. The project manager will need to be skilled at least in the following areas:

- *Effective people management*: this means that the project manager must identify the skills and expertise required to complete the project, and then recruit the staff. And, perhaps more importantly, he/she must then motivate and develop those people to their full potential to benefit not only the current development project, but also the whole organisation over the longer term.

- *Planning*: any project will always require careful planning. The project manager needs to plan each activity of the development so that resources can be made available when required and not too early or too late. The project plan will also give confidence to the project's client that the project is being properly managed.

- *Organisation*: the project manager must organise the resources available into an effective team or group of teams. Having planned the work, the use of resources with respect to the plan needs to be plotted, and any potential problems of slippage or overspend need to be identified early and remedial action taken.

- *Customer relations*: In many projects, liaising with the clients and users is a major activity in itself. The client will need to be reassured that the money they are investing in a new software system will bring the expected return on investment. Users will want to be reassured that the software will support their needs. On many, if not all, projects, requirements are constantly being changed and new ones introduced. This is not a criticism of the requirements capture process – any experienced project manager knows that requirements do change, that managing this is part of his/her job. Good project managers understand this and support their clients and users in this activity.

- *Technical leadership*: In many smaller projects, the project manager will be the person turned to for advice in devising and selecting solutions to technical problems. The project manager will not be expected to become involved in the details of these solutions, but must be able to spot the winners and losers. Alternatively a different technical leader or 'authority' might be appointed, perhaps called the 'system architect' or similar.

The human resource is the critical resource: successful teams and organisations empower people.

Summing up

In this chapter we have looked in some detail at how resources associated with software should be managed. We have focused mostly on human resources, on people, and how they are deployed within projects and their work monitored and guided. However we have also looked at the work environment and the use of tools. We saw that:

- a project is an important means of organising software-related activities and work to achieve defined outcomes under technical, financial, timescale, organisational, and other constraints;

- the project objectives or requirements need to be documented, covering project scope, with the expectation that they will evolve during the project;
- the cost and timescales for a project can be estimated, with these estimates updated and refined as the project progresses and generates more knowledge about the project;
- data from past projects must be collected and used to calibrate the chosen estimation model so that it fits local conditions;
- work is best scheduled using Gantt charts, taking care to balance resources so that all the work is properly resourced and resources are not overloaded;
- progress is best monitored using earned value, with frequent re-estimation and re-planning;
- tools should be used to help managing resources, but cannot automate the management task;
- the work environment is critically important as a motivator of people, and is worth investing in;
- overall it is the human resource that is the critical resource: successful teams and organisations empower people to produce their best.

Exercises

1. Collect all the 'laws' of software project management that you can find, in this book, in the various sources cited by us, and by searching on the Internet. For each of these determine the evidence upon which the law is claimed to rest, and make a personal judgement about whether the law really holds.

2. Look back at the library system in Chapter 7. Assume that this system forms part of a suite of systems that cover all of the schools administration and teaching – school timetabling, student attendance, financial management, lesson design, and lesson delivery. If you were managing this complete suite of systems as a single project, what project organisation would you choose? Draw the organigram (organisation diagram).

3. You are running a company that has established an offshore software development facility in South Asia, while retaining a small team back in your home country. You have clients in your home country wanting bespoke systems – at what point in the development life cycle should you transfer the work from your home team to the offshore facility? Give comprehensive reasons, if possible using case studies found on the Internet.

4. Estimating for software development is a very error-prone process – for example, we saw that COCOMO at its best could only estimate to within thirty per cent of the actual cost seventy-five per cent of the time. And yet one company in the UK is prepared to take a fixed price implementation contract for a system once the requirements have been fully specified – providing that they produced those requirements themselves in a preceding feasibility/specification study done under time and materials terms. Comment on how they could do this, bearing in mind that the implementation contract would have had to have been competed for in response to an open invitation to tender.

5. You have decided to obtain open source library management software for use in a Spanish-speaking country in South America. The software that best fits your client's needs is thought to be Koha (http://www.koha.org), which was originally developed in New Zealand and interfaces in the English language, based upon library practices common in the English-speaking world. While the functional match seems to be close, since library practices are largely governed by international standards, this will need to be reviewed, reverse engineering a high-level description of the software for comparison with the client's requirements, which will also need to be elicited in detail and then specified fully. Some changes to the software are expected. All the interface messages and help files will need to be translated into Spanish. Devise an estimation method for undertaking this work, noting that while software suffers a diseconomy of scale, translation work actually manifests an economy of scale as repeated translations become more frequent as the volume to be translated increases.

6. Making reasonable assumptions, plan the library project of Case Study 10.7 using a spreadsheet to balance resources and create the more detailed Gantt chart for the tasks D1 to D4, T1 to T3, and P1 to P6.

7. Draw the data model implicit in the use of spreadsheets for project management, as discussed in Case Study 10.9.

8. In a survey of UK project managers in the 1980s, the Butler Cox company discovered that newly appointed project managers performed considerably better than project managers who had been managing projects for several years, when measured in terms of bringing in projects within budget and timescale, achieving development at higher productivity levels. Explain this, writing around 1,000 words.

Endnotes

1. For example, H. Kerzner (2003) *Project Management – A Systems Approach to Planning, Scheduling and Controlling*. Wiley.
2. See http://www.sigsoft.org/SEN/.
3. H. Sackman, W.J. Erikson and E.E. Grant (1968) 'Exploratory Experimental Studies Comparing Online and Offline Programming Performance', *Comm ACM* 11(1), 3–11.
4. See, for example, Doug Norman (1993) *The Things That Make Us Smart*. Perseus Books.
5. A. Cockburn (1998) *Surviving Object-Oriented Projects*. Addison-Wesley, pp. 100–101.
6. From R.S. Pressman and D. Ince (2000) *Software Engineering – A Practitioner's Approach* (European edition, 5th edn). McGraw Hill, pp. 134–135.
7. B.W. Boehm (1981) *Software Engineering Economics*. Prentice Hall.
8. B.W. Boehm, C. Abts, A.W. Brown, S. Chulani, B. Clark, E. Horowitz, R. Madachy, D. Reifer, and B. Steece (2000) *Software Cost Estimation with COCOMO II*. Prentice Hall.
9. S. Chulani, B. Boehm, and B. Steece (1999) 'Bayesian Analysis of Empirical Software Engineering Cost Models', *IEEE Trans. on Softw. Engineering*, 25(4), July/Aug, 573–583.
10. T. DeMarco (1982) *Controlling Software Projects*. Yourdon.
11. A. Albrecht (1979) Measuring Application Development Productivity. *Proc. of the Joint SHARE/GUIDE/IBM Application Development Symposium*, Monterey, CA, Oct 14–17, published by the GUIDE International Corp., pp. 83–92.
12. See http://www.ifpug.org/publications/manual.htm.
13. This account is based on a paper by T. Fetcke, A. Abran, and T.-H. Nguyen (1998) 'Mapping the OO-Jacobson Approach into Function Point Analysis', *Proc. TOOLS USA 97: Technology of Object-Oriented Languages and Systems*. IEEE. They refer to the IFPUG method, and map OO methods to that, distinguishing different kinds of object.

14. From R.S. Pressman and D. Ince (2000) *Software Engineering – A Practitioner's Approach* (European Edition, 5th edn). McGraw Hill, p. 135.

15. Charles Symons (1991) *Software Sizing and Estimating: MkII Function Point Analysis.* Wiley.

16. United Kingdom Software Metrics Association (UKSMA), *MK II Function Point Analysis Counting Practices Manual* Version 1.3.1 Date: September 1998, http://www.uksma.co.uk/public/mkIIr131.pdf.

17. See Boehm (1981), p. 71.

18. Reference to papers with more elaborated models may be found by performing a web search for 'CRESTES'.

19. Roger Pressman (1992) *Software Engineering: A Practitioner's Approach*, (3rd edn). McGraw-Hill.

20. R.S. Pressman and D. Ince (2000) *Software Engineering – A Practitioner's Approach* (European edition, 5th edn) McGraw-Hill, p. 166.

21. See http://www.prince2.com/.

22. This agency is now called the Office of Government Commerce (OGC).

23. See http://www.openworkbench.org/modules.php?name=Product.

24. See, for example, M.I. Kellner, R.J. Madachy, and D.M. Raffo (1999) 'Software Process Modeling and Simulation: Why, What, How', *Journal of Systems and Software* 46 (2/3) for a fuller discussion of this.

25. This is a seventeen-part standard issued by ISO. Only sections of it are legally mandatory in the EU countries.

26. Tom DeMarco and Timothy Lister (1999) *Peopleware: Productive Projects and Teams.* Dorset House.

27. W.S. Humphrey (1997) *Managing Technical People.* Addison-Wesley.

28. Bill Curtis, William E. Hefley and Sally Miller (1995) 'People Capability Maturity Model', *Software Engineering Institute Technical Report, CMU/SEI-95-MM-02*, Carnegie Mellon University, Pittsburgh, September, 1995.

29. W.S. Humphrey (1997) *Introduction to the Personal Software Process.* Addison-Wesley.

Managing work-products and digital assets

What we will study in this chapter

During software development and evolution we produce many intermediate and final digital work-products. Digital assets are also produced within many other activities in an enterprise. All these digital assets are changed frequently, and these changes need to be managed. In this chapter we will focus on software work-products, and from that standpoint consider the more general issue of managing all other digital assets.

We will see that in general these digital assets evolve through a sequence of versions, with collections of these versions belonging together in configurations that together serve a coherent purpose. Some of these configurations form baselines within a project, from which further work takes place, some baselines become releases for use by customers.

These digital assets are under continuous pressure for change, and change needs to be carefully controlled to ensure that only changes which result in net benefit to the enterprise are permitted.

The processes involved are complex and benefit from computer assistance. A range of software tools are available, though not all provide the full support needed. There is much product differentiation between tools where common solutions could be beneficial.

11.1 Introduction

Digital materials now constitute important assets of an organisation. These digital materials could be:

- work-products created during the development of software;
- software items made available more widely as software components for reuse elsewhere;
- documents created using office systems like word processors and spreadsheets as part of internal and external operations;
- material that will be made available via the web.

These digital materials are often treated separately, but they have much in common and will be treated together here, though we will focus mostly on the first two because of their importance in software development.

The common ground is that these digital materials:

- need to be stored in some systematic way that enables their easy retrieval when needed;
- are made up of basic items that may need to be kept in groups that together constitute a meaningful collection;
- will be subject to change and update where earlier versions remain meaningful;
- may need to be processed through a number of operations in some constrained sequence.

We will start by focusing on software development work products because they are the most complex case, and from there consider what is needed for the other three cases, software reusable assets, documents, and web content.

11.2 Software configuration management

Software size and complexity can grow very quickly, only limited by the productivity of the people developing the software and the capacity of the computers which will execute it. We discussed software evolution in Chapter 9, and saw there that the vast majority of software actively used is subject to pressures for change. These pressures are present even before the release of the first operational version of the software. We saw how, as software is developed and evolved, its various component parts need to be changed and the changes need to be managed in a disciplined way to ensure that the software continues to function as intended. If such discipline is not present it is easy for incompatible versions of components to be put together into a release that yields subtle or even serious problems after delivery. We can conclude that 'managing software is managing change'.

This chapter takes a general view of the management processes for change, looking at the nature of software products and at management controls such as Change Control Boards (CCBs) that are important if we are to avoid, or at least minimise, configuration problems. Case Study 11.1 illustrates the kind of obscure problem that can arise. If the change control process is too complicated, change control can become a constraint on productivity, so developers and managers need to find a balance which suits the responsibilities and needs of their enterprise and their clients. Change management is a complex problem that requires suitable computer systems to support it, and we will look at the kinds of tools that are available to help.

Case Study 11.1 *Emergency software repair*

Pat Hall worked as a consultant in software development methods and standards. While on an assignment in the oil industry at a company located in Glasgow, one of the persons working with him, Joyce, was whipped off to troubleshoot an emergency problem that had arisen while printing the quarterly business accounts – the results were clearly incorrect, but none of the front-line maintenance people could understand why. Joyce knew the programs in detail, having worked on their original development and traced the problem back to changes made three months earlier when part of the system had been recompiled with a new compiler, but other parts had not been recompiled. There were incompatibilities between the two compilers, and recompiling everything with the then-current compiler cured the fault – after a weekend working very long hours.

The lesson from this was that not only do we need compatible source versions of software working together, we also need to be sure that the compiled and built versions are compatible, recording the names and versions of all tools used in the process. Thorough testing of everything after even a small change is essential to catch other functions that might no longer work as a consequence of this change.

11.2.1 What is configuration management?

Given the continual pressures for software change, the following problems are common when change control is not properly implemented:

- users may be sent the wrong version of the software that does not meet their requirements;

- changes to a component of the software can be implemented on the wrong version of that component, leading to the need for later rework to make good this error;

- time and effort can be spent in trying to find where a particular version of the code has been stored. For example, during the diagnosis of a defect, a considerable amount of effort may be needed in reconstructing the older version of software being used by those who have reported the defect.

Change needs to be controlled. Case Study 11.2 describes one simple way of doing this.

> Change needs to be carefully managed to ensure that after the change everything works as intended.

Case Study 11.2 *The Gold Copy system at GenRad*

GenRad, originally General Radio, was a company that made (among many other things) very expensive test equipment for electrical circuit boards in the 1980s. Circuits would be placed on the equipment, and test probes (known as 'nails', with the whole test bed known as a 'bed of nails') would be raised to contact particular points in the circuit that were then measured as a number of tests of the circuit were run. Associated with this hardware was complex software that would activate the probe nails and run the tests on the board, measuring outputs and comparing these measurements with what should have been expected, passing or failing the circuit board as a result.

The software was regularly updated and improved. To control these changes the company operated a 'gold copy' system, in which a single version of the complete software was maintained as the 'gold copy' and was controlled by the lead software architect. This lead software engineer was responsible for building and testing new contributions to the gold copy, only accepting these into the gold copy if everything was right. It was this gold copy that was shipped with their test equipment, and current customers were encouraged to move to the latest version of the gold copy, particularly if they had any problems with the version they had. During the development of the various parts of the software, engineers might build their own local copies, but this variety was not allowed to affect the policy of a single gold copy at any one time.

This part of GenRad was acquired by Teradyne in 2001.

Configuration management consists of the methods, tools, and standards for managing changes in a software product or other product as it is enhanced, adapted, and fixed over time. A configuration management system:

- authorises which changes should happen and which should not;
- ensures that the version or release of the software delivered is the one intended;
- ensures that when a change is made, all the changes necessary are made;
- identifies and records versions of components, and which collections of these versions belong together as a coherent whole.

Use a gold copy system to control changes to a single version of an evolving system.

It is an activity that must continue from the cradle to the grave through all phases of software acquisition and evolution for all types of software: it starts on the first day of an initial development project and ends when the software is phased out and ceases to be used. It is equally important for commodity software (software developed for a wide variety of users who will buy it in the marketplace) and for bespoke software (software developed for a single user who normally pays for its development and subsequent maintenance and evolution).

The simplest, but also the most limited, approach to change control is to store a single copy of the last version of each of its components, the 'gold copy' system we saw in Case Study 11.2. The gold copy system may be unsatisfactory for several reasons. First, different users may have different needs and software needs to be customised to each of these users – thus seeming to require multiple released versions, but look at Case Study 11.3. Second, as changes are implemented a series of releases are sent to users, but customers may not choose to move to the latest release and then, if a problem arises, the software supplier might not be able to give adequate support. This does not mean that the software organisation necessarily has to actively support all the previous releases of the software – this can be very expensive – but it is important that the software organisation can effectively retrieve earlier releases of the software if, for example, a query or a defect has been reported and needs to be investigated, diagnosed, and fixed.

Case Study 11.3 *Operating system customisation*

Going back to the 1970s and 1980s, the operating systems of most major suppliers were released as large generic packages which had to undergo a lengthy configuration process at the customer site. Each customer's configuration of hardware would be unique, with different choices of peripherals selected to meet the customer's particular needs. The software at installation had to be told about this hardware configuration, and other choices would also have to be made.

This practice needs to be contrasted with that of a major UK supplier who knowing what hardware they were shipping to their customer, would configure the operating system for them before shipment. However when one of their customers encountered a problem, they had to be able to construct the exact configuration of their customer – whereas in the alternative approach all those details of configuration were the customer's responsibility, and if a fault was encountered, they could conduct their tests on the generic software.

In addition to storing different versions of the code, you also need a change management process that will ensure that changes are satisfactorily implemented and delivered to those who need them. The records generated by a change management process provide an audit trail showing which changes have been approved, implemented, and validated. Such processes must follow the rules established by the organisation, either on its own or following a particular configuration management standard.

With the exception perhaps of software inspections (see next chapter), the introduction of configuration management is the one single process improvement which will have the most visible impact in helping to provide discipline and maturity to a process.

Configuration management is one part of the quality system of the software enterprise. In quality frameworks such as **CMMi**, covered in Chapter 12, the introduction of configuration management is one of the process areas that are mandatory for the important transition between level 1 (initial or chaotic) to level 2 (managed).

Activity 11.1   *Why configuration management?*

What are the advantages and disadvantages of using configuration management for a software enterprise?

Discussion

Software change is inevitable as long as a system is being used. Configuration management brings discipline to the management and implementation of change; for example, it reduces the likelihood of errors due to shipping the wrong version to a user, or in locating an old version that is needed in order to identify a defect. In general, the benefits of configuration management compensate for any disadvantages, such as the effort required to install and keep the configuration management tools running and up to date. Some organisations have appointed a dedicated librarian in charge of configuration management and this adds costs which are likely to be compensated through savings due to fewer defects. The change control process associated with configuration management can be costly to run and organisations need to achieve a viable trade-off between their responsibilities toward their clients and society, the criticality of the software being changed, and the constraints (e.g., costs and resources, schedules, technology) within which the enterprise operates.

Full configuration management systems enable multiple versions to coexist simultaneously without losing control.

11.2.2 The basic elements of a configuration management system

Let's start with a simple example which illustrates in more detail what the basic issues are. In Case Studies 11.1, 11.2, and 11.3 we saw the need for overall controls, so that the customer gets a stable system to work with, and the development team can reproduce any system released to a user in the event that defects are encountered and need repair. To be able to assert control over change and configuration we will need to dig a little deeper, and Case Study 11.4 illustrates in finer detail the problems that can arise.

Case Study 11.4 *Software for the disabled and illiterate*[1]

A small team is developing software to support people who are illiterate or who otherwise are unable to respond to written messages and information on the computer screen. The team is building a web browser which will work entirely through speech and images, enabling people to access information on the Internet, and also to contribute information to the Internet, without the need to read and write that is so fundamental to current technology.

A web page developed with this system contains images and speech, where the speech may explain images, or images may illustrate speech. Central to the system is a speech editor that enables non-technical people to record and then selectively change parts of the recorded speech, rearrange the speech, and so on. It also includes a text-to-speech (TTS) subsystem built using the Festival system, to enable both written commands in existing software to be read out, and to enable existing material from the web to be read to the user.

There are three overall technical areas:

- the overall architecture of the system and its integration into existing web technologies;
- the speech editor subsystem which can accept existing speech from the web or from the TTS system, and outputs speech for use within web pages;
- the TTS subsystem which reads written text and outputs speech, either for further editing or for playing to the user.

Each area is being undertaken by a different engineer, working together within an informal 'Agile' method, with much discussion and sharing of knowledge, working together to find solutions, laying down essential documentation such as overall system design, but otherwise letting the software code (in Java) represent the system directly. However, one area where management disciplines will be enforced is in change management, and the widely used CVS system is being used on this project.

While the TTS system clearly uses existing software, and in particular a Java version of Festival, it also uses locally created software, in particular to link the TTS system into the browsers and platforms on which it will run. The speech editor subsystem is being built in house but will also use existing software where possible, for example for changing the speed of speech readout; it will also need to integrate with the browsers and platforms, producing compressed speech in some standard format. The external software may be available as source code, but it may only be available as compiled binary code, or even in some instances as executables. The connections between the major subsystems are regulated by interfaces defined by the team, which are then wrapped to connect to the platform – this wrapping software may be browser- and platform-specific, and so may exist in several 'variants'. Wherever possible common software processes are produced once and shared between systems.

The system is exploratory, with frequent trials with a pool of illiterate users, with subsequent changes. An anthropologist is assisting the engineers in this aspect of their work.

These changes will happen in particular user interface routines (Java classes) of the software, and it is important to control these changes and make sure that different parts of the software do connect together even though they have been changed. Often several classes have to be changed together, and must be kept in step. Some of the components of the system are obtained externally and changes occur outside the control of the team – these changes need to be tracked and accepted at convenient times.

We see from Case Study 11.4 that individual items of software, in this case Java classes, need to be changed and that changes need to be coordinated and kept in step so that the overall subsystems and system remain consistent. But it is not just software that needs to be controlled: the key interfaces and overall architecture also need to be controlled. All of this is happening in an environment of existing software supported externally that may also be subject to change. The software being developed may have to integrate with completely different sets of software, leading to a number of variants of the software tailored to these different environments.

We will now abstract from this example to create a general model of software and how its evolution needs to be managed. In doing this we will introduce the terminology that has become established in configuration management and change control systems. However, we must also recognise that the specific terms and their meaning may vary from organisation to organisation and from tool to tool.

11.2.3 Configuration items

During the development of the software, a variety of items are produced, such as:

- data flow diagrams and data structure diagrams in traditional 'structured' development;
- use case diagrams, class diagrams, and other UML diagrams in object-oriented development;
- individual programs in source code files, or the compiled versions of these in object code files;
- requirements statements and requirements specifications;
- architectures and designs;
- test plans and test cases.

For each type of item, there may be a large number of different individual items produced. So there will be many data flow diagrams, many OO class diagrams, and so on. These items will be produced during the project, stored, changed, stored again, and so on. We shall refer to these items as **configuration items** or simply items. Each configuration item must have a unique name, and a description or specification which distinguishes it from other items of the same type. In Case Study 11.4 the Java classes, interface definitions, and architectural design, are our configuration items. However, following the experience of Case Study 11.1, all items of external software, including compilers will also need to be identified as configuration items.

Configuration items are atomic, in the sense that we would not be interested in the parts within them. The relative size of these atomic items is known as the **granularity** of the configuration items – for example, the set of all DFDs would be a large grain item, individual DFDs would be medium grain configuration items, while individual boxes or lines or text elements would be fine grain. While we would not go as far as individual elements in a DFD, we might make each paragraph in a requirements document into a configuration item, so granularity might vary across the system. Based on their current and future needs, the software organisation decides what items at what level of granularity will be put under configuration management. These generally include the source and object code, the high and low level designs, test plans and test cases, the user documentation and the user requirements. In Case Study 11.4 items are relatively coarse grained – so, for example, we are not interested in individual procedures (methods) within classes, and are only interested in the overall interfaces, not the individual parts.

Documents such as emails and personal notes of the developers are not likely to be placed under configuration management, despite providing a possible source for the rationale behind the decisions taken during the development. Ideally one would like to put under configuration management the rationale and the assumptions made by developers, but there are no widely accepted standards and tools for capture and management of rationale. Regrettably this valuable information is all too often lost, and designs that did not work may be repeated and again be found not to work.

The key thing that happens in the life of a configuration item is that it is changed, or revised, to produce a new **version** (or **revision**) of the configuration item. It is the versions of a configuration item that are stored and retrieved. We often talk informally of an item when we mean a version of an item, just as we often talk informally of an object class when we mean an instance of an object class. To avoid misunderstanding here, we shall adhere pedantically to 'version of an item', 'item', and so on. Versions of items are given version numbers, which are unique with respect to that configuration item.

We must also distinguish between **variants** of a configuration item; these are essentially the same item but differ in some well-defined sense. For example, the configuration item 'library data structure diagram' might be available in two variants, one for centralised libraries and one for distributed libraries with branches. Variants are distinguished by having different descriptive names, and also have descriptions characterising them. Variants themselves undergo revisions and thus have versions. In Case Study 11.4 we saw the need for variants of all the wrapping code that connected the project's software to browsers and platforms, leading in turn to variants of the actual system being produced.

As the software is produced, one item leads to another. A context data flow diagram may be analysed to produce lower-level data flow diagrams; a data structure diagram may lead to SQL code. This sequence is important information, since if we update a version of one item we might want to do something about all those versions of other items that were based on this item version. We call this relationship between versions of items **derivations** or **dependencies**, though the relationship may be generically true and thus hold between configuration items and not just their versions.

Figure 11.1 gives a data model for configuration items, their variants, and the versions of both. There are three entity types here: configuration items on the left, versions of configuration items on the right, and variants of configuration items in the middle and below. A configuration item may be related to many variants, and both configuration items and variants may have many versions. Also shown are the principal attributes of these entities, so configuration items have unique IDs, names and descriptions; variants also have unique IDs, names and descriptions; and versions have version IDs, date created and description. Note that a variant of configuration item is essentially a subclass (or subtype) of the configuration item and thus is different in kind from a version, which is an instance of configuration item.

> Configuration items are the atomic elements whose versions are being controlled.

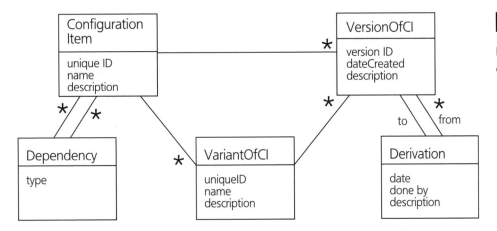

Figure 11.1

Data model for configuration items

Configuration items would normally be stored in machine-readable form in a project repository or library or database, which we shall refer to as the **configuration repository** (or just **repository**). Placing a version of an item into the repository is usually termed **checking in**, while retrieving a version of an item from the repository is usually termed **checking out**. The term 'checking' signifies that a record will be kept of this action.

When an item version is checked out, the current preferred version (usually the latest) is obtained unless a specific version number is indicated. The time of check-out and the person who did this is recorded. Several people may check out the same item simultaneously — many might only want to refer to the item, but some may also have the intention of updating it. If the item is updated, then at check-in, a new version would be created, and the originator of this version recorded together with the time it was created. This may seem all right, but what if two people check out the same version of an item, then both update it and later both check it back in? This is a classic problem in databases and transaction management and is known as the 'lost update problem'. In conventional administrative databases we would normally lock anything we intended to update — so if we took this approach, we would require that, on check-out, the users declared their intention to update, allowing only one person to make such a declaration. But in design databases, such as we are discussing here, we must recognise that we may only discover the need to update a version of an item we are using some time after checking it out. We might also want to keep the item checked out for a long period.

Here are ways we might control the situation where two people have changed the same version of an item and then attempt to check it in as a new version.

1. Accept the first one checked in only, and disallow any later check-ins. Only the new version is then allowed to be updated, after it has been checked out.
2. Elaborating on 1, notify other users of a particular version as soon as the first new version is checked in, to warn them should they be planning an update.
3. Allow later check-in actions to create different versions even though checked out from the same earlier version — usually this is done using a branching structure of version derivations.
4. Allow two (or more) parallel development streams, as in 3, to be merged later, either manually or using tools.

It is the last option that is usually chosen.

Figure 11.2

The data flow context diagram for version management process

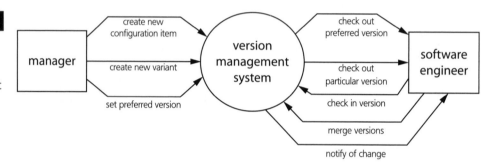

Configuration item versions are stored in a repository and checked out when needed and checked in after change.

The various actions can be documented as a data flow diagram, as in the context diagram of Figure 11.2. Only the manager can create new configuration items and variants of them, and set the preferred version on which all developers will work. Developers check out item versions, usually the preferred version though maybe occasionally a different one. When they check an item version back in after changing it, all check-ins after the first produce a branched line of versions which can be later merged.

The sequence of these activities and other will be constrained, so check out is followed by update, then test, before a check in results. This sequence forms a business process, and might be enforced using a workflow system.

11.2.4 Configurations and baselines

As we develop a number of configuration items, with their sequences of versions and derivations, we find that particular versions of items belong together. For example, we might have developed version 3 of a piece of software based on version 2 of the data flow diagram and version 7 of the data model. We want to mark selected versions of each item as belonging together to make a consistent whole. If this set of items includes the source codes for everything, then we can compile these and build a system that we should expect to execute successfully.

We call this coherent collection of versions of configuration items a **configuration version**, while the generic collection of configuration items would be a

configuration. We refer to the catalogue of configuration items and the versions used in a particular configuration version as the **build state** of the configuration version.

A configuration can also be thought of as configuration item, albeit consisting of a collection of other configuration items. Thus we can think of configurations as containing other configurations, which in turn can contain other configurations, and so on recursively.

Some configuration versions are singled out as special because they form a foundation from which further development can progress. These are called **base-lines** and are typically associated with the major milestones of a project. We talk of further development progressing from a baseline; note that the preferred version of an item checked out by developers might be implicit in this baseline. The config-uration versions delivered on completion of the project for use by the customer are called **releases** and are the baselines from which maintenance and evolution takes place.

Figure 11.3 pulls all this together in a data model elaborated from that of Figure 11.1. This is quite an elaborate data model, so read it carefully! This is the same as the data model in Figure 11.1 with four more entities added on top. Configurations are composed of many configuration items. Configurations have many versions each of which are built from many versions of configur-ation items. Some configuration versions become baselines, and some baselines are releases.

> Configurations are coherent collections of configuration items and their versions. Baseline configurations serve as a foundation for further work.

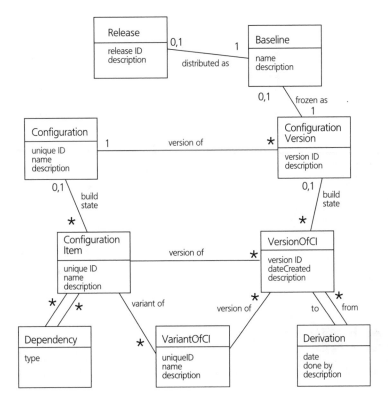

Figure 11.3

Full data model for configuration management

Case Study 11.5 *The KSI project*

Figure 11.4 presents the folder structure used to store the source files of an open source project, called KSI, which is a lightweight implementation of the Scheme programming language (a variant of LISP developed at MIT for teaching computing) and interpreter.

This figure has been generated using a special tool: on the left there are five levels marked, but only four are used, as described in the case study text.

The ellipses indicate folder names, the lines indicate the hierarchical relationships between folders and the number close to the line indicates the number of files stored in each folder (depicted by the folder name within an ellipse) immediately below the line. For example, the folder 'ksi-3.4.1/lib' stores thirteen files or configuration items. The full name of these items will include 'ksi-3.4.1/lib' as the first part of their identifier. In this particular case 'ksi-3.4.1' is the name of the project together with a release identifier and 'lib' is the component to which the items belong. The rectangular boxes on the left hand side of the figure indicate the position of the folder in the hierarchical naming structure, with 'level 1' representing the root folder 'ksi-3.4.1' and 'level 4' representing the lowest folder in the hierarchy, which in this case is 'ksi-3.4.1/gc/include/private'. The 'next level' box is generated by the tool used to present the diagram and for our purposes should be ignored.

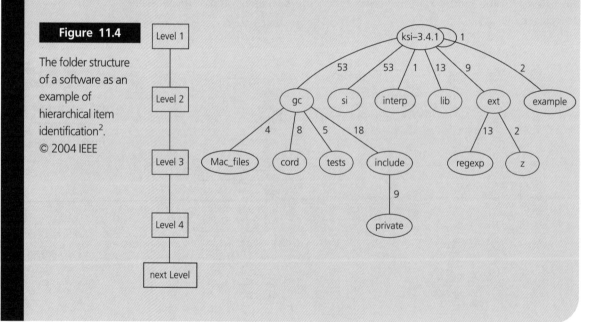

Figure 11.4

The folder structure of a software as an example of hierarchical item identification[2].

© 2004 IEEE

Activity 11.2   *Item naming*

List some of the advantages and disadvantages of the hierarchical naming of configuration items.

Discussion

Hierarchical naming offers the advantage that it can reflect the structure of the system and the mapping between items and the different parts (subsystems or modules) of the system. This way, given an item, you can tell from its name where it belongs.

However, it has the disadvantage that it makes difficult to locate items which share a particular property, such as all the items which were created in order to address a specific requirement. Furthermore, the naming of items based on their role in a particular project makes it difficult to locate them with the purpose of reuse for other projects.

In fact, embedding meaning into the identifiers of items violates a very basic information management principle – the identifier should indicate the unique existence of the object and nothing else. Any other information should be stored separately, accessed via the identifier as metadata – it is common practice to put this information within a computer file as a 'header'.

11.2.5 Release planning

In general, software organisations distinguish between major and minor releases of software in order to indicate significant changes in the functionality of the system and defect fixes, respectively. Some systems may have distinct sequences of releases that may consist of versions of the system for different user groups or markets. These can sometimes be evolved in parallel or in more or less intricate release trees. Release planning can involve branching, where new release sequences are generated, so as to address a particular market and set of customers. It can also involve merging several releases into one single release, for the purpose of reducing costs. Evolution of several largely independent parallel release lines tends to be costly, due to effort duplication when implementing concurrent changes and because developers need to understand and take into account the differences across release lines.

Releases should be carefully planned, with intermediate minor releases and patches as needed.

Release planning needs to take into account many factors, including risk mitigation. As we saw in Chapter 9, Lehman's fifth law suggests that if the scope of a release exceeds that of previous releases, a clean-up release should be planned in order to fix defects and re-engineer the code.

Activity 11.3 *Triggering releases*

In addition to those factors mentioned above, what other factors are likely to trigger the need for a new release of the software?

Discussion

Other factors that can trigger the need for a release include:

- the launch of new hardware and software platforms on which the released software must run;
- market competition;
- sales department commitments;
- changes in technical standards.

Developing a new release may involve considerable cost from the point of view of the software enterprise and the software users. It involves the steps traditionally found in development from scratch, from requirements analysis, design, implementation, integration, testing and documentation update. Some release development processes may skip some of the steps, such as documentation updates, at the risk of paying a high price in the long term as the documentation becomes progressively out of date and, hence, useless. The user also will need to become familiar with the additions and changes in the new release. In some domains, installation of a new faulty release may involve loss of business, require retraining and so on. A new major release is really justified for significant, useful changes that provide value to the stakeholders. Minor releases implement smaller changes and additions, usually defect fixes and minor functionality enhancements.

Small but nevertheless urgent changes – needed for mission-critical reasons, such as security or safety – are delivered as **patches**, whose distribution over the Internet has become inexpensive and easy. Patches are portions of executable code and sometimes data which can be incorporated into an existing executable (object) program as a partial update. In recent years, security patches for packaged software, such as the Windows family of operating systems, have become frequent and users are prompted to keep their software up to date with the latest patches in order to have some protection against the latest known software viruses and other malicious threats.

In newer development processes it has become common practice to make daily builds of the complete software as part of the process of continuous evolution of the software, as a way of validating the software development of that day. This would be done in Agile methods and in Open Source development, and is also the practice at Microsoft, as in Case Study 11.6. When activity is intense, builds may even be more frequent than daily. These frequent builds in turn lead to more frequent releases, and one company we know has weekly releases to customers – in our view weekly releases to customers is too frequent and only serves to confuse.

Daily builds help coordinate a team and mark progress.

Case Study 11.6 *Microsoft's build process*

Microsoft's software development processes have been documented in detail by Cusumano and Selby.[3] A key aspect of this process is the development of the various parts of software in parallel, but with a daily resynchronisation of all the parallel work through a daily build. The software development and build process is described below, summarised from Cusumano and Selby's Table 5.1 (pp. 264–267).

1. Check out software components into a private workspace ready for update.

2. Implement feature, changing software, and building new software as needed.

3. Build and test private release in own workspace, using new and updated software and other unchanged software from the central repository. Test this private release to make sure new features work properly. This may need to be done for each target platform, and may require an overnight run.

4. Synch code changes to the rest of software by comparing the changed code with the

code in the central repository, and if it has changed merge the two versions to make a composite version.

5. Rebuild and test private release including new merged code, testing this as in step 4. Then run a short regression test to make sure that the product is working overall.

6. Check in the changed and new code providing the tests of step 5 have been successful. This includes rechecking for compatibility between the changed code and the code in the central repository.

7. Generate daily build at some fixed time, recompiling and linking all the code to produce a system containing all the functionality developed so far. A series of automated system tests are run, and if it passes these

tests, the build is made available to concerned people in Microsoft.

The process between step 1, check out, and step 6, check in, may take several days or even weeks; the key thing is that when checked back in the code must be of high quality. The developers work under the pressure 'not to break the build', that is, not to check in a faulty component which makes it impossible to have a running version of the system the next day.

Having a daily build is seen as enabling Microsoft to be ready in principle to ship a system at any point in time, though of course they do not do that – the daily build marks the progress of the development process as new features are added and stabilised.

11.2.6 Other digital material

Reusable software assets

Software components and other material collected for reuse will have all of the properties described above for software and other work-products produced during the development of a particular piece of software:

- the components and other items need to be stored and later retrieved;
- individual components will be updated and these changes will need to be controlled as successive versions of these components;
- when used, the components may well be used in small configurations of component versions that need to be consistent with each other.

These reusable configurations may be built into some semi-compiled form for use in projects. Particular versions will be deemed suitable for others to use, and be released for that purpose.

The only significant difference is that the library of reusable components must be capable of being searched using fairly imprecise criteria. By contrast, in a software development project each component will have been produced with its place in the system in mind, and the component would be found in the database using this knowledge.

Documents

The various digital materials produced during normal operations using office software will mostly be ephemeral material like emails and memoranda, produced for a particular purpose and not subsequently updated. All that is needed for this material is their storage in case of some later audit.

However, there will also be many operational documents that are updated and revised, with successive versions needing to be retained. Examples might be human resource employment terms and conditions, information strategies, marketing policies, budgets, and so on. These will most commonly be word processed documents, but they may well contain non-textual material like figures and tables derived from non-word processing sources. This material requires all the facilities described above, including small-scale configuration management and release control.

Web content

The same applies to web page content, which is often generated from the underlying digital materials discussed under the previous heading. This web content will proceed through revisions and will pull together material from various sources that need to be kept track of.

We thus see that version and configuration management is not just applicable to software development, but to most of the digital resources of an enterprise. We have taken a common view of these materials – but as we will see later, they are often treated quite differently by organisations and by the suppliers of software tools to support them.

> Apply a uniform view of all the digital assets across your enterprise.

11.3 Change control

So far we have focused on configuration items: the versions that arise through change and configurations in baselines and releases. Our primitive actions of checking in and checking out go some way towards regulating change, but we really need something more formal, otherwise anybody could make a request for a new function for the system, a change to a digital resource, and a willing software developer or secretary could well respond by making the change uncoordinated with other changes taking place. We need a way to manage this situation.

We will focus initially on software development work-products, and return later to consider other digital assets.

11.3.1 Change control process

Baselines give us one instrument for control, and we talk of freezing a baseline, forbidding any further change to it. That would mean disabling further check in operations for the items in the corresponding configuration. But that well may be overdoing it, so we need to have some means of updating a baseline or generating a new baseline in a controlled manner. This is what change control achieves.

Before a change can be made, a formal request for a change to the baseline must be made. The person requesting the change may be a user or a software engineer working on the project; he/she might want some new facility or may have discovered what they believe to be a defect. The change request makes the case, with as much supporting evidence as possible.

On receipt of a change request, further information might be added: for example what needs to be changed (the main item concerned, and all the other things that must be changed in consequence, discovered through an **impact analysis**) and an estimate of the cost and timescale. This is then put to a designated authority — the project manager on a small project, perhaps, or a change control board (CCB) in the case of a large project spanning many organisations and enduring for many years. A decision to proceed with the change, or to defer or reject it, is made.

Once a change has been agreed, the change is undertaken when resources are available. Several changes to the same items may be grouped together, and some priority system may operate. To make the change, the work goes through a small-scale development process, rather like the one we saw in Chapter 7:

1. check out the versions of the configuration items required;
2. design the changes, updating the design diagrams as appropriate;
3. make the changes to the code;
4. unit test the changes systematically;
5. check changed versions back into a new configuration;
6. regression test the changes systematically;
7. gain formal approval for the changes;
8. make the new configuration into a new baseline or release.

Regression testing is a process that arises specifically in the context of change. Whenever any change to software is made, the specific changes need to be thoroughly tested, as with any software development. However, because the area of change is just part of a much larger system there may be unexpected consequences, and the rest of the software may get worse: it may regress. So it has become good practice to run a complete set of system tests, or perhaps selected critical parts of the tests, as regression tests, just to be sure.

Emergency repairs are a special case. Here some person in authority must still agree the change, with it being cleared retrospectively with the CCB or project manager in due course. Versions of configuration items are checked out, but changes may now be made immediately to the code, which is then tested and immediately put into service. Updated diagrams and documents and their incorporation into a new baseline come later, but still must be done. Undertaking changes in this way must only be done in exceptional circumstances.

Figure 11.5 shows the change control processes as a procedure. 'Impact analysis', as discussed earlier, is the process of finding out the likely effect of making the change, to estimate the amount of change required. 'Retrofit' means to revise the design diagrams to incorporate the revised code after the code has been changed – normally, code would be written to conform to an already designed model; here we are changing the code first and then amending the model to suit.

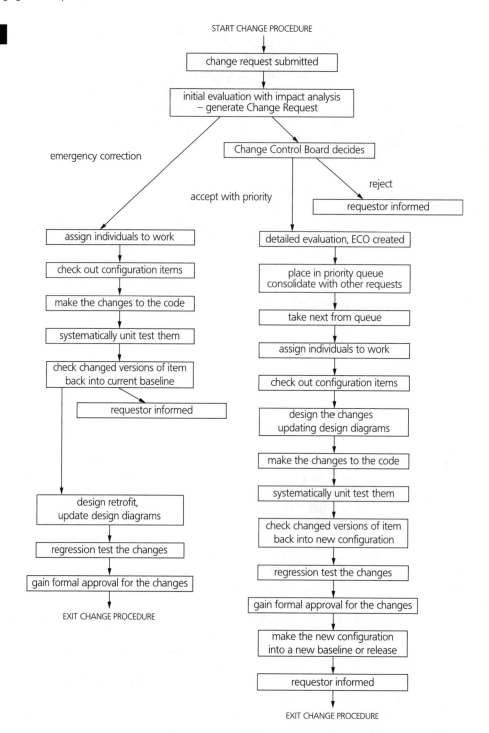

Figure 11.5

Change control
process

Let us work through one particular application of the procedure in Figure 11.5
in Table 11.1:

No.	Description
1.	Problem discovered and the user triggers a modification request.
2.	Suggested change is evaluated by an analyst, who elaborates a report, and sends a change request to the CCB.
3.	CCB meets to evaluate the change request and consider the technical details, quality, cost, and schedule aspects of its solution. A decision is made as to whether the change request will be addressed immediately as an emergency, be scheduled for later, or rejected. If the change request is to be rejected, the user needs to be informed and the process ends. Otherwise, the process follows as indicated below.
4.	Make a detailed evaluation of the actions to take, which will vary if the change request addresses a defect, if it is a new requirement, or if it is something else. The change request will be assigned a priority level, and then it waits until the resource needed is available, and then is assigned to a person or to a team for its implementation.
5.	The individuals responsible for the implementation check out the configuration items involved in the change.
6.	The responsible persons work on the implementation of the change request.
7.	The change is subject to a review or audit.
8.	The changed configuration items are checked in.
9.	In order to perform testing, a complete configuration is built.
10.	The necessary verification and validation takes place. This involves regression testing and other activities.
11.	The developer and the program librarian incorporate the changes into the next release.
12.	Formally accept the changes as part of the new release.
13.	Release new version to the users.

Table 11.1

List of steps for handing a modification request through a Change Control Board (CCB) or similar group

This change control procedure, and the underlying configuration management system described earlier, form an important part of the organisation's quality management system, and should be described in the quality manual. An individual project should declare in its quality plan when the baselines are produced, and who serves on the Change Control Board. Special circumstances in the project may simplify the general system described here — for example, variants may not be important, and all changes may be given the same priority.

Follow a standard process for agreeing and implementing changes.

11.3.2 Management processes

Successful configuration management also involves organisational issues, such as the definition of how the various tools will be used and the formal setting up of the Configuration/Change Control Board (CCB) or similar. The CCB considers each modification request and makes a decision as to whether it will be implemented or not. According to specific circumstances, the CCB may also alter the priority, the scope, and the actual process of implementing a change. The CCB should normally involve a number of different stakeholders, including developers, managers, sales personnel, and maybe even representatives of user groups. Users may or may not have a role to play at the CCB; for bespoke software where the user is paying directly for the system, the user clearly must have some involvement; under Agile methods and other rapid development paradigms, users are involved in the discussion and in the prioritisation of change requests that impact on the user-perceived functionality. For commodity software, users may not be present in the CCB, but sales department representatives at the CCB may represent users' points of view and needs.

Requests for modifications should be formalised through the use of a suitable form, such as that shown in Figure 11.6. The sources of modification requests are varied. They may emerge directly from users, from developers, or from sales and support personnel. In commodity software, developed for a large range of customers, users can send reports to the customer support team but users are not directly involved in the generation of modification requests. Incoming customer reports are analysed by a member of the customer support team, who will check whether the customer problem is likely to be due to a defect or could be due to a misunderstanding of the documentation, for example. If appropriate, the customer support team generates a modification request for the defect to be fixed, which will then be assessed by the CCB taking into account its severity and cost. Defects with low severity and low impact that require substantial effort to be fixed are likely to be given a low priority. On occasion it might be decided that the problem lies not in the software but with the use of the system, requiring user feedback and maybe user training.

Figure 11.6

Software problem report. *A change request form where the title does not presuppose that the problem encountered really requires a change to the software*

Software problem report	
SPR number:	Date raised:
Raised by (your name):	
Job title and location:	
Software system or subsystem where problem encountered:	
Description of problem:	
Severity of problem (Please indicate cost if this is possible.):	
Attachments supporting problem:	
Suggested possible solution:	

Some organisations may demand a business case for approval of larger changes, with analyses of costs and benefits to be estimated for the particular modification request to be approved.

Change control can be informal or formal. Informal change control is likely to take place at the beginning of a project when no items have been delivered outside of the team and no baselines have been accepted. At the beginning of development simple procedures may be put in place and developers are usually authorised to implement localised changes and fix local defects without need for involvement of the CCB. The developer can make his or her own judgement based on the specification of component, for example. However, for changes that impact on components developed by other teams, the CCB will need to be involved.

Software configuration audits examine properties of a configuration item and of the change request implementation. They check not only that a formal technical review has been conducted on that item, but also whether the established process for dealing with change has been followed and whether the change implementation has been verified and validated against the modification request. Audits need also to ensure that the change has been adequately propagated to other parts of the system and the enterprise dealing with the system, including notifying relevant stakeholders.

Audits or reviews are also undertaken in order to ensure that a baseline has the required functional and non-functional characteristics and is of sufficient quality to be released. The configuration management process itself can also be subject to an audit that will check the integrity of the change management process itself. Such audits will check, for example, that the identification and the content of a version or a release match and that there are no mismatches.

Excessive change control will affect the productivity of the developers. Three different levels of change control are commonly practised. Informal change control happens before an item becomes part of a baseline; a change may be authorised by a team leader, provided that the change does not impact on more than one configuration item or on the work of other teams. Project change control takes place after an item has become part of a baseline but before its release to users: the item is still in development. At this level, the CCB may become involved but changes are subject to a lesser degree of scrutiny than for items which have been released to users. Finally, formal change control applies to items which have been released to users; in this case the CCB is fully involved and the change is closely scrutinised. Configuration managers must decide the time and amount of resources applied to each level of change control. For each application and domain there is likely to be an optimum beyond which productivity can be seriously affected.

In general, there is a trade-off between speed of change and disciplined change control. Each software enterprise must achieve an appropriate balance. At one end of the spectrum one can find organisations developing safety critical software, for example, for software for aircraft engines, the strictest possible change control must be applied. At the other end one could find domains which may favour speed of response over change discipline and in which lighter change management approaches may be applied such as, for example, the rapid and continual updates that might be required by some e-commerce applications.

A process that uses daily builds generally involves a larger number of versions that need to be individually identified than when a traditional process is followed.

Formalise agreement about change using a request proforma and Change Control Boards.

Speed should not be confused with lack of discipline: rapid change needs disciplined control, otherwise developers may start losing track of the configuration items, the situation can easily get out of hand, and confusion could dominate the project.

11.3.3 Configuration management and quality certification

In order to achieve certification under ISO 9000 and also within CMMi (see Chapter 12), the software enterprise must define or select and then use standards which cover configuration management. The IEEE Standard 828 – 1998 is one of these. The software enterprise will need to tailor a generic standard like this to its specific needs and constraints. The quality management system should incorporate the configuration management standard being used.

One limitation of most configuration management standards is their assumption that the software enterprise follows a sequential, linear process, such as the **waterfall** model. Under this model, once the system has been implemented and the units or components tested, the responsibility for integration and system testing is passed to the system integration team, which may also be the configuration management team. If faults are discovered in a component, the development team fixes them and delivers a new version of the component to the system integration team. If the new version is of sufficient quality it is then incorporated into the new baseline for further development.

With daily builds, the latest version of each of the components of the software system are daily compiled and linked into the full system, with tests being run every day. Quality issues can be addressed more quickly than when the interval between builds is several days or weeks. However, the configuration management system needs to keep track of each daily build, leading to many more configuration versions that may need to be stored.

Activity 11.4   *CM for particular methods*

Based on what you have learned about Agile methods in Chapter 8, consider whether or not the change control process described above will be suitable for Agile methods. Justify your opinion.

Discussion

Agile methods do not include a formal process of change control such as the one described above based on CCBs. Small teams of developers working closely together, sometimes located in the same room and even sharing the same workstation as in pair programming, and relying mainly on informal communication, use simple system build and configuration management tools. In order to achieve rapid development and evolution of their software, they tend to avoid the formal documentation of changes, which is common in large software projects involving multiple development sites.

Individual projects need to have specifications regarding how they will manage their versions and configurations and changes to them. The Configuration Management Plan describes how configuration management is to be applied in a particular software organisation or project. It includes standards, definitions, and procedures, suitably adapted to fit the constraints of the particular organisation or project.

The plan should include at least the following information:

1. Indicate what items need to be under configuration management, how they will be identified, and what the relationships are between them.
2. Define the roles and responsibilities of all those involved.
3. Define the configuration management process.
4. Indicate the policies and rules to be followed for configuration management and, in particular, for change control.
5. Indicate what tools will be used for configuration management.

> Configuration management is an essential component of quality management.

11.3.4 Other digital materials

Clearly change within all digital materials other than ephemera needs to be controlled. Just as with software, you cannot allow just anybody to update organisational policy documents or web pages.

Using forms to document a request for change will be appropriate for software asset libraries, and maybe for web pages, but not for internal policy documents, since the number of people who could legitimately make a request for change would be relatively small and memoranda and meeting minutes would suffice.

Authorising the change should be formalised, though a single CCB would almost certainly be inappropriate. Some person or committee should be charged with authorising changes and updates to all critical digital resources.

> Control changes to all digital assets.

11.4 Configuration management tools

In addition to organisational processes, effective change and configuration management requires adequate tools. These tools enable:

- the storage of the configuration items, whether software development work products or other digital assets;
- control of access to and update of these resources;
- the building of systems or products from these items;
- the control of which versions of the code are released to users.

While we have seen that all digital assets are essentially the same in their requirements, different tools and toolsets are normally proposed for the different kinds of data:

- version and configuration control systems for software;
- document management and content management systems for other data, documents and web pages.

We will look at the systems for software control, and then look at systems for the control of other digital material.

11.4.1 Version and configuration management systems

Configuration repositories

All work products created during the development and evolution of a software system are stored as digital files, and together form a database or repository.[4] This database needs to be managed from the point of view of change and configuration control – this requires extra control information about the items and the configurations, the users of particular configurations, change requests, hardware and software execution environments, and so on. This extra control information could be integrated with the storage of the work products, or could be stored separately in a configuration management database. The way the control information is stored in relationship to the software gives us a first dimension of potential choice between tools.

This control information could follow the data structure diagrams earlier in this chapter; alternately, a specialised schema could be developed to document the requirements for this control information. For example not everybody might want to distinguish variants, or differentiate between baselines and releases. The details of how change requests relate to changes needs to be detailed, and other specific details of software development like the passing of tests, may need to be added.

As well as the data we would need to elaborate the functions that will be undertaken on this data. The context diagram (Figure 11.2) and flow diagram (Figure 11.5) would be a start, though clearly something much more detailed would be necessary to specify our configuration database system.

A second potential technical choice arises from how related files, particularly successive versions of files, are stored. When a file is updated, very little may be changed, and it can be much more efficient to store the differences between files rather than to store each successive file in its entirety. In fact, this is one of the ways Microsoft's Word system stores its files, but not now in order to save storage space (since only the latest version is offered), but for other technical reasons believed to be related to undo and recovery actions.

It is common that after the implementation of a change, a record is kept inside the component indicating the date of the change, the person responsible, and a description of the scope of the change. These are called change log records and contain the derivation history. Such records are normally stored as part of program headers or on the front page of documents. Figure 11.7 illustrates one such program header. If the format is sufficiently consistent one can then retrieve information about the change history by using scripts written in a language with regular expression capabilities such as Perl.

Software artefacts are created from scratch or by using previous versions as a template and subsequently changed. Software artefacts can also be renamed – then the question arises of whether they are still the same artefact or whether they have become a new one. Normally it will be assumed that changing the name or identifier of an artefact is equivalent to removing the old and generating a new artefact, even if the content remains the same. However, this is a matter of convention and different tools may follow different rules for defining and naming configuration items. For traceability reasons, some organisations may enforce a policy of not physically deleting any component. A component which is not used anymore in any configuration still remains in the repository for audit trail purposes.

```
#AUTHBUILD.c
#AUTHBUILD conversion program
#Author: Caroline Todd
#Purpose: to take release 7.0 file structure and make it
 into release 8.0 file structure.
#Date created: 01-Oct-1993
#Assumes that database integrity has already been checked
 by the USE REPORTs A
#and B. Reference USE conversion Technical Specification
#Change history
#11-Oct-1993 Guy Secretan
#Amended to include save stk and tk_kcv
#27th October 1993 Joanna Clore
#Automatically convert 16 char auth keys to 32 chars
#12th May 1994 Alan Statham
#A tidy exit if we try to read a parent route code that is no
 longer in the database
*Names have been changed to protect confidentiality.
```

Figure 11.7

An example of a
change log record*

It is possible to get much of the functionality required by simply using the file management system of the computer – grouping configurations in top-level folders that contain subfolders with the various components, and so on. This works very well for a gold copy system.

Whatever the system deployed, it must include sound systems to secure the data against unwanted access, and it must include a comprehensive back-up system to ensure that valuable data assets are not lost.

> For simple change control the disciplined use of a computer file system may suffice.

Configuration management functions

Implicit in data analysis is consideration of the functions that you want to undertake on the data, and we saw this in our analysis above. Basic functions of access and control of access would be supported by the storage technology. If you want more sophisticated controls, you need a more sophisticated system, a full version or configuration management system. This may be developed bespoke, but will more likely be purchased as a commercial configuration management system that more or less does what is required.

Despite considerable differences in the details of the different tools, the vast majority of them conform to the concepts and principles indicated in the preceding sections of this chapter – the only facility that we have not found in commercial systems is the handling of configurations: items and versions can be labelled as members of a configuration but that is not quite the same thing. It would require our making a significant compromise.

There are two types of version management tools: stand-alone and integrated tools. There are stand-alone tools for version management, such as CVS, RCS, and Subversion (see Case Study 11.7). Integrated tools are usually proprietary and expensive, such as ClearCase, which includes configuration management and system building, and ClearQuest for the configuration database. Both ClearCase and ClearQuest implement Rational's Unified Change Management process.

Case Study 11.7 *Subversion*

As an example, we give some details here of Subversion, which is a more recent tool than the popular CVS incorporating a number of enhancements with respect to CVS. Subversion is implemented using a client-server architecture as depicted in Figure 11.8.

The client-server architecture is based on two types of processes: servers, which provide access to functions or services, and clients, which make use of the latter. In general, many clients can be simultaneously supported, and a client does not have to be aware of the presence of others. This architecture is convenient for configuration management tools, since developers and other team members can run client processes on their computers that access the common repository, enabling parallel work. This, however, does not solve the problem of possible conflicts when the same configuration item is being modified by more than one person.

The figure shows some of the main elements of a configuration management tool: at the bottom of the figure you can see the software repository, which stores the configuration items

---

Figure 11.8

An architectural view of the Subversion CM tool[5]

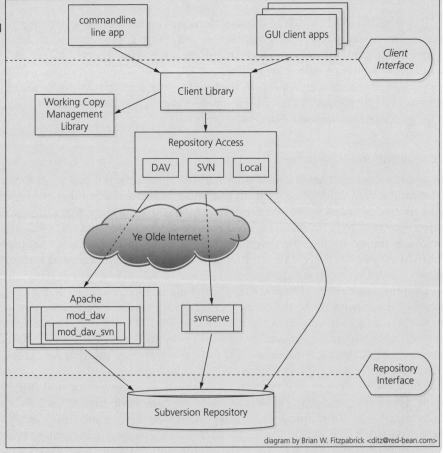

diagram by Brian W. Fitzpabrick <ditz@red-bean.com>

and which can be accessed through a repository interface. Several different models of access to the repository are possible through the Internet via the popular web server Apache, via a stand-alone server or directly via a local access. Both Apache and the stand-alone server provide mechanisms for authorisation and authentication. On the upper part of the diagram one can observe the client part of the system, which supports two modes of access: access through command line commands and via graphical user interface (GUI) applications.

After its creation and normally after validation and verification, an item is formally stored in the main software repository of the organisation or the project. This process is commonly referred to as checking in. If an item needs revision or modification it needs first to be checked out by an authorised person. Generally the members of the development team have read access to the repository. Writing access or check-in rights may be limited to those who can approve a change. Once an item has been modified and validated, it can be checked in again. In large teams, several team members may have checked out the same item. If this is so one needs mechanisms to deal with possible parallel modifications being done on the same item. This is called *synchronisation control*.

If each configuration item (or file) is stored in full at the moment of defining a new version, the size of the repository could grow very quickly. For reasons of efficiency, configuration management tools avoid storing the full changed item again. Instead, versions are described based on their differences with respect to some master version of the item. This is enough to be able to retrieve any version of the file from the master version. The name given to the differences is *delta*. Backward deltas can be useful in generating a previous version of a configuration item from the latest one available.

Change log records as seen in Figure 11.7 can also be a source of metric data which can be of use in effort estimation of long-lived software and in managing software evolution. For example, one of the measures that can be derived is the size of the system in components over calendar time. This can be done by extracting the names of the components together with their creation date. The number of changes can also be calculated in different ways in order to provide an indication of the level of changes being applied to the system. This information can be useful for managers in release planning, for example, as the past history of the system is likely to reflect the safe or stable level of work, beyond which the evolution process may become unstable (see Chapter 9 on software evolution for Lehman's laws and Case Study 9.2, related to the IBM OS 360 operating system, which exemplifies this phenomenon).

Some configuration management tools enable the storage of metadata associated with a configuration item, such as the names of the persons who have contributed to the item, the number and description of defects fixed, traceability, or derivation information so that the item can be related to a particular requirement in the requirements specification and so on. Metadata represents information which is not part of the configuration item itself but can be of help to managers and developers for purposes of queries, defect location, traceability among items, and process improvement.

> Version management and configuration management systems are essential for all but the most simple software development.

11.4.2 System building

System building involves the compilation and linking of all required components so that an executable version of the software is generated. For large and complex software systems, system building can be a complex task. You need to ensure that the appropriate version of the source code, data, and other necessary files are used, and that the appropriate compilers and linkers are executed with the required parameters. The wrong version of a single component can damage the whole system build. The activity of system building usually requires large computational resources and may take hours, even days, for large systems. Appropriate planning is then required. Configuration management tools provide support for system building. Usually a system-building script is written by the team in charge of this part of the process. The script specifies which versions of which components and which tools need to be involved. Then the system-building tool generates the executable of the system based on this script. In order to do so, it checks which source code files have been changed from the previous compilation, so that the new object (that is, machine executable) code is generated via compilation. When possible, it is recommended to have integrated tools for configuration management and system building in order to avoid possible mismatches between source and object files.

11.4.3 Management of other digital assets

Configuration management is also of interest in the engineering of complex systems involving hardware, software, and processes. In fact, configuration management was initially applied (and still is applied) in manufacturing and complex projects of all kinds, not just software. Manufacturers, for example, need systems that keep track of the set of parts that are needed to build a product. Increasingly software is being embedded in other artefacts (e.g., automobiles, buses, airplanes, trains, industrial machinery). Some configuration management systems need to deal with both hardware and software artefacts. The requirements are very similar to those of software development, excepting of course the actual artefact being controlled must exist outside the computer, and only a reference to it placed in the computer.

Version management and configuration management systems would also be typically used for software component libraries, though the component look-up needs would have to be added, perhaps as a separate indexing system on the side.

When you move away from software you find a completely different set of tools. These tools arose out of concerns for knowledge management and the realisation that a lot of an enterprise's competitive advantage lies in the knowledge it possesses, much of which is stored in documents that had traditionally been paper records looked after by librarians and archivists. With the rise of software systems and networks, new opportunities arose to store, correlate, and make available this storehouse of knowledge. Document management systems arose which focused on scanned images of old documents, content management systems for web materials, and integrated versions of these when specific content creation tools were involved. In all of these the core of the system was a repository that could be searched on a range of criteria, with a large range of fringe facilities like workflow to add value to the core and differentiate it in the market place. Look at Case Study 11.8 about a learning content management system to see how this differentiation happens; behind this educational expression of the system lies a standard content management system plus workflow system.

Case Study 11.8 *Moodle,[6] an open source content management system for education providers*

Moodle describes itself as 'a course management system (CMS) – a free, Open Source software package designed using sound pedagogical principles, to help educators create effective online learning communities. You can download and use it on any computer you have handy (including webhosts), yet it can scale from a single-teacher site to a 40,000-student University.' The development of this system began in Australia in the 1990s, and its first release was in August 2002, with university-level teaching in mind. Since then the development has spread worldwide, with versions of the system available in a wide range of natural languages and usage across the educational spectrum.

Descriptions of educational courses and their associated materials are stored in a database and made accessible via the Internet. These courses can be categorised and searched. The courses (or parts of them) can be presented to students in prescribed sequences. Tests can be administered at selected points in the sequence. There are extra facilities called 'forums' for the learning support of students, discussions of particular issues, and for student-to-student chatting.

A teacher is able to lay down a learning timetable, upload learning resources to the right position in the timetable, and set out a number of activities for the students:

- Assignments: a task for the student with a due date and a maximum grade, later enabling the student to upload answers and the teacher to assign grades and comments.
- Multiple-choice activities.
- Forums for single-topic discussion, a free-for-all general forum, or one discussion thread per user.
- Personal journals for students to reflect on the material they are studying, perhaps triggered by an open-ended question.
- Quizzes consisting of multiple choice, true–false, and short-answer questions.
- Predefined survey instruments for evaluating and understanding the class.

What stands out in these content management systems is the limited treatment that content origination (authoring) and evolution gets. Some systems talk of versions, but not in the full sense we encountered in software development. More limited is the support for configurations, even though in simple word-processed documents containing figures and special fonts, it becomes critical.

> Management of digital resources in general could use common software, though application-specific facilities lead to differentiation in the market.

Summing up

This chapter has provided a general overview of configuration management and change control, looking not just at software and its development, but at digital assets more generally. We have seen that:

- change needs to be carefully managed to ensure that after the change everything continues to work as intended;
- a simple system for controlling change is the 'gold copy' system, which tracks a single version of an evolving system, controls changes to the gold copy and then releases the gold copy to users;

- full configuration management systems enable multiple versions to exist simultaneously without losing control;
- the atomic elements whose versions are being controlled are known as configuration items;
- configuration item versions are stored in a repository, checked out when needed, and checked in after change;
- configurations are coherent collections of configuration item versions; baseline configurations serve as a foundation for further work;
- releases are baselines delivered to the users and should be carefully planned, with intermediate minor releases and patches as needed;
- daily builds help coordinate a team and mark its progress;
- all digital assets across your enterprise could be viewed uniformly;
- a standard process for agreeing and implementing changes should be followed;
- agreement about changes should be formalised using a request form and change control board;
- configuration management is an essential component of quality management;
- for simple change control the disciplined use of a computer file system may suffice;
- version management and configuration management systems are essential for all but the most simple software development;
- management of digital resources in general could use common software, though application-specific facilities lead to differentiation in the market.

Exercises

1. You and three friends have successfully built a first working version of a new system for playing music with pictures in a novel way. A demo at a local exhibition attracted a lot of interest with a very positive write-up in a PC magazine. However you need some financial backing if you are going to take this further, re-engineer it to make it robust, and package and market it to ensure large sales. You find a venture capitalist prepared to back you – providing that you implement a rigid change control system. The venture capitalist continues to insist this even though you protest that you follow an Agile methodology, and he proposes that you become responsible for system integration and change control, maintaining a daily build using the latest versions of the software. You must assign each part of the system to a single person who updates and enhances that part of the system, giving you the latest copies of all their software every day by mid-afternoon, ready for you to start your complete system build. Analyse this proposed system and write a short report on how it might be improved.

2. A university has developed an educational management system for its own internal use, and realises that it could sell this system to other universities. Should they do this as a low-volume, high-price, high-margin system, or should they commoditise it and look for large volumes with lower prices and

profit margins? Examine these options from a change control and configuration management perspective.

3. Expand the context diagram of Figure 11.2 to produce the first level data flow diagram for the system, showing the storage of the configuration items, versions, and other data, and the processes operating on these. Do not include the personal workspaces of the software engineers, but write a paragraph explaining how these would be managed.

4. Case Study 11.1 showed that recording the software used to automatically derive some items from other items, such as compilers, is important. Extend Figure 11.3 to include this information. You may need to distinguish between types of configuration items and make build states explicit.

5. What are the relative advantages of coarse grain as opposed to fine grain configuration management systems?

6. In writing this book we have had to control change as we commented on and updated our chapters, and have had to be concerned about keeping together both text and diagrams and other files that belonged together within a particular version of a chapter. We evaluated the use of a software version management system, but in the end simply used the MS Windows filing system to control our versions through naming conventions and configurations using folders. From your own experience of writing and updating documents, how significant a problem is the version control of documents from the authoring point of view?

7. A very large multi-organisation project is producing a complex system for a government agency. In order to control changes to the system they establish a hierarchy of Change Control Boards, one in each organisation contributing to the project, one at the overall project management level in the lead organisation (so that organisation has two CCBs), and one in the customer government agency who is funding the software development. Suggest what the hierarchical relationships between the various CCBs should be, what the scope of each CCB should be, what the criteria should be for passing on a change request for somebody else to decide on, what the meeting frequency should be, and when during the project life cycle they should first meet. Assume an evolutionary life cycle similar to those seen in Chapter 8.

8. Find detailed descriptions of one commercial or one Open Source configuration management system for software, and examine to what extent it does actually meet the complete requirements of such a system as explored in this chapter. Write a detailed evaluation of the chosen system. If you can find detailed descriptions of several systems, do a weighted scorecard for these and recommend a best buy.

9. Find an online encyclopaedia like Wikipedia, and look up 'content management', 'records management', 'digital asset management', 'integrated content management', and other 'integrated' forms; 'enterprise' forms of all of these, and so on, to gain an impression of the overlap between them. Write a short critique of these different management systems from the point of view of their use for managing the components produced during software development and evolution.

Endnotes

1. While some aspects of this case study are fictionalised to bring out the issues, the case study is based on a real project being led by Pat Hall and being undertaken in Nepal.
2. Source: A. Capiluppi, M. Morisio and J.F. Ramil, Folder Structure Evolution in Open Source Software. Metrics 2004 Symposium, 14–16 Sept 2004, Chicago, Illinois, USA, IEEE Press, Los Alamitos, California. © 2004 IEEE.
3. Michael A. Cusumano and Richard W. Selby (1995) *Microsoft Secrets*. Harper Collins.
4. These are equivalent terms, 'database' remaining in favour in Europe while 'repository' has gained favour in the US. We will use them interchangeably.
5. Source: http://subversion.tigris.org/project_status.html.
6. See http://www.moodle.org.

12 Managing quality

What we will study in this chapter

In acquiring and then evolving software it is easy for the quality of the software to degrade. As well as managing costs and timescales, it is also important to manage the quality of software. Quality is an elusive concept, difficult to define, and yet we know a lot about how to manage it.

In this chapter we will look at:

- a number of competing views of quality;

- how process quality relates to product quality;

- the use of metrics to guide software acquisition and evolution, covering both process and product metrics;

- quality economics;

- quality culture;

- ways the quality of software might be assured;

- quality frameworks and standards: ISO 9001:2000, CMMi, SPICE.

12.1 Introduction

This chapter presents quality management within the wider theme of managing a software enterprise. Look at Case Study 12.1, which shows the failure of a system. This example is used widely in education, mostly to illustrate management failure. This was clearly a poor-quality system, but why did the system fail, and what could have been done to avoid it? What do we mean by the phrase 'poor quality'?

Case Study 12.1 *London Ambulance Service computer-aided despatch system*

In 1992 the London Ambulance Service commissioned a computer-aided despatch (CAD) system. The system was intended to support the despatch of ambulances, optimising resources and monitoring call response progress. The system's requirements included the automatic location of the position of an ambulance, together with mobile terminals located in the vehicles for automatic communication with the crews. Soon after it was made operational, the system experienced serious problems: it could not cope with the demand. The automatic location feature did not work, leading to incorrect assignment of ambulances, with long arrival delays and multiple ambulances assigned to the same call. An increasing queue of exception messages made the system slow down even further. The ambulance crews were put under stress and delayed the notification of their position. Some of the crews did not use the mobile terminals and others made errors when entering information. The entire ambulance system was close to collapse. It is said that one ambulance arrived eleven hours after a 'stroke' call and five hours after the patient arrived at the hospital using independent means. Another ambulance arrived as undertakers were taking away the dead patient. The CAD system reverted to partial manual operation, and eight days later the system was discarded and the London Ambulance Service returned to manual operation. The head of the service resigned immediately.

There were many deficiencies in the management of the CAD project that led to its failure to provide a vital service.

The key issue is that the software failed to satisfy its stakeholders: the patients waiting to be brought to the hospital, the ambulance crews, the operators at the London Ambulance control centre, and the public at large. This is what we will mean by quality: high-quality software fulfils the purposes, in all its aspects, for which it has been acquired.

Producing high-quality, defect-free software is really very difficult, so much so that producers of software usually claim that they cannot be held responsible for any defects in their software or for any losses that arise in consequence. Look back at Chapter 5, Case Study 5.8, which shows an example. Liability for product defects and consequential loss is a matter for the law, as discussed in Chapter 5. In Chapter 9, we saw how software inevitably evolves; this evolution can also introduce defects.

Activity 12.1   *Customer perceptions of quality and liability*

Why do customers, and why does the law of a country, expect that food manufacturers, car manufacturers, and similar, achieve and maintain high standards of quality in their products, but tolerate software failures and non-liability agreements such as that in Case Study 5.8?

Discussion
The disclaimer statement in Case Study 5.8 suggests that the software industry, in general, has come to the same conclusions as Lehman in his uncertainty principle.

It is likely that as the computing discipline matures, society will progressively make higher demands of software systems. But this is a slow process driven by consensus within the professional community, by technological progress, and also by economic forces. As knowledge and understanding of software, computing, and software management advance, the minimum expectations of society, users, and stakeholders will in general increase. It is possible that one day non-liability statements such as that in Case Study 5.8 will be completely unacceptable. However, software is still a relatively young discipline compared with more mature disciplines such as mechanical or electrical engineering. In fact, some of the quality frameworks currently proposed for software have their origin in other disciplines, as in the case of the ISO series of quality standards examined later in this chapter.

In this chapter we start by looking at the general principles of quality, including quality cultures and the ideas behind **Total Quality Management (TQM)**. We will then look at specific quality frameworks and standards including **CMMi**, ISO 9001, and SPICE, which claim to ensure high quality. These frameworks claim to achieve a high-quality product through a high-quality process – this is a view which we will contest and discuss as we proceed.

High quality means fitness for purpose.

12.2 Quality and what it means

12.2.1 Defining quality

Quality is a difficult concept to define, yet we all know what it means. We all possess some intuitive understanding of what quality means in a particular context and for a particular service or product of interest. This is influenced by our individual backgrounds, our taste, needs, and surrounding circumstances. This is tacit knowledge, we cannot describe or define quality it, and yet 'we know it when we see it'.

This view of quality is sometimes called the 'transcendental view' of quality. However, this subjective approach is not adequate. We must be able to share our understanding of quality so that we can all agree that a piece of software does or does not have quality.

Let us start with something quite different, cars. We all have some experience of cars, and would agree that a Rolls Royce is a high-quality vehicle. What about a smaller car, like a Volkswagen? Is it of lesser quality than a Rolls? Many would agree that it is, but can you really compare them since the Volkswagen costs a lot less? Is a Volkswagen value for money? Would you also describe it as a quality car of its kind? How does this year's model compare with the equivalent model ten years ago? Would you accept today the kind of cheap car that you would have accepted as value for money ten years ago? How could you compare the quality of a heavy-duty lorry and a Rolls Royce? You wouldn't drive to a fashionable social function in a heavy-duty lorry, but then you could not carry a load of bricks in a Rolls-Royce.

From this simple example, we see that quality has various associations, about luxuriousness, about value for money, about appropriateness for the job at hand, about meeting standards, and about meeting standards that change over time.

Let us look at how the experts define quality.

The International Standards Organisation, in ISO 8402, *Glossary of Terms Used in Quality Assurance*, provides this definition:

Quality: the totality of features and characteristics of a product or service that bear on its ability to satisfy a given need.

The definitive guide to quality is Juran's *Quality Control Handbook*,[1] which provides a similar definition:

Quality consists of those product features which meet the needs of the customer and thereby provide product satisfaction

but also allows a much narrower view:

Quality consists of freedom from deficiencies

though what exactly is meant be 'deficiency' is not clear. A commonly used definition of quality that is concise and memorable was seen earlier. It is

fitness for purpose.

When we discussed the motor example, quality seemed to have a rather more complex and subtle meaning, for it means different things to different people, and we must understand this when we aim to provide quality software. This has been analysed by Garvin[2] to give five possible points of view:

1. transcendental view – felt rather than measured;
2. product view – number of features;
3. user view – fitness for purpose;
4. manufacturing view – conformance to requirements;
5. value view – quality at acceptable cost.

The user view is the one defined by ISO 8402 and by Juran's first definition, while Juran's second definition is closer to the manufacturing view, and is very technological. These different perspectives on quality will be picked up again later, and are crucially important. From the manufacturing viewpoint, it is quite acceptable to produce the software that was specified, even if this does not satisfy the customer's needs. Of course from the user's viewpoint this is totally unacceptable.

We will use the simple user view, 'fitness for purpose'.

It is important to maintain the quality of software while it evolves. Of crucial importance to quality are the stakeholders, those who benefit directly from the software or who are affected by its use. This includes the software users and their management, but also developers, testers, sales personnel, and so on. As when performing requirements analysis, quality management of a software product involves identifying who the major stakeholders are, understanding what their current and future needs are, and what they can expect from a particular software product.

> Quality software satisfies the needs and expectations of its stakeholders and does not frustrate or cause damage to them.

For us the quality of a software product is the presence of positive characteristics that will satisfy stakeholders' needs and expectations. Quality is also the absence of characteristics which could affect software use in a negative way, such as frequent crashing, which leads to work being disrupted while the system is rebooted. Poor quality software may lead to in serious consequences as in Case Study 12.1.

Activity 12.2   *Terminology for defects*

One view of quality is that the product should be free from defects. In general, a defect is anything that prevents a product from fulfilling its intended purpose or that makes it exhibit undesired behaviour or properties. Here we have used the word 'defect' but similar terms are, 'bug', 'error', 'fault', and 'failure'. There are no generally accepted definitions for these terms. Try to provide some definitions of your own.

Discussion
Here is a possible set of definitions:

- 'Errors' refer to any mistakes made by the analyst, designers, programmers, testers, or integrators.
- 'Bug' is the informal way of referring to an error in code. The term 'bug' to mean software error is believed by computing specialist to have been coined by Grace Hopper in the early days of modern computing, when she discovered that a machine-trapped insect or bug was the cause of program malfunctioning. This led to the term 'debugging' to refer to the search for software errors. However the use of the word 'bug' in this meaning can be traced back to long before computers to the laboratory of inventor Thomas Edison[3] who in 1878 explained bugs as 'little faults and difficulties' that require 'months of anxious watching, study and labor' to overcome in developing a successful product.
- The term 'defect' usually refers to errors identified before the artefact is delivered to the end-users or to the next activity. Humphrey advocates the use of the term 'defect' instead of the term 'bug', since it promotes a positive mindset: defects should be avoided or minimised and are not inevitable. A defect may be related, for example, to an implementation error in the source code itself, a coding defect, to errors in other documents and artefacts, such as ambiguities in the original requirement, or to errors in the user documentation.
- 'Faults' are errors identified after the artefact has been released or passed to a subsequent activity.
- 'Failures' are errors which actually prevent the artefact from accomplishing its intended mission or bring about any undesirable effects in the operational domain.

In some software organisations the term used to refer to any of the above is 'issues', 'problem reports', or simply 'reports'. One of the reasons for the existence of different ways for referring to defects is the difficulty in distinguishing between a genuine defect on the one hand, and a change request or a new requirement on the other. Sometimes what is reported as a defect in the software is in fact a misuse of the system, because the system is not being operated properly by a user who lacks appropriate training.

'Correctness' is also a term used frequently by software professionals. A program can be shown to be 'correct' with respect to a specification when it has been proven, by means of mathematical arguments, that the software fully satisfies the specification. Note that 'correctness' is relative to the specification, and if the specification is incomplete or wrong or contains incorrect assumptions the software may still be 'correct'.

12.2.2 Measuring quality

If the purposes – the needs – that the software must meet could be completely specified, then quality would be the degree to which the software product meets the specification. It could be measured. For the vast majority of software systems addressing real world applications, however, one cannot completely specify the requirements. The real world problem (for example, an air traffic control system or a word processor) may not be able to be completely specified, at least in advance. Even if it were, it would be subject to change. Moreover, the 'system' also involves the people using the computers, the business process, and other forms of technology such as communication networks.

It is common to quote Sir William Thompson (Lord Kelvin, 1824–1907) concerning the importance of measurement (from his lecture to the Institution of Civil Engineers, 3 May 1883):

> When you can measure what you are speaking about, and express it in numbers, you know something about it; but when you cannot measure it, when you cannot express it in numbers, your knowledge of it is of a meagre and unsatisfactory kind; it may be the beginning of knowledge, but you have scarcely, in your thoughts, advanced it to the stage of science.

From this it is often deduced that in order to be able to control quality, we must be able to measure it. But this is not necessarily true – the transcendental view would claim that in comparing two products you could judge which was better, even if you could not explain why, let alone put numbers on it. We can objectively determine relative quality, without being able to determine absolute (i.e., measurable) quality. For example, given a balance we can say which of two stones is heavier, even though we might not be able to say what the actual weights were. The comparison using the balance is objective.

Nevertheless, being able to measure absolute quality would be very useful. See Appendix B for a discussion of software metrics. It was suggested in the late 1970s, in the work of McCall[4] and Boehm[5] and their collaborators, that while quality could not be directly measured, we might be able to measure it through decomposing quality into a number of more basic **quality factors** which might themselves be able to be measured. The factors that are now generally considered to be appropriate are:

- Correctness/reliability – to what degree does the software meet its requirements and specification?
- Efficiency – how effective is the software's use of memory space and execution speed?
- Integrity – how secure is the software to attempts to breach its access controls?
- Usability – how easy is it for a user to learn to operate the software and interpret its results?
- Maintainability – how easy it is to make changes to the software, to keep it up to date, or to locate and fix an error?
- Testability – how easy it is to test the software?
- Portability – how easy is it to move the software to new hardware and software environment?

● Reusability – how easy is it to use all of the software or parts of it in other applications?

● Interoperability – how easy is it to connect the software to other systems to exchange data with them?

Thus we decompose the concept of quality into a number of *factors*. Each individual factor has a clear definition, which hopefully will make it measurable – if only by human judgement.

However it may turn out that these factors are not themselves directly measurable, and should be decomposed into another layer of factors, or directly into criteria that are directly measurable. It turns out that only one or two layers of factors is necessary. Associated with each criterion is an appropriate measurement or *metric*. This three- or four-layer view of measurement has now become widely accepted, not only for quality, but for any other complex attribute that we might wish to measure – see for example Figure 12.1. Simpler attributes might only use two levels.

Making the actual measurements may itself be very difficult. The precise definition of the metrics needs to be very carefully thought about, and the same definition consistently applied always. To illustrate this, consider the seemingly simple measurement of program size. Is it measured in lines, statements, or bytes? Does it include comments? Does it include non-executable code like declarations?

Having measured these quality factors, how do you combine them? Let us look at Figure 12.1 again. Suppose you have made the measurements on the right, to obtain values for the criteria. You then add them together, suitably weighted, to calculate the factors on the left. Another round of weighting and adding together finally yields the quality measurement on the far left. This is a linear combination in a manner similar the way we saw for cost estimates.

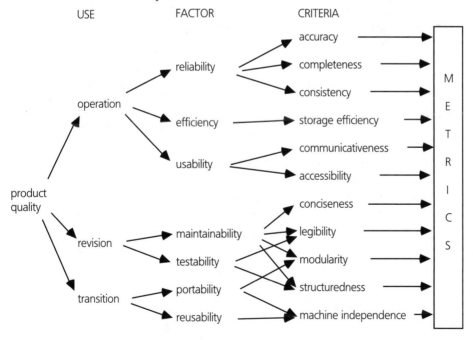

USE   FACTOR   CRITERIA

Figure 12.1

Software quality model[6]

Source: Norman E. Fenton (1991) *Software Metrics: A Rigorous Approach*. Chapman Hall, p. 12. With the kind permission of Springer Science and Business Media.

There are two difficulties with this simple and appealing approach. Finding the weights to use requires that we have lots of examples which we can measure and from which we can estimate the weights. We need some independent measurement of the factors and quality on the left, and from these get a number of equations which can be solved to obtain the weights. If the characteristics are interdependent in some way, we run into difficulties, though these difficulties are surmountable. We will not explore these difficulties further here.

If we proceed as above, we will end up with some measurement of quality. This may not actually quite match our intuitive notion of quality, but nevertheless the measurement is useful. It can help us to control a development process to ensure that a quality product is delivered. A more sophisticated approach would attempt to predict the final quality from intermediate products like design documents, but how to do that is beyond this text.

Decomposition of quality has even found its way into international standards, such as the ISO 9126 standard, briefly described in Case Study 12.2.

Case Study 12.2 *The ISO 9126 standard on software product quality*

Taken from Wikipedia, http://en.wikipedia.org/wiki/ISO_9126, in August 2005.

ISO 9126 is an international standard for the evaluation of software. It classifies the areas in a structured manner as follows:

Functionality – A set of attributes that bear on the existence of a set of functions and their specified properties. The functions are those that satisfy stated or implied needs.

- Suitability
- Accuracy
- Interoperability
- Compliance
- Security

Reliability – A set of attributes that bear on the capability of software to maintain its level of performance under stated conditions for a stated period of time.

- Maturity
- Recoverability
- Fault Tolerance

Usability – A set of attributes that bear on the effort needed for use, and on the individual assessment of such use, by a stated or implied set of users.

- Learnability
- Understandability
- Operability

Efficiency – A set of attributes that bear on the relationship between the level of performance of the software and the amount of resources used, under stated conditions.

- Time Behaviour
- Resource Behaviour

Maintainability – A set of attributes that bear on the effort needed to make specified modifications.

- Stability
- Analysability
- Changeability
- Testability

Portability – A set of attributes that bear on the ability of software to be transferred from one environment to another.

- Installability
- Conformance
- Replaceability
- Adaptability

The standard contains some definitions, such as: the quality requirements definition is based on the union of the implied needs of classes of users, appropriate metrics are selected and measurements carried out, but the individual user is left to construct his/her own rating level definition and assessment criteria definition.

ISO 9126 distinguishes between a defect and a nonconformity, a defect being the nonfulfilment of intended usage requirements, whereas a nonconformity is the nonfulfilment of specified requirements. A similar distinction is made between validation and verification, known as V&V in the testing trade.

Standards such as ISO 9126 can be useful. In practice, each software organisation needs to achieve its own definition and decomposition of quality, using metrics to measure and track the evolution of each of these attributes. For a given application domain some quality attributes can be more important than others. Risk analysis and management, discussed in Chapter 13, can be used to identify which attributes are critical for a given application and moment of time.

Quality can be measured to give more detailed guidance.

Activity 12.3   *Quality measurement of small programs*

Suggest how the quality of small programs could be judged by the number of lines of non-comment code, the number of comments, and a measure of complexity based the number of *if*, *loop*, and *case* statements. How could you calculate a quality index for such programs?

Discussion
We have three factors/criteria here that could be directly measured:

N = the number of lines of non-comment code,

C = the number of comments, and

X = a measure of complexity

which could then be combined in a weighted sum

$$Q = w_n \times N + w_c \times C + w_x \times X$$

We need to determine the values of the weights, which we could do from just three programs to which we assign quality measures that a group of experts agree together do properly represent the respective qualities. Of course we should use many more and arrive at 'averaged' or best-fit weights.

Note this does not include conformance to requirements, so that the very fundamental idea of quality, fitness for purpose, is missing.

12.2.3 Quality-enhancing activities

Quality of software, and any other product, can be enhanced by undertaking extra activities during the production process explicitly aimed at quality improvement and at defect removal. In addition various technical measures in the product itself can be taken to enhance the quality.

All these development activities and technical measures involve, in some sense, adding redundancy to the processes concerned: Figure 12.2 illustrates this. The redundancy can take two forms:

1. The alternative process can fully (or approximately) achieve the same results as the main process, and is switched on when the failure of the first system is detected.
2. All parallel systems are operational all the time and their results compared, with one chosen or the results combined in some way.

First, technical measures. Some safety critical systems are designed with fallback layers to ensure that the system remains safe and that the operators can cope with the situation and bring the failure situation under control. This is typical in plant automation, in which panels of electromechanical relays are installed as a back up in case of computer failure. The CAD process in the London Ambulance Service in Case Study 12.1 should have had a back-up system which would work when the main computer system failed though it was possible to fall back onto the manual system. In other systems the same net effect may be achievable by a number of different means – for example a word processor may offer you the automatic numbering of headings, but also permit you to number them yourself. This functional redundancy is visible to the user, and very useful in enhancing quality and usability. Other redundancy may be 'under the covers' and largely invisible, such as duplicate computer systems so that if one fails the other can take over operations. In all these cases the redundancy is of the first type. The second type also occurs when a disc drive is replicated as a 'hot standby' with data written to both drives and the failure of the main drive triggers the use of the standby, or when hardware circuits are replicated and their outputs sent to a voting circuit which selects the majority answer.

This idea of redundancy can also be applied to the development processes, to build in quality during design. The simple argument here is that process quality leads to product quality, and so it does, providing that you set off to produce the right product in the first place. So what are these redundant processes that we can adopt? Well, they have become so much part of standard processes that you may hardly think of them as redundant!

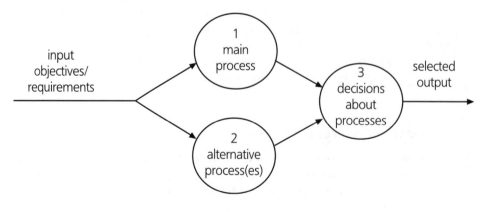

Figure 12.2

Improving quality through redundancy. *The final output depends upon decisions made in process 3, based on the outputs from the main process (1) and the alternative process(es) (2).*

| **Activity 12.4** | *Quality-enhancing activities* |

Based on your own experience as a user or a developer of a software system, what types of activities involved in the software development process help enhance the quality of the released product?

Discussion

One possible view is that achieving software quality and stakeholder satisfaction requires at least five types of activity:

1. Requirements elicitation and analysis: activities by which the problem to be addressed and the needs of the stakeholders are identified, the bounds of an application determined, the requirements specification is generated, including any relevant constraints related to technology, regulations and so on. This ensures that you set out to build the right product.

2. Implementation of the requirements into an operational software system, within budget, time and other constraints. This ensures that you build the product right, and that no defects are added during implementation.

3. Validation that the software continues to meet the requirements; this ensures that any changes in requirements are noted and incorporated into the product as it is developed.

4. Verification activities, those seemingly redundant activities of reviews and inspections and testing, that ensure that the development process remains producing the right product and the product right.

5. Activities which ensure that activities 1, 2, 3, and 4, above, are continually aligned towards ensuring quality: quality management and quality control.

   Requirements analysis and implementation, activities 1 and 2, are really mainstream software development activities, so should be set aside. The other activities are often seen as extra, done to ensure quality. The activities of type 5 ensure that nothing falls between the cracks of activities 1, 2, 3, and 4.

Those 'extra' quality-improving processes during software development and evolution are:

- reviews and inspections;
- testing;
- duplicate design and implementation.

We will work through these in turn, explaining as we go why in some sense these can be viewed as the exploitation of redundancy. The key thing is redundancy in parallel paths, where the work involved, or some aspect of it, is done in parallel in each path and the results are compared and may be combined.

Extra quality-improving processes should be included within the overall process.

Reviews and inspections

In a formal technical **review**, also called an **inspection**, an intermediate or final work-product is examined by a group of experts who look for defects and possibly make product improvement suggestions. Every time some document, program, or other item is produced, it is inspected to see if it is of sufficient quality to be delivered for use by somebody else. It fits in well with project management procedures – if an item 'passes' an inspection, then it provides evidence for the completion of an activity, evidence that the project has made progress.

The early practice in the 1950s and 1960s was simply for the line manager to read and approve an item. Some approaches realised that management reviewing one's work might not lead to an open consideration of quality, and this led to peer reviewing and 'ego-less' programming. Later it was thought useful to involve more people discussing the document in á review meeting. For software this led to the idea of a **walkthrough**, a giant 'dry run' or manual simulation, but this was found to be unsatisfactory.

And then an IBM engineer, Michael Fagin, began to use a form of stylised meeting which he called an 'inspection', which was successful. This was simply a well-run review. These inspections have been adopted by many companies now, with uniform claims of success.

An inspection focusses on a single deliverable, usually a document, with discussions about how it can be kept short. People will have read the document beforehand, taking a particular point of view or role. At the meeting the document is worked through systematically, and issues are raised and discussed just sufficiently to agree that a problem does or does not exist. The objective is to find problems, not solutions, and to find problems in the document or program, not fault with its author. Issues may be raised in other documents as well.

The meeting itself is important, for at the meeting new issues arise in discussion in a way that they do not arise when people comment independently on a document. A review meeting should not last more than a couple of hours, and it needs a firm chair to keep the discussion focussed.

After the inspection, the issue list is distributed, the author responds to these issues, and the moderator checks that actions have been carried out. Sometimes a reinspection may necessary.

Attendance at inspection meetings is limited to between five and seven participants, and excludes all management. Attendance may include:

- moderator (trained chairman);
- author of document under inspection;
- author(s) of source material used;
- engineers who will use the document;
- independent specialists;
- customer representative.

For example, for the inspection of a module design document, the participants could be:

- the moderator, a trained chairperson for inspections;
- the author of the specification to which the design has responded;
- a programmer who will have to code from the design;
- a test engineer who will have to test the code produced from the design;

- an expert in the platform on which the system will run;
- a quality assurance representative;
- a customer representative, only if the module contains algorithms or processes that are important for the customer (e.g., tax calculations).

Activity 12.5   *Inspections and reviews to spread good practice*

Design reviews and inspections offer the opportunity to spread good practice and enforce programming conventions that lead to software that is maintainable at a relatively low cost. Propose and justify ways in which reviews and inspections can be adapted to serve this extra need of a learning organisation.

Discussion
A mix of experienced and inexperienced staff will expose the less experienced staff to a wider body of knowledge. Similarly by involving a range of people, the inexperienced staff will be exposed to a wider set of perspectives about the software than they might otherwise have seen.

The advice for inspections is to only involve five to seven participants, since a discussion with more people can get out of control – the objective is to complete discussions while participants remain fresh and focussed, say within two hours.

However, we could include inexperienced staff as observers, with the explicit instruction to remain quiet during the inspection. For example, if a design document is being inspected, the lead designer for the team who produced the design, and the lead programmer from the team who will use the design to code the software, would be participants. However all other members of the relevant teams could be present as observers.

To fully participate in an inspection or review you must refer back to the documents and other work products used by the developers of the product under review, for they determine what the requirements of the product are. You must work from these and in effect duplicate the developers process, only this time you have their solution to consider and must simply check that it does properly respond to those input documents. This is a form of parallelism, with an alternative duplicate process being undertaken, albeit in rather reduced form. The comparison of results and decisions about what to output is taken at the meeting.

> Reviews and inspections are the single most important quality-enhancing activities.

Testing

We have already come across testing in some detail in earlier chapters of this book. In particular we saw the Vee life cycle model in Chapter 8, which placed more emphasis on testing than is usual. For example, a system specification would lead to a conventional implementation path of design and coding, ending up with a complete system claiming to meet that specification, while parallel to this test planning and then test case design would lead to a comprehensive set of tests which were then run against the system to see if the system produced what the tests expected.

Often instead of explicit test cases, a test case generator is produced so that very long-running tests can be conducted. Sometimes the new system is run in parallel with the old system it is replacing – this is a very well-established method in administrative systems.

In some cases, like aero-engine controller software, to test the software a complete simulation of the aero-engine might be made – building this simulator could be just as complex and as expensive as building the controller, maybe more so. To capture this the W lifecycle (as two Vee lifecycles joined together) has been proposed,[7] building the system software and the environment simulator in parallel but meeting at the system test stage.

Thus in system development the implementation path develops a representation of the system in one form, while test planning and preparation creates another representation in terms of a set a comprehensive test cases or even, sometimes, a complete simulation of the operational environment of the software. Technically we can view this as producing two equivalent representations of the behaviour, one intentional (the implementation) and the other extensional (the tests) or a system dual (the simulation). During the testing process these two representations are compared, and if they are found to be equivalent then all is well, if they mismatch in any way, then either the implementation or the test/simulation is wrong, or both are wrong, and changes must be made in the areas of mismatch.

> Testing creates a second complimentary view of a system which is then compared with that embodied in the implementation.

Design redundancy

A method proposed and tried out for systems which require very high reliability has been for several teams to develop the same system independently, with the resulting systems then being run in parallel with their results being compared and voted on. The trials proved not to be very successful due to common-mode failure – each team failed in its design in the same ways: as a result of a shared faulty specification or due to shared education and experience in this type of system.

But the idea is sound, taking the use of quality-improving redundant processes to the extreme.

12.2.4 Quality culture

Despite the many technological advances, software development is still a complex intellectual activity, with plenty of room for the use of human judgement. Because different people can make different equally valid judgements, there is a fundamental limitation to the repeatability of a software process. Further, because the process is iterative, the experience, knowledge, and understanding gained through the execution of the software process provides input to new iterations. People are of central importance in the process, and the most important resource in a software organisation is people.

Quality efforts must be focussed on sustaining and enhancing the abilities and skills of people, and the way they relate to each other. The successful assimilation of quality improvements requires more than management commitment and the appropriate levels of resources and technological means, it requires a **quality culture**. An organisation has a quality culture when quality is highly valued and when managers support employees who care for the less tangible aspects of quality, such as readability, adequacy of documentation, and so on, which are hard to specify explicitly. Everybody in the organisation feels ownership of the product and responsible for achieving the highest possible quality within the available resources. This has been acknowledged by mainstream software engineering.[8]

One approach to quality that is rooted in the idea of a quality culture is **Total Quality Management (TQM)** – see Case Study 12.3. To understand total quality, let us start with a little story, possibly a myth. A UK computer company decided to order electronic components from Japan. They prepared a conventional UK contract in which they stipulated a low level of defective components. When the order was delivered to them they found their components were just what they wanted, but packed separately from these were the stipulated level of defective components. The whole idea of shipping any defective components to a customer was alien to the supplier, but if that was what the customer wanted, then of course that would also be supplied. We see in this story the two ingredients – they would not accept failure and would never normally deliver defective components. But customer satisfaction was pre-eminently important, and if the customer asked for a certain level of defective components, then those would be supplied as well.

> Quality is everybody's responsibility as part of a quality culture.

Case Study 12.3 *Total Quality Management (TQM)*

TQM as a concept began in the US with Armand Feigenbaum's book *Total Quality Control*, first published in 1951.[9] This then was picked up in Japan in the 1950s, and gained popularity in the West in the 1980s where it subsequently went into decline but is now staging a comeback. In his book *Total Quality Management*,[10] John Oakland identifies two major causes of quality problems:

- acceptance of failure;
- misunderstanding of quality.

The particular view of quality picked up by Oakland is the *user* or *customer* view of quality, a view that has been very strong in Japan, where customer satisfaction has been placed higher than immediate profit. Why should this be? In the TQM movement, a frequent claim is that 'Quality is free', yet adding procedures to assure quality seems to add cost. There are two answers to this apparent paradox:

- In the long term what matters is having customers, and it is no good making a large profit from today's customers if they do not come back. Extra effort in supplying quality to your customers today, with reduced profit margins, is recovered later when the customer returns again and again.

- Making a concern for quality visible also makes the processes and procedures associated with assuring the quality visible, so a new source of expenditure is seen. What is not so visible are the savings that are made in consequence of this.

Thus we see that the critically important view of quality, that is the key to success, is customer satisfaction. This is fitness for purpose where both the fitness and the purpose are determined by the customer.

What about that other issue identified by Oakland, acceptance of failure? Let us motivate our discussion with an example from the software industry. You purchase an item of shrink-wrapped software in a retail shop in your high street. You take it home, and find one of the CDs is damaged and cannot be read. You then realise that the box had been soaked with water at some time and had then dried out. It had been sold to you damaged – the shop assistant that you had bought it from should have noticed it before putting it in a bag for you. You had intended to use the software over the weekend, and now your plans for the weekend have been frustrated, you must wait until Monday to return to the shop. By the time you get to the shop with your complaint, you are very angry, and display your anger to the

▶

shop assistant. But is it his fault? He should have noticed the damage and not supplied you with that box, but he had assumed that the damage was superficial, otherwise it would not have been put on the shelf. Besides, if it did not work and the customer complained, he would always replace it! The store manager who had unpacked the consignment from the supplier had noticed the damage also, but she had been very busy that morning and decided to chance it. The supplier, where the flooding had occurred, had also decided to chance it, even though he was covered by an insurance policy and could have reordered without loss. And so a defective package of software was passed on down the line, with a succession of people prepared to accept and pass on the fault until the customer complained.

We see here not only the acceptance of failure, but also a sequence of such acceptances. We have a **quality chain**, a succession of stages all of which are responsible for the final quality delivered to the customer. Each person in the chain should have felt responsible for the quality of goods passing through his/her hands – and should have taken a 'zero defect' attitude to his/her work, rejecting the damaged package before it ever reached the final customer.

How does TQM suggest that we should proceed? Quality management is seen as taking a customer view of quality, seeing yourself in a supplier relationship in which the provision of defective goods and services is not acceptable. You need to identify your customer and work at understanding what they want. You will establish whatever process seems appropriate to avoid passing on defects. One method is the inspection of goods prior to despatch. Quality management becomes *total* when this customer–supplier relationship is passed down the chain, so that every stage in the chain becomes a supplier for a customer who is the next stage in the chain. This must be true even for stages within the same organisation, so in our software supply story, the store manager who undertook the goods inward function was the supplier to her customer the assistant who stocked the shelves.

In summary then, the principles of TQM are:

- Quality can and must be managed.
- Everyone has a customer and is a supplier.
- Processes, not people are the problem.
- Every employee is responsible for quality.
- Problems must be prevented, not just fixed.
- Quality must be measured.
- Life-cycle costs, not front end costs.
- Management must be involved and lead.
- Plan and organise for quality improvement

TQM focusses on quality culture.

Within TQM there are a number of ways to help make total quality a success. One of these that have received wide publicity is **quality circles**. Quality circles are one important, albeit small, aspect of total quality management. A quality circle is a way of involving everybody in the production of quality products. Quality should not be simply the goal of management. A quality circle is a group of four to ten volunteers who meet regularly, say once a week, to identify, analyse, and solve their work-related problems. Note that it is the work-related quality problems that are discussed, not the work of individuals, let alone the individuals themselves. As Mike Robson explains:[11]

> At their most general, Quality Circles can help to change the culture of an organisation to one where there is a common ownership of corporate goals. . . . given the right conditions, many people in organisations will choose to use more of their abilities and experience to take part in solving work problems. (p. 4)

Quality circles, as in the whole TQM approach, take the view that we are all involved with the work of the company, and can all influence the quality of the product. It is not somebody else's problem or fault. We are all responsible.

In many instances this requires a change in company culture to become a quality culture, because quality and service must pervade all aspects of work. Making this change takes time, and costs money – the usual time suggested for the implementation of TQM is three years, but many companies cannot wait that long and there have been many programmes to implement TQM that did not succeed due to senior executives expecting too fast a return on investment. Many companies have successfully implemented TQM, like Motorola and Toyota.

> Quality circles enable individuals and the group to focus on quality.

> A concern for quality should be part of the culture of an organisation.

12.2.5 Quality economics

The concept of quality economics, primarily in engineering and manufacturing, emerged in the 1950s. It was present in Armand Feigenbaum's book *Total Quality Control* (cited earlier) and in Joseph Juran's *Quality Control Handbook*, also published in 1951.[12] Feigenbaum looked at all costs associated with quality, both those associated with quality improvement, and with the extra work associated with quality failure. He identified three classes of costs:

1. Prevention costs so that defects never happen: training staff, preventive maintenance, reviewing requirements.
2. Appraisal costs to catch the defect after it has happened but before it reaches the customer: inspections and testing.
3. Failure costs, where the defect is only found after it has reached the customer: rejects, rework, warranty claims, customer complaints, extra work carried out to get round the fault, loss of business, etc.

The normal engineering wisdom is the 1:10:100 rule – for every unit of money spent on prevention you spend ten times as much removing an undetected defect before it reaches the customer and 100 times the prevention costs if it reaches the customer. These general engineering figures are very similar to figures collected within software development by Barry Boehm and many others – see Table 12.1 – a defect which could be avoided in the very earliest requirements analysis stage would cost 200 times as much to fix if only identified during operational use of the software.

Let us look at how investment in quality (money spent on defect prevention and product appraisal) is related to savings in failure costs, the cost of

> Quality prevention and appraisal costs money, but saves on failure costs.

Stage	Relative repair score
Requirements	1
Design	5
Coding	10
Unit Test	20
System Test	50
Maintenance	200

Table 12.1

Relative cost to fix a defect in software within a waterfall development process (after Boehm[13]).

Figure 12.3

Balancing the costs of
defect prevention
and appraisal against
the savings from
reduced failure costs

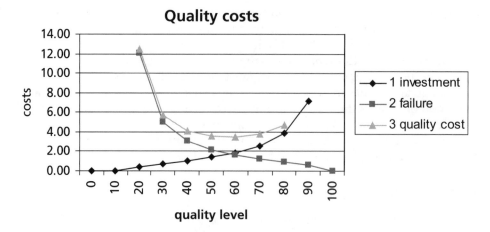

Figure 12.3

Balancing the costs of
defect prevention
and appraisal against
the savings from
reduced failure costs

'unquality'. This relationship is shown in Figure 12.3. The horizontal axis is the product quality, which for this purpose could be thought of as reliability. The vertical axis is cost. Curve 1 shows the investment in quality improvement: at zero investment we have low quality, and to get perfect software we require infinite investment. Curve 2 shows the savings from having quality software: if the software is very poor, the failure costs are very high; if the software is very high quality, the failure costs are very low. If we add together these two curves we get curve 3: the net cost of quality – and what we get is a very typical U-shaped curve, with some optimal level in the middle as we balance investment in quality with savings from quality.

In manufacturing and engineering there have been attempts to produce quality models which indicate the relationships within these costs. In general, these models show that as the investment in prevention and appraisal increases, defects should decrease, and thus also internal and external failure costs. The total quality costs, the sum of the categories should first decrease, reach an optimum (minimum total cost) and then increase again. The implementation of quality systems requires incurring extra costs and setting up an infrastructure and these are represented by the indirect quality costs. This effort can be recovered by means of reducing rework and improving customer satisfaction, leading to increased sales and revenue.

The point is that quality always involves compromises, and perfect software, or indeed any other engineering artefact, should not be expected. Phil Crosby made popular the slogan 'Quality is free'. His message was that expenses in quality are likely to be recovered by their positive impact which will eventually lead to better revenue. However he also used the slogan 'defect free', and while it is sensible to strive for this, we also realise that it is unattainable. It is the job of the software manager and the software engineer to balance carefully the expected benefits with the costs, and also to customise a general quality framework to the particular needs of their organisation. Organisations need a proper programme of data gathering, using metrics, so that they can monitor the levels of rework, costs and benefits, and justify the business case for the particular quality management practices they adopt.

Balance quality
costs and quality
benefits.

12.3 Quality frameworks

In most cases it is not sufficient to have a shared value in quality, it is also important to institutionalise quality management. Quality management systems (QMS) cannot eliminate the risk of software failure, or of the software failing to meet stakeholders' expectations, but many experts[14] consider that it certainly can mitigate it. Every manager and software engineer should be familiar with quality management systems.

In many industries, such electrical components or civil construction, selected standards are mandatory (e.g., the National Electric Code in the USA). However this is not (yet) the case for the software industry, and in many sectors software managers can pick and choose from the available frameworks and standards, some of which are covered below. In certain industrial sectors, such as the US military, compliance with a quality framework such as CMMi (to be discussed later) can be required for a contractor to be allowed to participate. Many safety-critical applications have to follow specialised strict standards. By contrast, in other domains, such as the software games industry, the application of specific quality systems may not be required, though even there human factors standards may become mandatory.

Quality frameworks encapsulate good practice and consensus as to what processes, activities and management systems should include and what quality level they are likely to achieve. (This is not a guarantee!) Quality frameworks are likely to evolve as our knowledge and understanding of processes in general, and of the software process in particular, evolve. However, there are basic enduring principles which are likely to stay.

> Quality management systems help establish quality in an organisation.

We will give high-level descriptions of three available quality management frameworks and standards: the ISO 9000 series, CMMi, and SPICE. Nominally these are independent of each other, but in practice they embody similar concepts such as continuous improvement, but also such differences as CMMi and SPICE providing a road map towards achieving higher maturity and capability while ISO doesn't. All three are subject to revisions and evolution themselves (e.g., ISO standards tend to be revised every five years or so), and the latest version should be obtained from the primary sources.

12.3.1 ISO 9000 series

The International Organization for Standardisation (ISO) defines quality as 'the degree to which a set of inherent characteristics fulfils the requirements' in its standard ISO 9000. ISO's approach to achieving and maintaining quality is through management systems. A management system '... refers to what the organization does to manage its processes, or activities in order that the products or services that it produces meet the objectives it has set itself ...'. The objectives cover at least three areas:

1. satisfaction of customer requirements;
2. compliance with applicable regulations;
3. accomplish environmental targets.

For a software enterprise, meeting the requirements of the users of the software is an obvious goal, as is the compliance with applicable regulations such as those seen in Chapter 5. An environmental target for a software company may include, for example, reduction in the environmental impact of its media, packaging and user documentation or removing print all together through providing documentation online.

ISO defines a quality management system (QMS) as a 'the set of interrelated or interacting elements to direct and control an organisation with regard to quality'. The basic elements of a QMS are:

- organisational structure;
- people;
- processes;
- documentation.

A QMS should document the way in which the enterprise achieves products that satisfy user demands, that is, with building quality into products and maintaining it. This documentation is referred to as the Quality Manual, and contains the company quality policy and all the relevant standards, procedures and quality controls to be applied in the whole enterprise. Based on this Quality Manual, each project needs to create its own compliant Quality Plan, and the project team then works within the boundaries of their Quality Plan.

In following a QMS we:

- plan before the start of the project how it will be executed and what quality controls will be put in place;
- keep sufficient records during the project execution so that it can be audited;
- conduct audits at specific intervals during the project and at the end of the project;
- avoid loopholes (such as having subcontractors who do not have a comparable set of quality controls); and
- aim at improving the QMS as a project progresses and after each project.

The ISO 9000 series of standards can be traced back to difficulties in defence procurement in the 1940s and 1950s, which led to the 1959 quality management programme for the US military, MIL-Q-9858. In the late 1960s this programme was adopted by NATO as part of the AQAP standard series (AQAP1, AQAP4, and AQAP9). In 1973 the UK defence industry created its own quality assurance standard DefStan 05-21, and then in 1979 commercial versions of these were published by the British Standards Institution (BSI) as BS 5750 parts 1, 2, and 3. And then, based on all these preceding quality standards, ISO 9001, 9002, and 9003 was published in 1987:

- ISO 9001:1987 – quality assurance in design/development, production, installation and servicing;
- ISO 9002: 1987 – quality assurance in production and installation;
- ISO 9003: 1987 – quality assurance in final inspection and test.

In 1994 revisions of the ISO 9000 series were published. The revisions addressed inconsistencies in the wording of some clauses. A further revision of the standards was made in 2000, and another revision must be due in 2006 or 2007.

ISO 9000:2000 covers definitions and terminology (a glossary). ISO 9001:2000 is a generic standard, applicable to all industries. Its focus is on processes and not on individual products. Its underlying assumption is that by improving the processes, the quality of the products can be also improved and controlled. A number of further standards guide the interpretation of the generic ISO 9001:2000 to a particular industrial sector – so for example ISO/IEC 9000-3:2004 gives guidance on the application to software development. ISO 9004:2000 deals specifically with process performance improvement.

ISO 9000-3:2004 – application to software

ISO addresses the specifics of the software industry in the ISO 9000-3 standard, first released in 1991 – Guidelines for the Application of ISO 9001(:1987) to the Development, Supply and Maintenance of Software. It was replaced by a 1997 revised version, which was called Guidelines for the Application of ISO 9001:1994 to the Development, Supply, Installation and Maintenance of Computer Software. The most recent revision is the ISO 9000-3:2004 standard. In order to give a general idea of its coverage, a list of the five requirements areas and twenty-two requirements subjects of ISO 9000-3:2004 is presented in Table 12.2.

Requirement class	Requirement subjects
4. Quality management system	
	4.1 General requirements
	4.2 Documentation requirements
5. Management responsibilities	
	5.1 Management commitments
	5.2 Customer focus
	5.3 Quality policy
	5.4 Planning
	5.5 Responsibility, authority and communication
	5.6 Management review
6. Resource management	
	6.1 Provision of resources
	6.2 Human resources
	6.3 Infrastructure
	6.4 Work environment
7. Product realisation	
	7.1 Planning of product realisation
	7.2 Customer-related processes
	7.3 Design and development
	7.4 Purchasing
	7.5 Production and service provision
	7.6 Control of monitoring and measuring devices
8. Measurement, analysis and improvement	
	8.1 General
	8.2 Monitoring and measurement
	8.3 Control of non-conforming product
	8.4 Analysis of data
	8.5 Improvement

Table 12.2

Requirements subjects for the ISO 9000-3: 2004 standard

Accreditation and certification

Organisations can establish a quality management system and seek certification that their QMS conforms to ISO 9000. To do this they contact a certification body, to whom they show their Quality Manual, and will have one or more audit visits to check that the organisation does actually operate according to their Quality Manual. If they pass the audit, the certification body issues a written certificate stating that the latter has audited the quality management system of the former and found that it conforms to the standard. The certification body then places the certificate in a register of companies that have been issued similar certificates. This step is called registration. Commonly certification and registration can be used as synonyms, with some preference worldwide for the first, and in North America for the latter. The register of ISO-certified companies is available for inspection by anyone interested in finding out, such as purchasing organisations wishing to evaluate their potential suppliers.

There is a mechanism termed accreditation by which a certification body shows that it is competent to perform ISO certification within a particular industrial sector. The certification bodies themselves must comply with certain requirements with regard to their management systems and to the level of competence of the personnel, the assessors or auditors, performing the ISO assessment. An organisation called the International Register of Certified Auditors (IRCA) maintains a register of assessors and a number of requisites have to be fulfilled for an assessor to be included in the register. These include experience in management and software development, and the successful completion of a course for auditors.

In the late 1980s a scheme called TickIT was introduced in the UK and Sweden in order to promote the concern for quality systems in the software industry and the adaptation of ISO 9001 to the software domain. At that time, ISO 9001 had been successfully applied to the manufacturing sector but not to software. TickIT and other efforts led to the present software-related ISO 9000-3 standard. TickIT is also authorized for the UK to accredit certification bodies within the software sector.

According to ISO, certification is not compulsory. Organisations can benefit from applying the standard without incurring in the costs of seeking external independent certification. The business decision of seeking such certification should consider, for example, the presence of market incentives or regulatory pressures, the achievement of the certification as a risk-reduction strategy or to motivate personnel.

ISO 9000 lays down guidance from which an organisation can obtain certified compliance.

With the publication of the ISO 9000:2004 series, there has been a shift in the focus of this ISO standard from conformity to performance. One of the goals behind the ISO 9000 series is to help organisations to avoid the production of low-quality products and work consistently. ISO 9000 embodies the concept of process improvement and in particular the organisational learning triggered by difficulties. However, the standard lacks the concept of relative competence and how to progress to increased levels of competence. Other limitations of ISO 9000:2000 are its focus on documentation and the lack of a road map for quality improvement. These aspects have been addressed in frameworks such as SPICE and CMMi which, as opposed to the ISO 9000 series that are industry-generic, have been specifically conceived with software organisations in mind.

12.3.2 CMMi

In the mid-1980s the Software Engineering Institute began to investigate how the capability of contractors in the area of software could be assessed. As a result of this work, the Capability Maturity Model (CMM) was introduced in the 1990s as a road map for software organisations to follow in order to achieve an increased level of capability. There were five levels of capability defined. A high level of capability indicates that the organisation is able to produce quality products consistently over a series of software projects or releases of an evolving system. It also implies that the organisation has mechanisms to improve its performance, not only in terms of average performance, but is also able to reduce the variation in that performance. Other related models, such as the People Capability Model (P-CMM) were introduced. CMM was widely disseminated and discussed in the software engineering community and has helped to move the topic of process improvement up the agenda.

More recently, in an attempt to integrate different related models and to address a number of reported limitations of the model, the SEI has developed an integrated capability model (CMMi), which supersedes previous CMM-related models. The model comes in two instantiations: staged and continuous.

The staged version is the closest to the previous CMM. It maintains a five-level classification of capability maturity, which permits the overall assessment of the software enterprise and a number to be assigned. It also provides a sequential progression between levels, which constitutes a road map for process improvement. The five-level scale is presented in Table 12.3.

CMMi maturity level	
(Staged instantiation)	Level name
1	Initial
2	Managed
3	Defined
4	Quantitatively managed
5	Optimising

Table 12.3

The five capability levels of the CMMi staged model

Each maturity level has a number of processes and specific goals related to it. For instance, the process areas associated with level 2 (managed) are requirements management, project planning, project monitoring and control, supplier agreement management, measurement and analysis, process and product quality assurance, and configuration management. In addition to the above, an organisation successfully assessed at level 2 must also have accomplished the generic goal of institutionalising the processes that are required at that level as managed processes.

Activity 12.6 *Drawbacks of CMMi*

The five-level CMMi staged model provides a sequence of stages for organisations to follow if they are interested in achieving products with higher levels of quality and in consistent performance. Could you think of any disadvantages of this approach?

> **Discussion**
> Navigating the five levels requires consistent and focussed effort. A possible shortcoming of this approach is that organisations may be inclined to introduce practices at the higher levels without having addressed issues at the lower levels. There might be process areas that an organisation does not really need because of their particular application domain and business environments. For example, an organisation which develops all its software without external suppliers does not require the process area related to supplier agreement management.

The continuous version complements the staged model by providing a finer-grain view that focuses on twenty-four process areas organised into four groups. Table 12.4 presents the CMMi process areas and groups. Each process area has goals and practices.

Goals are descriptions of the desirable state to be achieved by the software organisation. CMMi includes specific goals for each process area. For instance, a specific goal within the 'requirements management' process area is that 'Requirements are managed and inconsistencies with project plans and work products are identified.' It also includes generic goals which apply to the organisation as

Table 12.4		
Process area group		**Process area**
Process area groups and process areas in CMMi	Process management	Organisational process definition
		Organisational process focus
		Organisational training
		Organisational process performance
		Organisational innovation and deployment
	Project management	Project planning
		Project monitoring and control
		Supplier agreement management
		Integrated project management
		Risk management
		Integrated teaming
		Quantitative project management
	Engineering	Requirements management
		Requirements development
		Technical solution
		Product integration
		Verification
		Validation
	Support	Configuration management
		Process and product quality management
		Measurement and analysis
		Decision analysis and resolution
		Organisational environment for integration
		Causal analysis and resolution

a whole with regard to the institutionalisation of good practice. An example of CMMi generic goal is 'The process is institutionalised as a defined process.'

Practices are ways in which a particular goal can be achieved. For example, for the above goal, an associated practice is: 'Establish and maintain an organisational policy for planning and performing the requirements development process.' The practices are only indicative and not prescriptive: CMMi recognises that there is more than one way to achieve a goal and there is room for an organisation to choose their own practices. The CMMi model is very detailed and, in addition, includes typical work products, subpractices, notes, discipline amplifications, generic practice elaborations and references.

In CMMi, each of the twenty-four process areas is assessed and classified on a six-level scale, presented in Table 12.5. A key feature of the continuous CMMi model is that it provides the opportunity for organisations to achieve different levels of maturity for different processes.

CMMi focuses on process capability and provides a five-level road map to achieve higher levels of capability

Table 12.5

CMMi scale to assess process maturity

Level of maturity of every process area	Level name	Key features
1	Not performed	Lack of satisfaction of at least one specific goal associated with the process area.
2	Performed	Goal associated with the process area are met. Scope of work agreed and indicated to team members.
3	Managed	Organisational policies define process use. There are documented plans, resource management, and process monitoring procedures.
4	Defined	For each project, processes are tailored from a defined set. Process assessment and measurements collected.
5	Quantitatively managed	Use of quantitative analysis to control subprocesses.
6	Optimising	Process improvement driven by measurement, including trend analysis and continual process adaptation to the evolving wider business environment.

An ISO 9000 certified organisation is likely to be assessed at CMMi level 2, with some level 3 activities. The ISO 9000:2004 focus on performance has brought it closer to the CMMi philosophy: however, it is possible for ISO 9000 certified companies to still be rated at CMMi level 1.

12.3.3 SPICE

The Software Process Improvement and Capability dEtermination (SPICE) project[15] started in 1993 as a joint effort undertaken by ISO and IEC with the aim of achieving normalisation and standardisation of software process assessment approaches with worldwide applicability across a variety of industrial sectors.

In 1995 the SPICE project made available its version 1.0 report. This report became then the basis for the ISO/IEC TR 15504 standard, which appeared in 1998. The SPICE project was backed by the International Committee on Software Engineering Standards ISO/IEC JTC 1/SC 7 through its Working Group on Software Process Assessment (WG 10). The aim was to achieve an international standard and work has been carried out in the form of wider international revisions and formal trials from 1995 to 2000 involving a variety of organisations in different countries.

The goal behind ISO/IEC TR 15504 is the harmonisation of existing process assessment methodologies. It provides a detailed assessment model, with six levels of capability. The focus is on 'what' the deliverables of the assessment are rather than 'how' they are performed. It is intended to be of wide applicability to a variety of software organisations and to become an international standard.

Similarly to CMMi, SPICE also provides a road map for continual software process improvement. Strictly speaking, SPICE is an assessment model: its main purpose is the determination of the capability level of a software organisation. The SPICE assessment model is based on six capability levels, as seen in Table 12.6. The assessment of what level an organisation is at is based on the achievement of process attributes. The model indicates which attributes are required at each level. In order to maximise compatibility with other process assessment models such as CMM, the SPICE model focusses on 'what' is accomplished in a software

Table 12.6	Level number	Level name	Required process attributes
The SPICE assessment model and the required process attributes at each level	0	Incomplete	No process attributes. Informal process. None or little evidence of any planned process.
	1	Performed process	Process performance: processes are identified at the input–output level (black box).
	2	Managed process	Performance management: there are procedures which define process performance. Work products management: work products are documented and subject to control, including verification of compliance.
	3	Established process	Process definition: well-defined processes are consistently applied through the organisation. Process resources: the organisation controls utilisation of human resources and infrastructure.
	4	Predictable process	Measurement: the measurement of performance is linked to organisational goals. Process control: achieved via collection of process and product measures, analysis and implementation of corrections to the process in order to achieve process goals.
	5	Optimising process	Continuous improvement: the impact of process and managerial changes are regularly monitored via measurements to assess their success.

organisation rather than on 'how' activities have been done. Table 12.6 presents both the SPICE capability levels and an indication of the process attributes that are required.

ISO/IEC TR 15504 includes a reference model for processes and process capability. The goal was to make this model sufficiently general to be able to apply it in conjunction with any of the process models previously described in the literature including sequential models such as the classic Waterfall, and incremental models such as Gilb's Evolutionary Development or Boehm's Spiral Model, all described in Chapter 8.

SPICE makes a distinction between the 'what', activities present in a software organisation, and the 'how', the way in which the activities are accomplished. The 'what' and the 'how' are called base practices and generic practices respectively.

The SPICE process model includes twenty-nine processes which an organisation needs to deploy in a satisfactory manner in order to achieve the highest capability level (level 5). These processes are grouped into five subject areas: customer-supplier (CUS), engineering (ENG), support (SUP), management (MAN), and organisation (ORG). As an illustration, the engineering process category includes the seven processes or base practices indicated in Table 12.7.

Each process is subdivided into base practices. For example, process SUP.5 (perform peer review) includes the base practices indicated in Table 12.8.

Process	Description
ENG. 1	Develop system requirements and design
ENG. 2	Develop software requirements
ENG. 3	Develop software design
ENG. 4	Implement software design
ENG. 5	Integrate and test software
ENG. 6	Integrate and test system
ENG. 7	Maintain system and software

Table 12.7

SPICE process activities under the engineering process category (ENG)

Base practice	Description
SUP.5.1	Select work products (to be reviewed)
SUP.5.2	Identify review standards
SUP.5.3	Establish completion criteria
SUP.5.4	Establish re-review criteria
SUP.5.5	Distribute review materials
SUP.5.6	Conduct peer review
SUP.5.7	Document action items
SUP.5.8	Track action items

Table 12.8

SPICE base practices for performing a peer review

In the SPICE model, process assessment is conducted by a qualified team coordinated by an assessment leader. Key assessment activities are the determination of the ratings for the individual practices. A four-point scale is used to assess the adequacy of a base practice: fully achieved, largely achieved, partially achieved, not achieved. A binary classification is used to assess whether or not the base practice produces identifiable work outputs.

Activity 12.7   *CMMi and SPICE process assessments*

Based on what we have so far explained, compare and contrast the CMMi and SPICE process assessments.

Discussion
The SPICE assessment operates at the process level and looks at twenty-nine processes. It is more detailed and closer to the process level than the CMMi staged model. SPICE does not see maturing as a process of going sequentially through a series of plateaus. The SPICE assessment will require more time than the CMMi staged model. The result of the SPICE assessment is not a summary view as in the CMMi staged model: this means that under SPICE it is more difficult for organisations to achieve a global view of their processes. However, the CMMi continuous model has similarities with SPICE: both focus on how individual processes mature. CMMi, in general, is more elaborated and documented in more detail than SPICE and for this reason is more accessible.

> SPICE combines the advantages of both ISO 9000 and CMMi

12.3.4 Frameworks in practice

The quality standards and frameworks (ISO 9001, CMMi, SPICE) briefly presented above make explicit the learning and knowledge management processes within the software organisation that we referred to in Chapter 2. There have been some critics of the ideas of process maturity enshrined in CMM and its successor CMMi. For example, Keith Bennett wrote:

> Frameworks such as ISO 9001, CMMi, and SPICE provide guidance for implementing a quality management system.

> . . . there is little evidence in practice that improving software process maturity actually benefits organizations, and the whole edifice is based on the assumption that the success of the product is determined by the process. That this is not necessary is demonstrated by the success of certain commodity software. (p. 296)

Certainly CMMi cannot solve all the problems or explain all the successes but a high level of maturity is generally recognised as a characteristic of organisations with a concern for quality.

Case Study 12.4 *Quality at Infosys in India*

Infosys was founded in 1981 by six engineers, had grown into a 9,000-employee, ten billion-dollar company by 2001 had over 25,000 emloyees by 2004. From their modest begin-nings in Bangalore, they expanded across India in 1995, established their first European office in 1996 in Milton Keynes, UK, and their first North American office in 1997 in Toronto, Canada.

Their annual revenues topped the one billion dollar mark in 2004. They now occupy a large campus in Bangalore that would be the equal of anything in the US, and are seen as the model to which other companies in the region should aspire.

Infosys attributes much of its success to rigorous quality control and conducts most of its business offshore. Along with many other companies in India, Infosys sought and obtained registration under ISO 9000 in 1993 before moving on to gain registration at CMM level 4 in 1997 and then level 5 in 1999. The way this conformance to quality works out in practice has been described in an excellent book by their Quality Director Dr Pankaj Jalote.[16]

Of the forty-two organisations worldwide that had reached level 5 on the CMM scale in 2001, twenty-five were based in India.

Summing up

In this chapter we have taken a high-level view of software quality, the way quality is seen by different communities and stakeholders, the principles underlying quality systems, and how quality can be institutionalised and managed. The chapter has also looked at the various frameworks and standards which have been put forward in order to guide software organisations in pursuing quality products and processes. We saw that:

- high quality means fitness for purpose, so that quality software satisfies the needs and expectations of its stakeholders and does not frustrate or cause damage to them;

- quality can be measured, and though these measurements are only indicative, they can give guidance to management actions;

- extra quality-improving processes should be included within the overall process; the most important of these are reviews and inspections; while testing is always done it is also quality-enhancing, and creates a second complimentary view of a system which is then compared with that embodied in the implementation;

- quality is everybody's responsibility as part of a quality culture; Total Quality Management focusses on quality culture, with Quality Circles enabling individuals to focus on quality within the enterprise;

- quality prevention and appraisal costs money, but saves on failure costs, whch need to be balanced;

- quality management systems help establish quality in an organization; ISO 9000 lays down guidance for producing a quality management system, for which an organisation can obtain certified compliance; CMMi focuses on process capability and provides a five-level road map to achieve higher levels of capability; and SPICE combines the advantages of both ISO 9000 and CMMi – all give useful guidance for implementing a quality management system.

Exercises

1. In the shipbuilding industry in Europe during the 1960s and 1970s it was common practice to base a claim for quality on the engineering view of quality – conformance to specification. They would require a complete and precise detailed specification from their customer, and then deliver exactly what was specified. If the customer changed his mind, then a significant charge could have been required in order to build a modified ship. Comment on this as an acceptable definition of quality.

2. Individual work products during the development of software could have quality attributes measured. One of these was described in this discussion of Activity 12.3; another might be the 'fog index' for text; and another might be coupling and cohesion measures for designs. Explain how such measurements might be used in reviews and inspections during software development.

3. Consider the claim made by Edsger Dijkstra against testing that 'Program testing can be used to show the presence of bugs, but never to show their absence!'[17] Yet we have argued that testing is a quality-enhancing activity – write a short refutation of Dijkstra to justify the continued use of testing as an integral part of software development.

4. Consider the processes involved in sending and receiving faxes in a large archaic organisation. You give your fax to an administrator, who then takes it or sends it through internal mail to the fax office who transmit it. When an incoming fax arrives, the fax office telephones you, and if there is no reply, puts it in internal mail to the admin. Draw a diagram showing the quality chains and customer–supplier relationships. Are all of these clear? How could the system be improved?

5. Quality circles are meetings of five to ten people, and so are inspections, so what is the difference? Examine these carefully, if necessary accessing other sources of information, to characterise their differences. Quality circles are popular in Japan but inspections are not. Why?

6. Case Study 12.1 gave a very short account of the failure of the London Ambulance Service's computer-aided despatch system. Find out as much as you can about this, and then consider how expenditure earlier in the life cycle might have prevented this gross failure. What kinds extra investments in quality could have served to save the enormous cost of failure eventually endured?

7. Find out about the so-called 'quality gurus,' W. Edwards Deming, Dr Joseph Juran, Armand V. Feigenbaum, Dr Kaoru Ishikawa, Dr Genichi Taguchi, and Shigeo Shingo. What do they have in common? What differentiates them? Would any of them endorse quality frameworks like ISO 9000 and CMMi as the right way to introduce quality into a company?

8. Steve Hayes, an Australian consultant specialising in Agile methods, wrote in 2003: 'All Agile methods emphasise the production of high quality software, and extreme programming in particular adds a number of practices to support this objective.' Do you think this claim is correct? Hayes justifies his claim by quoting an example – could you explain why Agile methods might deliver higher-quality software in particular cases and why they might not do so in general?

Endnotes

1. Edited by Joseph M. Juran with Frank M. Gryna as associate editor, and published in the United States by McGraw-Hill as the fourth edition in 1988.
2. D. Garvin (1984) 'What Does Quality Really Mean?', *Sloan Management Review*, Fall 1984.
3. Our thanks to http://www.answers.com/topic/bug for this etymology.
4. J.A. McCall, P.K. Richards, and G.F. Walters (1977) *Factors in Software Software Quality*. 3 volume RADC report.
5. Barry Boehm, John Brown, Hans Kaspar, Myron Lipow, Gordon MacLeod, and Michael Merritt (1978) *Characteristics of Software Quality*. North-Holland.
6. Norman E. Fenton (1991) *Software Metrics: A Rigorous approach*, Chapman Hall.
7. This was suggested by Pat Hall, and is reported in Stewart Gardiner (ed.) (1999) *Testing Safety-Related Software: A Practical Handbook*. Springer.
8. See, for example, Sommerville's software engineering text, I. Sommerville (2004) *Software Engineering*, seventh edn, Pearson. We recall talking to senior management of a leading software house who proudly proclaimed their quality culture, and then complained that this was carried to excess in that staff insisted that even internal memos had to be perfect – they were right about their company, and about those memos – quality is not perfection, it is fitness for purpose.
9. First published as *Quality Control: Principles, Practice, and Administration*, in 1951 based on earlier articles, this is now published in its fourth edition simply as *Total Quality Control*, by McGraw-Hill Education (International Student Edition).
10. John S. Oakland (1989) *Total Quality Management*. Butterworth Heinemann.
11. Mike Robson (1982) *Quality Circles*. Gower.
12. Now in its fifth edition, at a massive 1,872 pages: Joseph M. Juran and A. Blanton Godfrey (1996) *Juran's Quality Handbook*. McGraw-Hill Professional.
13. Reported in his *Software Engineering Economics*. Prentice-Hall (1981).
14. For example, Deming and Juran in the wider manufacturing domain; Watts Humphreys in the software field.
15. See http://www.sqi.gu.edu.au/spice/.
16. Pankaj Jalote (1999) *CMM in Practice: Processes for Executing Software Projects at Infosys*. Addison-Wesley.
17. In O.-J. Dahl, E.W. Dijkstra, and A.R. Hoare (1973) *Structured programming* (second edn). Academic Press.

13 Managing uncertainty and risk

> ## What we will study in this chapter
>
> In Part I of this book, we considered the rich human and social context which surrounds the activities of the software enterprise. Part II discussed the various sources and processes to acquire and evolve software. Some of these processes recognised aspects of the uncertainty integral to software development and tackled them straight on. In Part III we are discussing 'how to make it all happen' through the managing of resources and the quality in software products and processes. There are different sources of uncertainty in software and software-related work. These uncertainties lead to risks that need to be acknowledged and addressed. In this penultimate chapter we considered these uncertainties and how to tackle them.
> This chapter will look at:
>
> - the types of risk and the causes and consequences of failure;
>
> - common software-related risks;
>
> - risks related to particular software sources;
>
> - risk management.

13.1 Introduction

As human beings we are aware of what risk means in a general sense. It is something that we learn from our own experiences when interacting with the world around us. As children we soon learn that both touching a hot water tap and staying too long in the sun can burn you. We all have an intuitive notion of risk, even though the risk perceptions of each person may be different. For some, high-speed car racing or skydiving are acceptable, even enjoyable, activities. Risk is part of their enjoyment. Others will consider them too risky. In Chapter 3 we saw that stability and security are some of the basic human needs identified in Maslow's hierarchy. We also saw how uncertainty avoidance varies across countries and cultures.

In software, risks are associated with undesirable events that represent a threat to the software stakeholders: these events, if they happen, are likely to lead to tangible harm or losses (e.g., damage to people, goods, loss of contracts, loss of revenue, decrease in market share, penalties in contracts) or intangible harm or losses (e.g., loss of trust, credibility and future business opportunities, damage to the reputation of people, organisations or trademarks, dissemination of confidential information, loss of intellectual property rights). Risks also include potential situations which are likely to emerge that will negatively impact the wider community within which the enterprise operates and to whom it is responsible (e.g., software defects impacting users).

Risks are part of doing business. Highly risky businesses tend also to be highly rewarded and may have a particular attraction for some entrepreneurs and venture capitalists. Codes of conduct, insurance premiums, national and international legislation and accepted professional practices (e.i., practices recommended by professional societies and trade unions or encapsulated in standards) regulate and promote different views of which risks are worth taking and which aren't. Public opinion, as reflected by the news industry and the media, has evolving perceptions of risk in different areas. Different communities of practice also have different perceptions of risk. These perceptions evolve over time as knowledge and understanding evolve. Perceptions of risk also evolve within the software enterprise and in software teams.

In general, a risk has two components: the **likelihood** or chance that an unsatisfactory outcome becomes real and its **severity** or **cost**.

The importance of a risk is given by the product:

$$\text{risk seriousness} = \text{likelihood} \times \text{severity}.$$

Seriousness of risks can be used to prioritise them, that is, to select the order in which they should be tackled when resources are scarce or constrained. In general, high-likelihood, high-severity risks should be tackled first. Low-likelihood, low-severity risks should be tackled last.

13.2 Types of risks

The software enterprise has to cope with different categories of risks. Software managers need to be aware of all the categories. Typically there are three different categories:

1. Organisational risks – these are potential undesired situations which can endanger the viability of the organisation and its business. These situations may emerge, for example, from changes in the market, law, financial context, or relationships with customers. Examples of this type of risks are: loss of a judicial trial, instability of share values, loss of trust of investors; or emergence of a new technology or a new competing product which is superior in terms of functional power and overall quality.

2. Project risks – these correspond to events which can affect the quality, cost, and schedule of a project or which may make it difficult or impossible to be able to deliver the software or other business solution on time or within budget. Examples include: high personnel turnover which can lead to loss of irreplaceable knowledge, skills, and experience; or underestimation of cost or schedule in order to win a contract.[1]

3. Technical risks – technological problems which can emerge at any time in the software lifecycle. Examples are: a new release of a third-party component which fails to comply with its specification; a serious defect in a software component which has been delivered to the users; a misunderstanding in a subset of requirements which led to the wrong type of functionality being implemented; or some tacit requirements being neglected during design and implementation.

Risks may not fit perfectly into one of the three categories. For example, a defect may have been introduced by a developer who was working overtime, in a project for which effort and schedule were underestimated. The introduction of a defect, which prevents full access to functionality or deteriorates non-functional characteristics, is primarily a technical risk. However, insufficient personnel allocated for the size of the task is primarily a project risk. The estimate may have been biased by financial and business circumstances (e.g., likelihood of not being awarded a contract), which could be seen as organisational risks.

Risks are inevitable for the software enterprise. They can be classified as business, project, and technical risks. Some risks belong in more than one category.

Activity 13.1   *Risk classification*

Based on the types of risks described above, classify the following risks:

1. An employee with highly specialised knowledge of the leading software product of a company may leave the organisation and join a competitor who may be trying to develop a similar software product.

2. The only copy of the source code may be erased as a result of a hard disk problem with the servers running the code repository. The tape back-ups, when checked, may not work.

3. As a result of an attempt to send the code for inspection to another team working on the project at an offshore location, the full code and the documentation of the proprietary system may be placed on the web by one of your workers.

4. Due to the excessive complexity of the code base of a legacy system and of lack of training, the developers may take much more than the agreed time to implement a change.

5. After the loss of a major contract, developers may have low morale, gossip may become frequent, and management may appear neither to be aware nor to take action.

6. A developer in a software company using open source code may mix proprietary and source code in such a way that it is no longer possible to recognise which is which.

Discussion
These risks can be classified as follows:

Risk (1) is both a project risk and an organisational risk. The projects in which the employee was involved may have to be delayed until a replacement is found. If not properly documented, some of the organisational knowledge may be lost. This is also a business risk because the competitor who has hired this worker may be able to use his or her knowledge in producing a competing product. As a result the organisation may lose market share and value.

Risk (2) is a technical risk because it has to do with a storage failure. However, it can also become a project and business risk, depending on the severity of the code lost.

Risk (3) is an organisational risk. Unauthorised third parties could have copied the code and all the confidential information it contains. This can have implications in terms of security: weaknesses in the software may be exploited by crackers. Competitors may have access to technological secrets, such as algorithms. Confidential identities of people and companies may have been revealed.

Risk (4) is a technical and a project risk. The issue of excessive complexity has a technical solution: refactoring, restructuring, and inclusive redevelopment of the whole system. The progress of the work is being affected, so this is also a project risk. It may even become a business risk if the system which is difficult to evolve is business-critical.

Risk (5) is a project and an organisational risk. In Chapter 3 we saw that lack of motivation can represent a risk because it will impact negatively on productivity. Low morale and loss of managers' respect may endanger the future of the business.

Risk (6) is a technical and a project risk. Developers dealing with proprietary and open source code need to be trained so that the two are not mixed – with the potential loss of rights on proprietary code (see Chapter 6). Applications which involved proprietary and open source should be architected, and their configuration managed, in such a way that the two types of code are always identifiable.

13.3 Causes and consequences of failure

This section presents some general lessons learnt from the investigation of accidents, making special reference to the notions of **routine** and **radical design**, previously discussed in Chapter 10.

13.3.1 Failure in radical design

Radical design tackles problems which have not been solved before, whereas normal design addresses problems which have been solved in previous instances. Examples of radical design include NASA's Apollo space program, which enabled humans to walk on the Moon for the first time in history; and the Concorde, the first supersonic passenger aircraft.

Routine design is illustrated by the design of, for example, a new version of a compact car or the design of a conventional bridge. In computing, radical design is involved when new algorithms will need to be developed, when the system integrates elements which have not been made interact together before or when the solution involves new design ideas not tried before. One can argue that there is an element of radical design when those implementing the software have not done it before, even if the problem has been successfully solved by others. For example, the IBM OS 360/370 mainframe operating system developed in the 1960s, and 1970s (referred to briefly in Case Study 9.2 in Chapter 9) included aspects of radical design. Radical design has two aspects: the trial of new ideas and the trial of existing ideas in new contexts. Case study 13.1 referring to the Tacoma Narrows bridge collapse tragically demonstrates the consequences of failure in radical design.

Case Study 13.1 *The Tacoma Narrows bridge collapse*[2]

The history of engineering has cases of radical design which failed, such as the Tacoma Narrows suspension bridge in Tacoma, Washington, USA, which collapsed in November 1940, after having been in use for only a few months. A moderate (42 mile per hour) wind storm made the bridge oscillate in an uncontrolled way. The dramatic scenes before and during the collapse were recorded for history by an amateur film maker. Some changes in the design would have prevented this. Previous to this accident, engineers considered only the static load of the wind, but not its dynamic effects on the bridge structure. The Tacoma Bridge disaster led to a new discipline called bridge aerodynamics. A new, much safer suspension bridge was opened in the same place in 1950.

Figure 13.1

The collapse of Tacoma Narrows bridge

Soource: © 2006 The Camera Shop, Tacoma WA, USA. http://www.ketchum.org/bridgecollapsepix/tacobreak-298x400.jpg. Reprinted with kind permission of Ed Elliot.

Routine design projects also entail risks, but the ones that are likely to predominate are of the project and business types. As indicated in Chapter 10, the fact that software is invisible makes it more difficult for managers and developers to track progress of a software project and anticipate risks. The complexity and functional richness of software makes it impossible to exhaustively test the software against all possible conditions, as has already been seen in Chapter 12. Software failures can be as dramatic as the Tacoma Narrows bridge collapse. In recent years software has become pervasive: it is present everywhere. Voice and data networks and, in particular, the Internet are controlled by software. This implies that even software fault events with a small likelihood can have serious negative effects for society. The use of software is increasing at a higher rate than the ability of system and software engineers to design *systems of systems*, including socio-technical elements, which are fault tolerant. There is no accepted theoretical basis for the design of reliable systems of systems upon which society increasingly relies. These can be seen as examples of radical design.

In domains which are not well understood or for which there is not yet a standard engineering practice, there are processes such as the variants of early prototyping and incremental development (e.g., Boehm's spiral model, see Chapter 8) which focus on testing design hypotheses and mitigating technical risk early in a project through iterations of the 'specify–build–evaluate' idea.

Nevertheless, routine design is not absent of risks, as we can see in the next section.

> Software development is inevitably risky and more risky if the development is radical and innovative or if you have not done it before.

13.3.2 Failure in routine design

Earlier in this book we referred to the failure of the Therac-25 radiotherapy machines (Chapters 1 and 4) and of the software to automate the London Ambulance Service (Chapter 12) as two examples of *software failures*[3] and some specific lessons derived from them. Neither of these two cases were clear examples of radical design – it could have been 'radical' in the sense that the individuals involved had not done it before. Let's briefly look at the lessons learnt from the analysis of a number of accidents.

Case Study 13.2 *Safeware: System Safety and Computers*

Nancy G. Leveson, from MIT, has analysed a number of accidents involving computer-controlled equipment. Results of her investigations are published in a book entitled *Safeware: System Safety and Computers*, published by Addison-Wesley in 1995. The following summary is taken from Professor's Leveson's website.[4]

> *Contents: This book examines past accidents and what is currently known about building safe electromechanical systems to see what lessons can be applied to new computer-controlled systems. One lesson is that most acci-*

dents are not the result of unknown scientific principles but rather of a failure to apply well-known, standard engineering practices. A second lesson is that accidents will not be prevented by technological fixes alone, but will require control of all aspects of the development and operation of the system. The features of a methodology for building safety-critical systems are outlined.

Professor Leveson is preparing a new book on the same topic as *Safeware*. A draft of the new book can be obtained from her website.

One of the 'outline design' accidents that have been analysed by Leveson is the destruction of the Ariane 501 rocket, briefly described in Case Study 13.3.

Case Study 13.3 *Ariane Rocket Flight 501*[5]

On 4 June, 1996, the Ariane 5 Flight 501 rocket with a payload of four satellites and a total cost of US$500 million moved out of the intended ascension trajectory and was destroyed by a remote command issued by the ground controller less than one minute after being launched. This was the maiden flight of Ariane 5 (Flight 501). The board created to investigate the accident determined that an inadequate handling of an exception by the Inertial Reference System computer (SRI) triggered the chain of events which eventually led to the rocket's destruction. Part of the software for Ariane 5 was reused from the previous version of the launcher, Ariane 4. The two launcher versions had different flight dynamics and planned ascension trajectories. The reused software was not adequately tested with the different trajectory characteristics of Ariane 5. Due to these differences, an internal variable went out of range. This triggered an exception, which was not properly handled, leading to the shut-down of the SRI computer and the loss of trajectory control for the rocket and to the decision of the ground controller to destroy the rocket.

The report of the commission created to investigate the accident presented in total fourteen recommendations, including improvement of the design and testing processes and improvement in the organisation and cooperation of the partners involved in the Ariane 5 programme.

Figure 13.2

Ariane 5 rocket explosion as a result of a software failure. Copyright owned by ESA/CNES.

The rocket exploded seconds after launching

In her investigations, Leveson has arrived at the conclusion that many accidents result from the lack of application of well-known standard engineering practice. This is called Levenson's first law:

> most accidents are not the result of unknown scientific principles but rather a failure to apply well-known standard engineering practices. (Nancy Leveson, http://sunnyday. mit.edu/book.html)

The immediate consequence is:

> In safety-critical applications, make sure that those executing the project are the most qualified for the job and apply state-of-the-art techniques. They must be familiar with the scientific principles of the domain and also know the standard engineering practice well.

In routine design and well-understood technological domains, the likelihood of technical risks can be decreased if during design, risks are identified, assessed, quantified, and mitigated in a systematic and detailed way. For example, there is sufficient knowledge and historical data of the operation of oil refineries that experts can quantify the likelihood and severity to different events, such as the explosion of a pipe due to excessive pressure or a lightning strike affecting a storage tank. There are methods by which experts review the components of a technological system (e.g., a chemical plant or a car), ask questions about possible malfunctioning, quantify the risks of failure, and make decisions regarding how to assess them. One of the methods to achieve this is called *failure mode analysis*. In some cases, this exercise leads to redesign in order to make the system *'fail-safe'* for particular types of failure. Fail-safe means that in case of any malfunction the system should end in a state which does not represent actual or potential danger to people or to equipment. The type of failures tackled through these approaches fall mainly into the category of technical risks.

In well-understood technological domains, risk can be assessed and quantified in a detailed way.

There is yet another important lesson emerging from accidents such as the explosion of Ariane 501. There have been two predominant ways of analysing the causes of an accident or a failure. One was based on the *single cause* or *domino-effect* view of accident causality. One event leads to another event and to another, as when the first of several dominoes placed in a line falls, knocking down its neighbour until an accident happens. Though simple, the domino-effect view is insufficient to explain accidents such as Ariane 501. An alternative, more realistic, view to look at accident causation is to see accidents as triggered by *multiple causes*. This view takes a systemic view of the accident. In addition to recognising the role of individual events, it looks at wider factors such as organisational practices, management policies, directives and quality systems (see Chapter 12). Complex situations need to be analysed using the multiple-causes view, as the accident investigation board of the Ariane 501 rocket explosion did. Leveson's work supports this view.

Within the multiple-causes view, the causes of accidents can be classified as hard, human, and system-based. This classification of causes complements the classification of risks into technical, project, and organisational given earlier in this chapter. Hard causes can be explained in terms of physical objects, technological devices and their interactions. Human causes involve actions or inaction of operators, users, and other people interacting with the system, including their cognitive and reasoning processes. System causes involve how organisations, teams, and groups organise themselves, their plans, their manuals, their authority and responsibilities, and the businesses processes they follow in order to accomplish their aims.

Activity 13.2   *Ariane 501 accident*

Download and read the report of the Ariane 501 accident from, http://sunnyday. mit.edu/accidents/Ariane5accidentreport.html. What would be the explanation of the accident if one takes a single-cause, domino-effect view? Alternatively, what would be the possible explanation under a multiple-cause view? Read the recommendations and try to classify them into hard, human, and system causes.

Discussion

The single-cause explanation focusses on the failure of the software and how it propagated through the Ariane's trajectory control system, loss of control, followed by a human operator-issued self-destruction command.

The multiple-cause explanation focusses on process issues and addresses the lack of sufficient validation and verification activities to detect the problem before the actual release of the software and the actual launch of the rocket.

The classification into 'hard/human/system causes' of the recommendations is not absolute and some recommendations can be seen as addressing simultaneously more than one type of cause. The point emphasised here is the complexity of the systems that involved people, hardware, and software and the multiple design and operational factors which could impact on the system's behaviour as a whole. As Leveson's law says, 'accidents will not be prevented by technological fixes alone'.

'Accidents will not be prevented by technological fixes alone, but will require control of all aspects of the development and operation of the system.' (Nancy Leveson, http:// sunnyday.mit.edu/ book.html)

Software risk management has learned from the wider field of risk analysis and accident prevention. It involves the assessment and control of possible threats or unsatisfactory outcomes in a systematic way using a variety of approaches and techniques. The next section presents a view of software risk management by one of the leading software engineering experts.

13.4 Software risk management

Software risk management involves the assessment and control of possible threats or unsatisfactory outcomes. Risk management can be tacit or explicit. Figure 13.3 presents the steps proposed by Boehm[6] as a methodical and explicit approach to risk management.

Figure 13.3 presents the steps or activities in the form of a data structure diagram, which is relevant because each step is represented by a document or other data artefact which summarises the plan and the results of the activity. Some of the elements in the figure such as simulations, cost models, and analysis of assumptions have been covered in previous chapters of this book. For reasons of space, the lower level of the figure shows only a subset of the steps given by Boehm.

There are two basic risk management strategies: reactive and proactive management. Under the reactive strategy, unsatisfactory outcomes are tackled after they happen. These include strategies which are similar to those pursued by a firefighting squad trying to control and put out a fire. In some circumstances there is no other way to approach an undesired event than reactively, but proactive approaches are better in the majority of cases. One of the limitations of the reactive approach is the inevitable delay between the occurrence of an undesired event and when it is actually handled. Losses may occur during that period of time. Moreover, reactive approaches involve moving resources and attention from other activities to the tackling of the risk, with undesired rippled effects through the organisation. For example, the assignment of a software team to fix a serious defect

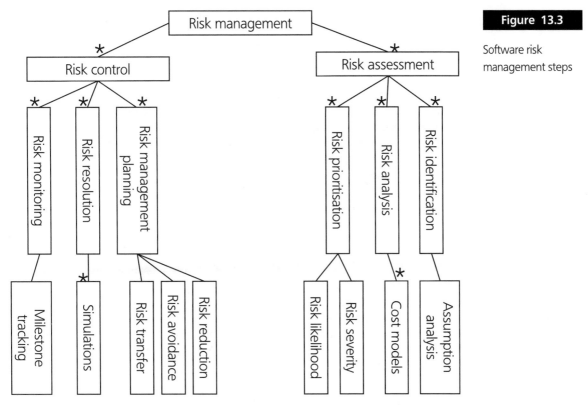

Source: Adapted from B. Boehm (1991) Software Risk Management: Principles and Practices. *IEEE Software*, January, pp. 32–41.

which has been detected may compromise progress in other activities for which they had a commitment.

On the other hand, the proactive strategy involves anticipating risks, planning and, in some cases, taking actions before the risk becomes real in order to counteract its effects. This is clearly the most desirable approach.

Within the proactive approach there are four basic strategies to manage risks. These are risk avoidance, risk reduction, risk retention, and risk transfer.

1. Risk avoidance – this strategy seeks an alternative arrangement which does not involve the risk at all.
2. Risk reduction – this strategy accepts the risk but also takes measures so that the loss is reduced.
3. Risk retention – this strategy involves accepting the risk and doing nothing to prevent it.
4. Risk transfer – it passes the costs of the event to some other party.

Risk management involves identifying risks, assessing their likelihood and severity, and creating a risk register. The next step is their prioritising the risks. Following this, actions are taken in order to manage, at least, the top priority risks. The risks which are located near the top of the priority list need to be handled by adequate policies. These policies need to be executed and their successes assessed. This cycle repeats as the risks themselves evolve with the project and the software enterprise.

One possible approach is for project managers to compile and maintain registers of the most evident risks for their project. Regular project meetings may discuss each of these risks and the strategies to handle them. During the meetings, any newly identified risks should be recorded. A usual technique for the identification of risks is **brainstorming**. In some domains (e.g., safety critical software) formal techniques such as fault-trees and failiure mode analysis can be used with the purpose of identifying and assessing risks.

The explicit recording of risks is a common activity in organisations dealing with safety-critical and business-critical applications. Nobody in the organisation will question this activity or will feel it is inappropriate. In other organisations, the explicit management of risks may not be seen as natural (e.g., the term 'risk' is rarely used) or is done implicitly rather than explicitly. For example, project meetings may record items and actions which are risks and risk management policies, respectively. However, they may not be explicitly named as such. This implicit management of risks has the weakness of being a piecemeal approach: important risks may be left without proper consideration.

Whatever the approach used, it is impossible to compile complete lists of risks affecting the software enterprise. Risk identification needs to be carried out continually. The experience of the managers and team members are a key contributor to risk identification.

Activity 13.3 *Some typical software risks*

Based on what you have already read in this book and your experience as a software manager, developer, or user, give examples of software risks for each of the different management strategies.

Discussion
Risk avoidance – if outsourcing is seen as a loss of control and autonomy, this risk can be avoided by developing and evolving the software in house. Risk avoidance is the safest but is not always available as a feasible option.

Risk reduction – increasing the motivation of the personnel is likely to reduce the risk of high personnel turnover.

Risk retention – accepting that the estimates are over-optimistic and uncertain and doing nothing to obtain more precise estimates.

Risk transfer – this can be achieved through taking out insurance or by inclusion of contractual clauses which pass certain costs to the other party. For example, time-and-materials contracts which remunerate according to amount of effort and the transfer the project risks to the client. This is in contrast to fixed-price contracts in which an increase in actual effort spent may not be considered in the amount being paid.

Many other examples for each category are possible.

Risk management is one of the responsibilities of software enterprise managers. Ideally, all those involved with software will share part of the responsibility of risk management by looking at what they and others do, at their surroundings, and by sharing information quickly and accurately about any risk. This state of awareness and communication should be one of the elements of a **safety culture**.

13.5 Risk identification

We distinguish between risks which are common to all software-related activities and those which emerge when particular sources of software are used. This section starts with a reference to the common ones and ends covering some of the risks associated with the sources of software which we discussed in Chapter 6.

13.5.1 Common software-related risks

We saw in the first part of this book that software development and evolution take place in a rich human and social context. Many risks are related to the nature of software and its relationship to its context. There are several sources of uncertainty that can be managed but never completely removed:

Source 1:   This is related to our limited knowledge about the context, the domain and environment in which the software enterprise operates and where its software products are installed and executed. Part I of this book presented some of the challenges emerging from the rich and complex contexts for software and for the software enterprise. From that discussion it became clear that the context within which the enterprise operates is rich and dynamic and that we find it difficult to reduce it to a simple description.

Source 2:   This is related to Lehman's principle of software uncertainty, discussed saw in Chapter 9, which states that it is not possible to guarantee absolutely the successful execution of the software in a real-word domain, no matter how many times the software has successfully been executed in the past. The reason for this statement lies in the inevitability of assumptions which are reflected in the code and other software artefacts. The case of the software error that triggered the Ariane 501 disaster, referred to above, and the case of the CERN accelerator software, mentioned in Chapter 9, illustrate the possible impact of invalid assumptions. The environment is fundamentally unknowable and impossible to document, so any documentation is necessarily partial. This leads to assumptions, and the descriptions and assumptions may even be wrong, others may become wrong as the environment changes.

Source 3:   This relates to the difficulty of anticipating all changes in requirements. Software requirements evolve and such evolution is, generally, impossible to predict in full accuracy.

Risk management tackles risks before or after they materialise, by avoidance, reduction, retention, or transfer.

Source 4:   This involves scoping, estimation, planning, and scheduling. All these activities involve uncertainty. Over-optimistic estimates and plans are particular sources of uncertainty.

Source 5:   A fifth source is determined by human involvement in software related activities at all levels and by the nature of human action and decision. This common wisdom is captured by the phrase 'To err is human.'

There are areas of risks common to all software-related activity. These risks are related to the nature of software and its relationship to its context.

In principle, any of these risk sources can lead or be associated to technical, project, and organisational risks. These five sources are related. Limited knowledge forces software managers, developers, and all those involved to make explicit or implicit assumptions about the users, the domain, the requirements, the machine, and all the elements involved. Some of these assumptions may be invalid or some may become invalid as a consequence of changes in the domain. New requirements may be triggered by the realisation that assumptions have become invalid.

13.5.2 Risks related to specific software sources

In Chapter 6 we discussed different software sources including comments on their possible advantages and disadvantages. Chapter 6 is now helpful in determining specific risks associated to each of the acquisition modalities. Some of these specific risks are presented in the activities below.

Activity 13.4   *Software acquisition risks*

Skim through Chapter 6, to identify specific risks that are likely to be associated with specific software sources. List at least one specific risk for each form of software acquisition described in Chapter 6.

Discussion

- Wrapping of legacy software: wrapping software may not be able to address all the technical issues.
- Component-based approaches: errors in documentation of components; high defect rate in components.
- Use of open source software: lack of single source for support during installation and maintenance.
- Outsourcing of software development: loss of control of the evolution of the software; contractor may not have incentives to maintain the quality of the application.
- Offshoring of software development: misunderstandings and cultural issues.
- Acquisition of software as a service: possible loss of data; lack of control of the performance or level of service.

This is a partial list. Other risks can be identified or inferred from Chapter 6 and from the background knowledge of the reader.

Activity 13.5   *Risks and proprietary software*

Visit the websites of large software organisations such as Microsoft, Oracle, SAP, and Adobe. Search for the term 'risk' or browse the pages seeking to identify risk-related items. Do the suppliers alert the users of any risks in using their products? Do they publish any data regarding defect density, for example? Are there any common risk-related themes when you compare the different websites?

Discussion

One of the risk-related aspects which is frequently mentioned is the issue of security and the threat of software viruses. Another one is the phasing out of old releases, by which users may be literally forced to adopt new versions of the software if they are to continue receiving support from the developer (i.e., planned obsolescence). Little or nothing is known about the risk management processes followed by the large software developers.

Activity 13.6   *Open source risks*

Visit a website or mailing list where free/open source developers share their experiences and proposals regarding the evolution of a popular free/open source software such as the web browser Mozilla or the Linux operating system. Look for instances of risk management. Compare and contrast what you have found here with what is normally given in websites for commercial software (see previous exercise).

Discussion

In general, discussions in open source bulletin boards and mailing lists expose all the known technological vulnerabilities. There is, however, no separate function of 'risk-management' as part of the open source software development process. The 'risk management' concern is embedded into the wider discussion about the requirements that should be implemented first, defects that need to be fixed.

Activity 13.7   *Practical risk identification*

You are being interviewed for the post of manager of a project which has the following planning documents: a list of requirements, a work-breakdown structure, a Gantt chart indicating the major deliveries, a set of estimates at the macro (full project) and at the micro (individual activity) level, and an architectural diagram showing the distributions of responsibilities for the development of the individual components. The interview panel asks you to explain what you would be looking at when inspecting each of these documents in search for possible risks.

Discussion

Some guidelines:

- Look for critical path activities and for activities whose resources or time are likely to have been underestimated, such as component and integration testing.

There are specific
risks which are
likely to affect
different modalities
of software
acquisition and use.

- Examine, if the process model is waterfall, whether it is likely to be inappropriate due to the nature of the application or problem.
- Ask how estimates have been obtained.
- Look for evidence of validation of the requirements.
- Look for any elements of radical design at the macro (e.g., architectural) or micro (e.g., functional) levels of the system.

13.6 Risk mitigation

Many of the recommended practices by software engineering experts that we have mentioned in this book – Boehm, Brooks, DeMarco, Gilb, Humphreys, Lehman, and Parnas – can be rationalised as guidelines for risk reduction in the software process. For example, when Brooks says that 'adding people to a late project makes it later' he is, essentially, telling us that there is a risk of not meeting the scheduled delivery date if one chooses the strategy of adding people instead of removing unnecessary functionality from the scope. Lehman's emphasis on the need for recording and management of assumptions (Chapter 9) can also be seen as a risk reduction approach. Formal methods are particularly useful in safety critical systems, stressing, however, that the safety of these system should be addressed at the 'system level' (that is, humans + hardware + software) and not only at the software level. Regression testing and other types of testing can be seen as risk reduction activities, together with daily builds and the 'eat your own food' approach – essentially using your own developed software, so that you will be amongst the first to detect a problem. Process simulation models can be used to identify certain types of risk, but only a few software organisations can afford the expertise and effort required. In fact, risk management is not 'gratis'. The cost of developing software for safety-critical systems is believed to be ten times or so of that of developing non-critical software. Whilst in some domains certain practices are mandated by standards and the law, in other domains managers and developers can use their discretion in selecting the level and type of risk reduction they will apply.

13.6.1 Industry-specific risk management

There are certain 'critical' domains which have evolved sets of practices and standards. The actual demonstration that all risks have been reduced to a level 'as low as reasonably practicable' (ALARP) may change from domain to domain. For example, the safety-case approach is followed for validation and certification of software in aviation, nuclear industry, chemical industry, and medical devices. Leveson's book includes in the appendices a description of some of these industry-specific approaches.

Software is everywhere nowadays, including the plant floor, embedded in machines and running control centre consoles. This can make software developers liable in case of accident which is caused by software failure. In every situation, the software organisation should seek legal advice. For example, in the UK, there is legislation which may form part of the 'context' of safety-critical applications and developers must know about them. This legislation may be particularly relevant for applications in industrial facilities in which hazardous substances and processes are handled: the UK Health and Safety at Work Act 1974, Control of Substances Hazardous to Health (COSHH) Regulations 1988, Management of Health and Safety at Work Regulations 1992, and the Control of Major Accident Hazards Regulations 1984. Other countries may have comparable legal instruments.

Activity 13.8   *Mitigating the risk of high staff turnover*

Assume that you have been appointed manager and need to deal with the risk of high staff turnover. What are the implications of this risk of high staff turnover for the way projects and the organisation are managed? When possible, make reference to human and social factors described in Chapters 3 and 10 of this book.

Discussion

In Chapter 3 we saw that higher financial reward covers basic needs and is a 'hygienic factor'. People have high-order needs, such as respect, esteem, belonging to a community of practice, and self-transcendence. In Chapter 10 we saw that the needs and the relative importance that people place on status and office space differently as they become older. Some professionals will value a motivating and challenging job more than the quality of the office space. All these suggest that risk reduction strategies need to address both hygienic and high-order needs of personnel, with the latter dominanting.

Activity 13.9   *Managing risks in software development*

Suppose that you are the manager of a software organisation that has been subcontracted to develop a new air traffic control system. Your organisation has been basing its work on the specification and interface description of a radar system provided by another subcontractor. Identify one possible technical risk which may apply to this situation and how it could be tackled.

Discussion

One possible risk is misunderstanding the documentation and communications issued by the other subcontractor. As a manager you should take action to ensure that the documentation is validated and that your team has all the information needed. You also need to check that the contract indicates how to handle the situation in case errors in the documentation are located. For example, formalisation of the radar system – using some appropriate tool - may help to identify ambiguities and errors.

Risk management may involve trade-offs and balancing between alternatives. For success, decision-makers must continually use their judgement and expertise.

If you work in a specific safety-critical domain (e.g., medical, airspace and naval, nuclear, or oil and chemical plants) you need to know the industry-specific approach to safety, including standards, conformance criteria, and the regulatory and certification bodies.

Activity 13.10   *Managing risks in software maintenance*

Suppose that you are appointed manager of software maintenance in a medium-sized software enterprise that has undergone cost-cuting and personnel reduction. When taking the job, before being briefed by your new team, you decide to review the literature in search of standard approaches to risk management during software maintenance. Using your information retrieval skills – or with the help of your library – find a paper reporting on a case or a similar study which is relevant to your current situation. Read the paper and provide a summary of the main points made in the paper. Outline the approach to risk management that the authors have followed. Based on your experience, provide a critical analysis of this paper: which parts do you agree with and which points would you question?

Discussion
A possible answer is presented in Case Study 13.4.

Maintenance and evolution differ from development in terms of the specific challenges for institutionalising a risk management process.

Case Study 13.4 *Managing risk in software maintenance*

The paper entitled 'Managing Risk in Software Maintenance', by R. Charette, K. Adams, and M. White, in *IEEE Software*, May/June 1997, pp. 43–50, reports on a business re-engineering effort, started in 1994, within the US Navy Maintenance Support Office. The authors worked to provided a formal risk management process, which was to be part of a new project management plan. The approach is based of the following seven steps: identify, estimate, evaluate, plan, obtain resources, control, and monitor. For the identification step they used the Software Engineering Institute risk taxonomy. A risk baseline was created at the beginning of a project which was selected as a pilot. During the life of the project, 168 risks were identified. Based on consensus, the severity of the risks was rated and the risks were ranked. Requirements-related risks were the most frequent. Mitigation plans were designed for the five top risks only because of lack of resources for more. (The authors recognised

that this was itself a risky strategy.) Risks were re-assessed every six to eight weeks, along with major project milestones. Risk reviews were performed weekly. The successful pilot was followed by efforts to institutionalise risk management across the organisation. This involved what the authors called a cultural assessment, success benchmark definition and the tailoring of the process used in the pilot. The cultural assessment indicated that NMSO's knowledge of risk management was rudimentary. Risk wasn't a term that appeared frequently in meetings or communications. After identifying root causes in the maintenance process, the risk management was tailored: it was made more user-centric and involved the NMSO Change Control Board. Risk assessment involved considering impact of actions or inaction in the next release, and a release profile for each release was created. A training program was put together to support the risk management process. A survey is periodically conducted to get the opinion of the developers and other participants about the effectiveness of the risk management process. At the moment of writing, the institutionalisation of risk management was still in its early stages.

The Main points are:

- The paper reports on the experience of institutionalising risk management in a large US Navy software organisation.

- Common risks for maintenance and development are requirements volatility, staff inexperience, and tight time constraints.

- The authors observe that risk management in maintenance differs from that in development because there is a higher diversity of risk sources, risk opportunities are more frequent, and projects have less freedom (i.e., projects are constrained by the existing set of users, the application, the code).

- One important risk in maintenance: possible deadly side-effects of changing code which is poorly documented, complex and which has interfaces to a '...myriad of systems that the developers never even conceived of'.

- Attention to users who already depend on the system is important.

- All developers participated in risk management.

- The standard process enabled the team to communicate risks to upper management without feeling at risk and without the need to blame.

- The maintenance organisation is not monolithic, hence the difficulty in institutionalising the risk management effort.

- The study found that the root causes of maintenance risk were lack of control, lack of information, and lack of time.

- 'Lack of control' in maintenance occured because the process was driven externally by user requests.

- The year 2000 issue was another symptom of lack of control.

Adapted from R. Charette, K. Adams and M. white (1997) 'Managing Risk is Software Maintenance', *IEEE Software*, May/June, 43–50.

Summing up

This chapter has given you some concepts which can be useful when dealing with the wide topic of uncertainty and risk in software and software-related activities. These are the main points that have been made in the chapter:

- risks are inevitable for the software enterprise; they can be classified as business, project, and technical risks, and some risks belong to more than one category;

- software development is inevitably risky, and more risky if the development is radical and innovative or if you have not done it before;

- 'most accidents are not the result of unknown scientific principles but rather a failure to apply well-known standard engineering practices' (Nancy Leveson, http://sunnyday.mit.edu/book.html);

- in safety-critical applications, make sure that those executing the project are the most qualified for the job and apply state-of-the-art techniques; they must be familiar with the scientific principles of the domain and also know well the standard engineering practice;

- in well-understood technological domains, risk can be assessed and quantified in a detailed way;
- 'accidents will not be prevented by technological fixes alone, but will require control of all aspects of the development and operation of the system' (Nancy Leveson, http://sunnyday.mit.edu/book.html);
- there are multiple sources of risk in software, which tend to be difficult to assess and quantify;
- there are areas of risks common to all software-related activity; these risks are related to the nature of software and its relationship to its context;
- there are specific risks which are likely to affect different modalities of software acquisition and use;
- risk identification, prioritisation, and handling must be performed continually; lists of prioritised risks and the actions to tackle them must be reviewed periodically, particularly during project meetings;
- risk management is the tackling of risks before or after they materialise; there are four main approaches to tackling risks: avoidance, reduction, retention, and transfer;
- risk management may involve trade-offs and balancing between alternatives; for success, decision-makers must continually use their judgement and expertise;
- there are established approaches to tackle well-known, recurrent risks in software engineering activities through the recommendations of software engineering experts;
- if you work in specific safety-critical domains (e.g., medical, airspace and naval, nuclear, or oil and chemical plants) you need to know the industry-specific approach to safety, including standards, conformance criteria, and the regulatory and certification bodies;
- maintenance and evolution differ from development in terms of the specific challenges for institutionalising a risk management process.

Exercises

1. Discuss the statement 'risks are part of doing business' from the point of view of ethics and professionalism. Do you think that it is justified to take risks, provided that the outcome leads to profit? In your discussion use some of the concepts you encountered in Chapters 3 and 4 of this book.

2. Radical design addresses problems that have not been solved before. Review the concept of double-loop learning discussed in Chapter 2 (Figure 2.12). Indicate whether such a concept can help minimising risk during radical design, and how.

3. A software-development company specialising in safety-critical systems, wishes to reduce the risk of 'failure during operation' of any of the software in their portfolio of application by fifty per cent. Advise this company on how they should proceed and what they should do in order to attain such a goal.

4. In Chapter 1 you saw the analogy we made between building architecture and software with regards to the crisis of modernism and the limits of rationality. The design of bridges seems to be mainly driven by advances in science and technology, which are 'less social' forces than those driving building architecture. Use the concepts of 'fixed' and 'variable' software to extend the analogy of software to both building architecture and bridge design.

5. A colleague of yours is running a small software company. She has heard of your interest in software management and has asked you how she should proceed in order to introduce risk management in her company. Give her advice, justifying this advice.

6. Choose a safety-critical domain, for example the manufacture of devices for chemical plants, and find out about the industry-specific approach to safety. You may start by looking at the guidelines given by the relevant international and national regulatory and standards organisations.

7. Search for articles which propose techniques and methods for risks management in software organisations. You might consider starting with the following paper: B. Boehm (1991) 'Software Risk Management: Principles and Practices', *IEEE Software*, January, pp. 32–41. This is available via links at: http://sunset.usc.edu/classes/cs510_2003/notes/risk.pdf.

8. Find out about software hazard analysis and apply it to a software system or a critical component that you are working with.

9. Write a short essay discussing how the principles of software risk management relate to quality management. Write not more than 700 words.

10. Should all safety-critical software controlling potentially dangerous systems and critical processes (e.g., chemical plants, ambulance service) one day be made open and available to the public for scrutiny? Justify your answer in no more than 500 words.

11. Develop summary risk management plans for the library system described in Chapter 7.

Endnotes

1. This is what Barry Boehm (*Software Engineering Economics*, Prentice-Hall, 1981) refers to as 'price to win' estimation. We have already referred to 'price to win' in Chapter 10. There are at least two possibilities here. One is that the estimator is biased by the desire to win the contract and unconsciously underestimates the work. The other possibility is that the organisation consciously decides to offer a price which is lower than the cost in the hope of recovering the difference somehow in the future or because intangible gains (e.g., increased business reputation because of being awarded a contract).

2. See http://www.ketchum.org/tacomacollapse.html.

3. For further examples, see W. Wayt Gibbs (1994) 'Software's Chronic Crisis', *Scientific American*, Sept, p. 86. Also available as a web version at: http://www.cis.gsu.edu/~mmoore/CIS3300/handouts/SciAmSept1994.html.

4. See http://sunnyday.mit.edu/book.html.

5. See   http://www.esa.int/esa-mmg/mmg.pl?b=b&keyword=ariane%20501&start=1.   Reproduced with kind permission from the ESA/CNES.

6. B. Boehm (1991) 'Software Risk Management: Principles and Practices', *IEEE Software*, January, 32–41. Available via links at: http://sunset.usc.edu/classes/cs510_2003/notes/risk.pdf.

14 The way forward

What we will study in this chapter

We now pull together the various threads of this book, viewing the material from different perspectives to see how the parts fit together and point a way forward. We start by summarising the problems that the software industry has faced, that change is inevitable, before looking at the failure of managerialist responses of ever tighter control. Instead we see the solution in a partnership between people and software technology, as software technology becomes ever more pervasive. We cannot control this movement, but we can accept and guide it.

14.1 Beginning with problems

Computers, and the software that makes them useful and effective, have become central to our society and our own lives. This has happened over the past half century, since the computers that were developed in the 1939–1945 Second World War[1] were moved from scientific calculation and other military purposes into supporting administration and business, and so into their widespread use today.

In the beginning the focus was on automating clerical processes, looking for savings through labour displacement and reduced storage costs for data. Software was developed by examining those clerical processes and through that determining what the computer system should do, what its requirements were. We saw an illustration of this in Chapter 7, where we walked through the development of a school library system to identify all the activities that are undertaken in developing software systems. This simple sequential process worked in the 1950s and 1960s, and still works today for some simple systems. In Chapter 7 we identified the work-products that were delivered by each activity, and looked at examples of the notations used.

If we were developing such a simple system today we wouldn't really need to make these activities so explicit or produce those intermediate abstractions – we could hold the design simply in our heads, as a tacit agreement among those developing the system, and express the solution directly in the finished product of interconnected hardware devices and software written in some high-level 'self-documenting' programming language. But back in the 1950s when we were still finding out how to do these things we might well have sketched pictures of our intended solution before we built the hardware specifically to meet our purpose, using some low-level assembly language to program the computer.

Thus one characteristic of developments since the 1950s has been the solution of ever larger and more complex problems, aided by higher level languages and standardised hardware. However, these advances were not sufficient.

An early recognition of difficulties that could be encountered with software was documented in meetings in the late 1960s, such as the much celebrated NATO-sponsored conferences on software engineering in Garmisch, Germany, in 1968 and 1969. And it was found in reports from IBM of the difficulties they were having with their major operating systems. We saw some of the analyses of these difficulties in Chapter 9, which became embodied in 'Lehman's laws'. But the major impact came with Fred Brooks' book *The Mythical Man-Month*,[2] first published in 1975, and described below in Case study 14.1. His book struck an immediate chord with software developers and managers around the world. These software engineers were also having problems, and now that they knew that the largest software company in the world at that time was also having problems, they had a problem shared. But in this case a problem shared was not a problem halved. Even today the book finds resonances with newer generations of software engineers and software managers: the problems are perennial.

Case Study 14.1 *The Mythical Man-Month*

In the mid 1970s, Fred Brooks wrote a book called *The Mythical Man-Month*, which discussed a number of software development issues from the point of view of a battle-scarred project manager. Fred Brooks had managed the development of the major IBM operating systems during the 1960s, involving at its peak over 1,000 software designers and programmers and other staff, about 5,000 person-years from 1963 through to 1966. This book is a classic and is regarded by many as essential reading for any would-be project manager, even today thirty years later. The primary thesis of the book is that 'persons' and 'months' are not interchangeable, hence the title of the book: if one person takes two months to complete a task, it does not follow that two people will only take one month to complete the same task. Two people are likely to take significantly longer than a single month. Putting more people onto a software project requires more training and more communication with other people. Even if the developers are experienced, they must still get to know the new problem they are working on and learn to work within the project's organisation. Adding an extra person to a team increases the number of communication paths; there is one communication path between two people, there are three communication paths between three people, six between four people, ten between five people, and so on.

Hence the much quoted saying from the book, 'adding people to a late project just makes it later', now viewed as an immutable law of software development, 'Brooks' law'. Brooks describes many other problems associated with software development, such as the uncertainties in the process causing him to suggest 'build one to throw away'. When first published in 1975, this book gave voice to the growing realisation in the software industry of just how complex the software development process is. Developing software is not easy. It needs good management, and that management is not easy either.

14.2 Change is inevitable

More or less at the same time that Fred Brooks was writing *The Mythical Man-Month*, another analysis of the software problem emerged from observations of the long-term evolutionary behaviour of the IBM OS 360 and other systems. Lehman and Belady's 1985 book[3] includes papers which summarise the research findings in IBM OS 360 and other systems in the 1980s.

Case Study 14.2 *The evolving nature of 'variable' software*

If Fred Brooks focussed on the problems of development from the inside, Lehman and Belady took an external view and look at the 'system' formed by developers, managers and the software being evolved. In 1972, when commenting on a plot of the growth – measured in total number of instructions – of the IBM OS 360 over releases, they wrote:[4]

> *It displays clearly the linear growth of the system. In the present paper we shall not analyse the deviations from linearity, except to observe that the ripples on the data are typical of a self-stabilising process with both positive and negative feedback loops. That is, from a large-range point of view the rate of system growth is self-regulatory, despite the fact that many different causes control the selection of work implemented in each release, with varying budgets, increasing number of users desiring new functions or reporting faults, varying management attitudes towards system enhancement, changing release intervals and improving methodology. (p. 123)*

From Belady and Lehman's studies, the concept of 'software growth dynamics' and later, the concept

of 'feedback-driven software evolution' emerged. These concepts were not accepted as rapidly as Brooks', and it took several decades for these ideas to be taken in, but nowadays the problem of software evolution is well understood, though not so its solutions. Some, like Harry Sneed, have observed that Agile methods are a response to the problems identified by Lehman and Belady in the 1970s and 80s.

In Chapter 9 we saw how 'variable' software is the predominant type in the vast majority of infrastructure and application software. This type of software is destined from birth 'to change'. We also saw how the need for evolution of the software can be explained by the observation that 'variable' software models the real world but necessarily in a limited way. The software is limited and the domain isn't, so there is always a gap. This gap cannot be closed, but can be kept 'more or less' under control through feedback from the operational domain – of course at a cost.

The norm in software development is now evolution, not green-field development, and this is where the majority of the resources in software organisations will be spent.

In Chapter 9 we saw Lehman's laws and how they imply that the individual developer has limited ability to control the evolution of the system. Evolution becomes routine maintenance until the unexpected happens: observations show that the evolution of software is discontinuous and punctuated, no matter what amount of foresight is applied at the beginning. This contradicts management assumptions of regularity and stability (i.e., stable growth) which are usual management objectives. The empirical study of the evolution of software systems may help us understand the laws and other forces which govern the evolution of software as well as other complex artefacts built by humans.

14.3 The controlling response

What do many managers do when the enterprise they are managing does not deliver as intended? They introduce more controls, more discipline. And that is what the software industry and its pundits did.

Software development methodologies were introduced with very detailed procedures intended to cover all contingencies. We saw a flavour these in Chapter 8, though the only way to really appreciate these is to look at the metres of manuals and to work within a team enacting the mandated process.

Some of these methodologies were essentially sequential, the original way of developing software scaled up enormously. But things don't necessarily scale up; as can be illustrated with bridges. To bridge a small gap carrying people on foot a simple plank may suffice, but for large gaps carrying heavy transport the plank would break, and complex struts and cables are required. We saw that sequential methods break is at uncertainties, particularly with requirements, when we encountered two problems with large and complex systems, which:

- take a long time to develop, and what is needed or perceived as being needed may have changed by the time the system is ready for use;
- have requirements that are impossible to write down precisely.

Both these were noted as attributes of modern life in Chapter 1. The world is changing with increasing rapidity, and there are limits to rationality and our ability to reduce the world to formal descriptions through which we can control it.

We saw in Chapter 8 that both of these concerns can be counteracted with iterative and participative approaches. Iterative approaches enable us move in small steps towards an understanding and agreement about what is really needed, with the gap between final agreement and final delivery of the system being very short. If the iteration is in terms of an evolving prototype, the agreement will have been in terms of what the users see. Participation takes this further, with users drawing upon their tacit knowledge of what would work to guide the development in all its facets. By involving the stakeholders we are able to focus on 'good enough' solutions that will do, guided by that old observation that 'the best is the enemy of the good'.

In Chapters 10, 11, and 12 we saw other aspects of the use of controls to overcome problems. Chapter 10 included methods for more accurately forecasting costs and timescales, and the way these can be used to monitor and control software development. In Chapter 11 we saw methods for controlling the many thousands of individual components being produced and updated, controls that are essential if we are to avoid chaos and be able to build and deliver large working systems. In Chapter 12 we focussed on quality and how it can be managed, building quality into the product, so that 'quality is free'. While these controls were initially a response to the difficulties of software development, perhaps even a turn to heavy management, they remain equally relevant today as management becomes lighter.

In 1986, just over ten years after his *Mythical Man-Month*, Fred Brooks wrote a paper, published at a conference and then in a journal, entitled 'No Silver Bullet',[5] in which he postulated that

There is no single development, in either technology or management technique, which by itself promises even one order-of-magnitude improvement within a decade in productivity, in reliability, in simplicity.

If Brooks sees salvation anywhere, it is in 'great designers'. We agree, but much more broadly. The missing ingredient in these responses of turning to managerial controls has been the human element. Yes, it was there in participative development, but that focussed on but a small part of the overall process.

14.4 Value from the human component

In Chapters 2 and 3 we argued strongly for the important role of humans in all enterprises. We looked at learning organisations populated by learning people, together able to respond to their external changing world. We looked at human motivation and how important the opportunity to learn was for motivation.

And yet it has taken two generations of software engineers for us to learn that people matter, that they are the secret ingredient that makes success. We have known for a very long time now that some software developers are more productive than others, by factors of ten or more. We have tried on the one hand to remove these differences by routinising everything in the many methodologies discussed above (reducing everything to the lowest common denominator, some might argue). On the other hand, most projects do organise themselves so that people with ability and experience take leading roles, as system architects, design authorities, and team leaders. One particular project organisation, not covered in Chapter 8, was the Chief Programmer team investigated by Harlan Mills[6] in which one lead person, the chief programmer, was supported by a team aimed at facilitating his/her productivity. Mills' report was very favourable and encouraged others to try it out for themselves, but now, twenty years later, chief programmer teams are but a fading memory. Chief programmer teams just did not scale up for larger systems.

What can unlock the potential of those most able software engineers?

That amusing aphorism 'if you pay people peanuts, what you get is monkeys' just is not right. We saw in Chapter 3 that you must be 'hygienic' with respect to pay, sufficient to avoid personal money worries, but thereafter it is 'growth need' and 'social-need' that motivate. And it is being cared for and trusted, as seen in the Hawthorn effect, and it is the removal of unnecessary management. Many fine books about the human side of software development attest to this, for example Fred Brooks' *Mythical Man-Month*, Tom DeMarco and Tim Lister's *Peopleware*,[7] and Watts Humphrey's *Managing Technical People*.[8]

Is this the secret of the success of Agile and Open Source methods we saw at the end of Chapter 8? These approaches grew out of the excitement of creating software in the laboratories of universities and the small enterprises of mythical garages. Open Source methods, particularly where the contribution is completely voluntary, removes all trace of coercive management, though it retains enough control over the ultimate product to assure quality and provide the motivation of acceptance of work by peers and acknowledged experts. We have yet to see how Agile methods evolve and take root; they too focus on product but at the moment they seem too constrained by ritual and approved practice. Both Open Source and Agile methods help liberate the individual programmer's potential.

It is not just on the software engineering side of enterprises that the human element is an ingredient for success. People are more flexible than software. If the software does not do what is needed they can work around this, being inventive and creative in their own parts of the business process. There is a balance between what people do and what software does, a balance that we have picked up repeatedly throughout this book.

14.5 Build on top of past great products

If what you need, or something very like it, already exists, why build it again? Why not just get hold of that software, adapt it in small ways to your needs if that is really necessary, and off you go. That is what we explored in Chapter 6, and what Fred Brooks endorsed in his response to Brad Cox's 'There is a Silver Bullet'.[9] After over fifty years of vibrant industry there is a great volume of software in existence that can be drawn upon.

We always use ready-made software, in the operating systems and office software on our PCs, in the communications software that drives the Internet. We saw that when faced with a need to evolve our enterprise we can:

- make the most of what software we already have, wrapping this legacy in a thin layer of software so that it will integrate with the new software we added;
- obtain software off the shelf, either from proprietary sources, COTS, or in open source as a public good;
- use remote services to execute specialist functions which we don't need in house;
- then integrate these to make larger systems to support our total enterprise.

It is only if these routes fail that we become involved in developing new software. We might do this in house within our own organisation or outsource this development to some specialist company. We might even offshore this work to the area of the world which specialises in this. We might offshore for the more dubious reasons of cutting cost by exploiting cheap labour, but even this has a positive side of developing emergent industries and helping nations develop.

In developing new software we can still build upon past experience, by using design patterns and frameworks to guide software construction, and by acquiring software components. We saw this in Chapter 8, where we also saw the way similar systems could be repeated by building them within product lines.

Much software production is no longer about programming new software, but about integrating existing software so that it does useful work for us.

14.6 Pervasiveness, mobility, and nomadic IT

Whilst we ponder theoretical concepts, the world moves on. In Chapter 13 we discussed the issues of uncertainty and risk, which permeate software and software-related work. At the technical level, we cannot absolutely guarantee that our programs will work as expected, no matter what the level of testing or the use of formal proofs. At the enterprise level, with the exception of a few organisations, the standards of estimation, planning, and achieving budget/schedule/quality targets are appalling, with the consequence that we cannot know whether the software will be released on time. At the society and economy levels, software still raises many issues which have not been fully understood or conceptualised, for example the debate about intellectual property described in Chapter 5, which probably has more to do with maintaining the economic supremacy of some nations than the protection of creative work. Despite all of this, software is making its way deeper into the fabric of society and human activity at all levels. An example of this, the Internet, was a visionary dream a few years ago. Messerschmidt and Szyperski[10] describe this new world of pervasive computing, mobility and so-called nomadic IT with this example:

> The ideal home security system should automatically close the drapes and turn out the lights when you watch a movie on your home theatre, and the toaster should disable the smoke alarm while it is operating. The microwave oven should shut down while the cordless phone is in use to avoid interference. The stop sign and traffic lights at intersections should be eliminated, replaced by signals or automatic braking mechanisms within each automobile so that actions can be based entirely on the presence of conflicting traffic. The automobile horn (another car's initiating an alert) should be replaced by a signal in the car being alerted. (Of course, these ideas ignore the reality of pedestrians, bicycles, and so on.) (p. 356).

Perhaps this future is not so far away. In such a future, instead of huge software applications built in a disciplined top-down fashion, software will be distributed in appliances and devices which will interact transparently in a wireless environment and from which, hopefully, useful behaviour will emerge from which humans will benefit. The Internet does not support this nomadic and mobile usage of software and major technological advances are still needed. How will the software industry react to these challenges? Who will be the winners and the losers?

Paul Ceruzzi[11] observes that the history of computing is influenced not only by technological developments, but also by political and social forces (p. 349). He comments that each new development in computing is put forward by individuals who wish to redress imbalances of the past – just consider here the move towards object orientation in the 1990s. However, technology (also processes, methods, tools) moves faster than the ability of the organisation and society to cope with the all the consequences. We are, for example, still trying to address problems of Internet content and email spam. Each wave of technology, process and methods, and tools brings its new set of challenges and unanswered questions, with many of the fundamental questions still unanswered. At the end of his book, Ceruzzi ponders whether we are actually in control of computing or computing is, in fact, shaping society and becoming the 'master'(p. 350). This is another philosophical question that software managers should keep at the back of their minds when making decisions or simply reacting 'to follow the flow'.

14.7 Going with the flow

We ended Chapter 1 by posing the paradoxical question:

> How can we use rational precise and certain software applications and management methods to control and guide an organisation operating in an uncertain and unpredictable and changing world?

The recognition in Chapter 1 that the world is changing fast, that returns on investment were difficult to demonstrate, that the world is too complex for us to plan its future in every detail was not a counsel of despair; it was not a call for us to stop attempting to control and guide our future through software. Rather, it was a call to recognise the nature of our enterprises as a blend of people and software together enacting the business processes of our enterprise. We need to recognise the relative strengths and limitations of these two components. People may appear to be rigid but they are flexible and adaptive, the creative source of enterprises. Software may appear to be flexible, but it is inflexible, rigidly bound to other software in configurations in which if one part shifts the whole falls apart.

The central part of this book, Part II, has shown how we can create software that is appropriate for organisations and draws upon the creative strength of its developers. But we also saw that these methods still need to develop and mature. In Part III we saw how this software creation process can be managed and guided so that we do get predictable results. But we must beware of over-managing, and still have much to learn. And in Part I we saw that the way we produce and use software is but part of larger movement in society over which we have no control and within which we must fit. We must understand these wider social and political and cultural movements, lest we find that we are trying to move software use and production against this flow. Only by going with the flow will we succeed.

Endnotes

1. This is a very Euro-centric view of this tragic upheaval. In the US, Russia, and Japan the dates are different since they entered and left the war at different times, and give the conflict different titles too. Cultural relativism has been one of our themes.
2. Frederick P. Brooks Jr (1975) *The Mythical Man-Month: Essays on Software Engineering*. Addison-Wesley. A new edition was published in 1995 with four new chapters. The original book and the four new chapters are all well worth reading.
3. M.M. Lehman and L.A. Belady (eds) (1985) *Software Evolution – Processes of Software Change*. Academic Press. This book is out of print but will be soon available in digital form on the Internet. A search using the title should find it!
4. L.A. Belady and M.M. Lehman (1972) An Introduction to Program Growth Dynamics. In W. Freiburger (ed) *Statistical Computer Performance Evaluation*. Academic Press, pp. 503–511. Reprinted as Chapter 6 in M.M. Lehman and L.A. Belady, cited above.
5. Fred Brooks (1986) No Silver Bullet: Essence and Accident in Software Engineering. *Information Processing 1986*, H.-J. Kugler (ed.) Elsevier. pp. 1069–76.
6. Harlan D. Mills (1971) Chief programmer teams, principles, and procedures. *IBM Federal Systems Division Report* FSC 71-5108, Gaithersburg, Md. Also described in Fred Brooks' *Mythical Man-Month*, cited above.
7. Tom DeMarco and Timothy Lister (1987) *Peopleware: Productive Projects and Teams*. Dorset House.
8. Watts S. Humphrey (1997) *Managing Technical People*. Addison-Wesley.
9. Brad Cox was a pioneer of object-oriented methods and software components – the note to which Fred Brooks was responding was Brad Cox (1990) There is a Silver Bullet. *Byte*, pp. 209–218.
10. D.G. Messerschmitt and C. Szyperski (2003) *Software Ecosystem – Understanding an Indispensable Technology and Industry*. MIT Press. p. 363.
11. P.E. Ceruzzi (2003) *A History of Modern Computing* (2nd edn). MIT Press.

A Modelling notations

What we will study in this appendix

Diagrams are important as a means of modelling the parts of a system and their interaction abstractly. The system being modelled could be composed of people and/or software undertaking administrative and business tasks, or computing and communications hardware. This appendix describes two classical notations, data-flow diagrams and data-structure diagrams, which together enable us to model all the systems covered in this book.

A.1 Modelling with diagrams

It has become the standard practice in the development of complex systems to describe the system at a number of levels of abstraction using diagrams. We usually refer to the abstraction set out using diagrams as a **model** of the system. It represents the major elements that make up the system and the interactions between these elements. Typically there is an overall diagram together with a number of other diagrams that expand on the elements in the higher level diagram. These expansions may continue recursively[1] for many levels. Diagrams may also connect to other diagrams at the same level.

Since computers were first applied to administrative and business problems in the 1950s, a range of notations have been developed, extended, and replaced as software systems become ever more elaborate and complex. During the 1970s and 1980s a whole range of notations arose, some differing just in the shape of the boxes that were drawn, some being very complete in the range of software specification and design concerns they tackled, while other just focussed on the essentials. The notation that we will describe here is a composite of two of the earlier notations pioneered respectively by Tom De Marco and by Charlie Bachman, two of the great thinkers and innovators of computing. These notations just focus on the essential features of systems and their models, sufficient for most of our purposes here.

During the 1960s and 1970s practitioners thought about systems from two complimentary perspectives:

- the activities performed by the people and software and hardware of the system, with data or other things flowing between these;
- the data or information itself, what its elements are and how these are related.

Developments in the US were characterised by the focus on activities and the flows between them, **data-flow diagrams**; while in Europe they were characterised by a focus on data that was flowing and being stored, **data-structure diagrams**. However there was a lot of interchange of ideas between the communities, and notations of both type were developed and became established in practice in Europe, the US, and elsewhere. In sections A.2 and A.3 below we describe simple variants of both of these, while referring readers to more complex alternatives where these are accessible in books. Regrettably, many really insightful modelling methods were only ever captured in proprietary manuals and have now been lost.

These notations typically use a combination of circles and boxes interconnected by arrows. Thus sometimes these are referred to as arrow–box–circle or ABC diagrams. However, modelling ideas did not rest there, and from the 1980s onwards **object-oriented (OO)** methods began to be developed and then extended to become the foundation of full blown development methods like **UML**.[2] The idea here is that every thing or object in the model has the actions it can perform associated directly with it, and a system model consists of a number of objects and their interactions. The separate description of data and process (data flow) is seen as not necessary. However there are difficulties in applying these modelling approaches to anything other than software, a limitation that is so severe that these methods often end up ignoring the many wider issues that must be covered and which have been addressed in the main body of this book. For that reason we have not adopted object-oriented methods in this book, seeing these important methods as relevant primarily to software.

A.2 Data-flow modelling

The basic elements of a data-flow diagram (DFD) are shown in Figure A.1. All data-flow modelling methods have these basic elements; they differ only in the particular shapes and styles of the boxes and arrows used.

We divide up a system into processes, which are parts of the system performing functions and undertaking activities. These processes are represented by circles in our diagram, with the name of the process (or function or activity) written inside it. Sometimes these process 'bubbles' might be numbered to enable easy cross-reference to them.

These processes interact by sending data to each other, represented by an arrow connecting together the processes, with the arrow labelled by a name or description of the data flowing along it. These are called **data flows**. Sometimes we show the arrows converging, in which case the data flowing is combined, and sometimes we show the arrow splitting so that some of the data flows in one direction and other data flows in another direction. Sometimes we show the arrows as bidirectional to emphasise that the interaction goes in both directions.

Often we don't draw a separate environment (as seen in Chapter 1), but instead show elements of the environment as **terminators**, representing these as squares or rectangles in the diagram. We distinguish terminators where data originates and flows into our diagram as **sources**, and terminators where data flow ends up after flowing out of our diagram as **sinks**. This is particularly useful where we are using a DFD to describe a computer system interacting with people in its environment.

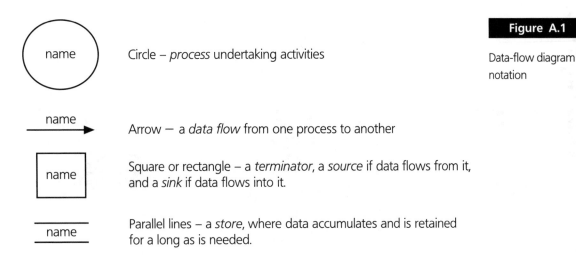

Circle – *process* undertaking activities

Arrow – a *data flow* from one process to another

Square or rectangle – a *terminator*, a *source* if data flows from it,
and a *sink* if data flows into it.

Parallel lines – a *store*, where data accumulates and is retained
for a long as is needed.

Organisations and systems frequently retain data for long periods, using this
data as the basis for further actions: we call these **stores**, or **data stores**, and represent these by a pair of parallel lines with the name of the store written between
them.

When drawing these diagrams we try to keep them simple, maybe no more
than ten process bubbles in a single diagram. If we want to give further detail, we
can then expand one or more processes into subdiagrams, and we see examples of
this throughout this book. Occasionally we expand a process *in situ*, but usually
only where we want to emphasise particular process decompositions.

Note that the notation above has conformed to the widespread convention of
using circles to represent processes, even though these can give difficulty when
placing text inside, or even placing other processes inside – in these cases rectangles would make much more sense, and have been used in many proprietary
notations and supporting software tools.

Data-flow diagrams can be too precise for some purposes, and in the approach
to understanding organisations and information systems known as soft systems
methodology,[3] the practice is to draw 'rich pictures', very informal cartoon-like
pictures that depict the situation being studied. Rich pictures are very powerful
devices for engaging non-technical people in meaningful discussions about technical systems.

We will now look inside an activity by looking at a simple example, the assembly of a toy, described in Case Study A.1.

Case Study A.1 *Assembly of a child's toy*

Figure A.2 shows the instruction leaflet for a simple LEGO® toy. Given a set of parts supplied, the
recipient assembles the toy following the very
clear instructions. The complete set of instructions

would start with selecting the part required, and then following the instructions in the sequence set out.

Note that the assembly of the figure and of the airplane can be done in either order or even concurrently by two separate children.

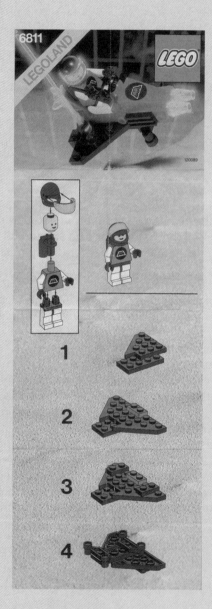

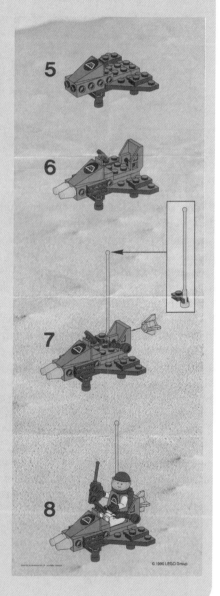

Figure A.2

Instructions for a LEGO toy. © 2007 The LEGO Group. LEGO is a trademark of the LEGO Group.

Such a sequence of activities are often represented as data-flow diagrams, and Activity A.1 challenges you to use the notation you saw earlier in Figure A.1. In this example the flows are actually of physical objects rather than of abstract data, but they do illustrate the use of our DFD notation very effectively.

Activity A.1   *Creating a data-flow diagram*

Produce a data-flow diagram for the assembly of the toy person and aircraft shown diagrammatically in Figure A.2.

Discussion

We will produce three DFDs to represent this, using a two-level hierachy of processes. The first DFD in Figure A.3 places the assembly process in the context of a parent giving the child the kit, and the child then assembling the kit and then playing with it. A diagram like Figure A.3 is usually known as a **context diagram**. It shows a single circle with the overall activity named within in, and on either side are the two participants or 'terminators' in the activity. The arrows show the flows between the participants and the activity – in this case the LEGO kit and its parts. Note that it is debatable whether the child should be shown as a terminator in the environment, as the parent is shown – the child is part of the process, the 'engine' which makes it happen.

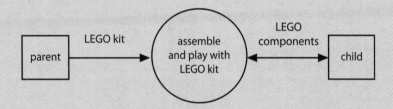

Figure A.3

Context diagram for playing with a LEGO kit

The central process must now be decomposed to show what happens in assembling the toy and then playing with it. This leads to the 'level 1' DFD in Figure A.4. We have assumed that not only does the child assemble and play with the toy, but also tidies it up at the end, placing it in the toy box depicted as a store.

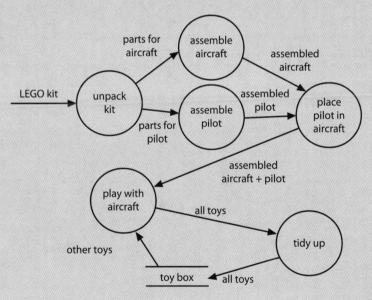

Figure A.4

The level 1 DFD for assembling and playing with the LEGO kit

This is about as large as we like DFDs to be. There is a lot on this diagram, including several uses of the notation that need discussion.

1. The relationship to the higher-level context diagram is maintained by the title 'assemble and play with LEGO kit' and by the data-flow 'LEGO kit' coming in from the left matching precisely the data flow on the context diagram. Note that the flow on the right of the context diagram has not been replicated, adding weight to the argument that the child should not have been represented there.

2. We have recognised that the assembly of the pilot and the aircraft can take place in either order or concurrently, though there is a small dependency not noted here – they both share the same set of pictorial instructions. Thus if we had two children with one working on the figure and one working on the airplane, they would both need to refer to the set of instructions of Figure A.2. The details of how to assemble the pilot and the aircraft are shown respectively in Figures A.5 and A.6.

3. An internal store has been identified, the toy box, from which other toys, presumably mostly LEGO sets, are taken, and to which everything is returned at tidy-up time.

4. We can assume that some of the processes are self-evident and need no further expansion, but we do need to expand the two assembly processes further as in Figure A.5 and A.6.

Figure A.5

The level 2 DFD for assembling the LEGO pilot

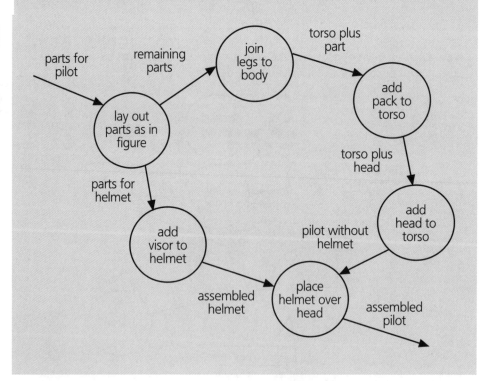

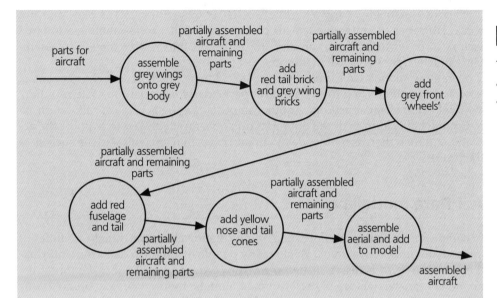

Figure A.6

The level 2 DFD for assembling the LEGO aircraft

Activity A.2 *The value of DFDs*

Just how useful do you think DFDs are for describing activities and processes? Relate your reflections to the LEGO set example, and any other examples you think appropriate.

Discussion

Clearly they do give us a basis for breaking down a complete process into smaller parts so as to understand it the better. At its simplest we saw this in the overview of a system interacting with its environment, but in the LEGO set example we saw a much more complex problem. The DFDs did help us to decompose the process into smaller and more understandable chunks.

However it is clear that DFDs can be taken too far, as was seen in the LEGO set example. The assembly of the pilot is understandable, referring to clearly recognisable parts and carrying out the assembly of the helmet in parallel to the assembly of the rest. However the assembly of the aircraft is pretty difficult to follow, and we would really be better off presenting this whole detail in text, or indeed using that pictorial diagram. This is one place where words cannot replace pictures.

Moreover the decomposition of processes in this way forces the separation of things which may not be beneficial. A couple of kids working on that LEGO kit model would not share the work as implied by the figure, one doing the pilot and one the aircraft; they would rather work much more fluidly together, maybe doing the assembly in some other order. Maybe they would just work from the pictures of the finally assembled kit, as one boy we know does.

Decomposing a process as in DFDs is reductionism, and our comments illustrate well why being reductive has its drawbacks.

Clearly, assembling a toy as in the LEGO set Case Study A.1 is play, and not work. However assembling a toy for play is very similar to assembling a toy in a factory in order to produce complete toys for sale, and is even similar to assembling much larger items like motor cars.

Data-flow models will typically need to address other issues. One is control flow, to be distinguished from data flow, particularly important in systems where external events trigger actions. Another important issue is resource allocation, to indicate what resources of the organisation are being deployed to support the activity. And then there is timing, delays in processes that are critical to the success of the process.

A.3 Data modelling

In computing systems we record data or information about the things or entities of interest and importance to us. While many people distinguish data from information which in turn is distinguished from knowledge, we will not make those distinctions here. We will simply refer to **data models**, though we may on occasions talk about recording information in the data model.

The primary element of a data model is the **entity**. Entities may be related to each other. In the basic notation that we will adopt, entities are represented as rectangular boxes, while **relationships** are represented by lines joining the boxes, as shown in Figure A.7.

Entities are given identifying names or identifiers, like 'employee' or 'purchase item' or 'contract', written inside the box. We will call these entity names.

Each entity will have a number of characterising **attributes** like 'employee name' or 'contract number' which have values taken from some set of possible values. One or more of these attributes will uniquely identify particular entities, in which case we refer to these combined attributes as keys. Attributes are written inside the entity box, as we can see in the example in Figure A.8.

Note that in the previous paragraph we have been a little casual about the way we talked about entities and attributes and values, in line with normal practice in the software industry. We should really distinguish between collections of entities of the same **entity type**, and the particular entities actually existing in an information system at one time, in which case we refer to an **entity instance**. Further, an attribute is an abstract concept consisting of the attribute name (or attribute identifier) and the value set (or domain). But we usually know what is meant from the context.

Figure A.7

Data modelling notation[4]

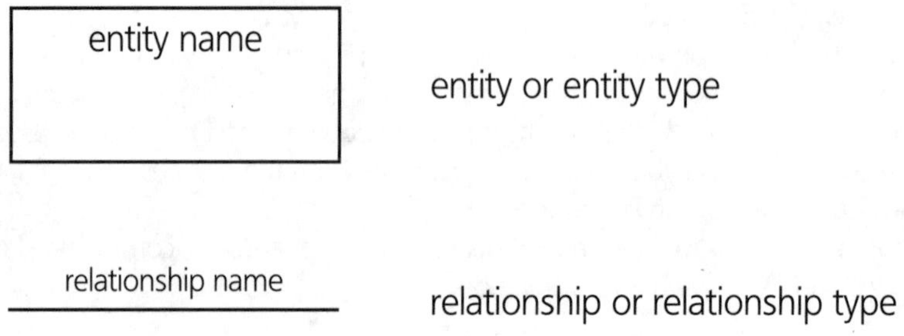

entity name

entity or entity type

relationship name

relationship or relationship type

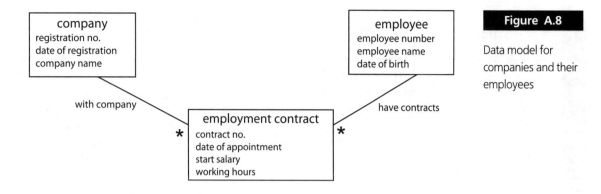

Data model for companies and their employees

Relationships between entities are also given names or identifiers, which we will refer to as relationship names. Consider the following statement about a company: an employee may have an employment contract with a company. 'Employee', 'employment contract' and 'company' are all entities (entity types) while 'have' and 'with' are relationships. This is shown in Figure A.8.

Note that in Figure A.8 we have placed a * at one end of the relationships. This denotes that each employee may have many employment contracts and that a company may have many employment contracts. The absence of any * at the other end indicates that an employment contract can only involve one employee and one company. We refer to these relationships as *one-to-many*; most relationships are one-to-many or many-to-one, and while *one-to-one* and *many-to-many* relationships are in principle possible, they are very unusual.

We could have, for example, drawn a model in which a company was directly related to an employee through a many-to-many relationship 'contracted to'. However our modelling rules would not enable us to record any attributes for the contract, and hence the need for the 'employment contract' entity. This need for an 'intersection entity' is so common that each time when data modelling a many-to-many relationship arises, you need to think carefully about whether there should not be an entity in between.

Often on relationships we want to specify that not every instance of an entity must have a particular relationship – we call this *optional*, as opposed to *mandatory*. The simplest way to denote the combination of optional or mandatory and one or many is to write a pair of symbols at each end of the relationship, thus:

- 0,1 – optionally one entity, and only one entity at this end may be related to an entity at the other end;
- 1,1 – the relationship is mandatory, one and only one entity at this end must be related to an entity at the other end;
- 0,* – optionally one or more entities at this end may be related to an entity at the other end;
- 1,* – one or more entities at this end must be related to an entity at the other end.

To see how this works out consider the stock control system described in Case Study A.2.

Case Study A.2 *Data model for a stock control system*

The BrainBox Computer company assembles a range of computers from components that it holds as stock items in a warehouse. Departments that assemble particular computers request items from stock, and are either supplied with these items immediately, or are informed that the items are out of stock and need to be re-ordered. When items become out of stock, or the stock falls to a low level, the items are re-ordered from a preferred supplier in multiples of some standard quantity sufficient to fill all outstanding requests. When the reordered items arrive from the suppliers, all outstanding requests are immediately filled and the remainder are placed in stock.

Figure A.9 shows a data model of the various entities involved in this stock control situation.

In developing this data model we have made various assumptions, for example that a stock item can only be supplied by one preferred supplier – a different organisation might have allowed multiple preferred suppliers. We have also separated the initial requests from the unfilled requests – this did not need to be done. Note that most of the relationships are many-to-one.

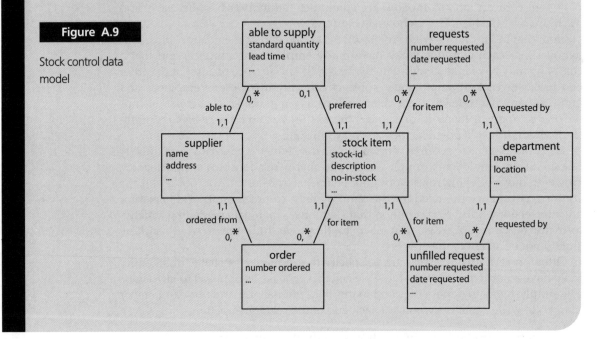

Figure A.9

Stock control data model

Other modelling conventions might use special ends to the relationship lines to indicate the one-to-many status, etc. A particular different style of modelling has been the entity relationship diagrams of Peter Chen[5] where the relationship is a diamond box – these diagrams get bulky and thus have not been used in this book, though they have been widely used in practice.

Endnotes

1. We say that a modelling notation is recursive when models of the same type can be contained within it.
2. UML or the Unified Modelling Language, has become the standard notation for object oriented methods, with a complex array of notations. See for example http://www.uml.org.
3. See Peter Checkland (1981) *Systems Thinking, Systems Practice*, Wiley; and Peter Checkland and Jim Scholes (1990) *Soft Systems Methodology in Action*. Wiley.
4. This simple notation dates back to the late 1960s when Charlie Bachman started using them for describing the complex databases he was working on at GE. See C.W. Bachman (1969) 'Data Structure Diagrams', *Journal of ACM SIGBDP'*, 1(2), March, 4–10.
5. Peter Chen (1976) 'The Entity-Relationship Model – Toward a Unified View of Data', *ACM Transactions on Database Systems*, 1(1), 9–36.

Measurement theory

> **What we will study in this appendix**
>
> Measurement and metrics must conform to the well-established principles and theories described in this short appendix.

This appendix is about measurement in general. Measurement is of such great central importance in both science and engineering that it has been the focus of much research and theorising such that it is now well understood. Here we draw upon this measurement science, choosing the bits that are relevant to management and to software. In software measurement is usually discussed and applied under the title of 'metrics' – the book by Norman Fenton and Shari Pfleeger[1] on metrics gives an excellent introduction to measurement theory. It is difficult to avoid jargon and technical terms here, so please be sympathetic to the following account of measurement theory.

Whenever we measure something, we must express this measurement in some particular *measurement units*. These units might be **qualitative**, like 'big' or 'small', 'cheap' or 'expensive', or the units could be **quantitative** and numeric. Numerical measures might be integral whole numbers, or they might be 'real' numbers which include fractional parts; they might also be subject to constraints, such having to be positive, or lying within some range.

We need to be certain that the measurement is useful and relevant. It can always be claimed that there is a 'something' that it does measure, but we need to be sure that the actual measurements and what we can do with them relate to our tacit understanding of that 'something' and its properties. So let's look at what we might want to do with measurements.

Given two measurements we may need to compare them, and say whether they are the same, and if not place them in some order such as larger or smaller. To be able to do that requires that the measurement units permit this comparison. In making comparisons we will talk of one measurement being 'equal to', 'less than', or 'greater than' another measurement. All the example measurement units we gave above permit such comparisons, so that:

- 'big' is greater than 'small';
- 'cheap' is less than 'expensive';

- '3' is less than '7';
- '4.82' is greater than '4.428'.

All this is stunningly obvious, isn't it? But not all measurements can be compared. For example we might record hair colour as one of 'brown', 'black', 'fair', 'red', or 'white' – while we could say whether two people have the same hair colour, it does not make any sense to say that one of these is less than some other one. Indeed the idea of even calling these 'measurements' seems wrong. The ability to compare is fundamental to the idea of measurement.

Sometimes we might turn a qualitative measure into a quasi-numerical one. An example of this practice is the Likert scale frequently used in questionnaires and surveys, for example where people are asked to say whether they agree or disagree with a statement, as illustrated in Figure B.1.

6.3 How important is it to have a spell checker with standardised spellings for your own language?				
unimportant, would not use	unlikely to use	don't care either way	likely to use	essential, certain to use

Figure B.1

Example of a Likert scale used in a recent survey of language needs in South Asia

If two measurements are not the same, we might want to say by how much they differ. We cannot do this for qualitative measures like 'cheap' and 'expensive' or in the Likert scale of Figure B.1, but we can do this for numbers simply by doing some arithmetic. If our measurement is the purchase price of an item of software, and we are investigating two otherwise comparable items of software, the difference would represent the potential saving from purchasing one rather than the other. Related to this is scalability and ratios – it is meaningful to talk of one software package costing twice as much as another. But differences and ratios are not always meaningful, and it would be quite wrong to assign numbers to the Likert scale in Figure B.1 (often these are assigned numbers -2, -1, 0, $+1$, $+2$) and then do arithmetic on these, for example finding the average opinion in a survey.

Measurement can be obtained using an appropriate instrument directly upon the item concerned. The instrument depends upon what it is that is being measured, and could be a ruler, an electrical meter, a questionnaire, or even an expert judgement.

But often a property cannot be measured directly and we combine other directly measurable quantities to calculate the derived measurement for the property concerned. Figure B.2 illustrates what we have in mind. Ideally the process in the

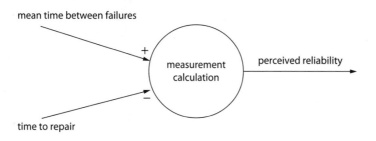

Figure B.2

Combining direct measurements to create a derived measurement middle would calculate the property measurement from the input measurements. The example is taken from reliability measurement, where we are estimating *perceived reliability* from directly measurable *mean time between failures*, and *time to repair*. What we have shown here is an **influence diagram**, showing that if *mean time between failures* increases, *perceived reliability* increases, indicated by the '+' sign on the arrow; but that if *time to repair* increases, the *perceived reliability* decreases, shown by the '−' sign on the arrow.

Endnotes

1. Norman E. Fenton and Shari Lawrence Pfleeger (1998) *Software Metrics: A Rigorous Approach* (2nd ed). PWS.

Glossary

The following define the key terms of the book in the sense that we use these terms in this book. In many cases these are the normal meanings, but in some cases we use the term in a more restricted or specialised way. The numbers in brackets at the end of each entry show the chapter and section where the term is principally used. Where a term refers to another term in this glossary this is shown in bold.

acceptance test a set of tests or trials on the basis of which the stakeholders who normally pay for the system, or their representatives, will formally accept the system. It also refers to the process phase during which such tests are being conducted (7.13)

accomplishment-cost see **earned value**. (10.4)

adaptive maintenance changes to existing software that respond to changes in the world outside, intending to make the software continue to work successfully. (9.2)

affordance principle of human-centred design where the action you take on a technical artefact is implied by the visual appearance – for example a handle on a door suggests pulling, and plate of metal on a door suggests pushing. (8.3)

Agile Alliance an organisation that promotes **agile** methods. (8.8)

Agile methods that seek to respond rapidly to users' changing needs and are kept as free from bureaucracy as possible. (8.8)(9.1)

algorithmic estimation estimation using a formula in which parameters have been derived from historical data. (10.3)

alpha test trial use of the software in house within the same organisation that produced it. (7.13)

applications software software that does useful work for the user, such as

supporting a business process. See also **systems software**. (6.1)

architectural design the major components of a software system and their interconnections. (7.6)(8.1)

architectural styles the principles upon which particular **architectural designs** are created. (7.6)

aspect-oriented software development an aspect addresses a cross-cutting concern that can be handled in a manner similar to components, except that the software to implement the aspect may be dispersed across the software. Each aspect can be separately described with the aspiration that the aspect can then be implemented across the software using automatic processes. (8.6)

assumptions inevitably not everything will be known that needs to be known in order to define a project precisely, and in these areas a best guess or assumption will need to be made, and need thorough documentation. (10.2)

attribute a named property of an **entity**. (Appendix A)

balanced scorecard an extension of the weighted scorecard approach, which takes into account business values to guide all decision-making. (2.4)

baseline a **configuration version** that is used as the basis for future work. (10.4)(11.2)

basic needs part of Maslow's theory of motivation – the needs that all people normally have, like food, shelter, and security. Herzberg called these 'hygienic'. (3.1)

benefits the value gained from a particular activity, possibly expressed in monetary terms. (2.4)

bespoke development developing a system and its software to meet a particular purpose. (6.1)(6.6)

beta test before the **software** is widely distributed or released publicly, trial use of the software within some external organisation on some preferential understanding with the organisation who produced it, taking **feedback** from the beta user to modify the software before full release. (7.13)

bottom-up estimation see **micro estimation**. (10.3)

BPR abbreviation for **business process re-engineering**. (2.3)

brainstorming a method of seeking requirements and risks divergently in which ideas are sought freely unconstrained by any initial evaluation of them. (7.2)(13.3)

build the act of **linking** components together to create a deployable or executable system or subsystem. (7.11)

build state the **versions** of the **configuration items** that together make up a version of a **configuration**. (11.2)

business process the set of activities and their interrelations, such as precedence, priority, and sequence, that carry out particular parts and aspects of the work of an organisation. (2.2)

business process re-engineering (BPR) changing a **business process** in order to accommodate new ways of doing things, the use of new technology, or to meet new business objectives. (2.3)

business rules constraints on aspects of a business process that assert business structure or influence the behaviour of the business, often focussing on access control. (2.2)

capital goods goods that are durable and are used, along with resources, in the production of further goods or services (3.4)

captive market imperfect competition where the cost of repeat purchases is considerably lower than for the initial purchase. (3.5)

capture-replay software that will record user input to create a **test script** which can later be run automatically. (7.12)

CASE Computer-Aided Software Engineering. The development of software using tools such as version control systems, configuration repositories, editors, testing and building tools, which are used to support different needs of software developers.

change charter a definition of what can be potentially changed when developing a new system. Closely related to **scope**, with which it will often be treated as synonymous. (2.3)(7.2)

change management the analysis, planning, and control of proposed changes to a system, approving or prohibiting them, and then ensuring that the approved changes are executed fully with the result intended. (2.8)

checking in placing an updated version of a **configuration item** back into the **configuration repository**. (11.2)

checking out taking a copy of a **configuration item** out of the **repository** for the purposes of changing it. (11.2)

client see **client-server architecture**. (7.6)

client-server architecture a configuration of computers and software where the client runs the software which presents the software functions to the user, connected via some **network** to the server which undertakes the data storage and processing operations required. (6.5)

CMMi 'Capability Maturity Model integrated', a framework for process quality improvement and assessment that recognises levels of attainment, the ability to improve ('mature') with a road map for organisations to focus their improvement efforts. See section 12.3.2 for discussion. (10.5)(11.2)(12.1)(12.3)

code of conduct a set of rules or code laying down what members of a group, often a professional society, should and should not do. (4.3)

code of ethics a set of rules or code laying down a number of ethical principles to be followed by a group, often a professional society. (4.3)

coding writing of the computer programs in response to specifications and designs created previously. (7.10)(8.1)

co-evolve evolution of more than one part of the overall system, such as the software, the hardware, and the **business processes**, in harmony with each other. (9.2)

cohesion a design evaluation principle which expects all the parts within a **component** to be closely related so that they can be **encapsulated** together. (7.8)

command economy an economy where central planning determines what will be produced and hence consumed. (3.4)

commercial off the shelf standard commodity software – see **packages**. (6.3)

commodity a standardised and undifferentiated non-perishable good, with an abundant supply and a potentially fluctuating price, capable of being traded both for current ('spot') delivery and for future delivery. (3.4)

Common Object Request Broker Architecture a standard architecture for the communication between applications over a **network**, promulgated by the **OMG**. (8.6)

commons see **public goods**. (3.4)

community architecture designing buildings in consultation with the people who will inhabit or use the buildings in such a way that the buildings themselves promote a sense of community and respect their personal and social values. (1.4)

community of practice group of people engaged in a form of social learning, sharing knowledge and experience. (3.3)

component a coherent part of a system that can be implemented independently and for which plug compatible replacements could in principle be produced.

configuration a collection of **versions** of **configuration items** that together make up a consistent and meaningful whole. (11.2)

configuration item the smallest individual item that is part of a software artefact produced during a project, that is stored, changed, stored again, and so on. (11.2)

configuration management managing changes (see **change management**) in software or another product as it is enhanced, adapted, and fixed over time. (9.2)(11.2)

configuration repository a **database** or **repository** containing **configuration items** and their **versions**, together with their configurations and other records. (11.2)

configuration version a new **configuration** created as the items in the original configuration are changed. (11.2)

constructionism the philosophical view that reality is subjective and is socially constructed by people as they make sense of the world. (1.4)

consumables goods that are not durable and once purchased are consumed and no longer available for further use. (3.4)

context diagrams the highest level of process model in the data-flow convention, showing the interactions between a system and its environment. (2.1)(Appendix A)

contract formal agreements between two (or more) parties that are legally binding and that normally involve mutual duties and benefits. (5.3)(6.7)

copyright protects the expression of the ideas in written works, drawings, music and similar, but it does not protect the ideas themselves – see **patent**. (5.2)

CORBA abbreviation for **Common Object Request Broker Architecture**. (8.6)

corrective maintenance changes that fix defects found during operational use. (9.2)

cost the resource (e.g., money) spent on carrying out a particular activity. (2.4) (13.1)

cost-accomplishment see **earned value**. (10.4)

COTS abbreviation for **commercial off the shelf**. (6.3)

coupling the degree of interdependence between **components** or **modules**. (7.8)

coverage analyser measures the effectiveness of a set of tests by measuring the relative amount of software actually exercised by the test (7.10)(7.12)

coverage measure a **metric**, the proportion of software constructs of a particular type which are executed or used in a particular testing process. (7.12)

critical path analysis a way of identifying the sequence of activities that will take the longest time overall, and thus determine the overall duration of the project. (10.4)

cultural relativity view that morality is not absolute and universal, the same for all, but rather morality varies relative to the culture concerned. (4.2)

data flow a connection between two processes for transferring data; on a **data-flow diagram**, the line from one process to another representing the flow of data. (Appendix A)

data-flow diagram a diagram for representing a process model, consisting of processes and the data that flows between them. (Appendix A)

data models abstract description of the information or data used by an organisation and the relationships between the individual elements, focussing on the data themselves rather than in their generation or processing. (2.1)(Appendix A)

data protection legislation that restricts the use of data in a computer and physical filing system to be solely for the purpose for which the data was collected. (5.4)

data store a place in a **data-flow diagram** where information is stored for later use. (Appendix A)

data structure diagram a diagram for representing a data model, typically composed of entities and their relationships, or classes and their relationships. (Appendix A)

database a collection of data items and their interrelationship as stored in the computer. (7.6)

defamation see **libel**. (5.4)

deliverable a **work-product** that has the formal status of being a required output of a particular activity whose delivery may form a milestone on a project. (7.1)(8.1)(10.2)

Delphi method a method for reaching consensus between experts about any matter of interest. (10.3)

deontological ethics approach to ethics that considers duties and the rights of others as the source of morality. These duties should be undertaken regardless of their consequences. (4.2)

dependencies relationship between **versions** of **configuration items** showing that they are dependent upon each other and if a version of one is changed the others should be reviewed. (11.2)

derivations relationship between **versions** of **configuration items** showing that one item version was created using the other items: it was *derived from* them. (11.2)

design the process of determining how something will work or look in terms of its parts and their configuration or arrangement. (7.6)(8.1)

design abstraction see **design recovery**. (9.4)

design recovery abstracting the underlying software **design** from existing software **code**, one aspect of **reverse engineering**. (9.4)

detailed design the decomposition of a large subsystem, module, or

component into smaller **modules** and their interrelationships. (7.8)

development for reuse the production of software components not only for the immediate project at hand but also for later reuse via a component repository. (10.2)

direct cost cost that can be directly attributed to the activity concerned, like the labour costs of those working on the activity or the purchase of capital equipment for use in the activity. (2.4)

discounted cash flow see **net present value**. (2.4)

diseconomy of scale the opposite of an economy of scale where large size or volume leads to a reduction in unit costs – in a diseconomy of scale large system size leads to disproportionally greater cost. (10.3)

distribution a combination of software, both executable and source, and associated documents, made available by the 'gatekeepers' (e.g. the core development team) to the wider user and co-developing community, a **release** within the **FOSS** world. (6.4)

domain model a model for an **application** area or domain. (8.6)

double-loop learning learning involving two feedback cycles, one which changes the way we learn on the basis of experience, with a second cycle within this through which the actual learning takes place. (2.7)

earned value a way of assessing progress of a project in terms of the value of the **work-products** completed to date. (10.4)

economies of scale situation where the larger the volume of production the lower the price of goods and hence the tendency to create a monopoly. (3.5)

embedded part of a system contained within some larger system, usually used to refer to software which forms part of a larger engineering artefact, and even a **socio-technical system**. (2.5)

emergent behaviour behaviour (or properties) of large and complex systems which we did not predict, and maybe could not have predicted, from our knowledge of the parts and how they were composed. See also **emergent properties**. (1.4)

emergent properties properties of large and complex systems which we did not predict, and maybe could not have predicted, from our knowledge of the parts and how they were composed. See also **emergent behaviour**. (1.4)

encapsulation a software design principle which collects together everything that is closely related into a single **module** or **component**. (7.8) (9.4)

enlightenment project philosophical movement starting in the late 1600s with its main adherents continuing throughout the 1700s, though it is still referred to, and strongly debated today, particularly in the **postmodern** movement. The enlightenment project regarded observation and reasoning as the basis for knowledge and understanding that can lead to progress, improving society, and making people free. (1.4)

entire agreement a legal phrase used to restrict a contractual agreement to just what is in the contractual document concerned. (5.3)

entity the basic thing about which data is collected, to become the elementary building block of **data models**. (Appendix A)

entity type the generic form of similar **entities** which have the same **attributes** and **relationships**. (Appendix A)

entity instance a particular **entity** belonging to an **entity type**. (Appendix A)

escrow arranges for a copy of the source code to be held by some third party, perhaps a bank, to be released if certain conditions such as the bankruptcy of the supplier arise. (5.3)

estimation cost estimation, predicting the cost of developing or changing software before the work starts or early in the development process. (8.1)(10.3)

estimation by analogy estimation undertaken by comparing a description of the proposed system with descriptions of other systems for which the costs are known. (10.3)

ethical decision-making making a decision based not just on cost and benefit but also other factors such as whether the goods being considered were produced with exploited labour and whether their production could have a negative impact on the environment. (2.4)(6.7)

ethics consideration of the effect of our behaviour on others, and constraining our behaviour as a consequence. (4.1)

evolution synonymous with maintenance, normally refers to progressive changes to the software which are small relative to the whole, which are done after its first **release**. (9.1)

evolutionary method an **iterative** process that produces successive versions of the system, exposing them to users and taking into account their feedback before changing and evolving the system until a satisfactory solution has been created. (8.3)

excludability the usage of a good by one person immediately denies the use of the same good by another person. (3.4)(5.2)

explicit knowledge knowledge that has been made explicit, written in paper documents or other form of media. (2.6)

externalised placed outside any individual person, particularly for knowledge that has been documented to make it accessible to other people. (2.6)

externalities situations where agents are affected indirectly, beneficially or detrimentally, by the trade in goods but are not directly participating in the trade as buyer or seller. (3.5)

eXtreme Programming (XP) the best-known of the **agile methods**

developed by Kent Beck, focussing on code developed incrementally in association with test cases. (2.2)(8.8)(9.4)

failure mode analysis failure mode and effect analysis examines potential failure of products or processes, evaluates their likelihoods and consequences, and through this helps determine how to avoid the failures or their consequences. (4.4)(13.3)

feasibility study an investigation of a proposed solution to assess whether it can be implemented with existing knowledge and at acceptable cost. (2.4)

feedback (a) a process whereby discrepancies between an expected or desired result and an actual result is used to modify the processes that produced the result; thus feedback is taken to constitute a good model of learning. (2.7); or (b) any situation in which the output affects, intentionally or otherwise, the input of a process or system. (9.3)

focus group a convergent method of determining requirements where one or more proposals are put to a panel and discussed in general terms. (7.2)

force majeur circumstances under which a contract may fail for reasons that the parties to the contract cannot be held responsible for. (5.3)

fordism synonymous with **taylorism** (2.2)

formal methods the application of mathematics or mathematical-like reasoning to the development of software. (8.4)

forward engineering developing software from requirements statement through to executable code. (9.4)

FOSS abbreviation for **Free and Open Source Software**. (5.2)(6.4)(8.7)

frameworks a proven **software architecture** for a particular class of **applications** or services that can be filled out in detail to fulfil a particular need. (8.6)

Free and Open Source Software (FOSS) software that is available without payment with access to the source code which can be adapted as needed. (5.2)(6.4)(8.7)

Free Software Foundation the original organisation that created **Free and Open Source Software** and developed the GNU license, founded by Richard Stallman. (8.7)

free-rider a person who, through a positive externality, benefits from **goods** or **services** while not being party to the trade in those goods or services. (3.5)

Gaia hypothesis following James Lovelock, the whole planet Earth functions as a single organism in which all parts are interdependent and survive or die together. (1.4)

goods the material products produced and consumed within an economy. (3.4)

granularity the relative size of the configuration items being controlled. Also applied to items in general. (11.2)

gratis literally, free; a gratis economy is one in which goods and services are offered without payment. Rewards and compensations can come in different ways, such as the fulfilment of a social obligation or the full enjoyment of the use of goods and services freely provided by others. (3.5)

growth needs part of Maslow's theory of motivation – the needs that motivate people by enabling them to learn and develop themselves and gain self-fulfilment. Herzberg called these 'motivational'. (3.1)

guilds medieval organisations that took an interest in the regulation of society, industry and trade. (4.3)

health and safety (a) legislation which holds employers responsible for the health and safety of their employees, concerning the arrangements made in the workplace. (5.4); (b) more widely, legislation and industry-specific knowledge and practices concerning the protection of people, property and environment against the negative side-effects of technology and industrial production.

high-level design see **architectural design**. (7.6)

IDE abbreviation for **Integrated Development Environments**. (8.1)

impact analysis an analysis of all the places in a system that might need to be changed as well if a change is made to a particular item. (11.3)

imperfect competition one or a few players can determine price and rig the market, making the market imperfect. (3.5)

implicit knowledge what must have had to be known to produce a particular artefact or undertake a particular activity but which has not been spelt out in manuals or other documents. (2.6)

incremental a number of interconnected **waterfall**-like life cycles each delivering an increment of an overall system so that together they deliver the full system. (8.2)

indirect costs costs that are incurred as a consequence of the activity concerned, but cannot be directly attributed to the activity, such as the cost of senior management. (2.4)

individualism–collectivism Hofstede's concept about intercultural differences in the relationship between an individual and those around him/her. (3.2)

influence diagram a special **data-flow** like diagram in which the process are calculations or similar relating **inputs** to **output**, with the inputs marked to show how they influence the output in the same direction (+) or in the opposite direction (−). (Appendix B)

information hiding a software implementation principle that only makes visible outside a software **component**, those aspects that are necessary for its successful use. (7.8) (9.4)

infrastructure software see **system software**. (6.1)

in-house development developing a software system within the enterprise or organisation who will then use it. (6.6)

inspection a particular kind of review meeting following clear procedures which promote good quality improving results from the meeting. (7.15)(12.2)

intangible costs and benefits that cannot be directly described and assessed but which nevertheless can be attributed, such as customer goodwill. (2.4)

Integrated Development Environments computer programs (such as Eclipse for Java) that provide compiling, editing, and testing functionality 'under the same roof', plus specific aids to help developers using a particular language. (8.1)

Integrated Project Support Environment (IPSE) a comprehensive set of **CASE tools that interoperate and support different activities and needs from inception to release of the product. Unless carefully customised and evolved, an IPSE can become a straitjacket for developers.** (8.1)

integration building a system and making sure that the parts fit together without necessarily executing the software. (7.11)

integration testing testing an integrated system, running test cases as appropriate. (7.11)

intellectual property property that arises as product of the intellect, such as writing, music composition, designs, software, and similar. Intellectual property rights are the legal right to ownership of intellectual property and its economic exploitation. (5.1)

interoperate two more items of software interoperate if they work together successfully (6.7)

IPR abbreviation for **intellectual property** rights. (5.1)

IPSE abbreviation for **Integrated Project Support Environment**. (8.1)

ISO 9000 the original internationally recognised **quality framework** promulgated by the International Standards Organization. Enterprises are required to establish a quality system documented in a Quality Manual, and then get certified as complying with ISO 9000, this certification being given by some accredited agency. (12.3)

IT procurement see **software acquisition**. (6.1)

IT provision see **software acquisition**. (6.1)

iterative a **process model** involving a number of cycles of development producing a part of the system, or perhaps a full system, in order to resolve some uncertainty about what is required and what is possible. (8.3)

joint venture an organisation that is specially formed jointly by two or more other organisations. (6.6)

jurisdiction the legal system and set of laws that apply to a particular contract. (5.3)

knowledge management management focus explicitly upon the organisation's knowledge which can take two forms: to store, manipulate and retrieve externalised representations of the knowledge, or to cultivate tacit knowledge and its sharing through meetings and similar social processes. (2.6)

law of scarcity there are not enough resources to be able to produce enough commodities to meet each and every demand, and hence resources are attracted to use in products that produce the highest profit. (3.4)

learning organisation an organisation that acquires knowledge and learns, and through that improves its performance, as a practical business approach to how organisations should change and do change. (2.7)

legacy data data that is old but still of value, and must be retained, possibly also for legal reasons, see **legacy systems**. (6.2)

legacy software software that is old but still of value, providing a valuable service, see **legacy systems**. (6.2)

legacy systems established systems incorporating **business processes** that do not change, often with the consequence that the technical systems become outdated while they remain essential. (2.3)

Lehman's laws eight general principles abstracted by Manny Lehman from the observation of industrial software development by him and Les Belady in the early 1970s. These laws are believed to characterise and constrain the evolution of variable software. (9.3)

letter of intent a letter stating that a contract will be drawn up, thus enabling work to commence in anticipation of the contract. (5.3)

libel material published which gives offence and leads to other people holding the person or organisation referred to in low esteem. (5.4)

license agreement a legal contract that permits the use of software without transferring ownership. (6.7)

life-cycle model see **process model**. (8.1)

likelihood the probability that a particular event will happen. (13.1)

link connecting together separately developed components at points where one component expects input and another component generates appropriate output. (7.11)

localisation modifying any good so that it is appropriate for a local market – in software this typically means translating all the text into the local language. (3.5)

macro estimation cost estimation based on a description of the overall system, from which estimates are made by analogy with other similar systems; high-level features are counted to give a functional size from which cost can be calculated; or other macro

characteristics are used as the basis. (10.3)

market economy an economy where the type, amount, and prices of goods that are produced is determined by the free interaction between consumers and their demands, and producers and their supplies. (3.4)

masculinity–femininity Hofstede's concept about intercultural differences in the way men and women respond differently or the same on a range of questions. (3.2)

measurement the length, volume, weight, or other numerical (or non-numerical) assessment of the size of something. (2.1)(Appendix B)

metric a **measurement**. (12.2)

micro estimation cost estimation based on the small elements from which the system will be built, requiring some initial analysis and design in order to identify those small elements and produce the base level costs, which are then added for the overall cost. (10.3)

milestone key event in a project plan, typically the completion of a **deliverable** by a certain date. (8.1) (10.2)

mission statement the overall purpose of the organisation and its products, services, and markets, implying some order of priorities, which clearly separates the mission of the organisation from other organisations. (2.1)

model an abstract representation of an aspect of the software or of the domain within which the software is intended to operate. (8.1) (Appendix A)

modernism a movement in the arts, music, literature, design and architecture, which emerged around 1900, rebelling against the preceding academic and historical traditions. For example in architecture, modernism is epitomised by glass-encased skyscrapers with gleaming metal adornments, and with systematically laid out cities of rectangular blocks with housing segregated from shopping malls segregated from office zones and light industry. We use this term in the broader sense of everything associated with the 'modern world' particularly science and technology. (1.4)

module a small subdivision of a system, possibly a **component**, which could be implemented by a single person in a reasonably short period, independently stored (e.g., in a file) from the rest of the code and separately compiled. (8.1)

monopoly imperfect competition where a single agent controls the market. (3.5)

moral philosophy debates what should be the basis for our behaviour, what actions are good and should be encouraged, what actions are bad and should be discouraged. (4.2)

negative feedback feedback in which the changes in the process that take place as a result of the feedback have the effect of *reducing* the discrepancy between the expected or desired result and the actual result. Compare with **positive feedback**. (2.7)

net present value a method of analysis which takes into account that money has more value today than in the future because of inflation and interest rates, and also takes into account opportunity costs, so that future costs and benefits over many years can be properly compared. (2.4)

network (abbreviated net) a set of computers and other devices and their software which can communicate through communications protocols and share information and other resources.

normal design also known as routine design, design problems that are well known with similar ones having been tackled many times in the past with solutions that can be drawn on for solving the current problem. (13.2)

normative views of behaviour, what we ought to do, looking to agreements within a social group. (4.2)

NPV abbreviation for **net present value**. (2.4)

object the basic building block of **object-oriented** systems, consisting of data and the operations that manipulate that data. (Appendix A)

Object Management Group (OMG) a collaboration of various industrial organisations to produce standards in the object-oriented software development area. (8.1)

object-oriented a 'paradigm' or basic principle for software development that arose in the 1970s but gained popularity from the late 1980s onwards. In this the problem is analysed in terms of 'objects' that store information and offer a number of operations (often called 'methods') upon that information. (7.1)(8.2) (Appendix A)

offshoring transferring the software development and maintenance, full or in part, to some other country, often in the developing world, via the creation of a subsidiary, and outsourcing contract or other modality. (6.6)

OMG abbreviation for **Object Management Group**. (8.1)

onshoring outsourcing to a local company that uses labour recruited offshore, usually at cheaper rates. (6.6)

OO abbreviation for **object-oriented**. (8.2)

open source software development the process of developing software where the source code is open for anybody to make a contribution – where access is via the internet, these contributions could be from anywhere: once a contribution has been offered, it is reviewed by the specialist(s) guiding the process. This is the basis for **FOSS** software. (8.7)

operating system programs that manage the computer hardware and present this to the applications software and to users in such a way as to make this usable. (6.1)

opportunity costs the benefits that would have been gained had the money been spent on another activity. (2.4)

organisation any group of people and their associated **systems** that have some permanence and share a collective purpose. Examples are administrative institutions and commercial companies, but also parts of these where this is appropriate. Organisations are distinct from teams, which may have a relatively short life. (1.2)(2.1)

organisational learning academic area of research characterised by Argyris that should question the very idea that an organisation can learn – however in this book we do not problematise this, and assume organisations can learn because their constituent human members can learn. (2.7)

outsourcing arranging for an external organisation to undertake the work required. (6.6)

packages standard commodity software available off the shelf, possibly then customised to the particular needs of the user. See **commercial off the shelf**. (6.3)

parallel running trial use of new software where an older system and the new system are run in parallel duplicating the work so that the results of the old and the new systems can be compared. (7.13)

participative design (PD) design in which the intended beneficiaries of the design process also take part in the design process, along with technical experts. (8.3)

participative development see **participative design**. (8.3)

patches a change to a system distributed so that a small part of the overall system is replaced by new code in the field implemented directly upon the live system. (11.2)

patent legal mechanism to protect inventions and their subsequent economic exploitation in manufacture, protecting the idea itself and not just its expression – see **copyright**. (5.2)

patterns standard solutions to **design** problems expressed abstractly so as to gain wide applicability, usually associated with **object-oriented** approaches. (8.6)

PD abbreviation for **participative development** or **participative design**. (8.3)

perfect market an economy in which salaries, prices, supply, and demand are kept in balance, leading, it is claimed, to an optimum use of resources. (3.4)

perfective maintenance changes to existing features to make them better, or adding features left out previously, without adapting the system to its changing environment, making the system easier to maintain, or fixing manifest defects. (9.2)

performance how well or badly an organisation fulfils its mission. (2.1)

performance indicators a measurement of performance, such as return on investment or profits. (2.1)

planned obsolescence product differentiation by artificial ageing, planned so that replacement goods are required before the good is no longer of serviceable quality. (3.5)

positive feedback feedback in which the changes in the process that take place as a result of the feedback have the effect of *increasing* the discrepancy between the expected or desired result and the actual result. Compare with **negative feedback**. (2.7)

post-implementation audit a review at the end of a project or period of investment to assess whether the intended benefits were achieved, the costs were held to the amount originally budgeted, and thus whether the return on investment that justified the investment was achieved. (2.4)

postmodernism the philosophical movement that arose in response to the limitations of the **enlightenment project**, **modernism**, and science, recognising the important role of humans in what constitutes knowledge and scientific truth. (1.4)

power distance Hofstede's concept about intercultural differences in the relative power and authority of individuals. (3.2)

preventive maintenance changes, like **reverse engineering**, that avoid problems in making future changes. (9.2)

private goods a good where the property rights reside in one individual or a group of individuals for their exclusive use and benefit. (3.4)

pro bono services such as legal advice given **gratis**. (3.5)

proactive initiating any action without external stimulus or instruction. (2.1)

process models abstract descriptions of a collection of activities undertaken by an organisation and their interdependencies and the sequence undertaken. (2.1)(7.1)(8.1)

product differentiation making one product different from a similar product so that the products are not substitutable, leading to imperfect competition. (3.5)

product line a number of closely related applications that can be met by small variations on an underlying **framework** and a set of **components** such that any new application in that class can readily be produced. (8.6)

professional society a society formed by people within the same profession in order to further the interests of the profession, providing criteria for membership and mutual support through training and seminars. (4.3)

progress monitoring keeping track of what is actually being achieved relative to what was planned. (7.9)

project a collection of activities which together have a defined outcome and possibly also have a defined timescale and cost. (2.1)

project plan in the broad sense, a comprehensive set of documentation that will facilitate the management of a **project**, including project objectives, resources, timescale, activities, schedules, and so on. In the narrow sense this could mean just the activities to be undertaken and the schedule of when they will be undertaken, together with the assignment of appropriate resources. (10.1)

project requirements see **requirements documents**. (10.2)

property rights the right of ownership of goods and commodities and the right to benefit from the use of these, usually protected by the law. (3.4)

prototyping a variation of the **evolutionary** process where a mock-up of the system is produced and discussed with the **stakeholders** before producing the real system, possibly following a **waterfall** approach, or possibly an **evolutionary** approach. (8.3) (10.2)

public goods goods where the ownership is held in common by the community with no exclusive right of use by any individual or group. (3.4) (4.1)(5.2)

qualitative usually contrasted with **quantitative** measurement, where matters are characterised numerically, *qualitative* measurement focusses on descriptions in words and symbols to describe experiences and values. (2.1) (Appendix B)

quality a property of a product or process, generally understood as 'fitness for purpose'. (12.2)

quality chain the recognition that a product undergoes a sequence of stages with each stage capable of degrading, preserving, or enhancing the quality of the product as it passes. In **TQM** each stage must never knowingly pass on a defective product, aiming for the highest quality possible. (12.2)

quality circles a meeting in which people from across the organisation discuss quality issues, without focussing on particular cases let alone the competence of the people concerned. Not the same as an **inspection**. (12.2)

quality criteria precisely defined means of measuring basic attributes of a system or software, these **measurements** are then combined to give measurements for **quality factors**. (12.2)

quality culture an attitude to quality held by everybody in a group, valuing high quality with everybody feeling responsible for it. (12.2)

quality factors the component properties that together make up **quality**. Ideally factors could be measured, and these **measurements** combined to give an overall measurement of quality. (12.2)

quality framework a management system aimed at facilitating the management and control of quality. (12.3)

quantitative a numerical measurement of how much of something there is, usually contrasted with **qualitative**. (2.1)(Appendix B)

RAD abbreviation for **Rapid Application Development**. (8.5)

radical design also known as innovative design, design problems that are new, very different from previous problems, with no similar problems to draw inspiration from. (13.2)

Rapid Application Development a **timeboxing**-based **process model**, also described as **Agile**. (8.5)

Rational Software Corporation an organisation created to promote the **object-oriented** approach to software development, bringing together many of the leading exponents of the day. (8.2)

Rational Unified Process a sequential process model created by the **Rational Software Corporation** for developing object-oriented software. (8.2)

reactive responding to a external situation or stimulus and then undertaking some relevant action (2.1)

redocumentation recreating the supporting documentation that should accompany software into service, maintenance, and **evolution**. **Design recovery** and **reverse engineering** are aspects of this. (9.4)

reductionism every complex phenomenon can be decomposed into its constituent parts, with this decomposition continuing until the parts can be well understood, and when recomposed the whole can similarly be understood in terms of the parts and their interactions. Reductionism is a cornerstone of modern natural science along with experimental methods supported by statistical analysis. The term *reductionism* is used in a derogatory sense by some social scientist following **constructionism** principles. (1.4)(2.1)

re-engineering recreating existing software in more up-to-date form, consisting of **reverse engineering** followed by **forward engineering** to produce an equivalent system. (9.4)

regression testing the execution of a comprehensive set of tests following a change to a system, to test not only that the change has been implemented correctly but also that no other part of the system has been accidentally changed. (11.3)

relationship an association between **entities** showing that they are related, and in what way. (Appendix A)

release the **baseline** of a **system** that is made available to external parties and customers. (6.4)(11.2)

repository see **database**. (7.6)(11.2)

reproduction the most fundamental of intellectual property rights, the right to control how copies are made and by whom. (5.2)

requirements analysis same as **requirements engineering**. (7.1)

requirements creep the process of gradually gaining more requirements as a result of enthusiasm on the behalf of either technical staff or stakeholders, a phenomenon that needs careful control. (10.2)

requirements document a document setting out the requirements for a **project**, usually produced in two stages: a **requirements statement** and then a **requirements specification**. (10.2)

requirements elicitation the process of understanding what system is needed, interviewing **stakeholders**, harmonising conflicting views, and recording the outcome. (6.1)(7.2)(8.1) (10.2)

requirements engineering the process of understanding and describing what system is needed, consisting of two parts, **requirements elicitation** and **requirements specification**. (6.1) (7.2)

requirements specification a description of what a system or project should achieve, typically including the relationship between the system and the organisation that it is intended to support; or the activity that produces this. (2.5)(7.2)(8.1)(10.2)

requirements statement an informal description of the requirements, produced by the **requirements elicitation** activity. (7.2)

requirements validation the process of checking that the requirements as documented match the needs of the stakeholders. (10.2)

resource balancing ensuring that the resources needed for particular work are available while no resource is overloaded. (10.4)

resource levelling see **resource balancing**. (10.4)

resource profile the way the number and type of resources, human and machine, vary over the duration of a project. (10.4)

restraint on trade a clause in a contract that is intended to restrict what one of the signatories can do either during or after the period of the contract in order to protect the interests of the other parties. (5.3)

return on investment (ROI) the difference between the benefits gained and the costs incurred by a particular investment. (2.4)

reuse a cost-saving practice through the use of **components** developed by previous projects or elsewhere, and kept in a component repository or similar. Sometimes referred to as **development with reuse**. (10.2)

reverse engineering the process of abstracting designs and specifications from the executable code of a software system. (8.3)(9.4)

review meeting to consider a **deliverable** in the context of the deliverables that were used to produce it, and the processes that will use the deliverable. (7.15)(10.2)(12.2)

revision a change to a **configuration item** to produce a new **version**. (11.2)

risk what can go wrong, outcomes that are harmful or deleterious in some way. (13.1)

risk assessment consideration of all places in a process where assumptions have been made and things could go wrong, followed by consideration of how the effect of the risk could be mitigated. (2.8)

risk avoidance seeking an alternative arrangement which does not involve the risk at all. (13.3)

risk mitigation reducing the severity or likelihood of risk, or managing it by some other means – by **risk avoidance**, **risk reduction**, or **risk transfer**. (13.5)

risk reduction accepting the risk while taking measures so that the loss is reduced. (13.3)

risk retention This strategy involves accepting the risk and doing nothing to prevent it. (13.3)

risk transfer consists in passing the costs of the event to another party. (13.3)

ROI abbreviation for **return on investment**. (2.4)

round-trip software engineering the complete cycle of producing software and other artefacts by **forward engineering**, followed by **reverse engineering** back to the specification, enabling changes and further forward engineering. (8.3)(9.4)

routine design see **normal desgin**. (13.2)

rules agreed **normative** behaviour. (4.2)

RUP abbreviation for **Rational Unified Process**. (8.2)

SaaS abbreviation for **software as a service**. (6.5)

safety culture an organisational culture in which everybody is safety conscious, concerned that by their actions or through their products they should not put people or the environment at risk. (13.3)

scenarios example uses of the intended system. (10.2)

scientific method a systematic process used by scientists for discovering the nature of the universe, consisting of observation leading to the formulation of a hypothesis from which predictions are made which are then tested by suitable experiments. (2.1)

scope defines what can be potentially changed, what cannot be changed, and what can be analysed, during a software development project. See **change charter**. (2.3)(7.2)

server see **client-server architecture**. (7.6)

services in economics the non-material equivalent of **goods**. (3.4)

service level agreement a legal agreement concerning a service offered to a client in return for appropriate payments or other compensations. (6.5)

service-oriented architectures an extension of the **client-server architecture** where a server offers its services on a network for other servers or for clients to connect to as required. (6.5)

severity of a risk, the loss that would be incurred should this event happen. (13.1)

short-termism an approach to investment that expects a return on investment within just a few years. (2.4)

sink a terminator into which data flows out of a **data-flow diagram**. (Appendix A)

single-loop learning learning within a single feedback cycle that changes behaviour based on the discrepancy between the desired and actual behaviour. (2.7)

situated action responding to a situation with an appropriate action contingent upon that situation, rather than executing some pre-planned activity which might not be completely appropriate. (2.8)

socio-technical system a system made up of engineering artefacts, technology, and people or social groups. (2.5)(8.3)

software in a strict sense is the set of instructions that control the behaviour of a programmable computer. In a wider sense, as used normally in this book, software involves all artefacts (see **software artefact**) that **stakeholders** need for useful computing.

software acquisition the process of obtaining software by whatever legitimate means. (6.1)

software artefact a generic way of referring to any asset produced during the the software process, including code in all its forms and all forms of documentation.

software as a service the use of software rented to undertake a particular function or service, traditionally offered through a bureau, but nowadays offered via the internet. (6.5)

software crisis the observation that demand for software is ever increasing and yet so often found to fail, at a time when there is a shortage of suitably qualified software engineers. (10.1)

software decay software deteriorates with the passage of time and successive changes that degrade its structure. (9.3)

software development project a **project** that will develop or modify software. (10.1)

software maintenance updating and modifying software after its first **release**. It is the stakeholders' satisfaction with the software that is maintained. (9.1)

source a terminator from which data flows into a **data-flow diagram**. (Appendix A)

SPICE Software Process Improvement and Capability dEtermination, a project aimed at achieving normalisation and standardisation of software process assessment approaches worldwide and industry-wide. (12.2)

spiral process model an abstract view of **iterative** process models created by Barry Boehm. (8.3)

SSADM Structured analysis and design method, a traditional bureaucratic method based on a sequential process, once popular in the United Kingdom. (4.4)(8.1)

stakeholders the people or groups of people who have an interest or stake in a particular system, project, or organisation, either as an investor or as a participant. (2.1)

standards specification or procedures to which all participants in a particular economic sector are expected to conform and follow in the interest of higher-quality products and the free operation of the market. (4.4) (6.1)

store same as **data store**. (Appendix A)

stub a dummy component which can stand in for a component that is not yet ready so that a partial system can be integrated and tested. (7.11)

subject to contract a clause in a letter of intent saying that commitments in the letter will only be legally enforceable if the contract is duly prepared and agreed and signed. (5.3)

subsidiary an organisation that is legally part of a parent organisation. (6.6)

sustenance a word used in some organisations for **evolution** or **maintenance**, though because of its association with food, this is not a term used by us. (9.1)

system any configuration of independent but interrelated elements – humans, business procedures, hardware, software, and other equipment – that serves some combined and common purpose. (1.1)(2.1)(8.1)

system dynamics a method of simulating a process to explore aspects of its behaviour originally proposed by MIT's Jay Forrester. The method is inspired by control theory ideas and focuses on the identification and modelling of **feedback** loops which are believed to influence the behaviour of many organisational and other systems. (9.3)

system test test of a complete system, typically running comprehensive tests to make sure that the system meets its specification and is technically robust. (7.12)(8.1)

systems software software that provides computers with basic operations needed for their work (e.g. operating systems, network drivers), also called **infrastructure software**. (6.1)

tacit knowledge what people know, but may not be able to describe or document. (2.6)

tangible costs or benefits that can be directly assessed. (2.4)

Taylorism or taylorism a characterisation of the management theories of Frederick Taylor that views workers simply as machines, with work decomposed into small steps which workers then enact repeatedly and mechanically. This characterisation treats Taylor's theories very unfairly, leaving out a lot of the humanity and support for labour that he embodied. (2.2)

technology knowledge and understanding of tools and crafts to serve human needs and the tools themselves.

TCO abbreviation for **total cost of ownership**. (2.4)

TDD abbreviation for **Test-Driven Development**. (8.8)

terminator the points at which a data-flow process model connects to its environment – typically agents or devices or other systems. (Appendix A)

test case an example of **inputs** to software together with the expected **outputs** or results, used to test the correct execution of the software. (10.2)

Test-Driven Development part of the **XP** agile method, focussing on test cases as the way of incrementally developing the software. (8.8)

test harness software which helps to test the software-under-test by supplying it with the required input and capturing the outputs generated. (7.10)(7.12)

testing executing the software with a number of sample inputs checking to see whether the expected outcomes were produced. (7.10)

test-script the coding of a sequence of test cases and the actions to be taken depending upon the result of the test case, so that the testing process can be automated. (7.12)

Theory X part of McGregor's theory of motivation, which contrasts this theory X, that reluctant workers need to be coerced to work at all, with his **Theory Y** (3.1)

Theory Y part of McGregor's theory of motivation, which contrasts this theory Y, that willing workers only need encouragement and support, with his **Theory X** (3.1)

thrashing a process of **negative feedback** that overcompensates, leading to a discrepancy in the opposite direction, which in turn is followed by negative feedback that again overcompensates, and so on. (2.7)

timeboxing an approach to software development which fixes the time to delivery (the timebox) and the resources to be applied, and allows variation in the actual functions to be delivered. (8.5)(10.4)

top-down estimation see **macro estimation**. (10.3)

total cost of ownership (TCO) the accumulated costs over time of all direct and indirect costs for the ownership of **technology**, or more generally any investment, this concept is important because it shows that choosing low initial costs may cost more in the long run. (2.4)

Total Quality Management an approach to quality in which everybody is responsible for quality working within **quality chains**. (12.2)

TQM abbreviation for **Total Quality Management**. (12.2)

trademark any word, name, symbol, or other device, which identifies and distinguishes the goods of one manufacturer or seller from goods manufactured or sold by others. (5.2)

trustworthiness in decision-making, selecting suppliers or contractors is inevitably based on trust: confidence that the person or organisation concerned will deliver what is promised, and will be in business in twenty years' time to support you. (2.4)

UIMS abbreviation for **user interface management software**. (7.6)

UML abbreviation for **Unified Modelling Language**. (2.1)(Appendix A)

uncertainty avoidance Hofstede's concept about intercultural differences in which people in some cultures like a predictable future, and in other cultures relish the unexpected. (3.2)

uncertainty principle a principle in quantum physics, first enunciated by Werner Heisenberg, that there is a limit to how precise physical measurements can be; if we want to measure the location and momentum (mass times velocity) of a particle, the more precise we want to be about one the less precise we can be about the other. (1.4)

Unified Modelling Language a series of design notations for use in object-oriented software design and programming, produced by **OMG**. (2.1)(8.1)(Appendix A)

use cases the interaction between a user or actor and the system of interest in undertaking some general business process using the system. (10.2)

user interface management software software which defines the screens with which the user will interact, captures the user responses to these and organises what the next interaction will be. (7.6)

utilitarian ethics based on the argument that your actions should not harm others because that action if undertaken by others could harm you. (4.2)

V&V **verification** and **validation**. (8.1)

validation making sure that the software as produced fulfils the real user need, characterised as 'building the right system'. (7.15)

variants **configuration items** that are essentially the same but differ in some small principled way. (11.2)

VDM the Vienna Development Method, invented in the Vienna laboratories of IBM, a **formal method** written in a programming-like notation. (8.4)

Vee life cycle a sequential **waterfall**-like process model that focusses on testing as an important part of the process. (8.2)

verification making sure that the software as produced conforms to an earlier specification of what it should do, characterised as 'building the system right'. (7.15)

version as a **configuration item** undergoes change, a new version of

that configuration item is produced. (11.2)

Vienna Development Method see **VDM**. (8.4)

vision statement the desired future state of the organisation and world and the destination of the group's work together, formulated in a way that inspires the members of the organisation. (2.1)

walkthrough a particular kind of **review** in which a system is 'simulated' by those who have designed it, looking for defects. (12.2)

waterfall the traditional process model in which the activities follow each other in sequence with the assumption that each activity follows on the from the previous one only when that is complete, and that there will be no need to repeat an activity to do rework. (8.2) (9.1) (11.3)

weighted scorecard a method of guiding the selection between alternatives based on setting out a number of criteria that are independently scored, which are combined by multiplying the individual scores by weights that represent the relative importance of the criterion, and then adding these together. (2.4)

work-arounds a means of working when the system fails to support work in the way intended, a way of coping with a system as it actually is and appropriating this into the relevant business processes. (6.7)

work breakdown the decomposition of the work that must be undertaken on a project into smaller parts, possibly in a hierarchy. (7.7)

workflow systems support for work as a sequence of activities that must be undertaken on a number of documents or information items in a particular order, using the computer and communications to ensure this. (2.2)

work-product an item that is produced as the result of a particular work activity. Though distinct from a **deliverable**, in this book they will be treated as largely synonymous. (7.1) (8.1)

wrapping adding a minimal amount of software at the interfaces of a component so that it can connect to new software following the protocols of the new software. (6.2)

XP abbreviation for **eXtreme Programming**. (8.8)

Z a **formal method** created at Oxford University based on mathematical set theory. (8.4)

Index

Note: Page numbers in bold refer to material in tables and diagrams and to examples and activities. Case Study material is in regular font.

accidents *see* software failure
accomplishment-cost *see* earned value
accreditation 356
ACM Sigsoft 263
Adams, K. 382
adaptive maintenance *see* software evolution
affordance 202
Agile Alliance 216
Agile Manifesto 216, 217
agile processes 9, 15, 215–19
    and change control **324**
    compared to open source development **218**
    and human factors **217–8**
ALARP 380
Albrecht, A.J. 173
Alexander, Christopher 208
Allied Quality Assurance Publications *see* AQAPs
alpha test 183
Aoyama, Mikio 247
Apache 143. 329
API *see* application program interface
application bounding 230, 268
application frameworks *see* frameworks
application lifecycle 230–1
application program interface (API) 70, 140
application software *see* software, types of, application
AQAPs (Allied Quality Assurance Publications) 88, 354
Arango, Guillaume 41
architectural design **174**, 174–6, 191
architecture 11–15
    community 14
    specification 211
Argyris, Chris 41, 43
Ariane Rocket Flight 501 372
    cause of **373–4**
Arthur, L.J. 245
As-Is system 166, **167**
as low as reasonable practicable *see* ALARP
asset repository *see* component repository
assets, digital materials as 303–4
    management of 325, 330–1

ATM *see* automatic teller machine
attribute 402
audit
    post-implementation 33
    for conformance to standards 89
    of configuration management process 323, 326
    for quality certification 354, 356
automatic teller machine (ATM) 6–7
automation boundary 171

Baan 156–7
Bachman, Charlie 22, 395
Bainbridge, David 103
balanced score card 35
    see also weighted scorecard
bang 175, 279
Barnum, Carol 202
baseline 288, 313
    change of 318
basic needs 57
bazaar 213
Beck, Kent 217
Belady, Les 229, 232, 389
benefits 31–5
    tangible 31
    intangible 31
    and knowledge 38–40
    qualitative 23
    quantitative 23
Bennett, Keith H. 247, 248, 362
Berne Convention 98, 106
Berry, John 62
bespoke software *see* software, types of, bespoke
best performance 297–8
beta test 183
Biggerstaff, Ted 239
body shopping 152
Boehm, Barry 203, 218–19, 340, 351, 374–5
Boehms's Spiral Model 203–4, **204**, **207**, 363
Booch, Grady 195
bottom-up estimation 271
bounding see application bounding

brainstorming 168, 376, 378
brands 108–9
Brewer, David 196
British Standards Institute (BSI) 87–8, 354
Brooks, Fred 153, 229, 231–2, 263, 388, 390–1
Brooks' law 232, 263–4, 388
BSI *see* British Standards Institute
bug *see* software failure
build
    process of Microsoft 316–7
    daily build 324, 380
    state 313
Buschmann, Frank 209
business processes 24–9, 25, 42
    tacit 36
    explicit 36
business process reengineering (BPR) 29–30, **30**,
      41, 142, 241–2
business rules 24

CAD *see* computer-aided dispatch
calibration **281**
call centre 154
call graph 238
Capability Maturity Model (CMM) 357
capture-replay 182
Carmel, E. 155
Castells, Manuel 1, 2
The Cathedral and the Bazaar 213
CBEMA (Computer and Business Equipment
      Manufacturers' Association) 86–7
CEPIS (Council of European Professional
      Information Societies) 82
CERN particle accelerator 234
certification
    of configuration management 324
    marks 109
    of quality management systems (QMS) 356
    of software development process 89
Ceruzzi, Paul 393
change 7–9
    basic processes of 228–9
    and digital materials 325
    inevitability 389
    and learning 41–3
    log records **327**, 329
    and new and evolving systems 29–30
change charter 29, 168, **169**, 268
    see also application bounding
change control 318–25, **322**
    levels of 323
    processes 44, 305, 319–20, **320**
    see also configuration management
Change Control Board (CCB) 304, 321–2
change management 46–7
    see also configuration management
change request **321**, 322, 323
change scenario 44, 46

Charette, R. 382
checking in 311, 329
checking out 311, 329
Chen, Peter 404
chief information officer (CIO) 40
chief programmer teams 391
Chikovsky, E.J. 238
CIO *see* chief information officer
Clement, A. 201
client 175
    see also client-server architecture
client-server architecture 149–50, 328
CMM *see* Capability Maturity Model
CMMi 157, 298 307, 357–9, **357**, **358**, **359**
    compared to SPICE 362
    drawbacks of **357–8**
COBOL 132–3, 135–6, 225
Cockburn, Alistair 272
COCOMO 276–8
COCOMO II 277–8
code production *see* coding
codes
    of conduct 76–80
    personal 79
    of practice 85
    see also ethics; regulation; standards
coding 179–181, 191
    pseudo-code or programme design language
      179, **238**
co-evolution 226–7
cohesion 177
Coleman, D. 244
collaborative work *see* CSCW
collective marks 109
commercial off the shelf software (COTS) 112,
      139–42
    advantages and disadvantages 137
    selection 137–9
    integration of 139–42
    technical 139–40
    through customisation 140–2
commodity 65–6
Common Object Request Broker *see* CORBA
commons *see* public goods
Communications of the ACM 15
communication to the public 107
community of practice 40, 64
    see also knowledge, sharing of
competitive advantage 34
component approach, limits of 212–3
component repository 68, 211, 329, 330
    see also product line
composition *see* integration
computer-aided dispatch (CAD) 336
Computer and Business Equipment
      Manufacturers' Association
      see CBEMA
computer misuse 122–3

Computer Support for Collaborative Work *see* CSCW
configuration item 309–12, **311**
    hierarchical naming of **315**
    variant of 310–12
    version of 310–12
    repository of *see* configuration management tools, configuration repository
configuration management 47, 228, 304–18, **313**
    advantages and disadvantages of **307**
    and baselines 312–3
    basic elements of 308–9
    and data model 315
    of digital material 317–18
    plan 324–5
    processes 321–5
    quality certification 324–5
    tools of *see* configuration management tools
    see also change management; version management
configuration management tools 325–31
configuration repository 311, 326–7
    functions 327–9
    system building 329–30
    and other digital assets 330–1
configuration repository *see* configuration management tools, configuration repository
constructionism 15
    see also social construction of technology
consultancy 152
content management system (CMS) 146
contingency **287–8**, 289, 292
contracts 111–17, **113**–5, 152, 159
    cost plus 116
    for outsourcing 152
control theory 37
Cookfair, Arthur S. 107
Cooper, Alan 202
copyright 97, 101–7
    court decisions on 103–4
CORBA (Common Object Request Broker Architecture) 210
corporate schema 175
corrective maintenance *see* software evolution
correctness 339
cost-accomplishment *see* earned value
cost-benefit analysis 32
cost drivers *see* effort multipliers
costs 31
    direct 31
    indirect 31
    opportunity 31
    reduction of by weakly coupled subsystems **278**
Council of European Professional Information Societies *see* CEPIS
COTS *see* commercial off the shelf software

'Counting Practices Manual' 279
coupling 177
coverage analyser 180
coverage measure 182
Cox, Brad 392
critical path analysis 286
Crosby, Phil 352
Cross, J.H. 238
CSCW (Computer Support for Collaborative Work) 28
cultural relativity 76–7
culture, Trompenaars' fundamental dimensions of *see* Trompenaars' fundamental dimensions of culture
Curtis 380
customer support team 322
customisation
    of software 140–2
    of operating system 306–7
Cusumano, Michael A. 316–7
CVS 308, 328

database 175
    see also configuration management tools, configuration repository
data-flow diagram *see* diagrams
data protection legislation 117–8
defamation *see* libel
defects 343
    terminology for **339**
deliverable product 164, 185, 192, 267, 289
Delphi technique/method 171, 271, 273
DeMarco, Tom 22, 173, 279, 296, 396
dependencies 310
derivations 310
design
    detailed 177–8, 178, 191
    participative *see* participative design
    redundancy 350
    see also architectural design
design abstraction *see* reverse engineering
design recovery *see* reverse engineering
development impact assessment *see* impact analysis
DFD *see* diagrams, data-flow (DFD)
diagrams
    arrow-box-circle (ABC) 396
    context **25**, 399, **399**
    data-flow (DFD) 396–7
    limits of **25**
    data structure 396
    influence 408
    see also modeling
discounted cash flow *see* net present value
diseconomies of scale 270, 276
Display Screen Equipment directive 120–1
distance education 5–6, 24, 30
distributions 144

document management 330
draft for development *see* intercept standard
domain
    analysis 211
    model 211
    and variable software 230–1, **231**
Draft International Standard (DIS) 86
Drucker, Peter 26
DIS *see* Draft International Standard
DSDM *see* Dynamic Systems Development
    Method
Dutton, Bill 37
Dynamic Systems Development Method
    (DSDM) 206–7, 216

earned-value 289
economies of scale 68
economy 65–71
    market 65
    command 65
    gratis 71
Effective Technical and Human Implementation
    of Computer-based Systems *see* ETHICS
effort multipliers (EM_i) 277
effort *see* person-months
80/20 rule 206
Elements of Software Science 244
EM_i see effort multipliers
embedded software *see* software, types of,
    embedded
emergency repairs 319
emergent behaviour 15
emergent properties 15
encapsulation 177, 237
encryption 122
Endres, Albers 264
enlightenment project 11
enterprise resource planning (ERP) 8, 34, 131,
    141–2, **142**
entire agreement 116
entity 402
escrow agreement 116
estimation 191, 270–8
    algorithmic 273–5
    by analogy 273
    of cost, models of **275**
    see also COCOMO; function points
    expert 272–3
    function point-based 279–81
    and basic change processes 228, 321
    of maintenance and evolution 281–2
    models for 245
    of resources and duration 270–1, **284–5**
ethical reasoning **78–9**
ethics 76–79
    of cost estimation **271**
    and decision-making 158
    and decisions about investment 34

deontological 76
    normative approach to 77–8
    utilitarian 77
ETHICS (Effective Technical and Human
    Implementation of Computer-based
    Systems) 200–1
evolutionary method 199
evolutionary process model *see* process model,
    iterative or evolutionary
evolvability *see* maintainability and evolvability
excludability 66, 67, 96
execution tracer 238
externalisation 38
externalities 67–8, 94
    see also free-rider
external threats 122–3
eXtreme programming (XP) 27, 217, 218, 239

Fagin, Michael 346
fail-safe 373
failure mode analysis 88, 373
fair dealing 106
fair use *see* fair dealing
feasibility study 32–3
Fedora project 144
feedback 42–3
    double-loop 42–3, **43**
    single-loop 42, **42**
    and software evolution 230–1, **230**, **231**
Feigenbaum, Armand 349, 351
Fenton, Norman 405
Fetzer, James 15
Finkelstein, Anthony 226
fitness for purpose *see* quality
Fitzgerald, B. 145
Flores, Ivan 15
Flowers, Stephen 2
focus group 168
fonts 95
force majeur 116
Fordism (fordism) *see* Taylorism
forward engineering 240
    see also reverse engineering
FOSS *see* Free and Open Source software
Fowlers, Martin 239
frameworks 210
    quality of 353
Franke, R.H. 2
Free and Open Source software (FOSS) 70–1,
    110, 142–3, 158–9
    acquisition of 142–8
    costs and benefits of 145–8
    development methods of 213–4, **214–5**
    motivation for 71
    project management tools for 294–5
    support for **148**
Free and Open Source software movement
    143–5, 213

free-rider 67, 94, 147
Free Software Foundation 70, 110, 213
Free Software movement *see* Free and Open
    Source software movement
Friends of Development 99–101
function points (FP) 173, 279
    see also estimation, function point-based
Future Shock 7

Gaia hypothesis 15
Gantt charts 286, **287**
Garlan, David 175
Garvin, D. 338
GATT 98–9
General Agreement on Tariffs and Trade *see*
    GATT
Gilb's Evolutionary Development model 361
GenRad 305
globalisation of software 9
Glossary of Terms Used in Quality Assurance 338
GNU licenses
    General Public License (GPL) 70, 110
    Free Documentation License 110
GNU manifesto 70
gold copy 305–6, 327
goods 65–6
    consumables 66
    capital 66
    private 66
    see also public goods
Gordon, Thomas T. 107
GPL *see* GNU licenses, General Public License
    (GPL)
granularity 310
graphical user interface (GUI) *see* interface,
    graphical user
gratis economy *see* economy
Group of Friends of Development *see* Friends of
    Development
groupware *see* CSCW
growth needs 55
GUI *see* graphical user interface
guidelines 85
guilds 79–80

hacking 24, 145, 213
Hagemeister, J. 244
Hall, P.A.V. 238
Halstead, M. 244
Hamel, Gary 26
Hampden-Turner, C. 61
A Handbook of Software and Systems Engineering 264
hardware/software co-design 38
Hawthorne effect 54, 56, 296
    see also motivation
health and safety legislation 120–1
Heisenberg's Uncertainty Principle 235
    see also uncertainty principle

Herzberg, F. 54
Hewlett-Packard 244
high-level design *see* architectural design
historical records 243–4
Hoare, Tony 10
Hofstede, Geerte 57
Hofstede's four dimensions of people 57–59, **60**,
    62
Hopper, Admiral Grace 133
HTML (Hyper Text Mark-up Language) 90–1
human resources 291
    and best performance 297–9
    development of 63–5
    and failure of **297–8**
Humphrey, Watts S. 296–7

IBM OS 360 231–2, 263, 339, 369
IDE 193
IEC (International Electrotechnical Commission)
    85–6, 361
IEEE *see* Institute of Electrical and Electronic
    Engineers
IFIP Working Group 2.3 on Programming
    Methodology 9–10
IFPIG *see* International Function Point User
    Group
impact analysis 228, 319
imperfect competition 68–71
    and patents and trademarks **109**
incremental process model *see* process model
information hiding 177, 237
information society **6–7**
Infosys 362–3
in-house development *see* software
    development, in-house
innovation 63–4, **90**
innovative design 371–3
innovative expertise **63–4**
inspection *see* review
inspection meeting 346–7
Institute of Electrical and Electronic Engineers
    (IEEE) 83–4, 86–8
institutional memory 41
insurance industry, evolution of 7–8, 34
Integrated Development Environment *see* IDE
Integrated Project Support Environment (IPSE)
    193
integration 8, 181
    of COTS **140**
intellectual property law 95–123
    necessity of 95–6
intellectual property rights (IPR) 96–111, **107**
    economic 105–6
    exceptions and exemptions 105–6
    exhaustion of 106
    international organisations and agreements
        on 97–101

(Continued)

intellectual property rights (IPR) (*Continued*)
  moral 104, 108
  need for **96–7**
interface 56, 134, 310
  and design 204
  graphical user (GUI) 134, 329
  between software and organisation 38
  user 69, 150, 174–5, **194**, 309
International Function Point User Group
    (IFPUG)
International Organisation for Standards *see* ISO
International Register of Certified Auditors
    (IRCA) 356
International Telecommunications Union *see* ITU
Internet Explorer 90
interoperation 158
invitation to tender (ITT) 264, 265
  see also tender
IP law *see* intellectual property law
IPR *see* intellectual property rights
IPSE *see* Integrated Project Support
    Environment
IRCA *see* International Register of Certified
    Auditors
ISO (International Organisation for Standards)
    85–7, 338, 359, 354
ISO 8402 340
ISO 9000 series 353–6, **355**
ISO 9001 88–9
ISO 9126 342–3
ISO/IEC TR 15504 360–1
ISO/TC176 86
iterative method 199
iterative process model *see* process model,
    iterative or evolutionary
IT procurement *see* software acquisition
IT provision *see* software acquisition
ITT *see* invitation to tender
ITU (International Telecommunications Union) 86

Jacobson, Ivar 195
Java 140, 237, 310
Jencks, Charles 11
joint venture 156
Jones, Caper 173
JTC1 86–7
  subcommittees for software development **87**
Juran, Joseph 338, 313
jurisdiction 116

Kelen, Andras 71
Kenny, T. 145
Kidder, Tracy 36–7
KLOC (thousands of lines of code) 276
KM *see* knowledge, knowledge management
knowledge
  explicit 36, 38–41
  knowledge management (KM) 40, 330, 362

sharing of 40
tacit 36, 38–41
  and patterns 208
  see also community of practice
knowledge-creating company *see* learning
    organisation
knowledge creation cycle 39–40, **40**
  changes to **44–5**, **45**
Knuth, Donald 56
KSI project 314
Kuniavsky, Mike 202

Laboratory Life 15
Landauer, Thomas 1, 2, 9
Latour, Bruno 15
law, necessity of 96–7
law of scarcity 66
learning
  organisational 41, 356, 362
  best practice 42, 141, 213
  and patterns 210
  software enterprise 43–7
  see also feedback; work-arounds
learning organisation 41
  and inspection 349
legacy data 134, 135
legacy software 132–6
  difficulty in changing 133–4
  wrapping of 134–6, **136**, 160, 308, 310
legacy system *see* system
Lehman, Manny 10, 229, 230, 232, 251, 389
Lehman's laws of software evolution 233, 233,
    315, 389
Lehman's Software Uncertainty Principle 234–6,
    336, 377
LEO *see* Lyons Electronic Office
letter of intent 116
Levenson, Nancy G. 3, 371
Levenson's 1st law 372
liability 118–20, 336, 380–1
  limits to 116
libel 118
library privilege 106
license agreement 158, 215
licenses
  public goods 110
  creative commons 110
  versus service **151**
  see also GNU licenses
Likert scale 407, **407**
lines of code-based method *see* COCOMO
link 181
Linux 5, 70–1, 110–1, 113–15, 143, 144
LISP 314
Lister, Timothy 296
localisation 9, 70–1
lost update problem 311
Lyons Electronic Office (LEO) 4

Macintosh 6
macro estimation 270–1
Madrid Protocol 1
maintainability and evolvability 242–7
    index 244
    measurement of 243–5
maintenance extension 245, 281
maintenance organisations **253**
managing resources *see* project
'Managing Risk in Software Maintenance' 382–3
Managing Technical People 297
Manifesto for Agile Development see Agile
        Manifesto
Marian, Petre 63–4
market economy *see* economy
masculinity-femininity 58–9
Maslow, Abraham 55
Maslow's hierarchy of needs 55, **55**, 296
mathematical approaches 9–10, 15, 205
McCabe, T. 253
McCall, J.A. 340
McGregor, D. 53–4
McIlroy, Doug 130
Meaning of Working 62–3
mean time to change (MTTC) 243
measurement 23, 406–8
    see also performance indicators; earned-value
mergers 8
Messerschmidt, D.G. 393
metadata 329
metrics *see* measurement
MFN *see* most favoured nation
micro estimation 271
Microsoft 6, 90, 110–11, 119–20, 316–17
milestones 192, 267, 290
millenium bug 225–6
Mills, Harlan 391
mission statement 23
MK II Function Point Analysis 281
Model Driven Architecture (MDA) 195, 211
modeling 192, 395–404
    data 22, 402–4, **403**, **404**
    data-flow 396–402, **399**, **400**, **401**
    with diagrams 395–6
    of knowledge *see* knowledge creation cycle
    of organisations *see* organisations,
            modeling of
    process *see* process model
    soft systems methodology 397–8
    see also Vee lifecycle; waterfall lifecycle; staged
            model of software lifecycle
modernism 11
modules 177, 191, 239
moral philosophy *see* ethics
motivation 53–67
    global view of 57–63
    motivation-hygiene theory 54, 71
    organisational 65–7

and prototyping **202–3**
and XP 217–18
and working environment 296
model-view-controller pattern 208–9, **209**
modification request *see* change request
modules 179, 193, 242
monopoly 68, 100
Moodle 331
morality *see* ethics
most favoured nation (MFN) 99
MTTC *see* mean time to change
Mumford, Enid 200
The Mythical Man-Month 229, 232, 263–4, 388, 389

negligence *see* liability
Neilsen, Jakob 56, 202
net present value (NPV) 33
Netscape 90
Neumann, Peter 2
Nonaka, Ikujiro 39
normal design *see* routine design
Norman, Don 202
NPV *see* net present value

Oakland, John 349
Object Management Group (OMG) 192, 195
object-oriented (OO) method 195, 279
    and refactoring 239
    maintenance **247**
    modeling of 396
offshoring 154–7
    advantages and disadvantages 155, **157**
    forms of 156
Oman, P. 244
onshoring 154
open loop 230
Open Source movement *see* Free and Open
            Source software movement
Open Source Software (OSS) *see* Free and Open
            Source software movement
open source software development 213–15
Open University 5, 142
Open Workbench 294–5
optimal project duration 276
organisation of work *see* Taylorism
organisations 5, 22–30
    Hofstede's classification of 57–61
    and interaction with environment **23**
    modeling of 22–30
    and relationship with software 35–38
    work of 24
OSS *see* Open Source Software (OSS)
outsourcing 152–3
    advantages and disadvantages 152–3
    core competencies for **153–4**

packages *see* commercial off the shelf software
pair programming 296

parallel running *see* acceptance test
Parikh, Garish 237
Paris 1971 Protocol 106
Parkinson's law 271, 287
Parnas, David 237, 246
participative design/development (PD) 200–2
Pascal 238
patches 316
patent 97, 107–8, **108**
Patent Fundamentals for Scientists and Engineers 107
patterns, software design 208–10
    and reverse engineering 238
peer reviewing 348
People Capability Maturity Model (P-CMM) 298, 357
PeopleSoft 8, 34, 112, 142
Peopleware 391
perfect market 66, 67, **67**
perfective maintenance *see* software evolution
performance indicators 23, 31, 39
    see also return on investment; cost-benefit analysis; weighted scorecard
pervasiveness of software *see* ubiquity of software
Perl 146, 326
person-month 276, 284–5, **285–6**
PERT charts 285–6
Peterborough Software 4
Pfleeger, Shari 405
planned obsolescence 6, **69**
Plans and Actions 46
postmodernism 11, **13**
power distance 57
Pressman, Roger 285, 290
preventive maintenance 236–42
price to win 271
PRINCE (Projects in Controlled Environments) 292
prior art 107
proactive interaction 22
pro bono *see* social contract
process model 22, 164, 192, 193–213
    design-driven 207–13
    evolutionary or iterative 199–207, **200**
    incremental 198–9, **198**, 271
    for product-lines **212**
    prototyping 199, **199**
    sequential 193–8
    limits of **197–8**
product differentiation **69**
product line 70, 210–11
    process model of **212**
    see also component repository
productivity 1–2, **2**
    and change control 304, 323
    labour 1–2, 56
    multifactor 1

of software engineers 269–70
    and working environment 296–7
professional **81**
professional societies 81–3, **82**
programming languages 237
    and mathematical approach *see* mathematical approach
    programming methodology *see* IFIP Working Group 2.3 on Programming Methodology
    and refactoring 239
    see also COBOL; Java; LISP; Pascal; Scheme; SQL
project 22, 164, 264–300
    assumptions 267
    budgeting for 269–85
    business analysis of 264–5
    establishment of requirements for 267–9
    see also requirements
    estimation of resources and duration 272–287
    see also estimation
    management 291–9
    laws of 263–4
    skills for **298–9**
    standard practices of 292
    tools for 292–5
    monitoring and controlling progress of 178–9, 288–90
    performance 23
    plan 265–7
    progress monitoring *see* monitoring and controlling progress
    organisation 265–6, **266**, 291, **291**
    scheduling 285–8
    remedial actions if behind **290**
    set-up 264–9
    software development 262–3
    features of 262–3
Projects in Controlled Environments *see* PRINCE
Projistics 149
property rights 66
prototype 199, 267, 271
prototyping process model *see* process model, prototyping
public goods 66–7, 96, 109–11
    software as 109–10

quality 337–63
    accreditation and certification 356
    assurance 185
    chain 350
    circles 350
    culture 348–9
    customer perceptions of **336–7**
    definitions of 337–40
    economics 351–2, **352**
    enhancement activities 343–5, **345**
    factors 340–1

frameworks 353–5
   in practice 362–3
   investment in 249–50, 351–2
   management system (QMS) 321, 354
Quality Plan 354
Quality Manual 354, 356
   measurement of 340–3, **342**, **343**
   and reviews and inspection *see* reviews and
      inspections, quality
   and savings on initial development **249**
   software quality model **341**
   and testing *see* testing, quality
   and the uncertainty principle 234–5
   see also ISO 9000 series; CMMi; SPICE
Quality Control Handbook 338, 351
'quality is free' 352
Quintas, Paul 37
QMS *see* quality, management system

radical design, failure of 369–71
Rajlich, V.T. 247
Rapid Application Development (RAD) 206, **207**
rationality, limitations of 9–15, 198, 205
Rational Software Corporation 195, 196
Rational's Unified Change Management 327
Rational Unified Process (RUP) 195–6, **195**, **196**
Raymond, Eric 213, 216
reactive interaction 22
recursion *see* refactoring
Red Hat Linux *see* Linux
redocumentation *see* reverse engineering
reductionism 14, 24, 46
redundancy 344
reengineering 240–2
   and business process reengineering (BPR)
      241–2
   versus new software **242**
refactoring 239–40
reflective practitioner 64
register of ISO-certified companies 356
regression testing *see* testing, regression
regulation
   as a public good 76
   self-regulation 80–4
   see also standards
Reifer, Don 31
releases 144, 313
   management of, Lehman's recommendations
      251–2
   planning of 229, 315–7
   triggering of **315–6**
repository *see* component repository
reproduction 104–5
requirements
   analysis 165
   and routine and radical design **269**
   creep 226, 263, 268
   document 265

elicitation 131–2, 165–71, 191, 267
   engineering 131
   specification 38, 166, 171, 191, 267
   cost-benefit estimation of 173
   and prototyping 199, 267–8, 269
   and review 269
   statement 152, 166
   validation 267
   volatility **224–5**, 264
return on investment (ROI) 31–5, **33**, 66
   and intellectual property rights 97
   and evolution and maintenance costs 249–50,
      250
   see also performance indicators
resource balancing 285
resource leveling *see* resource balancing
resource profile 285
restraint on trade 116
restructuring 239–40
retrofitting 319
reuse *see* software reuse
reverse engineering 70, 203, 237–9
   directive on 139
   and reengineering 241
   see also forward engineering
reviews and inspections 185, 267–8, 345–7
   to spread good practice **347**
revision *see* configuration item
risk 366–84
   analysis 268
   assessment 46
   avoidance 375
   classification **368–9**
   floodgate 121
   identification of 377–80, **379–80**
   management of 374–7, **375**, **381**
   mitigation of 380–3, **381**
   reduction 375
   retention 375
   and software **379**
   transfer 375
   types of 367–8, **376**
Robson, Mike 350
Rombach, Dieter 264
round-trip software engineering 203, 239, 241
routine design, failure in 371–4
Royce, W.W. 193
Rumbaugh, James 195
rules 80

SaaS *see* software as a service
safety critical systems 2, 89, 249, 251, 373
   and change control 323
   and redundancy 344
   and quality standards 353
   and risk mitigation 380–1
safety culture 377
Safeware; System Safety and Computers 371

SanFrancisco Project (SFP) 140–1, 210
SAP 8, 34, 141, 142
scaffolding 181
Scheme 314
scenario 267
    change 44, 46
Schneidermann, Ben 202
Schoen, Donald 43
Schwalbe, Kathy 33
scientific management approach *see* Taylorism
scientific method 12, 24
scope 29, 170
Selby, Richard W. 316–7
Senge, Peter 42
sequential process model *see* process model
server 175
    see also client-server architecture
service marks 109
service level agreement 151
service-oriented architecture 150
services 65, 148–50
SGML (Standard Generalised Markup
    Language) **90**
Sharp, Helen 202
Shaw, Mary 175
shelfware 200
short-termism 33
simulation tools **295**, 348
Singapore Computer Misuse Act 123
situated action 45–6
Sneed, Harry 389
social construction of technology 36–7
    see also constructionism
social contract 71
social obligation 71
sociology of technology *see* social construction of
    technology
socio-technical system 38, 200
software acquisition 129–60
    decisions about 157–60
    risks of 378–80, **378**
    see also legacy software; commercial off the
        shelf software; Free and Open Source
        software
software aging phenomenon *see* software decay
software artifacts 326
software as a public good *see* public goods
software as a service (SaaS) 148–51
    costs and benefits 150–1
    standards for 150
    versus license 151
software complexity metric 253
software component library *see* component
    repository
Software Copyright Law 103
software crisis 263
software decay and death 229–36
software development 44–5, 164

aspect-oriented 212–3
of bespoke software 131, 151–7
in-house 139, 152
methodologies of 9
mathematical modeling 9, 15, 207
open loop **232**
open source *see* open source software
    development
risks in 380
standards of 89
team 152, 265, **266**
aspect-oriented 212–3
Software Engineering Institute (SEI) 300 357,
    382
Software Engineering notes 263
software enterprise learning *see* learning
software evolution 223–254
    cost drivers of 245–7, 279
    decision-making about 248–50
    empirical studies of 229–32
    laws of 233
    maintainability and evolvability of *see*
        maintainability and evolvability
    management guidelines 251
    Lehman's recommendations for **251–2**
    process model of 247–8
    risks in 382–3
    standards for 253
    types of maintenance and evolutionary
        activity **227–8**
    and types of software 230–2
    see also Lehman's laws; maintenance
        organisations
software failure 1–4, 31, 263, 336
    causes and consequences of 369–74
    and ethics 75, 89
    and lawsuits for breach of contract **112**
    in radical design 369–1
    in routine design 371–4
software flaw *see* software failure
software house *see* consultancy
software lifecycle *see* staged model of software
    lifecycle
software maintenance *see* software evolution
software marketplace 130–2
Software Patent Institute 108
software problem report **322**
Software Process Improvement and Capability
    Determination (SPICE) *see* SPICE
software production 164
    and user design 204
software product line 70, 212
    development of 213
    see also component repository
software project management *see* project,
    management, laws of
software quality model *see* quality, software
    quality model

software recovery and rejuvenation *see*
    preventive maintenance
software reuse 68, 209–10, 267
    development for reuse 267
software sustenance *see* software evolution
software tools 214, 238, 266
    for managing resources 291–9
    open source project management 294–5
    and round-trip software engineering 241
    see also call graphs; execution tracers;
        spreadsheets
software, types of
    application 131, 175
    bespoke 131, 306
    business-critical *see* legacy software
    commodity 306
    embedded 35–7, **37**
    see also hardware/software co-design;
        socio-technical system
    layered 175
    fixed (type S) 230, 268
    flight control 37
    free open sources *see* Free Open Source
        Software
    generic 306–7
    infrastructure software 131
    legacy *see* legacy software
    long-life 225–6
    for payroll systems 4–5
    pliable (type P) 232
    project management 138–9, 149, 164
    difficulties in 263
    reusable 317
    variable (type E) 230–1, **231**, 268
    well-engineered 237
    wide impact **159**
The Soul of a New Machine 36
source code 116, 144–5, 215
SourceForge **143**
specifications 85
spreadsheets 293–4
SPICE (Software Process Improvement and
        Capability Determination) 359–62, **360, 361**
    compared to CMMi 362
spiral process model *see* Boehm's Spiral Model
spyware **123**
SQL 179
SSADM (structured systems analysis and design
        methodology) 89, 192
staged model of software lifecycle 248–9, **249**,
        252, 282
stakeholders 23
    interaction with software 226–7
Stallman, Richard 70, 213
standards 84–91
    actual 84
    for configuration management 324
    de facto 84

de jure 84
functional 85
generic 88–9, 357
for hardware 131, 136
for information representation 131
intercept 85
interface 85
military 88
process 85, 212
products 85
for project management 292
prospective 85
quality 353–63
reference model 84
retrospective 85
for service-oriented architecture 150
for software
maintenance and evolution 253
technical 88
see also CMMi; ISO 9126; ISO 9000 series;
        regulation; SPICE
standards-making bodies 85–7
Strassmann, Paul 1
stub 181
subject to contract 116
Subversion 328–9, **328**
Suchman, Lucy 46, 217
Symons, Charles 281
synchronisation control 329
system building *see* configuration management
        tools
systems house *see* consultancy
systems of systems 373
system 1
    architect 176
    building *see* configuration management tools,
        system building
    dynamics 232
    integration of 8, 10, 191–2, 324
    legacy 30, 241, 242
    operating 130
    testing *see* testing, system
systems of systems 371
system software *see* software, types of
Szyperski, C. 393

Tacoma Narrows suspension bridge 370
Takeuchi, Hirotaka 39
Taurus 31–2
Taylor, Frederick Winslow 26
Taylorism (taylorism) 26–7, 28
    see also ETHICS
technical disclosure 108
technology transfer 100
tender 116
Test Driven Development (TDD) 217
Test-First design *see* Test Driven Development
        (TDD)

test case 268
test harness 179, 182
testing 179–84
    acceptance 183–4, 192
    integration 181, 191–2
    quality 347–8
    regression 229, 319, 380
    and uncertainty **235**
    system 182–3, 192, 235
    unit 179–80
test-scripting 182
text-to-speech (TTS) system 308–9
Theory X 53
Theory Y 53–4
Therac-25 2–3, 79–80
Thompson, Sir William 340
TickIT 356
Tija, P. 155
timeboxing 206, **207**, 289
timesheet **288**
To-Be model 171, **172**
Toffler, Alvin 7
top-down estimation 270–1
Torvalds, Linus 143, 213
total cost of ownership (TCO) 33
Total Quality Control 349, 351
Total Quality Management (TQM) 337, 349–50
Total Quality Management 349
trademarks 108–9, **114**
Trade-related Aspects of Intellectual Property
    Rights *see* TRIPS
tragedy of the commons 67, 70
TRIPS 99
Trompenaars, Fons 57, 61–2
Trompenaars' fundamental dimensions of
    culture 61, **62**
The Trouble with Computers 1
trustworthiness 34
TTD *see* Test Driven Development
Turner, Clark 3
typographical right 105

ubiquity of software 4–7, 371, 392–3
UCC *see* Universal Copyright Convention
UK Data Protection Act 117–18
UMIS *see* user interface management software
UML (Unified Modelling Language) 22, 171,
    192–3, 195, 208, 396
uncertainty 15, 203
    avoidance of 59
    resolution of 198–207
    using formal methods 205, **235–6**
    sources of 236, 377–8
    and testing *see* testing, uncertainty
    see also Heizenberg's Uncertainty Principle;
        Lehman's Uncertainty Principle
Unified Modelling Language *see* UML
Universal Copyright Convention (UCC) 98

Unix 6, 147, 213
unquality 352, **352**
usability 9, 156–7, 202
US Patent Act 107
Use Cases and Class Models 267, 279–80
user-centred
    design *see* design
    methods 9
    see also usability
user interface *see* interface, user
user interface management software (UMIS)
    175

V&V *see* verification; validation
validation 185, 192
    ways of 269
Van den Besselaar, P. 201
variant *see* configuration item
Vee lifecycle model 196, **197**, 199, 347
version *see* configuration item
version management 312–3, **312**
    tools of 327
    see also configuration management
verification 185, 192
Vienna Development Method (VDM) 205
viruses **123**, 145
vision statement 23
voluntary codes *see* regulation, self-regulation

W lifecycle 348
walkthrough 346
warranty 115
    disclaimer on 119–20
waterfall lifecycle 193–4, **193**, 327, 363
    and configuration management standard 324
Watson, T.J. 231
Wegner, Peter 130–1
weighted scorecard 35, 35, 138, **139**
    see also balanced scorecard
Wenger, Etienne 64
WfMC *see* Workflow Management Coalition
White, M. 382l
Winograd, Terry 13
WIPO *see* World Intellectual Property
    Organisation
WIPO Copyright Treaty 99
WIPO Performance and Phonograms Treaty
    99
Woolgar, Steve 13
work-arounds 43, 158
work breakdown 176–7, 266–7
    bottom-up 282–4
    see also PRINCE
work centrality 63
Workflow Management Coalition (WfMC) 28
working environment 120–1, 295–7
    improvement of **296**
workflow systems 27–9, **28**

work-product 164, 192
World Intellectual Property Organisation
        (WIPO) 99–101
World Trade Organisation 100, 112–13
World Wide Web Consortium (W3C) 90
The Worshipful Company of Information
        Technologists 82
wrapping *see* legacy software, wrapping of
WTO 98–9, 110–1
WTO *see* World Trade Organisation

X3 committee 88
XML 90, 135–6, 150
XP *see* eXtreme programming

Y2K *see* millenium bug

Z 179, 205
Zachman, Tom 175
zero defect 350
Zvegintov, Nicholas 237